Fetter'd or Free?

Woman in Chains, anonymous Pennsylvania artist. Courtesy of Bryn Mawr College Library, Special Collections.

BRITISH WOMEN NOVELISTS,
1670-1815

Edited by

Mary Anne Schofield and Cecilia Macheski

Ohio University Press
Athens, Ohio
London

Copyright © 1986 by Ohio University Press.
Printed in the United States of America.
All rights reserved.
Reprinted, 1987. First paperback edition, 1987.

Library of Congress Cataloging in Publication Data

Main entry under title:

Fetter'd or free?

   1. English fiction—18th century—History and criticism—Addresses, essays, lectures. 2. Women in literature—Addresses, essays, lectures. 3. English fiction—Women authors—History and criticism—Addresses, essays, lectures. 4. English fiction—Early modern, 1500–1700—History and criticism—Addresses, essays, lectures. 5. English fiction—19th century—History and criticism—Addresses, essays, lectures. I. Schofield, Mary Anne. II. Macheski, Cecilia.
PR858.W6F48   1986   823'.009'9287   85-8869
ISBN 0-8214-0799-6
ISBN 0-8214-0868-2

for our families and friends

Contents

IV. MORAL AND POLITICAL REVOLUTION

V. FICTIONAL STRATEGIES

VI. THE NOVEL AND BEYOND:
CRITICAL ASSESSMENTS

List of Contributors

PAULA R. BACKSCHEIDER, professor of English at the University of Rochester, is the coeditor of *An Annotated Bibliography of Twentieth-Century Studies of Women and Literature, 1600–1800*, and is the editor of *Probability, Time, and Space in Eighteenth-Century Literature.* She has published numerous articles on Daniel Defoe and has written the introduction to *Defoe's Life of Marlborough* for the Augustan Reprint Society.

JERRY C. BEASLEY, professor of English at the University of Delaware, is the author of *The Novels of the 1740s, The Checklist of Prose Fiction, 1740–1749,* and *English Fiction, 1660–1800: A Guide to Information Sources.* He coedited Garland Publishing Company's monumental *The Novel In England, 1700–1775,* and has published articles in *Studies in the Novel, Ariel,* and *Studies in English Literature.*

DIANA BOWSTEAD, has taught at several colleges within the City University of New York since 1965. She is now teaching at Hunter College and the College of Staten Island.

MARTHA G. BROWN, instructor of English at High Point College, is the editor of Fanny Burney's *The Wanderer, or Female Difficulties* to be published by Scholars' Facsimiles and Reprints.

KATRIN R. BURLIN, assistant professor of English and head of the Freshman English Composition Staff, Bryn Mawr College, is the author of " 'The Pen of the Contriver': The Four Fictions of *Northanger Abbey*," *Jane Austen: Bicentenary Essays*; she is active in the Jane Austen Society of North America and has addressed numerous professional organizations on Austen and her work.

ROBERT ADAMS DAY, professor of English at the City University of New York, is the author of *Told in Letters: Epistolary Fiction before Richardson*; he has published numerous articles on eighteenth-century figures in *PMLA, Studies in Bibliography,* the *Augustan Reprint Society Publications,* and the *New Cambridge Bibliography of English Litera-*

ture. He has just completed his critical edition (the first ever done) of Smollett's *History and Adventures of an Atom*, a book-length prose satire on midcentury England.

MARGARET ANNE DOODY is professor of English at Princeton, and author of a new book on Fanny Burney, and well-known for her many books and articles on Samuel Richardson, including the introduction to the Penguin edition of *Clarissa*. Her detective novel, *Aristotle Detective*, is soon to have a sequel.

DEBORAH DOWNS-MIERS, associate professor of English at Gustavus Adolphus College, is the author of the forthcoming *Labyrinths of the Mind: A Study of Sarah Fielding.* She has held three NEH Summer Seminar fellowships and is currently serving a four-year term for the Minnesota Humanities Commission.

RHODA L. FLAXMAN, assistant professor of English and assistant dean at Wheaton College, is presently preparing a study for publication entitled *Victorian Word-Painting and Narrative: Toward the Blending of Genres.* Her interests include nineteenth-century visual arts and literature and the new scholarship on women. Professor Flaxman works on the Balanced Curriculum Project at Wheaton and has conducted workshops and faculty seminars on innovative critical frameworks for the teaching of literature.

LINDA C. HUNT, Director of Women's Studies and Assistant Professor of English at Ohio University, has published articles on women writers in such journals as *Tulsa Studies In Women's Literature, Colby Library Review,* and *Victorian Institutes Journal.* She has also delivered papers and given presentations on women and literature at various conferences. A recent article, on Maxine Hong Kingston's *The Woman Warrior,* will appear soon in *MELUS.*

GARY KELLY, professor of English, University of Alberta, is the coeditor of the forthcoming *Women of Their Time,* an anthology of overviews of eighteenth-century women writers, and is the author of *The English Jacobin Novel.* He has published articles in *Eighteenth-Century Life, Women and Literature, Etudes Anglaises,* and *English Studies.*

JEAN B. KERN, emerita professor of English, Coe College, has been active in the eighteenth-century field for several years. The author of *Dramatic*

Satire in the Age of Walpole, 1720–1750, she has written numerous articles on eighteenth-century dramatists and novelists alike for the *Philological Quarterly, Eighteenth-Century Studies, Studies in Eighteenth-Century Culture*, and *Modern Philology*.

APRIL LONDON, assistant professor of English, University of Ottawa, has contributed numerous articles for *A Dictionary of Women*, the chapter entitled "Patronage and the Musæum Tradescantianum," in *The Catalogue of the Tradescant Collection*, and has written review articles on the picaresque novel, and nineteenth- and twentieth-century poetry.

ROGER D. LUND, assistant professor of English and chairman, LeMoyne College, is the author of *Restoration and Early Eighteenth-Century English Literature, 1660–1740: A Select Bibliography of Resource Materials*; he has published articles in the *Bucknell Review, Dickens Studies Annual*, and the *Denver Quarterly*.

CECILIA MACHESKI is assistant professor at Fiorello H. LaGuardia Community College of the City University of New York and is planning a full-length study of needlework imagery in women's literature.

CATHERINE E. MOORE is associate professor of English at North Carolina State University at Raleigh where she has recently completed a five-year term as a director of freshman composition. She teaches courses on the eighteenth century, particularly the eighteenth-century novel, and has published articles on Daniel Defoe and Mrs. Barbauld.

MITZI MYERS, instructor, University of California, Los Angeles, has been very active in women's studies, most especially those of the eighteenth century. Publishing in the *Mary Wollstonecraft Journal, Studies in Eighteenth-Century Culture*, and *Studies in Romanticism*, she has also contributed to *The Lost Tradition: Mothers and Daughters in Literature*, ed. Cathy N. Davidson and *E. M. Broner and Women's Autobiography: Essays in Criticism*, ed. Estelle C. Jelinek. She is currently coediting *Women of Their Time*, an anthology of overviews of eighteenth-century women writers.

TWILA YATES PAPAY is Director of Writing Programs at Rollins College. Her articles have appeared in ERIC and *College English Notes*, and she has presented papers at the Modern Language Association, CCCC, CEA, and NEASECS conferences.

MARY ANNE SCHOFIELD is an associate professor at St. Bonaventure University and the author of *Quiet Rebellion: The Fictional Heroines of Eliza Haywood.* She has edited a collection of four of Haywood's novels (Scholars' Facsimiles and Reprints, 1982) and has written a book on Haywood for the Twayne English Author Series (1985). She has published articles in *ELN, Studies in Eighteenth-Century Culture, Ariel,* the *Windsor Review,* and other journals.

SARAH W. R. SMITH, formerly an assistant professor of English at Tufts University, has also taught at Northeastern and Boston University. She was Field Editor of Twayne's English Authors Series for the period 1780–1840. Currently she is director of documentation at LMI, an artificial-intelligence firm in Cambridge, Mass.

PATRICIA MEYER SPACKS, professor of English at Yale University, is the author of numerous books and articles on the eighteenth century and women's studies, including *John Gay, An Argument of Images: The Poetry of Alexander Pope, The Female Imagination,* and *Imagining a Self.* She has edited *Late Augustan Poetry* and *Contemporary Women Novelists.*

SUSAN STAVES, professor of English at Brandeis University, is the author of *Players' Scepters: Fictions of Authority in the Restoration* and has co-edited the *Index to the Prose Writings* and *The Prose Works of Jonathan Swift.* She has published articles in *Studies in English Literature, Studies in Eighteenth-Century Culture, Eighteenth-Century Studies, Modern Philology,* the *Texas Quarterly, Revue de Littérature Comparee,* and *Comparative Literature.*

IRENE TAYLER is associate professor of English at Massachusetts Institute of Technology and well known for her *Blake's Illustrations to the Poems of Grey.* In addition to her work on Blake, Professor Tayler has published articles on women and eighteenth-century literature, including "Gender and Genre: Women in British Romantic Literature" (coauthored with Gina Luria), and "The Woman Scaly," a study of Blake's view of the female.

List of Illustrations

Preface

In making the case for female authorship, Virginia Woolf created Judith, Shakespeare's sister, and imagined her life, a grim mirror image of her brother's, to show how different the lot of an Elizabethan daughter was from that of a son. Had Woolf chosen to write about the eighteenth century, her task might have required less toil and yielded more optimistic results. Had she chosen Fielding rather than Shakespeare, for instance, Woolf would have found a sister ready-made—Sarah, the accomplished novelist. If she sought a playwright whose life was not ruined by seduction, she might have met Mrs. Inchbald. Women poets, letter writers, essayists, pamphleteers, and painters—most long forgotten—managed to earn a living by their pens from 1670 to 1815.

Many recent studies have begun to revive interest in women writers of the nineteenth century and have met with great appreciation by readers eager to know more about "Shakespeare's sisters": Ellen Moers's *Literary Women*, Elaine Showalter's *A Literature of Their Own*, and Gilbert and Gubar's *The Madwoman in the Attic* all illustrate the growing market for scholarly but readable books on women writers. No work has focused exclusively on the earlier novelists—the antecedents of Jane Austen. Most books, like Showalter's, dedicate an early background chapter to acknowledging the existence of eighteenth-century women, but immediately move into the better known texts of Austen, Brontë, Gaskell, and later authors.

Fetter'd or Free? is a collection of twenty-three essays designed to aid both specialist and general readers of eighteenth-century British literature to learn more about the women authors whose reputations have suffered as much from social prejudices as from lack of literary merit. The essays link the early "scandalous" novelists—Behn, Manley, Haywood—with the later, more sanctioned writers—Burney, Radcliffe, Austen—and encompass such lesser known but equally noteworthy figures as Mary Davys, Jane Barker, Frances Sheridan, Elizabeth Inchbald, Charlotte Smith, Jane West, Mary Brunton, Maria Edgeworth, and Hannah More. Organized thematically, the collection examines such issues as gender and genre; feminine iconography; sexual relationships; social and political motifs; and literary strategies. It concludes with critical assessments and bibliographic apparatus designed to provide unique opportunities for continuing dialogue.

We wish to express our thanks to the English departments of St. Bonaventure University, LaGuardia Community College, City University of New York, and the College of William and Mary and the staffs of the following libraries: Bryn Mawr College Library; the University of Pennsylvania Rare Book Library; the Graduate School and University Center Library of the City University of New York; New York Public Library; Kingsway-Princeton College of Further Education, London; and the Victoria and Albert Museum Collection.

Our very special thanks to Jim Pearce of Wyeth Laboratory; Jimmie Smith of Chilton Publishing Company; Rosemarie Prinz, Florence Pasternak, and Ida Mintzer of the English Department of LaGuardia Community College; and Lori Linderman of St. Bonaventure University.

And, to our friends, family, and colleagues for their kindnesses, cooperation, and endless cups of tea, most especially Susan Barone, John M. Buckley, Theresa Covley, Bryne R. S. Fone, Michelle Lawler, Arthur and Theresa Macheski, Cathy Myers, Janet Saunders, Anne Schofield, Cathy Stern, Geoffrey Thomas, and Sr. Mary Anthony Weinig.

Acknowledgments

Several of the *Fetter'd or Free?* essays have been presented at regional and national conferences. The editors and the contributors wish to thank the many host institutions for providing an arena where early versions of our ideas could be aired, disputed, and developed.

For illustrations, we would like to thank Bryn Mawr College Rare Book Library for permission to reprint our frontispiece; Brandeis University Library for permission to reprint "Mrs. Skinn with Mr. Brown"; and the Bodleian Library for permission to reproduce the engraving prefacing "Frances Sheridan: Morality and Annihilated Time."

"The Woman of uncommon understanding, and superiority of parts, ought not to be tied in fetters by the rules of honour or the forms of established custom. . . . it is a mark of true spirit to break through such servile and ridiculous chains, fit to be imposed only on the vulgar and illiterate."

(Sarah Fielding,
The Cry 2: 266)

Introduction

In *A Room of One's Own*, Virginia Woolf observes that women's writing cannot be considered in isolation from the social, political, and economic situation which dictates and defines woman's position; it is an observation which applies to all centuries of women's writing. Like her male counterpart, the female author neither lives nor produces in a vacuum. And though the facade of the female most frequently presented to the outside world—that of passivity and subordination—is often assumed to be the real female self, an exploration of feminine literature of any period reveals the fallacy of such an assumption.

This Janus-like quality forms the predominant characteristic of the female writers of the minor fiction of the eighteenth century. Writing at a time of extreme social subordination, as Patricia Meyer Spacks observes, these authors and their books "necessarily refract the effects of that subordination in ways hardly possible for a man to duplicate."[1] So it is that Jane Barker, Mary Davys, Eliza Haywood, Mary Manley, Elizabeth Inchbald, Sarah Fielding, Charlotte Lennox, Hannah More, Charlotte Smith, and Mary Brunton, among others, write during the early and late decades of the eighteenth century detailing and reacting to their subordination and exploitation under the cover of their fictions. In the guise of their sentimental heroines, their aggressive female manipulators, and the like, these novelists explore the perimeters of their being and that of the female self in general, leading us to ask the question, are they fettered by literary conventions, social mores, and economic limitations, or are they free to invent a female rhetoric, to express a selfhood, and to develop economic independence?

The essays in *Fetter'd or Free? British Women Novelists 1670–1815* provide a forum for examining this important question. In doing so, the essays illuminate not only the literary but the larger environment in which the novelists lived and worked, a culture oftentimes envisioned as a prison. The essayists are concerned with investigating the freedom and artistic integrity of their respective novelists when confronted by the myriad and subversive forms of entrapment and enslavement manifested in eighteenth-century England. This inquiry raises many questions, six of which form the basis for the organization of *Fetter'd or Free?*

We begin by asking (I) how does one separate concepts of gender from

1

those of genre? (II) Are the novelists fettered by conventional iconography or are they free to invent new patterns of distinctly feminine imagery? (III) Are they circumscribed by societal categories, thus unable to be salubrious sluts or happy old maids? (IV) When the novelist moves her scene from the boudoir to the bi-election, does she risk forfeiting her readership by venturing into the political arena, a traditionally male sanctum? (V) Do female writers design their own stories in conscious imitation of dominant male patterns or in revolt against such forms? (VI) And finally, have critics been shackled by excessive reliance on conventional methodology unsuited to feminine writers working independently of these traditions?

In asking whether the eighteenth-century woman novelist was fettered or free, each essayist represented in this collection provides one more figure in the carpet, one more answer to the nagging question. In the first section, *Gender and Genre*, Linda Hunt places Jane Austen's fiction solidly in the courtesy and conduct book tradition, exploring "late eighteenth and early nineteenth-century social changes and cultural attitudes concerning women," arguing that Austen's early heroines defy the fictional conventions of the female novel of the time because Austen herself was seriously committed to realism. In her last three novels, she grapples with the difficulties involved in reconciling the feminine ideal with that commitment to realism in literature. As Austen uses the conduct-courtesy book tradition, so Fanny Burney's novels, Martha O. Brown argues, are indebted to the romance tradition from which she drew heavily for plot, character and theme, although it is only in *The Wanderer*, her last novel, that Burney addresses herself to peculiarly female difficulties. In the Mary Brunton world, according to Sarah W. R. Smith, these difficulties become purely economic: two Brunton heroines, Laura Montreville and Ellen Percy, both become professionals—Laura a painter, Ellen a governess and small business woman—thus providing one solution to the female difficulties that plagued the Austen and Burney heroines, respectively. Conduct books, romance tradition and female difficulties each in its own way offers one writer's solution to the dilemma of gender and genre; the courtesy-conduct book, romance structures and financial obligations help each heroine to define her gender while each writer must at the same time shape her genre to her individual perception of gender.

The next group of essays addresses the issue of feminine identity through patterns of imagery rather than attention to form. Katrin R. Burlin and Cecilia Macheski focus on writers' choices of topoi, icons and allusions to the sister arts to underscore and elucidate the female dilemma. Burlin examines the topos of choice, illustrated both by Prodicus' "Hercules at the Crossroads, between Virtue and Vice" and Reynolds' "Garrick as Hercules

Hesitating Between Comedy (Pleasure) and Tragedy (Virtue and Duty),"
while Macheski investigates heroines' choice between chastity and lust as
mirrored in writers' use of needlework as a uniquely feminine signature in
the fiction of Lennox, Smith, Inchbald and Austen. April London and
Rhoda Flaxman shift our attention from tactile icons to metaphoric touch-
stones. In the case of London, we find the metaphors informed by "the
myth of the garden and directed toward ratifying the source and significance of power." The recurrent use of the garden image, she argues, "ultimately leads to the formulation of a rubric of erotica in which pervasive
sexuality is achieved by the conflation of human and natural," while Flaxman urges that the fiction of Ann Radcliffe attempts to establish a fictional
language which "articulates an aesthetic of particularity and passion." The
four essays taken together detail a positive response to the question raised
earlier: women have indeed freely invented symbolic matrices of their own
that define the female self when the male structures no longer sufficed.

In searching for feminine symbols and a language of female experience,
writers inevitably looked toward love, sex, and marriage. The third group
of papers focuses on dualities juxtaposing meritricious characters with villainous ones in order to express, through familiar patterns, the women
authors' unwillingness to accept those very patterns. Patricia Meyer
Spacks examines sibling relations in Austen, Lennox, and West and concludes that the "complex relation of sisters to one another, to parents, and
to the world without functions . . . in the three novels . . . as a metonym for the moral density of all relationship." Paula Backscheider in turn
looks at a score of eighteenth-century novels by women to conclude that
they reveal "a quiet but definite re-working of the definition of sexual and
marital pleasure." Society offers women ambivalent messages, on the one
hand requiring duty and on the other encouraging pleasure, but in the end
the heroine must choose, and the ideal marriage offers the answer to the
Herculean dilemma: virtue is its own reward. Susan Staves, in contrast, in
her study of Ann Masterman Skinn, says that the author of *The Old
Maid; or, the History of Miss Ravensworth* "seems to smash all the
eighteenth-century icons of female decorum and sensibility." Focusing on
actual litigation records from the sensational Skinn divorce case, Staves
counters the idealized marriage of fiction with a documented case history
of an unhappy marriage. From the well-publicized details of Skinn's divorce case it is an easy transition to the "salubrious sluts" of Eliza Haywood's fiction, who offer healthy alternatives to the circumscribed roles
society proscribes for fallen women. Through close reading of several
Haywood novels, Mary Anne Schofield examines the taxonomic structure
of Haywood's beleaguered heroines, concluding that stereotypic paths do

not inevitably lead to satisfactory self-definition as more conventional novelists would have us believe. Jean Kern continues to explore unconventionality in her study of the "old maid" in fiction. Like Schofield she uses a taxonomic approach to identify various types of old maids who occur in such writers as Jane Barker, Elizabeth Inchbald, Mary Collyer and Jane Austen, but concludes that "while they show sensitivity to, and empathy with the old maid, they also make clear that she is still fettered by a society which condones only marriage as the ultimate destiny of women."

Does the novelist who abandons the conventional goal of marriage as her heroine turns instead to the wider political arena risk forfeiting her readership as she moves into the undercover world of the covert text? Jerry C. Beasley affirms that works of prose fiction "regularly addressed political issues and events" and that because "women novelists were so numerous they reached a very broad audience" and that "collectively they did at least as much as any other group of writers to keep the contemporary ideals of public and private virtue before the consciousness of the British people." Moving to the politics of the 1790s, Diana Bowstead and Gary Kelly examine the relationship between domestic conflict and political upheaval. While Kelly sees the debate largely as one over "rights versus duties," Bowstead explores the relationship between nature and art and concludes that the very spirit of popular romantic fiction is analogous to that of revolutionary fervor. Kelly concludes that Austen's "attempted resolution" is "closer by far to Anti-Jacobin than to Jacobin models of the relationship between self and society," but Mitzi Myers discovers a "middle-class progressive ethic" is to be found in Hannah More's *Cheap Repository Tales*, thus rendering her work surprisingly radical in its subtext.

Subversion manifests itself not only politically but also rhetorically in female novels. Sarah Fielding's concern with "the labyrinths of the mind" becomes Deborah Downs-Miers' critical focus: "the liminality of women, the suspension of this consciousness between being object and becoming subject constitutes the real subject of and provides the structure and methodology for Fielding's work." In the novels of Frances Sheridan, Margaret Anne Doody uncovers yet another strategy for feminine fiction, namely, Sheridan's treatment of time. As Doody states, "in all of her major fictions she is interested in the recurrence of the past, the illusory quality of present activity, and the inability of the past to die." She goes so far as to suggest that Sheridan's work "is an influence on *Wuthering Heights*, and perhaps even at several removes, on Proust," and concludes that "the treatment of time is a feminine if not feminist contribution to the novel." Twila Yates Papay concludes this section with an analysis of yet another experiment in fictional artifice by revealing in Maria Edgeworth's *Harrington* evidence of the author's preoccupation with the psychological novel. Even though the novel "misses" as a "first-rate psychological study," Edgeworth nonetheless offers the modern reader evidence of the richness and intricacy of the female text in the eighteenth century.

It is this very wealth and confusion of the female novel from 1670–1815 that inspires the ongoing critical assessment that forms the basis for our last chapter. Beginning with a re-evaluation of Aphra Behn by Robert Adams Day, and moving ahead to Anna Laetitia Barbauld's criticism in the *British Novelists* (1810) by Catherine E. Moore, we end with a detailed bibliographic essay that assesses critical studies on eighteenth-century women novelists. Roger Lund offers descriptive analysis of works from 1960–1980.

Underlying this book is an ongoing dialogue addressing the title question, are the novelists fettered, or are they free? The myriad range of ideas, argument and evidence presented suggests that while no simple answer is possible, raising the question has at least brought recognition to the many women whose novels have for too long been neglected. Moreover, taken together, the essays in *Fetter'd or Free?* offer persuasive evidence that within the subtexts, if not the very texts themselves, of novels by eighteenth-century women writers, there exists the basis for defining a female tradition in literature. By posing the dichotomies of gender and genre, of freedom and enslavement, as the matrix for *Fetter'd or Free?* we hope to suggest that not only are the questions thus raised worth asking, but that asking the question is itself part of the answer.

1. Patricia Meyer Spacks, *The Female Imagination* (New Haven: Alfred A. Knopf, 1975), p. 50.

I. GENDER AND GENRE

A Woman's Portion
Jane Austen and the Female Character

LINDA C. HUNT

Many readers approach Jane Austen's later novels after a long and happy acquaintance with Elizabeth Bennet of *Pride and Prejudice*, and consequently are startled by Fanny Price of *Mansfield Park* and Anne Elliot of *Persuasion*. They would be similarly surprised by the approach to womanhood found in *Emma* if they were to read it carefully and not allow themselves to be distracted by Emma's energy and intelligence. Elizabeth Bennet refused to adhere to conventional decorum, running breathless along muddy lanes to visit her sick sister. She is obviously independent-minded, as well as witty and vivacious. In marked contrast, Fanny is exceedingly proper, silent, passive, and physically weak. Fanny Price has been the subject of much critical concern, and is, without a doubt, Jane Austen's most unpopular heroine. Although she has her defenders, many readers are impatient with her passivity and moral perfection, and even find her something of a prig. Kingsley Amis, for one, calls her "a monster of complacency and pride."[1] Tony Tanner asks, "What, then, was Jane Austen doing in this book?"[2]

For readers knowledgeable about the cultural milieu in which Jane Austen lived and wrote and the novelistic tradition out of which she grows, however, the figure of Fanny should be very familiar. Fanny is an exemplary heroine, a heroine who embodies the characteristics widely viewed by Jane Austen's contemporaries and immediate predecessors as essential aspects of ideal womanhood. To find models for Fanny Price we can look to the fiction written by women in the last three decades of the eighteenth century and the first decade of the nineteenth, novels by writers such as Mrs. Griffith, Clara Reeve, Charlotte Smith, Maria Edgeworth, Elizabeth Inchbald, Fanny Burney, Jane West, and Elizabeth Hamilton. As girl and woman Jane Austen read such fiction avidly; in terms of qualities of character both Fanny Price and Anne Elliot resemble the heroines of the novels by women written in this period.

If we turn to the numerous conduct books for women written at this time we find similar models for Fanny and Anne. Books like Dr. Gregory's *A Father's Legacy To His Daughters* (1774), James Fordyce's *Sermons To Young Women* (1776), Mrs. Chapone's *Letters on the Improvement of the Mind, Addressed to a Young Lady* (1773), Lady Mary Walker's *Letters from the Duchess de Crui* (1776), Mrs. Griffith's *Essays Addressed to Young Married Women* (1782), the Reverend John Bennet's *Letters to a Young Lady* (1791), Thomas Gisborne's *An Inquiry into the Duties of the Female Sex* (1797), the Edgeworths in their book on female education and Jane West's *Letters To a Young Lady* (1806) advise women on their duties, morals, and manners, and suggest educational regimes appropriate to "the sex." It is not surprising to find that many of these conduct book writers, especially the women, also write novels.[3] It is not surprising because the line between the conduct books and the female novels of the period is often quite thin; the two genres at times virtually shade into one another. Because both were usually epistolary in form, it was easy for an author to make the shift from one to another.

In an important essay published in 1950, Joyce Hemlow describes the period 1760 to 1820 as "the age of courtesy books for women" (she uses the term "courtesy book" instead of "conduct book"), and observes that "courtesy book material was diverted into the rising novel of manners." As the novel developed, the courtesy book could not compete with the novels from the circulating library which were so much more entertaining, and so the courtesy book writers attempted to liven their teachings by fictional devices borrowed from the novel. At the same time some of the novelists attempted to justify and dignify the new genre by including the moral and utilitarian material of the courtesy books.[4] The result was what Hemlow calls the "courtesy novel"—a novel whose central purpose is to define, in fictionalized form, the ideal woman, either by offering an exemplary heroine or, sometimes, by showing the vicissitudes of an imperfect heroine who must learn to correct her errors in conduct and attain perfection before she can win a husband.

My essay explores such novels and conduct books in the context of late-eighteenth- and early-nineteenth-century social changes and cultural attitudes concerning women, and places Jane Austen's fiction in the tradition of writing which focused on how to be a woman. The relationship of Austen's approach to women to that of her predecessors and contemporaries cannot be grasped without an understanding of the main currents of thought on womanhood in her era. The restrictive nature of the feminine ideal of the period causes some critics to assume it harks back to the past.[5] They select certain aspects of the ideology of womanhood as moments of

forward-looking clarity amid darkness. Actually, the view of women offered by most of the advice manuals and novels of Austen's day, rather than
being traditional, is a new approach generated first by changes in the domestic role of affluent women, and then by shifts in the structure of society
created by the challenge of the middle class to the old aristocratic order,
which expressed itself in part through religious reform.

Jane Austen's attitude toward the concept of female character is not
easily apparent because in her first three novels she resists the conventional
heroine as a model for her protagonists. My argument is that the heroines
of her early novels defy the fictional conventions of the female novel of the
time not because Austen ever rejected the feminine ideal, but because she
was seriously committed to realism; during the first stage of her artistic
development she did not feel able to render the ideal realistically. As Jane
Austen matured as a novelist, the accepted feminine ideal became a challenge. By the time she wrote *Mansfield Park* she was both more firmly
convinced than ever before of the importance of the social definition of
femininity and also more confident artistically. In her last three novels she
grapples with the difficulties involved in reconciling the feminine ideal with
a commitment to realism in literature.

I

Jane Austen and the other female novelists of the late eighteenth and
early nineteenth centuries were writing at a time when the positions of
women were undergoing significant changes. Growing affluence and the
removal of much domestic drudgery from the home led to increasing leisure for women of the middle ranks and above. It is likely that, even in the
early part of the eighteenth century in London and the larger provincial
towns, spinning and weaving, making bread, beer, candles, soap, and so
forth, were no longer necessary household tasks because most necessities
were manufactured and could be bought in shops; gradually this important
change was to spread throughout England.[6] Thus when Thomas Gisborne,
writing primarily for the landed classes in which many men too had considerable leisure, sets out to "ascertain the characteristical impressions which
the creator has stamped on the female mind," the difference between the
sexes is largely *temperamental*. He asserts that the female mind is unrivaled
"in powers adapted to unbend the brow of the learned, to refresh the overla-
boured faculties of the wise, and to diffuse throughout the family circle the
enlivening smile of cheerfulness. . . ."[7] According to the new ideology,
women exist to contribute to the welfare of the household as daughters,
wives, and mothers—but not, as in the past, by performing or supervising

complex domestic tasks. Gisborne's assertion of woman's function is typical in its emphasis on how women can bolster the egos of others. Divested of their traditional domestic responsibilities, women of means were offered an important new role in the family, one for which, it was felt, they were uniquely fitted.

Moreover, the Evangelical movement for regeneration of the Church of England which emerged at the end of the eighteenth century emphasized that women were moral beings responsible for themselves and to society. The religious reformers were middle-class moralists, and in the 1790s they argued that aristocratic views regarding women had had a corrupting effect on the social order. Dr. Gisborne, an Evangelical clergyman, insisted that women were made for God's purposes, not man's, and chastised, for example, Dr. Gregory for advising women to dissimulate to please the men in their lives. Hannah More similarly rejected the idea that women were made for men's pleasure, arguing that through stringent self-control women could develop their moral and intellectual powers, thus attaining power in society through moral influence.[8] Women writers responded favorably to these ideas.

Both novel and conduct book contributed to the codification of a distinct notion of female character. The model that emerged was made up of ideals which had long been part of the culture, but in earlier epochs other, even contradictory concepts of femininity had also held currency (misogynistic charges in earlier periods had often focused on woman's desire for domination as well as her excessive sexual appetites). In the eighteenth century, the female *role* became a subject involving much controversy. There was considerable debate on the amount of learning a woman could absorb without becoming "masculine" as well as disagreement on just what subjects of study were suited to the feminine mind. People argued about the place of the "accomplishments" (fine needlework, drawing, singing, the ability to converse in French, and so forth) in a woman's education, they debated endlessly over the potential conflict between filial obedience and a woman's right to marry for love, and they took diverse positions on whether it was appropriate for women to develop a knowledge of or interest in politics. Some thinkers even argued the necessity for women of gentle backgrounds to develop an art or profession lest they ever need to support themselves, and there was criticism of the existing marriage laws and of woman's legal status.[9] In spite of the various positions taken on these topics, positions which reflected deeply divergent philosophical assumptions, there developed a striking degree of consensus on what constituted the female character. According to the ideology which crystallized in the last part of the eighteenth century, women are characterized by such qualities as meekness, submissiveness, chastity, modesty, physical frailty, reserve, delicacy, affection, gentleness, and sympathy. Innately religious, they are emotional, self-abnegating, and have a unique capacity for self-control and self-knowledge, qualities which give them a quiet strength.

The only novelists and thinkers who dissent are those who belong firmly in the romantic-revolutionary tradition. Jacobin novelists like Mary Wollstonecraft (*Mary, A Fiction*, 1788; *The Wrongs of Women*, 1798) and Mary Hays (*Memoirs of Emma Courtney*, 1802) do not assume any natural reserve, delicacy, modesty, or timidity on the part of their heroines, nor do they see the lack of such qualities as the cause of their sad fates. Such books were few in number and were quickly met by a tide of "antiphilosophic" novels such as Elizabeth Hamilton's satiric *Memoirs of Modern Philosophers* (1800), especially after the anti-Jacobin reaction in England which followed upon the Terror and the rise of Napoleonism. The female character undeniably remained triumphant, even in the works of novelists who were on the *fringe* of the revolutionary circle, "liberals" such as Charlotte Smith, Mrs. Inchbald, and Mary Robinson.

It is in their novels, perhaps more than in any others, that we can clearly see the hold the new ideology of femininity had come to have on the imagination of England. Charlotte Smith, who in *Desmond* (1792) could argue strenuously for the right of women to an interest in politics, express resentment at the contempt in which men held women's minds, and point out the oppression of the marriage laws, nevertheless portrays Geraldine, the model of female perfection in the book, as first and foremost a dutiful wife and daughter (to a selfish mother and a vicious, dissipated husband), and a very loving mother. She even nurses her children—at a time when most babies were sent out to wet nurses. Her unhappy marriage makes her pale and languid, but she remains "compassionate," "modest," "tender," and "sweet." The adjectives are significant because they are part of the diction of the ideology of womanhood.

In *A Simple Story* (1791), Mrs. Inchbald shows us the sad fate of the basically good, but improperly educated, Miss Milner, whose vivacity and propensity for repartee are symptoms of the fact that her training as a woman did not include the inculcation of the principles of proper female conduct. She lacks reserve, self-discipline, and (evidently) the proper delicacy, for when her husband is forced to be away for a prolonged period, she "giving way to that irritable disposition which she had so seldom governed, resolved, in spite of his injunctions, to divert the melancholy caused by his absence, by mixing in the gay circles of London." This leads to an affair and eventually to her death. Her daughter, Matilda, wins through to a happy ending because she, in contrast, is characterized "by the delicacy of her sex" and "the extreme tenderness of her heart."[10] Her upbringing secluded her from the glittering world of fashion, her education was carefully supervised, and as a result her character is marked only by physical weakness (she swoons several times), intense emotion, and strong filial piety. Matilda is a "courtesy-heroine," as Hemlow would say, in spite of the author's liberal sympathies and irregular life (Elizabeth Inchbald ran away from her family to become an actress, temporarily lived apart from her husband, and received the attentions of men as different as William Godwin and Dr. Gisborne!)[11]

Thus writers of varying life-styles and diverse opinions were generally quite sure about the nature of women—at least in their public writings. However, all the writers mentioned (with the exception of Dr. Gregory) do stress women's capacity for rational thought and sound understanding, urging their lady readers to read and study so as to be fit companions for men. Fordyce is typical of conduct book writers in that he does not want women to be "metaphysicians, historians, special philosophers or Learned Ladies of any kind," but recommends poetry, drama, biography and memoirs, books of voyages and travels, geography, and the more obvious aspects of astronomy. He acknowledges that "these require solidity of judgment," but believes "there are women in no way deficient in these qualities."[12] Almost all thinkers on the question of women's nature and role wished women to acquire some solid education and were critical of the shallow education girls were offered. Hannah More, certainly an ideologue of female character, argues adamantly against the memorization of trite aphorisms and clichés and against the emphasis on "accomplishments," urging that women be taught to cultivate their understandings.[13] Hannah More was also an opponent of excessive sensibility, a concern she shares with Thomas Gisborne, who devotes a large section of his *Inquiry into the Duties of the Female Sex* to this topic. Many novels deal with this theme. Jane Austen is not at all unique in creating intelligent women who take themselves and their responsibilities seriously, nor is she alone in satirizing women who are intellectually and morally shallow or victims of "sensibility."[14]

II

In Jane Austen's first three novels, conceived in her early twenties, we see an interest in the development of a female personality well-equipped to handle the domestic relationships which will be central to the heroine's role as a woman in society; her themes are not dissimilar to those explored by her sister novelists. Thus Marianne Dashwood must learn to control her excessive sensibility, Catherine Moreland must learn to view the world realistically rather than through a romantic filter, and Elizabeth must learn to restrain impulsive character judgments while Lydia provides a negative example of the dangers of giving in to unregulated passions.

Nevertheless, in the heroines of these early novels there is a unique disregard for the stereotyped pattern of feminine character. Certainly Elizabeth does not conform to Dr. Gregory's pronouncement that "one of the chief beauties of a female character is that modest reserve, that retiring delicacy, which avoids the public eye, and is disconcerted even at the gaze of admiration. . . ."[15] One thinks of Elizabeth self-confidently flirting with Wickham, coolly rejecting Mr. Collins, and courageously standing up to Lady Catherine de Bourgh, and it is quite clear she is not the kind of girl he has in mind. She completely lacks the timidity which the conduct book writer John Bennett feels "arises from the natural weakness and delicacy of your frame. . . ."[16] Furthermore, Elizabeth's most salient quality is her wit. Yet one finds Gregory and Fordyce both asserting that wit is a dangerous talent. Fordyce explains how the husband of a witty wife would feel: "He sought a soft friend, . . . he found a perpetual satirist or self-sufficient prattler." He describes his dislike of "her who has contracted a certain briskness of air and levity of deportment!"[17]—certainly an accurate description of Elizabeth! At least one contemporary reader of *Pride and Prejudice* actually voiced such objections. Mary Russell Mitford, novelist and essayist, comments in a letter written in 1814 that she finds a "want of elegance" in Jane Austen. Significantly, she mentions not having read *Mansfield Park*, but regrets that in *Pride and Prejudice* "so pert, so worldly a heroine" should be "the beloved of such a man as Darcy." She goes on to praise Austen, commenting, "she wants nothing but the beau-idéal of the female character to be a perfect novel-writer."[18]

Sense and Sensibility is in some ways even less concerned with conventional ideals of womanhood than *Pride and Prejudice*. In the latter novel we at least have Jane Bennet. She is the foil for Elizabeth's rejection of conventional feminine character. As we might expect, she is physically less robust, catching a severe cold after a ride in the rain, and compensating for Elizabeth's self-assertion by her own excessive sweet reserve (Mr. Darcy cannot tell that she loves Bingley), making up for Elizabeth's satiric bent by her gentle tenderheartedness. *Sense and Sensibility* shows a closer relation to the conduct book tradition by its more didactic polarization of contrasting personality types, but it offers no model of "ideal" femininity. Eleanor's virtues—common sense and sobriety—are asexual, and the heightened sensibility which endangers Marianne is just as much an aspect of her admirer, Willoughby.

In *Northanger Abbey* we have a heroine who as a girl was "fond of all boys' plays, and greatly preferred cricket . . . to dolls."[19] By the time we meet her she is concerned about propriety and a chief interest is the admiration of young men, but she remains healthy and adventurous, not afraid of taking a journey of seventy miles alone in a coach, only upset by its circumstances. She continues to be uninterested in domestic accomplishments to the exasperation of her mother. Catherine Moreland is certainly not the figure who steps delicately through the pages of the conduct books.

Fanny Price of *Mansfield Park* is Austen's first attempt to place at the center of a novel and render realistically a heroine modeled on the feminine ideal of her time. Jane Austen was in her late thirties when she wrote *Mansfield Park, Emma*, and *Persuasion*; she had been in her early twenties when she conceived her first three novels. Yet just before she began *Mansfield Park, Pride and Prejudice* was rewritten for publication, and in January 1813 Austen could say in a letter to Cassandra Austen, "I must confess she [Elizabeth] is as delightful a creature as ever appeared in print, and how I shall be able to tolerate those who do not like *her* at least I do not know."[20] Thus I am not claiming that Austen did an about-face in her views on women during the years in which she passed from youth to maturity. Just as we are encouraged to respect and admire the angelic Jane in *Pride and Prejudice*, the mature Austen still wants us to delight in Elizabeth's comparative freedom of personality at a time when she has come to see the feminine ideal as more important than she once did. The change is more a shift in priorities than a shift in values. Jane Bennet, the conventional feminine ideal, was largely exempted from the pervasive satire of *Pride and Prejudice*; only very occasionally does Elizabeth poke fun at her, and then the teasing, aimed at her inability to see any bad in people, is gentle and tinged with admiration.

The freedom from stereotype which we see in the protagonists of the earlier novels is primarily the result of Jane Austen's very serious concern for realism. The depiction of the ideal went against her deepest artistic instincts. Her remarks on the fiction of her time are often mocking in tone, yet it is clear she was very influenced by these novels, and the qualities which characterize their conventional heroines are never repudiated. What Austen did not like in the fiction of her predecessors and contemporaries is their departure from plausibility. In a letter to Cassandra written in October 1813 she mentions Mary Brunton's *Self-Control*, about an exemplary heroine for whom strength of character is self-restraint, commenting, "in spite of its being an excellently meant, elegantly written work," it was "without anything of Nature or probability in it."[21] She goes on to ridicule the fact that the heroine "is wafted down an American River" (evidently an

improbable episode), and in another letter threatens to improve on it by
sending her heroine across the Atlantic in the same way.[22] Even without
such adventures, depicting an ideal heroine obviously involved problems of
verisimilitude.

In a letter to her niece, Fanny Knight, written in 1817, Austen remarks,
"Pictures of perfection, as you know, make me sick and wicked," and in the
same letter she says about her own Anne Elliot, "You may perhaps like the
Heroine, as she is almost too good for me."[23] The advice she gives her niece,
Anna, who had taken to writing fiction, is all in favor of the realistic as a
mixture of the good and the bad. "Cecilia continues to be interesting in
spite of her being so amiable. . . . I like the beginning of D. Forester very
much—a great deal better than if he had been very good or very bad." And
a few months later: "In some former parts Cecilia is perhaps a little too
solemn and good. . . ."[24] The interesting thing about this advice is that it
was given in 1814, just after Jane Austen had completed *Mansfield Park*
and the solemn and good Fanny Price was about to appear before the
world. It also happens that Fanny is the only heroine about whom Jane
Austen's extant letters reveal no remarks. All this leads me to feel that her
creation was a literary and moral exercise, a first attempt to resolve the
conflict which existed between her artistic principles and the increasing
seriousness with which she had come to view the feminine ideal of her day.

In the years which intervened between her two periods of high creativity,
the mood of England had grown more conservative. The spread of the
Evangelical movement certainly contributed to the sobriety of the climate
and may have stimulated in Jane Austen more concern for the family and
woman's role in society. The seriousness with which she views the clerical
role in *Mansfield Park* suggests that she was responsive to at least some of
the concerns of Evangelicalism. Whatever the reasons, she evidently came
to place more value on conventional womanliness. *Mansfield Park* rings
with the diction of the conduct books and "courtesy novels." Fanny is described as "well-principled and religious," possessing "true generosity and
natural delicacy," and "sensibility which beautified her complexion and
illumined her countenance . . ." (p. 235). Mention is made of the "gentleness, modesty and sweetness of her character," her "diffidence, gratitude
and softness." We hear of her "timid nature," and observe her love of being
silent in company, most evident at the Grants' dinner party when she is so
pleased at "the happy flow of conversation prevailing in which she was not
required to take any part" thus leaving her "the fairest prospect of only
having to listen in quiet, and of passing a very agreeable day" (p. 223). A
reader familiar with Dr. Gregory would immediately think of his dictum:

"this modesty will naturally dispose you to be rather silent in company, especially in a large one,"[25] and of Fordyce, to whom "boundless loquacity is disgusting in a woman."[26]

We see the beginnings of the nineteenth-century apotheosis of women as the nobler half of humanity, whose function was to elevate men's sentiments and inspire their higher impulses. Edmund is convinced that Fanny will be the making of Henry Crawford. "A most fortunate man he is to attach himself to such a creature—to a woman, who, firm as a rock in her own principles, has a gentleness of character so well adapted to recommend them. He has chosen his partner, indeed with rare felicity. He will make you happy Fanny, I know he will make you happy; but you will make him everything" (p. 351). Henry agrees, saying to Fanny, "You are definitely my superior in merit. . . . You have some touches of the angel in you. . . ." In this vein, Gisborne asserts that the female character can have important effects on society by, among other things, "forming and improving the general manners, dispositions and conduct of the other sex, by society and example."[27]

Edmund sees Fanny as an ideal woman and says: "You have proved yourself upright and disinterested, prove yourself grateful and tender-hearted; and then you will be the perfect model of a woman, which I have always believed you born for" (p. 347). According to the ideologues of female character, firm principles are as important as generosity of heart so Fanny must walk a delicate tightrope in situations where these two poles of femininity might conflict. Henry Crawford is not all he should be, morally speaking—Fanny's soft heart belongs to another—yet her constancy to Edmund and to her principles must not under any circumstances look like an unyielding hardness. Fordyce puts it well, recommending "fortitude where virtue, duty and reputation are concerned," but in other areas, "a timidity peculiar to your sex; and also a degree of complacence, yielding and sweetness."[28] And so Fanny is adamant about not acting in the Mansfield theatricals (an important moral issue in the novel, and the issue upon which Fanny shows herself to have the most reliable moral sensibility of anyone) yet yielding enough to help in any other way she can with the production, and possibly not strong enough to keep resisting their entreaties were it not for Sir Thomas's timely return. When she helps Mary with her part by reading Edmund's lines, we are told that her rendition of Anhalt is inadequate for all her efforts because of her "looks and voice so *truly feminine* [emphasis added], as to be no very good picture of man" (p. 169); such overt attention is frequently drawn to Fanny's femininity.

Again, she is firm enough in her refusal of Henry Crawford to resist the persuasive powers of Sir Thomas Bertram, for whom she feels the utmost gratitude and filial devotion. Nevertheless Jane Austen goes out of her way to tell us that

> her influence over him [Henry] had already given him some influence over her. Would he have deserved more, there can be no doubt that more would have been obtained. . . . Would he have persevered, and uprightly, Fanny must have been his reward, and a reward very voluntarily bestowed, within a reasonable period from Edmund's marrying Mary. (p. 467)

This passage makes clear that Fanny's true sphere, for all her love of books, for all her strength of character, is the area of the heart—that which is dominated by "sympathizing sensibility, warmth and tenderness . . . the glory of the female sex."[29]

We see Fanny constantly giving of herself, sacrificing out of the generosity of her heart, even to hateful Aunt Norris, the person responsible for most of her misery at Mansfield Park. "Fanny's disposition was such that she could never even think of Aunt Norris in the meagerness and cheerlessness of her own small house, without reproaching herself for some little want of attention to her when they had last been together . . . ; (p. 282). When Fanny is invited to dinner at the Grants' (her first invitation anywhere), Aunt Bertram's initial instinct is that she cannot spare her for the evening. Our heroine responds, "in a self-denying tone—'If you cannot do without me, ma'am' " (p. 217). When Mary Crawford goes out riding with Edmund on Fanny's horse and they forget to return on time, thus interfering with exercise necessary for Fanny's health, the self-effacing girl thinks "it rather hard on the mare to have such double duty; if she were forgotten the poor mare should be remembered" (p. 68). This type of response does much today to make Fanny Price Jane Austen's most unpopular heroine. Jane Austen is not entirely successful in her first attempt to bring to life a protagonist who embodies the conviction that personality is best realized through adherence to one's social role.

In *Mansfield Park* Austen uses the acting of dramatic roles as a metaphor that suggests the dangerous pressures of the modern world which subvert the coherent personality grounded in deeply internalized moral values. On the literal level, Austen may also have felt that such entertainment was not good for young people, in spite of the fact that amateur home theatricals were a popular form of amusement in her family when she was a girl. Thomas Gisborne, whose book Jane Austen praised and with whom she often seems to agree, warns that the tendency of such amusement is "to encourage vanity; to excite a thirst of applause and admiration . . . to destroy diffidence, by the unrestrained familiarity with persons of the other sex, which inevitably results from being joined with them in drama. . . ."[30] The elopements of Julia and Maria may indicate that Austen shared Gisborne's fears, but more importantly playacting must be dangerous in this novel because Jane Austen is here concerned with the modern problem of identity, the difficulty of creating and maintaining a coherent self. Clearly, Jane Austen is rejecting the Romantic notion that the self can come to a full realization of itself through experiments in different roles.[31] It is also relevant to consider the nature of *Lovers' Vows*, the play the young people choose to perform at Mansfield. It is Continental political radicalism expressed in the conventions of sentimental comedy; the aristocracy as a class is denounced as villainous, and in general the play reflects the fact that Mrs. Inchbald, while not a Jacobin, has been influenced by the ideals of the French Revolution. The play reveals her belief in the natural goodness of the individual which can emerge only when he or she is freed from despotic institutions.[32] The fact that this play is at the center of the playacting episode is evidence of Austen's hostility to the tradition of eighteenth-century rebellion against established values. *Mansfield Park* is about the importance of rejecting such currents in contemporary thought which would encourage the individual to pursue fulfillment at the expense of fidelity to social roles.

Henry and Mary Crawford, sophisticated, urban people, approach the question of identity by taking on many different masks. Lacking any core of values, they act and think one way in London, another in the country; of course by rejecting steady principles they are in fact importing London ideas to Mansfield Park. Their values are no more stable than their places of residence—and they like it that way: "To anything like permanence of abode, or limitation of society, Henry Crawford, had, unluckily, a great dislike . . ." (p. 41). An early conversation between Mary and Edmund shows the relationship between this fluid superficiality of values and the question of feminine personality. They are discussing the issue of proper female behavior before and after "coming out" into the social world (a standard topic of the conduct books and "courtesy novels"). Mary has been unable to determine Fanny's status, confused by her reticence, and says:

'Girls should be quiet and modest. The most objectionable part is that the alteration of manners on being introduced into company is frequently too sudden. They sometimes pass in such very little time from reserve to quite the opposite—to confidence!'

Edmund replies,

'The error is plain enough . . . such girls are ill brought up. They are given wrong notions from the beginning. They are always acting upon motives of vanity—and there is no more real modesty in their behavior before they appear in public than afterwards.'

'I do not know,' replies Miss Crawford, hesitatingly. (pp. 49–50)

Mary is incapable of grasping Edmund's concern for "real modesty." For her, manners are more important than morals—in fact, morals, as such, do not exist except in relation to what is expected in the society in which she finds herself. When Maria Bertram ultimately elopes with her brother, Mary cannot understand Edmund's horror; she can only talk about saving appearances. It is precisely this vacuum in regard to values, afflicting most acutely fashionable young people like the Crawfords, which Jane West, in *Letters Addressed to a Young Man*, explains provides the need for books like her own.[33]

The reactions of both Henry and Mary to Edmund's choice of the clerical profession are significant in relation to these questions of unified identity and internalized principles. In *Mansfield Park* ordination becomes a symbol of commitment to a life role. Mary is surprised that Edmund takes his profession seriously; he intends to be true to its essence, really serving his parishioners to the best of his ability, not merely wearing the title and collecting the living. Henry acknowledges that while he might *occasionally* play the role of clergyman, delivering a sermon to an admiring congregation, he "should not like to engage in the duties of a clergyman always for a constancy" (p. 343).

Jane Austen is here making a distinction between two kinds of role playing: the acting of multiple temporary roles at which Henry is so good, and the real, permanent commitment to a role which is then absorbed into the deepest reaches of the personality. Edmund's choice of the clerical role is of the latter type—and so is Fanny's total acceptance of the female character. The novel seems to suggest that by 1811 the bounds of conventional femininity did not seem needlessly restrictive to Jane Austen. *Mansfield Park* seeks to demonstrate that freedom and self-definition can only come about through self-limitation.

Jane Austen's next novel, *Emma*, contrary to wide belief, does not show a return to the relatively iconoclastic position on female identity seen in *Pride and Prejudice*. Emma has been compared by Frank Bradbrook to both Miss Milner of Inchbald's *A Simple Story* and Charlotte Smith's Isabella from *The Old Manor House*. To Bradbrook, "all three heroines reflect changes in ideas on women's role in society"; he is struck by their wit, confidence, and independence and even goes to the extreme of seeing them as examples of "the New Woman." He quotes from *A Simple Story*: "Miss Milner thought that 'as a woman she was privileged to say anything she pleased; and as a beautiful woman, she had a right to expect that whatever she pleased to say should be admired' " and adds "This is Emma's attitude too."[34] Bradbrook is right in seeing a resemblance in these three characters, but he fails to perceive that this attitude is a severe *defect* in both Miss Milner and Emma. Miss Milner's boldness leads to her disgrace and death, and Austen, less melodramatically, shows us that Emma's inclination to say whatever she pleased permits her to make the thoughtless and hurtful remark to Miss Bates which shocks her into a reassessment of the moral direction in which she has been drifting. Less attention is directed to the moral regeneration of Isabella, Charlotte Smith's heroine, but when she appears in a second novel, *The Wanderings of Warwick*, she is no longer spirited and thoughtlessly vivacious; she has become meek, loving, dutiful, and devoted to the man of her choice.

In *Emma* Austen has produced the alternative type of "courtesy novel," a variation on the genre which was also popular. Fanny Burney's Camilla, in the novel by that name, must undergo a painful re-education under the guidance of her male mentor and come to understand her errors before she is allowed a happy ending. Similarly, Emma is a seriously flawed heroine who must be educated toward true womanhood. Because Austen is a convincing realist, Emma, of course, actually learns far more from experience than from her mentor, Mr. Knightley, although he is proven right in everything.

Emma asserts that she does not ever wish to marry; clearly she is a woman who is strongly attracted to autonomy. She makes a great deal of trouble for herself and others because she wishes to control other people through the power of her will. Emma is one of those managing women men still make jokes about. She tries to claim credit for Mrs. Weston's marriage, she makes up absurd daydreams about Jane Fairfax, and she almost manipulates Harriet into a tragedy.

Emma is a woman of tremendous energy and talent with no healthy outlet for her abilities. She indulges in fantasy about other people and tries to impose her fictions on life for lack of anything better to do. Her yearning for activity is obvious. "Harriet would be loved as one to whom she could be useful. For Mrs. Weston there was nothing to be done; for Harriet everything" (p. 27). As indicated above, in courtesy novels of this "corrective" type the flawed heroine is provided with a mentor; Emma has Mr. Knightley to point out her errors. With his aid Emma must learn to fill her life with the duties of her sex and social position, and this means accepting her limitations, and subordinating her will, in order to achieve the best possible happiness a woman can hope for, as a good wife to a good man.

A conversation between Mr. Knightley and Mrs. Weston makes clear this necessity for women to submit. Mr. Knightley says:

> 'And ever since she was twelve Emma has been mistress of the house and of you all. In her mother she lost the only person able to cope with her. She inherited her mother's talents and must have been under subjection to her.'

He goes on to tease Emma's former governess:

> 'You were preparing yourself to be an excellent wife all the time you were at Hartfield. You might not give Emma such a complete education as your powers seem to promise; but you were receiving a very good education from her, on the very material matrimonial point of submitting your own will, and doing as you were bid. . . .' (pp. 37–38)

And so Emma must learn, in the course of the novel, how to be a good wife. Emma accepts her humiliation and is grateful for Mr. Knightley's wisdom. She does not sacrifice her vivacity and energy, but they become subordinated to the conventional social identity which she chooses by choosing Mr. Knightley. The distance between *Emma* and *Pride and Prejudice* is noteworthy: Elizabeth never effaces her will. She will learn from Darcy, but he in turn will learn from her how to laugh and live more flexibly; each will, to some extent, remake the other in his/her image. *Emma* suggests that by 1817 Jane Austen had learned how difficult such mutuality really is. More significantly, however, Austen has come to see as dangerous an individual's inclination to make private judgments of reality. Emma's private judgments are always distortions. Although Jane Austen's continuing understanding of the friction that *must* exist between the individual's needs and society's expectations lifts her art way above didacticism and mere conventionality, ultimately her concept of society in her later novels depends on the assumption that its members best realize their individuality through their social roles.

In her last novel, *Persuasion*, Jane Austen tries again to put a womanly woman at the center of her novel. Anne is modest, generous, submissive, sympathetic and self-denying, and she possesses moral sensitivity. She is even rather frail physically, easily fatigued, and past her first bloom. The tension that exists between her personal emotional needs and the demands made upon her by her acceptance of her social role is at the heart of the novel, and in spite of eight years of unhappiness, Anne makes it perfectly clear at the end that she in no way regrets her initial decision to reject her lover out of "filial" obedience. Wentworth's mature love for Anne has more depth than his youthful passion because it is now based on an understanding of the truly feminine nature of her strength of mind. Wentworth declares at the end of the novel that Anne's character is "perfection itself, maintaining the loveliest medium of fortitude and gentleness." He comes to realize that strength of mind can consist not in "self-will," but in "steadiness of principle" (p. 24).

The reconciliation of the real and the ideal in the character of Anne constituted a major artistic accomplishment for Jane Austen. Jane Bennet, Austen's one attempt at embodying conventional qualities of female character during her first creative period, is a lifeless paragon. Like the heroines of most of the conduct novels, Jane Bennet simply is the way she is by virtue of authorial fiat. In contrast, Fanny Price's personality, while problematical in important ways, is grounded in social facts.

In *Mansfield Park* Austen gives the so-called female character a realistic basis by showing that rather than being a biologically innate aspect of woman's nature, such qualities as gentleness, meekness, delicacy, and physical frailty are dependent on certain material conditions. Fanny Price discovers on going to Portsmouth that her mother is slatternly, vulgar, fretful, and unloving. Austen makes it clear that this is the result of too many children and too little money. In affluence, we are told, her nature might still be "easy and indolent," but "she might have made just as good a woman of consequence as Lady Bertram." Susan, Fanny's sister, must be taken out of the Portsmouth environment. Jane Austen has no doubt that her loud voice will soften when efficient servants make it unnecessary to shout. She will have no temptation to lose her "imperfect temper" when she is not surrounded by dirt, noise, and squalling children.

Austen does not have Susan take on Fanny's personality once she is at Mansfield Park: she does not become timid, highly sensitive, and extremely sweet. These are not the qualities of all women. Yet Susan too becomes a satisfactory companion for Lady Bertram. The two sisters are not alike in disposition, but they become more alike when living under the same conditions. Jane Austen sees that women who share the same objective social reality will have certain things in common because personalities adapt to circumstances. Fanny Price can be a companion to Lady Bertram because of her "sweetness of temper and strong feelings of gratitude," but Susan will function well in the same role because of "a readiness of mind and inclination for usefulness." They are different people, but shared circumstances bring out in both submission, gentleness, and self-denial.

One believes in Fanny Price far more than in Hannah More's Lucilla or Maria Edgeworth's Belinda. Fanny's submissiveness is motivated by the fact that she is a kind of Cinderella, brought up at Mansfield Park to remember that she is "the lowest and the last." Her behavior and her feelings when she visits her squalid home at Portsmouth are particularly believable. Nevertheless Fanny Price is seriously flawed as a character. Rather than creating a realistic model of ideal womanhood, Jane Austen creates a young woman who emerges as somewhat believable but whose self-abnegation appears neurotically excessive and whose holier-than-thou attitude is unpalatable. Yet Austen wants us to like and admire Fanny, her values and her personality: Fanny embodies the self-limitation the novel is about.

Perhaps because Austen did not entirely resolve the conflict between her realism and her commitment to the feminine ideal in *Mansfield Park*, in *Emma* she partially retreats from the problem of rendering a "perfect" heroine realistically by approaching the ideal of womanhood instead from the direction of correcting a central character who is imperfect, as discussed above. She goes back to the pattern she had used successfully in *Pride and Prejudice*: the embodiment of female character, Jane Fairfax, is kept in a minor role. But now she supplies motivation for Jane Fairfax's feminine personality, an indication that in *Emma* the author is again trying to deal seriously with the problem of how to depict such a woman. Jane Fairfax is pallid of complexion, given to headaches and poor appetite. Reserved and gentle, she is close to the conduct book stereotype (despite certain defects, primarily aloofness and the willingness to keep her engagement secret), but she is quiet and unassertive essentially for the same reasons Fanny is; she has always been in an inferior role socially, grateful for any recognition.

Anne Elliot of *Persuasion* also lacks a strong social position. Although the daughter of a baronet, she is not loved by him nor by his favorite, her elder sister, and she suffers from the liability of being twenty-seven and unmarried. When we meet her she is regarded as being "over the hill" from the perspective of the marriage market and has been relegated to the role of spinster aunt by her family and friends. In addition, her spirits have been quenched by the loss of her youthful love. Thus Jane Austen provides realistic motivation for yet another womanly woman, and this time she tries once more to put her at the center of the novel.

It is instructive to compare Fanny and Anne. In a sense Anne is even more conventionally feminine. Certainly she is more yielding. The effect is not didactic, however, in part because Austen softens a major convention of the "courtesy novel": the use of foils by which good behavior is made to stand out by proximity to the excesses and defects of negative deportment.[35] In *Mansfield Park* all the other young women are in deliberate negative contrast to Fanny. Maria and Julia Bertram lack her natural delicacy, her ability to accept restraints; they are the victims of an education that has stressed "the accomplishments" while she has learned solid virtues from experience. Mary Crawford is explicitly compared to her again and again by Edmund who keeps insisting they are alike as it becomes more and more apparent to the reader that they are not. The three other young women in the novel, then, are as bad and "modern" as Fanny is good and "traditional." On the other hand, in *Persuasion*, Louisa and Henrietta Musgrove have nothing pernicious about them. They lack Anne's depth of character, and Louisa is rather silly to go fall on her head at Lyme, but they are nice enough girls. Of course Elizabeth Elliot and sister Mary are negative characters, but they are presented so one-dimensionally that we never have to take them seriously at all.

Most important, Jane Austen does not allow Anne to get carried away with goodness. Kind and compassionate as she is to her little nephew and her sick friend, Mrs. Smith, and patient as she is with her hypochondriacal and selfish sister, Mary, she is not a martyr. We do not have to endure any longings to do good to her nasty father and sister Elizabeth; they are mean to her and she wishes not to be with them. Anne does not make moral judgments about others unless she is forced to in order to assess the kind of relationship she should have with them (as, for example, Mr. Elliot, her suitor). Fanny, in contrast, is given to correcting the behavior of others, such as her sister Susan, and expressing outrage at subtle abridgements of her code, such as Mary's open criticism of the uncle with whom she had lived. Anne does not counsel anyone to follow her model of submission and forbearance; she simply is the feminine ideal without fanfare. We are open to her gentle passivity because it is in tune with the mellow, autumnal tone of the novel.

We *see* her offering sympathetic understanding to Captain Benwick and others; we are not told again and again by the narrator and admiring characters that she possesses these qualities. Jane Austen's biggest mistake with Fanny is to constantly tell us what she is—her attributes are mentioned ad nauseum. I suspect this is because the author is unsure of herself in this first attempt to focus on an ideal heroine; Fanny does not really *live* in her imagination. The author, self-conscious about breaking away from her previous, more individual style of characterization, is too aware of her experiment and falls into didacticism. But Jane Austen does finally succeed in *Persuasion* in creating a thoroughly credible heroine who is both attractive as a personality and yet totally conventional in her femininity. She renders an ideal heroine satisfyingly because she provides solid motivation for Anne's characteristics in her personal history, rejects the convention of crudely contrasting good and bad types, emphasizes dramatization over exposition, and shows that she understands how circumstances form feminine character. Anne Elliot explains the womanly virtue of constancy in

love: " 'We live at home, quiet, confined and our feelings prey on us' "
(p. 232).

The solution that Jane Austen found to the problem of working within a
novelistic tradition which has at its heart a universal of female character is
an impressive technical achievement. However, it was not available to writers of the nineteenth century who also had to come to terms with literary
conventions and social stereotypes of women which continued to dominate
the social imagination, perhaps even more totally. For Jane Austen, role
and personality can cohere without necessarily doing violence to verisimilitude or depth of characterization because, for her, external reality—the
reality of society—does not conflict with the reality of inner personality.
Anne Elliot's identity *is* defined by her rank and sex and the duties these
two social facts entail. One feels that she has chosen to shoulder the responsibilities of her role, and this conscious awareness of what it means to accept a "woman's portion," expressed so movingly in the conversation with
Captain Harville at the end of the novel, gives her great dignity. Characters
who are less true to the dictates of the female role in its ideal form are not
more "free." They are either selfish, weak, or foolish; or, like Mary Crawford, they became subject to the buffeting of the various winds rather than
being faithful to the promptings of the inner truth of, say, a Jane Eyre. In
short, in Jane Austen psychological reality is limited to the rational, the
social. To probe into psychic recesses is necessarily to render false any universal model of feminine virtue. Thackeray may regard Amelia Sedley as "a
dear little soul," but he understands that she is a "tender little parasite"
(*Vanity Fair*, chapter 67), that abysses of selfishness lie under her sweetness
and passivity. For a later writer not to probe into the hidden recesses of the
mind results in the creation of a character who, like Mrs. Gaskell's Molly
Gibson in *Wives and Daughters* (1866), may be credible but is inevitably
very naive and childlike. Molly Gibson, probably the most realistic of later
nineteenth-century "angels," seems to be unaware of something she should
be conscious of if we are to regard her with respect: the possibility of an
independent inner life (Thackeray does not expect us to respect Amelia).
Thus the continuing existence of the ideology of femininity created a more
complex artistic problem for writers after Jane Austen. Later writers, especially women who had been brought up themselves in the ideals of female
character, who felt themselves part of the feminine fictional tradition I have
been exploring, and who wished to put an interesting heroine at the center
of their novels, had to work out new modes of coping with the problem: the
conventional ideal could not simply be made real in a world where the split
between private and public reality was a major fact of consciousness.

NOTES

1. Kingsley Amis, "What Became of Jane Austen?" in *Jane Austen: A Collection of Critical Essays*, ed. Ian Watt (Englewood Cliffs, N.J.: Prentice-Hall, 1963), 144.

2. Tony Tanner, Introduction to *Mansfield Park*, Penguin Edition, 8. Tanner argues that the qualities Fanny embodies—stillness and selflessness—are the basic values of the novel. Lionel Trilling, in his essay on *Mansfield Park*, points out that Fanny's combination of physical weakness and moral strength is in the tradition of the Christian heroine, as in *Clarissa* or *Wings of the Dove*. "The tradition which affirmed the peculiar sanctity of the sick, the weak, and the dying." (Trilling's essay appears in the collection edited by Watt cited above.) Both explanations are no doubt true but do not adequately explain the character of Fanny Price.

3. For example, Mrs. Griffith wrote *The History of Lady Juliana Harbly* and Jane Austen wrote *The Advantages of Education, or the History of Maria Williams* and *A Gossip's Story*: Maria Edgeworth, of course, wrote many novels and "moral tales."

4. Joyce Hemlow, "Fanny Burney and the Courtesy Books," *PMLA* 65 (1950): 732, 756−57. Hemlow does not mention Jane Austen as part of the courtesy novel tradition, and, although she defines the subgenre, she does not discuss any specific examples except the novels of Fanny Burney.

5. See Frank Bradbrook, *Jane Austen and Her Predecessors* (Cambridge: University Press, 1966); and Lloyd Brown, "Jane Austen and the Feminist Tradition," *Nineteenth-Century Fiction* 27(December 1973):321−28.

6. Watt makes this claim; see *The Rise of the Novel* (Berkeley: University of California Press, 1962), 44.

7. Thomas Gisborne, *An Inquiry Into the Duties of the Female Sex* (London: reprint, Philadelphia: J. Humphreys, 1798), 11.

8. Nancy Cott, "Passionlessness: An Interpretation of Victorian Sexual Ideology, 1790−1850," in *A Heritage of Her Own*, ed. Nancy F. Cott and Elizabeth H. Pleck (New York: Simon & Schuster, 1979), 166−67.

9. See A. R. Humphreys, "The 'Rights of Women' in the Age of Reason," *Modern Language Review* 41 (July 1946):256−69.

10. Elizabeth Inchbald, *A Simple Story and Nature and Art* (London: Thomas de la Rue & Co., 1880), 212, 241.

11. W. B. Scott, *Introduction to A Simple Story and Nature and Art*, xxvi.

12. James Fordyce, *Sermons to Young Women* (London: T. Cadell, 1792), 273.

13. Hannah More, *Strictures on the Modern System of Female Education*, vol. 1 of *Works*, (New York: Harper's, 1825), chap. 14. The theme is also taken up by Elizabeth Hamilton in *Popular Essays* (1812), in Gisborne's *Inquiry*, and in a review of a conduct book by Thomas Broadhurst which appeared in the *Edinburgh Review* 15 (1809−1810):306.

14. Lloyd Brown, in a article on Jane Austen and feminism, goes astray in see-

ing Jane Austen as an anomaly of her epoch, concealing within her decorums a
rejection of conventional attitudes and a subtle sympathy for the Jacobin fringe (see
Brown, "Jane Austen and the Feminist Tradition").

15. Ibid., 16.

16. John Bennett, *Letters to a Young Lady* (New York: Printed by John Buel
for E. Duyckinck & Co., 1796), 1:7.

17. Fordyce, *Sermons to Young Women*, 193.

18. Mary Russell Mitford to Sir William Elford, 20 December 1814, in *Jane
Austen: The Critical Heritage*, ed. B. C. Southam (London: Routledge & Kegan
Paul; New York: Barnes & Noble, 1868), 54.

19. Jane Austen, *Northanger Abbey*, 13. All quotes from Jane Austen's novels
will be from *The Novels of Jane Austen*, ed. R. W. Chapman (London: Oxford
University Press, 1948–1954, vol. 1, 1953).

20. Jane Austen to Cassandra Austen, 29 January 1813, in *Jane Austen's Letters;* ed. R. W. Chapman (Oxford: Clarendon Press, 1932), 297. All further references to Austen's letters will be to this edition.

21. Austen to Cassandra Austen, 11 October 1813, 344.

22. Austen to Anna Lefroy, November or December 1814(?), lx, 423.

23. Austen to Fanny Knight, 23 March 1817, 436–37.

24. Austen to Anna Austen, May or June 1814, 387. Ibid, 9 September 1814,
402.

25. Gregory, *A Father's Legacy to His Daughters* (1774), 16.

26. Fordyce, *Sermons to Young Women*, 197.

27. Gisborne, *Inquiry into the Duties of the Female Sex*, 9.

28. Fordyce, *Sermons to Young Women*, 223.

29. Gisborne, *Inquiry into the Duties of the Female Sex*, 16.

30. Ibid., 127–28; Austen praises his book in a letter dated 30 August 1805.
Gisborne was an evangelical clergyman, a member of the influential Clapham sect;
the fact that Austen read and liked him is, perhaps, further evidence that she was
influenced by the Evangelical movement.

31. Lionel Trilling in the essay on *Mansfield Park* cited earlier explains the
hostility to home theatricals in that novel in this light.

32. See Elizabeth Inchbald, *Lover's Vows* (London: Printed for G. G. & J.
Robinson, Paternoster Row, 1798).

33. Jane West, *Letters Addressed to a Young Man* (Charleston, Mass.: Printed
by Samuel Etheridge for Samuel H. Parker, 1803), viii–ix.

34. Frank U. Bradbrook, *Jane Austen and Her Predecessors* (Cambridge: University Press, 1966), 110.

35. Hemlow, "Fanny Burney and the Courtesy Books," 758.

Fanny Burney's "Feminism"
Gender or Genre?

MARTHA G. BROWN

Reading older literature with modern glasses is a pervasive tendency. In the nineteenth century, this approach resulted in a propensity to judge eighteenth-century poetry by Romantic standards and to find it wanting. The novel too, has suffered from this sort of self-congratulatory measurement in the twentieth century, in which the yardstick was Jamesian realism. In the past few years, a different manifestation of this approach has been gaining in popularity as critics sift through the fiction of the eighteenth- and nineteenth-century women novelists, looking for evidence of latent feminism. Recent interpretations of Fanny Burney's novels, in which feminist readings are becoming fashionable, reflect this tendency.[1] Critics point to the trials the heroine in each novel endures, including her loss of fortune, and to the marriage at the end as expressions, however repressed or even unconscious, of the frustrations and resentment Burney felt in her role as a woman in a male-dominated society. Each heroine does suffer a series of trials in which she falls prey to an assortment of villainous males who attack her virtue, her heart, or her purse; each novel is also concluded with a marriage. This is, however, a matter of genre, rather than gender, since these plot features, which some critics trace to feminism, are instead debts to the romance tradition, from which Burney drew heavily for plot, theme, and character.

All feminist readings of Burney's fiction center around one recurring theme—dependence. All stress three central plot features that these critics see as evidence that Burney visualized women as dependent—economically, physically, and psychologically—on men. The first of these arguments for Burney's feminism is that the heroine in each novel is denied her proper rank and fortune—at least until the end, a fact which they interpret as a feminist resentment of women's financial dependence on men. Rose Marie Cutting argues that "all are cut off from their rightful inheritance—a situa-

29

tion that serves as a good metaphor for the historic poverty and economic dependence of women."[2]

The first part of this statement is undeniably true. Evelina, the unacknowledged but legitimate daughter of a nobleman, has been abandoned by her father, a libertine who burned the marriage certificate. Aware of her questionable parentage, Evelina calls herself an "orphan," "motherless," and "worse than fatherless." Throughout the novel, as she is forced to live in the vulgar world of Madame Duval and her Branghton relatives, the possibility that she may be accepted by her true father seems remote, as Villars recognizes when he asks, "only child of a wealthy baronet, whose person she has never seen, whose character she has reason to abhor, and whose name she is forbidden to claim; entitled as she is to lawfully inherit his fortune and estate, is there any probability that he will properly own her?"[3]

Cecilia's situation also focuses on the question of inheritance. Orphaned young, she has been reared by an uncle whose recent death has left her alone except for three guardians. Unlike Evelina's, Cecilia's pedigree is public. Cecilia, however, is marked by a different stigma—the name clause, which requires her to retain her family name forever and her husband to relinquish his. Since the Delvilles' pride in their family name makes it impossible for them to approve their son Mortimer's taking Cecilia's maiden name of Beverly, this clause blocks the lovers' marriage. After an abortive first attempt at a secret marriage, they are finally married secretly, but with Mrs. Delville's approval. A condition of the marriage is, of course, that Cecilia must give up her fortune of £ 3,000 per year rather than Mortimer his name, making her "portionless, though an HEIRESS."[4]

In *Camilla*, the inheritance theme takes a different form. No mystery surrounds Camilla's birth; no clause blocks her inheritance, which is denied her instead through an even more bizarre circumstance. The daughter of a poor clergyman, she is heir to her uncle's estate until a series of accidents that leave her sister terribly crippled cause her uncle to make this unfortunate niece his heiress. Dependent on a small allowance from her father, Camilla, because of her own imprudence, is in economic distress throughout the novel, distress which is alleviated only through her union with the wealthy Edgar Mandlebert.

In *The Wanderer*, Burney returns to a more traditional use of the inheritance theme. Juliet's birth and identity are shrouded in mystery. The daughter of a nobleman by his first and secret marriage to a commoner, she has been reared in France by a bishop in an arrangement that stipulates that she inherit only if she remains in France, keeping her identity secret. Escaping a forced marriage, she comes to England where she is forced to conceal her name as she struggles to support herself in a series of demeaning occupations until she is acknowledged by her father and receives the standard reward—name, money, and a husband.

Although inheritance is an important focus in all four novels, the assertion that this "serves as a good metaphor for the historic poverty and economic dependency of women" is unconvincing. Fielding's Joseph Andrews and Tom Jones are both cut off from their rightful inheritance; so is Smollett's Humphrey Clinker. Are we, therefore, to assume that Fielding and Smollett meant this as a "metaphor" for men's "economic dependence"? Of course not. The inheritance theme in so many eighteenth-century novels is clearly traceable to the romance tradition, a tradition whose influence on the novel has recently been recognized by several critics.[5]

The typical romance plot, beginning with the Greek prose romances of Heliodorus, Longus, and Tatius, centers on an infant who is abandoned, or "exposed," by his parents, rescued and reared by a kindly shepherd. After the child reaches maturity, he falls in love, a romance that is blocked, often by the mystery surrounding the hero's birth. After a series of trials, the lovers are finally united when their true identities are revealed, their inheritance is restored, and they are married. Variations on this story have supplied the plot for prose and verse romances for many centuries; they continued to do so in the eighteenth-century novel.

In Burney's novels, as in romance in general, the denial of the hero's birthright has important implications for plot and theme. At the superficial level of plot, the hero's mysterious origin and lack of both rank and fortune make possible the adventures so necessary for romance. Evelina and Juliet are forced on their journeys or quests by the dubious circumstances of their birth and by their rights to inherit. The economic plights of all four heroines make them vulnerable, which is necessary to set them up for the trials and tests that they must endure. Mr. Villars says of Evelina's vulnerability, "The supposed obscurity of your birth and situation makes you liable to a thousand disagreeable adventures" (p. 116). The "disagreeable adventures" multiply in *The Wanderer*, where Juliet's namelessness and poverty subject her to humiliation and danger.

The disinheritance of the heroines also has important thematic implications, and these are moral and psychological, rather than economic. The quest for identity ending in the self-recognition so central in romance is really, as Northrop Frye suggests, "attaining one's original identity."[6] This attainment is especially apparent in *Evelina* and *The Wanderer*. Because Evelina has been stripped of her fortune and her name she must seek to discover who she is before she can claim her place in society. She must also seek to discover where and to whom she belongs. Her position makes her all *potentia*. Because she is nobody and belongs to nobody, she may be anybody and belong to anybody. Her quest for identity involves a series of moral tests and moral choices through which she proves herself worthy of the inheritance and name she has been denied. Juliet, too, must undertake such a quest in order to discover her proper identity and claim her fortune. Because her name and fortune have been denied her, she is forced to leave her home and is thrust into the world, nameless, friendless, and fortuneless, to undergo a bizarre series of trials, including the obligatory incest threat, which tests her prudence, courage, and virtue. Her well-deserved reward is the return of her rightful identity and fortune. Since Cecilia's paternity is not in question, the idea of inheritance becomes even more urgently connected with the theme of identity, which is underlined by the name clause. And when Camilla is stripped of her inheritance, confusion arises about which of the Tyrold daughters is the true heiress—a question that helps to reveal motive and character. A heroine who is secure in both her identity and her inheritance would simply not be an effective heroine of romance, where the quest is essential to both plot and meaning. Romance demands instead a heroine who is poised at the threshold of initiation into experience, who is ready to undergo the symbolic *rite de passage*, which involves testing and self-discovery. The lack of name and fortune are necessary plot devices embodying central thematic concerns.

And finally the economic distresses of all four heroines serve to reinforce not only the theme of identity, but also a second major theme—prudence. Characters in Burney's novels are judged by the way they handle their money as well as by the way they order their passions. Each learns in the course of the quest the financial prudence that will enable her to be a careful mistress of her fortune. Although this is not a pressing concern in *Evelina*, it becomes an increasingly urgent theme in each succeeding novel. Cecilia, who like her friend Mrs. Calton has a "generous foible," is seduced into supporting Mr. Harrel's decadent extravagance. By the end of her quest, however, "she had learnt the error of profusion, even in charity and beneficence" (2:471). Camilla's misguided generosity has even more dire consequences, resulting ultimately in her uncle's ruin and her father's imprisonment. And Juliet's lesson is hardest of all; she must learn not only to save money, but also to make it. It is not surprising to find the question of inheritance linked so closely with prudence since wealth or treasure as a symbol central to romance often, according to Frye, "means wealth in its ideal forms, power and wisdom."[7]

A second argument for Burney's feminism—closely related to the first— is that the heroines in the novels suffer abuse because they exist in a world where women are powerless and oppressed. Cutting sees the cruelty in Burney's novels "as a manifestation of feminine sensibility: she was, after all, describing a world in which women had little power."[8] It is true that each heroine suffers abuse at the hands of a malicious man. Evelina is at the mercy of her chief tormentor, Sir Clement Willoughby, throughout and occasionally falls prey to a cast of minor villains who accost her physically in the alleys of Vauxhall and Marylebone gardens. Cecilia is the victim of the machinations of an arch villain, Mr. Monckton; the greed of Mr. Harrel and Mr. Briggs; and the pride of Mr. Delville. In *Camilla*, the heroine's tormentors, Sir Sedley Clarendel and her own brother Lionel, are less wicked than the utterly vile Bellamy, who heartlessly tortures Eugenia. Because of her deformities, which are the result of her uncle's carelessness, Eugenia is constantly brutalized.

Feminist readings of the cruelty in Burney's novels have two main weaknesses. First, the heroines are victimized by women as often as by men. Evelina's wicked "stepmother," Madame Duval, uses and abuses her as often and as maliciously as Sir Clement. In *Cecilia*, each male tormentor has his female counterpart—Mr. Monckton's cruelty is rivaled by that of Mrs. Monckton, Mr. Delville's by that of Mrs. Delville, Mr. Harrel's by that of Mrs. Harrel. In *Camilla* Eugenia is frequently victmized by women, such as Indiana or the nameless country women, who taunt her about her dwarfed and crippled body. And finally, in *The Wanderer*, Juliet's nightmarish trials are caused largely by Mrs. Ireton, Mrs. Maple, Selina, and other vicious women.

If the malice is general, we must seek a source other than feminism; that source is the romance tradition, where the hero's mettle is tested by a series of trials. In the Greek romance, the heroine undergoes a bizzare series of adventures in which she is shipwrecked, kidnapped, tortured by pirates and savages—who are, by the way, males. Does this suggest that Heliodorus, Longus, and Tatius were avant-garde feminists? The idea is too absurd to entertain. But it is no more reasonable to attribute the trials of Burney's heroines to feminism when they are so clearly a feature of the genre in which she was working. As Frye explains, the quest in romance has three stages: "the stage of the perilous journey and the preliminary minor adventures, the crucial struggle . . . and the exaltation of the hero."[9] Burney's novels, all of which fall roughly into three parts analogous to these three stages, concern the "perilous journey" of the heroine. The "preliminary minor adventures" are typically social skirmishes, while the "crucial struggles" are moral and spiritual.

The quest is necessary for the heroine's moral growth because each is, at the beginning, virtuous but untried. All four heroines have been reared in seclusion and are of just that age when their innocence must be tested by experience. The theme of the initiation or *rite de passage* is implied in the title *Evelina; or, The History of a Young Lady's Entrance into the World,* and it is made explicit by the narrator who says in the first chapter of *Camilla*:

> The experience which teaches the lesson of truth, and the blessings of tranquillity, comes not in the shape of warning nor of wisdom; from such they turn aside, defying or disbelieving. 'Tis in the bitterness of personal proof alone, in suffering and in feeling, in erring and repenting, that experience comes home with conviction, or impresses to any use.[10]

Each heroine, then, must be thrust out of the rural world of innocence into the urban world of experience so that her virtue can be tried and perfected. On one level the tests involve manners, as the heroine is placed in social situations in which her choices are invested with symbolic and ritualistic significance. In speaking of the perilous journey of romance, Kathleen Williams says, "the hero's fate depends upon whether he takes a certain seat, asks or answers a certain question."[11]

On another level, the tests are moral. Basically virtuous, each heroine has only to add good judgment to a good heart. *Prudentia*, involving the ability to make moral choices leading to virtuous action, is what each heroine must acquire. And she can acquire this only through a series of tests in which her failure to judge well and to act wisely brings her perilously near disaster again and again. The more serious assaults on the heroine are a necessary part of the ritual initiation in which the quester must meet and slay the dragon. Frye explains that in romance, "the hero travels perilously through a dark labyrinthine underworld full of monsters" and that this often becomes "a structural principle of fiction."[12] In Burney's fiction the obligatory dragons and monsters of romance are transformed into a gallery of fops and rakes; the labyrinth becomes the dark alleys of Marylebone and Vauxhall.

The centrality of the quest to romance also provides the refutation for the third feminist argument, which is that the marriage at the end of each novel suggests a surrender to male power. Judith Newton calls Evelina's entrance into the world an "entrance into the marriage market" and argues that by marrying she abdicates adult responsibility and power.[13] Cutting asserts that "if a woman's whole life (and 'fortune') depend on pleasing and winning a man, then Camilla's story is also a fitting parable for the general fate of women."[14] And Patricia Meyer Spacks argues that in Burney novels, the heroine's " 'growth' leads her back toward childhood" and that "the 'happy endings' of Burney novels reassert the charm and irresponsibility of the child as the greatest achievement to be hoped for by adolescents."[15]

These are odd criticisms to make of Burney; indeed, they would be odd criticisms to make of any eighteenth-century novel, since, with the exception of *Clarissa*, all major novels of the period end in just this way—happily, and with marriage, or better yet, a set of marriages. In the romance tradition in all its different incarnations, including the eighteenth-century novel, marriage signifies in two essential ways. First of all, marriage and treasure are the two standard rewards awaiting the hero at the end of the successful quest. With the exception of Juliet, who is perfect from the beginning, each of the heroines is unfit at the onset of the quest to manage either marriage or money; these are rights that must be won. The marriage is also a way of placing the hero's individual moral maturation into a social and communal context, making it more symbolic than personal. As Henry Knight Miller suggests, "romance and comedy traditionally conclude with the celebration of a marriage, not because that marks the end but precisely because it celebrates a new beginning, the sacramental emblem of a new world of maturity and hope, the assertion of life and continuity as against the 'reality' of isolation and death."[16] Marriage, then, is not a matter of giving up, but of growing up.

And Burney is no more fettered by the tradition in which she was working than her heroines are fettered by the tradition of marriage that they all enter. In fact, working within a tradition is freeing for an artist in a very real sense. Because the romance tradition supplies plot and character types, Burney was freed from these decisions, which enabled her to concentrate on other narrative areas, such as dialogue and setting. Of course another way a writer may use tradition is to react against it openly or, more subtly, to turn it to his or her own purposes. So that if one accepts the contention that these plot features—the heroine's lack of her rightful rank and fortune, her trials, and finally her marriage—are drawn straight from romance, it is possible to argue that Burney took these stock features of romance and put them to feminist uses. There is, however, no evidence, at least in the first three novels, to support this; there is instead ample evidence to refute it.

In the first place, as I suggested earlier, the numbers of villainous men and women are roughly equivalent. The moral types, too, are as often men as women. Each heroine has her chivalrous knight to protect her. Evelina is guarded and guided by Orville, who is a paragon of courtesy and morality. Cecilia has Mortimer Delville, Camilla has Edgar Mandlebert, and Juliet has Harleigh—all of whom are versions of Orville. In addition, there are several wise, kindly, father figures—the Reverend Villars in *Evelina* and the Reverend Tyrold in *Camilla*—and a variety of decent men who befriend the heroines—Mr. Macartney in *Evelina*, Hal Westwyn in *Camilla*, Mr. Arnot in *Cecilia*, and Lord Melbury in *The Wanderer*.

In addition, in each novel, Burney creates one more-or-less liberated

lady and clearly disapproves of her. Mrs. Selwyn in *Evelina* is such a character. Although she serves the positive function of occasionally protecting
Evelina, she is too aggressively outspoken to suit Burney. Evelina says of
this intelligent, independent, and sharp-tongued woman, "her understanding, indeed, may be called *masculine*; but, unfortunately, her manners deserve the same epithet; for in studying to acquire the knowledge of the other
sex, she has lost all the softness of her own" (p. 269).

Lady Honoria in *Cecilia* is a free-spirited, strong-willed woman, whose
wit and charm are outweighed by the confusion and embarrassment she
causes. That Fanny Burney sternly disapproved of such behavior is amply
evident in her early diary where she writes of a Miss Allen, "she is too
sincere: she pays too little regard to the world; and indulges herself with too
much freedom of raillery and pride and disdain toward those whose vices
and follies offend her."[17]

In *Camilla*, Mrs. Arlery, who flaunts convention and is "guilty of no
vices, but utterly careless of appearances," has sullied her reputation by her
lack of prudent behavior (p. 194). Again the early diary evidences Burney's
distaste for this sort of behavior among women. Writing of a certain Miss
Bowdler who lives "exactly as she pleases" and scandalizes all by visiting
single men, Burney declares herself in agreement with Mr. Rishton, who
believes that a woman "who despises the customs and manners of the country she lives in must, consequently, conduct herself with impropriety." To
this Burney adds, "I can by no means approve so great a contempt of public
opinion."[18]

The most complex and interesting example of this type of "new woman"
is *The Wanderer*'s Elinor Joddrel, who is a spokeswoman for personal and
political freedom. An ardent admirer of the French Revolution, she declares, "I hold no one thing in the world worth living for but liberty!" But if
her love of freedom is attractive, it is also dangerous and destructive. The
narrator explains that what "was termed by Elinor the love of independence" is actually "the spirit of contradiction," and that although she has
"a solid goodness of heart," "quickness of parts," and "liberality of feeling,"
she is also "alarming and sarcastic, aiming rather to strike than to please, to
startle than to conquer."[19] She is so headstrong and so saturated with a sort
of self-destructive willfulness that she cannot love Albert's brother, Dennis,
who loves her, but only Albert, who does not. Not only does she take masochistic pleasure in her unrequited love, but she also delights in her own
histrionics, especially her theatrical suicide attempts.

Although Burney certainly does not completely approve of Elinor and
does not intend her as a model of female virtue, there is some sympathy and
even admiration in her portrayal of this "new woman," who is complex

and interesting, although finally unsatisfactory. Many of her comments are perceptive and fair. She says, for example, "the Rights of Woman . . . are the Rights of human nature," and rebukes Juliet when she is complaining of the difficulties of being an unprotected female by saying, "Debility and folly! Put aside your prejudices, and forget that you are a dawdling woman, to remember that you are an active human being, and your FEMALE DIFFICULTIES will vanish into the vapour of which they are formed" (3:36).

This ambivalent attitude toward Elinor is indicative of a subtle change in Burney's attitude in *The Wanderer*. Although this novel is clearly influenced, as the first three are, by the romance in plot, character, style, and theme, there is a new note of anxiety and dissatisfaction with women's lot in life and a new focus on problems that are particularly female. This new concern is evidenced from the beginning by the subtitle, "Female Difficulties," which seems to have gynecological connotations, as well as social implications. Although Juliet is accomplished and educated, there is simply no way she, as an unprotected and unknown female, can make her own way in the world. First of all, Juliet's situation draws attention to a woman's dependence on social status, especially that provided by men, to ratify her worth. She observes:

'How insufficient . . . is a FEMALE to herself! How utterly dependent upon situations—connexions—circumstances! how nameless, how for ever fresh-spring are her DIFFICULTIES, when she would owe her existence to her own exertions! Her conduct is criticized, not scrutinized; her character is censured, not examined; her labours are unhonoured, and her qualifications are but lures to ill will! Calumny hovers over her head, and slander follows her footsteps!' (2:197)

If social ostracism is humiliating to the unprotected female, economic distresses are still more pressing and dangerous. Juliet, who is well-educated, talented, and intelligent, is forced to undertake a series of degrading and poorly paid occupations. First, she gives harp lessons, which is respectable but hardly lucrative, since her pupils refuse to pay and are incensed that she expects to be paid "just as if she were a butcher, or a baker; or some useful tradesman" (2:314). Next, she is saved from the humiliation of a public performance only by Elinor's suicide attempt, after which Juliet employs herself with needlework of various kinds. Finally, she is forced into the most devastating occupation of all as she becomes Mrs. Ireton's "toad-eater," which is, as Mr. Giles Arbe defines it, "a person who would swallow any thing, bad or good; and do whatever he was bid, right or wrong: for the sake of a little pay" (3:337). It is significant that Juliet is the only one of Burney's heroines who is forced to work for a living.

If there is indeed such a change, however subtle, in Burney's attitude and intentions in *The Wanderer*, there are two possible causes for it. The first is that in the years between the writing of *Camilla* and *The Wanderer*, Burney suffered many personal defeats and disappointments that may have seemed to her especially womanly ones. For one thing, she watched her favorite sister Susan abused by a cruel husband. She also experienced pain and humiliation when her brother James abandoned his wife and children to run away with his half-sister, Sally. Burney herself had been crushed by economic hardships, by a painful separation from her family, and by poor health. In 1811 she underwent a mastectomy, performed with no anesthetic; this was a female difficulty which may have scarred Burney emotionally as well as physically.[20] A second explanation may be found in a shifting social consciousness and intellectual climate typified by the publication—twenty-two years before *The Wanderer* was written—of Mary Wollstonecraft's *A Vindication of the Rights of Woman*.

Perhaps this apparent "feminism" in *The Wanderer* has led some critics into reading these tendencies, if they actually exist, back into the earlier novels. Because the novels are so similar on the surface in basic plot, characterization, and even in theme, it is tempting to lump them together and to generalize about them almost as though they were one novel. To do so, however, is reductive and slights the richness, the complexity, and the diversity of Burney's work. The young girl who wrote *Evelina* was different in many and important ways from the mature woman who wrote *The Wanderer*, which embodies new concerns and new attitudes.

NOTES

1. Examples of feminist readings include Rose Marie Cutting, "Defiant Women: The Growth of Feminism in Fanny Burney's Novels," *Studies in English Literature, 1500–1900* 17 (1977): 519–30; Judith Newton, "Evelina: Or, the History of a Young Lady's Entrance into the Marriage Market," *Modern Language Studies* 6 (Spring 1976): 48–56; Patricia Meyer Spacks, *The Female Imagination* (New York: Alfred A. Knopf, 1975) Susan Staves, "Evelina; or Female Difficulties," *Modern Philology* 73 (May 1976): 368–81.

2. Cutting, "Defiant Women," 521.

3. Fanny Burney, *Evelina; or the History of a Young Lady's Entrance into the World* (London: Oxford University Press, 1970), 19. Page numbers for Burney's works are supplied in parentheses in the text.

4. Fanny Burney, *Cecilia, or Memoir of an Heiress* (London: George Bell & Sons, 1882), 437.

5. See Sheridan Baker, "Humphrey Clinker as Comic Romance," in *Essays on the Eighteenth-Century Novel*, ed. Robert Donald Spector (Bloomington: Indiana University Press, 1965); "Fielding's Amelia and the Materials of Romance," *Philological Quarterly* 41 (1962): 437–49; "Henry Fielding's Comic Romances," *Papers of the Michigan Academy of Science, Arts and Letters* 45 (1960): 411–19; Margaret Dalziel, "Richardson and Romance," *Australian University Modern Language Association* 33 (1960): 5–24; Henry Knight Miller, "Augustan Prose Fiction and the Romance Tradition," in *Studies in the Eighteenth Century III: Papers Presented at the Third David Nicol Smith Memorial Seminar, Carbera, 1973*, ed. R. F. Brissenden and J. C. Eade (Toronto: University of Toronto Press, 1973); *Henry Fielding's Tom Jones and the Romance Tradition*, English Literary Studies Monograph Series, no. 6 (Victoria: University of Victoria, 1976).

6. Northrop Frye, *The Secular Scripture: A Study of the Structure of Romance*, Charles Eliot Norton Lectures, 1974–1975 (Cambridge: Harvard University Press, 1976), 152.

7. Northrop Frye, *Anatomy of Criticism* (Princeton, Princeton University Press, 1957), 193.

8. Cutting, "Defiant Women," 520.

9. Frye, *Anatomy of Criticism*, 187.

10. Fanny Burney, *Camilla, or a Picture of Youth* (London: Oxford University Press, 1972), 8.

11. Kathleen Williams, "Romance Tradition in *The Faerie Queene*," *Research Studies* 32 (1964) reprinted in *Edmund Spenser's Poetry*, ed. Hugh McClean (New York: W. W. Norton & Co., 1968) 561.

12. Frye, *Anatomy of Criticism*, 190.

13. Newton, "Evelina," 53.

14. Cutting, "Defiant Women," 521.

15. Spacks, *Female Imagination*, 129.

16. Miller, *Henry Fielding's Tom Jones*, 40.

17. Fanny Burney, *The Early Diary of Fanny Burney, 1768–1778*, ed. Anne Raine Ellis (London: George Bell & Sons, 1913), 1:134.

18. Burney, *Early Dairy*, 1:325–26.

19. Fanny Burney, *The Wanderer, or Female Difficulties* (London: Longman, Hurst, Bees, Orme, & Brown, 1814), 1:243, 109, 160–61.

20. Joyce Hemlow, *The History of Fanny Burney* (Oxford: The Clarendon Press, 1968).

Men, Women, and Money
The Case of Mary Brunton

SARAH W. R. SMITH

Writing about a literary group out of the mainstream, whether it is a modern ethnic minority or the female writers of the early nineteenth century, brings with it a certain awkwardness about the problems of form. The perception of form by itself becomes an issue, an intrusion of possible bias into literature where it might be irrelevant, where form may become a means to deny content rather than a method of criticism. "Exquisite form and presentation," "a fully realized world," "realistic and well-rounded characters," "variety of incident" should strike us not as criteria but questions when we judge the work of some groups of minor writers. What ideas about fiction do we expect to have fulfilled by these fictions? Need we be comfortable with them, or may disapproval or distaste be as appropriate literary reactions from us to them as the approving comfort we find in more traditional writers? What social bias do we imply by our judgment of "the real"—for instance, in a book by and about women of the lower classes or rural areas, is "variety" reconcilable with "realism"? The work of many female minority writers is supposedly marked by literary clichés; but how do writers in a literary minority use their cliches—simply as page-fillers, or as a system of social signs, the subtle variations of which can transmit their own messages?

Jane Austen and Walter Scott, mainstream writers of the early nineteenth century, nevertheless suggest such questions through their alliance with literary minorities: Scott with the regional Scottish novel, Austen with women's fiction. Austen, of course, is Austen, there is no one better at the subtle delineation of relationships; and if Scott is only Scott, he is, nevertheless, the creator of a national mystique, the man who replaced the Johnsonian conception of Scotland with the heroic and tragic figure of the Highlander. But their alliance with literary minorities has also been used to explain "deficiencies" in them, particularly the relative inability of either to create a believable relationship between a fully developed female character and an equally developed male.

Is this problem due to their roots in the provincial woman's novel or the Scottish novel? Perhaps not. We cannot give the counterexample of equally skilled writers in the genres who *did* create believable male-female relationships. But one writer, not otherwise remarkably skilled, happened to belong to both literary minorities, and her work provides a thoroughgoing and probably conscious criticism of male-female relationships in fiction of the period, a criticism particularly applicable to Austen and Scott. She is not a major novelist. But her originality in two areas is delightful: in her definition of work and social value, and in her almost uniquely unromantic attention to the subject of money.

In comparison with many of her contemporaries, Mary Brunton is a slim pole to fly such large critical flags from. She was not a literary professional like Charlotte Smith or Elizabeth Inchbald; not an impressive intellectual like Hannah More or Anna Laetitia Barbauld. In comparison even with Susan Ferrier or John Galt, her talents are modest, and to compare her with Scott, as her contemporaries did, or with Austen, she felt would be to mock her. She wrote only two books and part of a third; of the two finished novels her husband, Alexander Brunton, could write, only four months after her death, "They rose very fast into celebrity, and their popularity seems to have as quickly sunk away."[1]

Most of her early life must be read between the lines of her husband's memoir, published with her fragmentary last novel, *Emmeline*. She was born Mary Balfour on Barra, in Orkney, on November 1, 1778. Her father was Col. Thomas Balfour of Elwick; her mother, Frances Ligonier, was the sister of the second earl of Ligonier. The *Memoir* is a model of discretion; it is possible, but not certain, that Frances Ligonier Balfour was the source of the "early unkindness"[2] and the informal education from which Mary Brunton suffered, and which contributed to her portraits of later female cruelty and miseducation. At sixteen, with her mother still alive and apparently in good health, the daughter took over the running of the household. At nineteen or twenty she was offered the chance to go to London to live with her godmother, Viscountess Wentworth; instead she chose marriage to the twenty-six-year-old minister of the church at Bolton, a scholar who would eventually be the author of a Persian grammar, Alexander Brunton.[3]

"Marriage is like sin," wrote Mrs. Brunton; "if we often allow it to be presented to our view, we learn to look without starting."[4] It is the remark of a woman sympathetic to the unmarried; but the Bruntons' seems to have been a model marriage, literally the model for the enlightened and friendly relationships between hero and heroine in her books. "It has been for twenty years my happiness to watch the workings of her noble mind," her husband said of her, "my chief usefulness to aid its progress, however feebly."[5] The young couple read together a formidable course of criticism, belles lettres, "the philosophy of the human mind," theology and history—he mentions Read, Robertson, Froissart, and the ethical classics of the Established Church. She learned some German and would eventually learn Gaelic; at Bolton, which was in East Lothian, she was stimulated by a landscape very different from that of the Orkneys to learn to draw. From this good beginning for an intellectual life, Alexander Brunton was called in 1803 to the New Greyfriars Church in Edinburgh, where he would serve until removing to the Tron Church in 1809.

In Edinburgh Alexander Brunton had less time for their intellectual pursuits together, and Mary Brunton began friendships with intellectual women; several close women friends and influences are mentioned in the *Memoir*. She began writing about 1809, and, like her heroine Laura Montreville, she seems originally to have been inspired by not only the possibility of succeeding in her art, but of selling the results. She was a professional from the beginning, setting herself a goal of a certain number of pages a day. Her first novel, *Self-Control*, was published in early 1811, anonymously, but was soon known to be hers. It is a story of virtue rewarded, with an ideal heroine, Laura Montreville (whom Brunton found tedious—"if ever I undertake another lady, I will manage her in a very different manner.")[6] *Discipline*, in which her talent for irony is first evident, appeared in 1814, with a very different type of heroine, the self-willed Ellen Percy. Brunton researched it thoroughly, taking advantage of a trip to London and making special expeditions to the Highlands. It seems clear that she would have written more on the Highlands, if it had not been for Scott and *Waverley*; her study of Gaelic had given her special insights and she was continuing it systematically. But although she greeted the appearance of Scott's novel with generosity, his heroic Highlands interfered with her more modern, egalitarian, women-dominated stories. She wrote nothing for several years, while contemplating a more "feminine" subject, a series of moral tales along the lines of More's or Edgeworth's. *Emmeline*, what we have of it, has the undramatized summary quality of many of these moral tales. But the subject, a divorced, helplessly feminine woman, and the burning irony of Brunton's approach to the romantic novel have no parallel in tales for children.

The couple had raised Alexander Brunton's two East Indian wards but had had no children of their own. In early 1818, at thirty-nine, Mary Brunton became pregnant. She had completed less than seventy pages of a first draft of *Emmeline* when she gave birth to a stillborn child. She died of childbed fever on December 19, 1818.

To understand Mrs. Brunton's feminist qualities, it is necessary to examine her religious background. Many writers of the period claim a religious motivation for their entertainment; Brunton is both firmer and less obtrusive than most. She writes to her brother in 1815:

> The great purpose of the book is to procure admission for . . . religion . . . . Though I love money deeply, money is not my motive for writing as I do; not for the complexion and sentiments of my books. On the contrary, I am quite sure I might make twice as much of my labour, if I could bring myself to present to the public an easy flexible sort of virtue . . . .[7]

She is not theologically feminist; her religion includes a patriarchal moral orientation with which some current theologians would be dissatisfied. Her heroines are satisfied with a social duty that is defined (though not exclusively) in terms of duty to fathers and husbands. Laura Montreville is pleased to earn money for her father's needs, not her own, and she makes the presentation of her first wages as an artist an occasion for asserting her social dependence. "I have no wants, no wishes," she says, refusing to keep any of the money for her own, "and when I have . . . let their gratification come from you, that their pleasure may be doubled to me."[8] Ellen Percy characterizes her final social state as "the mother of [the Graham] chieftain."[9]

But Brunton is a Scottish Calvinist; and while her religion makes a patriarchal and marital orientation almost inevitable, it does not consider it the *only* way to fulfill duty, and it allows her women to escape from the passivity that so often goes along with a purely social patriarchal and marital orientation. Calvinism postulates a church *and* state government, a democratic theocracy, in which leaders are elected for virtues and abilities, not for social qualities such as breeding and money. Divine love is expressed through *all* the possible social relationships, through human beings in interchange with one another. "Love" therefore includes not only the relationship between man and woman (husband-wife, father-daughter), but also those between aunt and niece, beggar and almsgiver, friend and friend, employer and employee. Ethics, political and moral problems, and Christian economics are all of concern to the serious Christian, who must form her life to the service of this plan of love.

The system is essentially egalitarian because it makes a distinction between priestly functions and administrative ones. Priestly functions are universally shared among all members of the Church; the Church itself, consisting of all its members, is a priesthood of all for all, in which God moves all to minister to each other. Priesthood, of course, is the far more important function.

Administrative functions, including the official ministry, are given to certain members because they have a certain ability to perform a task, such as preaching. They are purely functional appointments, not sacred or spiritual distinctions. Almost everyone has such functions, more or less wide-ranging according to "circumstances . . . made by Him to accomplish His promise, that all shall work together for good to them who love Him."[10] Some are almsgivers; some are beggars. In social terms, all social distinctions—wealth, property, and at least for Brunton the social aspects of maleness and femaleness—are or should be mere recognitions of ability to perform a task for the common good, not judgments about the sacredness of the priestly individual.

Thus Brunton's religious orientation allows her to be comfortable with the passivity that had come to be associated with all "good" novel heroines, and many heroes, in the later eighteenth century, the Sentimental passivity of the Richardsonian and post-Richardsonian good person who asserts "I am not in my own power." But to a far greater degree than many of her English fellow novelists, Brunton can meld it with social activism. The typical heroine of Sentimentalism spends her time being kidnapped by a bad man and rescued by a good one, sacrificing herself for one good cause or another, and suffering passively while she waits for her vindication. Her suffering shows her moral rightness.[11] For Mary Brunton's Laura Montreville and Ellen Percy, however, suffering in itself is not necessarily either good or bad, and it can coexist with a high degree of social and economic activity. It is often Laura's or Ellen's own activity, rather than fate or a good man, that help not only her but also other characters.

The two novels are similar—so similar that *Discipline*, the second, may in some ways be taken as a comment on the relatively conventional heroine-hero relationship of the first—and both spend a remarkably large amount of time discussing how the heroines make their living, and refusing to make the expected social judgment of it. The heroine of *Self-Control*, Laura Montreville, is poor, the daughter of a half-pay officer and of a nobleman's daughter with a small fortune and large tastes. Her mother has died and she is the only child of her father, who has recently laid out almost all of his money on an annuity for her.

At the beginning of the book she is courted by a Colonel Hargrave, whom she loves until she discovers with horror that he plans to make her only his mistress. Although he changes his mind, she sends him away for a two-year probation, concerned that her father will find out about the incident and feel himself obliged to "defend her honor." Through a legal mistake her annuity is lost. She is "no mean proficient" in painting and is surprised when a critical friend suggests that she might make a living at it. In the circumstances "this excites an interest which no other earthly subject could have awakened." As she and her father go to London to try to regain her annuity, she continues with her painting, and after many disappointments sells not only her large painting, the *Farewell of Leonidas to his Family*, but gets a commission for a companion piece.[12] She does not realize, however, that both have been bought by Montague de Courcy, a good man who has been taken with her story and her appearance. They make acquaintance (the families are old friends) and are pleased with each other's company.

Laura's father is unhappy at her earning money; it is "hard, very hard" for a woman of her descent to be "dependent on your daily labour," he complains, and although she says it is her "only real independence" she bows to her father's will and no longer paints for pay. She still considers herself deeply in love with Colonel Hargrave and hopes that he will reclaim his faults, but paints for Montague de Courcy a picture of the Choice of Hercules in which he is pictured as Hercules choosing between Pleasure, a fancied portrait, and Virtue, for which she poses.[13] She is unaware of the sense in which Courcy might take this until he proposes to her, at which she sends him away.

By doing so she unwittingly leaves herself and her father almost penniless; Courcy, as a friend of the family, has been secretly paying part of their rent, and his arrangements for covertly continuing this go awry. Unknown to her father, Laura takes up art again, supporting him by selling chalk sketches. He falls ill and dies. Now alone, she has difficulty in practicing her profession, which is too likely to put her into ambiguous situations; she becomes a companion to her mother's sister, Lady Pelham, a domestic tyrant who has quarreled with her own daughter and means, by default, to make Laura her heir. Mr. Warren, the fop who has been withholding her annuity, is persuaded to rectify the legal error—the sum, as Austen fans would like to know, is £100 a year—and she is again approached by Colonel Hargrave, who insists that he has reformed. Not likely. Exposed in another affair, he kidnaps Laura (all the way to America!) to have his wicked will of her, but when he realizes that she is no longer capable of loving him, has a rather Byronic change of heart and kills himself. Laura makes her way back from America to do Lady Pelham's daughter justice and be married to Montague de Courcy.

"What channels do the customs of society leave open to the industry of women?"[14] Ellen Percy, the heroine of *Discipline*, does not feel the urgency of the question so quickly as Laura Montreville. The only child of a doting father, she will have £200,000 on his death. Self-will and frivolity are her sins; though her father seems to intend her for the serious Mr. Maitland, she has been given only a fashionable education. Her companions are the idle rich and the nobility, including Juliet Arnold, "educated to be married," and Frederick de Burgh, whom Ellen finds fascinating. Frederick tries to kidnap Ellen, actually compromises her, and finally talks her into planning an elopement to Gretna Green. Meanwhile Maitland has fallen out of love with Ellen; he is deeply involved in the slavery question, plans to devote his life to those who are still in slavery, and cannot marry a woman who thinks his vocation merely amusing. After his departure, Ellen's father goes bankrupt and commits suicide.

Ellen is now as penniless as Laura, and less prepared. She is rescued and given a home by Miss Mortimer, a friend of her mother's whom she has previously rejected. Miss Mortimer, a poor spinster dying of cancer, brings Ellen back to life and starts her education. After Miss Mortimer's death, Ellen goes as a governess to Edinburgh and meets a Highland woman, Cecil Graham, whom she aids. Her second job as governess is with a domestic tyrant, Mrs. Boswell, so jealous of her husband's timid admiration of Ellen that she has Ellen put in a madhouse. By exercising self-control, Ellen persuades her keepers that she is not mad.

Back in Edinburgh, Ellen meets her old companion, Juliet Arnold, now the unacknowledged wife of a nobleman; Ellen takes on the care of Juliet and her baby, a task in which she is helped by a new acquaintance, Charlotte Graham, chief woman of Cecil's Highland clan. After Juliet's death Ellen goes to visit Charlotte at the Graham ancestral home, to find that her old friend, Maitland, is coming to take up his ancestral duties under his real name, Henry Graham. He and the now-educated Ellen are happily married.

Readers familiar with the minor fiction of the late eighteenth century will notice its use, and criticism, in Brunton's novels. The story of Colonel Hargrave in *Self-Control* is one more in a long series of novelistic arguments against the maxim that "a reformed rake makes the best husband,"[15] while the romantic histories of most of the good women are part of the equally venerable novelistic warnings against first love.[16] The contrast of Ellen's fate and Juliet's exemplifies the frequently used "sister plot," in which one young woman gains fortune and married happiness through a sound education while the other's triviality leads her to misery and death.[17] The books follow the late eighteenth-century preference for heroines rather than heroes, and to some degree the men in them represent the tendencies in the heroines' lives, their potential for self-help and self-damage.

But Brunton's men are far more independent than the norm, as we shall see, and in several other important ways her work is distinctive. The usual eighteenth-century popular novel locates will and individuality in the heroines, but social activity in the heroes. For instance (to take two scenes almost omnipresent in the fiction of 1780 to 1800) a woman makes a bad judgment; as a result, she is kidnapped by an active bad man and rescued by an active good one. Or, after she makes a similar false judgment, an active bad man challenges another man for her hand or honor. If she is a good woman (that is, sufficiently passive), the man who responds refuses to duel the challenger, but persuades him that fighting is wrong. If she is "bad," that is, passionate, the man who responds compromises her or is killed.

Both scenes have as their subtext the quarrel between self-restraint and passion—a subtext that appears frequently in fiction of the period and that has other associated emblems, such as the Choice of Hercules. The kidnapping scene dramatizes the emblem of the hand of reason holding back the horses of passion. The kidnapper invariably takes the heroine toward inappropriate sexual experience, a rape or forced marriage; the male rescuer not only holds back the horses but also, in most versions of the scene, "holds back" himself, refusing to make the scene into a fatal quarrel and refusing too sudden an involvement with the heroine.

Brunton uses both scenes but alters the sex roles. Instead of restraint and reason, as well as passion, being externalized in male figures, the women themselves take over not only the blame but also much of the activity. There are three kidnapping-chariot scenes in the two books. Early in *Discipline* Ellen Percy is rescued from a kidnapping attempt, but it is one in which she plays a far more active role than the usual heroine; merely advised by a mysterious man (who does not appear again), she does not enter the kidnapper's carriage.[18] Earlier still, *she* plays the bad character letting loose the reins of passion, as she races in a coach with friends and almost kills an elderly woman. Maitland, the hand of reason, reins in the horses for her; but the original bad judgment, instead of being externalized through a character like Richardson's Sir Hargrave Pollexfen, remains solidly located in Ellen herself.[19] The female character is freed from emblemata, and Brunton is able to explore realistically the subjects of female self-will and female desire for domination.

The corresponding scene in *Self-Control* is so thoroughly a reversal as to be a comment on the type of scene. The already disciplined Laura, kidnapped by a Mr. Warren, simply reasons with him with "ineffable scorn," then takes the job of rescuing herself into her own hands: "Laura now rose from her seat, and seizing the reins with a force which made the horses rear, she coolly chose that moment to spring from the curricle, and walked back toward the town . . . ."[20] Perhaps significantly, in view of the novels' concern with money, she finishes her journey in a hired hackney coach.

Because Brunton's women act for themselves, Brunton's male characters can attain a far more independent existence. Laura's father, Captain Montreville, is a character in his own right—admiring his daughter, set in his ways, hypochondriac—but he is not any of these things, except admiring, *because* of Laura or anything she has done. Rather, his character presents a problem and a challenge to Laura's self-control, allowing Brunton to explore more facets of women's psychology: the "contagious depression" that infects a woman as she nurses a member of her household; the fear of destitution she feels at her father's death; her wish not to survive him. Montague de Courcy's character, which is by no means overdeveloped, is still not merely a reward for Laura's; Brunton delights in exploring the delicate combination of restlessness, admiration, and imprudence that involves a good man with a good woman before he has fully understood the state of her feelings.

In *Discipline* the male characters are even better. Mr. Percy, the rich Bloomsbury Square merchant, huffing and puffing with pleasure as he rejects noble aspirants for his daughter's money, would not have displeased Thackeray. Mr. Boswell, terrified by his wife and responding with timid lechery to Ellen's "pretty hair," is hardly developed, but he is understood; we feel he has a character. We are less close to the Richardsonian-fictional idea of minor characters as simply emanations of the central character's virtues and vices or *boîtes à confidences* for them, and closer to an essentially Victorian idea of fiction as social exposition and analysis.

Thus Brunton can look in an essentially realistic way at the connections between money, power, and human values. Women's economic oppression becomes, not merely a question of "virtue rewarded" or of a necessary progress toward education, but a social fact, one of the ways in which society rightly or wrongly confers value.

Realism is a powerful tool in Brunton's work. But she is essentially an idealist, influenced by Calvinism and judging value by social utility. Do her male and female characters use their talents for the good of all, whatever those talents are? Then they are good characters. It is a conclusion that many feminists have come to since, often on radical economic grounds. The psychological realism of all of Brunton's characters allows her to balance their (and her) social conservatism neatly against a radical reevaluation of some aspects of her society.

One of the most surprising of these, to readers trained in Romantic literature, is her characters' and Brunton's own attitude to art. For the male artist of the period, in life and in fiction, the experience of art is often one of transcendence, an escape to some higher reality in which the artistic self lives. Perhaps, of course, we are merely dealing with more Philistine artists in the female fiction of the period. But it is not only Mrs. Brunton who distrusts such ego-defining "glories of the brain." Brunton has her female characters speak about self-education, but in mathematics, chemistry, Gaelic—not art. Art is a craft, for making money and for making sense. Brunton echoes her own sentiments in her good heroine, Laura Montreville, who takes her art seriously because it gives her some "real independence" (which can be used to help others) and because it has a moral content.

We might generalize: the female artist does not encourage herself to value art for its effect on herself. She values it for social utility—the ability to help people, through giving them a useful moral message or through making money for their needs. She values it, as well, because, instead of freeing her from society, it establishes her within it; it allows her to make her living. (As soon as the label "artist" would put Laura in a bad social position, she gives it up and becomes a paid companion instead.) In terms of English male Romantic art, these reasons are illegitimate; they put the female in the category of false artists. But clearly, in dealing with the literary minority of female novelists, we are dealing with another group of social and class interests. The Romantic poets generally feel themselves members of a social establishment that they may criticize from within. But for the female novelists, "art" is a form of work, a legitimate occupation through which they can gain the place in the social establishment that they do not yet have. Art becomes a business, an accumulation of value and an exercise in power like any other business; its legitimate reward is money. Thus Mrs. Brunton's resolutely Philistine attitude to art and her occasional strange lapses in discussing Laura's—we never get any sense of whether, in artistic terms, it is any good, although we hear a good deal about whether and why it is salable.

But because Mrs. Brunton's definition of "social value" is not secular, art is even more radically redefined. Art has no special value in comparison with any other kind of business. Laura Montreville paints historical subjects but feels no artistic pang at giving them up for less ambitious chalk drawings and, eventually, for the quite inartistic job of paid companion. Art in the self-educating and self-ratifying sense is simply not an issue. Her progress in and past art is meant to be exactly parallel to Maitland's progression from India merchant, to member of Parliament and anti-slavery spokesman, to Highland chieftain. "Abstract" social utility is not the issue either, or Maitland would have remained an abolitionist agitator; the point is what *these* people should be doing at *this* time. Laura's progress and Maitland's are clearly presented as steps along the road to full social utility; each step has value.

The full scale of Brunton's revaluation can be judged by the third progress, Ellen Percy's from heiress to small businesswoman. Ellen Percy's very small business, the manufacture of what modern commerce would call "gift items," is, as Ellen herself admits, a trivial occupation and extremely boring, as well as not very profitable. But Brunton's whole point is that neither art nor business, of whatever legitimate nature and whatever size, can be judged by its size alone, its ability to educate and develop the persons pursuing it, or any facet of its secular glamour. None of these can confer value on the sacred individual; they are valuable only as they support the individual's priestly function.

The effect is to separate any question of worth from those of the nature of work, its glamour value, or its scale. Persons who value themselves on the scale of their business/art, or the amount of money at their disposition, are in Brunton's eyes generally fools or villains. Their folly is in valuing only the secular worth of the act—whether it is art, benevolence, or agitation against slavery. Goodness on a small scale is exactly as valuable as goodness on a large scale—because concepts such as "scale" and "valuable" (in a secular sense) have no meaning in the context. Again, Brunton's ideas are effectually feminist; women's liberality, which tends to the small-scale, may be precisely as worthy, or as worthless, as men's.

Her rich merchant character, Mr. Percy, is used to make the point. Men's ideas of liberality and women's, he says, complacently, must be very different. "When a man has thousands, and tens of thousands [of pounds], passing through his hands every day, it gives him a liberal way of thinking. But as for a woman, who never was mistress of a hundred pounds at a time, what can she know of liberality?"[21] After Mr. Percy has reacted to his bankruptcy by committing suicide, leaving his daughter unprotected, the "woman who never was mistress of a hundred pounds" restores that daughter to useful life.[22]

Fortunately, it is this kind of liberality that Ellen learns; she in turn will rescue Cecil Graham, getting back for the Highland woman not only the hand-woven winding sheet she wants but also the household goods and tools that will help her to keep her economic independence. Earlier, Maitland has preached this liberality to her; when Ellen wishes to give a young woman £50, he suggests that Ellen instead employ her as a seamstress, at the risk of having to wear an unfashionable gown. Later he embodies it: when his clan is left without a head, he gives up his important and satisfying work with slaves to advise and head the Grahams.

Art, business, and money are all tools for social utility. But social utility does not merely mean *gaining* power and money; it is a standard by which the good characters judge when to give them up. Willed self-limitation and self-restraint are appropriate for both women and men. The real villains in Mary Brunton's work are those who cannot dissociate themselves from their secular "worth" and "scale." Mr. Percy criminally deserts his daughter because he cannot bear bankruptcy. Lady Pelham, dispenser of bounty, with £40,000 to give away, spends her time planning how the money can be used to make her daughter and son-in-law destitute.[23] Juliet Arnold, starving and tubercular, dependent on Ellen for every mouthful she and her child eat, cannot escape thinking of how bountiful she will be as Lady Glendower: she "overwhelm[ed] me with promises which were to be performed when she should be restored to her rights and dignities. . . . It was heart-breaking to see her spending her last breath in devising schemes of vanity or revenge. . . ."[24] But she does not have enough strength of mind to help Ellen in the work that feeds them, comparatively "trifling" as that work is.

Any form of social valuation—money and talent as well as the implicit social valuation of maleness or femaleness—does not measure any character's ability to be socially useful, to perform the social administrative tasks that support the Calvinist priestly functions. At best it only indicates the form of officeholding the service will take. Male and female, artist and business-person, poor and rich have directly comparable functions. The question is whether the officeholder properly fills the office.

Mary Brunton's strength as a novelist is the ability to combine this idealistic view of society with the social reportage embodied in her realistic characters, not letting either unbalance the other. Her religious purpose does not keep her from a considerable sensitivity toward the ways women really feel about money. If money is, religiously, an index of what one can be called on to do, its presence in however modest amounts is a guarantee that one can do something. "Independence" is a word that means a great deal to all the female characters, from the best to the worst; and independence is money as well as a quality of spirit. Indeed, it is almost not too much to say that Brunton thinks every woman, even the worst, is better with a little money.[25] Repeatedly in her books, money allows women, whether bad or good ones, to do effective good. Money allows Lady Pelham to confront and defeat Mr. Warren over the annuity. Money changes Laura's relationship to Lady Pelham from complete dependence to something a bit nearer equality; she can consult her benefactor's wishes with her own money and make small gifts where her benefactor would not think to. Ellen's ability to earn money allows her to forgive Juliet effectively, and her earning power is deeply interwoven with her ability to make Juliet feel forgiven. Miss Mortimer's annuity allows her to save Ellen, as Ellen's earning power helps to make Miss Mortimer's deathbed more comfortable when the annuity is gone. There are no "old maids" in Brunton's works, no one like the poor Miss Bates, because there are no unmarried women without some competence, however small. Miss Mortimer and Charlotte Graham, who are not married and not young, are not penniless and not powerless either. They are defined, and think of themselves, in positive terms of social power rather than through the "negative" of their unmarried state.

In fact, there are only three dependent female characters in Brunton's works, and all are married. One is dying; one is mad; one is in an isolation so complete that it has the flavor of Hell. Juliet Arnold, the unrecognized Lady Glendower, is Mrs. Brunton's answer to her romantic-fictional sisters such as Olivia in *The Vicar of Wakefield*; she is neither repentant nor "interesting," but peevish, lazy, and sordid even on her deathbed. Mrs. Boswell, the jealous wife for whom Ellen Percy works in Edinburgh, is a case study in the psychopathology of dependence. "Dependence! heavy, heavy are thy chains," Mary Brunton quotes from Charlotte Smith to introduce her story; and though the lines are meant to refer to Ellen's situation, much more clearly they describe the wife's. "She was capable of a perseverance in sullenness, which no entreaties could move, and no submissions could mollify. . . . All her talents for rule . . . were exerted upon Mr. Boswell."[26] Neglecting her children to torment him, she will not speak to him for days together, or speaks "without deigning to turn her eyes or her head." Only one quality of his will move her; he is restored to momentary favor not because she is sorry for his sexual and social frustration—or, consciously, shares it—but because "Mrs. Boswell wanted money."[27] Untrained and uneducated for anything but marriage, Mrs. Boswell has chosen marriage as the only avenue to power. But the only power she can exert is through her husband, or over him. She is a great villain, but Brunton creates in her a moving and frightening portrait of the middle-aged woman without resources, turning to sadism and corrosive jealousy because she cannot bear being wholly without independence.

The final case, worse if that is possible, is the heroine of Brunton's fragmentary last book, *Emmeline*. Emmeline, the sweet dependent female ideal of a certain kind of novel, first appears to us on her wedding day to her first and only love, Sidney de Clifford. He has loved her as immutably as she loved him. It should make no difference that both had been married to others, that both have had children, and that finally they could stand no more and divorced their spouses to be with each other. But what it means— for Emmeline and her husband—is that, alone and loving in a house and gardens like Paradise, they are completely cut off from being useful. They are, as it were, outside the priesthood. Sidney will never again be able to lead a regiment, to serve in Parliament, even to be local justice of the peace. Emmeline, in the most powerful position a woman of her century could aspire to, is powerless: she will never be able to do anything that the squire's lady should, because her tenants stand off from her.

Here Mrs. Brunton shows what money cannot do; her treatment of Emmeline's is of a piece with her conception of money as a counter of social value. Emmeline has an immense amount of money and her husband is equally wealthy. But both are as "dependent" as Mrs. Boswell—dependent on each other for *all* society, *all* love, and cut off from everyone else; they will never do the most ordinary social service, and their money is no more use to them than dead leaves. The book, fragmentary and unfinished though it is, is a sketch for a nightmare.

Through her Calvinist heritage Mrs. Brunton is able to make a thoroughgoing critique of the novels of her contemporaries and immediate predecessors. In effect, if not by conscious intention, her novels become feminist and egalitarian. By judging moral behavior by criteria other than the scope of the characters' actions, she equates the larger sphere of male social activity and the more glamorous spheres of art and public service with the more modest and "female" duties of small business and local charity; essentially, she says, men and women have the same moral duties, though they are likely to hold different offices. This separation between priesthood and office turns the officeholder into a public servant, an egalitarian conception. Social power, once equated with male activity and female suffering, is for Mrs. Brunton essentially sexless. As a result, her novels present a conservative view of society, but read into it a quiet sexual radicalism.

Mrs. Brunton's novels do not "reverse" or "overturn" traditional sexual roles; her Highlands are not a Herland. However, sex is no longer the only metaphor for social relationships, and many social relationships are simply treated realistically, with no metaphorical qualities at all. Female protectors and friends do not take over the traditional novelistic role of male protectors; they augment it. Female artists and females adept at law and business are not "like" males, or "unlike" them; they are women dealing with realities. It is not that there is no sex present; Brunton's heroines are, if anything, rather too inclined to fall in love with handsome villains, and her heroes' hearts are involved while their heads are still shaking "No." But many relationships that, in other authors, would be addressed in sexual terms are here irrelevant to sexuality.[28] Apart from relationships that actually involve sexual attraction, sexuality is stripped of much of its social functions, and Brunton instead treats most "sexual" relationships as studies of social power, utility, and dependence.[29]

Both men and women are judged by their social usefulness. Brunton's good characters consider that women are attractive because of seriousness, intelligence, a sexual morality of honesty and faithfulness, social responsibility and economic integrity; and so are men. Ellen respects the Highlandwoman Cecil Graham for faithfulness to her husband and because, though she is destitute, she will not break into a pound note given her for someone else. Sidney is shocked at his beloved Emmeline because she accepts money that is not strictly hers; Mrs. Villiers will not visit Emmeline, though she pities her deeply, because Emmeline has broken the connection between social and sexual morality. Marriage, family, and friends are tied together by the same sorts of relationships, of mutual respect and trust, and can substitute for one another. It adds up to a rather idealistic-sounding picture of relationships, but Brunton is saved by her ability to show these "ideal" relationships realistically and by her clear sense of how her men and women actually act. Her "good" men and women feel sexual attraction, even inappropriately, and her worst feel a pride at being able to marshal their economic power.

Here at last we can begin to use Brunton to read her more distinguished contemporaries, Austen and Scott, and to show the effect on contemporary British fiction of the weakness her work points out. It is not, after all, that Mary Brunton is distinguished *as a novelist*. In a society of novelists all of whom looked closely at female economics, she would sink to a very modest level indeed. She shows her intelligence (as do a few, but not many, of her contemporaries in popular women's fiction) by taking women's economics as a subject; and the very fact that this distinguishes her shows how sketchily the subject is usually treated in the mainstream.

Her strength as a Highlands novelist is that she shows women as fully social beings. Scott's Highlands seem to include no conception of the role that women must play in a society in which many of the male leaders have been banished or killed. Brunton's Highlands picture a society more familiar to historians of other cultures torn by war, in which women hold considerable political, social, and economic power, often by proxy for male leaders; she believably shows how the patriarchal and hierarchic society changes under post-Rebellion stresses. Charlotte Graham, the powerful chief woman of the Graham clan, has a believable social relationship with Cecil Graham, an illiterate woman of her tribe; if Scott dramatizes the clans in crisis, Brunton shows them in the everyday, as women call on other women, engage in the work of farming together, discuss money, or make decisions about their lives. The heroic Scott concentrates on the chiefs; Brunton's Cecil Graham is colorful and quaint, but she is clearly the same sort of character and involved in the same kind of decisions as Charlotte or Ellen. Brunton's Highlanders are not in a world wholly other from that of Edinburgh; some of them have lived in Edinburgh and even in London, and Maitland has lived in the West Indies. They have a coherent moral life and a relationship to the Scottish past; their heroism under the difficulties of defeat is more adult, if less vivid, than Scott's heroical-tragical rodomontade.

With Austen the contrast is more subtle and more profound. Notoriously, for Austen, money is a given, a quality of heroism and not a means. It is bestowed by men on women—by, for instance, the Dashwood males on Elinor and Marianne—as one more form of social value. It is almost genetic; "Emma Woodhouse, handsome, clever, and rich," is the last as she is the first two. She has inherited her money, it is among her qualities in the same way that handsomeness and cleverness are. And she does not think about it. We do not know where it comes from, what alternative investments and uses might be found for it, what rights and responsibilities—outside of the field of marriage—it will admit her to. It is a quality that exists independently of her, a form of social value that will be handed by her father on to her husband and children, leaving her an undefined settlement of some portion of it that she will spend on herself, like a bad woman in a novel, or, like a good woman in a novel, will give away. It cannot be imagined that Emma, clever as she is, will talk over with Mr. Knightley the comparative social merits of investments in India, the Midlands, and Consols. In social terms, Emma's money is an important part of herself; it is the means through which she will exert an important effect on her society; it defines and limits her social sphere. But she is not in the least clever about it.

Is this what we miss in the narrowness of Austen's concerns, the domesticity of her heroines, the weakness of her heroes? Within their sphere they are complete. But there is something curiously absent from the picture of Darcy at Pemberley. He is an accomplished friend, brother, landlord, master; he has arranged for the house to be decorated to please his sister; his taste in landscaping is impeccable. But this is Saturday work; Elizabeth could do it herself. What does Darcy *do*? What are his social ethics? What are his politics? Darcy, to be what Austen says he is, must have them, and being Darcy must spend some significant part of his time in passionate advocacy of them. Can he share this with Elizabeth? Let us hope so; but in the context of mainstream fiction as Austen writes it, he cannot visibly do so.

The qualities of the heroine thus imply the weakness of the hero. The heroine exclusively concerned with the domestic sphere, without knowledge of the ways she fits economically into society, can have a relationship with the hero only on the traditional novelistic grounds of "love." The hero can exert his heroism only through "winning" her and through exerting himself in the domestic sphere; thus we have Grandison and his kind, active enough but in a curiously limited field.[30] The corollary of such limited heroism is the character of the rake—the man who can exert social power, but by turning the novelistic love-relationship into one of social oppression. It is left for such writers on the margins of mainstream literature as Mary

Brunton to make the myth realistic and thus to explode it. Her good man, Maitland, speaks to the typical female of romantic fiction, Ellen:

> . . . It would be misery to obtain [your love] . . . . After the raptures of a lover are past, the husband has a long life before him, in which he must either share his joys and his sorrows with a friend, or exact the submission of an inferior. . . . Who that seeks a friend would choose one who would consider his employments as irksome, his pleasures as fantastic, his hopes as a dream![31]

At the beginning of this essay I spoke about the problems of literary form. Mrs. Brunton exemplifies them. She is not a "complete" novelist, one who like Scott or Austen creates a world; she is instead reacting to theirs and to the world of fiction. She is without myth. For most novelists, love is a metaphor for all the possible relationships among men and women in the novel; but Brunton rejects the metaphor. The variety of her characters' experiences is that of bad fiction; it is instead their continuity that interests us, the abiding interest her men and women have in the ways that they make a living. She is fascinated with the tinsel of the bad romantic novel; she uses it constantly; but she plays with it as an intelligent naive mind does, showing her fascination by pulling the thing apart.

And this is her strength. For Brunton, love as a fictional metaphor, love in the simple domestic sense, is not enough. The active ethical person is happiest with his or her kind. Men who do all that men should must be happiest with women who, in however more modest an office, engage in the same sort of social utility. The true heroine must be actively useful and legitimately care about the most important means for exercising social utility, money. Brunton recognizes that economic independence is a social issue: to want to "do good" is to want an economic role; and she makes it a literary issue as well. In her modest way, by making money a part of her novels, Mary Brunton helps to expand the potential of the novelistic hero and heroine.

NOTES

1. Alexander Brunton, "Memoir," in Mary Brunton, *Emmeline. With Some Other Pieces* . . . (New York: A. T. Goodrich, 1819), lxxxvi.
2. Ibid., p. lxxxvii.
3. There is some uncertainty here, although Alexander Brunton implies none. Apparently they first went to Bolton after the wedding and spent six years there, leaving in 1803; but that would put the date of their marriage as 1797 instead of, as he dates it, 1798. Perhaps the trip to London was meant to prevent the wedding.

4. Mary Brunton, *Discipline* (London: Bruce & Wyld, 1844), 20.

5. Alexander Brunton, "Memoir," ix.

6. Ibid., xxix.

7. Ibid., lxvii.

8. Mary Brunton, *Self-Control* (London: N. Bruce, 1844), 37.

9. Brunton, *Discipline*, 161.

10. From an important letter to Mrs. Izett in which Brunton discusses her own skills as a novelist and ascribes them to a (clearly male) Higher Power; "Memoir," lvii. Clearly she thinks of her own novelistic work as an administrative function (though just as clearly she is glad to have the money).

11. See for further comments on this my introduction to *Samuel Richardson: An Annotated Bibliography*, Boston: G.K. Hall & Co., 1984. Heroines who make suffering synonymous with sanctity include Harriet Byron, Sidney Biddulph, Julia de Roubigné and, of course, Anne Elliot.

12. We cannot tell whether Laura's paintings are particularly interesting or outstanding. That, though, is the point; Mary Brunton makes no attempt to persuade us that they are interesting *as art*, and doesn't in fact tell us much about them, but is interested in the way they form a part of Laura's social life, particularly in how they help her earn money. This attitude to art is rare in the period, and generally, I think, in the work of male novelists who portray artists—offhand I can think only of Wilkie Collins's *Hide and Seek* (1854, 1861), where the question is far less sensitively treated. But it is very close to Brunton's own attitude. See later in this essay for further comments on the role of art for minorities.

13. Compare Katrin R. Burlin's essay on the use of the Choice of Hercules in Austen, "At the Crossroads: Sister Authors and the Sister Arts" in this volume.

14. Brunton, *Discipline*, 92.

15. The original treatment of the idea, at least as far as novelists of the period were concerned, was in *Clarissa*; it had been treated earlier, however, in both fiction and drama. From a later rake, Sir Hargrave Pollexfen in *Sir Charles Grandison*, Colonel Hargrave no doubt gets his name.

16. *Grandison*, if not the first, was the most exhaustive treatment of the theme; cf. Austen's treatment of it in *Sense and Sensibility*.

17. In, for instance, Anne Dawe's *The Younger Sister*; the anonymous *History of Julia Benson* (1784); the anonymous *The Twin Sisters; or, The Effects of Education* (1788); and William Dodd's *The Sisters; or the History of Lucy and Caroline Sanson* (1754). William Park discusses the "contrast plot" in his "Fielding *and* Richardson," *PMLA* 80 (1966), 381–88. Notable foreign examples of the sister plot include, of course, Sade's *Justine* and *Juliette*. Austen treats it, in a minor key, in *Pride and Prejudice* and *Sense and Sensibility*; in all her books there is a contrast of sensible and frivolous heroines, although (like Brunton's heroines) they are not necessarily actual sisters.

18. The mysterious man may be Maitland's agent, but the scene is Ellen's.

19. Brunton, *Discipline*, 44, 20. Additional "expostulation" is provided by a female character, Miss Mortimer.

20. Brunton, *Self-Control*, 52.

21. Brunton, *Discipline*, p. 33. Compare this attitude with the more usual reverence for the benevolent merchant.

22. In a nice touch, she sees that the jessamine keeping the sun out of Ellen's room is cut back before the girl arrives. Such domestic touches draw Brunton close to Austen and to Richardson.

23. Laura, who eventually gets the money, acts in a way that humorously criticizes the usual novelist's good person. She duly transfers most of Lady Pelham's inheritance to the daughter, but figures that her services as the lady's companion were worth about £2000, and keeps that. Brunton is full of touches like this, recognizable criticisms of novel conventions. For instance, Laura has been told by her mother never to give up a miniature. To relieve her father's wants, Laura sells the miniature. Nothing, either good or bad, happens to her as a consequence, and she does not get the miniature back. Captain Montreville has forbidden Laura to sell her paintings, but when he is ill she sells chalk drawings to support them. Again, nothing happens. The sanctity of a promise to a parent is no more abstractly sacred to Brunton than is the "absolute value" of art.

24. Brunton, *Discipline*, 136.

25. There is an exception, as we shall see, that shows what Brunton means by "having money."

26. Brunton, *Discipline*, 111.

27. Ibid., 112.

28. Ellen's study of chemistry with Dr. Sidney, a man whom she has gently rejected, would continue to be a sexual situation in almost anyone else's hands. In Brunton's it leads to precisely nothing.

29. "Our grandmothers used to warn us against the arts of men. They represented lovers as insidious spoilers . . . I fear the nature of the pursuit remains the same, though the pursuit is transferred from our persons to our fortunes." (Brunton, *Discipline*, 23.) Frederick de Burgh, unlike more conventional villains, drops Ellen flat as soon as she loses her money; he does not even attempt to make her his mistress.

30. Grandison, about whose economic pursuits we know more than about Darcy's, helps only other Grandisons, real or honorary.

31. Brunton, *Discipline*, 62–63.

II. FEMININE ICONOGRAPHY

"At the Crossroads"
Sister Authors and the Sister Arts

KATRIN R. BURLIN

Most readers of Jane Austen know that after publishing *Pride and Prejudice*, she complained of feeling "fits of disgust" at its "rather too light, and bright, and sparkling" style. It wanted "shade," "a long chapter of sense, if it could be had." Although some of her suggestions for improving the novel are facetious, her discontent seems genuine; she was, she declared, in her next novel going to "try to write of something else, & it shall be a complete change of subject—ordination. . . ."[1] For the first and only time, Austen, in *Mansfield Park*, chose a masculine subject and something of the grand manner of history painting, rather than the miniature, to express it.

My title alludes to the famous topos of choice, "Hercules at the Crossroads Hesitating between Virtue (Duty) and Vice (Pleasure)," familiar to eighteenth-century producers, critics, and consumers of painting and literature.[2] I will here suggest that it is this topos, especially in its reinterpretation by Sir Joshua Reynolds,[3] that helped Austen, at the crossroads of her career, to work out her anxieties about the nature of her own genius. In his portrait of the Herculean actor David Garrick—*Garrick between Tragedy and Comedy*—Reynolds had dramatized the central moral choice as between *genres*, with Tragedy as Duty and Comedy as Pleasure.[4] By painting Comedy as a temptation to pleasure and Tragedy as the challenge of duty, Reynolds may have exacerbated Austen's uneasiness about the direction of her work. Had she, by writing comedy, taken the easier path?

What evidence have we that Austen knew the topos? Although its presence in *Mansfield Park* is unmistakable to a reader whose eye has been educated to detect the presence of the device of *ut pictura poesis* in literary art, it is not specifically named in the novel. However, in *Emblem and Expression*, Ronald Paulson tells us that as a major "structure of choice," the Choice of Hercules was "a part of every schoolboy's, every educated man's consciousness." In fact, it was one of "two basic school texts in eighteenth-century England for verbalizing the visual and visualizing the

60

verbal." Its popularity in England, he suggests, had to do with its subject, "choice" having "deeply English and Puritan sources."[5] Most important, for this argument, is that two prominent contemporary women novelists made provocative use of the topos. Mary Brunton's *Self Control,* a novel Austen read twice, offers an artist heroine who paints the hero as Hercules at the Crossroads (and herself as Virtue); Maria Edgeworth's *Belinda,* a novel Austen singled out for praise in *Northanger Abbey,*[6] makes Reynolds's portrait of Garrick as Hercules hesitating between Comedy and Tragedy of central dramatic significance. (Brunton was an admirer of Edgeworth's, as was Austen.) Brunton exploited the great male topos to question masculine assumptions about women's art; Edgeworth used it to challenge received critical assumptions about genre. As Jean H. Hagstrum has pointed out, the eighteenth-century English writer "carried about in his head what Malraux has called a *musee imaginaire,* composed of recollections of some of the leading master-pieces of European art."[7] It is the contribution of the more minor women writers to reconstruct that gallery for us, so that in turning to the art of their greater sister, we can read her with a fuller, richer responsiveness and greater accuracy. Thus Brunton and Edgeworth in their pointed naming and provocative deployment of the Hercules topos alert us to its presence in Austen's novel. The discovery of her witty allusions to the Choice of Hercules, I will suggest, can resolve some of the perplexities its puritanical heroine and tone have aroused in modern readers.

The Judgment of Hercules or the Choice of Hercules (the titles seem to be interchangeable) is, of course, a history painting, defined as a genre by its "preference for the heroic" and its "grand manner." Before examining the particular use our sister artists make of this heroic mode, we need to take a brief look at the larger question of how women novelists of Austen's time used the sister art of painting to define their own art. *The Oxford Companion to Art* tells us that "William Hogarth had in his 'modern moral subjects' developed a new and lively form of *genre* painting, which, with its emphasis on narrative, appealed greatly to the literary instincts of the English at the moment when the English novel was rising in importance."[8] Paulson argues that, in fact, "the great English artists of the eighteenth century (including Reynolds himself) were not the high-flying history painters but painters who continued to develop the possibilities of humble or intermediate subjects" and that "above all, the great *novelists* who revolutionized prose fiction" followed "the Hogarthian visual-verbal complex." Paulson celebrates Hogarth for "in some sense making fun of traditional iconography, and subverting and fragmenting it to make new meanings of his own. . . ."[9] As we shall see, women novelists make their own subversive contributions in this line.[10]

Many English women writers made the "humble" ground of genre painting theirs, some in conscious rejection of establishment views. Excluded
from full participation in masculine art, denied free admission into the
institutions of male art, there are women novelists who set up a playful
iconography of their own which not only satirizes patriarchal art and the
assumptions of its critics, but through a series of mutual allusions begins
delightfully to establish a female aesthetics and ethics.[11] Such women novelists are sophisticated in their knowledge of the received theories and criticism popularized in the art treatises of their day. They know the practice,
they have mastered the philosophy, they have handled prints. They are
ready to demonstrate their expertise by the knowledgeable skill with which
they both exploit and subvert the popular topoi. They are not afraid to
satirize the pompous sexism of the Earl of Shaftesbury or the moral evasiveness of Sir Joshua Reynolds. We can, in fact, trace the development of
the female novel along two lines, showing how the conscious adoption of
the ideals of "high-flying" history painting by such minor novelists as Mary
Wollstonecraft (and, to a degree, Mary Brunton) destroyed their female
inventiveness by turning their novels into copybook versions of received
masculine thought and taste, while the happy choice of genre painting freed
the comic invention of Austen and, less consistently, Maria Edgeworth.[12]

Most readers of Jane Austen know that she described her art as "the little
bit (two Inches wide) of Ivory on which I work with so fine a Brush, as
produces little effect after much labour."[13] Few readers, and this includes
most twentieth-century critics, understand that Austen was thus identifying herself as a miniature-portrait painter. Fewer readers yet may be aware
of the conscious defiance expressed in such a choice of genre by a woman
who, whatever her sense of her own merits, took the art of the novel seriously. From the point of view of so great an authority on aesthetic matters
as the Earl of Shaftesbury, miniature painting involved "no workmanship,
no labour, no not so much as thought." Portrait painting he dismissed as
mere "face painting," miniatures as art objects he thought to be effeminate:
"Ladies hate the great manner," he declared in contempt, "love baby sizes,
toys." The painter who wished for distinction must express himself in the
grand manner, must produce history paintings. "But when a subject is
given to a real painter, a heroic great subject: Good heavens! What toil!
What study! What meditation requisite!"[14] Shaftesbury exclaims, and the
"real painter" is, of course, a man.

Sadly, the miniature portrait as a metaphor for women's art received no
friendlier attention from the feminist Mary Wollstonecraft.[15] She is eager
to disassociate herself from the works of other women writers. Hungry for
intellectual equality with men, in reputation as well as in achievement,

Wollstonecraft actually uses her novel *Mary* to attack, with withering contempt, a genre of female fiction (and its notion of heroism) she defined by its characteristic exploitation of the miniature as a symbolic device: "The picture that was found on a bramble-bush . . . which caught the swain by the upper garment, and presented to his ravished eyes a portrait.—Fatal image! It sent . . . a new kind of a knight-errant into the world."[16] To her it seemed that the choice by women writers to associate their art with a "confined" art (the term is Reynolds's[17]) actually trivialized their achievement. The prose presenting the symbolic miniature expressed "pretty" thoughts rather than sublime; the action of such a novel portrayed "delicate struggles," not epic events. *Her* heroine—rather slavishly—champions the received aesthetic prejudices of the day: "*She* was particularly fond of . . . history-paintings [sic]." In this Mary is set apart from other women who as a gender are too ignorant to "descant" on the subject of history painting. Their interest in art is simply narcissistic: "as the ladies could not handle [the subject of history-painting] well, they soon adverted to portraits; and talked of the attitudes and characters in which they should wish to be drawn."[18]

Disassociating herself from such ladies, Wollstonecraft chooses the grand style and subject matter of history painting as *her* guiding metaphor and is, consequently, unable to write a novel. The generalized idealism of history painting is not sympathetic to the genius of the novel proper. Indeed, in *The Theory of the Novel*, Philip Stevick uses the analogy of "Hogarthian visual particularity" to stress the empirical nature, the specificity of eighteenth-century prose fiction.[19] History painting cannot serve as a functional analogy to novel writing since the "Grand Manner" in painting "demand[s] subordination of the particular and emphasis on the generic."[20] Eighteenth-century critics of the novel were quick to point out that the distinguishing quality of the novel was its closeness to "real life."

Measured by any standards, *Mary* is a failure. What makes it most disappointing, however, is its lack of originality. Thus although it purports to be feminist in taking a "Mind" for its heroine—to "display" the mind of a woman in its "thinking powers" ("Advertisement":4)—it subverts that end by filling the Mind with nothing but the most conventional masculine ideas.[21] As a novel, *Mary* has no art, no craft, and no invention.

Unlike Wollstonecraft, Austen parodies mindless exaltation of the epic scale. When the Prince Regent's librarian suggested that she write a historical romance, she repudiated the idea by pointing out that both romance and epic were alien forms to her imagination: "I could no more write a romance than an epic poem." She would deal in such modes for no "other motive than to save my life; and if it were indispensable for me to keep it up and never relax into laughing at myself or other people, I am sure I should be hung before I had finished the first chapter." That she knew her refusal to conform to the heroic ideal was radical is indicated in the hanging metaphor. Her independence is sturdy: "No, I must keep to my own style and go on in my own way. . . ." In the same letter in which she describes herself as a miniature portrait painter, the playfulness of her minimizing her own art is indicated precisely by the *comic* nature of her praise of her nephew's "strong, manly, spirited Sketches, full of Variety and Glow."[22] The joke here, as Donald Greene has firmly established, is that this "modest" woman is actually writing from her position of great authority, as a published author, to a mere "schoolboy" with literary ambitions.[23] While Wollstonecraft and her heroine wished to be discriminated from the rest of the sex, Austen deliberately associated herself with the art of novelists she called her "sister authors."[24] Like the women in *Mary*, though without their narcissism, she preferred portrait painting to history painting; in embracing her sister novelists, she redeemed the miniature as a central symbol and metaphor in and for women's art.

Such sublime artistic self-confidence could only come, of course, after a great struggle to define her "own way." Study of Austen's development reveals that *Mansfield Park* was the crisis point. Austen found herself in the position of Hercules, having to make a crucial choice about what path to take. She was, then, particularly responsive to what Paulson terms the "structure of choice" emblematized in the history painting Hercules at the Crossroads.[25] Partially, she followed in the track of other women writers. Two of these, Mary Brunton and Maria Edgeworth, may have stimulated her imagination precisely because they had provocatively dramatized the theme of choice by taking on the challenge in their feminine art of that great male topos of choice, and had, in the process, questioned male authority in aesthetics and ethics.

To understand the women writers' critical interpretations and reworkings of the Hercules topos, we need to know something of its subject, its structure, and of how it was conventionally rendered. The Earl of Shaftesbury's essay, "A Notion of the Historical Draught of Hercules," is here most helpful, because most generally known. In explaining his theories of how the topos ought to be painted, Shaftesbury drew on the Hercules story as it was narrated by Prodicus and recorded by Xenophon. In that account, Hercules, coming to the age when a young man must declare for either the virtuous or the vicious path of life, is approached by two statuesque women, the goddesses Virtue and Vice. Each goddess in turn urges Hercules to take *her* path. Pleasure (" 'My friends . . . call me Happiness, but those who hate me, give me, to my disparagement, the name of Vice' ")

offers Hercules " 'the most delightful and easy road,' " while Virtue promises that if he takes her path, he " 'will become an excellent performer of
whatever is honourable and noble.' " She will engage to show him " 'things
as they really are,' " to help him see that " 'of what is valuable and excellent
the gods grant nothing to mankind without labour and care . . .'."[26]

In directing the painter of this topos, Shaftesbury suggests that Hercules,
as "the first or principal figure of our piece," be "placed in the middle,
between the two goddesses." He should be "so drawn" that not only his face
but "the very turn or position of the body alone" would indicate that he
"had not wholly quitted the balancing part." Though turned toward Virtue,
his body ought to reflect a lingering, even a promising regret for the other
goddess. I will consider these and other aspects of the topos relevant to the
discussion in the context of the specific novels. One further point Shaftesbury makes, however, is of special interest to all our novelists. It is Hercules, he insists, who is "in reality the party judged"[27] here; the choice he
makes is a measure of his moral stature. The goddesses, of course, are
allegorical figures. To judge them would be irrelevant and absurd. And yet,
as we shall see, the women writers *do* judge them—when their interest shifts
from the central male figure to the feminine types.

The women writers exploit fully the moral and aesthetic values of the
topos; at times they seem comically subversive. We see something of this in
Mary Brunton's *Self-Control* when her highly talented and nobly contoured artist-heroine Laura attempts to interpret the Choice of Hercules.
Virtue, as Shaftesbury explains she should be painted, though elegant and
graceful, is too modest and sober in dress and behavior to offer sexual
temptation to the hero; Pleasure, or Vice, however, is a highly sexed temptress: "fed to plumpness and softness, but assisted by art . . . in her complexion, so as to seem fairer and rosier than she really was. . . . [S]he had
her eyes wide open, and a robe through which her beauty would readily
show itself."[28] Laura is well trained in the manner recommended to young
artists by Reynolds; she has learned to paint in the high style by imitating
the great models. She ambitiously attempts history paintings. But when she
comes to try her hand at painting the Hercules topos, her feminine modesty
makes her interpretation as pathetic as it is comic.

The problem of modesty does not arise, as we might imagine, when
Laura decides to use De Courcy as her model for Hercules, or to copy "the
form and countenance of Virtue" from the "simple majesty of her own." It
arises from the feminine delicacy that shrinks from depicting female
sexuality—indeed, from even conceiving it. To imagine Pleasure "cost the
fair artist unspeakable labour" because she "could not pourtray [sic] what
she would have shrunk from beholding—a female Voluptuary." The con-

sequence is a ludicrously proper goddess: "Her draperies were always designed with the most chastened decency; and after all her toil, even the form of Pleasure came sober and matronly from the hands of Laura.[29] Brunton laughs at Laura's prudery, but also establishes that a young lady's moral education will necessarily interfere with the successful practice of what is termed the higher art. The novel, in fact, treats the problems of a woman artist with some complexity and emphasis.

The "Montague De Courcy" mentioned in the cited passage is Laura's as yet undeclared lover. She thinks she has only platonic feelings for him. Having discovered that he has been anonymously buying her paintings, she has painted him as Hercules in gratitude for his courage in supporting her art. Brunton, however, slyly tells us that although De Courcy admires Laura for her enterprise, he almost instinctively hides her productions from public view. To him, as to Laura's father, there is something degrading in a woman's earning her living by the labor of her hands. And yet the money Laura makes through secretly painting and selling her pictures not only saves her father from the consequences of abject poverty, but also actually supports such of his luxurious habits as chocolate for breakfast; this she provides him through great physical self-denial, starving herself so that he might be deprived of no physical comfort.

Thinking marriage the only respectable profession for Laura, her father regards her painting room as a place of potential amorous intrigue rather than of artistic performance. Alert to how the Hercules portrait might strike De Courcy, he smuggles him into Laura's painting room. Prowling around the room, De Courcy unveils the painting and immediately reads the iconography as a species of proposal, rather than as a learned compliment. To De Courcy, that Laura "should have painted his portrait in a groupe [*sic*] where it held such a relation to her own," suggests the "conviction that he was beloved" (1: 251-52). It is popular topos, after all; he knows which goddess Hercules chose. Her reluctance to let him see the unfinished picture he reads as her shame at betraying her unsolicited feelings for him. He is so enflamed by what he interprets to be Virtue's sexual overtures (after all, Laura has covered Vice with more drapery than she has Virtue!) that he very nearly assaults the innocent artist. Like Fanny Burney in *Evelina*, Brunton dramatizes through her besieged heroine's dilemma the warning that for a woman to practice or criticize art in the presence of men leads inevitably to sexual harassment. When Burney's heroine dares to laugh at a man's ignorance of standard iconography, she is immediately and severely punished for her boldness by being mistaken for a prostitute. If De Courcy did not secretly think that Laura's professional life is somehow shameful, he would not so promptly have read her painting as an expression of personal passion. As a man viewing a woman's painting of which he is the subject, he cannot maintain a level of abstraction, cannot read the iconography as expressive of "fortitude,"[30] but brings it down to the very specific, egotistical level of "this woman loves me and wants me to choose her."

For Brunton, the spirit of the age seems to preclude heroism in men.[31] The same brutality that makes it dangerous for Laura to go alone to the art gallery to sell her paintings—seeing a well-dressed, attractive, and independent woman walking alone, men accost her and jeer at her as if she were a prostitute—has conquered heroism. Men's novels, Brunton suggests, have contributed to the lowering of the moral tone. Laura's earlier attempt to paint a history painting of the Spartan hero Leonidas, admittedly modeled on a former lover who later proves to be a rake, leads an admiring young lady to identify the hero as Tom Jones! The modern Hercules proves his heroism through his sexual prowess, violently embracing Pleasure. The mistake allows Brunton to dramatize a culturally significant moment: the "modern" consumer of art can no longer be expected to recognize the old iconography. He is likely to take his heroes from novels now. Interestingly, in both *Self-Control* and *Sense and Sensibility*, the artist-heroines, themselves of Herculean moral strength, have lovers who declare themselves decidedly un-Herculean in conventional masculine terms. Both young men protest that they have no ambition, no wish to leave the comforts of home by following Virtue's pointing finger to the rocky regions demanding fortitude.[32]

Brunton's constant stress on Laura's "labouring" to produce her paintings is echoed in Austen's phrase "the labours of art." Both women delight in the triumph over self that such hard labor necessitates. Like so many of the artist-heroines invented by women, Laura has no difficulty accepting the fact that art is the product of hard labor. She glories in her work, for it brings her strength through discipline, the "self-control" celebrated in the novel's title. It frees her from her natural susceptibility to passion, and allows her, while painting, a measure of control over her life. It is, however, in her sexually charged world but a short-lived consolation, possible only while there are men in her life to protect her from other men. After her father's death, Laura discovers that she must give up painting professionally because of her sex. Her "personal charms," she discovers, disqualify her for being an artist. As a lady, she must shrink from "the intrusion of strangers" and the "public observation" that her profession would demand. Indeed, she knows she would not be safe: "Besides, it was impossible to think of living alone and unprotected, in the human chaos that surrounded her" (p. 218). Brunton is herself deeply interested in the repressed sexuality of her heroine and she cleverly uses many of Laura's paintings to point out that a society that does not permit its women to be acquainted with their own passions and emotions will inevitably produce radically flawed women painters—especially if it only rewards painting in the high style. Laura's two history paintings are absurd. Men's art as well as man's nature will not permit a woman to paint in the masculine style and to follow masculine iconography. Though herself a figure for "Fortitude," Laura cannot paint herself as Hercules (although the more self-complacent painter Angelica Kauffmann did just that) because she has no choices to make. She is fixed in the ideal form of Virtue. Brunton comes to mock her heroine's rather pathetic attempts to reform the men in her life by idealizing them through high art. To cure Laura, to clear her head of outdated iconography, in the second volume of her novel, Brunton sends her down a Canadian river without a paddle, her educated eye condemned for days to see nothing but the primitive Canadian shores rushing by. But if Brunton satirizes her heroine through the medium of the Hercules topos, she also disapproves of how male artists, critics, and connoisseurs have interpreted Prodicus's story—as a seduction of the "enamoured hero" in (Shaftesbury's language).[33] Because of this introduction of the sexual tension into the topos of choice, her heroine could not handle the subject innocently.

One reason *Self-Control* is not the good novel it might be, given its clever insights and wonderfully comic moments, is that Brunton herself cannot resist the temptation to elevate her genre by offering—especially in the heroine—large-scale idealizations. With exceptions, Laura is a figure posturing theatrically in a history painting, not the portrait of a probable, individual woman. To Austen, Brunton's novel seemed "excellently-meant" and "elegantly-written" but having "nothing" of "Nature" or "Probability" in it.[34] High intentions and high style have destroyed it as a novel for her. Finally, Brunton shows herself rather insensitive to the novel as a genre. For while, like Austen, she defends the novel as a literary form— "Why should an epic or a tragedy be supposed to hold such an exalted place in composition, while a novel is almost a nick-name for a book?" she complains—her notion of the form betrays real aesthetic and critical weaknesses.[35] Imagining a novel "Milton himself need not have been ashamed of," she can only suggest a species of pastiche, based on various models (the advantages of imitation, of using models, is cited by Reynolds in his *Discourses*).[36] Her "novel" is a patched-together job, of male and female imaginations bundled indiscriminately into a single composition: "Let the admirable construction of fable in Tom Jones be employed to unfold characters like Miss Edgeworth's—let it lead to a moral like Richardson's—let it be told with the elegance of Rousseau. . . ."

Now the question of genre is of vital importance to Brunton's two greater sister novelists; doubtless, this is why they are yet more interested in Sir Joshua Reynolds's reinterpretation of the topos[37] as a choice between the genres, Comedy and Tragedy, than in the more conventional rendering of Hercules as hesitating between moral choices. In the Reynolds painting, Hercules is now the popularly admired actor David Garrick; the goddess Vice-Pleasure is Comedy; the goddess Virtue-Duty is Tragedy. The painting brilliantly exploits Shaftesbury's rather pedantic instructions to his painter. Garrick, his body inclining toward the sensuous and comely figure of Comedy, clinging playfully to his arm, looks back with an expression of rather cheerful regret at the formidable figure of Tragedy who grips his wrist while pointing sternly upward to the rocky path of fame. Horace Walpole offers a persuasive contemporary reading of Garrick's choice: "Comedy drags him away, and he seems to yield willingly, though endeavouring to excuse himself, and pleading that he is forced."[38]

Tragedy, then, retains the posture, costume, features, and general iconography of Virtue; Comedy takes the luscious form of Vice. Paulson's reading of the portrait differs. He suggests that the presence of the Hercules topos in Garrick's portrait is Reynolds's learned compliment to the actor, to his Herculean talent. He explains that Reynolds meant to suggest that the actor, unlike the hero, need not choose between his goddesses—for he is great in either mode. He is, according to Paulson, choosing between "equal goods."[39] It seems to me, however, that because of the inevitable moral resonances of the old topos, Reynolds's clothing and posing the women in the mode of Virtue and Vice, the painting cannot help but make a statement about the comparative ethics of the genres and, consequently, of the one who chooses. Walpole's language indicates *his* perfect comprehension that generic discrimination is implied. He points out that Tragedy "exhorts" Garrick to "follow her exalted vocation" before Comedy "drags" him away.[40] This aspect of the portrait, whether the product of Reynolds's conscious deliberation or not, this weighting or judging of the genres, seems to have made a deep impression on Austen, and affected Edgeworth's response to the topos.

On first reading, the introduction of the Hercules topos in Edgeworth's *Belinda* seems pure burlesque. In this novel, in a deliberately reductive feminizing of a heroic male topos, Hercules is become a lady's maid and the important drama of choice is between two ball gowns. In the chapter titled "Masks," announcing that "masquerade [is] the order of the day," the secretly tragic Lady Delacour, "forcing . . . an air of gaiety," asks Belinda: " 'Tragedy or Comedy, Belinda? The masquerade dresses are come.' "[41] As the women debate the virtues of the dresses in terms of their own generic "genius" and "taste," Lady Delacour wittily identifies her maid, Marriott, as Garrick in the Reynolds's portrait. Seeing her maid "with the dress of the comic muse on one arm, and the tragic muse on the other," she exclaims: "But whilst we are making speeches to one another, poor Marriott is standing in distress like Garrick between tragedy and comedy" (1:17). Edgeworth satirically assures us that Marriott, like Hercules, is "a person of prodigious consequence," and "judge in the last resort," though only "at her mistress's toilette." The maid's declared principle for choosing which lady will wear which mask comically reflects just how diffused the knowledge of such generic inconography had become, and how easily it was emptied of meaning: " 'Your ladyship's taller than Miss Portman by half a head. . . . and to be sure will best become tragedy, with this long train. . . . Tragedy, they say, is always tall, and, no offence, your ladyship's taller than Miss Portman by half a head' " (1:17). In a further comic feminizing of the topos, Edgeworth lets us see that neither woman aspires for the more "exalted" role; each prefers the comic dress as more becoming, more attractive to the hero for whom *they* compete. Thus they establish their own familiarity with the Reynolds's painting in which the hero, after all, chooses Comedy. And, as in Austen, the problem of choice is, finally, the women's—the goddesses', if you will,—in a significant displacement of the male hero from his centrality in this famous "structure of choice."[42] Indeed, in Edgeworth's verbal painting, *all* the members of the topos are women!

But Edgeworth's use of the Hercules topos is not pure burlesque. Underlying the comedy are hints of tragedy. The women writers may adopt Reynolds's generic rather than Shaftesbury's ethical version of heroic choice as model, but it is important to them to stress that generic choice *is* moral choice, that the choice of genre is vitally informed by ethical concerns. *Belinda* is a novel of a young woman's entrance into a world of masks, of hidden pain, intrigue and disease, of the dangerously close correspondence between social and stage performance. Here people are valued only as long as they are entertaining. On the social stage, when a woman ceases to be amusing, she becomes an object of pity and contempt. Lady Delacour forces Belinda to choose the dress of Tragedy, the "tragical disguise" (1:22) which for herself would be no disguise; she is afraid to let her mask fall, to let the world know that she is dying. She would *rather* die than take the inevitably public measures needed to cure her. The history of her dilemma is this: on a dare, Lady Delacour, dressed as a man, has fought a duel with another woman and suffered a serious wound in her breast which will not heal. She lives on the strength of opium and a series of "comic" disguises, exhorting Belinda, too, to "keep on the mask." But when this tragic woman refuses to acknowledge her own serious mode and wants to masquerade as the muse of Comedy, she violates the rigorous moral values of a novel that demands total self-recognition as the means of release from the domination of masks. When she insists on wearing the dress of Comedy she is, to Edgeworth, inescapably tragic.

Edgeworth, then, exploits Reynolds's version of the Hercules topos partially to satirize her society. Her point throughout is how much the appearance of both virtue and vice is a matter of theatrical performance. Paulson suggests that Reynolds's painting makes clear that all its figures—Hercules and his attendant goddesses—are actors "playing" at choice.[43] Lady Delacour is basically a good woman, but bored by the pretensions to morality of indifferently bad people, and by the badness of conventional moral style, she pretends to be wicked: " 'I never read or listened to a moral at the end of a story in my life—manners for me, and morals for those that like them' " (1:38). Shaftesbury's more standard "notion" of the Choice of Hercules also figures here. If Lady Delacour, placed in the position to choose, presently decides for what the world ignorantly terms Pleasure, she knows that only to the uninitiated can that choice suggest the delicious, untaxing path of life. In fact, Pleasure exacts far more from its votaries, than does Virtue, of emotional wear and tear, and physical stress.

Edgeworth also uses Lady Delacour to suggest the possibility that the Hercules topos, as it is rendered in "Garrick Hesitating between Comedy and Tragedy," may be irrelevant to actual human experience. It is a meaningful choice only for the professional actor. She declares: " 'Life is a tragicomedy!—Though the critics will allow no such thing in their books, it is a true representation of what passes in the world; and of all lives mine has been the most grotesque mixture or alternation, I should say, of tragedy and comedy!' " (1:66). Life does not offer a clear generic choice between modes of being. After the great choosing scene, where Lady Delacour is blackmailed by her punitive maid into wearing the tragic dress, the two women simply stop off at a friend's house and exchange dresses. If the muses are but disguises for truth, are not all received generic modes suspect? A woman, then, might freely invent her own more accommodating form. Despite the strictures of contemporary critics, Edgeworth thought that the novelist, in rendering ordinary experience, could not make a choice between the genres: the topos, as Reynolds interpreted it, was become irrelevant. Austen was not so sure, but the "mixed" form of *Mansfield Park was* a reaction against the "pure" comedy of *Pride and Prejudice*.[44] She may have been temporarily influenced by Edgeworth. Like Belinda, offered a choice of masks, she tries on both.

As a writer concerned with the moral seriousness of her art, Austen was, as I have suggested, most vulnerable at this time to the suggestion implicit in Reynolds's painting that Tragedy is the nobler mode, and that Comedy is a species of self-indulgence, an undemanding, superficial genre. Certainly the topos haunts the novel, as if Austen saw herself in Garrick's role in the painting and is deeply disturbed by the suggestion that, like his, her choice is of the less ambitious genre. At this crossroads of her career, the choice of Comedy may have come to seem too easy to satisfy her increasingly rigorous demands on her genius. Ought she to take the rockier, because new (to her), path of Tragedy? *Mansfield Park* is the only one of Austen's novels in which she herself is not certain that her genius is comic and that she can do most good in choosing Comedy as her genre. Consequently, it is a novel *about* this conflict, with the topos as a central configuration.

As a product, however, the novel suffers from the uneasy conflict between the genres. Garrick complained that the new self-consciously moral "weeping comedies" of his day were ruining drama by their attempt to place "the steeple on the playhouse."[45] *Mansfield Park*, in which Austen makes a sermon out of the playhouse of her imagination, seems such an awkward edifice, despite its undeniable grandeur and complexity. Austen chose a masculine subject in the grand style: "all that is of the first importance to mankind, individually or collectively considered, temporally and eternally." She has thus made herself responsible for "the guardianship of religion and morals, and consequently of the manners which result from their influence (3:93)."[46] If modern critics, unhappy with the achievement, ask plaintively "What Became of Jane Austen?" the answer that suggests itself is that she tried to write like "Jack."[47] The happy self-confidence implicit in the miniature metaphor earlier cited is not yet achieved.

Fortunately, this flirtation with the elevated mode is a temporary aberration. Working her way through the Hercules topos, especially as it is manifested in the works of her female colleagues, Austen comes to terms with herself as an essentially comic writer most comfortable in the company of the sister authors with whom she has from the first identified. Meanwhile, her use of the topos itself is ingenious, as *functional* as it is wittily precise and resonant with ironies.

Paulson tells us that "Hercules was a favourite figure in the iconography of English country houses.[48] The union in the Hercules topos of the drama of choice and its Puritan moral resonance is no doubt another reason Austen exploited it in *Mansfield Park*, her own country house novel, to consolidate the major themes of choice. Her characters' rehearsal of Kotzebue's weeping-comedy, *Lovers' Vows*, and the ordination of Edmund Bertram, her young hero about to enter upon his path of life, raise questions of generic and moral choice. The question of choice is the central moral issue of the novel, and all the central romantic triangles through which Austen explores her theme take the configuration of the Hercules topos. She offers us two Hercules. One could be painted by Shaftesbury's artist; the other is both Reynolds's Garrick and Shaftesbury's Hercules. The novel's hero, Edmund Bertram, is Hercules choosing between the heroine, Fanny Price, as the goddess of Virtue, and her rival, Mary Crawford, as the goddess of Pleasure or Vice. The villain or cad, Henry Crawford, a superb actor who can perform Garrick's best roles,[49] is Reynolds's Hercules, choosing between Fanny's cousins, Julia Bertram as Comedy and Maria Bertram as Tragedy. But he is also Shaftesbury's Hercules, choosing between Virtue (Fanny) and Vice (Maria). Like Crawford, Maria appears in both paintings: she is both Vice and Tragedy. How do the men perform in their heroic capacity? In the first volume, Edmund invites each "goddess" to take an arm and then vacillates between them until, in the last volume, an exacerbated Virtue actually loses her temper and angrily exhorts him to "Fix, commit, condemn yourself," even if it should be to the wrong goddess! As a man of "heroic" appetite for sexual intrigue, Crawford greedily tries to choose both goddesses, Fanny (Virtue) and Maria (Vice).

For *Mansfield Park*, Shaftesbury's interpretation of the topos of Hercules as mainly pedagogical in thrust is particularly relevant: "It is on the issue of the controversy between these two [goddesses], that the character of Hercules depends. So that we may naturally give to this piece and history, as well the title of The Education, as the Choice or Judgment of Hercules." His very language concerning the topos could be applied as usefully to explain the "subject" of *Mansfield Park*, the hesitation of its hero between ordination and the more fashionable life that his choice of Pleasure would entail. Like the "young" Hercules, Edmund must "deliberate on the choice he [is] to make of the different ways of life"[50] under the influence of two women. The first volume of the novel is dominated by great scenes of choice that seem especially indebted to Shaftesbury's directions to his painter. In the gardens of Sotherton, Mary and Fanny, like the goddesses of Prodicus, take opposing sides on the question of whether the hero should take the path of Virtue, of spiritual ambition, or the path of Pleasure, of worldly ambition. Back at Mansfield, we are offered the great scenes of choosing the play and casting the actors, the latter of which follows the structure of the topos as closely as the Sotherton scenes. *Generic* choice is here dramatized as the characters identify themselves and others according to generic type. But whether they see themselves as "comic" or "tragic," they have clearly lost all sense of the *moral* implications of choice; they care only about expressing their own aesthetic genius.

Austen seems scrupulously to follow Shaftesbury's guidance in identifying her heroines as Virtue and Vice (Pleasure). Thus Fanny has the requisite "modesty of look" and "sobriety of demeanor" Prodicus described in

Virtue; Mary has the vivacity of Vice or Pleasure. As Vice, too, it is appropriate that Mary should mock Fanny's virtuous harangues with her own
anticlerical taunts, her coarse puns on "rears and vices." Prodicus's Vice
makes wicked fun of Virtue's long-windedness. In turn, as Virtue, Fanny
must censor Mary's views and character.[51] To condemn her for her censo-
riousness, as modern readers have done, is a mistake contemporary readers
would not have made: they would have understood her role in the allegory.
To recognize Fanny's function in the topos, then, helps resolve the perplexities her apparent humorlessness and consistent goodness have created in
modern critical minds more used to Austen's ironic view of character.

To continue the list of telling correspondences, it is Fanny who, like
Prodicus's Virtue, consistently points out to the hapless hero "the way
which leads to honour, and the just glory of heroic actions."[52] This is the
significance of Fanny's most rhapsodic speeches, like the one in Sotherton
chapel in which she celebrates the old way of worship—trumpets and
banners blowing, arches and aisles contributing to the air of melancholy
grandeur (p. 85–86)—to an erringly amused Edmund. It is Fanny who
glories in the significance of Edmund's name—"There is nobleness in the
name of Edmund. It is a name of heroism and renown" (p. 211)—a glory
the worldly Mary cannot see unless the name were preceded by a "Lord" or
a "Sir." The care with which Austen followed conventional iconography is
also indicated in her heroines' responses to the Arts. Hagstrum has established that in standard versions of the topos, Pleasure is associated with the
Arts.[53] Mary, of course, is an accomplished harpist. That her performance
is seductive Austen makes clear by painting us a picture of a pretty Mary at
her pretty instrument in a sultry season playing love songs to an infatuated
Edmund.

In contrast, in a rare gesture of will that has puzzled modern critics,
Fanny has from childhood refused to learn either music or drawing. She
even makes speeches against the Arts (p. 113). Her attitude, of course, is
consistent with her allegorical role. The contrast is dramatized in the novel's famous "star-gazing" scene (pp. 112–13) in which Fanny, as Virtue, in
an attempt to make Edmund leave Mary and the pleasures of the house,
points to the stars in "the scene without."[54] Mary, however, as Pleasure,
through the manipulation of the arts, the performance of the glee, tempts
him back in her "way": Edmund turns his back to the window, to Virtue,
"moving forward by gentle degrees toward the instrument," to Pleasure
(1:113).

Most renderings of the topos suggest the potency of its hero by painting
the scene of choice as a species of moral seduction by the goddesses. Mary
as Pleasure-Vice is shrewd enough to manipulate Edmund by a challenge to

his sexuality: she signifies that the question of his profession is really a question of his manhood. At Sotherton, where Edmund's choice of language—he talks about the "proportion of virtue to vice throughout the kingdom"—signals the presence of the topos, Mary tries to persuade him that a clergyman's worldly position is so low that the profession ought not even to figure as a choice: "For what is to be done in the church? Men love to distinguish themselves, and in . . . other lines distinction may be gained, but not in the church. A clergyman is nothing" (1:92). Fanny, of course, takes the opposite view. Austen exploits the sexual tension implicit in the topos by showing that although Edmund intellectually understands the falseness of Mary's views, he is so powerfully attracted to her physically, that in touching her he forgets the claims of Virtue: "the gratification of . . . feeling such a connection for the first time, made him a little forgetful of Fanny" (p. 94). As each woman influences him, Edmund mirrors psychologically the conflict Shaftesbury instructed his painter to express through the hero's face and body position: He inclines toward one goddess even as he is choosing the other. Near the end of the novel, even as Edmund looks toward Fanny (Virtue), he regrets Mary (Pleasure).

Austen follows the topos neither slavishly nor humorlessly. She offers some significant reversals of the Prodicus story and makes a silly joke in response to Shaftesbury's directions. In Prodicus, it is not Vice but Virtue who exhorts the hero to be active and ambitious. Austen gives those speeches to Mary. Why? As a woman she seems thus to challenge received assumptions about the real nature of "fortitude"—Hercules's virtue.[55] It is in the inconspicuous service of humanity, she suggests, that real heroism lies. Mary's notion of heroism is even naive: she wants a stage hero, a glittering soldier. And Prodicus's Virtue does little to challenge worldly notions of heroism when she tempts Hercules with fame. Shaftesbury is wiser; he understands the character of Virtue: "The energy or natural force of Virtue, according to the moral philosophy of highest note among the ancients, was expressed in the double effect of forbearance and endurance."[56] These, of course, are *feminine* virtues[57] in Austen's novel, and preeminently Fanny's. It is as if Austen were more interested in studying the character of Virtue than of the Hero; as in Edgeworth, the focus of attention in the topos has shifted from the man to an attendant woman.

Another significant difference in Austen's rendering of the topos is that she paints Vice-Pleasure as the active, energetic figure, and Virtue as close to supine.[58] But Mary's energy, as many critics have pointed out, leads to no active good, and Fanny's passivity, I would argue, is largely enforced. In the privacy of an empty room, she practices her dance steps all along the wall; when she thinks deeply, she *paces* her room. In the absence of real, kind, active interest in her by women, she has been largely brought up by two highly conventional men—the severe patriarch Sir Thomas, who can frighten her into obedience, and her cousin Edmund, who bribes her with love. These men teach her the man's idea of a perfect woman: weak, dependent, fragile, timid, and passive. They almost destroy her naturally strong character. Anxious for love from Edmund, and fearful of alienating her uncle, Fanny adopts the feminine role extravagantly. Thus Austen uses the Hercules topos to challenge her society's assumptions also about womanly virtue. Fanny's side of the topos is seriously weakened as long as Virtue is too timid to urge her cause aggressively to the confused hero. Austen's subversive response to the topos includes the mockingly learned allusion to Shaftesbury's directions as to how Virtue should be dressed—in "purest" and "most glossy white" apparently.[59] Thus Austen has her Hercules admire not only the whiteness, but the "glossy spots" on Fanny's ball dress!

The Choice of Hercules was attractive as a moral emblem to Austen because of its very simplicity. It advertised her point in *Mansfield Park* that moral choices *are* simple: we complicate their psychology to evade the responsibility of choice. Fanny sees this very clearly, but it takes Edmund the length of the book to find his way back to her moral simplicity. Austen's interest in the Reynolds's Hercules seems at least partly prompted by *its* moral evasiveness. For, if we accept Paulson's reading, the actor is enabled to avoid the responsibility of moral choice by his painter's having translated the moral into aesthetic opposition.[60] Interestingly, this is precisely what Austen's actor, Henry Crawford, attempts for himself. Unlike Reynolds, Austen will not permit it—as we shall see.

Crawford is caught between opposing generic goddesses while casting *Lovers' Vows*, but the actors have been polarized by the issue even earlier. What condemns them in the genre-choosing scenes is that they play at what, to Austen, is a radically serious matter. From the first, they reveal their vanity by imposing their egoistic need for self-display on whatever text is chosen. They show no respect for the generic integrity of the play itself, demanding that it "be at once both tragedy and comedy" (p. 130). (That Austen should find this absurd reveals that she had decided against Edgeworth's ideal of a "mixed" form.) But when it comes to choosing the actors, Austen's characters suddenly become very nice in their ideas of generic type. Each, of course, has a personal stake in the available roles. Maria and Julia are "typed" generically not only by Crawford, but also, repeatedly, by their brother Tom. Like the maid in *Belinda*, he displays a pretty superficial understanding of genre. He judges aesthetic fitness primarily by his sisters'—and Mary's—physical type, and by the rule of his own will and convenience, rather than by their acting prowess. "Oh Yes, Maria must be Agatha. Maria will be the best Agatha. Though Julia fancies she prefers tragedy, I would not trust her in it. There is nothing of tragedy about her. She has not the look of it. Her features are not tragic features, and she walks too quick, and speaks too quick . . ." (p. 134).

According to Tom, poor Julia's physique is equally against her in Comedy: now, she is "too tall and robust" (135). Comedy, Tom declares, and his description corresponds exactly to Reynolds's painting of Comedy, should be a "small, light, girlish, skipping figure," like Mary (p. 135). Austen thus shows off a skill in iconography parallel to Reynolds's, since at least one of her figures for Vice (Mary) is, like his, also the figure for Comedy. Austen's characters selfishly exploit their expertise in the jargon of generic modes to manipulate each other; all their fine talk about aesthetic fitness—"Tragedy may be your choice, but it will certainly appear that comedy chooses *you*" (p. 135)—is simply sexual intrigue. This is what the topos has culminated in, Austen seems to suggest: from its inception in Prodicus, it's been translated into a series of scenes of seduction. Austen offers her own.

Both Bertram sisters are hopelessly infatuated with Crawford. Because Maria is already engaged, Julia feels that she has a greater moral right to Crawford. But it is Maria he wants precisely because she *is* engaged, and he hopes, in choosing her, not to have to choose. Caught between the women when he must choose one to "play" opposite him, he attempts to resolve the tension—like Reynolds—by translating the moral into a generic choice. Julia, he argues, is by nature Comic, while Maria is Tragic, and his own role in the play they are about to perform, demands that he choose Tragedy: " 'I must entreat Miss *Julia* Bertram,' said he, 'not to engage in the part of [Tragedy], or it will be the ruin of all my solemnity. You must not, indeed you must not (turning to her). I could not stand your countenance dressed up in woe and paleness. The many laughs we have had would infallibly come across me . . .' " (p. 133). Austen's verbal picture of Crawford hesitating between the Comic and Tragic actresses, then, is a comic reversal of Reynolds' painting where Comedy seems to triumph. (Not as skillful an actor as Garrick, Crawford betrays *his* preference in an indiscreet glance to Maria.) But Austen will not allow *her* actor the delusion that for an artist to redefine the moral into the aesthetic choice is to avoid responsibility for making right choices.[61] Crawford and Maria are forced to act out the tragedy they so lightly chose in their disastrous elopement.

To reinforce this point, Austen also places Crawford in the original paradigm, as Hercules between Virtue and Vice (Pleasure). After playing at love with the tragic Maria, he has fallen seriously in love with Fanny, and is, apparently, given a chance at reform. When Maria discovers that he is more committed to the play than he is to her—he would stay at Mansfield to finish the performance but not to court her—she marries another, in a jealous rage. Fanny, as Virtue, makes Crawford conscious that as a landowner he has powers for good he ought to exercise. He is about to embrace the virtuous life in the country when Maria, as Pleasure, tempts him to remain in London. Greedily, he attempts to choose both women, both goddesses. He yields to Pleasure under the illusion that he can always return to the straight path from the serpentine: "the temptation of immediate pleasure was too strong for a mind unused to make any sacrifice to right." But his choice has cost him Virtue, "the way of happiness" (p. 467). Virtue has found the true Hercules in Edmund, who has "set out, and felt that he had done so, on this road to happiness," "where there was nothing on the side of prudence to stop him or make his progress slow" (p. 471). For *her* part in the topos, Maria is explicitly identified as Vice: "Maria had destroyed her own character, and he would not . . . sanction vice" (p. 465). Austen has revenged herself on Reynolds for *his* identification of Comedy with Vice. Crawford, as Garrick-Hercules, in choosing Tragedy, has chosen Vice.

In *Belinda*, the heroines' appropriate choice of generic mode has been seen as a necessary stage in their moral development. In *Mansfield Park*, Austen severely holds even her minor characters to the generic mode through which they either identify themselves or are identified by others. Thus, Maria chooses the tragic role and is forced to perform it; Julia, identified as comic by Crawford and her author, and as untragic by her brother, consequently avoids the more terrible fate of her sister. In sly allusion to the secondary status of Comedy, Austen suggests that such a position can be morally redeeming: Julia had "held but second place," a "little inferior to Maria. Her temper was the easiest of the two, her feelings, though quick, were more controllable" (p. 466). Guilty only of "folly," Julia is readmitted into the happy temple of the virtuous; guilty of "vice," Maria is banished. In a punitive version of Fanny's early, morally refining life, she is destined to live with an aunt as a dependent niece. Now we understand why, when the curtain came down on *Lovers' Vows*, it disappeared into Aunt Norris's cottage.

Why *does* Austen insist on this rigid conformity between the roles the women act and their destiny? It is as if her own preoccupation with the right generic choice for herself, and her anxiety about such a choice being a *moral* choice, led her to allegorize her internal debate in the scheme of the novel. While she does not identify with the rather mean-minded and selfish Julia, through her fate she does seem to suggest that mistakes committed in the comic mode are finally less terrible than those one makes in the more ambitious mode. If Comedy receives less recognition, it is also less dangerous. The conclusion to *Mansfield Park* may finally testify less to moral than to aesthetic rigidity.

And thus in *Mansfield Park*, Austen with astonishing inventiveness and economy renders the Hercules topos in multiple permutations. Before she is through, she has worked out the topos in terms laid out by Shaftesbury, reworked it to try out Reynolds's ideas, and "outwitted" her sister authors in the multiple resonances that inform her deployment of its moral-generic functions. The consequence is that she succeeds in identifying for herself the nature of her own genius and comes to terms with it. There "can be no Virtue without Choice."[62] There *is* virtue in generic purity. She decides to "let other pens dwell on guilt and misery"; she will quit such "odious subjects" (III:461). As her clergyman achieves moral heroism only through choosing, so Austen achieves her comic masterpiece, *Emma*, through choosing *her* genre: Comedy.

NOTES

1. Austen, letters 77 and 76, quoted in *Jane Austen's Letters*, 2d. ed., edited by R. W. Chapman (London: Oxford University Press, 1952), 299, 298.

2. I am greatly indebted for guidance in reading the Hercules topos in the context of eighteenth-century English art and literature in Ronald Paulson, *Emblem and Expression: Meaning in English Art of the Eighteenth Century* (London: Thames & Hudson, 1975); Jean H. Hagstrum, *The Sister Arts: The Tradition of Literary Pictorialism and English Poetry From Dryden to Gray* (Chicago: The University of Chicago Press, 1958); and Frederick Hilles, ed., *Portraits by Sir Joshua Reynolds* (London: William Heineman, 1952). These critics attest to the popularity of the Choice of Hercules topos, making it all the more likely that even mildly educated women would have been familiar with it. None of these works is concerned however, with the contribution of women novelists to the creative reinterpretation of the topos. I owe my knowledge of Prodicus, and of a contemporary critical response to the topos, to the Earl of Shaftesbury's "A Notion of the Historical Draught of Hercules," in his *Second Characteristics or The Language of Forms*, ed. Benjamin Rand (Cambridge: The University Press, 1914), 29–61. Paulson points out that Shaftesbury's interest in refurbishing the topos to make it fresh and topical potentially suggests its value for novelists (*Emblem and Expression*, 38–39). Hagstrum and Paulson analyze the meaningful gestures and iconography of standard renderings of the topos. Paulson is particularly helpful in his interpretations of William Hogarth's and Sir Joshua Reynolds's creative responses to the topos.

3. The presence of the topos in Reynolds's portrait of David Garrick, "Hesitat-

ing Between Comedy and Tragedy," is attested to by Paulson, *Emblem and Expression*, 86 ff.

4. Here Paulson and I differ, for although he points to the complex function of the topos in Reynolds's painting, he does not read it as inevitably coloring the ethical resonance of the genres. I will be commenting on this issue later in the argument.

5. Paulson, *Emblem and Expression*, 73, 30.

6. See Austen's defense of the novel through her praise of her sister authors, in *Northanger Abbey and Persuasion: The Novels of Jane Austen*, ed. R. W. Chapman, 5 vols., 3d ed. (London: Oxford University Press, 1933); 5:37–38. For her admiration of Maria Edgeworth's novels, see Austen, *Letters*, letter 101, p. 405. All future references will be cited by volume and page numbers in parentheses in the text.

7. Hagstrum, *Sister Arts*, 162.

8. *The Oxford Companion to Art*, Harold Osborne, ed. (Oxford: Clarendon Press, 1970; reprint 1978), 488, 375.

9. Paulson, *Emblem and Expression*, 10, 9.

10. My discussion of the subversive themes and techniques of the women writers is indebted to Paulson's complex analyses of how Hogarth "subverted" the Hercules topos (and Shaftesbury's "Notion" of how it ought to be painted). That I found many of my independently formed ideas of the women's satiric views and practices anticipated in Paulson's interpretation of Hogarth's work, seems to me to confirm the women writers' very real place in the satiric tradition. J. M. S. Tompkins points out that "a strong satiric vein runs through the domestic novel, "*The Popular Novel in England* (London: Constable & Co., 1932), 113.

11. Irene Tayler and Gina Luria suggest that during the Romantic period "genre was . . . to some extent a function of gender" and that the novel became women's art because, unlike poetry, it did not demand from the writer that she have a classical education. Austen, they argue, in following the style of the Flemish painters— "representing quotidian reality consciously shaped to reveal the richness of individual life"—made "art of the 'new' women's novels." See ("Gender and Genre: Women in British Romantic Literature," in *What Manner of Woman: Essays on English and American Life and Literature*, ed. Marlene Springer (New York: New York University Press, 1977), 99–123. Sandra M. Gilbert and Susan Gubar offer a rich and extended discussion of how nineteenth-century women artists "tracing subversive pictures behind socially acceptable facades . . . managed to dissociate themselves from their own revolutionary impulses even while passionately enacting such impulses." Thus they also argue that "nineteenth-century women writers frequently both use and misuse (or subvert) a common male tradition or genre"—a subversive technique, I would add, anticipated by their eighteenth-century sisters. See *The Madwoman in the Attic: The Woman Writer and the Nineteenth Century Literary Imagination* (New Haven: Yale University Press, 1979), 82–83. Such research sufficiently contradicts Elaine Showalter's claim that "the early women writers refused to deal with a professional role, or had a negative orientation toward it," and that "they did not see their writing as an aspect of their feminine experience, or

an expression of it." See *A Literature of Their Own: British Women Novelists From Brontë to Lessing* (Princeton: Princeton University Press, 1977), 18–19.

12. In evaluating the significant contributions of eighteenth-century women writers to the " 'new' novel," I am in agreement with Tayler and Luria about the valuable contributions of Austen and Edgeworth—and to a degree about Brunton—but we disagree strongly about Mary Wollstonecraft's. Tayler and Luria argue that Wollstonecraft's *Mary* "provided a prophetic vision of the emerging genre, and that its achievement was "to redirect the energies of the novel." See "Gender and Genre," 109. I see no evidence in the works of the women writers I scrutinized of such direct and "radical" influence, and find the style and thought of *Mary*, except in its explicitly feminist passages, to be trite imitations of received masculine thought and taste. For a more charitable view of "a fine theme in inexperienced hands," see Tompkins, *The Popular Novel*, 345–46.

13. Austen, *Letters*, letter 134, p. 469.

14. Shaftesbury, Treatise 4, "Plastics or the Original Progress and Power of Designatory Art" in *Second Characteristics*. Cf. esp. 131:134–36.

15. For an equally hostile response from modern feminine critics, see Gilbert and Gubar, *Madwoman in the Attic*, 63 ff; 107–8:661.

16. Mary Wollstonecraft, *Mary, A Fiction* (New York: Schocken Books, 1977), 7.

17. Sir Joshua Reynolds, *Discourses on Art* (London: Collier Books, 1966), 66.

18. Wollstonecraft, *Mary*, 7, 48 (italics mine).

19. Philip Stevick, ed., Introduction, *The Theory of the Novel* (New York, Free Press, 1967), 4.

20. Osborne, *The Oxford Companion to Art*, 488.

21. Tayler and Luria also suggest that Wollstonecraft's "intended emphasis" is on "perception"—the potential 'grandeur' of a young woman's 'thinking powers,' directed towards an understanding of her own existence." See "Gender and Genre," p. 109. But only sisterly goodwill could prompt their impulse to give Wollstonecraft credit for realizing her declared intentions.

22. Austen, *Letters*, letter 126, pp. 452–53. See Donald Greene, 136.

23. "The Myth of Limitations," in *Jane Austen Today*, ed. Joel Weinsheimer (Athens: University of Georgia Press, 1975), 151.

24. She uses the expression in *Northanger Abbey*, 111.

25. For an extended argument concerning the relationship between verbal and visual meanings, see Paulson, *Emblem and Expression*, 8–10. I am indebted to his suggestive language—"structures of meaning" and "structure of choice"—for an insight into Austen's use of graphic art—the Hercules topos—to structure the verbal art of *Mansfield Park*.

26. Shaftesbury, *Second Characteristics*, 31, 32.

27. Ibid., 39.

28. Ibid., 31.

29. Mary Brunton, *Self-Control: A Novel*, 2 vols. (New York: Garland Publishing, 1974), 1:247. All future references will be cited in the text.

30. Shaftesbury claims "fortitude" as Hercules' chief virtue, in "Notion," 58.

31. For a discussion of the women writers' protest against male sexual coarseness, and their invention of a new, "feminine" hero, see Tompkins, *The Popular Novel*, 131–33.

32. Shaftesbury, according to Paulson, "disparaged" the "old enigmatic" deployment of iconography. He was arguing, in "Notion," for a "new, probable use." Contemporary history-painters ought to render the Choice of Hercules "so as to appear . . . 'modern' " (*Emblem and Expression*, 38–39). Brunton seems to suggest that it is already too late; the time is past for refurbishing the topos. Cf. Shaftesbury, "Notion," 40. Cf. also Paulson, *Emblem and Expression*, 38 ff. for a discussion of Shaftesbury's ideas, reinterpreted by Hogarth.

33. Shaftesbury, "Notion," 141.

34. Austen, *Letters*, letter 86, p. 344.

35. Brunton, quoted by Gina Luria, Introduction, *Self-Control* 1:8. All future references will be cited by volume and page number in parentheses in the text.

36. Reynolds, *Discourses in Art*, 85–101.

37. I am variously indebted here to Paulson's discussion of Reynolds's "adaptation" of the Choice of Hercules topos. Even where we disagree, his interpretation of Reynolds has stimulated my thinking about the contribution of *women* writers. Paulson establishes that "Reynolds keeps close to his topos: the scene is in the country, the figures obviously allegorical . . . and even Virtue's arm is raised in the proper way pointing toward the hard, steep path." Unlike Hogarth, Reynolds has found a topos that fits in most particulars; he has emphasized the congruence rather than the difference . . . and where there is a difference, it is a flattering one to the contemporary subject." Thus he paints Garrick as Hercules, an effusive compliment to his powers, while exploiting the theatrical resonances of the scene to point his moral (*Emblem and Expression*, 80; 86 ff.). Austen, too, exploits the topos most fully in those scenes in her novel where her actors are choosing roles.

38. Walpole, quoted in Hilles, *Portraits by Sir Joshua Reynolds*, 82.

39. "Unlike Hercules, he has *not* chosen; in fact though his head is turned toward Tragedy, his smile shows that his thoughts are on Comedy, toward whom the lower part of his body inclines; he seems to be striding in her direction but is stopped mid pace by Tragedy. The topos has been reshaped . . ." Thus, "the polarity of good and evil in Virtue and Pleasure has been subtly transformed . . ." (*Emblem and Expression*, 80).

40. Walpole, quoted in Hilles, *Portraits by Sir Joshua Reynolds*, 82.

41. Maria Edgeworth, *Belinda*, vols. 49 and 50 in *The British Novelists*, ed. Mrs. Barbauld (London, 1820) 49:16. For convenience, I will here term vol. 49, "1" and 50, "2." All future references will be cited by volume and page number in parentheses in the text.

42. In this they were apparently anticipated by Hogarth. Paulson points out that in his subversive reinterpretation of Shaftesbury's Hercules, in "A Harlot's Progress," Hogarth had "essentially made the chooser not a sturdy Hercules but a weak young girl, as if turning the tables on the male-female relationship of the original story" (*Emblem and Expression*, 39).

43. Cf. Hogarth's "A Harlot's Progress," which, according to Paulson, exploits

the Choice of Hercules topos to make a similar point of social criticism: "the real situation of Heroic Virtue in modern London" is that "choice is largely vitiated by fashion" (ibid., 40). Paulson claims Reynolds's figures are "obviously actors and the whole is a scene from a play. Comedy and Tragedy are *playing* Pleasure and Virtue, as Garrick is playing Hercules . . ." (ibid., 80).

44. Paulson offers an interesting analysis of how the "structure of choice itself is emphasized" in Hogarth's satiric Hercules paintings "until it is seen as something that oversimplifies the complexity of real life" (ibid., 73). I would suggest that this is the direction in which Edgeworth and Austen also move. Having used the Hercules "structure" of morality in *Mansfield Park*, Austen rejects the simple opposition of Virtue and Vice. Characteristically, in her next novel, the complexly ironic *Emma*, Austen also explores as doubtful the achievements of ambiguity.

45. Garrick, quoted by George Sherburne and Donald F. Bond in *The Restoration and the Eighteenth Century: A Literary History of England* (New York: Appleton-Century-Croft, 1967), 1042.

46. I am quoting Edmund Bertram on the importance of his chosen profession; his argument suggests the tremendous significance Austen saw in the question of "ordination." Characteristically, she chose a fictive character—and a man—to express her philosophy on so great a matter.

47. Title of Kingsley Amis's essay on *Mansfield Park*, *The Spectator*, no. 6745 (4 October 1957) 339–40.

48. Paulson, *Emblem and Expression*, 30.

49. For evidence that Garrick was in Austen's mind, see "Explanatory Notes" in *Mansfield Park: The Novels of Jane Austen*, ed. John Lucas (London: Oxford University Press, 1970), 439. See also Austen, *Letters*, letters 105 and 106, pp. 414, 415, 417. Crawford is acknowledged by all to be the best actor; even Fanny forgets her dislike in her admiration of his ability to act Shakespeare. See also Sherburne and Bond, *The Restoration and the Eighteenth Century*, 1035–49.

50. Shaftesbury, "Notion," 330.

51. Ibid., 31–32.

52. Ibid., 45.

53. Hagstrum, *Sister Arts*, 192.

54. Shaftesbury advises that Virtue be painted to express "her aspiring effort, or ascent towards the Stars of Heaven," thus indicating her "victory and superiority over fortune and the world" ("Notion," 44). This, of course is precisely Fanny's final victory, in the novel.

55. Cf. Paulson, for a contrast to Reynolds who did not question the "dangerous and destructive side" of heroic values (*Emblem and Expression*, 80–81).

56. Shaftesbury, "Notion," 58.

57. Cf. Tompkins, *The Popular Novel*, 130.

58. Paulson points out that the topos was commonly interpreted as the choice between Industry and Idleness and that Hogarth, in his "A Harlot's Progress," subverted both Prodicus and Shaftesbury by painting his Virtue as "inattentive," and his Vice as energetic and active in a bad cause. Thus Hogarth "reversed the roles of rational industry and irrational idleness" (*Emblem and Expression*, 73).

59. Shaftesbury, "Notion," 51. Thus also Shaftesbury tells his painter that Virtue should be dressed without much "ornament" ("Notion," 48). Austen makes much of the point that Fanny's single ornament is the little cross her brother has given her. Presented with additional ornaments, she is distressed as to how to wear them, and whether they are properly hers.

60. Cf. Paulson's discussion of the eighteenth-century assumption that ethical choice is "bipolar," and of the growing restlessness with this assumption, betrayed in the subversive readings of the Choice of Hercules by such artists as Hogarth (*Emblem and Expression*) 73. Paulson reads the painting to suggest that Garrick-Hercules is "unable to choose between his two charmers." But because Comedy and Tragedy are equally good, his hesitation is not "indecision." Thus he argues that "whereas the proper choice for Hercules was Virtue, for Garrick, the accomplished actor, it is the highest praise to show him unable to choose" (ibid., 80). Austen's Garrick, Henry Crawford, boasts, "I feel as if I could be any thing and every thing, as if I could rant and storm, or sigh, or cut capers in any tragedy or comedy in the English language" (*Mansfield Park*, 123).

61. Paulson suggests that there was a "rise of aesthetic appreciation with the Earl of Shaftesbury and Joseph Addison who distinguished between reading and seeing a picture," and who "did (despite their own moralism) play down moral structures of meaning of any complexity. . . . Meaning in the object is replaced by aesthetic appreciation in the viewer or by the artist's self-expression" (*Emblem and Expression*, 9). This surely is applicable to Reynolds's portrait of Garrick; Paulson himself suggests the self-congratulatory element in Reynolds's painting (ibid., 80). Austen would have objected strongly to such a reversal of priorities.

62. Joseph Spence, *Polymetis* (1747), quoted in ibid., 73.

Penelope's Daughters

Images of Needlework in Eighteenth-Century Literature

"The pen is almost as pretty an implement in a woman's fingers as a needle"

CECILIA MACHESKI

In the Aran Islands off the western coast of Ireland, where flocks of sheep and nets of fish summed up the eighteenth-century economy, knitters were renowned for the intricate, patterned sweaters they knitted for their fishermen. Each knitter varied her design, inventing new combinations of shapes and patterns as she worked in traditional techniques learned since childhood. Not merely for ornament, these garments served a more practical end; so unique was each knitter's code of stitches that should the wearer drown, the sweater was relied upon to identify the body when the rough seas washed the remains ashore. An encyclopedia of knitting recently commented that it "has never been discovered where the people of Aran derived their knitting . . . . the patterns themselves are unique to this small island and have never been found in any other part of the world."[1]

The skilled and subtle craft of the eighteenth-century needleworkers was much like that of contemporary novelists; women were moving into a territory that had previously been dominated by men and reshaping it to suit their own tastes. The development of both needlework and the novel owed much to domestic necessity and to the special female perspective of the emerging artists. Thus, we should not be surprised that conventional historians have neglected both forms. But there is another reason for the neglect. So artful was each worker's hand, that her finished product, whether sweater or novel, often conceals its origins from modern observers who are inclined to overlook the presence of an encoded language of either stitches or literary imagery and to see only the superficial pattern. Thus eighteenth-century women's work, whether with pen or needle, is frequently dismissed as insipid or innocent, artificial or romantic, by those who have overlooked its feminine, or frequently feminist, subtext. In looking more closely at several late-eighteenth-century women's novels against the background of their more classical male forebears, I suggest that the women writers in fact share patterns of imagery and ideas based on their common experience of needlework, and that this special use of language constitutes a subtext on female experience. Even when male authors use scenes with needlework, moreover, their art shows distinct differences in perception. Men have only observed the work while women have engaged in it, and as a result the imagery that evolves in each case is a key to the author's sex and some evidence that gender may define and influence a writer's choice of language. Like the initiated knitter, then, who could interpret a lost identity in the intricate panels of moss and diamonds, stag's leap, and feather stitches, readers must learn to recognize and decipher the special pattern of language in women's fiction if they are to unmask its meaning.

The tedious but soothing rhythms of spinning, knitting, and sewing were the very pulse of women's lives before the industrial revolution. Only if we remember that needlework was a shared experience between women of all classes and ages in the eighteenth century will we understand how natural it is to find it used as imagery in novels and poetry. From the spinners and silk winders who worked in Spitalfields for as little as three shillings a week[2] to wealthy women and their servants who employed idle hours embroidering silk flowers on waistcoats and firescreens, the needle was a common denominator. In the term "needlework," then, I include the broadest range of occupations from spinning yarn and weaving fabric to the making of clothing and household goods to such ornamental and fashionable pursuits as lacemaking, beadwork, and embroidery. So intrinsic to women's lives were these skills and tasks that, as my examples will show, the word "work" when applied to women in the eighteenth century generally means needlework. Because stitchery in all its forms was so closely identified as women's work, we should not be surprised that in literature of the era needlework is associated with chastity. In order to understand how Charlotte Smith, Charlotte Lennox, and Elizabeth Inchbald use this imagery, we must begin by glancing back to earlier eighteenth-century readings of that prototype of both chastity and women's craft, Homer's Penelope.

The double meaning of "craft" for the English writer neatly sums up the Greek weaver's attributes. Not only is she most skilled and subtle with her loom, but she is, also, like Odysseus, clever and cunning. Her work is designed, as Pope's translation reminds us, to protect her chastity:

> Elusive of the bridal day, she gives
> Fond hopes to all, and all with hopes deceives.
> Did not the sun, thro' heav'ns wide azure roll'd,
> For three long years the royal fraud behold?
> While she, laborious in delusion, spread
> The spacious loom, and mix'd the various thread.

In translating Homer's epic, Alexander Pope worked in a decidedly male voice as he interpreted the queen's motives and her work. His language as he presents her gambit to delay the suitors continues to emphasize her cunning to a degree not present in other translations.[3] Penelope, determined to maintain her celibate life, explains her wish to postpone marriage until she has finished weaving the burial robes for Laertes. She counters the suitors' demands on her duty as a woman and a queen to marry with the only argument that will carry weight with her audience, her duty as a daughter and her concern about her reputation:

> Lest when the Fates his royal ashes claim,
> The Grecian matrons taint my spotless fame.

And so we are told the story of her deception more forcefully:

> Thus she: at once the gen'rous train complies,
> Nor fraud mistrusts in virtue's fair disguise.
> The work she ply'd; but studious of delay,
> By night revers'd the labour of the day.

The clever scheme is successful in keeping suitors at bay, as Pope says, for three years. Discovered at last, the queen is forced to finish weaving the shroud, a project Pope salutes as "A won'drous monument of female wiles!" There is no question in Pope's lines that, whatever her motives, Penelope is as sly as her husband, at least where her honor is at stake; such phrases as "the royal fraud," "delusion," "virtue's fair disguise," and "female wiles" all emphasize Pope's suspicions of female wit. So distrustful is he, it would seem, that he condemns her cunning even when it is in defense of that most proper citadel, her chastity. But closer consideration of the queen's situation removes the apparent ambiguity from Pope's portrait. Penelope, from the suitors' point of view, was using Odysseus's absence as an excuse for remaining independent and celibate, thus keeping the kingdom in her own control during her son's nonage. By wishing to marry her, the suitors express more than a selfish wish to acquire political and royal wealth; their interest may be interpreted as opposition to a female regent. Thus her needlework is crafty indeed.

As Pope's couplets balance and counterbalance Penelope's chastity and her cunning, the reader is led to accept unquestioningly the connection between female sexuality and deception. Pope's references to women's craft at once weave together needlework and cunning, chastity and deceit. But Pope's Penelope may be a misreading of Homer's queen, as earlier lines by Dryden suggest. In contrasting the two versions of Penelope that exist in the early part of the eighteenth century, we begin to see how rich the needle-work imagery can be, and how complex were ideas on the role of women by the 1780s and 1790s when women transformed the imagery in their own novels.

Dryden's version of Penelope in "To the Duchess of Ormond" is far more conservative than Pope's. In praising his subject for her devotion and loyalty to her absent husband, Dryden compares the Duchess with Homer's queen:

> All is your Lord's alone; ev'n absent, He
> Employs the Care of Chast *Penelope.*
> For him You waste in Tears your widow'd Hours
> For Him Your curious Needle paints the flow'rs . . .

Clearly Dryden is more sympathetic to Penelope than Pope is, and ascribes more weight to Homer's epithet of "faithful" than the later poet chose to do. The Duchess's needle is "curious," or as the *Oxford English Dictionary* suggests, skillful, and as he continues the tribute it is apparent that Dryden associates needlework with women's duty and fidelity:

> Such Works of Old Imperial Dames were taught;
> Such for Ascanius, fair Elisa wrought.[4]

Dryden, then, elevates his heroine by ranking her not only with Penelope, but also with Dido, conveniently overlooking the illicit and tragic circumstances in favor of her devotion, as he willingly overlooked Penelope's deception for her faithfulness. So strong is the association of needlework with virtue that Dryden can be sure the duchess will find comparison to the Imperial Dames nothing but flattering.

Yet Dryden's and Pope's use of the imagery share common assumptions that distinguish them from women writers. First, for both men, the needle-work is a classical allusion, with little or no concern with realism. Surely the Duchess of Ormond did "paint flowers," but Dryden is more interested in the Homeric echoes than in whether her "curious needle" worked in chain or satin stitch. Similarly, Pope may use Penelope to make satiric remarks on women's wiles, but his primary interest, like Dryden's, is to re-create the classical heroine for his audience. The needle, for the male writers, is almost always used, then, as an allusion, or a symbol, part of a clever scheme or as idle employment, but never to achieve realism.

Surely one must allow for the differences in genre between Pope and Dryden and the later novelists, but even as one moves from poetry to fiction, it becomes apparent that Richardson has more in common, in his adaptation of needlework imagery, with Pope and Dryden than with the women writers who follow him. Richardson, for all his innovation and reputed feminism, has many firm attachments to the male tradition, as his use of this imagery reveals. Before looking at the female novelists who owe so much to the new ideas and structures developed in *Pamela, Clarissa*, and *Sir Charles Grandison*, it is worth looking briefly at perhaps the best known example of eighteenth-century literary needlework, Pamela's waistcoat for Mr. B.

At one point early in *Pamela*, Mr. B., irritated at the heroine's prudery and her incessant scribbling, chides her for her concern with finishing his waistcoat: "You mind your pen more than your needle; I don't want such idle sluts to stay in my house."[5] The illogical nature of Mr. B.'s outburst must be apparent to the reader; Pamela is engaged in precisely the kind of proper domestic work that makes her a seeming model of virtue. For the novel reader, of course, the situation is rich in irony, for Pamela has indeed only just stashed away her pen and paper and taken up her embroidery in an attempt to disguise her epistolary labor. For the reader familiar with Pope and Dryden, moreover, this scene, and the many like it throughout *Pamela*, suggest that however forward-looking Richardson was, and however much he lacked the formal classical training of many of his contemporaries, his heroine owed much to deeply rooted perceptions about female virtue and female guile. For Pamela's embroidery, like Penelope's "splendid web" is a ruse. Like the Greek queen's weaving which was unraveled at night and used to preserve chastity, Pamela's stitching also comes between her and Mr. B.'s illicit advances; Richardson uses the flowered waistcoat as Homer uses the burial shroud. But in the eighteenth-century analogue, the needlework extends and even invites courtship by lengthening the young servant's tenure at Lady B.'s; Pamela offers the rather flimsy excuse, we recall, that she cannot properly escape from her perilous situation because the vest is incomplete. That she frequently puts aside her needle for a pen suggests that like Penelope, Pamela knows that the needlework is a scheme, a work that encourages the appearance of virtue while at the same time actually defending her chastity from illicit suitors. Like the Ithacans, Mr. B. fails to press his suit with any success while Pamela is intent on her embroidery, charmed, as it were, by the magic in her web. When he finds Pamela writing, on the other hand, Mr. B. is far more inclined to express impatience and to attempt to seduce the heroine, almost as if he is punishing her for daring to write.

Whether Richardson consciously borrowed from Homer in using needlework as an emblem of Pamela's virtue, his heroine's credibility is enhanced by the parallel for readers familiar with the genuine loyalty and honor of Penelope. If, like Fielding, we are suspicious at times of Pamela's "vartue," we might find in the allusion to Penelope evidence that Richardson, at least, was very sincere in his belief in the girl's best intentions. As even Pope recognized, a woman could be clever and still be chaste.

Dryden, Pope, and Richardson spread the warp, so to speak, for the patterns woven into literature later in the eighteenth century. The association of a woman at her needle with Penelope-like virtue becomes a commonplace. In *School for Scandal*,[6] for instance, Sir Peter Teazle, in Act 2, reminds his wife that his earliest good impressions of her owe as much to her needle as her wit; he recalls a prelapsarian world of courtship. "Recollect, Lady Teazle, when I saw you first, sitting at your tambour, in a pretty figured linen gown, with a bunch of keys at your side, your hair combed smooth over a roll, and your apartment hung round with fruits in worsted, of your own working." Similarly, in *She Stoops to Conquer*, Miss Hardcastle, disguised as the barmaid, attempts to persuade Marlow of her innocence and virtue, but in this comic example Marlow twists her meaning and attempts to seduce her in Act 3 when he asks her, "Do you ever work, child?" Her answer, that there is hardly a "screen or a quilt in the whole house but what can bear witness to that" confirms that she reads "work" to mean needlework. Marlow then begins his seduction by mockingly suggesting, "Odso! Then you must show me your embroidery. I embroider and draw patterns myself a little." After he grabs her hand, Miss Hardcastle virtuously responds that "the colours don't look well by candlelight. You shall see all in the morning," revealing that she understands his implied meaning, and further that she has a plot of her own in hand, as the audience knows, to test his virtue and maintain her own. In short, Pope's astute reading of Penelope as a woman almost too clever to be trusted has given way to the more innocent and conventional reading. A woman at her needle is, in the mainstream literature, an emblem of virtue. For Goldsmith's comic spirit, it is not a large step to see in the embroidery a double entendre; it is a simple inversion that the very symbol of virtue becomes a tool for seduction.

For the male writers, the work of Penelope and her literary daughters is primarily symbolic rather than realistic; had Homer crafted his queen as a portrait painter or a pastry chef, in this guise she no doubt would have manifested herself in Pope, Dryden, Richardson, Sheridan, and Goldsmith. Men, we may infer, seldom used needlework for any intrinsic reason, it being an experience that was generally alien to their lives. Men seldom did needlework; they only observed women doing it, and they read Homer. Their subsequent uses of needle imagery, as the previous examples show, often do not reflect the actual practice of the craft; Sheridan's is the exception in its specificity of reference to worsted.[7] When we turn to works by women, we discover a decided change, for women truly engaged in needlework, labored from their youth to perfect the skill that so definitively classed them as women, and, as a result, when they adapt the Penelope legend to their own ends, their writing reflects the different experience and perception of women. So closely is the needle a symbol of female identity, and by the nineteenth century, of female drudgery, that Elizabeth Cady Stanton would use the bitter rhetoric of the suffrage movement to proclaim: "Woman has relied heretofore too entirely for her support on the *needle*—that one-eyed demon of destruction that slays its thousands annually; that evil genius of our sex, which in spite of all our devotion, will never make us healthy, wealthy, or wise."[8] Or, like Charlotte Brontë, women saw needlework as the direct antithesis of creative writing: "I have endeavoured . . . to observe all the duties a woman ought to fulfill . . . . I don't always succeed, for sometimes when I'm teaching or sewing, I would rather be reading or writing."[9] For many women, the needle became not the symbol of innocence and chastity that Richardson portrayed, or the painless idle labor Dryden's duchess passed the time with, but, more realistically, a symbol of the roles and responsibilities that fettered women. Obviously, the later writers reflect the differences in class between the duchess and working-class seamstresses as well as the differences between epic poetry and the novel, but this change is similarly apparent in the growing middle-class reading public. Anne Bradstreet, Dryden's contemporary, best described the difficulties faced by women writers when in "The Prologue" she complained:

> I am obnoxious to each carping tongue
> Who says my hand a needle better fits;
> A poet's pen all scorn I should thus wrong,
> For such despite they cast on female wits.
> If what I do prove well, it won't advance;
> They'll say it's stol'n, or else it was by chance.[10]

If the more radical poets and writers saw pens and needles as symbols of the conflict between women's traditional roles and their desire for creative expression, other more conservative eighteenth-century writers bridge the century between Bradstreet and her nineteenth-century sisters. Taking up their pens in the half century between Richardson and Jane Austen, writers like Charlotte Lennox, Charlotte Smith, and Elizabeth Inchbald turned to firsthand experience with the needle and to each others' novels to weave the Penelope allusions into a new female iconography. If women vented their frustration at the drudgery of needlework in real life, they found in the familiar instrument a rich source of imagery that gives their novels a distinctly female voice. Without their groundwork, it is difficult to imagine how one could explain the development from Pamela's waistcoat (a project any eighteenth-century woman probably recognized as even more time-consuming than the impossible pace of letter writing), to that memorable moment when we learn about Mansfield Park's mistress. "To the education of her daughters Lady Bertram paid not the smallest attention. She had not time for such cares. She was a woman who spent her days in sitting, nicely dressed, on a sofa, doing some long piece of needlework, of little use and no beauty. . . ."[11] They are, the cloying Pamela and the dangerously insipid Lady Bertram, close cousins, and in turning to Lennox, Smith, and Inchbald we begin to trace their lineage.

Lennox's *Sophia* (1762), Smith's *Emmeline* (1788), and Inchbald's *A Simple Story* (1791) share thematic as well as structural elements: each is a story of a young heroine's falling in love and overcoming obstacles to marriage; each is *not* an epistolary novel; and each attempts to provide young female readers with more realistic portraits of a woman's life than earlier novels had created. These three novels were selected from among many possible examples because they are representative of the development of narrative techniques in the latter half of the century. The three authors are skillful at portraying women in domestic settings, women concerned with marriage, with education, and with maintaining personal dignity in the face of social pressures that encouraged women to conform to fashion. One strand that links their work is their use of needle imagery. If Pamela plied her needle furtively as an excuse for prolonging her residency with Mr. B., in women's novels knitting, embroidery, weaving, tatting, netting, and bead-work are all familiar occupations, practiced openly, as part of the very texture of daily life. Although these tasks often take on symbolic or psychological overtones, or provide succinct clues to character, they are never presented abstractly; the reader is aware of the concrete presence of the needle and yarn in the heroine's fingers.

In Charlotte Lennox's novel *Sophia*, for instance, the needle is often the heroine's recourse when she is embarrassed, confused, or distressed, especially in the presence of her suitor, Sir Charles. "Sophia was in the room, and rose up at his entrance in a sweet confusion, which she endeavored to conceal, by appearing extremely busy at a piece of needlework." Later, when Mrs. Darnley (a foolish mother who anticipates Mrs. Bennet) leaves Sophia alone with Sir Charles, the awkwardness is tangible as "he stood fixed in silence for several minutes, leaning on the back of her chair, while she plied her needle with the most earnest attention, and felt her confusion decrease in proportion as his became more apparent."[12] The repetition of the word "confusion" in both scenes of needlework clearly reveals Lennox's concern with creating psychological realism. The heroine, her eyes riveted on her work, can blush but is relieved of the need to look directly into the hero's eyes, clasp his extended hands, or take any more suggestive action. The embroidery functions as a barrier to passion. Like Penelope's weaving, Sophia's work allows her to observe the conventions of hospitality, but to affirm, at the same time, her chastity, as long as she has reasons to question her suitor's motives.

After many trials and disappointments, we reach the final scene of the novel and find that, once again, Lennox locates in needlework a convenient device for reflecting Sophia's mental state. Her lover unexpectedly enters the room in which Sophia sits working. Upon seeing him, "she started from her chair, her work fell from her trembling hands, she looked at him in silent astonishment, unable, and perhaps unwilling to avoid him."[13] If the scene is typical in its sentimental language of so much earlier drama and fiction, nevertheless the artistic merit of the novel is enhanced as we recognize the needlework dropping from Sophia's lap as a symbolic gesture; she drops her shield, her "work," the emblem of chastity, and as Lennox hints, acknowledges her sexual desire. The use of the needlework makes the abstractions far more concrete than they would have been in many sentimental novels of the period; this is not just another happy ending, but a resolution of the heroine's conflict, and her recognition, expressed symbolically, of her growth into womanhood. In contrast to Pamela, Sophia does not use her work as a ruse. For her, the needle is an innocent occupation; it is the author who makes us aware of the design behind Sophia's activity. Putting it another way, for Richardson, female work is external to self, and is devious. For the women writers, the work is intrinsic to self, and suggests introspection. If the needlework is a mirror of sexuality, then it is fair to say that the men perceive women as deceptive while women portray sexuality as deeply important to self-definition and self-respect. Just as Pamela's needle reveals her hypocrisy, Sophia's alerts us to her true merit. Lennox seems to like and to trust her heroine more than Richardson does his.

A later heroine, Charlotte Smith's Emmeline, shares Sophia's preoccupation with her needle and her chastity. In an early scene, Emmeline is passing the afternoon in company with Mr. Rochely, an elderly man whose sexual interest in her she suspects, but tries to misinterpret as paternal affection. Her suitor, Delamere, arrives unexpectedly and finds her "at work by a little table, on which were two wax candles." She is not alone, however, as he anticipated, but "by her side, with his arm, as usual, over the back of her chair, and gazing earnestly on her face, sat Mr. Rochely." Emmeline hears someone enter the room, but cannot see who it is; she assumes it is a servant with tea. Thus Delamere can approach quite close to the table at which she works before she sees him, and then the "work dropped from her hands; she grew pale, and trembled; but not being able to rise, she only clasped her hands together, and said faintly, "Oh, heaven!—Mr. Delamere!"[14] Once again, the language owes much to the sentimental dramas of Cibber and Rowe. Yet, here, as in *Sophia*, the author is using needlework to reflect the psychological state of the heroine. Emmeline's surprise, her guilt, her fondness for Delamere all act like gravity pulling the work from her trembling hands. The reader is again given a concrete image of the mental state to counterbalance the barrage of sentimental expressions. The similarity of this scene to Lennox's also suggests just how closely the later author read her predecessor.

Smith's scene in contrast to Lennox's also shows an increasing interest in domestic realism. The later scene (1788) is much longer, the length resulting to a large extent from the addition of domestic, concrete details: the little table, the two wax candles, the position of Rochely's arm, the servant expected with tea. In Lennox's scene, on the other hand, the language is decidedly more vague and sentimental, relying on action and emotion more than physical detail: *stood fixed, leaning, plied, felt confusion, tender accent, hastily, started, trembling, astonishment, silent.* The earlier scene (1762) relies more on the readers' response to charged sentimental phrases than to descriptive adjectives. The needlework is virtually the only anchor for Sophia's emotions, while Emmeline's work, in falling, seems to highlight the very real and comfortable domestic setting. (The modern reader may find this technique anticipates Virginia Woolf's in *To the Lighthouse* where Mrs. Ramsay knits a reddish brown sock and the process reveals the interior of both the summer house and her mind.)

Emmeline plies her needle through the novel. At a scene toward the middle, she finds herself with Delamere's friend Fitz-Edward, whose presence reminds her of her unhappy situation at having lost Delamere. She uses her work this time to conceal her feelings: "She blushed deeply the moment she beheld him, and arose from her chair in confusion; then sat down and took out her work, which she had hastily put up; and trying to recover herself, grew still more confused, and trembled and blushed again." Here Smith, like Lennox, attaches needlework to the word "confusion" and illustrates the heroine's nervous and ambiguous state by her inability to decide whether to work or not. In this case, the heroine is partly attracted to Fitz-Edward, but unwilling to admit her feelings; thus she "flirts" with her work, sending uncertain signals. In the final scenes of the novel Emmeline discovers her true love, Godolphin, and when he proposes, we know not only from the expressed sentiments, but also from her actions with her needlework, that this is indeed a happy moment. "With deepened blushes, and averted eyes, she at first sought for refuge in affecting to be intent on the netting she drew from her workbox; but having spoiled a whole row, her trembling hands could no longer go on with it."[15] Like Sophia, Emmeline yields the emblem of her chastity as she accepts her lover's vows. Netting was a popular late-eighteenth-century pursuit which produced a mesh of varying density depending on the fiber and the shuttles used. By the 1790s it had become fashionable to net cloaks and gowns, but the technique was also used to more domestic ends, such as cherry nets for garden use and as snares for rabbits.[16] We can only speculate on how consciously Smith sketched Emmeline in the posture of snaring her man.

Needlework is one way women writers occupy their heroines' hands when the epistolary quill is removed. Heroines' mental states find concrete expression in the feminine "work" they do as novelists seek a more realistic device for representing emotion than the hyperbolic language of sentimental drama. It is no surprise that women took their iconography from the experiences they knew best. A needle, to an eighteenth-century woman, proved an ideal symbol: uniquely representative of woman's sphere, readily understood by female readers, and alluding to the noble tradition of Penelope's curious wiles.

Elizabeth Inchbald's use of the same motif highlights her skill for creating realistic domestic scenes and brings the novel to the doorstep of Jane Austen. In *A Simple Story*, published in 1791, Inchbald sets a scene in which the heroine Miss Milner and her companion Miss Woodley are working together when the hero Dorriforth joins them. The trio talk upon "indifferent subjects" until, sensing Miss Milner's dejection, Dorriforth says, "Perhaps I am wrong, Miss Milner, but I have observed you are lately grown more thoughtful than usual."[17] Indeed she has, for like Emmeline and Sophia, Miss Milner is in love; her dejection arises from her mistaken belief that Dorriforth will not, or cannot, marry her. But what is striking about this little vignette aside from its similarity to the scenes by Lennox and Smith is its feel for domestic setting. The heroine, unlike her predecessors, is not alone, or alone with her suitor. She is in the midst of a busy household, plying her needle along with her companion, the spinster Miss Woodley. Dorriforth's dwelling is filled with a variety of characters—Miss Woodley, an elderly priest named Sandforth, neighbors, servants. It is an active and realistic eighteenth-century home, and at the same time reflects Inchbald's experience as a dramatist who saw the scenes in her novels as they might have been played on the stage. This bustling set reminds us, too, of how often women's lives lacked privacy during this era. The rooms inhabited by many romance heroines are far too private and egocentric to mirror the real lives of women.

Yet Inchbald's heroine shares the love problems of her literary sisters even if not their rooms. At the moment that Dorriforth hints at his affection, our heroine "turned pale, and could no longer guide her needle—in the fond transports of her heart she imagined, the sensations to which he alluded, was his love for her—."[18] These last two quotations suggest Inchbald's further refinement of the needlework motif. Miss Milner does not drop her work and surrender herself as passionately as do her forebears, Emmeline and Sophia. Her gesture, loss of control of her needle, more precisely reflects the psychological dilemma Inchbald develops throughout the novel, that Miss Milner senses her love for Dorriforth is ill fated, and that yielding may in fact be a fatal mistake. When the couple do get hastily married, this theme again emerges as Dorriforth inadvertently places a mourning ring on his bride's finger. Slowly, then, a subtle language of female psychology emerges from the common imagery of the needle. Precisely how a heroine uses, or loses, her needle tells a good deal about her situation.

One can appreciate in Inchbald's scenes, as I mentioned, her success as a playwright. The sentimental language appears infrequently in her novels. Instead, she often reveals psychological states through well-crafted stage business—how characters look, what they do, what they do not say. Miss Milner's needlework is taken for granted by the reader; it simply exists as part of the domestic scene Inchbald carefully evokes. We do not see the heroine consciously pick up her work as Dorriforth enters. Instead, she is already working along with Miss Woodley. Later when she turns pale and cannot guide her needle, we realize that for the duration of the scene she has in fact been stitching and the symbolic value of the needlework is no less effective than in Lennox's or Smith's novels. Inchbald's talent rests in her ability to make us see by carefully realized glimpses like these the entire domestic scene. We accept it. The author has captured the household with such apparent naturalness that we overlook the very skillful art concealed in her narrative.

The next step in the development of needle imagery takes place when we move into Jane Austen's novels. So important are fashion, needlework, and related subjects to Austen's work that only a few brief references are possible here.[19] What we recognize if we approach the later characters with an awareness of their ancestry in the novels of writers like Lennox, Smith, and Inchbald is that Austen owed a greater debt than we might have imagined to the Emmelines, Sophias, and Miss Milners. Significantly, the needlework in *Pride and Prejudice, Mansfield Park,* and *Emma,* to cite only a few examples, brilliantly reveals not only the worker's immediate state of mind, but also her very character. Lady Catherine de Bourgh at one point examined the work of Elizabeth Bennet and Charlotte Collins and "advised them to do it differently." Fanny Price, we recall, is frequently at Lady Bertram's side arranging her work for her or "endeavouring to put her aunt's evening work in such a state as to prevent her being missed." In Fanny's room we may visualize "the table between the windows . . . covered with work-boxes and netting-boxes." But evidence of Austen's debt to the earlier writers is more apparent in scenes where romantic "confusion" is illustrated through a character's almost instinctive turning to her needle. In *Emma,* we find an important dialogue staged with very precise parallels to the earlier novels by women. Mrs. Weston prepares Emma for the news about Frank Churchill's engagement to Jane Fairfax, but the former governess erroneously believes that Emma's heart has been lost to Churchill, and so, in order to tell her gossip, she must arm herself with a woman's shield as she speaks: ". . . 'I will tell you directly;'(resuming her work, and seeming resolved against looking up.) 'He has been here, this very morning, on a most extraordinary errand. It is impossible to express our surprise.' " She might as well have used the more familiar word, confusion. She, too, speaks in a "trembling voice." Only Emma's reassurance that her heart is not lost to Frank Churchill allows good Mrs. Weston to look up from her work. The final example, from *Pride and Prejudice,* finds Elizabeth in romantic "confusion" when Darcy pays an unexpected visit. Not yet prepared to yield herself to his love, she defends her honor and pride, taking her needlework up as a symbol of her intentions; she "sat down again to her work," after Darcy's entrance, "with an eagerness which it did not often command."[20]

Through needlework imagery, then, we can trace the evolution of female characters and female authors through the eighteenth century. For Dryden and Pope, needlework meant allusions to Penelope, overt references to the classical tradition. Used in poetry, these references illustrate the male writers' identification with the Homeric past and their modification of the epic mode to accommodate and satirize modern mores. Penelope emerges from the Augustans' pens as not so much a heroic queen as a comfortable and scheming dowager. Her "curious needle" is portrayed as either a device for deception or a tool for idling away lonely hours, but never as a useful end in itself, an intrinsic part of domestic life.

Richardson's epistolary novel presents Pamela as un-self-consciously Penelopean. By her stitching, her scheming, and her obsession with her virtue, she represents an eighteenth-century analogue that is almost a parody of the Homeric original. The change in genre, from poetry to the novel, and the focus not on the past but on the contemporary world of domestic and fashionable life, opened a corridor into the literary marketplace for women excluded from the earlier tradition by lack of classical education and prejudice against women writers.

Women imitated the epistolary novel in both form and content for many years after the success of *Pamela* and *Clarissa*. Lennox herself wrote *The Female Quixote*, a comic novel in letters, and Inchbald first drafted *A Simple Story* in imitation of Richardson's method.[21] Yet characters in these novels seldom sew or pursue any domestic activities; they are too busy writing letters to bother with the trivial concerns of food, sleep, or family. In abandoning the novel of letters for third-person narrative techniques, novelists eschewed the artificiality of the epistolary conventions in favor of more naturalistic structures. Among the early writers to reject the Richardsonian method are Lennox, Smith, and Inchbald. Each favored a style that allowed her to portray women convincingly with increasing psychological insight and attention to realistic detail. The novelists used no direct allusions to Penelope, yet each heroine is a reincarnation of the classical figure. Skilled at her needle, confused by suitors, proud of the self-respect that preserves her chastity, each young woman claims her title as Penelope's daughter. The female novelists used the image of the queen to define a new presence in the novel: a heroine who is sufficiently feminine to meet the rigid standards of her audience, yet touched with enough energy, wit, independence, and common sense to foreshadow the heroines of the nineteenth- and twentieth-century women's fiction.

Women writers for two centuries after Lennox, Smith, and Inchbald continued to evolve patterns of imagery that used needlework to reflect, interpret, and enrich the lives of characters and readers alike. If the use of needlework imagery becomes increasingly sophisticated in the works of Jane Austen, the Brontës, Elizabeth Gaskell, George Eliot, Emily Dickinson, Amy Lowell, Virginia Woolf, Agnes Smedley, Dorothy Canfield, Ellen Glasgow, Alice Walker, and many, many others, it is because women ceased to perceive "the *needle*" as "that one-eyed demon of destruction," but instead recognized in needlework a uniquely female signature. Just as the Aran knitters made the intricate patterns their own, so women writers encoded their texts with clues to female history and experience. Penelope bequeathed her daughters a rich heritage of pens and needles, and as they explored and developed it in their fiction they gave Pope's phrase a new reading, for, between the lines of novels we find indeed "A wond'rous monument of female wiles!"

NOTES

Samuel Richardson to Lady Bradshaigh in *Correspondence*, ed. Anna Barbauld (London, 1804), 6:120, n.d.

1. *Oldham's Knitting Encyclopedia* (London: Hamlyn Publishing Group, 1968), 10.

2. M. Dorothy George, *London Life in the Eighteenth Century* (New York: Capricorn Books, 1965), 183.

3. Alexander Pope, trans. *The Odyssey* by Homer, *The Twickenham Edition of the Poems of Alexander Pope*, ed. Maynard Mack (New Haven: Yale University Press, 1963), 9: Book 2, lines 99–104, 111–12, 115–18, and 126. Other translators have paid less attention to the deceit in Penelope's scheme, emphasizing her cleverness but not unduly suggesting its connection to sexuality or her political power. See, for instance, the Butcher and Lang, or the T. E. Shaw translations, which speak of her "knowledge of all fair handiwork, yea, and cunning wit, and wiles" or that "Athene has bestowed on her an armoury of graces (skills in all housewifely crafts, and such arts and airs as her guileful wit adeptly turns to personal advantage) beyond parallel among the famous beauties of old time . . ." respectively. Butcher and Lang, trans. *The Odyssey* by Homer (1879; reprinted New York: Macmillan, 1930) and T. E. Shaw, trans. *The Odyssey* (London, 1935).

4. John Dryden, "To Her Grace the Duchess of Ormond," *The Poetical Works of John Dryden*, ed. George P. Noyes (1909; reprinted Boston: Houghton-Mifflin, 1950), 752, lines 157–62.

5. Samuel Richardson, *Pamela*, M. Kinkead-Weekes, Introduction (New York: Everyman's Library, 1962), 35, letter 22.

6. Richard Sheridan, *The School for Scandal* and Oliver Goldsmith, *She Stoops to Conquer* in J. M. Morrell, ed., *Four English Comedies* (London: Penguin Books, 1983) 335, 280, respectively.

7. In Elizabethan times, knitters' guilds were composed exclusively of men, as were most weavers' guilds throughout the nineteenth century. Both men and women knitted on Aran, but needlework and especially knitting remained predominantly women's tasks. Men continued to be associated with the mechanized and professional knitting and weaving industries while women did their work primarily at home, and for home use and ornament only. See Elizabeth Gaskell's novels, especially *North and South* and *Wives and Daughters* which portray the problems of the industrial revolution in the mills of the north, and where female characters

are revealed through the type of work they do; good English women pursue sturdy British worsted work while frivolous French women do elegant but useless silk embroidery, much in the school of Austen's Lady Bertram.

8. Stanton, quoted in Karen Peterson, "Many Never Signed Their Craft Work," review of *Women Artists of the Arts and Crafts Movement, 1870–1914*, by Anthea Callen, *In These Times*, 16–22 Jan. 1980, p. 21.

9. Brontë, quoted in Sandra M. Gilbert and Susan Gubar, *The Madwoman in the Attic* (New Haven: Yale University Press, 1979), 63–64.

10. Anne Bradstreet, "The Prologue," *The American Tradition in Literature* Vol. I ed. Sculley, Bradley, *et. al.* (New York: W. W. Norton and Co., 1956), 34–36, lines 25–30.

11. Jane Austen, *Mansfield Park*, ed. R. W. Chapman (Oxford: Oxford University Press, 1982), p. 19. All subsequent references to Austen are by volume and chapter to the Chapman texts (see n. 20).

12. Charlotte Lennox, *Sophia* (1762; reprinted New York: Garland Press, 1974), 4 vols., 1:72, 74.

13. Ibid., 2:206.

14. Charlotte Smith, *Emmeline, The Orphan of the Castle*, ed. Anne Henry Ehrenpreis (London: Oxford University Press, 1971), 93.

15. Ibid., 231–32, 447.

16. See the brief but useful monograph, Penelope Byrde, *A Frivolous Distinction* (Bath: Bath City Council, 1979), which discusses fashion and needlework in the works of Jane Austen, and provides a glossary of terms on textile history and needlework tools. This pamphlet is beautifully illustrated.

17. Elizabeth Inchbald, *A Simple Story* ed. J. M. S. Tompkins (London: Oxford University Press, 1967), 109.

18. Ibid., 110.

19. Again, see Byrde, who identifies needlework scenes in the novels and also illustrates Austen's own skill as a needleworker with photos of her embroidery on display in Chawton. Byrde's work is useful for it calls attention to the exactness of Austen's references to netting, carpet work, etc. She quotes Edward Austen-Leigh's description of a piece of her needlework, noting that it "shows that the same hand which painted so exquisitely with the pen could work as delicately with the needle" (33). While there is no logical connection between the two skills, the point I wish to make is that only because Austen was so familiar with needlework could she use it in her novels as imagery with more intimacy and skill than, say, Richardson, who knew such work only secondhand.

20. *Pride and Prejudice* 2, chap. 7; *Mansfield Park* 2, chap. 5, 1, chap. 16; *Emma* 3, chap. 10; and *Pride and Prejudice* 3, chap. 11.

21. For a discussion of Inchbald's rejection of the novel in letters, see Cecilia Macheski, "The Feeling Mind: The Early Literary Career of Elizabeth Inchbald" (Ph.D. diss., Graduate School and University Center of the City University of New York, 1984), chap. 3.

Placing the Female

The Metonymic Garden in Amatory and Pious Narrative, 1700–1740

April London

In one of the most perceptive analyses of pre-1740 narrative, John J. Richetti traces the contemporary rendering of experience as "secular" or "religious."[1] While this distinction clarifies the psychological appeals made by fiction and the authors' concern with reader response, it to a degree obscures the shared concern of amatory and pious novels with the fundamental issue of authority. Secular and religious can, in fact, be seen not as contrary, but complementary, responses to a world envisioned as ineluctably hierarchical. Although in each genre the chosen code fixes the limits of the fictional world, both structure experience to admit exclusive adherence to the favored model of dominance. This, in turn, delimits possible action as characters exist largely in order to yield control to a superior divine or sexual force. The subordination of character thus works both structurally and thematically; the predominantly female protagonists are bound by the interchangeable codes of gender and genre to realize their subject status.

This generic congruity extends to a shared vocabulary which supplements intellectual and emotional dependence through a recurrent pattern of physical enclosure. Both amatory and pious narratives employ metaphors informed by the myth of the garden and directed toward ratifying the source and significance of power. In the development of circumscribed structures of time, ethics, and action, the garden thus serves as a metonymy within the text for the world the text signifies. Contemporary authors drew upon the multiple meanings of the garden in their evocation of a world of necessary subordination: a place of Edenic innocence or transgression, of the intercession of a benevolent providence or of chaotic possibility, of divine presence or human skill, of natural passion or concealed sin, and of sacred or secular time. Coexistent with these moral and aesthetic perspectives, the garden retains its material status as property, with the attendant issues of ownership, consumption, productivity, and improvement. Within narratives that are often rambling, digressive, and of wavering didactic intent, the sure grasp of the garden image stands in sharp relief. To the early eighteenth-century writer, it was an accessible and often exploited metaphor; to the twentieth-century reader its variable functions provide a key to the ideological assumptions that underlie the rise of the novel. The attempted seduction of Pamela in the garden, then, works within a formulaic tradition of heroines set in apposition to an enclosed "natural" world. Granting the individual will a measure of integrity in accordance with Puritan doctrine involves for Richardson, however, the transposition of intellectual for physical subordination. Pre-1740 narratives rarely make such a distinction. Women writing about women—Mary Delariviere Manley, Eliza Haywood, Penelope Aubin—adapt the actual and symbolic terrain of the garden to stand analogically for the condition of their heroines and their relation to the world beyond.

I

Mary Delariviere Manley was among the most successful practitioners of amatory fiction, combining this career as an author with propagandizing for the Tory cause. Her alliance with the politics of the Scriblerian circle, collaborating, for example, with Swift in defense of the landed interest in *The Examiner*, did not exempt her from personal attacks by its members. In a letter to Lady Mary Wortley Montagu, Pope labels her a "noted common woman"[2]—one of the originals of the "Sappho" of the *Imitations of Horace*: "P_x'd by her love, or libell'd by her Hate."[3] The vehemence of his attack, despite their common satiric targets, stemmed from opposition to her narrative method. In a series of *chroniques scandaleuse* extending from *The Secret History of Queen Zarah* (1705), through *The New Atalantis* (1709), *Memoirs of Europe* (1710), and *The Adventures of Rivella* (1714), Manley offers political scandal leavened with erotic fantasy. It was the combination of these two elements that Pope and his contemporaries censured as an affront to social order and to the "true" nature of women. A footnote to *The Dunciad* directed at Manley's successor, Eliza Haywood, compounds the criticism by equating private life with public expression. "In this game is expos'd in the most contemptuous manner, the most profligate licenciousness of those shameless scribblers (for the most part of That sex, which ought least to be capable of such malice or impudence) who in libellous Memoirs and Novels, reveals the faults and misfortunes of both sexes, to the ruin or disturbance, of publick fame or private happiness."[4] Censorious evaluations of scandal chronicles consistently linked the content of the novellas with personal lubricity.[5] In presenting her own veiled autobiography, *The Adventures of Rivella,* in the form of a *chronique scandaleuse* Manley tacitly accepts this association, but asserts conversely that the eroticism of her works serves a positive social function.

The Adventures of Rivella begins with a discussion between the Chevalier d'Aumont and Sir Charles Lovemore of novelists who "treat well of love"[6] in which Rivella (Manley) is distinguished as preeminent among the successors to the Ovidian tradition. D'Aumont circumvents the conventional charge that her novels offer no more than gratuitous scandalmongering by concluding a list of her consummately erotic scenes with the comment that these

> are such Representatives of Nature, that must warm the coldest Reader; it raises high Ideas of the Dignity of Human Kind, and informs us that we have in our Composition, wherewith to taste sublime and transporting Joys. After perusing her Inchanting Descriptions, which of us have not gone in Search of Raptures which she every where tells us, as happy Mortals, we are capable of tasting. But have we found them, *Chevalier,* answer'd his Friend? For my Part, I believe they are to be met with no where else but in her own Embraces. (2:740)

The final line with its oblique self-compliment makes a subtle point about the ability of such fiction both to arouse and answer erotic fantasy. Manley admits that her novels respond to the reader's craving for vicarious sexuality and defends this on the grounds that passion is one of the higher human faculties. It has played a dominant role in her own life, but for those less fortunate, *Queen Zarah, The New Atalantis,* and *Memoirs of Europe* provide abundant recompense. Treating her own attractiveness as objective fact and sexuality as universally fascinating effectively ratifies the presentation of amorous adventures as something of a public service.

Among the episodes cited by d'Aumont as most provocative in Manley's works is "Chevalier Tomaso *dying at the feet of Madam* de Bedamore, *and afterwards possessing Her in that* Sylvan *Scene of Pleasure the Garden*" (2:740). The passage referred to is from the second volume of *The New Atalantis*:

> It was the Evening of an excessive hot Day, she got into a shade of *Orange* Flowers *and Jessamine,* the Blossoms that were fallen cover'd all beneath with a profusion of Sweets. A *Canal* run by, which made the retreat as *delightful* as 'twas *fragrant.* Diana, full of the uneasiness of Mind that Love occasion'd, threw her self under the pleasing Canopy, apprehensive of no *Acteon* to invade with forbidden Curiosity, her as *numerous perfect Beauties,* as had the *Goddess.* Supinely laid on that Repose of Sweets, the dazling Lustre of her Bosom stood

> reveal'd, her polished Limbs all careless and extended, showed the *Artful* work
> of *Nature*. (1:759–60)

The tacit association between the features of the garden and a kind of physical and psychological laxness inverts the relation between the mythic
Diana and Acteon. Diana de Bedamore is enveloped by shade, narcotized
by scent, and embedded by flowers; un-self-consciously she adopts the receptive pose of the female considered as both sexual and aesthetic object.
The reader in turn assumes the position of the absent Acteon, the secret
observer of a forbidden scene; except, of course, that one sees not the active
huntress but the helpless victim enclosed within sensuous nature.

The langorous tone conveying this passivity quickens when Roderiguez
enters the garden and seizes her. Diana's quiescence, defined initially as
corresponding to the lush beauty of the garden, now alters under the force
of the seducer's dextrous mental and physical art, his "*Rhetorick*" and
"*strange bewitching* Force" (1:760). The subsequent change in Diana's narrative role turns upon the transposition of natural features on to the female
figure; instead of evoking details like the "Canal," Manley writes of the
"rich *Meanders* of her Bosom" while Roderiguez "drinks her dazling naked
Beauties" (1:760–61). This collapse of consciousness and context into a
virtual identity between figure and setting completes the structure of ideological meanings. These develop within the passage through two stages.
First, conflating the female self with the setting denies her a capacity to
assert a separate will; woman is no more than an objective adjunct, the
"*Artful* work of *Nature*." Second, deflecting attention from Diana as an
individual to the sensuous order of the garden identifies this condition of
subordination as "natural." Roderiguez capitalizes on the seductive atmosphere of the garden to exploit his desire for Diana; his control over both
affirms prescriptive right.

The consequences of the seduction scene reinforce this point. Despite the
emphasis on her passivity and his aggression, the account concludes that
Roderiguez has done no more than assert a natural territorial imperative.
Her beauty did not simply provoke but actually invited the violation, and
she must, therefore, accept full guilt for the seduction: "She ought to be
enclos'd, to be locked up from all desiring Eyes, since in looking on her,
[men] must *necessarily* Sin!" (1:761). The punishment meted out to the
mythic Acteon is accordingly evaded by Roderiguez, who abandons Diana
to public shame and dishonor. The scene summarily incorporates three
central features of the amatory novel: titillation of the reader through selective detail, the exercise of power, and the punishment of the female for
failing to resist; vicarious eroticism and moral rectitude collapsed into a
persistent myth of sexual politics.

Manley's successor in the amatory genre, Eliza Haywood, self-consciously adopts this technique of fusing character with setting as an oblique representation of intercourse. Haywood, like Manley, clearly recognizes that the appeal of her novels lies in their evocation of passion, and if virtue finally emerges triumphant, it is only after a long series of attempted seductions have been lavishly described. This often leads to ludicrously distorted narrative conventions, especially of character. In *The British Recluse; or, The Secret History of Cleomira* (1722), for example, Belinda and Cleomira separately recount their unhappy histories, discovering only at the end that they were undone by the same man. Cleomira's narrative is relatively subdued, but Belinda's character undergoes a rather remarkable change as she describes her seduction. The two lovers have met in a wood:

> We were wandred, insensibly, perhaps, to *either* of us, at least to *me* I am sure it was so, a great Distance from the House, and into the thickest and most obscure Part of the *Wood*. But it was in vain that I reminded him how convenient it was that I shou'd return; he was too pressing, I too transported to be able to refuse him so small a Favour as my Company a few Moments longer. Never was a Night more delectable, more aiding to a Lover's Wishes. The arching Trees form'd a Canopy over our Heads, while through the gently shaking Boughs soft Breezes play'd in lulling Murmurings, and fann'd us with delicious Gales; a thousand Nightingales sang amorous Ditties, and the billing Doves coo'd out their tender Transports—every Thing was soothing—every Thing inspiring. The very Soul of Love seem'd to inform the Place, and reign throughout the whole.[7]

The passage divides neatly into two parts. Belinda begins to describe in a measured and pragmatic tone the context of her seduction, including a glance at self-justification. But when she starts to specify her surroundings, the analytical voice gives way to a rhapsodic cadence of lulling murmurings and cooing doves. In fact, Belinda as a character recounting her downfall in a confessional mode has disappeared and the narrator steps in, ransacking her vocabulary for appropriate images. Nature now functions euphemistically: the supine forms and pressing insistence of sensory detail figuring the physical seduction.

On those rare occasions in amatory novels when the garden assumes a positive moral function, it still retains the primary characteristic of enclosure. Manley's *The New Atalantis* adopts as the pretext for the lengthy representation of political scandal and erotic fantasy the descent to earth of Astrea, who tours Atalantis with Lady Intelligence and the banished Virtue. Lady Intelligence recounts the gossip; Astrea and Virtue comment; and the narrative as a whole resolves itself into a complex play of aggression, seduction, occasional repentance, and virulent attacks on the Whigs.

The volume was dedicated to Henry, Duke of Beaufort, who appears in the novel as the paragon Beaumond, "he that dares be Honest; that dares be Loyal, when it is so much the manner to be otherwise" (1:728). Manley chooses Beaumond's garden as an emblem of his virtue but significantly adjusts the design of Beaufort's actual estate to complement her didactic intent. Beaufort's property at Badminton was organized around "twenty radial avenues stretching far into the country."[8] Its fictional counterpart emphasizes not the illusion of spatial extension, but the enclosed or "labyrinthine" aspects, shrinking prospective view to contained garden.

> Shall we not be lost in this Wilderness of Beauty? These Verdant Labyrinths, that returning in themselves, and at once please and amaze, with a delightful wandring Error. See how those Rows of goodly well-shap'd Trees defend the inquisitive Rays of *Phoebus*, from darting into the sacred Recesses of this forbidden Scene! Hark! How Artlessly! yet Melodiously! we are saluted from above by the feather'd *Natives* of the Wood. . . .
>   See! the crown or Garland of the whole, the auspicious *Beaumond* . . . .
> (1:730–31)

This description is marked stylistically by a breathless artificiality punctuated by exclamatory remarks and thematically by the idea that virtue exists in a "retreat" (1:727), in the "sacred Recesses" of the enclosed garden. The garden blends art with nature; but art to Manley is clearly the more important component, capable of re-creating the paradisiacal condition of "everlasting Spring" (1:731). Beaumond's moral integrity and distinction from political corruption here assume physical form.

If Manley's encomium on virtue tends to fulsomeness, her depiction of vice can be remarkably blunt and well-paced. In the second volume, Count de Biron (Godolphin) recognizes Madame de Caria (Duchess of Marlborough) under her disguise as a country maiden, sees her meet the Duke of Candia (Shrewsbury), watches "her enter the Garden, and observe[s] the duke to join her, and both of them to walk off into the *Labyrinth*" (1:660). The Duke of Candia, alerted to the presence of a stranger, departs and leaves the count to seduce Madame de Caria in the "most retired Part" (1:662) of the labyrinth. Her disgrace completed, the count emerges total victor as he reveals he knows her identity. The scene is played over and over in the scandal chronicles: immoderation is indulged to the vicarious delight of the reader and then punished to appease the forces of virtue and self-righteousness. The labyrinth is intended as a visual symbol of this immoderation, and the ethical connotations of an act performed in darkness, in secrecy, and in disguise (in this instance, a *class* disguise) are sharply drawn in Madame de Caria's unfortunate end. The labyrinth here is not set within a context of aristocratic order and so cannot "please and amaze, with a delightful wandring Error" as in Beaumond's garden. Its associations are instead duplicity, transgression, and the irretrievability of lost innocence.

Although the garden of seduction regularly recurs in the *chronique scandaleuse* and *roman à clef*, it is not a dominant motif. Some tentative explanations may be considered. First, a female figure like the Duchess of Marlborough important enough to merit extensive treatment is made grotesque by attributing to her the masculine qualities of aggression and exploitation, and not the passivity, real or feigned, necessary to a seduction scene. Second, the pace of the narrative with its rapid shifts from scene to scene, the discontinuity between the various encounters, and the lack of a central thematic focus (other than scandal) are incompatible with the leisurely garden seduction. And finally, in the case of Manley, a more specifically political motivation may have played a part. She wrote in the period when the Tories were actively engaged in the struggle for power, culminating in the Harley ministry of 1710–14. Not yet in the political wilderness, there was no need for the Tory propagandist to sing the joys of rural retirement.

In the works of Eliza Haywood (1693?–1756), and such anonymous novels as *The Generous Rivals*, significant thematic and structural advances over the disjointed satires of Manley anticipate *Pamela*. These include more complex characterization, with some attention paid to motivation and causality, an emphasis upon engaging the reader's sympathy and participation, and a more integrated narrative. Garden seductions also assume a new prominence. The frequency of their recurrence and the limited range of types presented suggest that authors relied on their audience's knowledge of a convention of erotic landscape. The topological frame of Henry Hawkins's *Parthenaiea Sacra* and Bunyan's *Pilgrim's Progress* confirm an active seventeenth-century tradition of "reading" the landscape. This shared awareness finds expression in such eighteenth-century critical treatises as Francis Hutcheson's *An Inquiry into the Original of Our Ideas of Beauty and Virtue* (1725).

> The Beauty of Trees, their cool Shades, and their Aptness to conceal from Observation, have made Groves and Woods the usual Retreat to those who love Solitude, especially to the Religious, the Pensive, the Melancholy, and the Amorous. And do not we find that we have so join'd the Ideas of these Dispositions of Mind with those external Objects, that they always recur to us along with them?[9]

Hutcheson significantly links kinds of scenes to emotional responses and implies that a single setting can provoke a chain of associations. This structure of analogies was adopted with varying degrees of sophistication by contemporary novelists. We will see that Haywood, for example, frequently plays with the religious connotations of the garden within a scene that is explicitly sexual. The following two passages from *The Generous Rivals* (1716) appeal to a more simple principle of association. Opposing models of human behavior correspond to specific natural constructs, and the moral superiority of the first presented then anticipates the fortunate conclusion. In the first scene the lovers, Dorinda and Panaretus

> were conducted . . . to an Agreeable Arbor, where the whispers of the Ambient Air, joyn'd with the sweeter Harmony of Chanting Birds, gave them a most engaging Welcome. . . . The fragrant Rose, the verdant Grass, and all the dazling Glories of a blooming Spring, entertain'd their every Sense, and left nothing wanting, that the most fruitful Nature, yet more refined by Elaborate Art, cou'd produce to give them fresh Delight.[10]

Nature refined by Art is here used as an analogue for the innocent love of Dorinda and Panaretus. In the second scene, the natural art of the garden is overshadowed by the artful cunning of the "Lascivious Admirer" (p. 219), Phylopones.

Dorinda has retired to a "very recluse Part of the Garden" when the young Lord enters and "began with all the couchant Fawning of a mean and abject Lust, to tempt her Vertue" (p. 219). When Dorinda scornfully rejects his advances, Phylopones appeals to the example of nature.

> 'See, Madam, the pretty Freedoms the little chirping Birds around us take; they bill, and quench each others amorous Fires, without any of those idle Fears, which you amuse your self withal, and seem, by their after warbling Notes, to triumph o'er the groundless Superstition of us, (for whose Pleasure they were made) in being more Timorous than they. Come then, Madam, cease these irksome Thoughts; this pleasing Recess seems purely made for Love.' (pp. 220–21)

A comparison of the two scenes clarifies narrative strategy. In the first, the garden is described at length by the narrator who provides all the details of natural life essential to the creation of an emblem of legitimate passion. The dominant imagery is that of light; "blooming Spring" and "fruitful Nature" suggest paradisiacal conditions, while the language evokes innocent pleasure: "agreeable," "sweeter," "refined," "delight." But in the second passage there is no general description of nature. The narrator is present only at the beginning to establish the tone of the scene by the language used to characterize Phylopones. After this he absents himself and Phylopones dominates. Vice, in other words, is dramatized and the villain made to damn himself by his appeal to nature (animal passion) as norm. The scene verbally approximates the disposition of character to setting noted earlier in Manley's garden seductions. The point at which her female protagonist merges with the surroundings marks the relinquishment of self and fall into sin; here, withdrawal of the narrator breaks the illusion of detachment and discrimination. In both scenes, the conflation of immediacy and emotion has purely negative connotations. But the prefiguring of a final harmony in the earlier scene indicated that this was a "comic" amatory novel. Accordingly, the two lovers conform to that pattern by reasserting distance in marriage and retirement to a "convenient Country-Seat" where they discover that "Happiness, real substantial Happiness, is only to be found in *Innocence* and *Vertue*" (p. 270).

Eliza Haywood's most successful novel, *Love in Excess; or The Fatal Inquiry* centers on the amorous adventures of two brothers, with a neighboring baronet and his sister drawn in during the second volume as an added complication. The eldest brother, Count d'Elmont, returns to Paris after two years spent in a military career and is immediately besieged by various young women. Unattracted by marriage, he sets out to seduce Amena Sanseverin, thus provoking the jealousy of Alovisa who has already sent him a series of anonymous *billets-doux*. Amena then sends word to the count that she has been forbidden to see him and that night he steals into the garden, releases her from her room, and together they go off to the Tuileries, where he soon demands proof of her affection.

> Twas now this inconsiderate Lady found herself in the greatest strait she had ever yet been in; all Nature seemed to favour his Design. The Pleasantness of the Place, the silence of the Night, the sweetness of the Air, perfum'd with a thousand various Odours wafted by gentle Breezes from adjacent Gardens compleated the most delightful Scene that ever was, to offer up a Sacrifice to Love. . . . The heat of the Weather, and the Confinement having hindred her from Dressing that Day, She had only a thin silk Night Gown on, which flying open as he caught her in his Arms, he found her panting heart beat measures of consent, her heaving Breast swell to be press'd by his, and every Pulse confess a wish to yield; her Spirits all dissolv'd sunk in a Lethargy of Love.[11]

Haywood carefully establishes the varying degrees of moral culpability in the scene. Amena is characterized as a victim rather than aggressor, and in this novel's code of values is thus labeled as no more than "inconsiderate." She does not initiate action and so becomes "sacrificial" prey to her own dangerous passions, the advances of d'Elmont, and the atmosphere of the garden. The steps to her downfall are charted along a path of her psychological responses to his physical presence. As the count grows more aggres-

sive, her resistance is "dissolv'd", reason and control yield to a lethargic
passivity, and it is only the interruption of a servant in the "moment betwixt
her and Ruine" (1:29) that keeps her virtue intact.

Overcome with remorse, d'Elmont resolves to escort her home: " 'Tis
better for you, Madam,' said he, 'whatsoever has happened to be found in
your own Garden, than in any place with me' " (1:30). The suspicion that
Haywood is playing here with an allusion to Edenic innocence and its loss is
strengthened when the two lovers return to find the garden door locked.
The serpent in this case is Alovisa, who has engineered her rival's downfall
by informing M. Sanseverin of the illicit meeting. The significance of
Amena's passivity and the reason for her brief appearance in the narrative
now becomes clear: she is intended as a positive counter to the portrait of a
vicious and unnatural woman. And Alovisa is unnatural precisely because
she has adopted the masculine role of aggressor, especially in sexual terms.

She is, however, permitted a brief interlude of satisfaction in the possession of d'Elmont in marriage, but jealousy soon subverts the victory of
wills: d'Elmont falls in love with his ward Melliora. The process of his
restoration to a positive character begins here as he extricates himself from
his unnatural wife and realigns with "true femininity." The presentation of
Melliora thus replicates in all its essential details the relationship with the
archetypal victim, Amena. Following a tempestuous scene with his wife,

> he flung out of the Room in spite of all her endeavours to hinder him, and going
> hastily through a Gallery which had a large Window that looked into the
> Garden, he perceived *Melliora* lying on a green Bank, in a Melancholy yet
> charming Posture. . . . he in a Moment lost all the Rage of Temper he had
> been in, and his whole Soul was taken up with softness. (2:24)

Haywood marshals her images carefully. Melliora's "Posture" is, of course,
more than "Melancholy yet charming"; it is the passive and susceptible
pose of woman offered up on a green bank in the natural profusion of the
garden. The window replaces the former barrier of a door, and, again, only
the interruption of a servant saves the hapless victim.

When the family retires into the country for the summer the characters
are similarly "typed." The roles of male aggressor, accomplice, victim, and
virago initially assumed by d'Elmont, Anaret, Amena, and Alovisa are now
taken up by d'Elmont, Baron d'Espernay, Melliora, and Melantha. The
subplot of the love between d'Elmont's brother, the Chevalier Brillain, and
Alovisa's sister, Ansellina, provides an additional complication, and by the
end of the second volume the resolution of passion has acquired the complexity of a Jacobean tragedy. Alovisa is dead, the baron has been stabbed

by the chevalier, Melantha is unhappily married, and the count has set off to travel in order to overcome his grief at Melliora's retirement to a convent.

The third volume introduces new characters and scenes through which d'Elmont, chastened by sorrow, moves without pleasure. "He prefer'd a solitary Walk, a lonely Shade, or the Bank of some purling Stream, where he undisturb'd might contemplate on his Belov'd *Melliora*" (3:5). The love-sick wanderer, a prominent figure in amatory novels,[12] permits the conflation of developing self-awareness with a singular appreciation of nature. The hero seeks out those images which reinforce his separateness and thus initiates a healing process which will end with achieved wholeness. After a few fortunate deaths to dispose of unnecessary characters, d'Elmont is finally rewarded with Melliora, while her brother Frankville is granted matrimonial bliss with Camilla. The novel's restoration of order has been predictably equated with the reassertion of conventional sexual mores.

The vicarious thrill to Haywood's readers clearly centers on a passionate encounter in exotic surroundings with all nature vibrating to the forces of love. As her career progresses, these settings become increasingly far-fetched, and Haywood lavishes a wealth of imaginative detail on the evocation of sexuality. *Love in Excess* (1719) is set in the relatively familiar grounds of France, *The British Recluse* (1722) in London, *Idalia* (1723) ranges further afield to Venice, while *Philidore and Placentia* (1727) reflects the vogue for travel literature in its movement between England, a desert island, and Persia. In each of these novels, amorous passion is given precedence over the defensive maneuvers for preservation which had been the stock-in-trade of the French *roman heroique*.[13] The formula was clearly a commercial success: *Love in Excess*, with *Gulliver's Travels* and *Robinson Crusoe*, was one of the three most popular works before *Pamela*.[14] Haywood was enough of a hack writer that having once struck upon the winning combination, she rarely deviated from it. And it is clear from the recurrence of certain motifs that she recognized sexuality as the chief source of her novels' appeal. In refining her techniques for provoking the desired reader response, she ultimately consolidated a kind of rubric of erotica—certain scenes in which setting, dialogue, and characterization would support an implicit model of human behavior. Chief among these is the garden seduction: a ritual enactment in which all features contribute to the pervasive sexuality. We note, then, that the hero alone is granted mobility and the right to exercise control, which in turn effects a virtual equation of female figure with setting—"all Nature seemed to favour his Design" we are told in *Love in Excess*. The entrance of the male into the enclosed garden is thus not merely the prelude to seduction, but also a symbolic enactment of it, a thinly veiled assertion of that power which these scenes endorse. Woman, like nature, may initially resist man's ordering hand, but the impulse to yield to his pressure is finally irresistible.[15] Only some fortuitous interruption can finally save the Haywood heroine from her "natural" inclination to surrender.

II

Pious novels of the period, written in response to this "Deluge of Libertinism which has overflow'd the Age"[16] claimed to excise eroticism in the interests of admonitory didacticism. But authors like Penelope Aubin, in fact, adapt the basic premise of the amatory novel as the paradigm of relationships. Innocence persecuted is a persistent motif, and in her pursuit of it, she far exceeds Haywood in imagining possible varieties of degradation. The localized danger of the seducer is thus supplanted in Aubin's world by endemic catastrophe. Victimization is no longer tied to individual aggression, but has become a social reflex directed against the heroine as exemplar of piety and virginity. The conflation of the two contemporary myths of the victimized female and the infidel heathen fuels this view of the beleaguered Christian. Innocence threatened was a staple of romance narratives, and the addition of infidel barbarians to the crowd of besiegers was a sensational twist.[17] Together the two provide a powerful context for the victory of innocence; the heroines emerge spiritually unscathed from captivity in Barbary, while a number of minor characters present the stark alternative of submission to brutal lust and conversion to Mohammedism.

Like Defoe's narratives, Aubin's works depend on the figuration of the world as a play of hostile forces. They differ radically, however, in the forms of defensive opposition permitted the protagonist. Comparison of two responses to adversity—Maria's in *The Noble Slaves* (1722) and Moll Flanders' in Defoe's novel—epitomizes this divergence. Moll's narrative chronicles survival through exploitation. By adopting the strategems of the enemy—"to Deceive the Deceiver"[18]—she opposes and ultimately surmounts the penalties of gender and position. A lurid retelling of the St. Lucy story in *The Noble Slaves* represents a more characteristic female response. Maria, importuned by the heathen emperor, answers his lust by declaiming, "My eyes shall never see my shame, said I nor more inflame mankind; these I offer up to virtue, and they shall weep no more in aught but blood. At these words I tore my eye balls out and threw them at him."[19] Her action graphically mimics the ethic of renunciation that shapes the pious novel. To be a woman in the Aubin world involves constant sexual intimidation: a punishment so perfectly instilled, and by implication justified, that the protagonists answer it with self-destruction. Aubin, like Manley in the Diana de Bedamore episode from *The New Atalantis*, sees femaleness as a covert invitation to violation. Maria thus achieves moral stature within the novel not by asserting a separate self in opposition to threat, but by mutilating the guilty source of sin: her own body.

Mrs. Aubin was a successful polemicist, keenly aware of the commercial aspects of novel writing. She records rather plaintively and with heavy irony in the Preface to *The Strange Adventures of the Count de Vinevil*:

> As for the Truth of what this Narrative contains, since *Robinson Cruso* has been so well receiv'd, which is more improbable, I know no reason why this should be thought a Fiction. I hope the World is not grown so abandon'd to Vice, as to believe that there is no such Ladies to be found, as would prefer Death to Infamy; or a Man that, for Remorse of Conscience, would quit a plentiful Fortune, retire, and chuse to die in a dismal cell.[20]

But having observed Defoe's popularity, she grafted elements of the travel narrative on to her romances. In *The Noble Slaves*, for example, the boat carrying Teresa and her slave is blown off the coast of Mexico. Three days later they are "cast on a desolate Island"[21] where they are discovered by a Japanese man with his wife and three children who speak Chinese. Subsequent explorations of the island turn up a French man and his wife, a Spaniard, and two Persians living in a hill. This flagrant distortion of geography and the train of marvelous coincidences that provide the semblance of narrative coherence clearly undermine Aubin's claim to verisimilitude. But read on the level of a near-allegorical projection of Christian endurance and providential design, the novels could be seen as models of desirable emotional responses to adversity. The problem in assessing Aubin's didacticism becomes apparent with any attempt to balance such an interpretation against the hysterically defensive tone of her works. Ultimately, the allegorical reading invited by the reliance on providential intercession is defeated by the sheer weight of the impossibly complicated plots and the eagerness with which her heroines embrace martyrdom. Reading the novels as an expression of hierarchical power structures yields, in fact, a grotesquely warped parody of their putative didacticism.

In the novels of Manley and Haywood, the relation of eroticism to enclosure depends upon the presentation of the garden as a displaced image of the susceptible female. To the Aubin heroine like Maria, even this nominal acknowledgment of subjectivity is denied: she is enclosed within, defined by, and perceived as, an erotic object. The only means of grace or escape from this intrinsic identity is mutilation of self *qua* object. The pious novels of Elizabeth Rowe direct attention away from this exclusively human sphere with its ritual exercise of power under the guise of seduction. Her efforts won her popular and critical acclaim: there were at least eighteen editions of *Friendship in Death in Twenty Letters from the Dead to the Living* (1728) by 1800, and three of *Letters Moral and Entertaining* (1729). Samuel Johnson applauded the "copiousness and luxuriance" of her "attempt to employ the ornaments of romance in the decoration of religion,"[22] and at the end of the century Mrs. Berington in Fanny Burney's *Camilla* is one among many fictional characters depicted reading *Friendship in Death*.

Influenced by physico-theological and neo-Platonic thought, Rowe stressed the wide-ranging power of God and the beneficence of the divine order. Nature, considered as both a paradigm of divinity and the context for the *beatus vir*, is the medial point which links the ways of God to man. Virtue takes the form of an enthusiastic participation in this universal harmony and immortal bliss in heaven is the promised final reward. Since the only "true" good can be spiritual, the focus is on the aesthetic rather than material value of nature. The letters are consequently dominated by landscapes apprehended as prefigurations of Paradise and as equivalents to the moral condition of character. In her pursuit of these themes, Rowe most often adopts a celestial viewpoint, choosing as its counterpart on earth, the country life. Both perspectives are associated with clear and comprehensive vision and the attainment of peace: that Paradise is simply an extension of the rural existence is implicit in both collections.

The "peculiar enthusiasm for posthumous studies of the universe" has been traced by Maren-Sofie Røstvig through the works of W. Hinchliffe, Joseph Trapp, and Henry Needler. Bishop Burnet's contribution to the tradition in *The Theory of the Earth* (1683–89) adopts a characteristic visual image.

> Yet the fairest prospect in this Life is not to be compar'd to the least we shall have in another. Our clearest day here, is misty and hazy: We see not far, and what we do see is in a bad light. But when we have got better Bodies in the first Resurrection . . . better Senses and a better Understanding, a clearer light and a higher station, our Horizon will be enlarg'd every way, both as to the Natural World and as to Intellectual.[23]

Despite Burnet's claim that the "fairest prospect in this Life is not to be compar'd to the least we shall have in another," he, like Rowe, chooses the perception of landscape to approximate the spiritual state and further associates it with "enlarg'd" understanding. The didactic function of nature similarly informs the aesthetic in Rowe's *Letters on Various Occasions.* Appreciation of the world is made contingent on knowledge of it: together they anticipate the perfect state of the immortal. The dominant metaphor of the natural world thus neatly conjoins sensation and spirituality—an ingenious and much practiced solution to the questions posed by contemporary science and philosophy. Empiricism is no argument against divinity: it supports, even confirms, it. Rowe thus envisions the ideal state as the contemplative man in harmony with nature.

> I have found a romantick Retreat, surrounded with a charming Variety of Woods, open Lawns, and flowery Vales, in their uncultivated Beauty. Here I rove unattended and free, with no Circumstance of Grandeur, but the Consciousness of a reasonable and immortal Being . . . I have try'd what Delights were to be found in Madness and Folly, and am now in pursuit of what Wisdom and Philosophy can yield. In the fair Creation I trace an Almighty Power, and see the immense Divinity impress'd on all his Works.[24]

Philander has been spectacularly successful in all worldly pursuits, but found his only reward was restlessness. Now in the country, the inheritance of virtuous peace ratifies his material estate. Only in the condition of nature does the "Consciousness of a reasonable and immortal Being" find sufficient stimulus. The "fair Creation" as both object of empirical enquiry and evidence of divine purpose answers the human need for an enduring source of intellectual and spiritual sustenance.

Rowe's novels evade the problematics of subjectivity through the engagement of her characters with ideal form. In orienting her fiction toward spiritual truths, the politics of power is subsumed within the controlling image of a providential divinity. But despite this distinction, her novels share a structure basic to Haywood, Manley, and Aubin. In developing an analogical mode, each places a premium upon moments of identity: the transformation of the particular into the emblematic. The procedure holds true in most pre-1740 narratives, but there are a number of works that evoke contrary principles of discrimination, detachment, and judgment. These principles are most often applied in isolated scenes, as in Mrs. Barker's *Exilius, or, The Banished Roman*, and only rarely, as in the anonymous *Adventures of Lindamira* and in Davys's *The Fugitive; or, The Country Ramble*, shape the entire narrative.

Barker outlines her didactic intent in the Preface to *Exilius*, advocating a return to the romance values of "Virtue and Honour". She concludes her introductory remarks with the commendations provided by friends who have read the novel in manuscript form, mentioning "one Description, (and but one) which is pretty long, and that is of a Garden; but it being added since the Book was compos'd, those who love not Descriptions may pass it over unread, without any Prejudice to the substantial Part of the Story" ([A5ᵛ]). The reference is to a set piece account of a highly artificial garden with boundaries marked by four pyramids. It is further divided into six enclosures, each of which is detailed at length, and within these, the city of Troy modeled in greenery. Here Exilius and Exilia meet to declare their love in what Barker seems to consider regal terms. "Go, (said she) conquer Lybia, receive your just Reward, the Princess *Philometra*, the Heiress of the *Egyptian* Crown, and in her Right, become in Time a happy King. That I cannot be (reply'd I) unless *Exilia* be my Queen."[25] The model of propriety Mrs. Barker sets is both visual and verbal. Distance and discrimination are the controlling principles: in the garden, the geometric shapes, rigid construction, and distinct boundaries; in the language, dramatic gesture, stilted speech, and the oddly impersonal declaration of love. The language used by the author to detail the appropriate landscape reinforces this relation of figure to setting and setting to genre. In the Preface, Barker characterizes amatory fiction through a series of phrases—"Deluge of Libertinism which has overflow'd the Age," "loose Gallantry"—which approximate the disorder of unrestrained emotion by reference to formless nature. The precise rhetoric of the encounter between Exilius and Exilia evokes the opposed value of propriety, associated here with disinterested behavior and respect for the "higher" claims of the state. In relinquishing the idiom of a distinctive *persona*, this speech works toward elevating the individual to an exemplar of moral rectitude. The appeal, then, throughout the passage is to an ethical code of sufficient distance and comprehensiveness to absorb the singular or distinctive.

Exilius exploits the contemporary craze for exotic settings through a spurious account of the ancient world. Just as Aubin's desert islands were seen as appropriate locales for her beleaguered Christian heroines, so was the ancient world associated with exaggeratedly noble displays of heroism. Settings distanced by time or unfamiliarity were clearly thought to be related by the reader with behavioral extremes: as Defoe notes in *Serious Reflections During the Life and Surprising Adventures of Robinson Crusoe* (1720), "Facts that are form'd to touch the Mind, must be done a great Way off, and by somebody never heard of."[26] The vicarious experience offered by Barker functions at the same level, though the opposite end of the moral spectrum from that of Haywood's novels. For both, specific landscape types hold an ethical content understood by reader and author—landscape, in other words, was one of the keys to response. The three works I would like to consider now break almost every narrative convention of early eighteenth-century fiction, most notably that of authority. Rather than conceiving of power as imposed and arbitrary, the first two—*Adventures of Lindamira* and *The Fugitive*—internalize it to allow expression of will; the third, Blackamore's *Luck at Last*, domesticates it to identify authority as the prerogative of the landed interest. Each atypically extends the spatial and linguistic formalism of *Exilius* to the province of self-knowledge. Landscape is correspondingly modified as identity of character and setting yields to an acknowledged distance between self and object. In *Adventures of Lindamira* and *The Fugitive* the protagonists exercise a control over themselves and their surroundings which was denied the Barker female; in both novels, this desire to organize experience in conformity to a distinctive *persona* and a valued clarity of language is matched by a more sophisticated response to landscape.

The Preface to *Adventures of Lindamira* records the intentions of the author through an appeal to the reader's pride:

> If the histories of foreign amours and scenes laid beyond the seas, where unknown customs bear the greatest figure, have met with the approbation of English readers, 'tis presumed that domestic intrigues, managed according to the humours of the town and the natural temper of the inhabitants of this our island, will be at least equally grateful. But above all, the weight of truth and the importance of real matter of fact ought to overbalance the feigned adventures of fabulous knight-errantry.[27]

For once the narrative bears out this promise to "domesticate" extravagance by "real matter of fact." The pragmatic tone and careful structuring of events can be largely attributed to the author's atypical emphasis on character rather than plot machinations. Lindamira is distinguished by her sensitivity to ordered discourse, and as this is an epistolary novel the happy consequence is attention to clarity: "I will give it to you in as concise a manner as I can" (p. 45), says the heroine. The same principle conditions the analysis of her various lovers, who are accorded merit to the degree that their rhetoric is free of cant. Her trenchant criticism pervades the work; one female friend is dismissed with the comment that she would "so confound one thing with another that there was no coherence in all her discourse" (p. 116). By adopting language as the measure of value, Lindamira consolidates her own position as ironic commentator while shaping a unified narrative. The "coherence of her discourse" both marks her superiority and provides the necessary distance for judging those who fail to meet the standard.

The characterization of Lindamira owes much to that figure of Restoration drama, the self-conscious and confident female whose chief weapon is her wit. Her view of the country reflects this "court" perspective. One of the diversions while visiting her relatives is "to hear the awkward, ill-contrived compliments that the clowns make on the little beauty of their mistresses, and their piping, squeaking, and dancing before 'em, and now and then out of an abundance of love I should see those two-handed clod-pates carry home their milk pails for 'em" (46). This antipastoral, however, is at least in part a characteristic flaunting of familiarity with literary convention. Throughout the narrative, Lindamira carefully notes similarities between what she sees and "descriptions I had ever read on" (p. 46). Here, parody of rustic ignorance seems designedly allusive, the pose of the urban sophisticate. What is original in this novel are the lengthy descriptions which precisely record the features of the landscape.

> The house was situated on the rise of a hill. At a convenient distance ran a river, which in the summer-time rendered the place very delightful. Not far from it was a wood encompassing some few acres of ground, and in the midst of it a path that led to a little rivulet, near half a mile long, and a row of high elms on both sides, so that in the midst of the day one might walk without the least inconveniency from the weather. At the end of this rivulet was a well that was paved about with broad stone, and benches round. . . . A few paces from this well, after some turnings and windings, you come into a little solitary valley, at the end of which stands a small cottage. (pp. 45–46)

A prefatory comment justifies the inclusion of this passage: "the knowledge of my adventures somewhat depends upon a description of this place" (p. 45). The technique may seem crude, but the attempt to integrate the various sections of the narrative is unusual. Comparison with more typical amatory gardens, like those of Haywood, reveals further innovations. In novels such as *Love in Excess*, the cumbersome machinery of exotic flowers and gentle breezes functions primarily as a backdrop to the seduction. Here the scene has depth: objects bear relation to one another, distances are calculated, and as we approach the end of the description the view itself terminates with the valley and its focal point, the cottage. Yet despite this technical proficiency, the passage is exactly contemporary in the significance it finally accords to the landscape. In drawing from it an awareness of the "innocence of country life" contrasted with the "empty noise and bustle of the town" (p. 46), Lindamira simply reiterates the conventional typology of the *beautus vir*.

The heroine of Mary Davys's *The Fugitive* (1705) decides that she must "with *Cain* (tho' for different reasons) turn wanderer".[28] Those encountered on her ramblings are subjected to careful scrutiny, and throughout she is unaffectedly vigorous in her censure of any who deny her uniqueness. The misogynist who harangues about "damn'd Women" (p. 116) is countered with pungent insult. "I can't, for my Life, but fancy that your Father was hang'd for lying with a Sow, and you are the unnatural Offspring, nothing else could make you of so Hoggish a Temper; had your Mother been a Woman, Nature would have taught you to have had, at least, common Civility for them" (pp. 116–17). The earthiness of her style is of a different order than Lindamira's, but for both the ability to manipulate language provides a semblance of power. In her descriptions of landscape we find a complementary voice that tacitly identifies nature as the measure of value. The first home she visits is that of a frugal woman, the second that of a profligate gentleman; between these paired opposites is inserted the following:

> I went to walk in the Gardens, which were very fine, and where I had much the pleasanter Consort; the Trees were dress'd in all their Gaiety, and the little Birds were in the height of all their Mirth, the Beautiful Flowers gave the greatest content to the Eye and Smell, and the little Fishes in the Ponds, peept out to see the rising Sun. This place, I own, delighted me very much, and made me some amends for my Nights Lodgings. (p. 14)

A natural order of a distinctly human type is evoked here: the trees are dressed, the birds mirthful, and the fish peep out to see the sun. Nature, in fact, is the protagonist's "consort"—in its tenderness and profusion is a simplicity of design and responsiveness with which she feels herself temperamentally allied. In a social context, language asserts her integrity through distance; in relation to nature, it marks out similitudes.

Just as *Lindamira* and *The Fugitive* are most fruitfully considered in relation to amatory narratives, so does the pious novel offer a standard against which the aims and quality of Arthur Blackamore's *Luck at Last; or, The Happy Unfortunate* (1723) can best be measured. Rowe's celestial wanderers, Barker's noble Romans, and Aubin's persecuted innocents represent extremes of the pious novel: virtue aligned with divinity or propriety, and against the carnal. *Luck at Last* effects a compromise in its more stolid definition of morality. The author identifies the landscape of the estate as the nexus of value, but in a form that differs significantly from his contemporaries. Rowe, to whom it also had symbolic importance, had simply grafted an empirical bias on to the Horatian ideal of the *beatus ille*. Blackamore's representation, however, draws on the social implications of the seventeenth-century genre of topographical poetry celebrating the country house:

And now, as it were by the finger of an overruling Providence directing, she was almost at the end of her travels. About noon she got near seven miles into the country and at the entrance of a little village, seated near the seat of a pleasant hill that arose with a gradual ascent to the top where stood a noble pile of buildings that overlooked the country all about and was the mansion of a gentleman named Liberius, who was a person truly deserving, being of known sense . . . courteous, affable, hospitable to strangers, and a master of all the excellent endowments that are requisite to make one truly great.[29]

The heroine has escaped from a tyrannical father through the garden, "locking the door after her and throwing the key over the wall" (p. 18). She leaves this garden debased by unreasonable authority and journeys toward Liberius's estate: a secular version of the pilgrimage toward the Heavenly City. The estate functions in the narrative as the locus of a complex of values ranging from "right reason" to the "charms of virtue"; these are seen to encourage "profoundest tranquillity" and "solid happiness" (pp. 79–80). The landlord's active beneficence (he is "courteous, affable, hospitable to strangers") is iconographically represented by his position of eminence. His ability to "overlook the country all about" thus serves a double function as an image of ethical and visual comprehensiveness.

A subsequent description details the "vast quantity of ground" around the "noble front" that is covered by a "great many outhouses and gardens"; stretching away from this, a "prospect of the country below for several miles together" (p. 68). The estate owner's controlling presence makes the distance cohere into a pattern of order as the "pleasant eminence" becomes a version of Wallace Stevens's jar in Tennessee. His claim to control derives, of course, from a collapse of the material and aesthetic into a single image of dominance; the privilege of position extends the right of ownership over all that he can see. Despite the superficial resemblance here to Fielding's favored symbol, Blackamore's emphasis upon communal order and the owner's active benevolence in fact accords thematically with the country house poems of the previous century. His contemporaries more often punctuate the given ideal of his novel with a qualifying sense that the estate exists as a conceptual, rather than actual model. The "polish'd pillars" and "roofe of gold" of "proud, ambitious heaps" frame, but do not significantly disturb, Jonson's encomiastic ode "To Penshurst."[30] Timon's "inverted Nature," on the other hand, insidiously informs Pope's "Epistle to Burlington" as a prescient universal.[31] Fielding's adaptation of the estate image as closural device in *Tom Jones* and *Joseph Andrews* in turn refers to a social context broadly analogous to Pope's. In a world of sharpers and swindlers, betrayal and deceit, comic resolution depends upon the figuration of a separate order: enclosure behind actual and metaphoric walls.

Marriage and retirement to the estate, then, serve Tom and Sophia, Fanny and Joseph, and to a certain extent, Mr. B. and Pamela, as a defensive and mutual retreat from corruption. For the female this assertion of domesticity, personal, spatial, and architectural, has a supplementary function; it permits subordination and "natural" weakness to be seen not as covert invitations to violation, but as socially approved and useful attributes. The post-1740 preference for the estate rather than the garden image, then, has profound ideological implications for the definition of female character. The Manley, Haywood, and Aubin heroines equated with the suppliant garden are in both senses "natural" victims and, therefore, negative archetypes. Fielding and Richardson acquire the dubious distinction of institutionalizing inferior status by collapsing the "nature" of women with a means of control which is construed as a positive force. The boundaries of the estate and the closed circle of marriage offer a protection which carries its own burden of meaning, a meaning fully realized in subsequent narratives. "Positive" female characters in the novels of Sarah Fielding, Charlotte Lennox, and Sarah Scott must accede to a control which at once defines and prescribes a severely limited potential. For to contravene normative values is seen as not only a denial of individual integrity, that is, the realization of self in subordination; but also as a threat to social order, the estate and marriage as related terms in a microcosmic hierarchy.

NOTES

1. John J. Richetti, *Popular Fiction Before Richardson: Narrative Patterns 1700–1739* (Oxford: Clarendon Press, 1969), 13.

2. The phrase in fact appears in a letter from the Earl of Peterborow to Lady Mary Wortley Montagu. I have followed George Sherburn's annotation to this passage: Pope "persuaded his friend to sign this letter that he either dictated or at least shaped." George Sherburn, ed., *The Correspondence of Alexander Pope III, 1729–1735*, (Oxford: Clarendon Press, 1956), 352.

3. Alexander Pope, "The First Satire of the Second Book of Horace" l. 84 in *Imitations of Horace with an Epistle to Dr. Arbuthnot and The Epilogue to The Satires*, ed. John Butt, 2d. ed. (London & New Haven: Methuen & Co. & Yale University Press, 1953).

4. Alexander Pope, *The Dunciad*, bk. 2, note to l. 149. ed. James Sutherland 3d. rev. ed. (London & New Haven: Methuen & Co. & Yale University Press, 1963). Behind the tangle of dismissive rhetoric can be detected here the Augustan concern with the appropriate voice. Political satire, as a highly serious art, demands the decorum of a public *persona* to foster the illusion of objectivity. In Pope's view, Manley and Haywood deflect satire's didacticism by eliciting from the reader a personal response of vicarious sexuality. His attack, however, clearly moves

beyond the conditions of public and private in accordance with genre to a second frame of reference: the public text as a reflection of private lubricity. In presenting *Adventures of Rivella* as a *chronique scandaleuse* Manley defers to the latter term of Pope's argument. The subversive tendencies of her fiction emerge in the deviation from his first term—the necessary integrity of the "public" satiric voice—and the consequent denial that sexual revelation is "ruinous" or "disturbing."

5. John Duncombe's *The Feminiad* (London: 1754), ll. 139–44 enforces the traditional association in his lines on Manley:

> The Modest Muse a veil with pity throws
> O'er Vice's friends and Virtue's female foes;
> Abash'd she views the bold unblushing mien
> Of modern Manley, Centlivre, and Behn;
> And grieves to see One nobly born disgrace
> Her modest sex, and her illustrious race.

In a footnote to this passage, Duncombe writes: "These three ladies have endeavour'd to immortalize their shame, by writing and publishing their own memoirs" (15). The "One nobly born" refers to Manley, daughter of Sir Roger Manley.

6. Mary Delariviere Manley, *The Adventures of Rivella; or, The History of the Author of the Atalantis* in *The Novels of Mary Delariviere Manley*, ed. Patricia Köster (Gainesville, Fla.: Scholars' Facsimiles & Reprints, 1971), 2:740. All further references to Manley's works will appear in parentheses in the text, with the pagination of the Köster edition.

7. Eliza Haywood, *The British Recluse: or, The Secret History of Cleomira, Suppos'd Dead. A Novel* (London: 1722), 112. All further references to this work will appear in parentheses in the text.

8. Edward Malins, *English Landscaping and Literature, 1660–1840* (London: Oxford University Press, 1966), 8.

9. Frances Hutcheson, *An Inquiry into the Original of our ideas of Beauty and Virtue* (London: 1725), 76.

10. Anon., *The Generous Rivals: or Love Triumphant* (London: 1716), 147–48. All further references to this work will appear in parentheses in the text.

11. Eliza Haywood, *Love in Excess: or The Fatal Enquiry, A Novel* (London: 1719–1720), 1:28–29. All further references to this work will appear in parentheses in the text. The association between a lapse from self-control, the dangers of imagination, and the atmosphere of the garden appears again in Haywood's *Philidore and Placentia*. See William H. McBurney, ed. *Four before Richardson: Selected English Novels, 1720–1727* (Lincoln: University of Nebraska Press, 1963), 162.

12. See, for example, M. D. Manley's *Memoirs of Europe*, 2:9.

13. See English Showalter, *The Evolution of the French Novel, 1641–1782* (Princeton: Princeton University Press, 1972).

14. William H. McBurney, "Mrs. Penelope Aubin and the Early Eighteenth-Century English Novel," *Huntington Library Quarterly* 20 (1957): 250.

15. See Carole Fabricant, "Binding and Dressing Nature's Loose Tresses: The Ideology of Augustan Landscape Design," in *Studies in Eighteenth-Century Cul-*

ture, vol. 8, ed. Roseann Runte (Madison: University of Wisconsin Press, 1979), 109–35. In her incisive analysis of the complementary responses to women and landscape in Augustan poetry, Fabricant reveals the "profound interconnections between aesthetic, economic, and sexual forms of possession" (117).

16. Jane Barker, *The Entertaining Novels of Mrs. Barker* (London: 1719), sig. [A4]. All further references to this work will appear in parentheses in the text.

17. See G. A. Starr, "Escape from Barbary: A Seventeenth-Century Genre," *Huntington Library Quarterly* 29 (1965): 35–52.

18. Daniel Defoe, *Moll Flanders* (Oxford: Oxford University Press, 1971), 77.

19. Penelope Aubin, *The Noble Slaves* (Belfast: 1812), 29.

20. Penelope Aubin, *The Strange Adventures of the Count de Vinevil and his Family* (London: 1721), 6–7.

21. Aubin, *The Noble Slaves*, 8.

22. George Birkbeck Hill, ed., *Boswell's Life of Johnson*. Rev. and enlarged by L. F. Powell (Oxford: Clarendon Press, 1934), 1:312.

23. Maren-Sofie Rostvig, *The Happy Man: Studies in the Metamorphoses of a Classical Ideal*, vol. 2: 1700–1760. (Oslo and Oxford: Universitetsforlaget, 1958), 2:32, 35.

24. E. S. Rowe, *Letters on Various Occasions* (London: 1729), 98.

25. Barker, *Entertaining Novels of Mrs. Barker*, sig. [A4].

26. Daniel Defoe, *Serious Reflections during the Life and Surprising Adventures of Robinson Crusoe: With his Vision of the Angelick World. Written by Himself* (London: 1720), sig. [A6].

27. *The Adventures of Lindamira* (London: 1702), 3. All further references to this work will appear in parentheses in the text.

28. Mary Davys, *The Fugitive; or, The Country Ramble* (London: 1705), sig. [A6].

29. Arthur Blackamore, *Luck at Last; or, The Happy Unfortunate*, in McBurney, *Four before Richardson*, 36. All further references to this work will appear in parentheses in the text.

30. Ben Jonson, "To Penshurst" ll. 3, 101, in *Ben Jonson*, ed. C. H. Herford and P. and E. Simpson, 8 vols. (Oxford: Clarendon Press, reprint: 1965).

31. Alexander Pope, "Epistle to Burlington" l. 119, in *Epistles to Several Persons* (Moral Essays), ed. F. W. Bateson, 2d ed. (London & New Haven: Methuen & Co. & Yale University Press, 1961).

Radcliffe's Dual Modes of Vision

RHODA L. FLAXMAN

The new scholarship on women has extended our sense of the novel tradition by bringing hitherto neglected works by women to the attention of critics. Although Ann Radcliffe's work has never been completely neglected, reassessment reveals her importance as a formal innovator in the history of the English novel. Often she is praised for her attention to setting and story and for softening and romanticizing the conventional Gothic novel's atmosphere from horrific effects to merely terrifying ones. But she has never been recognized sufficiently for establishing a new descriptive mode and technique for the novel. In so doing, she effectively expands the novel's rhetorical possibilities.

Radcliffe was one of the first English novelists to elevate extended, visually oriented landscape description—previously nearly the exclusive province of poetry—to a position of prominence in English fiction. In addition to establishing a new subject—subsequently developed by writers as diverse as Scott, Ruskin, Dickens, Hardy, Lawrence and Woolf—she was the first to apply a genuinely cinematic technique to these descriptions. This technique, which I have labeled cinematic word-painting, refers to landscape descriptions that borrow pictorial techniques from the visual arts, with one significant addition. From the visual arts word-painting adapts framing devices, a consistent visual perspective, and compositional strategies, such as attention to volume, mass, the contrast between light and dark, and careful application of coloristic effects. In addition, the mode relies on a narrator/viewer who scans visual data according to a coherent point-of-view allowing the reader to visualize the general compositional configurations as if through a camera eye. This cinematic technique renders a spatially coherent landscape and gives the illusion of kinesis that emerges from a clear spatial progression from foreground to background, much as a modern camera zooms over a scene. Obviously, Radcliffe knew nothing of modern cinematography, but her technique for capturing landscape in language closely resembles filmic "visualization through perspective" that combines object and seer.[1]

Although cinematic word-paintings often appear to "freeze" narrative progression, the viewer's metaphorical journey through a landscape represents kinesis within stasis and may amend Ephraim Lessing's famous distinction between poetry and painting.[2] It also allows novelists to integrate description with narration by relating the object being observed to qualities of the viewer or its mood to anticipations of future events. Although Radcliffe rarely achieves such a symbolic interchange of significance—indeed, she was relatively uninterested in these relationships—her landscape description sometimes achieves the effect of a "narrative of landscape." Such a technique implies progression from one element to another focused through the unique consciousness of a particular spectator and, echoing the form of narrative itself, may represent one of English fiction's first dramatizations of the visual imagination itself.

The "dual modes of vision" to which this essay's title refers acknowledges that Radcliffe only rarely achieves the consistency and kinetic effectiveness of a genuine word-painting. In her most famous work, *The Mysteries of Udolpho*, for example, descriptions mostly adhere to conventional stylistic eighteenth-century modes. Radcliffe's dominant descriptive mode presents static "catalogues" of elements in a landscape that are described in generalized, abstract terms and ordinarily rely heavily on contemporary formulas for the obligatory balancing of the sublime with the beautiful. The opening paragraph of the novel exemplifies such an approach.

> On the pleasant banks of the Garonne, in the Province of Gascony, stood, in the year 1584, the chateau of Monsieur St. Aubert. From its windows were seen the pastoral landscapes of Guienne and Gascony, stretching along the river, gay with luxurient woods and vines, and plantations of olives. To the south, the view was bounded by the majestic Pyrennees, whose summits, veiled in clouds, or exhibiting awful forms, seen, and lost again, as the partial vapours rolled along, were sometimes barren, and gleamed through the blue tinge of air, and sometimes frowned with forests of gloomy pine, that swept downward to their base. These tremendous precipices were contrasted by the soft green of the pastures and woods that hung upon their skirts; among whose flocks, and herds, and simple cottages, the eye, after having scaled the cliffs above, delighted to repose. To the north, and to the east, the plains of Guienne and Languedoc were lost in the mist of distance; on the west Gascony was bounded by the waters of Biscay.[3]

A disembodied voice opens the novel by enumerating elements characteristic of pastoral scene: gently winding river, noble mansion, cultivated slopes, and flocks grazing on soft, green mountain pastures near the cottages of simple peasants. The identity of the observer is not important, and our ability to visualize the scene is hampered by the illogical perspective and the inert passivity of the language. Although there is a faint attempt to move our mental eye from the chateau to the Pyrenees to the south and then to north, east, and west in turn, it is impossible to understand how the observer can describe the chateau and the view from its windows simultaneously. The passive voice allows no rhythmic enlivening of the stilted, choppy phrases that build complex, often confusing, sentences. Verbs, adjectives, and adverbs lack specificity and color, but all elements contribute to depicting a natural landscape of peace and harmony between human beings and nature where "the eye after having scaled the cliffs above, delighted to repose" at an appropriately moderate mid-height.

The passage, though inert, introduces two favorite Radcliffian framing devices borrowed from the visual arts. We often find the heroine, Emily St. Aubert, gazing through a window onto a beautiful scene. This window helps to limit and organize what the observer sees; in addition, as in the passage above, a line of trees, a body of water, or the horizon line demarcates the farthest limit of her vision.

Radcliffe's dominant descriptive mode is characterized by descriptions of beautiful landscapes expressed in generalized diction that fails to capture their uniqueness. Her cinematic word-paintings, however, contrast vividly with the technique illustrated above. Her imagination, when thoroughly aroused by her concept of sublime landscape, struggles to free itself from generalized description to achieve an almost scientific particularity of observation. Not only does she include acute visual detail in such passages, but she also works out a kinetic technique to make the reader believe she or he sees the wild scenes she so obviously loved. Interestingly, Radcliffe's word-paintings represent the only places in *The Mysteries of Udolpho* where I sense the presence of a unique, impassioned voice. It is clearly the voice of Radcliffe herself.

There are five major word-paintings in Udolpho inserted among long narrative passages and briefer descriptive ones.[4] Their distribution may be structurally significant, for one important word-painting appears in each volume of the novel except for volume 3. A major cluster of extended landscape descriptions occurs in volume 2 and visualizes the heroine's journey through the Alps to Italy, her first brief look at Venice, and her journey through the Apennines to the Castle of Udolpho, a climactic moment in the complex plotting of the work. Through a close reading of the journey to Udolpho itself, I hope to demonstrate my claim for Radcliffe: that, although we might consider her "fetter'd" by the formulaic plots, characters, and themes of the Gothic tradition, she felt relatively freer than her male counterparts to explore the unknown territory of the cinematic word-painting and to contribute an innovative subject and technique to the English novel.

A brief sketch of the three major settings for Emily St. Aubert's literal and symbolic journey toward knowledge and happiness orients us to the complicated plot of *The Mysteries of Udolpho*. The novel begins in La Vallée, Emily's childhood home, where Emily lives harmoniously with nature in a version of the pastoral ideal, and no terrifying mysteries intrude. Although the author pays lip service to its picturesque beauties, the second major setting, the forbidding Castle of Udolpho, set amid the splendor and sublimity of the Alps, is the one that fully arouses the author's powers of description. This setting also provides the context for Emily's most lurid trials at the hands of the villianous Montoni. In the third setting, Chateau-le-Beau, Emily encounters her most sophisticated test, for she is required to discriminate between subtle manifestations of good and evil as the pastoral and gothic, the rational and irrational intermingle. Once Emily has learned to separate reality from illusion, her education is complete and her reward is marriage to the pallid, imperfect, but nonetheless lovable Valancourt.

At La Vallée the mountains and cliffs, safely remote, rim the horizon, providing a useful contrast with the cultivated valley. The light in this valley is clear, bright, and gay, permeated by soft greens and blues. But, as the recently orphaned Emily, her aunt, and the menacing Montoni (her aunt's new husband), journey through the Alps toward Montoni's castle, the landscape changes dramatically, as do the organizing mode of perception and the general level of intensity in the language. Here, finally, Radcliffe's writing achieves the sweep and vivid detail of a cinematic word painting that distinguishes this mode from the static catalogue this essay previously examined.

The passage beginning "at length, they reached a little plain, where the drivers stopped to rest the mules" organizes the dramatic ascent of the Alps as a progression through vistas—framed "scenes"—that provide suspense as Emily and her group near their destination. The journey gives Radcliffe the opportunity to describe visual elements that almost always appear as part of a Radcliffian landscape of the sublime and that clearly excite her imagination in a way entirely different from landscapes merely beautiful. The pictorial motifs might well remind us of a canvas by Rosa, Claude, or Poussin, whose paintings provided Radcliffe's only idea of how the Alps looked at the time she was writing *The Mysteries of Udolpho*. The cult of the picturesque dictated recurrent elements in Radcliffe's descriptions such as forbidding precipices, gnarled trees abutting tortuous narrow paths into high mountains, and the pastoral landscape stretching into the mists below.

Often—though not in the passage before us—other sense impressions augment the visual, such as the perfume of flowers or the faint sounds of lute, oboe, or violin music wafting up from some unknown source. This characteristic merging of sense impressions to heighten the moment's emotion anticipates a favorite strategy of Romantic poets.

As the little group of travelers ascends, we are treated to magnificent panoramas that dramatize the landscape by a frequent reiteration of contrasts between heights and depths, and between sheltered and expansive spaces. In the first paragraph of the word-painting, the stilted abstract language of La Vallée suddenly gives way to more colorful and precise adjectives, adverbs, and verbs, a more coherent point-of-view, and a livelier sense of rhythm and movement.

> Beyond the amphitheatre of mountains, that stretched below, whose tops appeared as numerous, almost, as the waves of the sea, and whose feet were concealed by the forests—extended the Campagna of Italy, where cities and rivers, and woods and all the glow of cultivation were mingled in gay confusion. (p. 225)

Opening the description from the foreground anchor of the little band of travelers and their mules to the vista below, we understand the reference to the "immensity of nature" because the narrator describes, progressively, the foreground figures, mountain tops below them, forests at mountain base and, beyond the mountains, the countryside of Italy laid out in bird's-eye view. The little word-painting sweeps us along with its vivid, active verbs (stretch, mingle, bound, pour) in the sentence that follows. The rhythms of the syntax echo the necessary quickness of the eye in taking in such a breathtaking varied scene.

In spite of the series of visually confusing figurative clichés in which the mountains are described simultaneously as amphitheatre, ocean waves, and feet, Radcliffe's intention here is both bold and original. She is trying to write movement into a progressive description, first, of ranges of mountains, then their tops (like waves) and, finally their bases in forests. Her similes may trip her up, but the excitement and intensity of the writing is palpable! Three bodies of water frame the vista and contribute a further sense of motion to the scene. We are able to visualize how elements in this sublime landscape interrelate as the "camera eye" sweeps the scene. Radcliffe has applied an essentially cinematic technique to landscape descriptions here.

Repetition of the transitional phrase "at length" in the several preceding paragraphs constitutes a rather clumsy attempt to signal the passage of time. Both travelers and the reader enter a seemingly timeless realm as they ascend the Alps, for time and space seem to expand endlessly in the gradually multiplying vistas that unfold before our eyes. Unfortunately, the narrator's excitement about the scene fails to animate the heroine, whose loneliness only increases with the sublimity of the landscape.

As the party climbs higher into the Alps, and ever closer to the Castle of Udolpho, the description becomes progressively more exciting, vivid, and dramatic. It is a dangerous ascent, and clearly represents the approach of an important test in Emily's symbolic journey toward maturity. The second paragraph contains some of the most particularized descriptive writing in this word-painting, for here, at last, Radcliffe allows the magnificence of the scene to unroll before us, unimpeded by the balancing of the pastoral. Contrast between enclosed and expansive space again accentuates and dramatizes the progress through the very heart of the Apennines—a scene inherently dramatic.

First we see very little, other than the narrow pass that surrounds us, its wild overhanging cliffs, and gnarled, windswept oak clinging stubbornly to rock inimical to human intrusion. This narrow entry only intensifies the sense of freedom when daylight returns with the long perspective of mountain range and rolling mist, "a scene as wild as any the travellers had yet passed" (p. 225). Radcliffe's use of the word "perspective" here indicates she is thinking like a painter as well as a writer.

The alternation between the specificity of foreground details and dramatic background vistas, between darkness and light, enhances that very sense of movement and rhythm that characterizes Radcliffe's very best word-paintings:

> Still vast pine-forests hung upon their base, and crowned the ridgy precipice, that rose perpendicularly from the vale, while above, the rolling mists caught the sunbeams, and touched their cliffs with all the magical colouring of light and shade. The scene seemed perpetually changing, and its features to assume new forms, as the winding road brought them to the eye in different attitudes; while the shifting vapours, now partially concealing their minuter beauties, and now illuminating them with the splendid tints, assisted the illusions of the sight. (p. 226)

Here Radcliffe's language captures the visual excitement of forms that shift rapidly with the changing perspectives of the eye as it moves across a landscape. The specificity of diction reflects an active creative engagement with wild nature—words such as impending, hung, rose, rolling, shifting—that emphasize motion and drama. Although the final phrase of this passage reminds us that Radcliffe ordinarily prefers suggestive, rather than explicit descriptive language, the vivid particularity in her successful word-paintings represents an opposing aesthetic tendency.

As if to frame and contain the wild energy of this writing, the passage continues with two brief paragraphs that return us—in one case, in mid-sentence—to the sentimental "sweet picture of repose" that recalls the pastoral opening of the novel.

But, not content to rest on the "green delights" of the pastoral, "smiling amid surrounding horror," the narrator quickly turns her discriminating eye back to the landscape that thrills her. The pace and vividness move quickly toward the climax both of the descriptive writing and of Emily's journey. The novel's title reminds us that we are approaching the structural center of the work at last. A fully realized cinematic panorama represents the climax of this word-painting as well.

> Towards the close of day, the road wound into a deep valley. Mountains, whose shaggy steeps appeared to be inaccessible, almost surrounded it. To the east, a vista opened, that exhibited the Apennines in their darkest horrors; and the long perspective of retiring summits, rising over each other, their ridges clothed with pines, exhibited a stronger image of grandeur, than any that Emily had yet seen. (p. 226)

In her eagerness to help us visualize precisely how Emily moves through this dramatic landscape toward the castle of Udolpho, Radcliffe jams both light effects and compositional placement into a single long sentence. One feels her again straining to encapsulate motion in the essentially static medium of language.

> The sun had just sunk below the top of the mountains she was descending, whose long shadow stretched athwart the valley, but his sloping rays, shooting through an opening of the cliffs, touched with a yellow gleam the summits of the forest, that hung upon the opposite steeps, and streamed in full splendor upon the towers and battlements of a castle, that spread its extensive ramparts along the brow of a precipice above. The splendour of these illuminated objects was heightened by the contrasted shade, which involved the valley below.
>
> "There," said Montoni, speaking for the first time in several hours, "is Udolpho." (p. 227)

Montoni's announcement accentuates the importance of this moment, and light—particularly vivid here—dramatizes the contrast with encroaching darkness as the sun sinks behind the mountains and the landscape chills. At such moments, Radcliffe's evocations of the precise look of light on landscape are far superior to those of James Thompson, whose passages from *The Seasons* receive the greater critical praise. Radcliffe shares a fondness for setting climactic events at twilight with Victorian poets such as Wordsworth, Tennyson, Rossetti, and Swinburne. At the transitional moments of dusk or dawn strange visions sometimes occur, realities are blurred, and irrational fears may conquer rational thought. Twilight increases suspense and lends an air of drama to things seen.

The transitional nature of this moment between day and night provides a fitting context for the discovery of the castle, seen in all its picturesque and lurid detail. As Emily gazes "with melancholy awe" at Udolpho, the sloping rays of the sun shoot through, touch, and stream with splendor dramatically in contrast to the encroaching shadows of night. A moment of stasis allows Radcliffe to describe with care how the rays of the setting sun gradually travel up the castle wall to battlements and clustering towers, leaving behind "a melancholy purple tint." The "darkest horrors" of the Apennines—in the language of the Burkean sublime—and the darkening landscape foreshadow Emily's quasi-imprisonment in the sinister castle that hangs above her. Sublime and imposing mountains which have thrilled and terrified the narrator—if not Emily—find ominous echo in the castle—"silent, lonely, and sublime"—fitting emblem of the inscrutable and defiant Montoni.

Our example of word-painting—Radcliffe's second mode of vision—ends with the ascent of the carriages, but here ascent is simultaneously a descent into darkness, cruelty, superstition, and terror. Significantly, when Emily, at the chapter's end, sits at the window of her new home, all is "sunk in darkness" (p. 229); she can discern nothing. The next step in her education will depend on her learning how to see and to interpret both visual and psychological realities at Udolpho.

Radcliffe's Gothic narratives overwhelmingly participate in the eighteenth-century aesthetic preference for balance and moderation, for limiting the ecstasies and perils of the sublime with the orderliness of the beautiful. But, occasionally, as I hope I have demonstrated, when her imagination is completely aroused, she reaches for a proto-Romantic descriptive technique, where the emotions of the narrator—if not the heroine—color the reporting of precise visual detail. At such moments, Radcliffe abandons generalized description in favor of an aesthetic of particularity and passion and brings her framed landscapes to life through a cinematic technique. The new cinematic approach described here dramatizes a landscape as a kind of journey of exploration anchored by a precisely placed perceiving figure who is often part of the foreground of the scene.

For the most part, Radcliffe's word-paintings lack the interchange of significance with character, action and theme, highly metaphoric in nature, to which post-Modernist readers are accustomed. The description of the arrival at Udolpho, however, is one passage where extended visually oriented material cooperates with narrative to contribute structural coherence to a climax in the novel. Though the writer is uninterested in linking the thing seen with the emotions of the heroine, Radcliffe's landscape visions express the narrator's interest in capturing the visual sublime in a verbal medium, though the elaborateness of the description itself is not balanced by a similar weight in the writing of the narrative sections.

Radcliffe's word-paintings are among the most daring and innovative in the history of English literature, for she was one of the first to see the possibilities for a dramatized descriptive mode that accurately captures the look of a particular landscape. Radcliffe often struggles to find specific descriptive language to express her vision. At times of transport, she abandons conventional personification in order to suggest important new possibilities for using a cinematic narrative technique within landscape description, such as when she describes what she imagines the sublime features of wild mountains to be.

With Radcliffe's word-paintings, one begins to discern an interplay between narrative and descriptive modes that was to lead to a kind of blending of the genres of prose and poetry by the end of the nineteenth century. The primitive relationship between narration and description in Radcliffe's fiction establishes a base-line with which to compare later attempts to fuse or intermingle story and scenery in English fiction. Word-painting, beginning in the Gothic novel as an interruption in narrative flow, gradually invades the story in subsequent fiction, becoming inseparable from it, and alters the nature of narrative and the form of nineteenth-century fiction as it moves toward the more fused symbolic techniques of writers like Dickens, Hardy, and Virginia Woolf. The narrative of landscape contributes significantly to the development of so-called hybrid literary works of the late Victorian period.

In addition, word-painting may contribute to the attrition of narrative that is such a prominent feature of some recent phenomenological and "poetic" fictions that seem to have abandoned "story" altogether in favor of a dramatized descriptive mode, one that has taken narrative movement into itself. Radcliffe's word-paintings, in this sense, serve as forerunner to the prose-poems of Virginia Woolf, and the contemporary antistories of Robbe-Grillet, Barth, Pynchon, and Coover. Her interest in word-paintings—Radcliffe's second mode of vision—signals one of her most important contributions to the evolving forms of English fiction. Therefore, although one might see her as "fetter'd" by some eighteenth-century novelistic conventions, occasionally Radcliffe achieves a passionately emotive, sensual descriptive mode that demonstrates her freedom to explore new content and new techniques for fiction.

NOTES

1. Alan Spiegel, *Fiction and the Camera Eye: Visual Consciousness in Film and the Modern Novel* (Charlottesville: University of Virginia Press, 1976), 33.

2. Word-painting, which often appears to move verbal art into the realm of the spatial rather than the temporal, may be one element that blurs Lessing's famous distinction between poetry as exclusively a temporal and kinetic art and painting as exclusively a spatial and static one. See Gotthold Ephraim Lessing, *Laokoön*, ed. Dorothy Reich (Oxford: Oxford University Press, 1965).

3. Ann Radcliffe, *The Mysteries of Udolpho: A Romance* (Oxford: Oxford University Press, 1970), 1. The first edition was 1794. All subsequent quotations from Radcliffe are drawn from this, the authoritative modern edition.

4. Word-paintings are found on pp. 1–5, 175–76, 224–28, 263–70, and 596–604 of the authoritative Oxford edition.

SELECT BIBLIOGRAPHY

Bayer-Berenbaum, Linda. *The Gothic Imagination: Expansion in Gothic Literature and Art.* Rutherford: Fairleigh Dickinson Press, 1982.

Hussey, Christopher. *Picturesque: Studies in a Point of View.* New York: Putnam's Sons, 1927.

Kiely, Robert. *The Romantic Novel in England.* Cambridge: Harvard University Press, 1972.

Manwaring, Elizabeth Wheeler. *Italian Landscape in Eighteenth-Century England: A Study Chiefly of the Influence of Claude Lorrain and Salvator Rosa on English Taste, 1700–1800.* New York: Oxford University Press, 1925.

McIntyre, Clara F. *Ann Radcliffe in Relation to Her Time.* New Haven: Yale University Press, 1920.

Spacks, Patricia Meyer. *The Insistence of Horror: Aspects of the Supernatural in Eighteenth-Century Poetry.* Cambridge: Harvard University Press, 1963.

Varma, Devendra P. *The Gothic Flame.* London: Arthur Baker, and Morrison and Gibb, 1957.

III. LOVE, SEX, AND MARRIAGE

Sisters

PATRICIA MEYER SPACKS

In fairy tales, sibling rivalry works itself out in predictable ways. Two arrogant, powerful older brothers, a weak and foolish youngest; the foolish youth, responsive to inner logic, helps birds and insects, wins princess and kingdom. Two sisters beloved by their mother, a younger stepsister scorned; the youngest, helped by a fairy godmother, dons the glass slipper and marries the prince. Toads and snakes drop from the mouths of unkind elder sisters; the generous youngest scatters diamonds and pearls when she speaks. We know from the beginning who will achieve the happy ending, thus assuring us that young and weak can overcome—if only they remain "good." These stories implicitly reassure the reader about envious or rivalrous feelings toward sibling competitors by equating struggles between brothers or sisters with the ancient conflict of good and evil and by offering outcomes in which right always triumphs, outcomes both psychologically and morally comforting.

Dr. Johnson did not recommend fairy tales as instructive reading. His predecessor, Joseph Addison, believed such tales, like the superstitious fancies of old nurses, pernicious influences on the young; Johnson would probably have agreed. As the developing novel of the eighteenth century attracted ever more readers, however, Johnson also perceived dangerous possibilities in the ambiguous morality of realism. He strenuously opposed the mingling of virtue and vice in a single character: young readers might learn from such figures to excuse their own moral failings on the ground that virtues accompanied them. "I cannot discover," Johnson concludes, in *Rambler* 4, "why there should not be exhibited the most perfect idea of virtue, . . . the highest and purest that humanity can reach, which, exercised in such trials as the various revolutions of things shall bring upon it, may, by conquering some calamities and enduring others, teach us what we may hope, and what we can perform."[1] The fiction writer may legitimately depict vice, but only by making it disgusting. The threat of moral confusion should prevent the novelist from indulging a taste for "mixed" characters.

Although the great novelists of the eighteenth century ignored this advice and its implications—even Richardson's villainous Lovelace displays attractive qualities, and saintly Clarissa has her faults—less accomplished writers of fiction followed the course Johnson recommended. Many women novelists chose to dramatize the absolute separation of virtue and vice by evoking a pair of sisters, one, good in every respect; the other, utterly reprehensible. Such pairings generate predictable plots, versions of fairy tales. The contrasted sisters justify the threatening subject of female competition as novelistic material. If the outcomes of such competition, as rendered in eighteenth-century fiction, present few surprises, the dramatization of sibling rivalry yet affords opportunity for authors to explore opposing fantasies, to imagine the pleasures of self-indulgence as well as the rewards of self-restraint.

Jane Austen, whose letters testify to her reading of her novelistic predecessors, clearly perceived the fictional value of sisterly opposition. In *Sense and Sensibility* (published in 1811, written and rewritten in the late eighteenth century), she employs many elements of earlier plots, but transforms the meaning of the familiar contrast between siblings. No longer do good and evil neatly isolate themselves in one sister or the other. Instead, Austen explores suggestions latent in previous novels, but never fully confronted by their authors. To read the Austen work in relation to two earlier fictions about sisters paired and opposed clarifies the complexity of Austen's achievement. It also calls attention to unacknowledged implications of the eighteenth-century texts.

Austen in her letters alludes both to Charlotte Lennox and to Jane West. Lennox published *Sophia* in 1762; it had earlier appeared, as "Harriot and Sophia," in her periodical, *The Lady's Museum*. At the century's end, West published *A Gossip's Story*, in some respects an obvious model for *Sense and Sensibility*. (It contains a young female character named Marianne, victim of excessive sensibility, who, like Austen's Marianne, meets the man of her dreams when he rescues her after a minor accident.) Although both works rely on realistic detail and eschew the supernatural elements of fairy tale, they render a relation between character and event recalling the traditional structure in which blessings shower on the virtuous after a sequence of character-testing trials. Yet the intensity with which these novels dwell on the activities of their meretricious characters suggests that the "bad" as well as the "good" sisters in exemplary fictional pairings express important preoccupations of the authors.

One can tell the difference between a "good" and a "bad" sister by the way each looks. The morally inferior typically manifests greater—or more obvious—beauty. Lennox, the least skillful of the three writers, makes the point most explicit.

> Sophia . . . wanted [i.e., lacked] in an equal degree [to her sister] those personal attractions, which in her [mother's] opinion constituted the whole of female perfection. Mere common judges, however, allowed her person to be agreeable; people of discernment and taste pronounced her something more. There was diffused throughout the whole person of Sophia a certain secret charm, a natural grace which cannot be defined; she was not indeed so beautiful as her sister, but she was more attractive; her complexion was not so fair as Harriot's, nor her features so regular, but together they were full of charms: her eyes were particularly fine, large, and full of fire, but that fire tempered with a tenderness so bewitching, as insensibly made its way to the heart. Harriot had beauty, but Sophia had something more; she had graces.[2]

In three sentences Lennox here recapitulates the fairy tale structure in which elder sisters appear to have advantages which turn out to belong to the youngest: clean off Cinderella's dirt, she emerges as a beauty; contemplate Sophia's charm, it proves *better* than beauty.

This ambivalence about physical appearance—beauty both does and does not matter, since "graces" matter more—emerges also in the other texts. West and Austen similarly emphasize the contrasts in sisters' appearances. West's Marianne possesses features "formed with delicate symmetry, her blue eyes swam in sensibility, and the beautiful transparency of her complexion seemed designed to convey to the admiring beholder every varying sentiment of her mind."[3] Her sister Louisa can claim only a figure "tall and elegant, her eyes expressed intelligence and ingenuous modesty" (1:18). Intelligence receives more emphasis than beauty in the elaboration about Louisa; West's account moves immediately to Louisa's education and conversation, as if to avoid the superficial. Austen hardly describes the "sensible" sister in *Sense and Sensibility*: "Miss Dashwood had a delicate complexion, regular features, and a remarkably pretty figure."[4] "Marianne was still handsomer," the account continues, going on to offer abundant specific detail.

The importance of beauty consists in its effect on the beholder. Beauty thus provides a metaphor for female power, that is, capacity to attract and to control others. Despite all Sophia's "graces," her sister first appeals to the rich suitor; beauty provides the more potent lure. The "admiring beholder" who deduces Marianne's sentiments from her complexion will succumb to her charms; people talk of Marianne Dashwood's beauty and of her marital prospects far more than of Elinor's, recognizing in Marianne the capacity to bend others to her will. As the sister originally declared inferior in beauty begins to assert her own kind of force, perceptions of her change. Marianne becomes less beautiful, Elinor more so as the novel goes on. But the original lack of showiness in the more "sensible" or "intelligent" sibling amounts to an important disclaimer: she in effect declares herself not interested in manipulating others because she possesses no obvious means of manipulation.

The problem of power recurs in many guises, even within the family unit. Female power, in these fictions, must manifest itself indirectly in order to be effective. Women who openly express aggression, who make apparent their desire to control the behavior of others, occasionally achieve short-term success, but always fail in the long run. To be loved (and not only by prospective suitors) provides a woman's most effective form of power. If others love her, she may hope to get what she wants without having to demand it. The meaningful "others" in young women's lives include their parents. In all three novels, only one parent remains to watch over two girls. Sophia and Harriot, like the Dashwood sisters, have a mother; Marianne and Louisa, in West's novel, a father. The question of parental preference therefore becomes acute. Harriot and Sophia's mother, herself a woman with "no merit but beauty," much prefers her elder daughter, who "engrossed all her affection" because of her beauty; Sophia, on the other hand, "she affected to despise" (1:2). Sophia, in her virtue, remains unfailingly loyal and compliant to her mother; yet the mother's assessment of her daughters' relative merit creates for one of them a nightmare version of the ugly duckling's fate. For all her "secret charm," for all her goodness, Sophia cannot win her mother's love. The moral unworthiness of the mother does not alter the pain of that fact. The contest underlying sisterly relations in these fictions focuses partly on parental affection. Sophia "wins" eventually—that is, without ever acknowledging any desire to win, she outdoes her sister—by attracting the rich husband who attests her worth even to her mother.

A Gossip's Story complicates this pattern, revealing problematic aspects of parental love. Louisa's father prefers her—the more worthy daughter— over her romantic sister, although (unlike Sophia's mother) he remains unfailingly kind to both girls. He has educated Louisa himself, while Marianne, with her grandmother, experiences "all the fond indulgence of doating love" (1:16) and nothing in the way of intellectual discipline. When Marianne suspects that her father cares more about Louisa's marriage than about her own, she leaps to the (mistaken) conclusion that the fact reveals her father's inadequate love for her; she reacts with an intensity which declares the issue's importance: "If there be any reason, it must be that I have less of his affections, and if so, lost, undone Marianne!" (1:86). But in fact Louisa comes closer than Marianne to being "lost" and "undone," specifically as a result of her father's greater attention to her. Because he wishes her to marry for the sake of security (ill, he fears that he can no longer care for her), he urges on Louisa the attentions of disagreeable Sir William Milton. He invokes "judgment" (meaning, apparently, attention to the pecuniary) as his sanction and insists that "personal considerations are beneath your attention," since "defect in character is the unavoidable lot of humanity" (1:67). Solely out of devotion to her father, Louisa agrees, still finding her suitor unpleasant. A letter from an unknown woman, however, reports that Sir William has seduced and abandoned the woman's daughter, after fathering two children. Louisa's father gives his daughter's lover the benefit of the doubt until doubt seems impossible, then dismisses him. He does not, however, conclude that Louisa's initial attention to personal considerations had any merit.

Louisa's central problem, then, involves her effort to fulfill herself without *losing* her father's preferential love. She accomplishes this end by falling in love with the man who has helped her father in his economic distress. Her lover, Pelham, proves his benevolence only after Louisa comes to care for him; her choice demonstrates in a positive way what her distaste for Sir William revealed negatively: the soundness of her intuitive responses to people. She attains, as her sister does not, the privilege of watching over her father's deathbed. This differentiation, as well as the winning of a husband wealthy and devoted and identified with her father, declares Louisa's success. As the father's death symbolically indicates, success involves separation from as well as sanction by the parent. First her father must love her best, then he must allow her to leave him.

The same pattern emerges in *Sophia*, whose heroine wins her mother's approval, but also separates herself from the mother's value system. Similarly, in *Sense and Sensibility*, Elinor, initially less favored by her mother than is Marianne ("The resemblance between Marianne and her mother was strikingly great"; p. 6), enters not only on happy marriage but on a "confederacy" (p. 378) with the mother to produce an equally satisfactory resolution for the second daughter. Elinor has the satisfaction of having been right—righter than her mother—in all her judgments and opinions; she embarks on the adult role of marriage, free to act more fully on her own judgments (she has married a passive, depressed man) and proved both upright and successful as women have traditionally been proved so: by the match she makes.

The relationship to a parent in its final definition seals the achievement of the dominant sister, but the action of these novels centers on the dynamics of sisterhood: the shifting equilibrium which reveals the balance of forces between the siblings. The two earlier works offer simplified versions of tension and resolution; *Sense and Sensibility* problematizes the sibling relationship and complicates its implications. Yet *Sophia* and *A Gossip's*

Story, despite their relatively primitive plots, help to illuminate the deep structure of the later novel. They demonstrate how conflict resolves itself in a pattern of stability which definitively reveals the realities of power.

In these eighteenth-century texts, loving sisters and hostile ones alike engage in intense sexual competition, whether or not they know what they are doing. Sex provides the arena of conflict in a society which defines a woman's worth by her marriage. The "good" sisters—Sophia and Louisa— demonstrate virtually no interest in sexual matters, although they more or less dutifully anticipate wifehood. Their more reprehensible siblings, on the other hand, have sex on their minds, in somewhat disguised form. Their emphasized beauty has this meaning among others: Harriot and Marianne locate themselves as sexual beings.

Harriot manifests aggressive, Marianne, relatively passive, sexual behavior. From the very beginning of *Sophia*, Harriot engages in sexually provocative conduct. "Her beauty soon procured her a great number of lovers; her poverty made their approaches easy; and the weakness of her understanding, her insipid gaiety, and pert affectation of wit, encouraged the most licentious hopes, and exposed her to the most impertinent addresses" (1:19). The narrator's unambiguous disapproval manifests itself clearly at Harriot's indulgence of undiscriminating desire. Sir Charles Stanley, "a young baronet of a large estate, a most agreeable person, and engaging address," whom everyone agrees "to be a man of the strictest honour and unblemished integrity" (1:20), decides to make her his mistress; Harriot appears too stupid to understand the nature of his designs, or too depraved to care about the social sanction of marriage. As the plot develops, Sir Charles shifts his attentions; Harriot, wounded in her sexual pride, accumulates other admirers. Her "ignorance, vanity, and eager desire of being admired, exposed her to the attacks of libertinism, and excited presumptuous hopes" (1:47). She succumbs to one of the libertines, becomes prosperous as his mistress, and considers herself in effect elevated to high rank because of her aristocratic admirer. Her punishment for sexual looseness consists of the loss of her beauty and her condemnation to a restrictive marriage, in which her husband keeps her in "rigid confinement" (2:233) to control her sexual inclinations.

Both the narrator's language and the plot, in other words, condemn Harriot for her open sexuality. Yet the plot also allows her much greater freedom than her virtuous sister enjoys. Sexy, nasty Harriot does pretty much as she likes. She slams doors, storms at those who displease her, often controls her mother's actions; she openly expresses her rage at her sister; she acquires fine clothes and jewelry and flaunts her acquisitions as well as her beauty. She receives not only physical but social gratification in her love affair with a rich man, which enlarges her power and her opportunity for exercising it. Meanwhile, Sophia follows the path of meekness, too "innocent" to know any sexual feelings in herself, too docile to oppose her mother, always choosing restrictive courses, so eager for goodness that she allows herself little pleasure. She meets a country girl whose love for a worthy young man does not prosper. When Dolly tells the story of how she came to love this admirable youth, Sophia comments, "Suppose this young man whose person captivated you so much, had been wild and dissolute, as many young men are; how would you have excused yourself for that early prejudice in his favour, which you took in so readily at your eyes, without consulting your judgment in the least?" (1:162−63). In other words: when in doubt, repress! As Sophia's advice indicates, she does not trust her intuitions and she considers physical response an index of danger. If one takes in at the eyes a favorable impression, one should instantly distrust it; "judgment" warns of sinister possibility. The fact that Dolly's lover has actually displayed only admirable characteristics makes no difference; the experience of being "captivated"—that is, of sexual response—implies its own warning. Dolly's favorable reaction would have been *inexcusable*, in Sophia's view, if her lover had in fact proved "wild and dissolute."

Bad girls have more fun. Charlotte Lennox would not have acknowledged any such belief. But as her novel works its way to its didactic conclusion, it demonstrates precisely this. Harriot manifests no attractive characteristics, no redeeming qualities; she conforms to Dr. Johnson's notion that the vicious character should repel. No reader could envy her personality. On the other hand, her wickedness makes space for action. "Haughty insolent Harriot," full of "rage and envy" (1:86), flinging herself into chairs, "tormenting her sister" (1:60) ("Scornful and unjust reflections upon her person, bitter jests upon her pedantic affectation, and malignant insinuations of hypocrisy"; 1:61), allowing herself "tears, exclamations, and reproaches" against her mother (1:67) ("Her mother would have found it a difficult task to have pacified her"; 1:67)—this reprehensible young woman, although her own unpleasant feelings cause her pain, also finds much more opportunity for action and expression than does her virtuous sister. She feels and reveals her own sexuality and aggression—aspects of personality utterly unknown to Sophia. Lennox does not approve, nor will the reader; but the fantasy of unconstraint has attractions although the unconstrained character has none.

The Jane West novel, on the other hand, separates sexuality from aggression; no female character in it expresses open hostility or allows herself rage. Marianne proves weak rather than wicked. In one revealing sequence, her maid, Patty, tries to incite her against her sister by telling her of her father's financial distress and suggesting that he wants Marianne's fortune to help him support Louisa.

> Patty's speech, instead of awakening the angry malevolent passions in the bosom of her gentle mistress, as she designed it should, inspired the kindest sorrow for her unfortunate father; mingled with a regret too tender to be called envy, that his preference for Louisa was so visible. Her heart was really excellent, and she resolved not meanly to supplant, but heroically to emulate her sister. (1:106)

This summary sketches the theme of the entire novel. It will not *call* Marianne's emotion "envy," given its "tenderness," and it terms her competitive efforts "heroic." The competition, in this instance, involves the effort at goodness: Marianne decides to remain unmarried and devote her fortune (inherited from her grandmother) to her father, thus outdoing Louisa, who will presumably marry in order to obtain a fortune for her father. An "excellent" heart, in other words, transforms competition into a noble activity. It by no means eliminates the competitive impulse.

Marianne's competitiveness with her sister, however, also assumes less conscious forms. Like Harriot, although not maliciously, not angrily, she uses her beauty as a sexual lure and triumphs in her attractiveness and the freedom it allows her. She grants herself the right to indulge her romantic fantasies; she plays with a worthy suitor, finally dismisses him, and when she finds a man who conforms to her fancies, she flouts the rules of propriety (precisely as Austen's Marianne will do), confident of the power of her attractiveness. In this novel too, one sister behaves well, the other has fun. Louisa worries over her father, castigates herself (with a kind of judgment apparently endorsed by the narrator) for the slightest imaginative excursion ("wishes are the weak resort of a querulous, impassioned mind"; 1:71), and represses all feeling: "Politeness and attention were so habitual to her, that it was impossible for any of the guests to complain of neglect, though her bosom was throbbing with sensations of the most painful nature" (1:78–79). The assumption that "wishes" betray an "impassioned mind" underlies all the action. Marianne's passionate nature—her sexuality— plays itself out in her imaginative excursions; Louisa's repression of passion implies her consistent self-subordination. Marianne is not "bad," only self-indulgent. It amounts to the same thing.

The resolutions of these novels emphasize the importance of freedom and power as issues and redefine their relation to sexuality. When Harriot loses her beauty, she loses her power, and subsequently her freedom; the loss of beauty proves not only cause, but also symbol of these other losses. Her rich lover leaves her, with "a small settlement," after his relatives have arranged " a match for him with a young lady of suitable rank and fortune" (2:231), and Harriot promptly disintegrates. "The vexation she felt from this incident, threw her into a distemper very fatal to beauty. The yellow jaundice made such ravage in her face, that scarce any of those charms on which she had valued herself so much, remained. All her anxious hours were now employed in repairing her complexion, and in vain endeavours to restore lustre to those eyes, sunk in hollowness, and tinctured with the hue of her distemper" (2:231–32). The account's emphatic detail stresses the symbolic importance of beauty. All Harriot's anxious hours focus on impossible efforts at restoration; far more than beauty in fact requires restoring. On the next page, we learn of her marriage. Her husband, an officer, takes her to the colonies, places her in "rigid confinement" and making her suffer "all the restraint of jealousy" (2:233) without any compensating love. Her lot of deprivation, the final absence of all the metaphorical space she had enjoyed, marks the disappearance of her effective sexuality and the futility of her aggression.

Marianne, in West's novel, far less wicked than Harriot, suffers an only slightly less constricting fate. Early in her career, her father has warned her that marriage at best implies subordination for a woman; he offers this fact as an argument for giving up romantic fantasy in favor of an effort to make realistic discriminations about suitors. "You must know," he tells Marianne, "that marriage divests you of all this assumed consequence. Law and custom leave the husband master of his own actions, and in a certain degree arbiter of his wife's. . . . Think yourself unhappy if the kneeling slave does not change into the Tyrant, and compel you, in your turn, to endure without complaint, the whimsical indifference of caprice, or the sudden burst of petulance" (1:96). Marianne, predictably, pays no attention. She continues on her course of self-expression even after her marriage, trusting the power of her beauty, charm, and sensibility. That power, however, soon evaporates. Pelham, who has earlier courted her, begins to recognize the "superior loveliness of intellectual beauty" (2:193). When he sees Marianne again, "he beheld [her] beauty . . . withering under the worm of discontent, her features contracted by peevish melancholy, and her temper rendered irritable by disappointment. Though such an object moved his pity, admiration and love could only be awakened by the mild intelligence and unruffled sweetness of a Louisa" (2:212). The use of the indefinite article ("a Louisa") calls attention to the paradigmatic roles of these women. Louisa stands for all good (mild, intelligent, unruffled, sweet . . .) women; her sister represents all female self-indulgence. One "Louisa" (good woman) would serve as well as another to awaken Pelham's admiration and love.

Like Harriot's loss of beauty, Marianne's is declared, in effect, her own fault, deriving from her indulged feelings. Although her physical deterioration receives less graphic description than Harriot's, her fate has even more bitter aspects. Unlike Harriot, she has married for love, choosing the man who gratifies her romantic self-image by responding to her physical and emotional charms. The marriage sours because of her overestimation of her own potencies, her failure to realize that rational and moral qualities as well as physical and emotional appeal must sustain a relationship. The contrast between her situation and her husband's emphasizes her restrictive fate. He, increasingly disaffected, wanders ever farther afield, enjoying himself with male companions, exploring the possibilities of pleasure; she, confined to home, finds herself cut off from pleasure, narrowed into misery—deprived of freedom and power.

The "good" sisters' lives, in contrast, open up in marriage. "Sir Charles, who adored [Sophia], put it amply in her power to indulge the benevolence of her disposition" (2:235). Her freedom to shower graces on others symbolizes a larger freedom, the result of "the delicacy, the ardor, and the constancy of [Sir Charles's] affection" (2:236)—which he explains as entirely the result of her gifts. He attaches himself successively, he points out, "to one or other of those shining qualities, of which her charming mind is an inexhaustible source." Sophia's "charming mind" corresponds to Louisa's "intellectual beauty." Outsides matter less than insides, these novels insist. Yet their plots finally deprive the morally inadequate of physical beauty, a painful punishment which suggests that appearances in fact have considerable importance. If beauty implies female power, its loss symbolizes impotence.

Pelham turns his attentions from one sister to the other, ultimately attracted by intellectual beauty. The Lennox novel follows a comparable pattern: Sir Charles wooes Harriot first, with dishonorable intent; then he shifts to her sister, first proposing to make her his mistress, later realizing his honorable love. This duplicated pattern underlies the theme of sexual competition. The good sisters not only marry more prosperously and wisely than their counterparts, but they also actually marry men formerly under the sway of the "sexy" sisters' more meretricious charms. Lennox emphasizes the bitterness of such a development for the rejected sister; West leaves the emotional consequences to the reader's imagination. (Since Marianne has earlier dismissed Pelham, she has no one to blame but herself.) Neither triumphant sister acknowledges the pleasure of winning what another has lost, yet that pleasure covertly invigorates the novels' happy endings.

In the background of these fictions (as in virtually all eighteenth-century fiction) lurks sexual danger. In both cases, however, the actual outcome of

sexual laxness seems oddly muted. Harriot allows herself to become a
"kept woman"; the worst consequence she suffers is the "danger of being
wholly neglected" (2:168)—that is, of social ostracism as a consequence of
lost reputation. The narrator lavishes condemnation on the fallen woman:
"The fallen Harriot was proud! the diamonds that glittered in her hair, the
gilt chariot, and the luxurious table; these monuments of her disgrace contributed to keep up the insolence of a woman, who by the loss of her honour
was lower than the meanest of her servants, who could boast of an uncorrupted virtue" (2:169–70). But the hollowness of that rhetoric—Harriot
enjoys her diamonds, she never experiences her "lowness"—calls attention
to the relative *lack* of wretchedness here attending abandoned virtue. True,
Harriot loses her beauty; true, her marriage lacks fulfillment. But she manages a marriage of sorts; she does not die in misery; for quite some time she
enjoys herself. Even more surprising is the story, in West's novel, of the
woman seduced by Sir William Milton. She turns out to have been a conniving creature in the first place, who lured him into the liaison. After
Louisa rejects him, Sir William returns to this mistress and continues to live
intermittently with her and their children. She announces freely that she
can become Lady Milton whenever she wishes; the narrator does not deny
the allegation. The reward of sin, in her case, consists in getting exactly
what she wanted.

The relative lack of punishment for sexual deviation in these novels underlines the emotional ambivalence manifest in them. Although both insistently proclaim their didactic intent, emphasizing the moralistic, they
also suggest a kind of feeling they never avow. The implicit double assessment of beauty, both important and meaningless; the plots which reveal the
greater freedom of the weak or wicked even as the narrative voice insists on
the penalties of misdoing: these aspects of the novels, like their curious
treatment of actual sexual misconduct, convey more complicated attitudes
than the texts ever acknowledge. One conspicuous difference between
Austen and her predecessors involves the later writer's capacity to *use* the
ambivalence which Lennox and West betray, but do not openly admit.
Sense and Sensibility deliberately confuses simple polarities. At the beginning of the novel we learn that Marianne, the sister marked by sensibility, is
also "sensible and clever"—that is, she possesses sense too (p. 6). She needs
to learn to grant it more power over her actions. But her sister—who, despite her "sense," is characterized in these terms: "her disposition was affectionate, and her feelings were strong" (p. 6)—needs to learn something too,
unlike Sophia and Louisa, both of whom require only room to demonstrate their virtues and time to find them rewarded. At the novel's end,
Marianne begins to act sensibly instead of only dreaming about possible

actions. And Elinor runs sobbing from a room, allowing herself fuller expression of her strong feelings, no longer concerned merely to govern them. Although Austen follows eighteenth-century tradition in stressing the importance of sense, the necessity of control, she also acknowledges more openly than do earlier novelists the costs of such valuable capacities.

In *Sense and Sensibility* as in the other two novels, one sister appears to have the advantage in beauty which the other later acquires. But even this conventional pattern receives a new twist in Austen's treatment. The Dashwood sisters' half-brother John registers the girls' shift in relative attractiveness. "She was as handsome a girl last September, as any I ever saw," he observes of Marianne; "and as likely to attract the men. There was something in her style of beauty, to please them particularly. . . . I question whether Marianne *now*, will marry a man worth more than five or six hundred a-year, at the utmost, and I am very much deceived if *you* [Elinor] do not do better" (p. 227). A little later he remarks, to Colonel Brandon, "You would not think it perhaps, but Marianne *was* remarkably handsome a few months ago; quite as handsome as Elinor.—Now you see it is all gone" (p. 237). John's direct equation of beauty with economic potential creates an ironic perspective on physical attractiveness. In this novel centrally concerned with varieties of need and possibilities of fulfillment, the use of beauty as a counter in the game men and women play calls attention to the reductiveness of systematized marital bargaining. To focus on beauty's practical value in this way emphasizes the novel's double perspective. A realistic viewpoint, product of economic necessity, demands awareness of beauty's immediate usefulness for women; the narrator's more distant view makes one realize that beauty's value inheres only in convention.

The subject of sexuality acquires comparable complexity. The novel provides in the background of the main action a little tale of sexual misconduct, comparable to the story of Sir William Milton and his mistress. Colonel Brandon offers the account of the two Elizas: the first beloved by him in his youth, forced to marry another, doomed by her own subsequent sexual misconduct to early and miserable death, leaving a daughter, the second Eliza, who becomes Willoughby's victim and in turn gives birth to an illegitimate child. The narrative has the severity conspicuously lacking in comparable episodes of the other novels. But it also conveys links between sexual feeling and other forms of emotion. Both Elizas suffer maternal deprivation; the elder clings to her child, keeping it always with her. She has embarked on a career of sexual looseness only after suffering intense emotional frustration, first deprived of her lover, then married to a man who neglects and insults her. Colonel Brandon sympathizes with her plight, although he condemns her conduct; he attributes her difficulties to her lack of a man to take care of her. He even feels responsible for the second Eliza's fall: he has not watched over her closely enough.

Like the fable of lost beauty, this story demands two opposed interpretations. Colonel Brandon makes one explicit, offering the tale as an exemplum for Marianne, a warning about the danger of sensibility. Sensibility and sexiness, it turns out, in his moral vocabulary imply one another. Women like Eliza (and Marianne) need men to guard them from themselves, to keep their passions under control when no internal principle governs them. Sensibility makes them vulnerable to their own passional impulses and to the machinations of evil men.

The story also comments, however, on the social system which allows few outlets for female feelings, few possibilities for women to control their own destinies. Both Elizas exist at the disposal of men. Eliza I cannot make her own marital choice, cannot escape legitimately from the choice made for her, cannot survive after her illegitimate escape without selling her body. Eliza II, "placed" in a school and in the care of a worthy woman by her guardian, proves at the mercy of Willoughby and then utterly dependent once more upon her guardian. An aside by Mrs. Jennings suggests the alternative to Colonel Brandon's benign quasi-paternal care: the girl could be apprenticed to some tradesperson. In the light of these facts, the warning to Marianne becomes rather more sinister. Because men arbitrate female destinies, women must please them. Too much revealed passion may attract men, but—as the Lennox and West novels also suggest—men do not marry the sexy female. The warning implicit in that fact takes on rich overtones in Austen's treatment; knowingness about the dynamics of social power informs her moralism.

In *Sense and Sensibility* as in the earlier novels, the weaker sister has more fun. Unlike her predecessors, Austen faces the implications of this fact. Marianne's freedom of action repeatedly shocks Elinor and perhaps the reader: not her sexual misconduct (she never seriously misbehaves) but her flouting of propriety even when her actions offend or hurt other people. She and Willoughby whisper maliciously about others in the immediate company; they refuse to submit to minimal demands of politeness. Such freedom declares its moral dubiety in its every manifestation. Marianne's self-indulgence, her tendency to wallow in her own feelings, also seem unattractive in comparison with her sister's self-command. Her spontaneity and grace, however, and particularly her awareness of her own emotions, make her attractive to the reader and to those who encounter her within the world of the novel. Elinor's self-repression, her embracing of the fox gnawing her vitals, arouses admiration; yet we feel the deliberate self-limitation as limitation indeed. Throughout her own emotional ordeal, Elinor manages to present a brave front to the world only at the cost of interrupting real communication with her sister. Less on guard when Willoughby comes to offer his self-exculpation, Elinor unexpectedly succumbs partially to his charm —in spite of the fact that Marianne at the time lies apparently at death's door as an indirect consequence of her involvement with Willoughby. This brief vulnerability measures a new, tentative attractiveness in Elinor. For the first time she thinks less about how she should act than about how she actually feels. She soon pulls herself together; she does not fully report her softening to her mother or sister. But something has happened. By the time Edward presents himself as her suitor (the knowledge of his unexpected freedom precipitates her tearful flight) she has loosened up considerably; she can allow her intense emotion to manifest itself.

Marianne's education through her dangerous illness (an illness serving also as punishment for her indiscretion) follows a conventional moralistic pattern; Elinor's education charts more unfamiliar ground. *Sense and Sensibility*, for all its romance elements and its reminders of fairy tale, makes the demands of realism in life more insistent, and in some respects perhaps more important, than those of morality. The novel's way of disposing of Willoughby underlines the point.

> That his repentance of misconduct, which thus brought its own punishment, was sincere, need not be doubted;—nor that he long thought of Colonel Brandon with envy, and of Marianne with regret. But that he was for ever inconsolable, that he fled from society, or contracted an habitual gloom of temper, or died of a broken heart, must not be depended on—for he did neither. He lived to exert, and frequently to enjoy himself. His wife was not always out of humour, nor his home always uncomfortable, and in his breed of horses and dogs, and in sporting of every kind, he found no inconsiderable degree of domestic felicity (p. 379).

The "punishment" of Willoughby's misconduct consists in his loss of Marianne. His compensations, however, are not inconsiderable, given his character. If we "depend upon" the fantasy of his broken heart or habitual gloom, we rely rather on the fancies of fiction than on our knowledge of actuality. Life punishes everyone, but it allots rewards and penalties less neatly than fairy tales do.

As for Marianne, she "submits" finally to "new attachments" (p. 379) and to the restrictions implicit in her social role; she accepts the necessities of the real. One feels a faint sadness at her sensible marriage. She seems to have given up fun: certainly she would have had more of it with Willoughby. The narrative tone, despite the novel's insistence on the resolution's happiness, acknowledges the irony of Marianne's compliance, the immense gap between her imaginings and her experience. But reality, the novel says, is all we have.

And of course, in Austen's comedic scheme, reality is quite enough. Its force generates the melancholy wisdom of Colonel Brandon and Edward, who have learned to deal with restriction and loss, and finally of Marianne and Elinor, accepting as lovers slightly tarnished figures, coming to terms with a world in which—as distasteful John Dashwood understands—money measures value. Other measures also survive (John's failure to understand *that* marks his inadequacy), but to acknowledge the inescapability of economic and social constrictions comprises part of every rational mortal's responsibility.

For Lennox and West, didacticism derives from the structure of romance and from an unrealistic isolation of personal qualities. Austen's transformation of the female novelistic tradition involves accepting implications that her predecessors could not acknowledge. The sisters in *Sense and Sensibility* demonstrate ambivalence; the narrator allows herself comparable ambivalence—about the place of beauty and of emotional expressiveness in female lives, for example. Characters and narrator alike conclude with the necessity of realism. True morality, Austen implies, depends on acceptance of precisely those ambiguities that Dr. Johnson deplored. The complex relations of sisters to one another, to parents, and to the world without functions in the three novels considered here as a metonym for the moral density of all relationship. Only Austen, however, genuinely explores the metonym's implications. The boldness of her enterprise becomes vivid in comparison with the conventional moralizing of her predecessors. But she also illuminates unexpected aspects of their achievement. In the context of *Sense and Sensibility* one can realize that writers such as Charlotte Lennox and Jane West, despite their fiction's unrealistic structures, convey more psychological complexity than they can afford to acknowledge. They hint the force of the competitive impulse between siblings, the freedom and pleasure as well as the penalties of indulged sexual feeling, the power of beauty as well as the superior importance of intelligence, the need to grow beyond parents, and the need to win parental love. It remained for Austen to incorporate such suggestions more explicitly in her novels' plots and to call attention to the necessities of social actuality as well as the longings embodied in fantasy.

NOTES

1. Samuel Johnson, *The Rambler*, ed. W. J. Bate and Albrecht B. Strauss (New Haven: Yale University Press, 1969), vol. 3 of The Yale Edition of Samuel Johnson, 22; #4 (31 March 1750).

2. Charlotte Lennox, *Sophia*, 2 vols. in one (New York: Garland, 1974), 1:2–3. Originally published in 1762. Further references appear in parentheses in the text.

3. Jane West, *A Gossip's Story, and A Legendary Tale*, 2 vols. (New York: Garland, 1974), 1:18–19. Originally published in 1797. Further references appear in parentheses in the text.

4. Jane Austen, *Sense and Sensibility*, vol. 1 of *The Novels of Jane Austen*, ed. R. W. Chapman (Oxford: Clarendon Press, 1923), 46. Further references appear in parentheses in the text.

"I Died for Love"
Esteem in Eighteenth-Century Novels by Women

PAULA R. BACKSCHEIDER

For hundreds of years marriage was the most important event in a woman's life. Her husband could make her utterly secure or utterly miserable. He could open the world to her or he could keep her unfulfilled. The metaphors of marriage are those of life and death: the wife would bloom or wither, flourish or droop; the grace of God brought eternal happiness, the grace of a husband, a long life of happiness. Perhaps it is already a cliché to say that the eighteenth-century novel occupies a narrow path into which the didactic tales of the past funneled. Romances, conduct books, saints' lives, exempla, and autobiographies came together in the early novels by and for women. Refined and narrowed yet again by the English demand for morality, practicality, and middle-class events; battered by the criticism of the sensational novels of Behn, Haywood, and Manley; and defined by the great courtship novels of Richardson and Fielding, the eighteenth-century woman's novel became formulaic, and women writers worked delicately within a set of demands and expectations until the narrow path once again divided and divided yet again and again with the sublime genius of Radcliffe, the doubting eye of Austen, and the combined iconoclasm of George Eliot, George Sand, and the Brontës.

The narrow path which is the eighteenth-century novel by and for women has the ideal of a happy marriage as its central subject. As Jean Hagstrum and others have demonstrated, that ideal was fixed; the bases were strong physical attraction, mutual esteem, and steadfast companionship.[1] Upon esteem rested the other two. Without it, attraction became lust and companionship would never develop. In almost all of the novels I've read written by eighteenth-century women, the desire of the heroine to win the hero's respect is present and, in many of the novels, is one of the central preoccupations. Furthermore, a notably large number of the most popular

152

and longest lived novels by women are of this latter type. Fanny Burney's *Evelina* and Jane Austen's novels surely give instant credence to this statement. Above all, Evelina, Elizabeth, and Emma keep a running tally of gains, losses, and feelings attached to the opinions that Orville, Darcy, and Knightley hold of them. For all the heroines' assertions of indifference, the reader always knows they deceive themselves and that their future happiness (and the resolution of the book) depends upon the heroes' final judgments. Because this judgment is crucial outside *and* within marriage, yet functions in somewhat different ways structurally and thematically, I have divided my discussion into two parts.

I. *Courtship*

The opinion that satisfaction in marriage is impossible without esteem seems to be entirely accepted, one of the theorems of eighteenth-century life. It is not hard to understand the grounds for this belief. Women had almost no alternatives outside of marriage, and most people considered any other alternative unfulfilling if not unnatural. Women had been created to be a man's helpmeet and the bearer of children. A number of female medical conditions were ascribed to celibacy, and childlessness was considered catastrophic. In fact, grief over barrenness was often described in the same ways as mourning for a child's death; both were intense, lingered for years, and were never thought of without pain and regret. Because marriage was woman's destiny and would determine the perimeters of her existence, the choice of husband was the most significant decision of her life. Whether he wanted to share his pleasures, the diversions of the town and country, or even to talk to her had large implications.

In addition to the lessons of common sense and experience, women read about the necessity for winning and preserving a man's esteem. The countless domestic conduct books endlessly described the good husband as guide, friend, and protector and warned that women could not hope for these blessings if they did not deserve them. Many of the conduct books discussed courtship and cautioned women about making foolish choices; they were particularly admonished to avoid the lure of carriages and fine clothes. The fictions of Steele, Swift, and Fielding are but variants upon those in *The Compleat Servant Maid* (1677) and *Religious Courtship* (1722). Steele's *Spectator* no. 80 in which Phillis and Brunetta become irreconcilable rivals, Swift's "Phillis; Or, the Progress of Love" in which the novel-reading maiden elopes with the butler, and Fielding's interpolation describing Leonora's infatuation with Bellarmine's coach and French waistcoat in *Joseph Andrews* would not be out of place in conduct books. These women care only for admiration and seek a fantasy world: "[Leonora] had before known what it was to torment a single woman; but to be hated and secretly cursed by a whole assembly was a joy reserved for [her first meeting with Bellarmine]."[2] The risks of infatuation, bedazzlement, and superficiality seem particularly female in this literature. In the course of the century, the burden of decision of whom to marry shifts increasingly to the woman, but writers continued to treat a husband as woman's lot in life. In *Advice to a Daughter* (1688), Halifax tells his daughter how to cope with the various kinds of bad husbands, and in *Religious Courtship*, Defoe concentrates on miseries suffered by a young girl who discovers her new husband is a Catholic. By the second half of the century, women in novels and conduct books were expected to exercise detached, good judgment.

Other conduct books treated marriage rather than courtship and enumerated ways respect could be lost. Adultery was, of course, the most certain, but drink, careless household management, sloth, bad temper, improper social behavior, imprudent and even too intimate friendships, and frivolity never failed to damage the woman's position and lead to her unhappiness. No wonder, then, that the novel, that genre so often described and seen as an extension of instructive nonfiction, found important and engrossing themes in woman's attempt to win and hold a man's respect.

Patricia Meyer Spacks has said that women were not to work openly to bring about a good marriage; "Marriage would simply *happen* to the virtuous girl, perhaps partly the result of efforts by her family, mainly the reward of her passive goodness. . . ."[3] But they did make efforts to win esteem. Novelists soon extended to women characters the old idea that men displayed their parts in conversation and revealed their souls in correspondence.[4] Lord Orville describes Evelina's power in such terms:

> She is not, indeed, like most modern young ladies, to be known in half an hour: her modest worth, and fearful excellence, require both time and encouragement to show themselves. She does not, beautiful as she is, seize the soul by surprise, but, with more dangerous fascination, she steals it almost imperceptibly.

And in another tone altogether, Austen says: ". . . Darcy had never been so bewitched by any woman as he was by her. He really believed, that were it not for the inferiority of her connections, he should be in some danger."[5] The merit that Pope described in *The Rape of the Lock* as winning the soul is more "dangerous" to man than beauty. The heroines gradually come to engross the man's thoughts and to engage his solicitude. He has come to assume that place as guide, friend, and protector even before marriage. When Darcy joins the search for Lydia and Wickham and resolves the problem, he has assumed the role of husband. If the woman cannot succeed before marriage when her suitor's attention and desires are strongest, she has little hope after the ceremony. An established pattern of interested, serious, and caring conversation, however, outlasts such other attractions as physical beauty and desire for sexual gratification. Sarah Scott's Miss Melvyn says that "to enter into wedlock without any prospect of social happiness, seemed to her one of the greatest misfortunes in life" and her Miss Mancel insists that "his sincere respect for her, which certainly is the most powerful charm to a woman of delicacy, could scarcely fail to make an impression on a heart so tender. . . ."[6]

Although the Burney/Austen structure of having country girl meet socially superior man and win his respect offers more opportunities for incidents, discoveries, and social instruction, the more common pattern in novels by women is to have friendship metamorphose into love. The characters, Berina and Artander, in Mary Davys's *Familiar Letters* (1725) describe social situations and personal experiences and comment on politics and poetry. Their respect and affection grows, and their good wishes for each other's happiness increase. The novel ends with Berina's defensive teasing and Artander hurrying to "try" her indifference to marriage. Natura and Charlotte's acquaintance "ripened into a friendship, which is the height and very essence of love" in Eliza Haywood's *Life's Progress through the Passions* (1748). Their love—friendship becoming tenderness and based upon "a parity of principles, humours, and inclinations"—grows naturally into physical love and deep satisfaction. Even illicit love often began in friendship. Bernardo Henault enjoys the nun Isabella's company and has great esteem for her but does not suspect he loves her "because he regarded her as a Thing consecrate to Heaven."[7]

The contrast in centrality and treatment of the theme of esteem between novels by women and those by men is apparent. Defoe insists upon similarity of temper, age, social status, and piety.[8] He may portray a kind of lasting love as he does with Moll Flanders and Jemmy, a satisfying marriage as he does with Jack and his fourth wife, a deep affection and continued enjoyment of conversation as well as sex as he does with Roxana and the Prince, but he does not show us the development of mutual esteem. The issue in Richardson's novels is the justification of the heroine's right to violate social stratification and marry above herself. His intention is to have everyone acknowledge her worthiness—the Lady Daverses, Mrs. Howes, and Uncle Anthonys as well as the heroes—not merely to bring about a satisfying union of lovers. The lesson is larger here, and critics have been correct to spend their time on Puritan themes, the representation of the struggle between Good and Evil, the incorporation of contemporary social and economic issues, and the problems of power, selfhood, and equality.

Here we see the contrast between towering novels which encompass the most significant philosophical, religious, political, and social debates, and novels that are merely timely and successful. We also see, however, an important relationship between the greatest novels and the "popular" or "formula" fiction produced in an age. Popular fiction picked up small parts, individual issues, and explored them in a variety of ways just as the great novelists took the skeletons of formula fiction and covered them with magnificent bodies and rich clothes. Consider Fielding's *Tom Jones.* Surely a great part of Fielding's art and our fun is his self-conscious use of the conventions of narrative. The very plot of *Tom Jones* is a cliché, but whoever reveled in the description of the heroine or the reliance upon coincidence as he did? The Pamela/Joseph Andrews inversion which had Joseph fearing for his "virtue" has a variant in *Tom Jones* which depends upon the search for esteem. Tom, not Sophia, must earn the lover's respect before he can be adult, fulfilled, and happy. Fielding did not differ from his contemporaries in asserting that the risk was chiefly the woman's or in setting up a variety of incidents to discover the nature of the lovers, but his inversion of who bears the burden of proof does much to give his novel its vitality and range. After all, men performed on a larger stage and had infinitely more ways to disgrace themselves.

Fiction of the eighteenth century makes the conduct books appear static and narrow. The conduct books exhort women to piety, sobriety, good temper, and duty, but fiction shows women's complicity in their own ruin. The conduct books offer the lesson, "Merit wins the soul," and passive virtue seems promising. The most significant difference between novels and conduct books, however, is not in the causes of ruin (shrewishness, drink, and sloth will always have the same result) but in the treatment of causes. In courtship, the major behavioral (as opposed to character) faults are frivolity, lack of chastity, and errors in judgment.

A number of critics have analyzed the "fallen woman" in eighteenth-century literature. One of the best, Susan Staves, writes that "seduced maidens were so appealing because they embodied precisely those virtues the culture especially prized in young women: beauty, simplicity (or ignorance, to call it a harsher name), trustfulness, and affectionateness,"[9] and I believe this speculation is correct. Her statement, however, fits heroines, not another category of female characters. This other category is lascivious women. Driven by appetite rather than motivated by tenderness and desire to please, they may seduce the man and are certainly obsessed with thoughts of sexual enjoyment. They scheme and want to receive. The heroines who succumb often seem to have been swept too far along a natural path of developing intimacy. Eliza Haywood describes her heroine Placentia (*Philidore and Placentia*, 1727) as follows: "In fine, she was charm'd

with him without knowing she was so, and, insensible of the danger, suf-fer'd herself to become a prey to it without the least endeavors for defense."
"Reason grew intoxicated with the sweet enchantment, and had no more the power to give her aid."[10] Haywood's Emanuella (*The Rash Resolve*, 1724) delays her marriage until her fortune arrives because she does not want to be obliged to her husband. As the weeks pass, the intimacy between the lovers increases, and finally "rapacious, greedy Love, too conscious of his Power, encroached on all, and nothing left for Honour."[11] Many of these women have indulged in daydreams about the marriage to come. Mary Davys's Altemira goes to bed two hours early to "indulge" in fanta-sies about Lord Lofty; soon after, he seduces and abandons her.[12] Delariv-iére Manley's Charlot is corrupted so that "her waking Thoughts, her golden Slumber, ran all of a Bliss only imagin'd. . . ."[13] "By the magic of her passion she shortly found excuses for the man she loved," Elizabeth Inchbald says of Hannah.[14] Hannah soon has William's baby, becomes a prostitute, and is sentenced to death for forgery by William himself. Jane West in 1793 described the purpose of her *Advantages of Education* "to explode those notions which novel reading in general produces, by delin-eating human life in false colours, expectations are formed which can never be realized; the consequence of which is, that life is begun in error, and ended in disappointment." Of her heroine she writes, "mistaken, unsuspi-cious creature, how does your fond heart worship virtues of its own creation. . . ."[15]

The women characters in the novels by men more often conform to the stereotype of temptress and siren. *Tom Jones* abounds with lascivious, promiscuous women and even *Amelia* presents women as sexual predators. Fielding's women seem to *relish* sex; they smack their lips and run their eyes over men. Defoe, Sterne, and Smollett also emphasize women's sexual ap-petites rather than the gradual development of mutual respect and affec-tion. Although the heroines are virtuous and idealistic, the ordinary women like Colonel Jack's wives and Tabby Bramble who people the major novels are often like Fielding's Mrs. Waters and Lady Bellaston.

Although writers like Defoe insist that men who marry the women they seduced will become jealous and reproach their wives later, we see no ex-amples in fiction by women. Instead the man continues to court the woman, waits years and hopes for marriage, and feels great remorse. In every case, the anxiety the female character has is about loss of esteem. Emilia "despises" herself for being seduced and writes in her diary:

A lover might in the height of his passion excuse my frailty, but when matri-mony, and continued possession had restored him to his reason, I was sensible he must think of me as I was conscious I deserved. What confidence, what esteem could I hope from an husband, who so well knew my weakness. . . . I was determined not to depend on any one who was equally conscious of my guilt. . . . I saw that a generous man must act as he did, but no generosity could restore me to the same place in his esteem I before possessed.[16]

Few seductions end in marriage, but when they do, the lover has pursued the heroine relentlessly and begged her repeatedly to marry him. Aphra Behn's Bellamora runs away and hides. Pregnant and destitute she resists marriage until the week of the birth of her baby.[17]

A different kind of threat to the establishment of respect is female frivolity. Women writers do not mean that women are stupid or even trivial; rather they see high spirits and youthful desires for fun as deadly. The woman who flirts and plays throws away her opportunities to display her mind and heart. She obscures her merit. Hannah More's chilling admonition is borne out in the experiences of characters like Elizabeth Inchbald's Miss Milner and Jane West's Charlotte Raby.[18] More writes:

That bold, independent, enterprising spirit, which is so much admired in boys, should not, when it happens to discover itself in the other sex, be encouraged, but suppressed. Girls should be taught to give up their opinions betimes, and not pertinaciously to carry on a dispute, even if they should know themselves to be in the right. . . . It is of the greatest importance to their future happiness, that they should acquire a submissive temper, and a forbearing spirit: for it is a lesson which the world will not fail to make them frequently practise, when they come abroad into it, and they will not practise it the worse for having learnt it the sooner.[19]

The most serious threat to gaining esteem is humankind's susceptibility to making errors in judgment. Premarital sex is one form, another is mistaking the character of the fiance, yet another is marrying for wealth. Such errors are legion. In the fiction of the first half of the eighteenth century, the development of the ways these mistakes occur forms a major part of the plot, and the repercussions are clear. In the second half of the century, another type of error in judgment appears, but its treatment is more problematic. A number of heroines marry to escape destitution. Mrs. Herbert "to rescue her parents from impending want, had given up a lover whom she justly valued, and united herself to a man destitute of every recommendation, but the possession of wealth."[20] She is a model of virtue and endurance and teaches younger women to endure. Mary Wollstonecraft's Maria marries to escape the tyranny of her step-mother. Austen presents Charlotte Lucas as choosing marriage with cold calculation in *Pride and Preju-*

dice. She accepts Collins "solely from the pure and disinterested desire of an establishment." Austen explains that marriage "was the only honourable provision for well-educated young women of small fortune, and however uncertain of giving happiness, must be their pleasantest preservative from want."[21] Novelists are not so certain such marriages are errors in judgment. The awareness of the lack of alternatives and the state of mind of the heroines prevent any unequivocal judgments. These heroines are not presented as hysterical or driven; rather they spend time examining their situation and chafe against their chains. They suffer more acutely because they regret the action even as they commit it and feel doubly obligated to make the best of it.

The increase in the frequency of this type of economic marriage is an extension of the earlier themes about marriage and a reflection of a new social situation. The ideals for marriage based on mutual love and esteem meant that marriages contracted for financial reasons alone would be condemned and probably doomed regardless of whether the parents or the woman herself brought them about. In the early part of the century, the woman was either her parents' victim as Clarissa was or culpable because of her own blind greed. Later novels showed woman as victim but gave her altruistic reasons for consenting. The least sympathetic motive was a desire to be free of the malice of a step parent in contrast to the earlier bedazzlement with coaches. By this time, the woman's right to refuse a marriage partner was entirely accepted by society, and such social movements as Evangelicalism, the rise of the middle class and of individualism had changed woman's self-concept. As Defoe and Richardson had pointed out in their fiction, each man (and woman) was his own master and accountable to his own conscience. Defoe's host of judgmentally religious servants and Richardson's fiercely independently moral heroines were but the beginning of a tide of characters who were responsible for their own actions. Furthermore, as Lawrence Stone has pointed out, the ideal of holy matrimony was incompatible with patriarchal authority, and, as the ideal was accepted, patriarchal conflicts naturally decline as fictional subjects.

A strain of antimarriage sentiment has always been present in the novels by women. One of Jane Barker's heroines eschews men for poetry, and Eliza Haywood's first novel, *Love in Excess,* includes a warning to the heroine, "Oh, Melliora shun the Marriage Bed, as thou wou'dst a Serpent's Den, more Ruinous, more Poysonous far, is Man." Scott's *Description of Millenium Hall* is an idyllic society of celibate women, and the Preface to Jane West's *The Advantages of Education* states, "I do not chuse to hold up matrimony as the great desideratum of our sex; I wish them to look to the general esteem of worthy people, and the approbation of their own hearts, for the recompense of their merit, rather than to the particular addresses of a lover."[22] Stone has suggested that the proportion of unmarried people rose in the eighteenth century. The death toll from English wars and the numbers of men sent abroad to fight or man merchant ships seem to have led to an imbalance between numbers of men and women; younger sons increasingly remained unmarried, and inflation led other men to delay marriage. Stone calculates that approximately 5 percent of the upper-class girls remained unmarried in the sixteenth century and that 20 to 25 percent did so after the mid-eighteenth.[23] The novels reflect both the greater pressures on women to marry even marginally acceptable men and the desire to have the unmarried life accepted as a respectable alternative.

II. *Marriage*

A large number of eighteenth-century novels portray marriages and find their subject matter in the vicissitudes and aspirations of the institution. Charles Gildon, a prolific and successful hack writer, recommends "The Distresses of married Love" as the subject of literature because courtship scenes provoke "Indignation or Sleep."[24] Some scholars estimate that only 5 percent of the women in eighteenth-century England never married;[25] such a population would have intense interest in novels about marriage. Throughout literary history, novels about marriage tend to be darker than those about courtship, and the eighteenth century's are no exception. Women writers show considerable concern with the continued need for esteem. Within her marriage, the woman character struggles to retain her respect for the man and to create a satisfying life for herself. The novels tend to strip away youthful illusions. Once married, men turn their attention wholeheartedly to business, politics, and male friendships and pastimes. They leave for the Exchange, discuss taxes and elections, and resume hunting. Miss Milner in Inchbald's *Simple Story* insists, "If he will not submit to be my lover, I will not submit to be his wife—nor has he the affection I require in a husband." Sensible women, however, are like Scott's country girl who asks "which is more desirable, his esteem or his courtship? if you really love him, you can make no comparison between them; for surely there cannot be a greater suffering than to stand low in the opinion of any person who has a great share of our affections."[26] Esteem is hard won; husbands seem to notice their wives when the women displease them or when the wife's service is extraordinarily strenuous. Lady Barton in Elizabeth Griffith's novel nurses her insensitive, unattractive husband through one illness, hurries home to nurse him during a second only to be unjustly accused of being an adultress and a murderess. He locks her in her room, but she is finally vindicated. Sir William leaves his hunting, traveling, and business only to express outrage. His wife's devoted attention during his illness even when it strains her own health calls forth gratitude which eventually leads him to regret her death.[27]

The novels of marriage surrender the ideal of conversation about feelings, about personal needs and hopes, and about poetry and ideas for the reality of the wife's place as household governor and emotional anchor. The modern reader senses Christian stoicism and even a feeling of the triumph of moral superiority in the successful eighteenth-century wife. Griffith's Lady Barton and West's Mrs. Herbert have both become so immured to the deprivations and even brutalities of their marriages that they no longer seem to suffer but offer their lives up to others as triumphs. They have peace of mind and respect if not companionship or access to the wider world provided in happy marriages by the husband's conversation. Even in Gothic novels such as Ann Radcliffe's *The Italian*, the heroine is called upon to endure without compromising her principles. When Ellena interprets her choice as obtaining her freedom by renouncing Vivaldi or accepting him "in defiance of honourable pride," she is working toward establishing a marriage based on consent, open acknowledgment, and lack of unequal obligation.[28] In spite of Vivaldi's eagerness and the fact that marriage would protect her, Ellena holds out until problems of identity and honor are resolved. Her principles balance Vivaldi's amorousness and promise a solid relationship.

Lovers may write of politics and human foibles, but wives discuss the vicissitudes and mundane events of daily life. Felicia and Lucius's romantic dalliances give way to conversations about tenants, business trips, and the rearing of her husband's illegitimate child. Elements of the conduct books linger into the nineteenth century. Soon after her marriage, Lucius asks Collyer's Felicia to join him in thanking God for their blessings, and Elizabeth Helme's *The Farmer of Inglewood Forest* and Penelope Aubin's *The Life of Charlotte DuPont* are full of scenes of family prayer.[29] The novels also strip away illusions about the special attractions and powers married women have. A typical passage describes the outcome of a passionate courtship. in Haywood's *Love in Excess*, Alovisa will not quarrel with or disoblige D'elmont:

> She rightly judg'd that when People are Marry'd, Jealousie was not the proper Method to revive a decay'd Passion, and that after Possession it must be only Tenderness and Constant Assiduity to please, that can keep up desire, fresh and gay: Man is too Arbitrary a Creature to bear the least Contradiction, where he pretends an absolute Authority, and that Wife who thinks by ill humour and

perpetual Taunts, to make him weary of what she wou'd reclaim him from, only renders her self more hateful, and makes that justifiable which before was blameable in him.[30]

Women dream of pregnancy renewing their husband's protective instincts, tenderness, and esteem, but childbirth like marriage itself proves to be a lonely experience and a solitary joy. Hester Thrale in *Thraliana* but reflects their fantasies when she writes after assisting at the birth of her maid's child, "Oh might *I* hope to be once more in that State by the Man my Heart doats on—how little would I value Death or Danger!" "What! die in my Piozzi's Arms, & leave him a Pledge of my unbounded, my true Affection! No! No! let me indulge no such Dreams of fantastic Delight. . . ."[31] Ellen Moers has pointed out that women writers "who wrote of motherhood as a focus of power" were usually childless.[32] The fantasy is short-lived in the eighteenth-century novel.

Childbirth seems to be anticipated with uniform dread regardless of the heroine's status or hope to win renewed respect. Almost all mention the pain and most the risk of death. Haywood describes Alithea (*The Mercenary Lover*, 1726) as knowing "she must expect those Agonies which all, in becoming Mothers, feel. . . ."[33] Emanuella awaits "the dreadful Hour" (*Rash Resolve*, 95). Manley uses childbirth as a grim metaphor. "And when, upon the first opportunity, he caught me in his Arms to kiss me, I felt the same Ease, the same Release from Pain, as a Wretch took from the Rack; or from that more exquisite Torture, the Rack of Nature; the Ease a Woman feels, releas'd from *Mother-pains*. . . ."[34] Motherhood is scarcely more desirable in unhappy marriages than in the unmarried state. Lady Barton cannot bring herself to tell her husband she is pregnant, and he is enraged when he finds out only when she miscarries.

Some of the reasons that childbirth is treated this way are not hard to find. Pregnant women often are not attractive, and husbands often resent the inconveniences of having a pregnant or nursing wife and later having to compete with children for the wife's attention. The age treated childbirth as a condition in which the body was "neither manifestly vitiated, not altogether whole," and women often died.[35] One way of coping with the risks of childbirth was to detach oneself from the pregnant wife. Francis Osborne writes that women

do not only run the hazard of their own Contamination by Marriage, to draw men out of the sins no less than punishments impending the barren and unnatural delights of solitude, but alter their shapes, and embase their celestial Beauties, when by discharging their Husbands of the venom of Love, they swell themselves into the bulk and dangers of Childbearing.[36]

Fielding satirizes the frequency of childbirth deaths in fiction by having Mrs. Novel in *The Author's Farce* say, "He swore he would be [my husband]—Yes, he knows I died for love; for I died in childbed." Even as Fielding's satire is on target regarding formula fiction, he, too, distances himself from the reality.

Two of the most remarkable treatments of childbirth in the century are by major male writers: Richardson and Defoe. In the 1741 sequel to *Pamela*, Richardson devotes Volume 4 to the birth of Pamela's first child, to B.'s affair with a woman met at a masquerade, and the couple's reconciliation. The volume begins with Pamela's campaign to persuade B. to allow her to nurse. She argues from Scripture and concern for the child's health, and her views are quite ordinary. Earlier Defoe had complained about the trend away from nursing in *The Compleat English Gentleman* [1728]. He had grumbled that talking to modern women about their duty to give their children a religious education is as fruitless as recommending nursing, "a thing as unnatural now as if God and nature had never intended it, or that Heaven had given the ladyes breasts and milk for some other use." He compares this attitude to that of Queen Anne and argues for mothers' nursing their children on two grounds. First, he argues that milk mixes the blood of the nurse with that of the child and may affect its health and personality. Second, it is the duty of the mother to nurse her child for the same reason it is her duty to teach it Christian precepts: she should instill good principles and good blood and guard the child because "the evill part allwayes makes deeper impression than the good."[37] The unfortunate Emma in *The Farmer of Inglewood Forest* states quite unequivocally that she poisoned her infant by nursing it: "I will relate how I murdered my infant . . . administered poison in the salutary form of milk!"[38] All of B.'s objections are those of the husband-lover rather than the husband-father and must be evaluated in the context of these widely held moral views. B. does not want his rest disturbed, he disapproves of separate beds, he fears Pamela will be less physically and mentally attractive, and he concludes, "But when I am at home, even a Son and Heir, so jealous am I of your Affections, shall not be my Rival in them." The initial debate establishes the problem of Pamela's role conflict and introduces this new, troublesome aspect of B.'s personality. Significantly, he has turned Pamela's Scriptural examples against her by pointing out the acceptance of polygamy in biblical times,[39] and he continues to lay out plans for her continued education and travel with him.

The conflict recedes, and the narrative focuses on Pamela's fear of the "approaching Occasion." She, and all her circle, share the realistic fear that she might die, and she, like many fictional and actual women, writes a will. Pamela fears the pain as well as the risk. She has not forgotten God's curse,

"I will greatly multiply your pain in childbearing; in pain shall you bring forth children" (Gen. 3:16). She imagines that fallen women see their pain as the just punishment for their sins and describes God punishing them "in Kind." After witnessing Pamela's labor, Polly Danford writes that she will never marry for "a Husband's Account" (to continue his family and name); neither, she thinks, can be adequate recompense for the pain.[40] That childbearing is for the sake of the husband's name seems disputable, but those who attempt to add a romantic element to it are chasing rainbows. B. visits Pamela for ten minutes after the birth and displays "thankful and manly Gratitude and Politeness," and he soon resumes her French and Italian lessons, but he begins his affair with the Countess Dowager almost at once.

Within days of the birth, Polly Danford writes, "You desire to know, my honour'd Papa, how Mr. *B.* passes his Time, and whether it be in his Lady's Chamber? No, indeed! Catch Gentlmen, the best of them, in too great a Complaisance that way, if you can." B. goes to Parliament and "sups abroad." A few days later Pamela writes to Lady Davers that B. "is not so fond of [the baby], as I wish him to be." Once the affair is undeniable, Pamela finds consolation in the nursery, and the baby assumes a new role in the conflict. B. continues to be jealous and once says he "would hire a Nurse to overlay him" if Pamela becomes upset every time he is sick. Pamela fears a separation from B. would mean her loss of the baby, the heir to B.'s estate. The baby becomes Pamela's consolation and chain; she cannot leave B. and must seek a resolution within that constraint.

Richardson's account has expanded upon the three elements found in the narrative sequences of childbirth: relationship to father, fear and risk, and resolution of relationship to father. Many of the fictional mothers, married or unmarried, are overwhelmed with tenderness for the infant and find a more satisfying object of their affection than the lover. Most, however, continue to long for a return of the intimacy and supremacy they enjoyed in courtship.

Defoe's Roxana, too, fears she will die in childbirth and writes a will. The Prince teases her, "*So all the Ladies say,* my Dear, say he, *when they are with-Child.*" Roxana calls the Prince to her bedside *during* labor. "I sent Word, I would make as few Cries as possible, to prevent disturbing him; he came into the Room once, and call'd to me, to be of good Courage, it wou'd soon be over. . . ."[41] He gives Amy ten pistoles for delivering the news that he was father of a son and visits Roxana that day and the next. Unlike B., the Prince enjoys watching the baby sleep and play. The child, however, is soon left with a nurse, and Roxana and the Prince return to Paris.

Roxana uses her pregnancy to get more attention from the Prince. She introduces the subject but waits until the Prince can feel the child's movement to confirm her pregnancy. She prepares her will two months before her son's birth and discusses its details. She involves the Prince in repeated conversations about the child's future. Not only does she assure the care and support of her son and her own additional material increase, but she also underscores the Prince's obligations. He has threatened her life, caused her suffering, and fathered a child who causes her concern and guilt. The Prince finally says, "if once we come to talk of Repentance, we must talk of parting."

When marriages survive the hardships and adjustments of the early years and develop into the near-pastoral comfort and tranquillity of lifelong love, esteem occupies a central place. In *The Farmer of Inglewood Forest*, Fanny admonishes William that he is to teach his family fortitude in adversity and offer comfort even as he admires her for suppressing her own distress upon the death of her infant and her sister Agnes.[42] She and many of the other women are constant sources of encouragement and help. West's exemplary Mrs. Williams admonishes Maria on the evening before her wedding,

> Shew [your husband], my child, that you are his helpmate, not his incumberance. Let not his distress at any disastrous circumstance, be aggravated by the fear, that you will sink under affliction. Convince him that you have fortitude to bear the common ills of life, as well as patience to endure its common provocations. . . . Humility, which inspires a lowly mind and moderate desires, is the surest road to content.[43]

Those characteristics which won youthful respect remain: woman's intelligence, insight, judgment, virtue, common sense, and clear-headed sensitivity. Her sphere has contracted, however, and endurance seems the supreme excellence. She seldom comments on politics, poetry, gardens, plays, her reading in history and languages, or even on human nature. Engrossed in family problems, she has no leisure. Her statements tend to be judgments rather than observations. Although few go as far as Austen's Mrs. Bennet, the conversation is most often about the children and their prospects.

The novels of maturity show a different role for esteem in love. As hard as it is to deserve and earn esteem, surely it is harder to hold it for a lifetime. Youth shows man and woman at their best, and trials and temptations are limited by situation and time. Engagement, for example, will end in estrangement or marriage within a fairly short time. Marriage to a brute, however, can last fifty or sixty years. The courtship novels show the delighted lover discovering new reasons to prefer the lovely girl and the girl believing happily that she deserves this respect and appreciation. The marriage novels show self-esteem attacked in new, more devastating ways. They reiterate the truth of West's "How poor, my girl, is that woman's boast, who is conscious that she rather gratifies the vanity, than charms the heart of her husband. . . ."[44]

One of the most common objections made to women's novel reading was that it gave them an unrealistic idea of the world. The women novelists of the eighteenth century increasingly and explicitly resist this danger. Behn and Haywood and even Aubin allow women to be beautiful, passionate, fortunate, and then devastatingly evil and ruined. They meet men as exotic, as hypnotic, and as monstrous as they. Seductions set in jasmine-scented bedrooms and the deathbed agonies of the poisoned, pregnant mistress belong to this world of heightened emotion and hysterical fantasy. After midcentury however, the novels show the grinding problems of the middle-class woman. As Elizabeth Hardwick says of the bourgeois novel: "What is asked of the heroine is not always a grand passion, but a sense of reality, a curious sort of independence and honor, an acceptance of consequence that puts courage to the most searing test."[45] As Burney's Camilla is ready to live single rather than deal dishonorably to win Edgar, so Austen's independent Elizabeth becomes the harmonizing force that brings together not only Jane and Bingley but Darcy and his aunt Catherine and Mr. Bennet and Kitty. Elizabeth's vitality and self-knowledge bring about the optimistic resolutions for all her circle. Unlike the early novels by women, emphasis was on character rather than on ingenuity of plot, and the novels were not sensational and aimed at the young and idle who attended the theater. Even when characters are monsters as Edwin in *The Farmer of Inglewood Forest* is, their faults are the middle-class ones of getting ahead in business, not winning an ego-consuming power struggle. By 1816, Sir Walter Scott could record the change: "a style of novel has arisen, within the last fifteen or twenty years, differing from the former in the points upon which the interest hinges; neither alarming our credulity nor amusing our imagination by wild variety of incidest. . . ."[46] This change had been gradual and profound.

NOTES

1. Jean Hagstrum, *Sex and Sensibility* (Chicago: University of Chicago Press, 1980), 14, 24, 160, 185, and 190. David Blewitt, "Changing Attitudes toward Marriage in the Time of Defoe: The Case of Moll Flanders," *Huntington Library Quarterly* 44 (1981): 78. Eighteenth-century writers acknowledged Milton's influence;

see, for example, Elizabeth Griffith's *The History of Lady Barton* (London, 1771), 2:120–21.

2. Henry Fielding, *Joseph Andrews* (New York: Norton, 1958), 89–90.

3. Patricia Meyer Spacks, *The Adolescent Idea* (New York: Basic Books, 1981), 20.

4. Samuel Johnson wrote to Mrs. Thrale (27 October 1777): "In a man's Letters you know, Madam, his soul lies naked, his letters are only the mirrour of his breast, whatever passes within him is shown undisguised in its natural process. Nothing is inverted, nothing distorted, you see systems in their elements, you discover actions in their motives."

5. Fanny Burney, *Evelina* (New York: Norton, 1965), 329; Jane Austen, *Pride and Prejudice* (Boston: Houghton Mifflin, 1956), 38.

6. Sarah Scott, *A Description of Millenium Hall* (originally published in 1762), ed. Walter Crittenden (New York: Bookman, 1952), 90–91, 104.

7. Aphra Behn, *The History of the Nun* (originally published in 1689), in *Restoration Prose Fiction*, ed. Charles C. Mish (Lincoln: University of Nebraska Press, 1970), 106.

8. Cf. Daniel Defoe, *Conjugal Lewdness* (London, 1727), 213–28, 252–72.

9. Susan Staves, "British Seduced Maidens," *Eighteenth-Century Studies* 14 (1980), 118.

10. Haywood, *Philidore and Placentia* (London, 1727), 8.

11. Haywood, *The Rash Resolve* (London, 1724), 56.

12. Mary Davys, *The Reform'd Coquette* (London, 1724), 65–70.

13. Delariviére Manley, *Secret Memoirs and Manners of Several Persons of Quality of Both Sexes from the New Atalantis* (London, 1709), 67.

14. Elizabeth Inchbald, *Nature and Art* (London, 1797), 1:162.

15. Jane West, *Advantages of Education* (London, 1793), 3:224.

16. Scott, *A Description of Millenium Hall*, 169.

17. Aphra Behn, *The Adventures of the Black Lady*, vol. 5 of *Works*, ed. Montague Summers (London: Heineman, 1915).

18. See West, Advantages of Education, 2:184–86, passim and Paula R. Backscheider, "Woman's Influence," *Studies in the Novel* 11 (1979): 9–10, 17.

19. Moore, quoted in Spacks, *Adolescent Idea*, 120.

20. West, *Advantages of Education*, 2:100–01.

21. Austen, *Pride and Prejudice*, 93.

22. Eliza Haywood, *Love in Excess* (London, 1719), 2:65; West, *Advantages of Education*, 1:3–4.

23. Lawrence Stone's *The Family, Sex, and Marriage* (London: Weidenfeld & Nicolson, 1977) is the source for demographic information, 375–86. Compare also his discussion of individualism, 47, 258–67.

24. Charles Gildon, *The Post-Man Robb'd of his Mail* (London: Bettesworth, 1719), 247.

25. W. A. Speck, *Stability and Strife* (Cambridge: Harvard University Press, 1977), 64.

26. Scott, *A Description of Millenium* Hall, 145.

27. Griffith, vol. 3.

28. Ann Radcliffe, *The Italian* (Oxford: Oxford University Press, 1971), 69–70.

29. Mary Collyer, *Felicia to Charlotte* (London, 1744–49) and Elizabeth Helme, *The Farmer of Inglewood Forest*, 7th ed., (London: George Virtue, n.d.).

30. Haywood, *Love in Excess*, 2:19.

31. Katherine C. Balderson, ed., *Thraliana* (Oxford: Clarendon, 1942), 1:583.

32. Ellen Moers, *Literary Women* (Garden City, N.Y.: Doubleday, 1976), 216.

33. Eliza Haywood, *The Mercenary Lover* (London, 1726), 53.

34. Delariviére Manley, "From a Lady to a Lady" in *The Novel in Letters*, ed. Natascha Würzback (Coral Gables: University of Miami Press, 1969), 51.

35. Quoted in Delores Peters, "The Pregnant Pamela," *Eighteenth-Century Studies* 14 (1981): 435.

36. Frances Osborne, *Advice to a Son* (Oxford, 1656), 41.

37. Daniel Defoe, *The Complete English Gentleman*, ed. Karl Bulbring (London: Nutt, 1890), 71–75, 83.

38. Helme, *Farmer of Inglewood Forest*, 416–17. See also Randolph Trumback, *The Rise of the Egalitarian Family* (New York: Academic Press, 1978), 203–223.

39. Samuel Richardson, *Pamela*, Shakespeare Head Edition (Oxford: Blackwell, 1929), 4:13–14. Polygamy was a subject of current interest. See Alfred Owen Aldridge, "Polygamy and Deism," *JEGP* 48 (1949): 343–60; and "Population and Polygamy in Eighteenth-Century Thought," *Journal of the History of Medicine and Allied Sciences* 4 (1949): 129–48.

40. Richardson, *Pamela*, 4:114–15, 120–21; Polly Danford dies in childbirth.

41. Daniel Defoe, *Roxana* (London: Oxford University Press, 1964), 78–79.

42. Helme, *Farmer of Inglewood Forest*, 274.

43. West, *Advantage of Education*, 2:235.

44. Ibid., 115.

45. Elizabeth Hardwick, *Seduction and Betrayal: Women and Literature* (New York: Random House, 1974), 182.

46. Sir Walter Scott, review of *Emma, Quarterly Review*, 14 (1816): 192–93.

Matrimonial Discord in
Fiction and in Court
The Case of Ann Masterman

SUSAN STAVES

Ann Masterman Skinn was the author of *The Old Maid; or, The History of Miss Ravensworth* (1771), a remarkable novel that seems to smash all the eighteenth-century icons of female decorum and sensibility. She possessed a comic, satirical, even farcical talent and took no pains to suppress it. This novel is the only book she is definitely known to have published. Indeed, the December 1770 *Critical Review*, disagreeing with my estimate of the novel, noted: "We find in the address of Mrs. Skinn to the reader, that she intends favouring the public with a history of her own life; but as we feel a most melancholy presage, that her future work will prove as insipid as the present, we humbly beg of her to drop the design."[1] Mrs. Skinn, whose experience of both critics and life seems to have been an embittering one, apparently did drop her autobiographical design, but since I have found records that shed light on her troubles, I intend to carry out at least part of her plan for her here.

Ann Masterman's epistolary novel contains most of the conventional characters and situations familiar in eighteenth-century sentimental fiction: a young girl who has various adventures and finally marries in the third volume; another young girl, her confidant, who is in love with a captain and, after her family threatens to marry her to a vicious baronet, finally elopes to Scotland with the captain; a wicked lord who wants to abduct and forcibly marry the heroine, kidnaps her from a masquerade, and locks her up in a country house; a poor farmer's daughter who is actually seduced by this same wicked lord and then dies; and so on. The title of the novel has a double reference, indicating both the possibility that Emily Ravensworth, the young heroine, may become an old maid, and referring also to Miss Martha Ravensworth, her aunt, described as "the picture of ill-nature and envy."[2] A source of suspense is whether Emily will turn into a mean old

Mᵣˢ SKINN, *with* Mᵣ BROWN, *the Attorneys Clerk at Hull in Yorkshire*.

Frontispiece, "William Skinn, against Ann Skinn," in *Trials for Adultery: or, The History of Divorces*. By permission of the Harvard Law School Library.

spinster like her aunt. At the beginning of the story, various characters worry that she is too spirited to be attractive to men. One, for instance, writes, "Is it not a pity, CHARLOTTE, that nothing can break this little blameable spirit, which spoils an (otherwise) really amiable woman?" (1:35). Emily further aggravates everyone's concern about her future by expressing actual reluctance to marry: "Oh! 'tis a hideous thing to be married . . . a girl, who centers all her happiness in darling Liberty, as I do—Horrid, MARIA, I expire at the very thoughts of being controuled by a set of wretches, who were born to be slaves, if our sex, in general, had but spirit enough to assert their right, and keep the things in proper subjection" (1:59). The reader is not surprised when one of the older women writes, "Much as [Emily] rallies old maids in general, yet I don't know any body in a fairer way of becoming one than herself, if she does not very much alter her present opinion" (1:69).

At first we wonder if such a flippant and hostile young girl, a girl who refers to men in general as "wretches" and "things," can possibly be the heroine of a novel. But Emily certainly seems to occupy that structural niche, and Masterman goes to the trouble of adding such touches as Emily's rushing home to care for her sick grandfather by way of indicating that she is fundamentally a good-hearted creature. As the story progresses, Emily's consistent defiance of conventions leads one to suppose that she is likely to pay a heavy price, to endure some dire punishment, if indeed she is to be allowed to live and to repent—perhaps her fate will be the harsh one of Miss Milner in Elizabeth Inchbald's *A Simple Story*, who progresses from spiritedness and flippancy to adultery and death, or perhaps it will be something milder like the humiliation and painful fever Marianne endures in *Sense and Sensibility* before she marries Colonel Brandon. Quite early on, Emily arranges an assignation for her girl friend with the captain at a local ball. The two girls get dressed to go to the ball despite not having her grandparents' permission. When challenged as to where they are going, Emily snips, "Why now, suppose it should not be quite so convenient to tell you, grand-papa . . . for my own part I fairly own, I am going to meet my sweetheart," and the girls and their cousin simply go off in the family carriage (1:52–53). At another point, when her grandfather orders her to accept an invitation to visit the Seagroves, she refuses flatly and insists, "Now you must know, that I am as firmly determined as yourself, and as my resolutions are of infinitely more consequence to me, than yours can be, I shall most strictly adhere to them . . ." (1:34). The reader schooled in eighteenth-century fiction must ask: can such a girl possibly get to the end of a three-decker without enduring the agonies of brain fever, seduction, rape, repentance, and/or death? Ann Masterman, breaking with convention, answers yes.

Emily is in revolt against authority, both in her outspoken speeches and in her actions. Unlike the more usual heroines driven to disobedience, however, she does not defy adults soberly and painfully. Instead, she seems to defy them joyfully, quite heedless of the consequences of her behavior. More sentimental heroines are apt to justify disobedience to relatives or to husbands on moral grounds, as Clarissa does, but they usually advance their arguments hesitantly and with reluctance to disobey. Not Emily. She speaks out eagerly and with amazing confidence in what she says and in her right to say it. For example, when Mr. Seagrove asks her in the second volume why she has not yet married Richard Ravensworth, her cousin and her family's choice, invoking the spiritual authority of the fifth commandment, "Honor thy father and mother," Emily replies with all the assurance of the great Cham: "Sir . . . if one's parents command one to commit murder, it is no breach of the commandment to be disobedient in such a case; and why they should have a right to make one lye [presumably in the repetition of the marriage vows], more than kill, is a point of argument which requires some sophistry to support" (2:146–47). Masterman's concurrence in Emily's argument here seems clear, especially as she puts the argument for obedience in the mouth of Mr. Seagrove, who is attempting to force his daughter to marry a debauched rake.

Emily's low level of ambivalence allows her to act as well as to speak. Unlike the more usual heroines whose painful "helplessness" and "impotence" have recently been well discussed by Paula R. Backscheider, Emily elects direct action and fights her own battles.[3] Though she clearly lives in the same social world of England in the 1770s as Fanny Burney's Evelina, a world with the same taboos against feminine self-assertion, Emily is simply unterrorized, and, for the most part, unrepressed.[4] In the first volume she goes to London to assist her friend Mrs. Clayton during her lying-in. While she is in Mrs. Clayton's house, Mr. Clayton makes improper advances toward her and tries to silence her resistance by saying that if she does not keep quiet, she will endanger Mrs. Clayton's health. Quite unparalyzed by the possibilities of this scruple, Emily stabs him through the hand with her pocket scissors. This scene, of course, is reminiscent of the famous scene in which Clarissa, cornered by Lovelace, threatens to stab herself with her pocket scissors. The scene dramatizes Emily's ability to direct her anger outward against those who attempt to interfere with her independence and integrity, rather than, like her softer sisters, directing rage inward against herself. Emily describes this particular adventure to her girl friend with a complacency which also contrasts startlingly with the agonizings of Clarissa. Commenting on the scissors and offering a bit of practical advice, she writes to Henrietta, "Don't you find they are a pretty kind of weapon, my dear? they outdo the tongue a bar's length, I find: pray never go without a pair in your pocket . . ." (1:87).

Some of the best comedy in *The Old Maid* comes in the relationship between Emily and another admirer of hers, Lord Wilton, and this part of the story also seems to play itself off against the story of Clarissa and Lovelace. Wilton is reputed to be a rake, but Emily, declining to worry over the usual burning issue of whether a good woman should ever marry a former rake and refusing to share the scruples of the sentimental against such an alliance, simply announces not very seriously, "I shall have the honour of reclaiming him; reformed rakes you know, my dear, make the best husbands" (1:150). Lord Wilton does propose to her in a scene which Masterman renders as that of the affected and idiotic man proposing to the intelligent woman, a scene elsewhere rendered in Fanny Burney's funny diary account of Mr. Barlow's proposal to her and in Jane Austen's still more comic version of Mr. Collins's proposing to Elizabeth Bennet.[5] "Yesterday he made me a formal declaration of the most ardent passion, that ever inspired the breast of man," Emily writes, "talked much of flames and darts, and vowed he should never be able to survive my cruelty; but sooner than suffer the excruciating torments which would be the undoubted consequence of my disdain, he would put a speedy end to an existence, which without me would be rendered insupportable" (1:152). The silly declarations of Mr. Barlow and Mr. Collins seem silly to Fanny Burney and Elizabeth Bennet, but they are, nevertheless, somewhat embarrassed and anxious about how they ought to respond. Not Emily. She bursts out laughing and tells Lord Wilton he is ridiculous. Nor is her laughter the nervous giggle of the young Evelina who tries unsuccessfully to stop herself from tittering at Mr. Lovel; it is an uninhibited laugh of genuine enjoyment. She tells Lord Wilton, "fate had been unkind to the stage, in making a lord of one who seemed so every way calculated for the buskin . . . thanked him for the diversion he had afforded me, and whenever I found myself inclinable to the vapours, would send for him by way of antidote" (1:153).

The comedy is only heightened when Lord Wilton is not finally deterred by this rebuff. Seizing the opportunity of Emily's presence at a masquerade, the rake tries a familiar trick. He bribes her servant, and has her taken in a chair, not to her home as she expects, but to his lodgings. Apparently trapped in the lodgings of a vile man, Emily neither faints nor sinks to her knees to implore the assistance of heaven. Coolly, she turns to Lord Wilton and declares, "I fear you not at all; I am always for myself a sufficient guard . . . take my advice and be convinced, you are naturally ridiculous enough, without taking pains to appear more the ideot than you already are" (1:173). When this does not work, she grabs a pistol and shoots at him, remarking that self-defense is the first law of nature. She misses, but has subsequent recourse to boxing him on the ears, tossing a letter to her relatives out of a chaise window as he spirits her off to his country house, stabbing him with a knife, and finally jumping out of a second-story window to freedom. Emily's unconflicted vigor and courage in these adventures is even more refreshing by contrast to Clarissa's paralysis than Sophia Western's simply walking out of her father's house, though admittedly Masterman's comedy is rougher than Fielding's more subtle humor. Fittingly, we learn rather casually in the third volume that Emily has her own pet monkey—a man falls over it and it scratches him. Evelina, it will be remembered, by contrast, involuntarily jumps up on a chair when Captain Mirvan brings a monkey dressed like a fop into Mrs. Beaumont's drawing room.

Although Emily is involved in many of the stock situations of sentimental fiction, the letters in this epistolary novel are not much occupied with advice to her about what she should do in her various predicaments or even with her own ruminations on what her responses should be. Her situations are not felt to be distressingly problematic, so instead of offering careful analysis like that of Richardson or Elizabeth Griffith, these letters are more concerned with description of action or with Emily's advice to others, principally other women. This advice departs significantly from the usual conduct book or novel advice on similar issues. It apparently never crosses Emily's mind to tell her female friends to learn patience, to school themselves in suffering, or to expect happiness only in heaven. On the contrary, she counsels flight from oppressive parents or husbands. At the beginning of the novel, we see her encouraging the clandestine relationship between her friend Henrietta Seagrove and Captain Crosby. Throughout, she stands ready to arrange assignations for them and urges them to elope to Scotland where they can contract a valid marriage without the consent of parents. Masterman seems to want to diminish objections to Emily's assistance to this pair by making Henrietta's situation as repellent as possible. Henrietta does not agree to elope until after her family tries to marry her to the vicious rake Sir Robert Boyle and until after the reader has had the benefit of reading his letters, in which he depends on Henrietta's obedience to her father and declares, "she is all gentleness; so, when I am tired of her, I can break her heart in a month at least . . ." (1:108–9). Sir Robert is also described in very vivid language by Emily as a corrupted body, the quintessence of loathsomeness, indeed, described so as to suggest that he would be likely to infect a woman he married with venereal disease.[6] Also, though Emily does not actually urge Mrs. Sandham to run away from her brutal husband, after Mrs. Sandham has done so and when she is known to be living with her lover, young Mr. Oakham, Emily not only expresses sympathy for her plight, as many late-eighteenth-century heroines would do, but goes so far beyond the bounds of decorum as to correspond with her Writing to her grandmother, Emily comments, "if any body may be excused so desperate an action, it is the unfortunate lady in question. Had she possessed an independent fortune, or a relation, who to that title would have joined the name of friend, she would, I dare believe, have acted differently" (2:137–38). Masterman appears to share her heroine's feelings for this deviant woman, since, in the end, she forces Mr. Sandham to die a horrible death and allows Mrs. Sandham to marry Mr. Oakham.

Throughout *The Old Maid*, Emily wants to think of herself as an active agent rather than as a passive sufferer. She does sprain her ankle jumping out of the window and subsequently develops a fever supposedly consequent on this injury, but she does not recant her determination to be active or her hostility to sentiment. When the contemporary palette of female roles fails to offer one in a sufficiently vivid color, she imagines herself as a man. Vowing that her friend Henrietta shall never be made to swallow what she characterizes as a bitter matrimonial pill, Emily declares, "Horrid— No—HENNY shall never be forced, I'm determined; I'll turn Knight-errant in her defence myself first" (1:126). Later, noticing how passive one wife seems, Emily insists that she would behave differently were she ever to be married to a tyrant: "How I should enjoy the opportunity of revenging some of my own sex, by thwarting and breaking the hearts of two or three of those despotic wretches, who vainly give themselves the titles of our lords and masters . . ." (1:130).

It would, I think, be wrong to suggest that *The Old Maid* is a particularly realistic novel in the ordinary sense. Although in the story Emily finds Edward Blanche, in reality a young girl who went about London of the 1770s making sarcastic remarks about marriage and sentiment and stabbing and shooting at men could not normally expect to marry a nice young man who liked her just the way she was. (Aside from his surprising tolerance for Emily's behavior, Blanche is about as bland as his name implies; in fact, though Emily never faints, on two occasions he does.) Nor were courage and spunk alone enough to defend women against evils like rape or husbands like Mr. Sandham who knocked them down and wounded their breasts. *The Old Maid* is in part a wish fulfillment fantasy about how things might be if women had control of their lives. It is in this way like Sarah Scott's *Millenium Hall* in which a group of women secede from the world to form their own benevolent community.[7] Unlike Scott, however, Masterman keeps the issues of physical force and violence on the surface. Violence is directed at women, and Emily at least both expresses her rage when her autonomy is threatened and directs violence back at men.

Nevertheless, even in *The Old Maid* an element of female self-hatred

persists embodied in the character of Martha Ravensworth, familiarly
called Aunt Patty, and in the attitudes toward her. Emily is potentially an
old maid, but her aunt is actually such a despised creature. Bad old Aunt
Patty hates Emily, betrays Henrietta's romance to her parents, and plots to
let one of her enemies catch smallpox. Even at the beginning of the novel,
Emily thinks that the one thing that might force her to marry is her desire to
save herself "from that never enough to be dreaded reproach of an old
maid" (1:81). Throughout the novel, Martha is the victim of Smollett-like
humiliations, practical jokes, and general rough treatment. Jokes about
raping old women are frequent. In a cruel though funny episode, Lord
Wilton, still not finally discouraged from attempting Emily after her escape
from his country house, tries to have her abducted from her home, but in
the dark Aunt Patty is captured instead. Aunt Patty gives a spirited if unconvincing imitation of a heroine resisting ravishment. Lord Wilton exclaims to his own correspondent. "Represent to yourself, a pretty tall
woman, extremely thin—nay, in short, the best description I can give you
of her, is to suppose two deal boards before you nailed together, with a
death's head on the top, by way of indicating it's being of the human species. . . . Ravish you, ha! ha! ha! . . . why, I'd as soon ravish my
grandmother, who has been dead these twenty years" (3:49–50). Wilton,
who is a trifle concerned that he may be ravished by Aunt Patty, finally
gives up the pursuit of Emily disgusted at the trouble it has been. Masterman here enjoys the joke that an unattractive old woman is more likely to
want to be the object of a ravisher's desire than any man would want to
ravish her, exactly the same sexist joke Fielding enjoys when he has Mrs.
Heartfree insist on dragging out the story of Jonathan Wild's attempts to
assault her sexually. Hypocritical old Aunt Patty, at the advanced age of
about forty not entitled to sexual desire, is finally discovered in bed with the
old butler and turned off with an annuity of £50. One might say that this
abuse of the real old maid is motivated by her individual meanness rather
than by a more general feeling that old maids are ugly and undesirable, but
it seems truer to say that Masterman splits the figure of the woman alone in
two, allowing Emily to fulfill her wishes and leaving the self-hatred to be
projected out into Aunt Patty.

For the twentieth-century reader happening upon this rare novel, one
question immediately arises: who could have written it? Who was Ann
Masterman Skinn? The title page describes the author of *The Old Maid* as
"Mrs. Skinn, late Miss Masterman, of York," an unusual formula. A concluding "Address to the Reader" is tantalizing. There Masterman says she
is young and attractive, acquits herself of "any very particular passion for
scribbling" or "any very great opinion" of her abilities "in the literary way,"

saying instead that "some family reasons, which it is neither requisite or convenient at present to declare, were my chief inducements for publishing . . ." (3:144). Some passages in the novel she allows to be based on fact, but she denies any single character represents herself, adding:

> A character so perfectly original, I reserve for some future occasion. . . . I shall not spare Mrs. Skinn, any more than I would another, whose true portrait I meant to exhibit to public view: this will I dare say prove perfectly agreeable, as the tongue of *envy* and *malice*, have been very inveterate against me already, and only wanted genius for invention and elocution, to do me every kind of prejudice . . . (3:147–48).

As for Mr. Skinn, he is instructed that, should he like the character of Mr. Sandham the wifebeater and consider it "applicable to any of his friends," Mrs. Skinn gives him her "full permission to present them with the portrait" (3:145). In a final sour note she informs the reader that she once knew an amiable woman, but, "As for the men, I have endeavoured to make some of them tolerably decent in my book, for the sake of variety, as it is a form generally used in writing novels; but I must confess, they are entirely the children of my own brain; as I could not find one original to copy by" (3:151–52).

What could have happened to make this woman so angry? A fortunate discovery of an ecclesiastical divorce trial, "William Skinn, against Ann Skinn," has led me to some answers.[8] Ann Masterman and William Skinn were married at St. Giles's in the Fields in London on June 29, 1767.[9] At this time she was described as "a minor about twenty years of age" and the granddaughter and heiress of Henry Masterman, of Settrington, in the county of York. (She was thus only in her early twenties when she published her novel.) The Skinns lived first in Acomb and then in Bishopthorpe, both villages within a few miles of York. In November 1768, after about sixteen months of marriage, Ann left her husband, taking with her a servant about her own age, Elizabeth Morris, and the two of them settled in Hull. A servant witness for William deposed that William treated his wife "with the greatest love, tenderness, and affection." According to this account, she eloped out of motiveless malignity. In Hull at the play one evening, Ann met an attorney's clerk, Matthew Browne, who saw her home that night and who afterwards became her lover. Elizabeth Morris, the same servant, also deposed that "in or about the later end of April 1769," after a noise wakened her at night, she surprised Ann and Matthew in bed together. Elizabeth burst into tears, but Ann told her—sounding very much like Emily Ravensworth—"that nobody had any business with her conduct." About a week later the three of them went to Edinburgh, where Matthew and Ann lived together as Mr. and Mrs. Browne for at least a month. Another witness, a London woman who let lodgings in Great Rider Street, in the parish of St. James, Westminster, deposed that nearly a year later, in April 1770, Ann and Matthew hired lodgings of her for a fortnight using the names of Mr. and Mrs. Beaumont; another landlady in the same parish offered similar evidence.

In December 1770 *The Old Maid* was reviewed in the *Critical Review* and in the *Monthly Review*.[10] It would appear that Masterman wrote the novel after leaving her husband, and judging from her attitude in the "Address to the Reader," also that she had probably fallen out with her lover. The "family reasons" to which she alludes in that address probably included the necessity to contribute to her own support. They may also have included a desire to hire a proctor to make allegations against her husband in the ecclesiastical court or to defend herself against her husband's allegations.[11] On January 16, 1771, the *Daily Advertiser* announced the publication of *The Old Maid*, noting that it included "An Address to the Publick, very interesting to th: Work." Like the address, the epigraph on the title page of the new novel seems to throw down the gauntlet to Mr. Skinn:

> If any here chance to behold himself,
> Let him not dare to challenge me of wrong;
> For if he shame to have his follies known,
> First he shou'd shame to act 'em.

Less than one month later, on February 9, presumably undaunted, Mr. Skinn gave in his libel in the ecclesiastical court alleging his wife's adultery and asking for a divorce, a divorce he subsequently secured.[12]

There is some evidence, though it is less good, that Mrs. Skinn also complained of her husband at this time, indeed, that she may have initiated the divorce proceedings. According to the *Daily Advertiser*, "On Friday last the Complaint of Mrs. Skinn was opened against her Husband, in an Ecclesiastical Court, when some Charges were exhibited against him by her Counsel, which were answered by his; and Misdemeanors were alledged against her on the Part of Mr. S. The Determination of the Matter was then deferred to a future Day."[13] The *Town and Country Magazine* of February 1771 also seems to refer to the same litigation, though it too speaks only of Mr. S. and Mrs. S., rather than of Mr. and Mrs. Skinn. This account, however, asserts that Mrs. S. was a widow when she married, which judging from other evidence does not seem to have been the case. As the heiress of her grandfather, though, she may very well have possessed the £900 a year, the town and country house, elegantly furnished; and the equipage which they ascribe to her at her marriage. I am inclined to think the magazine simply mistaken about her previous marital status. Noting that "the depositions furnished great entertainment to the gentlemen of the long robe," they agree with the *Daily Advertiser* that Mrs. Skinn initiated the proceedings and add that she complained of her husband's impotence and cruelty. They attribute the following story to her side of the litigation:

> On the wedding-day they went with a number of friends to Salt-hill to celebrate their nuptials; and on the lady retiring after supper, the bridegroom followed her, and after expressing great uneasiness, explaining the coldness of his disposition; on which the lady declared, that as long as he behaved with politeness and good humor to her, she would never publish the secret he had trusted her with. About two years elapsed; during which time they to all appearances lived very happily, when Mr. S—, (as it is said) began to use his wife with great neglect, and sometimes beat her; on which she discovered her situation to a relation, who advised her to apply for a divorce, which she has accordingly done.[14]

There may be ecclesiastical court records better documenting Mrs. Skinn's allegations, but I have not yet been able to obtain them. The apparent sequence of events combined with the text of the novel and its concluding address suggest that at the time Ann Masterman wrote *The Old Maid* she was living in London and that not only her relationship with her husband, but also her relationship with her lover—if, indeed, we are to be convinced as the courts were that Matthew Browne was her lover—had deteriorated irretrievably.

From this point things went from bad to worse for Ann Masterman and Matthew Browne. Exactly a week after the ecclesiastical court proceedings opened, her husband successfully sued Browne for criminal conversation, that is, for civil damages for adultery. The *Daily Advertiser* reported:

> On Friday a Cause between a Yorkshire Gentleman, and a young Lad, lately a Clerk at Hull, was tried in Westminster Hall [i.e., King's Bench]. It seems the Gentleman's Wife took so great a Fancy to the Youth, that she left her Husband, seduced the lad from his Master's Service, and took him to Edinburgh, Aberdeen and other Places; but the Husband discovering where they cohabited, brought his action for Crim. Con. and after a full Hearing, the Jury brought in a Verdict for 200 l. Damages.[15]

Though no names are mentioned, this story almost certainly refers to the Skinns and Matthew Browne. The newspaper's account differs from the husband's witnesses in the ecclesiastical court in alleging that Ann left her husband because of her lover; its unreliability here is, perhaps, a reflection of resistance to believing that a woman would leave one man except for another. That William Skinn was awarded only £200, when £500 or £1,000 would have been a more normal verdict, may reflect simply that if Ann eloped from him before she even knew Matthew, Matthew could not be found solely responsible for William's loss of his wife's consortium.[16] The low award might also reflect a jury's judgment that William himself contributed to driving Ann away or that in some way he was not a model husband. It is very possible that young Matthew, by this point probably an unemployed attorney's clerk, was unable to pay so much as £200 and hence either had to go to jail or to become an outlaw. I have found no further trace of him.

After triumphing over Ann and Matthew in Doctors' Commons and King's Bench, William went on to a third victory in the House of Lords where he eventually secured a parliamentary divorce which would enable him to remarry. The Doctors' Commons sentence granting him his ecclesiastical divorce must have come a few months after the King's Bench verdict, perhaps at the end of April 1771.[17] On February 20, 1772, William had Lord Boston present his divorce bill in the House of Lords. This bill proceeded through the usual steps, some of William's witnesses who had already given depositions in the ecclesiastical court appearing again. The only additional witnesses to appear produced documentary evidence of the Skinns's marriage, of the criminal conversation verdict in King's Bench, and of the ecclesiastical court's sentence. Thomas Stirling, counsel for Mr. Skinn, testified that "he personally served Mrs. *Skinn*, at her Lodgings in *Buckingham Street* in the *Strand*, with the Order for the Second Reading of the Bill; and also delivered to her, at the same Time, a true Copy of the Bill; and that she then declared to him, she was satisfied with the Provision made for her, and would not oppose the Bill."[18] Masterman's behavior here seems typical of the behavior of women in her position. Reading through the eighteenth-century *Lords Journals* shows women were often not represented by counsel in divorce proceedings and very rarely contested their husband's allegations against them. One good reason for this was probably the expense of litigation in the House of Lords; husbands may very well have told wives that they would not or could not make decent settlements on them at the time of divorce if their estates were eaten up by attorney's bills and other costs of litigation. Another reason why wives so rarely contested must be that at the point of litigation in the House of Lords they usually already had one or two strikes against them in other courts: the husband had won an ecclesiastical divorce in Doctors' Commons and often also a criminal conversation verdict in the secular court. Resistance at this point probably often seemed useless.

William Skinn himself is described as "of the Middle Temple" in the *Lords Journals*, but he was not "of the Middle Temple" in the sense of having been admitted there as a student of law. He is not listed as ever having been admitted to any inn of court or to either university. He was instead an attorney, that is, not a barrister educated at the inns of court and admitted to plead at the bar, but a man trained through an apprenticeship system requiring a five-year clerkship and permitted to perform legal work short of pleading at the bar.[19] Though William does not seem to have been an active member of the Society of Gentleman Practisers in the Courts of Law and Equity, a new London mutual aid club for attorneys, he is recorded in a list of July 20, 1781, as a member complying with a general order that all members should pay one guinea for the support of the society. His name also appears in *Browne's General Law List* of 1790 as one admitted to practice in the Court of King's Bench, and his professional address is there given as King's Bench Walks, Temple.[20] William thus seems to have survived the difficulties of his domestic life with Ann.

Some hints of Ann's life after the divorce are given by obituaries, though these seem less than completely reliable. The *Gentleman's Magazine* of March 1789 noted briefly in its obituary column under March 23, "At Margate, aged 42, Mrs. Ann Emelinda Foster, grand-daughter of Henry Masterman, esq. of York." The *London Times* of March 26, 1789, reported: "On Tuesday [i.e., March 24] died at Margate, in great poverty, Mrs. Ann Emelinda Foster, aged 42, Author of The Old Maid, a Novel, and other Works. She was grand daughter to Henry Masterman, Esq. of York, and legal heir to his whole fortune. Her first husband was Mr. Skinn an attorney; her second, Nicholas Foster, Esq. an officer in the army, and son of an Irish baronet." Returning to the story in its April issue, the *Gentleman's Magazine* repeated the information in the *Times* and added:

> She was blessed by Nature with a beautiful person, and every shining talent, and had every advantage of education. . . . But such is the instability of all human attainments, that by one false step, *before she was sixteen*, she so enraged her grandfather, that he disinherited her of 3000 l. a year. Her last husband forsook and left her in extreme poverty. She supported herself by her pen and needlework for ten years past, and kept a day-school; but ill health; owing in part to exquisite sensibility and extreme poverty, lately reduced her to the greatest distress.[21]

Some of the obituary details match what we know from other sources; some do not. Ann was forty-two in 1789, she was the heiress of her grandfather, she did marry William Skinn, and she did write *The Old Maid*. Even knowing five different names she used, however, I have not been able to find any "other works" she wrote, though, of course, she may have published anonymously or under a name unknown to me. The colorful story that she was "disinherited for a false step at sixteen" does not fit with William's ecclesiastical court libel describing her at the time of their marriage as twenty and the heiress of her grandfather or with the *Town and Country Magazine* 1771 report of her wealth at the time of this marriage. It seems significant that the obituary, having overcome inhibitions about speaking ill of the dead, does not mention her involvement in divorce or criminal conversation proceedings. The story, I would think, is wrong and perhaps represents a later version of the gossip produced by her sexual misconduct as a young woman. If she died in poverty, the poverty was probably not the result of her grandfather's early anger, but in part, at least, of William's success in the divorce settlement.

This obituary in the *Gentleman's Magazine* has been noticed before by J. M. S. Tompkins in *The Popular Novel in England, 1770–1800*; she uses it uncritically to illustrate the proposition that "in the history of Mrs. Skinn we have a typical case of the circumstances that drove a woman into authorship."[22] The impression is given by Tompkins's account that Ann's poverty resulting from her alleged disinheritance at sixteen by her grandfather, from her having been widowed by Skinn, and from her alleged abandonment by Foster led her to become a novelist. We have seen that she was probably not disinherited by her grandfather before her marriage, and that she wrote *The Old Maid* at twenty-three before she could have been involved with Foster. Though the obituary does not say that William Skinn died before Ann married Foster and though, in fact, William survived her, Tompkins assumes that William was dead and says, "She married Mr. Skinn, an attorney, and on his death Nicholas Foster." James Foster, in *The History of the Pre-romantic Novel in England*, without citing either the obituary or Tompkins, repeats this story with some slight changes and embellishments. Ann's name becomes "Anne Amelia Masterman," she is "widowed" by Skinn, and Nicholas Foster is "a heartless Irish officer."[23] Foster's version is in turn repeated by Madeleine Blondel.

There seems to have been no Nicholas Foster who was the son of a recognized Irish baronet, but there was an Irish Nicholas Foster born in 1758 who could trace his lineage back to one Sir Humphrey Foster who fought for Cromwell in Ireland. Nicholas's older brother Thomas was later (in 1794) created a baronet, probably relying in part on this inheritance. According to Burke's *Baronetage*, this Nicholas rose to be a colonel in the army and died in 1805.[24] I can find no record of him in the English *Army Lists*, but he may have been in the Irish army. If there were such a Nicholas who married Ann, and if he abandoned her ten years before her death, they could not have lived together for very long, since he would have been only fourteen at the time of her parliamentary divorce. I doubt very much that "exquisite sensibility" contributed to Ann's demise, but it is not difficult to imagine her finishing her days at Margate in the 1780s, Margate by then having become a fashionable spa where drinking seawater and bathing in the ocean for one's health could be supplemented with walks on the sand, visits to the ships, and attendance at public balls and entertainments.[25]

Ann Skinn may have run away from her husband for what no eighteenth-century court would have considered good reasons, taken a lover, and then invented tales of her husband's brutality (and impotence) out of a desire for self-justification. Certainly the author of *The Old Maid* makes no profession of devotion to conventional morality; on the contrary, she seems to insist on a woman's right to do as she pleases. On the other hand, it is possible that Ann's complaints of William were founded on fact. It is even possible that William bribed his witnesses—servants and mistresses of lodging houses—to perjure themselves in testifying to Ann's adultery; perjury has frequently been common in divorce trials.

What we do know is that when she wrote *The Old Maid* at about age twenty-three Ann Masterman was living apart from a husband who eventually divorced her, that she rejected the conventional eighteenth-century restraints on female behavior, and that she was angry at men in general and at the social world they had created. The reviews which appeared of her novel were unlikely to soften her attitudes. Only two noticed her book, neither of them warmly. The *Monthly Review* said tersely—I quote their notice in its entirety—"Although there are defects in this work gross enough to disgust a critical reader, there are parts of it that will be far from disagreeable to a good-natured one, who is fond of novels, and not too nice in his choice of them." The writer in the *Critical Review* began by saying that he was disgusted with novels in general and that his "nausea" was not relieved in the slightest by *The Old Maid.* Emily—who I may say after reading the novel with my own undergraduates, strikes the twentieth-century reader as a rather natural girl and a very refreshing change from the more usual repressed and sentimental eighteenth-century heroines—this critic considers "so inconsistent a character, that we need not scruple to say, such a one never did exist in real life."[26] Such an initial response served effectually to bury *The Old Maid* and there were no further editions. It is now an extremely rare book, only the Houghton copy being recorded in the *National Union Catalogue.* Banished from the canon like most of the eighteenth-century novels by women, *The Old Maid* and Masterman herself get very brief and sometimes inaccurate mention only in comprehensive literary histories.

It may be that *The Old Maid* is at least as much worth our time as such secondary canonical texts as *Peregrine Pickle* or *Fanny Hill*. When critics are investing so much energy in exposing the patriarchal ideology implicit in popular eighteenth-century texts like *Pamela* or *Manon Lescaut*, we might spare some attention for Ann Masterman's spirited and comic protest against that ideology. And who knows what other lives of women, what other texts, having provoked initial nausea in male critics, still lie unread?

NOTES

1. *Critical Review* 30 (December 1770): 479.

2. Ann Masterman Skinn, *The Old Maid: or, The History of Miss Ravensworth*, 3 vols. (London, 1771). Further references appear in parentheses in the text.

3. Paula R. Backscheider, "Women's Influence," *Studies in the Novel* 11 (1979): 3–22.

4. For Evelina's situation see, Susan Staves, "*Evelina*; or, Female Difficulties," *Modern Philology* 73 (1976): 368–81.

5. *The Early Diary of Frances Burney, 1768–78*, A. R. Ellis, ed., 2 vols. (London: George Bell & Sons, 1889), 2:47–71; Jane Austen, *Pride and Prejudice*, Frank W. Bradbrook, ed. (London: Oxford University Press, 1970), vol. 1, chap. 19, pp. 93–98.

6. "He is a little, fat, bloated monster, about thirty—his face carbuncled, so as to render it dangerous to come near so fiery a phenomenon—his eyes are little, grey, sunk about half a foot into his head—his nose made of rather (if possible) more combustible materials than his face—his mouth is of the true sparrow kind, and when he grins, betrays too visibly the bad furniture within; for he seems not to have a sound tooth in his head" (2:139).

7. On *Millenium Hall* see, Edith Larson, "Early Eighteenth-Century Women Writers: Their Lives, Fiction, and Letters" (Ph.D. diss., Brandeis University, 1980), 141–66.

8. "William Skinn, against Ann Skinn" was probably published as a pamphlet about 1771, though I have found it only in the following connections: *Trials for Adultery: or, The History of Divorces. Being Select Trials at Doctors Commons . . . From the Year 1760 to the Present Time. . . .* , 7 vols. (London: S. Bladon, 1779–80), vol. 4; *A New and Complete Collection of Trials for Adultery: or a General History of Gallantry and Divorce . . . From the Year 1780 to the Middle of the Year 1797* (London, 1796), vol. 3. Trials in both collections are separately paginated; the later collection reprints the earlier trial.

9. "William Skinn, against Ann Skinn," p. 1, gives date; *Journals of the House of Lords* 33:284, gives place and same date. Subsequent statements in this paragraph are based on "William Skinn, against Ann Skinn."

10. *Critical Review* 30 (December 1770): 478–79; *Monthly Review* 43 (December 1770): 500.

11. In theory, the ecclesiastical courts could require husbands to pay their wives's costs and there is evidence that in some cases they did so; in practice, women may not have found it easy to obtain both court costs and fees to pay the proctors of their choice.

12. Libel so dated in "William Skinn, against Ann Skinn"; Randolph Trumbach, personal communication, reports he has seen the libel with this date in the Greater London Record Office. I plan at a later time to visit London, York, and Margate to look for additional material on the Skinns in archives and in local newspapers not currently available on film.

13. Daily Advertiser, February 12 [Tuesday], 1771.

14. *Town and Country Magazine* 3 (February 1771): 110; the same report, almost verbatim, appears in *Scots Magazine* 33 (1771): 107.

15. Daily Advertiser, February 19 [Tuesday], 1771.

16. For the principles of calculating damages and the usual ranges of damages in criminal conversation see, Susan Staves, "Money for Honor: Damages for Criminal Conversation," *Studies in Eighteenth-Century Culture* 11 (1982): 279–97.

17. The last two depositions in "William Skinn, against Ann Skinn" are dated April 22, 1771; the sentence is undated.

18. *Journals of the House of Lords* 33:251 (February 18, 1772); 256–57 (February 20, 1772); 276 (March 3, 1772); 284 (March 6, 1772); 288 (March 9, 1772); 291 (March 10, 1772); 341 (April 6, 1772); 372 (April 16, 1772); 284 (March 6, 1772).

19. For an account of the social status and work of attorneys see, Robert Robson, *The Attorney in Eighteenth-Century England* (Cambridge: Cambridge University Press, 1959).

20. *The Records of the Society of Gentlemen Practisers in the Courts of Law and Equity*, Introduction by Edwin Freshfield (London: Incorporated Law Society, 1897), 153. There are law lists beginning in 1757, but I have not yet seen them; Skinn is absent from the Browne's list of 1795, which suggests that he may have retired or died by that time.

21. *Gentleman's Magazine* 59[1] (March 1789): 281; London Times, March 26, 1789; *Gentleman's Magazine* 59[1] (April 1789): 373.

22. J. M. S. Tompkins, *The Popular Novel in England, 1770–1800* (orig. 1932; reprint, Lincoln, Neb.: University of Nebraska Press, 1961), 122.

23. James Foster, *The History of the Pre-romantic Novel in England* (New York: Modern Language Association, 1949), 154; Madeleine Blondel, *Images de la femme dans le roman anglais de 1740 à 1771*, 2 vols. (Lille: Atelier Reproduction des theses, Universite Lille III, 1976), 1:591, 604–5.

24. John Burke, *A Genealogical and Heraldic Dictionary of the Peerage and Baronetage of the British Empire* (London, 1842). Cf. "Foster, The Rev. Sir Thomas" and "Foster, Rt. Hon. Sir Augustus-John."

25. William Hugh Dalton, *The New and Complete English Traveller: Or, a New Historical Survey and Modern Description of England and Wales* (London: Alex. Hogg, n.d.), 29.

26. *Monthly Review* 43 (December 1770): 500; *Critical Review* 30 (December 1770): 478.

"Descending Angels"

Salubrious Sluts and Pretty Prostitutes in Haywood's Fiction

MARY ANNE SCHOFIELD

In 1731 Sarah Millwood, London prostitute, protests:

> I curse your barbarous sex, who robb'd me of [my virtues] e'er I knew their worth; then left me, too late, to count their value by their loss. Another and another Spoiler came, and all my gain was poverty and reproach.[1]

She expresses *the* feminine concern of the eighteenth century: the wholesale takeover of the female self by the male machine. But Sarah's plea is not a solitary one, nor was the whore a voiceless victim. Notables such as Jonathan Swift and Bernard Mandeville in *Essay upon Projects* (1707) and *A Modest Defence of the Public Stews* (1724) respectively had taken on the cause of the common prostitute, but their "defences" merely added to the feminine plight. Mandeville, for example, argues that civil authorities would do well to permit what they cannot suppress and suggests as an alternative the establishment of publicly licensed and medically supervised houses of prostitution; he proposes that government should staff, license, and operate such establishments as a monopoly serving the highest public interest. He notes in *A Modest Defense* that "public whoring is neither so criminal in itself, nor so detrimental to the society, as private whoring," for the "mischief a man does in this case is entirely to himself; for with respect to the woman, he does a laudable action, in furnishing her with the means of subsistence, in the only, or at least, most innocent way that she is capable of procuring it." Though he condescendingly admits that "they themselves in reality utterly abhor it," Mandeville concludes that "these women," their minds being "so corrupted by the loss of chastity," will not change, and, therefore, he offers a program that will "legalize" a situation that cannot (and, in his estimate, should not) be eradicated. As he had pontificated earlier in *The Fable of the Bees* (1714): "It is manifest, that there is a necessity of sacrificing one part of womanhood to preserve the other."[2]

Mandeville's opinion, fortunately for the female sex, had a large number of dissenters, even among the male population. Indeed, George Lillo, albeit unconsciously, would not submit to total female degradation, and, though Sarah Millwood and George Barnwell are publicly punished at the end of their drama, it is not as a fallen woman who gets her due that one remembers her; rather, Millwood is notable because of what she tells us about the power shift, a subtle transfer of authority from the male to the female, that prostitution, if managed correctly, involves. And it is this issue of power rather than the reform programs of Swift, Mandeville, Steele, Bishop Burnet, Josiah Woodward, and others that captures the attention of the woman novelists, most especially Eliza Haywood. Not content to reduce the female prostitute to an object of mere physical titillation and stimulation, these novelists stripped her of the "romance" the male had thrown up around the figure and proceeded to anatomize and catalogue the prostitute for feminine fiction. The prostitute, like far too many of her sisters, these novelists realized, was part and parcel of the all-consuming, male-controlled dehumanization of women.

Specifically, the major female novelists of the eighteenth-century—Eliza Haywood, Sarah Fielding, Elizabeth Inchbald, and Charlotte Smith— were very aware of the trivialization of women. Themselves the victims of this economic-social phenomenon of virtual feminine dehumanization, they watched as the majority of women suffered the same fate. With the growth of the cities (most especially, London), the effective closing down and closing out of women from the home industry—coupled with extremes of poverty and moneyed leisure time—the eighteenth-century female found herself shunted aside, turned into a mere sexual plaything, a commodity to be bid upon, bargained for, and bedded by the male.[3]

Although the age witnessed a change in family structure with daughters exerting more influence in regard to husband selection according to Lawrence Stone, Janelle Greenberg, W. L. Blease, and I. B. O'Malley, their legal and economic situation (and sometimes social state) remained at a subjugation level. The eighteenth-century woman had been "trivialized"; totally lacking in power and independence, she became the financial responsibility of the male with whom she lived. Not only nice women, but their not-so-nice cousins, the prostitutes, also became the responsibility of the male. Seymour-Smith notes that "by the end of the seventeenth century, it was estimated . . . that there were altogether 50,000 prostitutes in London alone, twice the number in Paris",[4] a figure that clearly emphasizes the existence of male patronage and use.

According to psychologist Claudeen Cline-Naffziger, women were and are reduced by the male-imposed "shrinking phenomenon"; forced into inferior roles and patterns of behavior, women were quickly diminished in their own minds and in those of the controlling male. Unfortunately, there were not many avenues of escape open to them. Short of destitution or death, they had recourse only to prostitution or fiction as a means of escape. In order to elude her male controllers, the leisured, upper-class married lady, for example, "prostituted" herself in order to relieve her boredom; her very lower-class cousin found similarly that selling her body was preferable to the utter damnation of selling body and soul to fourteen or sixteen hours of work in a sweatshop as a seamstress or a mantua maker. And some women, in order to escape the actuality and drudgery of their fate turned to fiction, to imaginary domains where their dispossessed, unfulfilled, stagnant lives soon took on new meaning.[5] In "romance," either physical or fictional, lives that had lost their meaning were suddenly transformed, and women, dispossessed economically and socially, could once again feel fulfilled.

Whether through sex or fantasy, the eighteenth-century female was looking for an antidote to relieve her fettered state. And, ironically enough, this freedom came, for the literate woman at least, through the greatest figure of female imprisonment and exploitation: the prostitute. Her verbal sisters, the novelists and hack writers of the period, recognizing that the source of their power lay in taking her tale and the male-created character of the prostitute and subverting both for their own purposes, wrote passionately vitriolic yet disguised stories of these exploited women. Aware that they must control "anything that looks like a threat or competition," Barbara Bellow Watson observes of women writers of all periods that their readers "must not expect . . . the literature written by women . . . to tell us much about so sensitive a topic [that of the female self] in the form of declarations, manifestoes, plot summaries, or even broad outlines of characterizations." Instead, she continues, "we begin . . . to look at such techniques as ambiguity, equivocation, and expressive symbolic structures."[6] John Dollard explains, in his landmark study *Frustration and Aggression*, that it is usual for the frustrated to turn this emotion inside, to cover it over; but like a sore, the frustration does not dissolve; it merely festers. He concludes that "the existence of frustration always leads to some form of aggression. . . . [Thus] although these reactions may be temporarily compressed, delayed, disguised, displaced, or otherwise deflected from their immediate and logical goal, they are not destroyed."[7]

It is just such "symbolic structures" that the sluts and slatterns of the minor fiction of the eighteenth century form when examined en masse. The women novelists turn these "questionable types" into militant symbols of feminine aggression. The prostitute becomes an avatar of their unspoken thoughts about the plight of women, and through this figure of the fallen woman, the novelist criticizes her fallen world. The male is responsible for her degraded circumstances just as he is to blame for her initial exploitation and her dehumanization. The male created the type to exhibit his control and power; the female novelist inverts the figure to display her own strength and to reclaim these seduced and seducing women.

Their power, however, had to be hidden, and the novels, like the prostitute figure herself, only revealed their true sentiment if read "femininely," parenthetically. Haywood explains her subversive technique when she writes in *The Female Spectator*: "A modest wife should therefore never affect the virago. . . . it is not by force our sex can hope to maintain their influence over the men, and I again repeat it as the infallible maxim, that whenever we would truly conquer, we must seem to yield."[8]

What is created through their use of the prostitute and her story is what Nancy K. Miller labels the "heroine's text," the "text of an ideology that codes femininity in paradigms of sexual vulnerability."[9] The prostitute is the most vulnerable of women. Continually raped, she is paid to acquiesce docilely to male power—that is what rape is: "man's basic weapon of force against woman, the principal agent of his will and her fear." Susan Brownmiller continues: "His forcible entry into her body . . . became the vehicle of his victorious conquest over her being, the ultimate test of his superior strength, the triumph of his manhood."[10] Prostitution is salaried rape. It is an act of assertion of male supremacy, and that is the male text, the male story. Decoded, deconstructed, and translated into the heroine's text, this exploitation of female vulnerability becomes, paradoxically, the female's greatest source of power and influence. Docility and submission are reconstructed into aggression and control. Converting the heroine's forced "growing down" back to her normal "growing up,"[11] Haywood takes the prostitute figure and reveals her inherent power and control. Through this grown-up figure, Haywood and the other women novelists legitimize their feelings of rage.

Hence, salubrious sluts. Through these slatterns, female novelists are able to express the anger and frustration of their enslaved position and are able to control the male. Sluts and prostitutes, slatterns and mistresses, become healthier figures than the docile, pale heroines who proliferate the pages of the popular romances. They "tell" women that it is all right to be angry, that it is right to sell out for the female self, that it is correct to prostitute one's self for other women but never for a man. In their very being, they express the suppressed sexuality and hidden power that is inherently found in being female.

Eliza Haywood as the most popular and prolific novelist of the period is

well aware of this revolutionary aspect of the prostitute and her use of this
figure is quintessentially that of the age. Each of her sluts (and there are
graduated scales of each, just as there are grades of prostitutes) is the embodiment of her anger and the incarnation of her sense of control and
power over the male. In each type, she "transmogrifies" her feelings of
anger into those of female control.

There is, first, the "merry" prostitute found in *Fantomina; or, Love in a
Maze* (1724), a very early novel, and then later as a slightly older figure in
*Anti-Pamela; or, Feigned Innocence Detected in a Series of Syrena's Ad-
ventures* (1741). These prostitutes are presented in a happy, healthy fashion; they control their men and have a grand time doing so. Fantomina, for
example is not a "true" prostitute, but just a young girl enjoying her first
"fling"! In direct contrast, the second type, is the woman who is physically
and mentally forced to become a mistress-prostitute to a man she does not
care for; there is nothing merry about *Lasselia; or, The Self-Abandoned*
(1724); *Idalia; or, The Unfortunate Mistress* (1723); or *The Fatal Secret; or,
Constancy in Distress* (1725); the woman here is totally controlled by the
male, and her only way to freedom is through death. The third type of
prostitute is the reverse of the first. Rather than buoyant good spirits reflected in her ability to control the male, prostitutes like Glicera of *The City
Jilt; or, The Alderman Turned Beau: A Secret History* (1726), Henrietta of
The Life of Madam de Villesache (1727), and Gigantilla of *The Perplexed
Dutchess* (1728) mercilessly persecute and torture men in their role as mistresses. These viragos express Haywood's most uncensored hatred of men
who have forced women into this position of "self"-selling.

Haywood's first experiments with the type are not brutal, yet they adequately display her anger. Here she reverses the rape-of-innocence theme
so prevalent in the literature of the period and has the far-from-innocent
Beauplaisir "raped" by an initially naive Fantomina. Bred in the country,
Fantomina is transplanted to London and was, as Haywood writes,
"young, a stranger to the World, and consequently to the Dangers of it."[12]
Observing various "ladies of fashion," Fantomina decides "to dress herself
as near as she cou'd in the Fashion of those Women who make sale of their
Favours, and set herself on the Way of being accosted as such a one, having
at that Time no other Aim, than the Gratification of an innocent Curiosity"
(p. 258). She is so successful in her disguise that soon "A Crowd of Purchasers of all Degrees and Capacities were in a Moment gather'd about her,
each endeavouring to out-bid the other, in offering her Price for her Embraces" (p. 258). She is even more pleased "when She saw the accomplish'd
Beauplaisir was making his Way thro' the Crowd as fast as he was able, to
reach the Bench she sat on" (p. 258). He addresses her in the usual fashion

of salutations for her pretended profession: "Are you engag'd, Madam?—
Will you permit me to wait on you home after the Play?—By Heaven, you
are a fine Girl!—How long have you us'd this House?" (p. 259), but, Haywood continues:

> perceiving she had a Turn of Wit, and a genteel Manner in her Raillery, beyond
> what is frequently to be found among those Wretches . . . he chang'd the
> Form of his Conversation, and shew'd her it was not because he understood no
> better, that he had made use of Expressions so little polite. (P. 259)

From the first, then, Fantomina has him in control. She has forced him to
change his style of address; she will ultimately compel him to give up soliciting prostitutes.

In the meantime, though, Beauplaisir is unaware that she is anything but
what she appears to be and, "presuming on the liberties which her suppos'd
Function allow'd," he clamors for her body. "In vain," Haywood writes,
"she endeavored to delay till the next meeting, the fulfilling of his Wishes"
(p. 262). Notice carefully Haywood's language, as she continues: "She had
now gone too far to retreat:—*He* was bold;—he was resolute: *She*
fearful,—confus'd altogether unprepar'd to resist in such Encounters.
. . . In fine, she was undone" (pp. 262–63). Beauplaisir is the victor; she,
the vanquished, but not for long. This is the male version of the story;
Haywood subtly inverts the persecuted innocence theme, and victim and
victimizer exchange roles in her effort to show how to control the male.
Fantomina creates her own fiction: "She therefore said she was the Daughter of a Country Gentleman, who was come to Town to buy Cloaths, and
that she was call'd Fantomina" (p. 264), and then continues the charade,
masquerading as Celia the chambermaid, then the Widow Bloomer, and
finally as the Fair Incognita. Fantomina was an extraordinary manager;
"She preserved an OEcomomy [sic] in the management of this Intreague
[sic], beyond what almost any woman but herself ever did: In the first
Place, by making no Person in the World a Confident [sic] in it; and in the
next, in concealing from *Beauplaisir* himself the Knowledge who she was"
(p. 266).

But Beauplaisir is fickle like all men. "He varied not so much from his sex
as to be able to prolong Desire, to any great length after Possession: The
rifled Charms of *Fantomina* soon lost their Poinancy [sic], and grew taste-
less and insipid" (p. 267). As Beauplaisir tired of one woman, she artfully
became another and continued to control him. Beauplaisir in his false sense
of male superiority thinks himself well rid of one female, and, in his journey
out of town, he begins looking around for another. In her "round ear'd

Cap, a short Red Petticoat, and a little Jacket of Grey Stuff" (p. 268), Fantomina looks every inch the innocent chambermaid. Beauplaisir "was fir'd with the first sight of her and he soon lost the power of containing himself. . . . [He] devour'd her Lips, her Breasts with greedy Kisses . . . nor suffer'd her to get loose, till he had ravaged all" (pp. 269–70). Yet Beauplaisir is the victim, not Fantomina. Haywood's rage is quite near the surface here. Neither Haywood nor Fantomina will be undone a second time. Though ravished here, Fantomina vows never to be trivialized, dehumanized, again. She claims to "have outwitted even the most subtle of the deceiving kind, and while he thinks to fool me, is himself the only beguiled person" (p. 277), and for a time, Haywood writes, "she had all the Sweets of Love, but as yet had tasted none of the Gall" (p. 277). Fantomina's entire attitude is a healthy one from the female novelist's point of view; she is aware of the fickleness of the male's affections and will not be undone by it. Rather she will control. Fantomina challenges "all neglected Wives, and fond abandon'd Nymphs;" they, too, can control. Were women to adopt her aggressive methods, "Men would be caught in there [sic] own Snare" (p. 283).

Fantomina triumphs over the male, and she does so gaily and with spirit. But she cannot get the best of nature and her mother (she is pregnant), for "now all her Invention was at a loss for a Stratagem to impose on a Woman of her Penetration" (p. 287). Ironically, Fantomina is trapped by that very sex she exercises throughout her tale. Though forced to confess at the conclusion of her tale and sent to a monastery in France, Fantomina does not seem to be at all subdued; the reader is left with the impression that Fantomina will continue her wiles on that continent as well.

There is something thoroughly delightful and refreshing about Fantomina. Though she is, in the strictest sense, a vitriolic embodiment of Haywood's own rage at female exploitation, there is an endearing quality about her. Haywood liked this "salubrious slut" and returned to the type several times in the course of her writing career. Perhaps the most famous is her 1741 creation of *Anti-Pamela* written to counter the pervasive Pamela myth, that popular "fiction" of willful, feminine submission. This time, however, the protagonist is a true "lady of fashion," but still a woman who can control men. Before she was out of her bib, she was instructed in the arts of intrigue and coquetry and "was trained up to deceive and betray all these whom her Beauty should allure."[13] But Syrena, like Fantomina, is an experienced dissembler, and Haywood writes that long before her thirteenth birthday, "she excell'd . . . in a lively assuming [of] all the different passions that find entrance in a Female Mind" (p. 2). Syrena, like Fantomina, was able to control not only the males, but several female types as well. Because Syrena "was capable of loving in reality nothing but herself" (p. 45), she was able to destroy male after male. Mr. W_____ calls her "a Fiend . . . under an Angel's Form" (p. 229) and cannot believe the depths of her prostitution. And yet, until her final encounter with Mr. E_____, Syrena is a happy avatar of Haywood's frustration and rage. She enjoys men too numerous to mention and moves from one bed to another with glee. She controls them all. Only toward the end, when she seems incapable of making new, unique fictions does Syrena Tricksy become the "monstrous incestuous Strumphet" (p. 229) Mr. W_____ labels her. Before, she is able to project the image the man expected and to control him. At the last, though, and this is Haywood's true assessment of the type, these women have been the product of a great hoax: "The Notion she had been bred up in, that a Woman who had Beauty to attract the Men, and Cunning to manage afterwards, was secure of making her Fortune, appeared now altogether fallacious" (p. 261). At the last, the prostitute who is unwilling to assert herself and demand more of herself, will remain a dupe. She is totally hoodwinked by the male's fictions.

As much buoyancy and life as there is in Fantomina and Syrena, so there is the corresponding amount of hatred and nastiness in the third type of prostitute. Here Haywood is unable to mask her own aggression and her hatred of the situation that she finds women in. Her hostilities surface in such characters as Glicera, Henrietta, and Gigantilla. Each woman prostitutes her body in order to gain wealth, power, and most especially, control which she exercises over the duped male. These women display no mercy: they intentionally sell their bodies in order to gain mind control over the lesser men. Fierce viragos, they rage through a large number of Haywood's novels. One of the most calculating is Glicera, the protagonist of *The City Jilt* (1726).

The story begins with the upcoming wedding of Glicera to Melladore; unfortunately, before the happy event can take place, Glicera's father dies leaving her virtually penniless. Glicera initially, however, is not savvy.

> She thought it yet a less terrible Misfortune to lose her *Father* than a *Lover* who was so dear to her, and by whom she believed herself so sincerely and tenderly belov'd, that she should know no want of any other Friend.[14]

With no money, she is far less attractive, and Melladore ceases to think of marriage and contemplates rape instead: "His nobler Inclinations all were fled, and brutal Appetite alone remained" (p. 7). He seduces and violates her, and Glicera becomes his mistress. Still content to see only what she wants, "O'er whelm'd in Tenderness, and lost to every Thought but that of giving Pleasure to the dear Undoer, was she for a time content with what she had done, nor once imagined how despicable she was now grown in his Eyes for that very Action which she had yielded to but to endear him more" (p. 7). Discovering that she is pregnant, she begs for marriage, "But he had now obtained his wanton Purpose, Desire was satiated" (p. 8), and she is spurned. "Never was rage carried to a greater height than hers,—she seem'd all Fury—and distracted with her wrongs, beholding the cruel Author of them rather exulting than any way compassionating her Misery, she said and did a thousand things which could not be reconciled to Reason" (p. 9). The virago, she writes to Melladore, has been unleashed—"what a dreadful Revolution has thy Ingratitude caused within my Breast—my Thoughts before serene as an unruffled Sea, now toss'd and hurried by tumultuous Passions, o'erwhelm my Reason, and drive me into Madness" (pp. 14–15). Her rape leads to a hatred of "that whole undoing Sex. . . . she never rejoic'd as much as when she heard of the Misfortunes of any of them" (p. 20). Glicera vows to get even. She does so by selling her body to all men. She smiles and smiles and yet is a villain to the race of men. "The Hatred which Melladore's Ingratitude had created in her Mind was so fix'd and rooted there that it became part of her Nature, and she seem'd born only to give Torment to the whole Race of Man, nor did she know another Joy in Life" (p. 29). She manipulates Alderman Grubguard until she is able to buy Melladore's mortgage and financially ruin him, then she discards Grubguard. Her prostitution has paid off, and Haywood has been able to vent her spleen on the horrible race of men.

Haywood's most memorable characters appear in this group of the third type of prostitute. She takes more than a special interest in these "mad women" because they become her most outspoken characters for her own vitriolic creed. Henrietta, the protagonist of *The Life of Madam de Villesache* (1727) is an even more aggressive manipulator and controller-prostitute than Glicera.

The story begins amiably enough as Haywood details the country life of the young Henrietta, her love for Clermont, and the idyllic quality of her life there. She is taught to use her mind and at an early age demonstrates great logic. Her pastoral retreat abruptly ends when her father refuses to allow her to rusticate any longer, and takes her to court. "Now begun the Heart of this young Beauty to be sensible of Disquiet."[15] Her new life at court creates doubts about her earlier life, and "By degrees she began to look back on all that had past with a kind of contempt: after which, 'tis needless to say she resented having so hastily dispos'd of herself" (p. 13). Soon Henrietta has thrown over her former existence and wishes to be known only as Madam de Villesache. She "prostitutes" herself, offers herself to the Marquis de Ab＿＿le and marries him, ostensibly, she tells herself to help Clermont. She offers Clermont a position at court; in reality, she has done it all for herself. Madam de Villesache is entranced with power, and when the ability to have such unilateral control is presented to her, she cannot resist. Madam de Villesache, however, only succeeds in manipulating for a while. Unlike others of her type, Haywood expresses some ambivalence with Henrietta; though she successfully manipulates and controls for many years, in the end, her tactics are too severe—she almost poisons her husband's body in order to destroy his mind—and she has to be punished. The marquis finally recovers his sanity and reasserts his rights. He

> stabb'd her to the Heart . . . rip'd her open with an unmanly Brutality, and taking thence the Innocent unborn, stuck it on the point of his remorseless Sword, then threw it down in Scorn by the bleeding Parent. (P. 59)

Then he goes mad.

Madam de Villesache's fate points the way toward the second type of prostitute; however, this model of the whore does not enjoy the power and control of women like Madam de Villesache.

The second type of prostitute found in Haywood's fiction is not only the most tragic sort, but she also makes up the majority number. With this kind, Haywood describes the utter destruction men have brought to women. Haywood has written a very large number of novels of this sort, and, clearly, here her anger is only thinly veiled. She writes in the Dedication to *Lasselia* (1724): "My Design in writing this Little Novel . . . being only to remind the unthinking Part of the World, how dangerous it is to give way to Passion."[16] Haywood carefully delineates the destructive folly women indulge in who sell their bodies in the misguided notion that it will lead to a freedom for their souls. It leads only to suffering and damnation as Lasselia's tale illustrates.

The story is set in the opulent court of Louis XIV. When the King suddenly turns his lecherous eye on the young, innocent Lasselia, a young woman who knows her own mind, "no austere Parent, or Guardian [could] . . . over-awe Aversion, and force her to receive with Smiles the Man she hated—No Hopes, no Tears, Suspence, Perplexity, nor racking Jealousies, disturb'd her Peace or Mind" (pp. 9–10). So in order to avoid scandal and an obvious rape, she leaves the court and goes to the country town of Collumiers. There, meeting Monsieur de l'Amye, she is quite captivated with him, but disguises her attraction since he is a married man. De l'Amye is not as discreet; he writes and declares his love. When Lasselia receives the letter "alternate Joy and Shame, Surprize and Fear, sometimes a Start of virtuous Pride and Indignation sparkled in her Eyes" (pp. 22–3). Haywood continues: "Thus born away with a Tide of Delight . . . all the Warnings of her good Genius were hush'd, and her whole Soul was over-whelm'd with Passion (p. 23). De l'Amye persuades her it is "no crime to bless a love so perfect as his" (p. 30), and they are soon embroiled in a tempestuous affair, for "She had now gone too far in the fatal Labyrinth of heedless Passion, to know how to Retreat; and the Arguments he had made use of to persuade her . . . had the same Effect they ordinarily work'd on all whom he endeavour'd to bring to his Opinion; to make her think as he did" (p. 30). De l'Amye has reduced Lasselia to the level of his mistress. Not only has he diminished her unique person to a mere sexual object used to gratify his own appetites, but he has also taken away her feminine selfhood.

Lasselia is punished not only mentally, but physically as well. Their affair is discovered—ironically enough, one of de l'Amye's former mistresses sees them together and tells his wife. Only Lasselia is punished and suffers. De l'Amye placidly returns to his wife; Lasselia is immured in a convent for the rest of her life.

But it is *Idalia* (1723), an earlier novel, that presents the most detailed examination of the female psyche in Haywood's early fiction and, without a doubt, in all of the minor fiction of the early period. It is one of the most gruesome, horrific portraits of the utter ruin and damnation man has brought to woman when he turns her into a prostitute.

Idalia's problems begin with her parents—their indulgent, doting acquiescence to her desires, her "greatness of Spirit, made her, in Haywood's words, "unable to endure Controll, disdainfull of Advice, obstinate, and peremptory in following her own Will."[17] Her father screens her suitors and attempts to order and control her future. Idalia, however, is not so acquiescent. "She began immediately to lessen her Regard for her too-long indulgent father, which by degrees repin'd to a contempt of him, and ended in a Resolution to act in every Thing according to her Inclinations" (p. 4). The overindulgence subscribed to by her parents, the false sense of self and power that they have given her, is quickly put to the test with Florez and his associates. When, for example, she agrees to an assignation with him, Idalia is convinced that she will be the controller; but when Don Ferdinand comes in Florez's place, rapes Idalia, and then discards her to Henriquez, Idalia is forcefully confronted with the extreme falseness of her education and her extreme vulnerability. But her parents' training has been so shallow that Idalia does not consciously recognize the extraordinary severity of her fate.

Idalia has been totally hoodwinked; no matter how much she is abused by men, she maintains her position of "new-made slave" (p. 77) and joyously seeks another union with a man. She is the rankest, grossest example of total female exploitation. When Don Myrtano, Henriquez's brother, comes to Idalia with the results of the duel (Henriquez and Ferdinand had fought over her)—they both die—he, too, is totally captivated by her and vows to take control. Myrtano is just about to succeed in perpetrating his desires (with conscious compliance on Idalia's part), when virtue, a characteristic that Idalia has developed on her own, surfaces, and triumphs over her desires. Though not physically raped at this time, she has been mentally violated; she has been "solicited for a Prostitute" (p. 53), has been turned into a possession, a mere plaything by Florez, Ferdinand, and Myrtano. Her cry—"can e'er the Days of Innocence Return" (2:63)—is one echoed by all Haywood's women. The idyllic retreat of self-refuge has been violated.

Idalia's entire existence follows the pattern of rape, escape, and return. Since she is Haywood's incarnate symbol of feminine exploitation, it is fitting that she is moved from one rape scene to another. As she runs away from Myrtano, for example, she is captured and again almost raped by Sea Captain Richamboll; she is saved from his embraces by the Corsair Abdomar, who is the only man who does not exploit her. Haywood interrupts Idalia's story to tell Abdomar's tale, but it becomes merely a pastoral version of Idalia's own story of innocence betrayed. In this world of betrayal, there is no place of safety or refuge, and Idalia is forced to move on. Disguised as a man, she is further persecuted by robbers and by Donna Antonia, ironically enough, Myrtano's wife, who falls in love with her as a disguised man. Idalia must prostitute herself once again. Her adventures continue in this fashion until Idalia finally becomes what all men had transformed her into: a courtesan. Haywood writes: "She began to curse the Cause which had reduc'd her to a condition, such as could give room for Liberties so contrary to what she had been us'd to receive, and could so ill bear:—She wanted Revenge on all who durst to use her in this Manner;—and not having it in her Power, was ready to burst with inward Spleen, and stifled Indignation" (p. 60). Idalia finally does take action: seeing a cavalier from her window, she thinks it is Florez. Enraged and wanting to punish him for all that she has suffered, she stabs him; it was not Florez but Myrtano that she killed; in utter dismay and disillusionment, Idalia then kills herself. Death is the only road to freedom after such wholesale abuse and exploitation of the female self. The only control Idalia can have over her life is her own choice of whether or not to continue it. This is the extreme position that women can find themselves in; *Idalia* is Haywood's most blatant revelation of this state and fate of the eighteenth-century woman. Haywood will no longer let her condition disguise itself, and she strips away the "mask" that women had been forced to adopt.

In a corresponding piece, *The Fatal Secret; or, Constancy in Distress* (1725), the beautiful Anadea is betrothed to marry the Chevalier de Semar. When she meets the Count Blessure, all other thoughts are cast from her mind. And "Love! all-conquering, all o'er-powering Love! triumphed over every other Consideration! and she consented to his and her own impatient Wishes."[18] She disregards her parental duty and secretly goes off with Blessure. He arranges a "secret marriage" (p. 231) and they indulge in a wicked, sensual passion. De Semar's discovery and subsequent exposure of their affair ends their idyll. Blessure stabs him and is forced to flee and leave Anadea. She hides herself in the country where in due course she is discovered by Blessure's father (he does not know who she is), who, thinking her a common prostitute, drugs and rapes her (p. 250). The younger Blessure returns, she stabs herself; the marquis shoots himself, and the younger son enters the Capuchins and dies shortly thereafter.

This, then, is what men have driven women to. Is it any wonder that suicide is preferable to such a state?

The salubrious sluts and pretty prostitutes provide the antidote for such real-life situations by providing the disguise which eighteenth-century female novelists adopt in order to speak freely and frankly about the feminine condition. In the guise of these "loose" women, Haywood is able to give a "loose" to her anger, concerns, and ideas. She writes to destroy the myth of aggressive, male victimizer and submissive, acquiescent, female victim. Women are not to be considered mere playthings, sexual objects; they are no longer to be trivialized; the rape of innocence must be stopped. And the best method for halting it is by subverting the male myth. Turning male stereotypes against him becomes the most effective method the woman novelist has to combat the wholesale rape and exploitation women are subjected to. Haywood's fictions are healthy, her prostitutes salutary as they help her reveal what is at the heart of being female.

NOTES

The term "descending angels" is from Eliza Haywood, *Love in Excess; or, The Fatal Enquiry*, in *Secret Histories, Novels, and Poems*, 2d ed. (London: Browne and Chapman, 1725), 3:187.

1. George Lillo, *The London Merchant*, ed. William H. McBurney (Lincoln: University of Nebraska Press, 1965), 64.

2. Bernard Mandeville, *A Modest Defence of Publick Stews* (1724; reprint Los Angeles: University of California Press, 1973), 8–9; Bernard Mandeville, *The Fable*

of the Bees: or, Private Vices, Publick Benefits (1714; reprint Oxford: Clarendon Press, 1924).

3. See W. L. Blease, *The Emancipation of English Women* (London: Constable & Co., 1910); Paul Fritz and Richard Morton, eds., *Woman in the 18th Century and Other Essays* (Toronto: A. M. Hakkert & Co., 1976); Marlene LeGates, "The Cult of Womanhood in Eighteenth-Century Thought," *Eighteenth-Century Studies*, 10 (1976–77): 21–40; I. B. O'Malley, *Women in Subjugation* (London: Duckworth, 1933); Ruth Perry, *Women, Letters and the Novel* (New York: AMS Press, 1980): and Susan Staves, "British Seduced Maidens," *Eighteenth-Century Studies* 14 (1981): 109–34, for discussion of the trivialization of women.

4. See Blease and O'Malley above. Also Lawrence Stone, *The Family, Sex and Marriage, 1500–1800* (New York: Harper & Row, 1977); Janelle Greenberg, "The Legal Status of the English Woman in Early Eighteenth-Century Common Law and Equity," *Studies in Eighteenth-Century Culture* 4 (1974): 171-82. Martin Seymour-Smith, *Fallen Women* (London: Thomas Nelson & Sons, 1969), 98.

5. See Edmond de Goncourt and Jules de Goncourt, *The Woman of the Eighteenth Century* (New York: Monton, Balek, & Co., 1927) and Jean E. Hunter "The 18th-Century Englishwoman: According to the Gentleman's Magazine," in Fritz and Morton, *Woman in the 18th Century and Other Essays*, 73–89. Claudeen Cline-Naffziger, "Women's Lives and Frustration, Oppression and Anger: Some Alternatives," *Journal of Counseling Psychology* (1974): 51. See Perry, *Women, Letters, and the Novel*, for an interesting discussion of fiction as escape.

6. Barbara Bellow Watson, "On Power and the Literary Text," *Signs* 1 (1975–76): 113.

7. John Dollard et al., *Frustration and Aggression* (New Haven: Yale University Press, 1939), 1, 2, 10.

8. Eliza Haywood, *The Female Spectator*, 7th ed. (London: H. Gardner, 1771), 1:179.

9. Nancy K. Miller, *The Heroine's Text: Readings in the French and English Novel, 1722–1782* (New York: Columbia University Press, 1980), xi.

10. Susan Brownmiller, *Against Our Will: Men, Women, and Rape* (New York: Bantam Books, 1975), 5.

11. See Annis Pratt, *Archetypal Patterns in Women's Fiction* (Bloomington: Indiana University Press, 1981), 14–16, for discussion of growing up and down.

12. Eliza Haywood, *Fantomina: or, Love in a Maze*, in *Secret Histories, Novels, and Poems*, 2d ed. (London: Brown and Chapman, 1725), 3:258. Further references appear in parentheses in the text.

13. Eliza Haywood, *Anti-Pamela: or, Feign'd Innocence Detected in a Series of Syrena's Adventures*, 2d ed. (London: F. Cogan, 1742), 3. Further references appear in parentheses in the text.

14. Eliza Haywood, *The City Jilt; or, The Alderman Turn'd Beau: A Secret History* (London: J. Roberts, 1726), 4. Further references appear in parentheses in the text.

15. Eliza Haywood, *The Life of Madam de Villesache* (London: W. Feales & J. Roberts, 1727), 5. Further references appear in parentheses in the text.

16. Eliza Haywood, *Lasselia: or, The Self-Abandon'd: A Novel*, in *Secret Histories, Novels, and Poems*, 3d ed. (London: A. Bettesworth, C. Hitch, D. Browne, T. Astley, and T. Green, 1732) 4:vi. Further references appear in parentheses in the text.

17. Eliza Haywood, *Idalia: or, The Unfortunate Mistress: A Novel*, in *Secret Histories, Novels, and Poems*, 2d ed., 3:2, 3. Further references appear in parentheses in the text.

18. Eliza Haywood, *The Fatal Secret: or Constancy in Distress*, in *Secret Histories, Novels, and Poems*, 2d ed., 3:221. Further references appear in parentheses in the text.

The Old Maid, or
"to grow old, and be poor,
and laughed at"

JEAN B. KERN

Old maids had great difficulty in the eighteenth century achieving even self-respect. As their numbers increased during the century,[1] they became caricatures in novels as soon as they were recognized as economic burdens on the families who supported them.[2] Nor could they easily support themselves unless they were born to wealthy families who could afford them separate maintenance. In middle- to lower-class families, they lived at home nursing aged parents, caring for small children, spinning (hence the term "spinster")—family servants who were passed on to relatives once their parents died. As men increasingly took over former female occupations such as midwifery, mantua making, or clerking in shops, these single women were left with no respectable role. Fettered by their economic dependence, their frustrated sexuality, and their inability to translate individual talent into a public role in their society, they soon appeared in men's novels as sex-starved, frustrated, and disagreeable stereotypes described by Defoe as "a set of despicable characters called Old Maids."[3] The model is familiar in Bridget Allworthy and Tabitha Bramble who harass their bachelor brothers in *Tom Jones* and *Humphrey Clinker*. Because women novelists were more sensitive to the problems of old maids rejected by the society in which they must live, these women writers modified the stereotype caricatures. It is the purpose of this paper to illustrate how they motivated the old maid's jealousy of the nubile young heroine, how they explained the resentment of dependence, and eventually how they suggested solutions to the older single woman's psychological isolation. In writing from a woman's viewpoint, they individualized their old maid characters beyond stereotypes.

Some of these women novelists were themselves unmarried, such as Jane Barker, Sarah Fielding, Jane Austen; some married when they were al-

201

ready past forty, such as Fanny Burney. The deficiency of biographical information, especially about early women novelists, is further complicated by the eighteenth-century practice of calling all women *Mrs.*, an abbreviation of *Mistress.* "Mrs." Jane Barker published her novels in 1713 and 1723, but as late as 1798 Mrs. Charlotte Smith referred to an old maid character as "Mrs." Grinsted. However, all the women novelists cited in this paper agree that a female unmarried by the age of twenty-seven is an old maid. Their spinster characters reflect the value system of the middle class from which the novelists themselves came; they had to be literate to write novels.

Elisinda in the anonymous *The Prude*, "a Novel by a Young Lady" who signs herself only as "MaA,"[4] is an example of an old maid who is apparently prudish about sex. While she pretends to hate all men and spends long hours secluded at prayer, actually Elisinda is shown as a promiscuous heterosexual older woman who is jealous of her younger sister's fiancé because Elisinda wants him for herself. Her apparent prudishness is hypocrisy; when she pretends to be at prayers, she is actually in bed with both a female friend and a manservant. Prudery is, thus, a social disguise for this unmarried woman's active sexuality. But Elisinda does not marry in the end like Fielding's Bridget Allworthy or Smollett's Tabitha Bramble; there is not even a Captain Blifil or a comic Lishmahago for this old maid. She remains a villainous "Cinderella's older sister," tutored by her friend Stanissa to turn tables on men by adopting their role of sexual satisfaction through seduction. According to Stanissa, all husbands are tyrants who require a wife "to move like clockwork at his Will and Pleasure" (pt. 1, p. 18). Furthermore, she warns Elisinda that the servants who are now her accomplices, would inform on her if she married. Thus Elisinda remains an old maid throughout parts 2 and 3 of this anonymous novel—an undercover manipulator who can indulge her sexual appetite because she is financially independent. Only her frustrated jealousy of her young sister (she even bribes a footman to rape the heroine sister) remains from the stereotype old maid.

The hypocrisy of "MaA" 's Elisinda is echoed by Mary M. Collyer who names an old maid "Prudilla" in *Felicia to Charlotte.* The irony of the name is evident when Prudilla, desperate for sexual experience, tricks the hero of the novel by slipping into his bed when he is forced by a storm to stay overnight at her brother's house. She does so by pretending to be a housemaid, thus hiding her identity in that of a lower-class girl. The old maid, dependent on a brother and no longer attractive to men, must add deceit to hypocrisy to satisfy her sexuality.

Women novelists also write of old maids not as prosperous as Elisinda who is left with a fortune after her parents die, or Prudilla who is comfortably cared for on her brother's estate; some are forced into service as paid companions or governesses. Cynthia in Sarah Fielding's *David Simple* defines the humiliation suffered when she was the "toad-eating" companion to a wealthy woman. Cynthia reports how she was never at leisure to indulge her own preferences over the slightest whim of her employer/mistress. Isolated by her status—slightly above the servants but without their in-group camaraderie—she was both lonely and subject to dismissal the minute she did not please her mistress. Cynthia learns to value her independence as the result of her experience as a paid companion. She is bitterly aware that it is her sex which forced her into service while her brother was sent to the university with no inclination for the learning she longs for.

Cynthia becomes the strongest character in this novel, as Downs-Miers's "Springing the Trap: Subtexts and Subversions" (also in this volume), reminds us, because she is molded by her female awareness of what her experience as a paid companion taught her. When Sarah Fielding later wrote *The Governess; or, The Little Female Academy*, she made her ideal governess, Mrs. Teachum, a widow rather than an old maid. She knew that an unmarried governess living in a family was underpaid, without final authority over her pupils, and socially as isolated as a paid companion. Therefore, she gives Mrs. Teachum economic independence and status as a widow.

The most unpleasant such governess in novels by women is Mme. Frajan in Agnes Marie Bennett's *Anna; or, Memoirs of a Welsh Heiress*. In vol. 1, Frajan is thirty when she is hired to teach the children French in the country house where the orphan Anna lives. Jealous of Anna, she plots with the dissolute Gorget to seduce the heroine. Foiled and dismissed, Frajan appears again in vol. 3 in a much wealthier city house where she manages to brand Anna as a thief. Bennett does not analyze the spinster's motives beyond her obvious jealousy of the younger woman's physical beauty. But she does make Frajan a stereotypical French woman who is dirty, painted, ignorant, and malicious, thus transferring a caricature of an unpleasant old maid to another nationality.

Charlotte Smith's "Mrs." Grinsted in *The Young Philosopher* is still another variation of the old maid. She is not economically dependent like the governess or paid companion, but she is a gossip and troublemaker who keeps Laura Glenmorris's inheritance from her out of jealousy. Charlotte Smith also takes pains to inform her readers that Grinsted's obvious conceit is caused by what she felt she had missed by being born female; for Grinsted "really imagined that if heaven had made her a man," she would have gained "considerable rank among the statesmen of her day and nation."[5] Thus while Grinsted fits the stereotype of the unpleasant spinster, Charlotte Smith has individualized her by showing her aware of the unequal status of women. If the same opportunities were open to spinsters as to bachelors, failure to marry would not be so devastating to self-esteem.

That the female novelist of manners was sensitive to the bitterness of old maids is illustrated in yet another way by Alicia Askew in *The History of Betty Barnes*. Alicia Askew is a "man-hater" after being deceived by a lover who later denied their secret false marriage. Out of her own experience she distrusts all men including the heroine's lover. If this novel is by Sarah Fielding (the title page states it is by the author of *David Simple*), it is interesting that she should document the reason for Alicia Askew's prejudice against men. The logical motivation for hatred of all men also fits the sexual deprivation of a spinster novelist who is squeamish about describing the consummation of Betty Barnes's marriage.[6] Yet despite the psychological motivation provided Alicia Askew, Sarah Fielding found no word for the opposite of misogyny, hatred of women. In this century of male dictionary makers, she was clearly aware that the greater sexual freedom of men might embitter an old maid, but because she, like Burney and Austen, accepted marriage as the destiny of her heroine, she failed to coin a sex-oriented terminology. She does not call Alicia Askew a misogamist, a hater of marriage, but a "man-hater" because one man deceived her into a false marriage.

My examples thus far are of the female variations on the male novelists' caricatures of old maids, but women writers also treated these lonely spinsters positively and compassionately. Jane Barker, early in the century, published two novels about Galesia, *Love's Intrigues, or, The History of the Amours of Bosvil and Galesia* (1713) and *A Patch-Work Screen for the Ladies* (1723).[7] Both novels define the pressure on girls to marry and their isolation during courtship. Galesia is the narrator in both, telling in the earlier novel of a disastrous love when her cousin Bosvil rejects her and marries another. Hers is the usual pattern of an eighteenth-century courtship with the initiative all on Bosvil's side. Galesia is attracted to him, but cannot encourage him or confide in her parents until she has a firm offer of marriage because, as she says, "if the Amour be secret, or without Parents consent, that good Pilot which conducts young Lovers to the safe Harbour of Matrimony" (*Love's Intrigues*, p. 9) there is no other route but ruin. Caught in an impasse, she must conceal her sexual attraction or sublimate it in farm management and learning, which she acknowledges as "being neither of Use nor Ornament in our Sex" (p. 53). When Bosvil announces his approaching marriage to another woman, her internalized despair requires a great effort at self-control, but she leaves the room without fainting by hanging onto the furniture. Only in the privacy of her own bedroom can she react to her disappointment: "I threw myself on the Bed, roll'd on the Floor, hop'd each Cramp I felt would be my Death's Convulsion" (p. 58).

What is unique about this early novel (1713) is its intense portrayal of pent-up emotion. The dedication of the novel to the Countess of Exeter hints that Barker was writing out of her own experience, for she hopes that the Countess "may never intangle her Noble Person in those Levities and Misfortunes the ensuing Treatise describes me unhappily to have struggled with." Whether Jane Barker was so tormented and rejected cannot be determined as fact, but the words of Galesia have the authentic ring of autobiography.

Ten years later Jane Barker published her second novel about Galesia. *A Patch-Work Screen* is a patchwork novel, really a collection of stories told to a traveling companion. Interspersed with verse, and Jane Barker is still anthologized as a poet, these stories are patches of Galesia's experiences following her rejection by Bosvil in the earlier novel. In her country home, before her father's death, she had been encouraged to read and write by her brother and his Cambridge friends who exchanged their poems for hers. One wonders whether she sent them "A Virgin Life,"[8] published in 1688, where she pleads for an understanding of old maids. However, her brother's sudden death has cut her off from any intellectual encouragement. With her widowed mother Galesia moves to London, where she feels gauche and out of place in urban society. Still smarting from the experience with Bosvil, she is uncomfortable at public assemblies, "for as I never affected the formal Prude, so I ever scorn'd the impertinent Coquette" (p. 40). But when she again takes refuge in books in her attic Parnassus, her mother forbids even that comfort, calling "a Learned woman at best but like a Forc'd Plant" (p. 11). To escape her mother's chiding, Galesia finally agrees that books "like Oatmeal or Charcoal to the depraved appetites of girls" keep her from "the Diversions and Embellishments of our Sex and Station" (p. 79). Has she really bought her mother's argument or is this Barker's ironic acknowledgement that learning is a detriment to a woman's social grace?

Almost immediately following this concession, Galesia reports that her mother baldly tells her she is growing old and must marry before it is too late, and "that we, in a manner, frustrate the End of our Creation to live in that uncouth kind of Solitude, in which she thought I too much delighted" (p. 79). Suddenly the real objection to books and spinsterhood is clear: they keep her from her biological duty to marry and have children. Nowhere is the eighteenth-century objection to old maids more explicitly stated. That it is stated by a spinster author denied even Parnassus is poignant testimony to the plight of the old maid. Barker's two novels give a record of the fine honing of a young woman's temperament. She must subdue any libidinous tendencies by a diet of oatmeal and charcoal, but she must at the same time avoid falling into "stoical Dulness and humersome Stupidity" by burying her sexual appetite in the acquisition of learning. She must avoid solitude, appear in public, and be attractive enough to get a husband, but she must conceal her sexuality from a man like Bosvil or she will become a mistress, not a wife. Jane Barker clearly understood this feminine trap and argued, in her novels as well as her poetry, for a better understanding of the single woman.

Jane Barker identified the chief problem of the unmarried female as economic, but devoting herself to books and writing failed to provide a viable solution. Sarah Scott in *A description of Millenium Hall* (1762)[9] suggested a more practical plan for old maids and women who had made disastrous marriages to live together, pooling their income, and devoting themselves to their "amiable family" of surrogate children gathered from the poor of their area. Their idyllic life, suggested by the title, is reported by a male narrator who is forced to take refuge from a storm and stays on in Millenium Hall to recount their way of life. To this visitor the five ladies of the hall confide their own stories. All five have been disappointed by men, but despair of reforming their principles, and thus they have set up their own society where they live simply but comfortably and occupy themselves by training every sixth child of the poor to learn skills of spinning and weaving.

Equating their limitations as women to actual physical handicaps, they choose servants who are maimed or deformed: the housekeeper has a useless hand, the cook is lame, the kitchen maid has sight in one eye, the dairy maid is stone deaf. The rules of Millenium Hall are also listed: (1) fortunes are pooled; (2) each has a separate bedroom but common meals; (3) music is encouraged daily; (4) hours are regular; (5) the women have a housekeeper and servants, already described; (6) they alternate presiding at table; (7) they limit themselves to £25 a year for clothes; (8) clothes are plain but neat; (9) illness is paid for out of pooled income; (10) dismissal of pupils is for impudence only and very rare; (11) they keep a table appropriate for gentlewomen (pp. 83–84). When the narrator is amused that they encourage their girls to marry after their own experiences, he is told, "We consider matrimony as absolutely necessary to the good of society" (p. 125), but they agree that if a girl fails to marry, she is better off living with other women than with her blood family.

Sarah Scott had good reason to write *Millenium Hall* because she had herself, after a miserable marriage in 1751, gone to live with a relative, Lady

Bab Montague, and had established a school for the poor at Batheaston. She also had reason for sympathy with the deformed since her own beauty had been marred by smallpox at age eighteen. Her husband treated her so badly that her family had to rescue her from his house and provide her with an annual income to live in retirement.[10] Thus, she was well motivated to write of a female society which devoted itself to the nurture and education of the poor. She had already suggested such projects for women in her earlier novel *Cornelia* (1752).

Running a school would appear on the surface to be a viable option both for women who left disastrous marriages like Sarah Scott and for old maids, but such a project demanded private income. Only an old maid from a family of considerable means could become independent of her family by pooling resources to live in a style "appropriate for gentlewomen." (The five ladies of Millenium Hall had an income of 86,000£ between them.) Besides, there was another danger of such communal life well documented by *The Ladies of Llangollen*[11] who chose to live together in Wales against the will of their families. Sarah Ponsonby and Eleanor Butler, two Irish ladies, were a model of perfect female "romantic friendship" for everyone from the Duke of Wellington to Josiah Wedgwood, but their system of self-improvement did not protect them from a charge of lesbianism in the public press of the day. Instead of being rewarded for showing what two determined and devoted old maids could do by themselves, they were branded as unnatural. The experience of these actual old maids is further evidence of why the fictional *Millenium Hall* was unlikely to become a popular solution for spinsters.

Yet as the century progressed, women novelists continued to write sympathetically about unmarried women. Elizabeth Inchbald, a successful married actress and playwright who turned to writing novels late in her career, included a Miss Woodley in her first novel, *A Simple Story*.[12] Miss Woodley, the opposite of the sex-starved Elisindas, Prudillas, or "Mme." Frajans, is a stable, moral and self-effacing dependent of the male protagonist of this novel. She is also the mother manquée to his ward, the rather giddy Miss Milner who eventually marries her guardian, bears him a daughter, and then has an affair with a former suitor in her husband's absence from England. When he returns and discovers the affair, Lord Elmwood banishes both his wife and daughter for the wife's infidelity, forcing his wife to leave all her property in his hands. Miss Woodley then becomes the companion of the disgraced wife and her baby, taking over Matilda's education after the mother's early death.

Inchbald is careful to describe Miss Woodley's good qualities as the novel begins. She is then thirty-five and lives with her elderly aunt who is

Lord Elmwood's housekeeper. We are told on page five of her cheerful temper and "inexhaustible fund of good nature" which has caused her to escape ridicule and even "the appellation of old maid." After thus denying the stereotype of old maids, Inchbald develops her character as a model of stability and compassion. In part 1 Miss Woodley serves as a fulcrum between the frivolous and passionate Miss Milner and the rigid guardian who marries his ward. Seventeen years elapse between the two parts of this novel. In part 2 Miss Woodley, now in her fifties, has become the surrogate mother/grandmother of the young Matilda whom Lord Elmwood refuses ever to see because of his wife's disgrace. While she protects, nurtures, and guides the young girl in her charge, Miss Woodley is endlessly patient with the stubborn father whom she calls "haughty, impatient, impervious, and more than ever *implacable*" (p. 240). Her saintly, self-effacing personality gives this spinster the most stability of any character in the novel despite her dependent economic status as an old maid. Notice that she has taken over the nurturing role of a mother like the ladies of Millenium Hall as one way eighteenth-century women novelists came to terms with the inevitability of numerous unmarried women.

Thus while Miss Woodley is presented as a sympathetic character, she does not alter the pattern of a spinster's role. We learn nothing from the novel about why she never married, but from her dependence on her aunt and Lord Elmwood, we can infer that she had no income of her own. She survives the pressure to marry before reaching the "grand climacteric" of menopause without the bitterness or sexual frustration of Collyer's Prudilla. She is not a "man-hater" like Alicia Askew though she is clearheaded about her employer. Nor does Miss Woodley speculate, like Smith's "Mrs." Grinsted, about what she might have accomplished if she had been a man. Instead, she calmly accepts her status and finds fulfillment in raising another woman's child. Her nurturing role is similar to that of the ladies of Millenium Hall without their financial independence. And Inchbald gives no hint that Miss Woodley was frustrated about her place in society.

The women novelists who tried to show how old maids felt or how they sublimated their frustration were more often themselves old maids—Jane Barker, Sarah Fielding, Jane Austen, or Fanny Burney who married at forty-one. Burney, however, is sharper in her *Diary* than in her novels at portraying dependent spinsters. When after the success of her first novel *Evelina* (1778), she was appointed as a Lady-in-waiting to Queen Caroline, she leaves no doubt in her *Diary* about regarding this as a dubious honor: "I am *married*, my dearest Susan," she told her sister, "I look upon it in that light—I was averse to forming the union, and I endeavoured to escape it; but my friends interfered—they prevailed—and the knot is tied. What then remains but to make the best wife in my power? I am bound to do it in duty, and I will strain every nerve to succeed."[13] This extraordinary use of the language of a marriage ceremony clearly indicates that Burney knew what she was sacrificing by entering the Queen's service. In transferring her dependence in her father's house to her dependence on the Queen, she lost her time for creative writing and was no better off than the "toad-eating" companion of a rich woman.

Burney wrote no novels between 1786 and 1791 while she was Second-Keeper-to-the-Wardrobe; her *Diary* alone documents the strain on her health and spirits. For the five years between the age of thirty-four and thirty-nine she suffered from lack of sleep, no freedom of movement, no leisure, and constant harassment from the German Lady-in-Waiting closest to the Queen. What was supposedly an honor nearly killed her before friends intervened and petitioned for her release from the Court position. As soon as she was again at home, her *Diary* reports the elation she felt at being able to renew her creative activity free from the restraint of her "marriage": "The day is never long enough, and I could employ two pens almost incessantly, in merely scribbling what will not be repressed" (p. 241). For a spinster like Fanny Burney, "scribbling" was as satisfactory a substitute for marriage as it had been for Jane Barker early in the century. That she suffered both physically and mentally during five years crucial to her steady development as a novelist is reflected by her later novels which never achieved the level of *Evelina* even after her marriage to General D'Arblay. Joyce M. Horner has observed of this period that "the successful woman writer, as a rule, is either a spinster or a widow."[14] Burney illustrates that writing could be a fulfillment of an old maid's life and art only so long as she was free to pursue her own talent.

Early in the century, women novelists attempted to explain the stereotype of the old maid by showing her economic dependence, her sexual frustration, or her loneliness. When they wrote out of their own experience as Jane Barker did, the sensitivity was poignantly sharp in illustrating "that a woman's observation of character starts with herself, and that she uses her feelings to test the feelings of others."[15] By the end of the century as female economic independence eroded and pooled-income solutions like Millenium Hall were options for too few of the increasing number of old maids, novelists had developed more skill and variety in presenting spinster characters. Charlotte Smith showed how just being female limited an ambitious woman of intelligence and turned her into a troublemaker like "Mrs." Grinsted. Elizabeth Inchbald showed how a stable, dignified old maid like Miss Woodley could be both crucial to the plot and command respect by educating a motherless child.

But was being a surrogate mother/governess a satisfactory life for a spinster? Inchbald suggests that it was, but Inchbald was writing as a married woman. Spinster novelists such as Sarah Fielding did not relegate unmarried women characters to the role of governess because it commanded no respect. And Fanny Burney who gave up her writing to be a companion to royalty considered it a "marriage" to duty. Jane Austen who never married, even late in life as Burney did, clearly preferred writing to caring for another woman's children. As she said in a letter, her novels were her children.[16] Thus, while she affirms marriage as a destiny for all her heroines,[17] she manages to objectify the plight of her old maid characters out of her own experience. Her method of presenting old maids merits closer examination.

"Gentle" Jane was understandably gentle toward her spinster characters even when she conceived a humorous character like Miss Bates, that memorably loquacious old maid in her best novel *Emma*. Miss Bates is even made a key figure in the education of the self-willed heroine. When Emma publicly makes fun of Miss Bates on the Box Hill excursion by implying the old maid will have trouble limiting herself to "three dull things at once," even Miss Bates feels the barb: "I must make myself very disagreeable or she would not have said such a thing to an old friend."[18] Emma's offense draws a sharp rebuke from Mr. Knightley: "How could you be so unfeeling to Miss Bates? How could you be so insolent in your wit to a woman of her character, age, and situation? Emma, I had not thought it possible" (4:413). When Emma tries to defend herself, Knightley points out the old maid's lower social position and dependence on the Woodhouse family. Emma, chastened and full of guilt, begins to lose some of her self-assurance and vows to make amends. While she does not actually apologize to Miss Bates, she does go to call on her the next day, and in her newly acquired humility, she shows for the first time some genuine interest in the affairs of Miss Bates's "unfortunate" niece, Jane Fairfax.

Miss Bates is an excellently conceived character who illustrates the faults of a spinster too anxious to please her social superiors. But Austen also knows the consideration owed to the old maid's vulnerable dependence. That she also uses Emma's thoughtless discourtesy to the old maid to discipline the intelligent but self-centered heroine shows how sensitive Austen is to the plight of the unmarried woman in her rural society. For she links Emma's call on Miss Bates, in lieu of an apology, to her first expressed concern for Jane Fairfax who lacks a dowry and is about to become a governess to support herself.

Austen's last novel *Persuasion* takes a different tack. Anne Elliot, the heroine, is twenty-seven—that dangerous age for the unmarried female—

as the novel begins. Eight years earlier she had rejected an offer of marriage from a young naval officer who had no money and was inferior in social position to her family. As the middle daughter of Sir Walter Elliot, Anne was *persuaded* not to marry a social inferior. Even her dead mother's friend Lady Russell urged her not to marry for love against the dictates of her father. In the eight years that have followed, Anne has been both neglected and ignored by her father and her older sister who never take her to London when they go for the season. Her younger married sister has exploited her to act as a nurse during Mary's hypochondriacal illnesses or as a "sitter" and disciplinarian of her two unruly little sons. Thus Anne has faded into a pale, thin version of her bloom of nineteen when she is thrown again into the company of her former suitor, the now prosperous Captain Wentworth. She suffers the anguish of overhearing him say he would not have known her—so altered is her appearance. Austen is careful to show Anne's uneasiness and embarrassment in the small social group of the rural extended family when she is constantly forced to observe Wentworth's attentions to Mary's two unmarried sisters-in-law.

Throughout the novel Austen is sensitive to the aging young woman who, at twenty-seven, is already considered a spinster by her family. All the unpleasant tasks are assigned to Anne; *she* is the one who must play the piano while the others dance at a family gathering; *she* is left behind when her father and older sister take a solicitor's daughter with them to Bath despite that lady's lower social position; *she* is the one to nurse her small nephew when he breaks his collarbone. Only Lady Russell values Anne for her taste in reading and her self-effacing personality. Yet Lady Russell has failed to approve Captain Wentworth for her beloved Anne, who even at the end of the novel when Wentworth has proposed a second time fears Lady Russell's disapproval.[19] However, Anne resists *persuasion* at twenty-seven when she was unable to resist at nineteen, because she knows now that marriage is preferable to being neglected and exploited as a spinster.

What, finally, is Austen's attitude toward old maids? The most revealing clue, I think, comes from an unfinished fragment called *The Watsons*.[20] It is another story, like *Pride and Prejudice*, of several sisters with no dowry. The eldest, who watched the man she loved marry another, is now an old maid doomed to care for her ailing father, yet she still tells her youngest sister, "You know we must marry. I could do very well single for my own part; a little company, and a pleasant ball now and then, would be enough for me, if one could be young forever; but my father cannot provide for us, and it is very bad to grow old, and be poor, and laughed at" (5:286). Again one is reminded of Miss Bates. Clearly Austen perceives the worst of spinsterhood as a lonely old age of poverty, neglect, and ridicule. But she also criticizes the Watson sister who pursues a man just to be married and have a situation in life. Such a young woman is called "too masculine and bold," to which she adds, "Poverty is a great evil, but to a woman of education and feeling, it cannot be the greatest. I would rather be a teacher at a school (and I can think of nothing worse) than marry a man I did not like" (5:287). Thus while her solution for all her heroines is to marry for love, she treats old maids sensitively and delicately. Writing for Jane Austen may be a substitute for female productivity—novels for children, as she said, but she is well aware of the economic and social pressures on unmarried women. Her heroines all find husbands though like Anne Elliot they may wait until they are twenty-seven to escape the unpleasantness of being a spinster, exploited and patronized by characters who are their moral inferiors.

Old maids, then, ended the century no better off than they began it. Women novelists who recognized their plight found few solutions for their economic dependence except in the nurturing roles of surrogate mother, governess, or schoolteacher. Denied sexuality, oppressed by their dependence on relatives, they lacked financial means to pool their income and govern their own lives like the ladies of Millenium Hall. In a society where female sexuality could be satisfied only by becoming a wife or a mistress, the old maid suffered less social stigma than the "fallen" woman, but she was both more neutered by her sex than the bachelor and more frustrated by the few sterile careers open to her as companion or governess. And if writing and teaching were satisfactory careers for the old maid, they do not appear so even in the novels of Jane Austen—the best of the spinster novelists—who marries off even a minor character like Jane Fairfax in *Emma* before Jane is forced to become a governess. "To grow old, and be poor, and laughed at" (5:286) sums up the loneliness and ridicule which the single, dependent woman must suffer, yet it is not a worse fate than a loveless marriage to achieve status in a male-dominated society. However sensitive they were to the problems of an unmarried woman, these women novelists did not resolve the problems which they defined from a feminine perspective. What the women novelists did do was to develop the old maid beyond mere caricature—explaining her motivation, showing her with qualities which would have been valued in men, and illustrating in their novels that creativity was both the best outlet for the single woman and the best document of her low social status.

NOTES

1. Lawrence Stone, *The Family, Sex, and Marriage in England, 1500–1800* (London: Weidenfeld & Nicolson, 1975), 44, estimates the increase at 25 percent.

2. See R. B. Utter and G. B. Needham, *Pamela's Daughters* (New York: Macmillan, 1936), 221.

3. Defoe, quoted in Ian Watt, *The Rise of the Novel* (Berkeley: University of California Press, 1957), 144 n. 4.

4. *The Prude, a Novel by a Young Lady* (London: J. Roberts, 1724; part 1 reprint, New York and London: Garland, 1973; all references to part 1 are to the reprint; parts 2 and 3, 2d ed., London: J. Roberts, 1725, are in the British Library).

5. Charlotte Smith, *The Young Philosopher*, 4 vols. (London: T. Cadell & W. Davies, 1798; reprints, New York and London: Garland, 1974), 4:361.

6. *The History of Betty Barnes*, 2 vols. (London: D. Wilson & T. Durham, 1753; reprint, New York and London: Garland, 1974, 2 vols. in one), 2:212.

7. Jane Barker, *Love's Intrigues or, The History of the Amours of Bosvil and Galesia* (London: E. Curll, 1713; reprint, New York and London: Garland, 1973): *A Patch-Work Screen for the Ladies* (London: E. Curll, 1723; reprint, New York and London: Garland, 1973 with *The Prude*). All quotations are from the Garland reprints; page numbers appear in parentheses in the text.

8. Quoted in Angelina Goreau, *Reconstructing Aphra Behn* (New York: Dial Press, 1980), 75:

> Fearless of twenty-five and all its train,
> Of slights and scorns, or being called old maid. . . .
> Ah lovely state how strange it is to see,
> What mad conceptions some have made of thee,
> As though thy being was all wretchedness,
> Or foul Deformity in ugliest dress.

Jane Barker, "spinster," inherited an estate of only £47, 10s after her Royalist father's death in 1715. See G. S. Gibbons, "Mrs. Jane Barker," *Notes and Queries*, 12th Ser., 11 (1922): 278–79.

9. Sarah Scott, *A description of Millenium Hall* (London: J. Newbury, 1762); reprint, ed. Walter M. Crittenden (New York: Bookman Associates, 1955). All quotations are from this reprint; page numbers appear in parentheses in the text.

10. There was even rumor that he tried to poison her and Mrs. Delaney, that soul of propriety among the Blue Stockings, spoke of him as "a very bad man." See *Dictionary of National Biography*, 17:1005.

11. See Elizabeth Mavor, *The Ladies of Llangollen* (London: Penguin, 1971; reprint, 1974), 73–74.

12. Elizabeth Inchbald, *A Simple Story* in Mrs. Barbauld, ed. *British Novelists* (London: 1830), 18. All quotations are from this edition; page numbers appear in parentheses in the text.

13. John Wain, ed., *Fanny Burney's Diary* (London: Folio Society, 1961), 155. All quotations are from this edition of the *Diary*; page numbers appear in parentheses in the text.

14. Joyce M. Horner, *The English Women Novelists and their Connection with the Feminist Movement, 1688–1797, Smith College Studies in Modern Languages* 11 (1930): 63.

15. Ibid., 142.

16. *Pride and Prejudice*, for example, Austen calls "my own darling child," in R. W. Chapman, ed., *Jane Austen Letters, 1796–1817* (London: Oxford Press, 1955), 131.

17. Patricia Meyer Spacks writes, "Women—eighteenth-century women—employ the writing of novels to affirm the social order that limits them." See *Imagining a Self* (Cambridge: Harvard University Press, 1976), 57.

18. *The Works of Jane Austen*, 6 vols. (New York: Bigelow, Brown and Co., reprinted from the Bentley's Library ed. of 1882), 4:409. All quotations are from this edition; page numbers appear in parentheses in the text.

19. Sandra M. Gilbert and Susan Gubar, in *The Madwoman in the Attic: A Study of Women and the Literary Imagination in the Nineteenth Century* (New Haven: Yale University Press, 1979), have a good discussion of Lady Russell's role in this novel, 177 ff.

20. *The Works of Jane Austen* 5:281–343.

IV. MORAL AND POLITICAL REVOLUTION

Politics and Moral Idealism
The Achievement of Some
Early Women Novelists

Jerry C. Beasley

It is a commonplace of English literary history that women novelists of the Restoration and eighteenth century—from Aphra Behn to Jane Austen—were interested mainly in telling stories of domestic conflict featuring blushing virginal maidens whose happiness is threatened by their own social innocence, by avaricious fathers and brothers, by treacherous sisters, rakish seducers, and all manner of hostile people and circumstances. Like most commonplaces of its kind, this one is only partially grounded in the truth. Women did indeed write such stories by the dozens, particularly during the earlier years of the eighteenth century. But, as a quantity of recent feminist scholarship has shown, they did not always do so merely for the diversion or titillation of their readers. It is clear that many women writers actually used their works to give urgent and meaningful expression to a female consciousness, much as the Brontë sisters were to do in the nineteenth century, though not with the same degree of bold sophistication and—it is probable—only rarely with the same deliberate awareness of purpose. There can be no doubt that even the most trite and conventional of eighteenth-century novels by women often dramatize a subversive affirmation of the dominant value of the female as the active embodiment of emotional sensitivity and moral integrity and as the chief force for domestic stability. The popularity of prose fiction, among female readers at least, may be in part attributed to this kind of affirmation, whose importance otherwise to the development of the novel as a literature of common life can hardly be emphasized too much.

What has not yet been sufficiently noticed, even by feminist scholars and critics, is the political content and appeal, and sometimes the explicit political value, of a great many of the early stories by women. The relationships between political circumstances and the rise of the novel during the first several decades of the eighteenth century were both close and important.

216

Works of prose fiction regularly addressed political issues and events, frequently in an emphatically topical manner; and even when they were neither overtly topical nor very direct in their approach to politics, the writers of popular narrative tended to center on moral and social concerns that were deeply affected by the political atmosphere of the period. We may find a singular example of just this kind of thing in Samuel Richardson's hugely successful first novel, *Pamela*. The moralizing heroine of this apparently apolitical work makes an unmistakably political proclamation of the value of the individual life when she writes to Parson Williams, "But, O Sir! my Soul is of equal Importance with the Soul of a Princess; though my Quality is inferior to that of the meanest Slave."[1]

The author of *Pamela* was by no means the first novelist to put such a political sentiment in the mouth of a female character, or to project a domestic heroine as the exemplar of all virtue—public as well as private. Most of those who had done so before him were women who, not surprisingly, wrote about females in a social and moral environment. In their stories, as in Richardson's, the example of female virtue typically prevails in the end over all the hostility that a wicked society can fling against it, with the result that harmony is at last wrought out of disharmony and the domestic world is made stable and safe. The female character, it must be admitted, is often presented as a hackneyed expression of a sentimental cliché. But in the best works she is more than that. She is the formal representation of an ideal of order, set against a reality made dangerous by the anarchic forces of power-mongering, lasciviousness, and corruption of all kinds in all realms of human endeavor. We should not underestimate the political relevance of such characters, and the stories told about them, in an anxious age constantly worried over perceived threats of arbitrary power and continually preoccupied with Lockean ideals of moral government, with the controversies and scandals of the Walpole regime, and with repeated rumors of Jacobite uprisings.

We know that political life in the early eighteenth century was beset by a collision between the emerging order of modern Whiggism and the old aristocratic ideals of political and class structure.[2] We know, too, thanks to the astuteness of some recent students of Whiggism and its supposed prophet and evangelist John Locke, that the leaders who dominated English politics during the several decades following the exile of James II did not really govern by the classical principles of public and private virtue as repeated in Locke's *Two Treaties of Government* (1690).[3] To these latter-day Whigs—Godolphin, Churchill, Stanhope, Sunderland, and (most important of all) Robert Walpole—the Revolution Settlement of 1688 gave license to reinvent the British Constitution and adapt it to the vision and purposes of particular administrations.[4] The effects of such policy were not all bad. The Whigs did help to secure a peaceful Succession following the death of Queen Anne in 1714; and the Walpole years (from the early 1720s to the early 1740s) were on the whole prosperous and untroubled by war, largely because of the dogged first minister's genius for controlling legislative action. But many people were deeply distressed by the discrepancy between oft-repeated Lockean principles of good government by consent of the governed and the frequently shameless behavior of rottenly corrupt administrations, especially Walpole's. Among the disgruntled we must count a large contingent of Jacobite sympathizers who dreamed—not altogether disinterestedly, of course—of a second restoration of the traditional order symbolized for them by the Stuart monarchy. This perceived discrepancy between proclaimed political philosophy and the actual practice of governing was a recurring theme in scores of satirical treatises against politicians, and it was a fixation of Opposition journalists during the Walpole years. Meanwhile, it became a matter of insistent repetition among writers of popular narrative, who directly or indirectly reflected their consciousness of it in story after story of virtuous men and women struggling alone in a society whose hostility to them belies public ideals of morality and the preciousness of the individual life.

Robert Harley's Tory government of 1710–14 came in for its just share of skepticism and severe criticism—though it never suffered quite the bombardment later inflicted so relentlessly on the Walpole administration. Even so, we may not say that the widespread, ceaseless agitation over the conduct of politicians was a matter of partisan feuding only. What people distrusted, really, was the habit of government by manipulation and fiat, the perceived disruption of proper constitutional balance of powers, and the failure of their leaders to join morality and politics together in a harmonious relationship. The visible moral shabbiness of important officials and, above all, the threat posed by the continued exercise of arbitrary power: these facts of the period's politics produced outrage and, if the varied public forms of expression may be trusted, a genuine cultural anxiety over the weakening moral structure of a perplexingly changing society. In all kinds of popular art—including countless ballads and satirical prints— the men governing the land are projected as agents of chaos instead of stable order, as treacherous servants of the villainous impulses in human nature— avarice, cruelty, power-lust, promiscuity, deviousness, and dishonesty— rather than the instruments of goodness they should be. The public obsession with these matters inevitably found its way into the most widely available forms of entertainment, the theater and prose fiction, where it was reflected and reinforced by writers eager to exploit it for polemical purposes, or for purposes of commercial opportunism, or both.

The issues and concerns I have been outlining figure importantly in the works of novelists like Daniel Defoe, Samuel Richardson, Henry Fielding, and the early Tobias Smollett. *Robinson Crusoe*, though it has often been understood as an apology for the individualistic philosophy and the laissez-faire economic policy of new Whiggism, nevertheless takes its quite ordinary hero to a remote island free of all possibility of political corruption and factional strife. Crusoe's experience as an isolated but civilized man culminates in his establishment of a benevolent "monarchy" founded at least loosely upon the principles of the Revolution Settlement. The book is in the end utopian, if only in a tentative way. Richardson's *Pamela* and *Clarissa* are novels of domestic conflict, but the conflict is political in the most fundamental sense. For both stories are all about the potentially dehumanizing effects of arbitrary power, and they plainly reveal their author's deep concern over the moral disintegration of English society—the "discomposition" of the world, to use Clarissa's term. The political relevance of these two tales of heroic female virtue could hardly have escaped Richardson's readers, who were accustomed to public denunciations of failed and corrupted political leadership as principal cause of the unsettling disorder of life and as pervasive threat to all ideals of human goodness.

Fielding, in writing *Tom Jones*, made Sophia Western the image of moral perfection toward whom the hero must travel through an environment rife with corruption and with hostility to his basic good nature. In this as in his other novels, Fielding often portrays the representatives of contemporary institutions, particularly the law, as insidious enemies to the social and political ideals of harmonizing Christian love. In *Jonathan Wild*, of course, he is altogether explicit in his identification of "statesmen" with "prigs." Smollett, in *Roderick Random*, becomes more insistent than either Fielding or Richardson in his display of moral rottenness and stupidity in the Navy administration, in the legal and penal systems, and among members of Parliament and the bureaucrats of government offices. The rest of society repeats the failures of these political institutions, so incompetently and cruelly administered, and Roderick's furious reaction to what he sees very nearly blinds him to all understanding of the excellences of the heroine Narcissa, whose example of beauteous virtue serves as an opposing standard of goodness.

A primary appeal made by these major novels to their first readers must have resided in the effectiveness of their dramatized reflections upon the troubling reality of early eighteenth-century life, and that reality was intensely political. But Defoe, Richardson, Fielding, and Smollett, despite the greatness of their achievement, constituted only a tiny minority in the larger community of fiction writers, which was much more vastly populated by women than by men—women who, it may be argued with some conviction (though it cannot be proven), anticipated and helped to shape the expression of political and moral concern found in novels like *Pamela* and *Tom Jones*. It has long been confidently assumed, not very wisely I think, that in this period women writers, especially novelists, felt bound to write like men if they were to have the smallest hope of success in the marketplace. Some female authors doubtless did mindlessly accept and work from this notion. In any case the culture was decidedly male, and few fiction writers of either sex were able or even inclined to avoid this fact when conceiving and composing their stories. But it ought to be remembered that Aphra Behn, Delarivière Manley, Jane Barker, Eliza Haywood, Penelope Aubin, and Mary Davys were popular novelists long before the arrival of Samuel Richardson upon the scene. The explicit political content of Behn's *Oroonoko*, and of the secret histories of Manley and Haywood, helped to make them conspicuous and controversial works while simultaneously encouraging other storytellers to occupy themselves with the problems of contemporary life instead of merely repeating the trivial fantasies of romance. Moreover, the ostensibly apolitical amatory novels of Haywood, Barker, Aubin, and Davys surely helped to establish in the popular mind the striking image of the virtuous female as the almost emblematic expression of all that was truly good and desirable in human life: order, love, purity of soul, happiness.

The portraits of female character painted by women novelists are often abstract and condescending; and the heroine of a typical fable looks limp and passive as her tender beauty is seen against all the sordid bustling hostility and violence she must endure before enjoying—which she usually does—her triumph in domestic bliss when the world at last becomes transformed into a reflection of what she represents. But even at their most passive, such heroines regularly succeed as rhetorically effective creations because of the contrast they provide to the wicked society that beleaguers them. And besides, they are not always soft and frail. Eliza Haywood's more interesting ladies sometimes behave with an erotic aggressiveness that comes close to challenging the usual (often complacent) ideal of chaste femininity, and when they prevail it is as much by their energy as by their will or the force of their moral example.[5] Penelope Aubin's women are in many instances similarly firm and lively, though never erotic.

The power and timeliness of the familiar image of the virtuous female may be judged in part by the fact that in the 1720s Daniel Defoe, that most alert of contemporary storytellers, adapted and inverted it in his portrayal of Moll Flanders and Roxana, two deep and complicated studies of the potentially devastating impact of environment upon character. Richardson, Fielding, and Smollett later mocked the feminine effusions of "modern Novel and *Atalantis* Writers," to borrow a phrase from *Joseph Andrews*.[6] Yet the actual originals of the fictional character types repeated in the portraits of Pamela Andrews, Clarissa Harlowe, Sophia Western, and Smollett's Narcissa appear in dozens of earlier narratives by gifted and prolific ladies. If all this be acknowledged, then the old conventional wisdom that women storytellers regularly imitated the men in hope of gaining favor and success seems both doubtful and facile. There is a certain riskiness in the observation, but something like the reverse may be closer to the truth. In other words one might say—and with more than a smattering of real justice—that male novelists, even innovative geniuses like Defoe, Richardson, Fielding, and Smollett, felt obliged to write with at least some resemblances to the work of their female counterparts, who had already won the attention of the reading audience by appealing insistently to its deepest and most abiding preoccupations.

Turning now to the works in which early women novelists actually achieved what I have been claiming for them, we may take up first the example of Aphra Behn's *Oroonoko: or, the Royal Slave* (1688).[7] This book, published in the very year of the Glorious Revolution, appears to have very little to do with English politics at the time, and in fact it is not at all topical. Nevertheless it is of deep political interest. As a characterization of the type of the noble savage (the first such characterization by a British writer, it is supposed), it almost allegorically projects the lately emerged political ideal of individual worth upon a black man, a native African brought in humiliating bondage to the West Indian plantations as an article of chattel. Oroonoko was a prince in his own native land, so of course he is no ordinary mortal. But in an age of smug white supremacy and cozy, prosperous trading in black human flesh, Behn's slave was among the lowest of the low, and her decision to portray him at all was a daring one. Romantic, artificially stylized, even sensational, *Oroonoko* dramatically places its hero in the hands of citizens, plantation owners and managers, and government representatives; they abuse him, torture him, drive him into flight, hunt him down, dismember him, and at last kill him—all because he insists on affirming his natural dignity and personal nobility. The book itself treats Oroonoko as an isolated man infinitely superior in every respect to those who murder him. Because his stupidly vicious enemies are the collective embodiment of transplanted Western culture in general and of British culture in particular—its institutions and laws, its prejudices and rampant corruptions of authority and place—they are vehicles for the indictment of all that they represent. In an interestingly ironic twist, we learn that Oroonoko had been educated at home by a French tutor, who taught him Western history and all the highest civilized principles of "Morals, Language and Science." Only Oroonoko himself, it appears, is able to sustain these principles intact.

Oroonoko is not a denunciation of the slave trade, as was once thought. Instead it is, despite its author's acknowledged Toryism and her long devotion to the Stuart monarchy, a powerful subversive commentary upon some of the most controversial political issues that were swirling about at the time of its composition and publication: the maladministration of king and government leaders, their violations of the people's trust, their undermining of the ideals of public virtue, and the consequences in individual human suffering caused by all these failings. Its effectiveness as veiled political criticism helps importantly to account for the book's great popularity, especially since (as every historian of the period has shown) there was at the time a great public expectancy that a new regime, with a renewed moral vision of the English constitution, would bring an end to the abuses so graphically portrayed in its pages.[8]

The story of *Oroonoko* is emphatically moralistic, and it is the first important work of English fiction to undertake serious development of the theme of the isolated figure of merit beset by a hostile environment whose wickednesses are the visible products of those who hold all the power it has to offer. In this respect at least, Aphra Behn's very popular book was seminal; for, as I have already suggested, the same theme was to recur in dozens of narratives by women and men alike during the several succeeding decades. Behn wrote other fictions, of course, several of them quite effectively in the mode of secret history, or scandal chronicle. In the first decade of the eighteenth century, Delarivière Manley donned her predecessor's mantle and published two scandal chronicles of her own, *The Secret History of Queen Zarah and the Zarazians* (1705) and the *New Atalantis* (1709–1710).[9] Manley was a skillful storyteller and an extremely able Tory polemicist. Her books are nearly libelous attacks on the Whigs who dominated the court of Queen Anne, and although they are episodic narratives organized into no configuration of organic plotting or structure, they fairly throb with racy anecdotes and nasty bits of gossip. The only real unifying principle in either work derives from the author's briskly energetic pursuit of moral as well as political purpose. Obviously written as exercises in opposition rhetoric, *Queen Zarah* and the *New Atalantis* offer nothing in the way of political theorizing. Instead, they present sensational exposés of public characters as seen from a perspective that allows close glimpses of their private lives: their maneuverings and deceptions, their money-grubbing and graft, their power-broking, and (most of all) their promiscuous sexual adventures.

Virtue is subjected to constant assaults in these allegorized pictures of human rottenness in high life. Here, of course, virtue is synonomous with Toryism, and wickedness with the Whig leaders who control the government. Seduced and ruined young maidens are strewn all over Manley's pages, and in fact the books gain rhetorical effectiveness by their insistent reference to the ideal of female virtue. In *Queen Zarah*, the author actually inverts that ideal, thereby doubly reinforcing it, and depicts her protagonist as a perfect monster of villainy—the exact and quite criminal opposite of what she ought to be. The character of Zarah is a viciously distorted portrait of Sarah Churchill, Duchess of Marlborough, who is projected as a relentless predator upon the innocence of Queen Anne (Albania). Madly ambitious for position and influence, Zarah had seduced the fashionable court gigolo Hippolito (John Churchill, Duke of Marlborough) into marriage, thereby gaining her entrance to the highest reaches of society in Albigion (England). And then this beautiful, artful daughter of a whore—her mother "mov'd in a low Sphere, but had a large Occupation" (p. 3)—intrigued and snaked her way into the inner circles of power, at last becoming confidante to the trusting princess and later queen. Manley deliberately unites Zarah's promiscuous sexuality with her insatiable lust for power, and the polemical effect is devastating: "Fortune" had cut her out "purely for the Service of her own Interest, without any Regard to the strict Rules of Honour or Virtue," we are told by the narrator; and she was "fill'd with *Love* and *Ambition*; for though she was resolved to gain the *Last*, she was one who left no Stone unturn'd to secure to her self the *First*, which has always made her Life one continued Scene of politick Intrigue" (pp. 40–41).

Queen Zarah is sprinkled throughout with personal anecdotes of other objects of the author's political satire besides the two Churchills. Godolphin, Sunderland, Kent, and Thomas Wharton all appear, in thin disguise, as wicked creatures of hideous perversities (mostly sexual) and deformities.[10] Sometimes the deformities are physical, so that the world of the power-brokers seems populated by a varied collection of subhuman types, grotesques both in moral character and in body. The *New Atalantis* echoes this same formula, but at much greater length and with a much larger cast of characters. In this work, Manley quite straightforwardly exploits the advantage to be gained by repetition of a fable of beleaguered female virtue. Time and time again, chaste and innocent young women are left by reckless seducers to suffer the cruel hardships of shame, misery, and ruin. Such episodes, many of them based at least loosely on fact, transparently associate perfect and beauteous womanhood with ideals of order and public morality while unmistakably branding the Whigs as unscrupulous exponents of arbitrary power, as anarchic, destructive, seductively clever rav-

ishers of the welfare of the English people. One lengthy episode—like many
of the others, it is really a small novella—proves especially dramatic in its
effects, and a brief look at its conclusion may serve to illustrate both the
shrewdness and the pathetic intensity of Manley's method of handling her
chief polemical device. A Machiavellian "Statesman" called "the Duke" (he
is a portrait of the Earl of Portland) patiently courts and then rapes his
young ward Charlot, toys with her forgiving and tender affections, tires of
her, and heartlessly casts her off in favor of marriage to a rich countess,
formerly Charlot's friend. The young girl, ruined but not corrupted, languishes painfully and finally dies, and the bitter words of the narrator upon
the occasion achieve a real poignancy.[11] "Her Solitude," we are told of
Charlot,

> was Nourishment to those black and corroding Thoughts that incessantly de-
> vour'd her: We may be sure she often exclaim'd against *breach* of *Trust*, and
> *Friendship* in the Countess, as well as Ingratitude and Faithlessness in the Duke:
> The remainder of her Life was one continu'd Scene of Horror, Sorrow, and
> Repentance: She dy'd a true Landmark: to warn all believing Virgins from
> shipwracking their Honour upon (that dangerous Coast of Rocks) the Vows and
> pretended Passion of Mankind.[12]

Queen Zarah and the *New Atalantis* were notorious in their day, but
quite successful. They earned their author the gratitude of her fellow
Tories, for their polemical effectiveness seems to have helped to topple the
Whig administration in 1710.[13] Numerous imitators followed Manley's
lead, among them Daniel Defoe and John Oldmixon[14]; and by the 1720s
Eliza Haywood, that most adaptable and prolific of female authors, was
writing controversial secret histories of the Hanoverian court and the administration of Robert Walpole. The most important of these, the *Memoirs
of a Certain Island Adjacent to the Kingdom of Utopia* (1725) and *The
Secret History of the Present Intrigues of the Court of Caramania* (1727),
are both pointed and energetic satires, and they skillfully apply the sensational devices and mannerisms of the *New Atalantis* to new subject matter.
Pope thought them virulent and slanderous enough to warrant an attack on
their author in the *Dunciad* (1728), and he almost ended her career as a
writer. But Haywood, though more gifted than most of Manley's imitators
and more ambitious than any of them, was nonetheless rather a slavish
copyist from her predecessor, and her secret histories lack the freshness and
the sting of their more interesting originals. They achieved a smaller success
as polemical weapons against their targets, and do not appear to have won
much applause from the Opposition whose cause they were intended to
support. Possibly Haywood was, in these works, not so genuinely commit-

ted to a political purpose as Manley. Still, her two lengthy chronicles of scandal, by the controversy they did arouse, surely helped to keep the moral dimensions of contemporary political life current as a subject of public discussion, while they reinforced conventional ideals of the virtuous society by locating and then exposing the apparent sources of corruption in the government itself.

Eliza Haywood reached her finest achievement as a political satirist when she turned to what was for her a new mode of polemical fiction, the oriental romance. The *Adventures of Eovaai* (1736)[15] is an outrageous orientalized fantasy that savagely attacks Robert Walpole as a private man and public figure. In this work the devices of character assassination resemble those of the secret histories, but there is no basis at all in fact. The story allegorizes England's first minister as a vile deceiver and lecher who preys upon the person and the kingdom of the lovely heroine Eovaai, Princess of Ijaveo. Against the background of the dying words of Eovaai's father the king, who warns his daughter about the ensnaring arts of "*Arbitrary Power*" and false corrupt ministers, Haywood tells the tale of how Ochihatou (Walpole) uses hypocrisy, magic, and cunning in his nearly successful efforts to demolish all opposition to his desires. As a grand villain of almost heroic proportions, Ochihatou is a grossly hideous, bestial creature upon whom no one could bear to look, except that he uses his sorcerer's powers to deceive all eyes into seeing him as beauteous. He is really a most vicious monster of lusty depravity, and in depicting the scenes of his confrontations with Eovaai Haywood neatly balances titillation with indignation, so as to provoke a kind of double fascination in her reader. The heroine bodies forth the familiar image of spotless femininity, but is herself energetic and quick-witted enough to avoid ruination at the hands of her protean tormentor—though she does need the assistance of Providence ("divine *Aiou*") in the end. The strength of Eovaai's character only heightens the erotic interest of her moments of danger while it adds intensity to her overall conflict with Ochihatou, thus making him a more powerfully sinister force for destruction and disorder than he might be otherwise.

Haywood's romance is very shrewdly and skillfully written, and as a work of idealistic polemics it imparts an almost mythic quality to its reflection of contemporary politics and its assessment of the threat to moral life posed by unscrupulous men possessing the supposed appetites of a Walpole. *The Adventures of Eovaai* must have been read by many people, and it made an important contribution to the cause of the Opposition coalition. When reprinted in 1741 (under the altered title of *The Unfortunate Princess*) it may have helped to knock Walpole out of his seat at the head of the ministry. Haywood's book is, in fact, one of the two or three best among several dozen anti-Walpole fictions to be published during the years of the

"Great Man's" supremacy.[16] As pure narrative, *The Adventures of Eovaai* surpasses the efforts of the more discursive secret historians, including Haywood herself, for it sustains real singleness of interest and unity of effect through a rather tightly constructed plot that requires some 225 pages for its development. Fantastic satire though it is, the work comes fairly close to the form and appeal we now associate with the novel.

Other works of popular fiction, the majority of them by women, dramatize their moralized reflections upon the conditions of contemporary life in largely apolitical stories of domestic conflict, of travel and amorous adventures, of danger on the high seas and at the hands of pirates, and so forth. Like the novels by Richardson, Fielding, and Smollett that were to appear beginning in the decade of the 1740s, the numerous tales of Jane Barker, Penelope Aubin, Mary Davys, and the versatile Eliza Haywood herself vigorously detail the spreading decay of English culture, showing how the felt disorder, violence, and cruelty that everyone knew actually threatened to destroy the moral idealism of the nation and its people. In these novelistic fables of virtue under stress, it is always the powerful who are most dangerously corrupt: the tyrannical fathers, the avaricious suitors, the aristocratic libertines, the conniving merchant chiefs, the pirate captains, the trading justices. The point is not that works like Haywood's amorous *Love in Excess* (1719) or Barker's didactic romance of *Exilius* (1715) are motivated by any hidden partisan interest, or that they set out to record in some veiled way the particular events of contemporary political history. Rather it is that, despite their characteristic brevity and occasional crudeness of composition, such narratives offer surprisingly timely and effective recreations of the moral texture of English society in a post-Revolutionary age. That texture, as it is woven, strikingly resembles what we find in the blatantly partisan fictions by Manley and Haywood, and the stories themselves very often parallel the novella-like episodes that make up the bulk of a work like the *New Atalantis*. The typical form of the popular novel was, of course, derived largely from venerable Continental types of novelistic fiction, but its subject matter had been thoroughly naturalized.

Brief discussion of a few representative examples from the works of important female novelistic writers should suffice to show their rhetorical maneuverings in a clear light. None of these narratives is what we would call a good novel, but several were inordinately popular; and since the price of novels was high (about two shillings, six pence to three shillings per volume), we may safely assume that the audience for them extended beyond the class of barely literate milliners and serving maids to whom they were no doubt principally addressed. Their appeal was real, and it was broad enough to engage the attention of a large and heterogeneous (if undiscriminating) group of readers. *Love in Excess*, a most frothy tale of tender passion, was second only to *Robinson Crusoe* in popularity during the decade of the 1720s. Eliza Haywood's many other novels of passion and intrigue published at about the same time—*The British Recluse* (1722), *Idalia* (1723), *The Distress'd Orphan* (1726), and *Philidore and Placentia* (1727), to name but a few—were similarly if not equally successful, and they all insistently, even heavy-handedly, exploit the familiar fable of beleaguered female virtue in some variation or other. Their sensationalism and titillations notwithstanding, Haywood's stories designedly reflect with some urgency a public preoccupation with decadence and licentiousness among the powerful; this, indeed, was surely a major source of their appeal, especially to female readers. In *Love in Excess*, the dazzling libertine Count d'Elmont clearly represents rickety but still potently disruptive aristocratic tradition as it threatens order and stability in moral as well as social life. This novel offers no systematic examination of or attack upon actual contemporary institutions, but it is obvious that only their own individual integrity—and not always even that—can save from utter destruction the several virginal maidens whose lives are blighted by the adventurous Count. One young Italian lady dies of poisoning after an encounter with him, and another girl, who had followed him disguised as a page named Fidelio, perishes of a broken heart. In the end the Count is reformed by means of some conventional theatrical manipulations on the part of the author. But it is the moral force residing in the exemplary persons of the two energetically passionate heroines, Amena and Melliora, that actually justifies his transformation.

Despite the extravagant names and Continental settings of *Love in Excess*, no reasonably alert reader in 1719 or 1720 could have missed its implication that the new order supposedly inaugurated by Whig leaders at the Revolution Settlement, and then renewed after the death Queen Anne and the fall of the Tory administration of Robert Harley, was no order at all. Eliza Haywood's other novels of this same type follow a similar formula, and to comparable effects. Sometimes the setting is English, sometimes Irish, sometimes on the Barbary coast; plots vary just slightly from book to book. But the rhetoric and the appeal of all the stories are insistently repetitious, and are essentially the same always. Haywood had found a message and a manner that touched the nerves of her audience. With little interest in character development or close circumstantial delineation of the details of time and place, she projected archetypal figures of good and evil locked in a moral conflict already familiar to her readers from their own experience in a real world of embattled idealsim.

Jane Barker's *Exilius: or, The Banish'd Roman*,[17] is a different kind of

work altogether. Written (according to the title page) as an imitation of
Archbishop Fénelon's great didactic romance of *Télémaque* (1699–1700),
it is a long, loosely structured, episodic narrative of intense moral
purpose—a conduct book of sorts, showing the proper behavior of young
ladies in all manner of real-life situations. Several plots run simultaneously
along, each designed to place its heroine in a context of adventures that will
test her resilience, or train her into the proper way of conformity to social
expectations, or punish her for transgressions against accepted norms. The
ideal of perfect womanhood developed throughout is most strict, and quite
beyond all possibility of successful emulation by any living, breathing female. As John J. Richetti has put it, the typical Barker heroine in *Exilius* is
"a divine messenger whose beauty and saintly presence both prove and
pre-figure the truths and joys of religion in this life and the next. Her qualities provide emotional affirmation of the religious verities that the world
commonly denies."[18] In other words Clelia, Clarinthia, Scipiana, and the
other suffering maidens whose virtue is at last rewarded by Barker are creatures of fable, not fact; and they are projected as inspirational figures whose
example sets them above the world's darkness and attracts the most noble
males to their sides as their rescuers from distress and, eventually, as their
husbands.

Jane Barker's women actually divide into two groups, the virtuous and
the dissolute. Her saintly girls suffer inordinately as victims of a wicked
world, and it is often their perfect sense of duty that makes them miserable.
A daughter must always obey her father, even if he forces upon her a husband who is a toad, a lecher, and a spendthrift; and she must persist in filial
love, even if her father attempts vile incestuous acts with her. Over and over
again the innocent female is nearly smashed in the collision between
absolute standards of goodness and society's cruel, often violent disregard
of those standards. The woman who falls, joining her environment in its
viciousness, receives no pity from the severe author. Clodius, one of the
numerous libertines whose presence so darkens the book, reproaches a
woman he has ruined with words of painful justice: "how could you
suppose," he asks, "I would make you a Lady, or a Wife, who could not
keep yourself a vertuous Maid, nor a dutiful Daughter? No, no, (continu'd
he) those who bridle not their fond Desires with the Curb of Reason, or
filial Duty, are only fit to be Wives to Monsters, or Mistresses to the least of
Mankind." A fallen woman, he concludes, is but "the broken Meat for lost
Vertue to feed upon, and be the miserable Support of a ruin'd Reputation"
(2:75–76).

Unlike its model *Télémaque*, which is overtly critical of the rampant
corruptions of French society and government under Louis XIV, *Exilius* is

never directly topical. The titular hero himself, the "Banish'd Roman" of impeccable virtue, courage, and wisdom, surely was understood by Barker's first readers as an oblique reference to the exiled Stuart Pretender, whose supporters staged a dramatic but unsuccessful rebellion in the very year that *Exilius* was published. The implied judgment against the disarray of English politics under the Hanoverians and the newly installed Whig leadership is unmistakable. But otherwise this "new Romance" develops as a sweeping indictment of British culture in general, attacking its prevailing values and institutions as morally bankrupt, disordered, hostile to ideals of social and political justice. The contemporary world as Barker portrays it is brightened only by the resolute Christian heroism of the lonely female saints who struggle to survive in it, although they cannot reconcile it to what they themselves are; and by the few striking figures of male virtue who rush to their defense, comfort and succor them, at last uniting with them in happy marriage. In this respect at least, the rhetorical strategy of *Exilius* as a reflection of the moral turbulence of a troubled age differs little from what we find in the *New Atalantis*, the *Adventures of Eovaai*, and *Love in Excess*.

Jane Barker's other works of fiction, *Loves Intrigues* (1713), *A Patch-Work Screen for the Ladies* (1723), and *The Lining for the Patch-Work Screen* (1726), depart from *Exilius* in form but not in degree or seriousness of sober didactic purpose. They are all, in Richetti's phrase, examples of the novel as "pious polemic." *Love in Excess* may in fact have been Eliza Haywood's reaction to the stifled humanity of the virtuous heroines of *Loves Intrigues* and *Exilius*, for in this and other tales Haywood projects females whose own passions provide part of the testing and stress they must endure. *Exilius* nods in the direction of such ambiguity of character when the chaste Scipiana cries out to the gods during a crisis of temptation: "Oh why have you given me an Interior bearing so great Resemblance to your own Divine Purities, and not given me the Power to act accordingly; but have left me in such a State, that my Actions must combat my Conscience, and my Conscience oppose my Reason, and all make a Civil War in my Affections" (1:165). Barker never seriously develops this suggestion of complexity in any of her personages. Haywood both introduces and develops it, but only by pursuing its erotic possibilities instead of its potential psychological interest. The Haywoodian stories of beleagured females may thus have been more appealing than Barker's, but they were hardly so edifying.

If Eliza Haywood reacted to the circumspect Jane Barker, then no doubt Penelope Aubin wrote her tales of piety in action as responses to the more raffish author of *Love in Excess*. The public outcry against the supposed lasciviousness of Haywood seems to have prompted such works as *The Life of Madam de Beaumont* (1721), *The Strange Adventures of the Count de Vinevil and His Family* (1721), *The Life and Amorous Adventures of Lucinda* (1722), *The Noble Slaves* (1722), and *The Life of Charlotta Du Pont* (1723). In these narratives of moral adventure on a worldwide scale, Aubin repeats Haywood's successful formula of amorous intrigue, but without the slightest hint of the erotic. Her stories reveal an optimistic faith affirming that those who are strong in pursuit of the Christian life, though they suffer the torments of isolation and persecution in a viciously antagonistic and chaotic world, will always emerge triumphant to enjoy the happiness that is their due. Aubin's characters, while they are never portrayed with the skill or sensitivity of a Richardson, prove more interesting than those of Barker or Haywood; her more ambitious and sophisticated didacticism requires that she display something of their interior lives as they struggle to resist temptation and fend off threats, and she endows her females in particular with a kind of moral energy that foreshadows what the author of *Pamela* and *Clarissa* would achieve with his heroines. This she manages partly by keeping everyone in almost constant motion through plots that show goodness and innocence tested everywhere—in France, Wales, Virginia, Madagascar, and the West Indies; on the Spanish Main, up the river Oroonoko, at Constantinople, in Gibraltar, and on board the vessels of marauding pirates.

Aubin's books certainly register the influence of Defoe's currently popular tales of travel and adventure, but they pursue their purposes of edification and censure with a single-minded vigilance. In these novels it is not only England, but all the known world that is corrupted by bad men, bad politics, bad institutions. Against such a dark backdrop of universal villainy, the goodness of a Belinda (in *Madam de Beaumont*) looks bright indeed; and this heroine's wholesome beauty is again and again thrown into the terrifying shadows of evil until at last Providence relieves her and rewards her with the hand of the noble-hearted Mr. Lhuelling, a Welshman by birth. The same pattern of experience is repeated many times over in Aubin's popular stories, so that the whole corpus of her work looks like a comprehensive picture of global amorality, corruption, and disorder—the whole made bearable (the resemblance to Barker's *Exilius* is striking) by the final successes of the genuinely saintly characters, most of them female, whose lives of courage and faith we are admonished to emulate.

The stories themselves are moral fables, or moral histories of private virtue given great public visibility. Aubin obviously conceived them in this way, and since her first object is always the vigorous abrasion of archetypal representations of good and evil against one another in a context of timeless conflict, she does not appear to comment very specifically upon the actual conditions of English life. And yet her novels reverberate with the same criticisms of the contemporary environment that characterize the works by Behn, Manley, Haywood, and Barker I have already discussed. A strong hint of Aubin's immediate preoccupation with the felt moral and political reality she and her readers knew may be found in the Preface to *Madam de Beaumont*. In the present age, the author says, "Men are grown very doubtful, even in those Things that concern them most"—that is, in the eternal truths that support faith and the Christian life. She follows with a comparison decidedly to the disadvantage of her fellow countrymen: "Wales being a Place not extremely populous in many Parts, is certainly more rich in Virtue than England, which is now improved in Vice only. . . ." This jab is sharp and cutting, for Welshmen, like the Scots, were at the time popularly regarded as a species of romantic barbarians. And here Aubin is more than just vaguely topical, for a common charge against the Whig government turned upon its manner of sinking the nation into vice and infamy. But another remark is even more pointed. "He that would keep his Integrity," Aubin complains with some bitterness, "must dwell in a Cell; and Belinda had never been so virtuous, had she not been bred in a Cave, and never seen a Court" (p. vii).

A pair of works by one other important author must be mentioned briefly. *The Reform'd Coquet: or, Memoirs of Amoranda* (1724) and *The Accomplish'd Rake: or, Modern Fine Gentleman* (1727), both by Mary Davys, are skillful blendings of comedy of manners with sentimental didacticism. At a much higher level of literary pretension than the efforts of any of her female contemporaries, Davys examines in these two companion novels, respectively, the vagaries of untaught innocence ensnared by the dangers of the world, and the decayed values of masculine society with its villainous disregard of justice and moral principles. *The Accomplish'd Rake* is of particular interest, for it anatomizes the ways of morally low characters in high places and focuses sharply on the faulty conditioning of a basically good-natured young fellow, Sir John Galliard, who turns into a rake and a rapist. Sir John's victim is the coquettish but virtuous Miss Friendly, and she is saved from ruin and disgrace only by the reformation of her ravisher and his willingness to marry her and give a name to their child. Several subplots reinforce the theme of female innocence under duress, and they all center on attempted abductions and rapes. Davys's novels are more explicit about the English landscape, and the actual customs of English domestic life, than other novels by women being read at the time. Otherwise they are less topically interesting, partly because they develop as comic studies of behavior in various character types. Still, their denunciations of contemporary reality for its cruel and destructive effects upon the good nature of some individuals, and for its encouragement of the wickedness in others, are as timely as the satiric thrusts of *Queen Zarah* or the didactic posturings of *Exilius* and *Madam de Beaumont*. Readers of the day would surely have recognized Davys's stories for their extreme relevance to familiar discussion—as carried on in the press, and in popular writing of all kinds—of the debasement of life as a consequence of morally impoverished institutions and bankrupt political leadership.

During the decade of the 1730s, none of the female authors whose novels had for years been amusing and edifying the public continued to publish new books except the irrepressible Eliza Haywood, whose only notable work of fiction was the *Adventures of Eovaai*. Aphra Behn, Delariviére Manley, Penelope Aubin, and Mary Davys were all dead by the year 1731, and though Jane Barker lived until 1743 she retreated into oblivion after the appearance of her last novel in 1726. With the end of all their great activity concluded the first generation of energetic novel writing in the history of English literature.[19] Elizabeth Rowe, author of two collections of pious epistolary vignettes, *Friendship in Death* and *Letters Moral and Entertaining* (both 1728), enjoyed a steady following throughout the new decade. Penelope Aubin's novels were assembled and reprinted together in an impressive gathering of 1739, just one year before the publication of Richardson's *Pamela*. But fresh editions of works by Aubin's female forebears and contemporaries were sporadic and scarce, and no significant careers began during this period. The continued popularity of Defoe's superior books, and the explosion of interest in French fiction, may help to account for the shorter supply of native stories by women. And yet, if we look quickly at the new novelistic narratives that did appear in the 1730s, we find that the major themes, the rhetorical strategies, the relevance to turbulent contemporary life and political circumstance that distinguished the works of Manley, Barker, and the other important female fiction writers of their day recur again and again with but little variation, in a kind of unbroken "tradition." Simple reference to several representative titles may hint at the degree to which this is so. These titles ring familiarly: *The Fair Concubine: or, the Secret History of the Beautiful Vanella* (1732); *The Perjur'd Citizen; or, Female Revenge* (1732); *The Happy-Unfortunate; or, the Female Page*, by Elizabeth Boyd (1732); *Modern Amours: or, a Secret History of the Adventures of some Persons of the First Rank* (1733); *The Temple Rakes, or, Innocence Preserved* (1735); *The History of Clorana, the Beautiful Arcadian or, Virtue Triumphant* (1737).

As I suggested at the very outset of this essay, and as every serious historian of the English novel has always acknowledged, Samuel Richardson and Henry Fielding were keenly aware of their female predecessors when they sat down to write their own masterly novels early in the 1740s. Both of these men, as we know, reacted scornfully to previous fiction, and both claimed to be purposeful innovators inaugurating a "new species of writing." Richardson worked very deliberately and very seriously in *Pamela* to capture the moral reality of a corrupt and disordered society complete with its own Luciferian exponent of evil authority in the person of the aristocratic seducer Mr. B.; and his epistolary manner dramatized with great conviction and effect how that society interacts with, and is finally reconciled to, his own projected example of the idealized heroic female. The story was designed, Richardson remarked in a letter to his friend Aaron Hill, to deflect attention away from the "pomp and parade of romance-writing."[20] But Richardson's very statement of intention in his letter implies a recognition of and dependency upon the works of authors like Haywood and Aubin, whose novels differ from his more in quality than in primary appeal. Fielding's *Joseph Andrews*, conceived in part as a study in heroic male virtue, offers a purposeful alternative to the popular tales of female innocence, and by so doing actually grants them their preeminence. *Joseph Andrews*, of course, and Fielding's other novels as well, develop as a detailed commentary on the often gruesome realities of social, moral, and political life in the world as the author knew it personally. In this respect, the appeal of Fielding's works coincides exactly with that of the very tales he attempts to displace.

In all their fictional tales, Fielding and Richardson drew resourcefully upon the example of many writers practicing in many narrative traditions, as I have tried to show at length elsewhere.[21] But in their desire to be read these two male authors seem to have been ready to exploit while transforming what women novelists before them had already made current; and their narratives insistently display moral idealism in dire conflict with a world darkened by the abuses of the wickedly powerful. In this connection, it is worth emphasizing anew that a majority of their truly exemplary characters, and Smollett's also, are young innocent girls. Much the same is true of the more accomplished minor storytellers who were at work alongside them in the 1740s, and who (it must be said) doubtless reacted as much to their great contemporaries as to their female ancestors in a native tradition of novel writing. These largely forgotten but quite able and serious minor authors were, by the way, all women—Mary Collyer, Sarah Fielding, Charlotte McCarthy, a rejuvenated Eliza Haywood.[22] Clearly, the women novelists whose works I have been discussing at such length left an important legacy to their immediate successors, major and minor alike, and their impact on the novel as a mode of literary expression during the crucial formative years of the 1740s was considerable. Indeed *Pamela, Joseph*

Andrews, and the other really triumphant new fictions of that singular decade might never have been written without the prior example of the female storytellers whom their authors simultaneously copied and repudiated.

* * *

In reacting to the political climate as it seemed to affect the possibilities of a fulfilling moral life, early women novelists were rarely explicit or specific; but they appear to have been sharply aware of the contexts within which their works would be read, and their consciousness of the popular obsession with widespread corruption in the halls of government and in the other critical domains of power helped to dictate what they wrote. They were intensely political people, these novelists, writing in an age during which, as H. T. Dickinson has put it, the "relationship between politics and literature" was closer than ever before or since.[23] The polemical effectiveness of the actual fictions by women is usually difficult to gauge. But it is hardly worthwhile attempting to gauge it, for few of their authors— Manley and Haywood excepted—were controversialists anyway. Instead, they were storytellers intent upon enforcing a moral point of view which was sometimes also a political point of view, though rarely identified with any party dogma. The important thing is to note the depth of these female writers' sensitivity to the contemporary scene, and the insistence with which they pursued some kind of reciprocal relationship between the real world they knew and the imaginary worlds they created. Their works vastly extended the reading audience for fiction and, by responding with such urgency to anxieties over broad social and moral issues as they were touched by political circumstance, they did much to form and then sustain current ideals of public virtue—this is true even of Eliza Haywood's panting tales of tender passion. And all of the important narratives by women, including the scandal chronicles of Manley and Haywood, participated influentially in the cultivation of the popular taste for characters, plots, and themes drawn at least indirectly from the materials of familiar life. Without timely reader acceptance of such subject matter, and of its moralized treatment in a context of imaginative fable, the emergence of the novel as we know it today would not have occurred as it did, and when it did, with the sudden brilliant achievement of Samuel Richardson and Henry Fielding.

NOTES

1. Samuel Richardson, *Pamela: Or, Virtue Rewarded*, ed. T. C. Duncan Eaves and Ben D. Kimpel (Boston: Houghton Mifflin, 1971), 141.

2. For detailed discussion of the complex tensions of early eighteenth-century politics see J. G. A. Pocock, *The Machiavellian Moment: Florentine Political Thought and the Atlantic Republican Tradition* (Princeton: Princeton University Press, 1975), esp. chap. 11; Isaac Kramnick, *Bolingbroke and His Circle: The Politics of Nostalgia in the Age of Walpole* (Cambridge: Harvard University Press, 1968); and J. P. Kenyon, *Revolution Principles: The Politics of Party, 1689–1720* (New York and London: Cambridge University Press, 1977).

3. Kenyon, *Revolution Principles*, 17ff., argues this point to particular effect. See also John Dunn, *The Political Thought of John Locke: An Historical Account of the Argument of the Two Treatises of Government* (London: Cambridge University Press, 1969).

4. See Kenyon, *Revolution Principles*, 206; and Kramnick, *Bolingbroke and His Circle*, 127ff.

5. A recent book by Mary Anne Schofield, *Quiet Rebellion: The Fictional Heroines of Eliza Haywood* (Washington, D.C.: University Press of America, 1981), argues just this point at great length and to considerable effect.

6. *Joseph Andrews*, ed. Martin C. Battestin, the Wesleyan Edition of the Works of Henry Fielding (Middletown, Conn.: Wesleyan University Press, 1967), 187.

7. Aphra Behn, *Oroonoko; or, The Royal Slave* (London: Will Canning, 1688).

8. Some years ago George Guffey argued a contrary point of view, namely, that Mrs. Behn, a passionate Jacobite, wrote *Oroonoko* in support of James II at the very moment when he was about to lose his throne. More recently, Angeline Goreau has taken a position at the opposite pole, suggesting that the revolutionary impulses of Mrs. Behn's later life simply overcame her ardent Toryism, dividing her mind but nonetheless driving her to write her finest work as a strident protest against all forms of personal enslavement by the forces of arbitrary power. See Guffey, "Aphra Behn's *Oroonoko*: Occasion and Accomplishment," in *Two English Novelists: Aphra Behn and Anthony Trollope* (Los Angeles: William Andrews Clark Memorial Library, 1975), 3–41; and Goreau, *Reconstructing Aphra: A Social Biography of Aphra Behn* (New York: Dial Press, 1980), 287–90. The truth about Behn's intention, ambivalent as she certainly was, no doubt lies somewhere between these two extremes, and it can never be ascertained with any certainty. One thing, however, is clear: the continued appeal of *Oroonoko* throughout the eighteenth century, both in its original form and in Thomas Southerne's dramatic adaptation of 1694, depended very largely upon the combined emotional power and political relevance of its compelling portrait of a lonely, virtuous hero beset by all the vicious consequences of political and social corruption in the highest places.

9. *Queen Zarah* came out in two parts, both dated 1705. The four volumes of the *New Atalantis* include two works originally published separately under different titles: *Secret Memoirs and Manners of Several Persons of Quality, of Both Sexes from the New Atalantis, an Island in the Mediterranean*, 1709; and *Memoirs of Europe, Towards the Close of the Eighth Century*, 1710.

10. Manley's secret histories were decoded for their readers by separately pub-

lished keys. These are reprinted in Patricia Köster's two-volume facsimile edition of *The Novels of Mary Delarivière Manley* (Gainesville, Fla.: Scholars' Facsimiles and Reprints, 1971).

11. Manley's narrator is a personification of the goddess Intelligence, who is the principal storyteller in the work as she guides Astrea, goddess of Justice, on a tour of the world.

12. The whole episode of Charlot and the Duke occupies Manley for more than thirty pages (*New Atalantis*, 1:50–83). For full and interesting discussion of this same episode as a study in the conflict between male and female virtue see John J. Richetti, *Popular Fiction before Richardson: Narrative Patterns, 1700–1739* (Oxford: Clarendon Press, 1969), 143–49.

13. See Gwendolyn B. Needham, "Mary de la Rivière Manley, Tory Defender," *Huntington Library Quarterly* 12 (1949): 253–88.

14. Defoe's best remembered efforts in the vein of scandal chronicling are *Atalantis Major* and *The Secret History of the October Club* (both 1711). Oldmixon published *The Court of Atalantis* (1714) as a Whiggish reply to Manley.

15. Eliza Haywood, *Adventures of Eovaai, Princess of Ijaveo* (London: S. Baker, 1736).

16. I have written at length about these fictionalized attacks in "Portraits of a Monster: Robert Walpole and Early English Prose Fiction," *ECS* 14 (1981): 406–31. See especially pp. 421–24 for fuller discussion of *Eovaai*.

17. Jane Barker, *Exilius: or, The Banish'd Roman* (London: J. Roberts, 1715). References appear in parentheses in the text.

18. Richetti, *Popular Fiction before Richardson*, 235.

19. Behn died early, in 1689; Manley died in 1724, Aubin and Davys in 1731. Interestingly, the death of Defoe also occurred in 1731, so that this year really does mark a period in the early development of the British novel.

20. Richardson to Hill, January 1741, in John Carroll, ed., *Selected Letters of Samuel Richardson* (Oxford: Clarendon Press, 1964), 41.

21. Jerry C. Beasley, *Novels of the 1740s* (Athens: University of Georgia Press, 1982).

22. Mary Collyer, *Felicia to Charlotte: Being Letters from a Young Lady in the Country, to Her Friend in Town*, 2 vols. (London: Joseph Collyer, 1744 and London: J. Payne and J. Bouquet, 1749); Sarah Fielding, *The Adventures of David Simple*, 2 vols. (London: A. Millar, 1744); Charlotte McCarthy, *The Fair Moralist: or, Love and Virtue* (London: R. Baldwin, 1745); Eliza Haywood, *The Fortunate Foundlings* (London: T. Gardner, 1744) and *Life's Progress through the Passions* (London: T. Gardner, 1748).

23. H. T. Dickinson, *Politics and Literature in the Eighteenth Century* (London: J. M. Dent, 1974), 1.

Charlotte Smith's Desmond

The Epistolary Novel as Ideological Argument

DIANA BOWSTEAD

Charlotte Smith's *Desmond* (1792)[1] is remarkable for being the only epistolary novel among the ten Smith published between 1788 and 1798. It is also remarkable for being among the most successful of early attempts at a fully realized political novel in English. Although the central plot of *Desmond* is firmly grounded in the sentimental tradition, and, in fact, is very similar to the plot George Eliot describes in "Silly Novels by Lady Novelists,"[2] the thrust of the novel is nonetheless realistic, radical, and incisive. Throughout the novel, the political debates and observations that fill many of the letters tie injustice in the government of nations to injustice in the government of families. Quite overtly, by way of the "sentiments"— that is, the ideas and opinions—expressed by each of the correspondents, the domestic tyranny of which Geraldine Verney, the putative heroine, is an acquiescent victim is treated as analogous to political tyranny in France prior to the Revolution. More insidiously, the striking juxtaposition of a sentimental narrative and lengthy discussions among the correspondents of evils implicit in autocracy induces a reflective reader to notice that the conventions of popular romantic fiction are themselves informed by questionable tenets about the exercise of power: that is, a notion of eroticism characterized by contemptuous dominion, on the one hand, and obeisant delicacy, on the other.

Epistolary fiction, although still popular at the end of the eighteenth century, was on the decline. The novel told in letters seems to have begun to lose ground as soon as writers in the 1780s and 1790s found and refined means to convey unarticulated thoughts and emotions by way of the indirect interior monologue.[3] Although articulated first-person set pieces— personal histories and soliloquys, for example, as well as letters—appear in all of Smith's novels, she habitually uses indirect interior monologue to

237

present vacillating states of mind. Drawn out in a series of letters, mixed or vacillating feelings require long, often tedious, documentation. Smith's usual narrative strategy allows her to summarize concisely and, equally important, precisely; it allows her to control nuances so as to report morally questionable inclinations without seeming to endorse them. Often justifiably, romantic novels in letters were open to censure for inadequately distinguishing indefensible rationales from conscientious self-examination. Hence, it would seem from the evidence that Smith did not consider letters an appropriate vehicle for many psychological and most emotional muddles.[4] Nor was she comfortable with the form; in the Introduction to *Desmond*, Smith expresses doubts about whether she has succeeded "so well in letters as in narrative" (1:1).

Smith does not state her reasons for using letters in this novel, but there is a significant observation to be made from which useful inferences may be drawn. As Allene Gregory first noted, the "letters devoted to the actual narrative would scarcely fill more than one of the three volumes. The rest is devoted to conversation and arguments about the [French] Revolution."[5] It would seem therefore that Smith's choice of the epistolary form has to do with the largely political and didactic import of the novel, and with advantages letters seemed to her to have over authorial narration in accomodating so weighty a burden of information and opinion. I suggest two reasons, one stylistic and the other tactical, for telling this story in letters. First, because so much of the substance of this novel is, of necessity, delivered as monologue or quoted dialogue rather than as narrative, the choice of a form in which every element is implicitly or explicitly a rehearsal or exchange of ideas is singularly apt. Second, in epistolary fiction particular opinions are never conveyed in the author's voice, but are always a function of character. Hence, Smith shrewdly offers what seems to be a compendium of distinctive views expressed by a variety of individuals so that the novel presents itself rather as disquisition than as tract.

Fully conscious of the expectations most readers bring to a work of "romantic" fiction, Smith anticipated objections about the wisdom of combining politics and fiction. She supposed that readers who "object to the matter, will probably arraign the manner, and exclaim against the impropriety of making a book of entertainment the vehicle of political discussions" (1:vi). She remarks too that, "if those in favor of one party have evidently the advantage, it is not owing to any partial presentation, but to the predominant power of truth and reason, which can neither be altered nor concealed" (1:iii). Smith's disavowal of *unwarranted* bias is of course a rhetorical trick; the novel is tastefully executed propaganda.

Contemporary reviews unanimously applauded what was seen as a plausible strategy for introducing substantive instruction into a work of entertainment. By 1792, Smith's stature in the literary marketplace was such that each of the four prestigious literary magazines carried a sizable piece on *Desmond*. The reviewer for the *European Magazine*, in fact, suggests that Smith is unduly defensive. He remarks that she "has thought proper . . . to apologize for the introduction of political matter in a work professedly of another kind. To those who think an apology is necessary, this will be sufficient. She is likewise supported by precedents by those of Fielding and Smollett, both of whom introduce more than *allusions* to the political state of their country."[6] It is not surprising that he places Smith in the company of Fielding and Smollett rather than identifying her as a lady novelist. In many respects, she is the George Eliot of her time, a writer on serious subjects whose femininity reviewers take into account only as one aspect of the distinctive intelligence she brings to a work of fiction.

The review in the *Monthly Review*, after noting that Smith has "ventured beyond the beaten track, so far as to interweave with her narrative many political discussions," enlarges on the social significance of her decision to do so, although careful to convey to readers that the novel is nevertheless structurally coherent, that its characters are vivid and amusing, and that its social insights are astute:

Being very justly of the opinion, that the great events which are passing in the world are no less interesting to women than to men, and that in her solicitude to discharge the domestic duties, a woman ought not to forget that, in common with her father and husband, her brothers and sons, she is a citizen; Mrs. Smith introduces, where the course of the tale will admit of such interruptions, conversations on the principles and occurrences of the French Revolution; and these conversations she enlivens with humorous strokes of character, which prove that she has observed the present state of society with an attentive and discriminating eye.[7]

Even the *Critical Review*, in the only politically conservative piece of the four, recommends the novel. The reviewer admires the "principal novelty in the conduct of the tale": that it skillfully introduces the manners and politics of France into fiction for pedagogical reasons. He admits that he does not share Smith's views on the Revolution, yet adroitly grants that "Mrs. Smith has spoken as she thought, and represented the conduct and sentiments of the democrats as they appeared to her. History may confirm her sentiments, and confute ours." The *Critical Review*'s reservations have to do solely with the writer's moral responsibility to untutored, uncritical readers:

> The principal subject of enquiry is how far [Smith's sentiments] ought to be introduced into a work of this kind. We have often had occasion to observe, that the opportunities for modern fine ladies for information are so few, that every means of their obtaining it, incidentally, should be approved of. On the other hand, it may be asked, ought not the state of the question, in such situations, to be given more impartially, or at least the arguments on each side fairly stated?

The reviewer quite rightly notes that, although Smith repeats opinions she does not endorse, "when the argument on the other side appears to be just, [she does not] enforce it with her usual energy."[8] Her bias disturbs him only because her avowed purpose is to address and instruct readers so likely to be persuaded by patently manipulative rhetorical and literary strategies.

Lastly, the reviewer for the *Analytical Review*, fully Smith's political ally, comments on the stylistic advantages of the epistolary form for purposes of propaganda. He points out that, in Desmond's letters, "the cause of freedom is defended with warmth, whilst shrewd satire and acute observations back *the imbodied* [sic] *arguments*."[9] In fact, all Smith's minor characters are little more than embodied arguments. Whereas even the *Critical Review*'s politically unsympathetic reviewer commends Smith for her "well developed, or artfully contrasted"[10] major characters, the *Analytical Review*'s partisan reviewer is especially interested in her "subordinate characters" because they are "sketched with that peculiar dexterity which shoots folly as it flies."[11] He calls attention to the pointed social satire in this novel as purposive as well as pervasive, a function of its political message.

Most of the overt—sometimes almost gratuitous—satire in *Desmond* appears in the first of its three volumes because of the deliberate manner in which Smith distributes her material among them. Political issues dominate the first volume, marital issues the second, and the two are brought together by both characters and events in the third volume.

The novel begins when Desmond sets out to visit France. He has two reasons for traveling. First, he wants to put distance between himself and the married woman he loves, Geraldine Verney. Second, he is something of a Jacobin, and wants to see at firsthand the consequences of the Revolution in France. The period of time that elapses in the course of the entire novel is from June 9, 1790, to February 6, 1792 (roughly from the time when hereditary titles were abolished to the time when Louis XVI agreed to a constitutional monarchy). The period of time covered in the first volume is until October 10, 1790, hence not characterized by civic disorder, as rumors in England would have it.

All the letters in volume 1 are exchanges between Lionel Desmond and

Erasmus Bethel, whose ward Desmond had been until reaching his maturity; six years later, they remain close friends. All but three letters among a total of fourteen are written by Desmond himself. This part of the novel shows a family resemblance to Humphrey Clinker's letters from Scotland (1771) and to the first part of John Moore's *Mordaunt* (1800): a record of Mordaunt's travels abroad and, as the subtitle advertises, a collection of *Sketches of Life, Characters, and Manners in Various Countries,* not very different from the numerous factual, journalistic travel books popular during the period.

Beginning the novel by geographically separating her main characters, Smith of course precludes conventional exposition of character and any initial complications of situation. Instead she begins with exposition of a different sort: of her political subject matter, in scenes that are peopled by "embodied arguments." Apparently unrelated encounters between Desmond and individuals he meets along his route incrementally define what Smith puts forth as the central issue in the politics of the period: the disposition of property. Later, the romantic action of the novel draws the institution of marriage into a, by then, carefully ordered "grouping" of opinions about the ownership and government of property and invites readers to compare analogues—that is, to consider wives, too, as a kind of property— and themselves make inferences about the moral implications of such comparisons. Smith's literary tact is such that only once in the novel is the connection overtly made: when Geraldine refers to herself, in passing, while describing her husband, the "unfortunate man whose property I am" (3:x, 148).

Smith's strategy is to establish thematic connections between what initially seem to be no more than narrated anecdotes. She does so by means of recurrent episodes that involve the consumption, distribution, and production of food so that the ideas her characters express seem, with a certain dramatic inevitability, to inform and determine their behavior. She uses table manners, gourmandizing, indulgence of sexual appetites, treatment of poachers, farming practices, estate management, and more to animate characters in ways that seem consonant with their political principles, and either attractive or repulsive to suit Smith's bias.

Smith begins with the very first stop Desmond makes before crossing the English Channel. It is in Margate, where he meets two members of Parliament: Lord Newminster, who sits in the House of Lords, and General Wallingford, in Commons. This event is reported in a letter to Bethel dated June 24, 1790, and is the first instance in which conservative opinion is presented to the reader. General Wallingford arrives at a house in which Desmond and Lord Newminster have spent the afternoon to announce the latest news from France, that, "by a decree passed the nineteenth of June, these low wretches, this collection of dirty fellows, have abolished all titles, and abolished the very name of nobility" (1:v, 60). As important in characterizing Lord Newminster's political posture as any more serious defense of privilege that he offers is the scene in which Smith shows him engaged with his dog. Before refreshments are cleared, Newminster orders his servant to bring him the remains of the hot chocolate and a plate of bread and butter. "The man obeyed, and the noble gentleman poured the chocolate over the plate, and gave it altogether to the . . . dog—'was it hungry?' cried he— 'was it hungry, a lovely dear?—I would rather all the old women in the country should fast for a month, than thou shouldest not have thy belly-full' " (1:v, 57–58). This speech expresses the insensitivity that Smith proposes is at the root of his politics. Conservative opinion about who should eat is subsequently shown as, at the least, socially irresponsible, if not also cruelly egocentric.

Those who are especially concerned with eating well are frequently shown indulging their appetites in consequences of some form of social injustice; sometimes Smith merely allows mention of such injustice as part of the conversation, trusting the reader to perceive the pertinence of the "association of ideas." Hence, Desmond's second stop, in Dover, during which he overhears a conversation between a newly made squire and a doctor of divinity. The two English gentlemen—who, Desmond tells Bethel, refuse alms to a starving young mother—agree that the Revolution has gone too far and that England ought to invade France in order, specifically, to restore game laws and church revenues. Their attention is, however, repeatedly drawn from matters of political concern to concern over the quality of fish and game available both at home and abroad, and to all that they each find disappointing about French cuisine. As the squire leaves the tavern at which they met, he invites the clergyman to share a turtle soup prepared under his supervision by a Negro slave from his estate in the West Indies. However incidentally the fact that he is a slave owner enters the conversation, it is an important aspect of "character" that he both exploits and patronizes the culinary talents of a human being who is, in fact, his property.

The theme that takes shape in these, Desmond's first two encounters, is sounded periodically all the way through to the end of the novel in nicely differentiated variations. In the middle of the third volume, for example, Desmond's uncle, the former Major Danby, is described by Bethel as follows:

> You know, that being an old batchelor, and somewhat of an epicure, he is at home, what the vulgar call a cot; and has laid down his spontoon for the tasting

spoon, converted his sword into a carving knife, and his sash into a jelly bag—It is not her youth or her beauty, that recommended his present favorite house-keeper; but the skill she had acquired in studying under a French cook, at the house of a great man, who acquired an immense fortune in the American war, by obtaining the contract for potatoes and sour crout [*sic*]—But even to this gentlewoman, skilled as she is in "all kinds of made dishes, pickling, potting, and preserving," and tenderly connected with her, as the prying world supposes the Major to be; he does not leave the sole direction of that important department, his kitchen; which, when he is at home, he always superintends himself. (3:xiii, 174–75)

In this permutation, Smith's theme assimilates references to war profits gained at the expense of a badly fed army and implications that gourmandizing goes with lechery: the suggestion that Danby's cook is also employed as concubine.[12] Epicureanism like Danby's is shown to affect policy at home; epicureanism like that of the squire in Dover is shown to affect policy in his West Indian holdings. Hence, each emergence of the theme impinges not only on the subject of self-indulgence as a private matter—both psychological and moral—but also on the effect of avid appetites on the government of private property.

All such variants on the theme of the greedy gratification of appetites by men of means anticipate or echo two set pieces about the abuse of large land holdings, one in England and the other in France. Bethel reports to Desmond on "improvements" initiated by Stamford, who, having begun as Bethel's lawyer, has become a member of Parliament and very wealthy: profiting from sinecures and shady investments. In order to sustain the lavish table that draws influential people to his house in London, he quite literally puts a modest, but elegant, estate—formerly the Verneys'—entirely in the service of appetite. Bethel writes:

The beautiful little wood which overshadowed the clear and rapid rivulet, as it hastens through these grounds to join the Medway, has been cut down, or at least a part of it only has been suffered to remain, as what he calls a collateral security against the northeast wind, to an immense range of forcing and succession houses, where not only pines are produced, but where different buildings, and different degrees of heat, are adapted to the ripening cherries in March, and peaches in April, with almost every other fruit out of its natural course—The hamadryades, to whom I remember, on your first acquaintance with the Verney family, you addressed some charming lines of poetry, because it was under their protection you first beheld Geraldine; the hamadryades are driven from the place which is now occupied by culinary deities—The water now serves only to supply the gardeners, or to stagnate in stews for the fattening of carp and tench; heaps of manure pollute the turf, and rows of reed fences divide and disfigure those beautiful grounds, that were once lawns and coppices—Everything is sacrificed to the luxuries of the table. (2:xix, 92–93)

To Bethel, this is certainly a grotesque notion of husbandry.

Both here and later, when Geraldine Verney's husband and his aristocratic friends employ his Yorkshire estate for a hunting party—which includes, as evening sport, gambling and entertainment provided by prostitutes in addition to sumptuous meals—Smith shows a sorry abuse of valuable property by men of privilege whether serving the decadent profligacy of men of family, like Verney, or the ostentatious extravagance of the plebian nouveau riche, like Stamford. She suggests, too, that autocratic and self-serving landowners produce all that is unlovely and unnatural in the countryside, so that, at the extreme, the great house threatens to deplete the land on which it depends.

In France, the home of the Compte d'Hauteville serves as an eerie image of the ultimate consequences of socially irresponsible land management: a magnificent gothic edifice within an agricultural wasteland. Desmond describes his approach to d'Hauteville's property as follows:

> The look of even ill managed cultivation soon . . . ceased; and over a piece of ground, which was grass, where it was not mole-hills, and from whence all traces of a road were obliterated, we approached to the end of an avenue of beech trees; they were rather the ruins of trees; for they had lost the beautiful and graceful forms nature originally gave them, by the frequent application of the ax; and were, many of them, little better than ragged pollards.
>
> A few straggling trees of other kinds, that had been planted and neglected, were mingled among the rows of beech on either side; but were, for want of protection, "withering in leafless platoons."—Not a cottage arose to break the monotony of this long line of disfigured vegetation. (1:xi, 203–4)

The castle itself is a meeting place for those aristocrats who refuse to accept the Revolution and who intrigue to enlist the aid of other European monarchs for a counter-revolutionary invasion of France. As such it is a "residence, where mortified and discomfitted tyranny seems to have taken up its full station; and with impotent indignation to colour with its own gloomy hand every surrounding object" (1:xi, 199). Thus, the house stands almost as an expressionistic emblem of the nocuous chagrin of its owner and tenants. (It is among these people, and not far from the d'Hauteville castle, that Geraldine Verney's husband is mortally wounded, having been drawn into their affairs by way of gambling debts rather than as a matter of political conscience.)

In contrast stands the estate of d'Hauteville's nephew, the former Marquis de Montfleuri, an aristocrat sympathetic to the spirit of revolution and in all respects an ideal "governor," even if himself something of an epicure. Desmond describes him as "a man in whom the fire of that ardent imagination, so common among his countrymen, is tempered by sound reason" (1:vii, 107). Montfleuri has begun a program of reform on his own estates, which Desmond visits, anticipating and precluding violence among his dependents by correcting abuses and amending iniquities in the traditional agrarian system. He has, for example, purchased a newly vacant monastery adjacent to his own property, and converted one of the buildings into

> an house of industry; not to confine the poor to work, for he abhors the idea of compulsion, but to furnish with easy and useful employment, such as by age, or infirmity, or infancy, are unfitted for the labor of the fields.—And here he also means that the robust peasant may, when the rigour of the season, or any other circumstance, deprives him of occupation abroad, find something to do within; nothing, however, in the way of manufactures is to be attempted, farther than strong coarse articles, useful to themselves, or in the cultures of the estate. (1:x, 184)

Montfleuri's reforms have been sound and effective because he understands the causes of disaffection among the lower classes as well as among the middle class, as he demonstrates in explaining some of them to Desmond.

Montfleuri's function as a character in this fiction turns on the fact that reforms on his estate are an expression of his radical beliefs. He first embodies, as exemplar, Smith's implicit thematic subject; then he articulates, as knowledgeable partisan, her explicit political statement in support of the Revolutionary cause. By way of Montfleuri's speech in defense of the Revolution, as Desmond records it, Smith gives her readers an extraordinarily concise review of French history from the Jacobin point of view. Montfleuri goes as far back in time as the reign of Henry III, and concentrates on the policies and practices of subsequent monarchs insofar as they affected the quality of life in France.

There is nothing naive about the political analysis that accompanies Montfleuri's history. He takes into account for example the influence of "Mary of Medicis" and her party at court on her son, Louis XIII, to explain that a gesture that might seem to have been democratic in intent was in fact made to conciliate a faction among the elite:

> The early part of the reign of the weak and peevish bigot . . . , Louis the Thirteenth, was marked by a faint attempt to restore something like a voice to the people, by a convocation of les etats généraux.

But this was rather an effort of the nobility against the hated power of the Italian favourites, the Conchinis, than meant to restore to the people any part of their lost rights. (1:ix, 145–46)

So conscientious an historian is Smith that she informs the reader in a footnote that this particular session was the "last assembly of that description that was called in France" (1:ix, 145).

Montfleuri traces iniquitous economic policies that originated during the reign of Louis XIV and persisted during the reign of his successor, when

the sums . . . extorted from the hard hands of patient industry, were either expended in disgraceful and ill-managed wars, or lavished in the debaucheries of the most profligate court that modern Europe has beheld. From the infamous means that to support all this, were then practised to raise money; from the heavy imposts that were then laid on the country, France has never recovered; but, perhaps, in the *discontents* which these oppressions created, silent and unmarked as they were, the foundation was laid for the universal spirit of revolt, to which she is now indebted for her freedom. (1:ix, 149)

Having reviewed both the political and economic history of France up to the time of the American war, he observes too that the intellectual heritage of Voltaire, Rousseau, Turgot, and "the application of [Turgot's 'political maxims and economic systems'] by Mirabeau, excited a spirit of enquiry, the results of which could not fail of being favourable to the liberties of mankind; and such was the disposition of the people of France, when the ambitious policy of our ministry sent our soldiers into America to support the English colonists in their resistance to the parent state" (1:ix, 150–51). According to Montfleuri, dissidence at home was one of the ramifications of so imprudent a foreign policy on the part of the French government. Because members of the French ruling class were

blinded by that restless desire of conquest, and their jealousy of the English, which has ever marked its politics, or government did not reflect that they were thus tacitly encouraging a spirit subversive to all their views; nor foresee, that the men who were sent out to assist in the preservation of American freedom, would soon learn that they were degraded by being themselves slaves; and would return to their native country to feel and to assert their right to be themselves free. (1:ix, 152–53)

Smith, by means of Montfleuri's "sentiments," offers her readers a persuasive essay on the political, economic, intellectual, and military circumstances in France that, from the radical point of view, invited rebellion and by implication condone it.

Unlike the monarchy that historically exploited the country at the expense of the populace, unlike Stamford in England and d'Hauteville in France who exploit the land at the expense of those who live on it, Montfleuri sees his own interests best served when the people who work his estate benefit from enlightened, morally responsible management. As a character, Montfleuri serves as an attractive, sympathetic spokesman for the Jacobin cause inasmuch as he is motivated by a humane, moral appreciation of the obligations a man of property ought to assume to promote conscientious government and far-sighted husbandry.

Just as the opinions and behavior of individual landholders serve, in this novel, as specific manifestations in the private sphere of its political subject, so too does its romantic plot illustrate the continuity between ideology and action. Ways of governing erotic and/or romantic inclinations and of cultivating equitable, consensual relationships between men and women are explored within Smith's unusually simple—both for her and for the time—narrative.[13] Rather than developing a large cast of paired lovers—her usual practice—Smith puts Desmond at the center of a romantic triangle of sorts, which provides the means for a simple contrast between the two women to whom Desmond is drawn. The dramatic structure of the novel, although significant for what it allows Smith to say about women and marriage, is not, however, totally successful.

Contemporary critics quite rightly took exception to a subplot that is, in fact, too much a function of thematic design and of too little use in promoting the narrative. In effect, Smith doubles her heroine, introducing Josephine de Boisbelle, Montfleuri's sister, midway through the first volume of the novel. She, like Geraldine, suffers in consequence of a marriage arranged for her without due attention to the character and principles of the bridegroom. Whereas Geraldine is chaste, even in thought, and the proper object of Desmond's deep and distant reverence, Josephine acknowledges her sensual feelings and freely enters into an illicit relationship with him; neither claims to love the other—Josephine too has a first love, from whom she has been separated since forced to marry de Boisbelle.[14] Smith uses Josephine to propose that the sentimental heroine may, herself, have sexual appetites and to imagine for her readers the consequences when she chooses to satisfy them: in this case, an unwanted pregnancy, but no public shame or private guilt because Josephine's enlightened brother and honest lover cooperate to protect her reputation. The price she pays for her indiscretion is no higher than that required of Desmond. Contemporary readers seem unruffled by the radical implications of Josephine's story, perhaps because it can be seen as merely confirming stereotypical notions about the moral lassitude of the French aristocracy.

Critics noticed, however, that the Josephine subplot serves only to justify Desmond's mystifying refusal to account for his movements in the second half of the novel while he sees to it that the child of this liaison is born in secret. According to the *Critical Review*, the "connection of Desmond with madame [*sic*] Boisbelle is unnecessarily introduced; for the only purpose it answers, viz. to increase the perplexity previous to the catastrophe, is scarcely perceived among the more affecting circumstances of the other events."[15] In general, Smith was faulted for having allowed what seems an awkward inconsistency, "want of keep,"[16] in Desmond's character. The *European Magazine* notes that Desmond's "connection with Josephine ought to have been avoided. . . . But our Authoress may say, she did not intend to make him perfect. Perhaps not, we are not advocates for perfect monsters, but where faults answer little good purpose, they may well be avoided."[17] Desmond is, indeed, too little a "mixed character," too much a moral paragon, for a casual affair to seem probable behavior on his part. As the *Monthly Review* remarks, in a novel in which the "principal characters are boldly sketched and consistently supported," one feels that "the virtuous and romantic Desmond should not in his tour through France, have been suffered so far to forget himself and his Geraldine, as to have fallen into a *criminal* amour with a married woman,"[18] when this is precisely what Desmond refuses to do at home. The *Critical Review*'s reviewer puts the same objection more subjectively, admitting that "we may be romantic; but we feel our esteem for Desmond in some degree lessened"[19] by the terms of his affair with Josephine.

Had Smith made Desmond a more lusty character, were Desmond less effusively idealistic and quixotic in his sentiments about Geraldine, it is not likely that the critics would have objected to the affair on purely moral grounds. There are, in Smith's other novels, illicit relationships that did not excite critical disapproval. The problem here has to do with whether Smith has achieved consistency of character, and the difficulty, I believe, lies in the fact that she is using the epistolary form. Smith could have developed the subtleties of an ambiguous erotic response; she did so, for example, in both *Emmeline* and *Ethelinde*. She clearly wanted Desmond's experience with Josephine to sound a note that would ironically undercut the sentimentality of his devotion to Geraldine; without the contrast, the tenor of his relationships with women seems either unrealistically gallant or absurdly adolescent. Restricted by the epistolary form, however, Smith can only report what Desmond consciously grasps about his feelings and what he is willing to report to an older gentleman, his former guardian. She cannot show the operations of an emotional and moral conflict in process, as she does in other novels so adeptly by way of third-person narration, except by imitating Richardson: something she either could not or would not do. Hence, Desmond's affair with Josephine seems forced, contrived for purposes only dimly apparent to most readers and neither economical nor necessary for readers as astute as her reviewers.

Smith did, however, put the resources of epistolary fiction to good use in otherwise controlling sentimental tendencies of both characterization and narrative. Gossip among the correspondents about Desmond's affairs serves as ironic corrective. As the points of view of each of several disinterested characters who comment on Desmond's romantic attachments converge on the high seriousness of his feelings toward both Geraldine and Josephine, they diffuse the heady atmosphere Desmond's letters create. Bethel, for example, before reporting news of Geraldine, says to Desmond, "I expect to have you enacting very soon the part of an English Werther; for you seem far gone in his species of insanity; and I fear what I have to say to you today will feed this unhappy frenzy" (3:vi, 60). Montfleuri considers his quixotic devotion to Geraldine "a degree of visionary insanity," which leads Desmond to want what his French friend sarcastically calls "the sublime pleasure" he experiences in the notion that he is "deputed to watch over this angelic woman, with the fond affection of a guardian spirit" (3:xxii, 256, 255). Josephine provides opportunity for a truly sardonic discourse by Bethel on the likelihood that a sexual liaison will cure a sentimental one:

> At your age, my good friend, a lovely and unfortunate woman—who probably tells you all her distresses—who leans on your arm, and [in] whose voice you endeavour to fancy the tender accents of Geraldine—will, I will venture to prophecy, soon cease to please you, notwithstanding you "bear a charmed heart," only in the semblance of another.—And as to any engagements, you know, such as her having a husband, and so forth, those little impediments "make not the heart sore" in France. In short, I look upon your cure as nearly perfected, and by the time this letter reaches you, I doubt not, but that you will have begun to wonder how you could ever take up such a notion, as of an unchangeable and immortal passion, which is a thing never heard or thought of, but by the tender novel writer, and their gentle readers.—Madame de Boisbelle seems the Woman in the world best calculated to win you from the absurd system you had built; and had you been a descendent of Lord Chesterfield's, and his spirit presided over your destiny, he could hardly have led you to a scene so favourable to dissultory gallantry, and so fatal to the immortality of your attachment as the house of Montfleuri. (1:xi, 189–90)

Such friendly cynicism undercuts Desmond's most saccharine declarations.

Aside from her function in the moral structure of the novel, Josephine affords Smith the opportunity for the kind of scene for which she was, from the first, famous (according to the *Critical Review*, "in all of her novels, the descriptions of scenery and situation are peculiarly excellent.")[20] The pervasively sensual effect of this scene is not unusual in Smith's novels, but it could not have been written for a woman as concerned with the appearance of propriety as Geraldine is. The setting is the top of one of the highest hills close to Montfleuri's home, on which there is, according to Desmond,

> the ruin of a large ancient building, of which the country people tell wonderful legends. . . . [I] have entreated my friend to preserve this structure in its present state—than which, nothing can be more picturesque: when of a fine glowing evening, the almost perpendicular hill on which it stands is reflected in the unruffled bosom of the broad river, crowned with these venerable remains, half mantled in ivy, and other parasytical plants, and a few cypresses, which grow here as in Italy, mingling their spiral forms among the masses of ruin. (1:x, 170–72)

Somewhat later Desmond tells Bethel about "a walk which Josephine engaged me to take with her last night to the ruin on the hill"; there,

> seating herself on a piece of fallen column, she began, after a deep sigh, and with eyes swimming in tears, to relate to me the occurrences of her unfortunate life.
> Could I help listening to such a woman?—Could I help sympathizing in sorrows which she so well knows how to describe?—Alas! when she complains that her mother betrayed her into marriage with a man, for whom it was impossible she ever could either feel love or esteem—When she dwells on all the miseries of such a connection, on the bitterness with which her life is irrevocably dashed—The similarity of her fate to that of Geraldine, awakens in my mind a thousand subjects of painful recollection, and fruitless regret—My tears flow with hers; and she believes those emotions arise from extreme sensibility, which are rather excited by the situation of my own heart.

They remain, both occupied with their own thoughts, until Desmond realizes that it is quite late and getting dark:

> When these circumstances occurred to me, I suddenly proposed to Madame de Boisbelle to return—She had then been shedding tears in silence, for some moments, and starting from the melancholy attitude in which she sat, she took my hand, and gently pressing it, said, as I led her among the masses of the fallen buildings that impeded our path—'To the unhappy, sympathy and tenderness, like your's, is so seducing, that I have even trespassed on the indulgence your pity seems willing to grant me—I, perhaps have too tediously dwelt on incurable calamities, and called off your thoughts too long from pleasanter subjects and happier women!' (1:xiv, 274–76)

Of course, Desmond has been thinking about a woman no happier than she.

So intimate a scene cannot be assigned to Geraldine, yet it is one of the elements Smith's readers expected to find in her novels. Smith's reputation in her own time rested to a considerable degree on her original and unique capacity to draw on a poetically realized landscape for the mood of an emotionally charged scene. This episode differs from most only in the intensity of its erotic overtones. Hence, one of the things Smith manages by providing Desmond with a French companion is to play her love story both ways: sentimentally romantic for Geraldine and sexually "realistic" for Josephine.

Thackeray is not quite accurate, in his Preface to *The History of Pendennis* (1850), when he ascribes Victorian prudery to novelists of the eighteenth century after Fielding. About his own novel, he quite rightly asserts that Pendennis should have had a *liaison*, a token one, for the sake of his credibility as a character. In Thackeray's words:

> Since the author of 'Tom Jones' was buried, no writer of fiction among us has been permitted to depict to his utmost power a MAN. We must drape him, and give him a certain conventional simper. . . . Many ladies have remonstrated and subscribers left me, because, in the course of the story, I describe a young man resisting and affected by temptation. My object was to say, that he had the passions to feel, and the manliness and generosity to overcome them. You will not hear—it is best to know it—what moves in the real world, what passes in society, in the clubs, colleges, messrooms,—what is the life and talk of your sons.[21]

Pendennis is like Desmond in several respects, and should have had the kind of sexual latitude Smith allowed her hero.

As for the kind of platonic, idolizing love that both Pendennis and Desmond feel for women they may not marry, and whose beds they are not allowed to share secretly, Smith has something to say in verse about the facts of such relationships, although she perpetuates the romantic fiction in her novels:

> Friendship, as some sage poet sings,
> Is chasten'd Love, depriv'd of wings
> Without all wish or power to wander
> Less volatile, but not less tender.

Nevertheless,

> . . . she, who years *beyond fifteen*,
> Has counted *twenty*, may have seen

How rarely unplum'd Love will stay;
He flies not—but he cooly walks away.[22]

Although Smith seems to acquiesce to generally accepted social and literary proprieties of her time in the broad outlines of Geraldine Verney's story, she introduces ironic overtones that color the effect of the novel by positing a second "heroine," equally sympathetic, whose behavior deviates significantly from approved norms.

The second volume of *Desmond* is largely given over to Geraldine and the romantic plot in which she figures as suffering heroine. Smith works here with and through conventions common in eighteenth-century sentimental fiction. Geraldine's story might well be what George Eliot satirizes in "Silly Novels by Lady Novelists" when she says that the typical heroine of such novels

> as often as not marries the wrong person to begin with, and she suffers terribly from the plots and intrigues of the vicious baronet; but even death has a soft place in his heart for such a paragon, and remedies all mistakes for her just at the right moment. The vicious baronet is sure to be killed in a duel, and the tedious husband dies in his bed requesting his wife, as a particular favour to him, to marry the man she loves best, and having already dispatched a note to the lover informing him of the comfortable arrangement.

Only two features of Geraldine Verney's situation differ from Eliot's typical plot. The novel begins, not when Geraldine enters society, but when she is already married, a phenomenon rare enough to have been considered a novelty of its plot even though it had been done first by Henry Fielding in *Amelia*. Second, Geraldine is never seen to sparkle as the reigning beauty and wit of her social set, nor is she ever seen so comfortably provided for that "we have the satisfaction of knowing that her sorrows are wept into embroidered pocket-handkerchiefs" and "that her fainting form reclines on the very best embroidered upholstery."[23] The Verneys' financial straits keep Geraldine at home; opulence is far beyond their means.

For all that threatens to become maudlin in a plot otherwise quite close to Eliot's summary, the thrust of the novel is nevertheless away from excessive sentimentality. Eliciting pity is in this novel a means rather than an end. The reader's pity for Geraldine is not supposed to become awe at virtue's transcendent capacity for self-immolation—the intent of the Griselda motif. Rather, it is supposed to become indignation on her behalf and on behalf of all victims of institutionally authorized oppression. And these emotions are supposed to motivate critical insight into wrongful and inhumane presuppositions that are used to rationalize servility on the one hand and to justify privilege on the other.

Inasmuch as Geraldine Verney's story is played off against the French Revolution, the domestic tyranny of which she is the victim has analogues in political tyranny in France. Hence the reader is forced to consider, insofar as he is sympathetic to her sorrows and distress, whether she should be submissive or rebellious. The subplot of the novel suggests an alternative to submission. Josephine leaves her husband (as Smith herself did). For Josephine, honor and integrity demand an assertion of self-worth and independence. What is more, her virtue is not, like Geraldine's, inviolable. Her audacity and ardor cast a none-too-flattering shadow over Geraldine's diffidence and chastity. The final effect of the romantic plot in *Desmond* derives from its ironic structure. Since a happy ending for Geraldine seems to be achieved at Josephine's expense, Josephine's bitter lot is a nagging reminder that all such stories need not end as the conventions of sentimental fiction dictate. Although Geraldine is a "distressed heroine" and suffers as nobly as any of her breed, the reader is finally not altogether certain that abjection is a heroic posture. The disposition of subject matter—the contiguity of two such similar stories—raises questions about the relationship between resignation and integrity in a morally responsible individual, even when that individual is a woman.

In spite of its conventional aspects, Geraldine's story serves to bring a kind of realism into fiction that was new to the novel in 1792. Although the tale of Geraldine's trials ends with spectacular melodrama, the distress this heroine suffers throughout most of the novel offers no appealing titillation. Admittedly, the threat of lascivious seduction and of rape echoes in the background of some scenes, but the possibility of either coming to pass is denied as often as it is suggested. Geraldine insists that such dangers are peculiar to the fiction of an earlier time—there are references to *Clarissa, Sir Charles Grandison*, and *Evelina*—and not to contemporary real life.

Geraldine's distress is circumstantial: tedious, wearing, even debilitating. First we hear that, during the period immediately after the birth of her third child, her home in London is under execution for debts amounting to almost £4,000. In December, when these are settled—quite discreetly by Desmond—Verney returns to town, but not to his home, coming there only to change clothes. During this period, he negotiates the sale of his estate in Kent to Stamford to acquire funds for new extravagances. In February, Geraldine's doctor insists that she leave London for the sake of her health and that of the child she is nursing. She intends to go to Verney's estate in Yorkshire, but he refuses her the use of the house. As Bethel tells Desmond:

He is himself gone into Yorkshire, . . . and it is reported, and I fear with truth, that he has established an hunt there, of which he bears the greatest share of the expence, though it is said to be at the joint charge of himself, Lord Newminster, and Sir James Deybourne. The arrangement at Moorsely Park, is said . . . to consist of three of the most celebrated courtezans, who are at this time the most fashionable, and of course, the most expensive—Every one of these illustrious personages appropriating one of these ladies for the time of their residence. (2:ix, 101)

And this group is the subject of common gossip in London, Bath, and Kent.

What is more, as Geraldine tells her sister Fanny, the cost of lodgings outside of London, an "additional expence, though pronounced to be absolutely necessary to my existence, and that of his child, is submitted to with reluctance by Mr. Verney" (2:viii, 78). As if immediate financial problems and the functional difficulties of poverty were not enough, Geraldine is also threatened by Verney's attempt to get hold of property settled on her as part of their marriage contract.

Also distressing, but not at all sensational, is the treatment she receives from Verney in front of both his friends and hers. One example will suffice to convey the tenor of his conversation with her. When Verney returns home after five weeks in hiding from creditors whom Geraldine must face, he arrives in the company of Lord Newminster while Bethel is visiting Geraldine. Bethel reports to Desmond:

> Verney, who had just heard that the creditors, who had the executions in his house, were paid, and the bailiffs withdrawn, was not in a humour to be reserved, or even considerate.—Without speaking to his wife, he shook hands with me, and cried—"Damme, Bethel, how long is it since I saw you last? I thought you were gone to kingdom come.—Here's Newminster and I, we came only last night from his house in Norfolk.—Damme, we came to raise the wind together; for I have had the Philistines in my house, and be cursed to them, who had laid violent hands on all my goods and chattels, except my wife and her brats; but some worthy soul, I know not who, has sent them off.—I wish I could find out who is so damned generous, I'd try to touch them a little for the ready I want now."

Geraldine tries to leave the room as quietly as possible with her children, but Verney notices, shouting, "away with ye all, . . . get ye along to the nursery, that's the proper place for women and children." Bethel continues, "The look that Geraldine gave him, as she passed to the door, which I held open for her, is not to be described—it was contempt, stifled by concern—it was indignation subdued by shame and sorrow" (2:v, 35–36).

Geraldine's distress is of a psychologically wearing kind: she worries about money; she worries about her children's present confusion about the absence of their father and the numerous changes in residence; she worries about their future security should Verney squander money they ought to inherit; she worries about whether she should go on nursing the youngest child since her anxiety seems to affect his health. In addition, she worries about her dangerously irresponsible brother, who, had he been otherwise, might have served as her protector.

Geraldine's predicament is not at all the kind that sentimental heroines suffer. Melodramatic resolution at the end of the novel notwithstanding, Geraldine's story is about the dismal facts of wretched marriages, and especially of those (like Smith's) that have been arranged by self-absorbed parents. Geraldine's difficulties are never, until the end of the novel, dramatic or extravagant enough to be captivating.

In the third volume of the novel, issues that until now have been treated quite separately: the merits of democratic government, the proper management of estates and the kind of arrangements that ought to exist between husband and wife are brought together in a rather remarkable sequence of three contiguous letters. Avoiding polemic, Smith instead relies on the reader to appreciate what is meaningful about the juxtaposition of subjects and about the imagery they share. The broad, political issue that link them is overtly aired in the third letter, although it is implied earlier: whether there is, or can be, any rationale for oppression—at the extreme, for slavery.

The first of the three letters is from Geraldine Verney, recently arrived in France, to her sister. She writes that circumstances in and around Paris are not as bad as rumors reaching England suggest, and that she is persuaded that reforms benefiting the French peasants are in progress. She then observes that her sympathy for those who effected a greater democratization of French politics

> must be from conviction, for it cannot be from the prejudice of education—*we* were always brought up as if we were designed for wives to the Vicars of Bray— My father, indeed, would not condescend to suppose that our sentiments were worth forming or consulting; and with all my respect for his memory, I cannot help recollecting that he was a very Turk in principle, and hardly allowed women any pretensions to souls, or thought them worth more care than he bestowed on his horses, which were to look sleek, and do their paces well. (3:x, 133)

The aside, in which daughters are equated with horses, seems gratuitous, but leads directly to the next letter, in which Geraldine perceives herself as legally held captive because she is, for all practical purposes, Verney's property.

Geraldine has, in the interim between this and the next letter, taken a house in the suburbs of Paris while waiting for her husband to arrange to have her brought to him. She has every reason to believe that he intends to sell her services to some of his powerful friends in return for the money and patronage he desperately needs, having already spent both his fortune and hers on various forms of debauchery, some of which are indistinguishable from depravity. If her husband does indeed plan to venture into the white slave trade, she is already on her way to market; against the advice of friends, she has insisted that it is her moral duty to join Verney in the interior of France when he summons her. While waiting to continue the journey, she writes to her sister:

> You, my Fanny— . . . have never been unhappy, and have never known . . . the strange and, perhaps, capricious feelings of the *irretrievably* wretched— Since I have found myself so, I have taken up a notion that I do not breathe freely, while I am within the house; and like the poor maniac, who wandered about in the neighborhood of Bristol, I fancy 'that nothing is good but liberty and fresh air.' (3:xi, 159–60)

Her claustrophobia is emblematic of a psychological rebellion against surrendering herself to Verney's purposes, even if morally she feels compelled to.

The notion that she is a prisoner is then developed indirectly by means of the creatures her son captures in the garden. Because Geraldine feels incarcerated indoors, she lives

> all day about the gardens; while the sun is high, Peggy attends me with the three children, in some shady part of them; and George often amuses himself with catching the little brown lizards which abound in the grass, and among the tufts of low shrubs on this dry soil—He brings them to me—I bid him take great care not to hurt them—I explained to him, that they have the same sense of pain as he has, and suffer equally under pressure and confinement—He looks very grave, as I endeavour to impress this on his mind; and then gently putting them down, cries, "no! no! indeed! I will not hurt you, poor little things!" (3:xi, 160–61)

Geraldine's fears, both for herself and for her children, develop around the analogy to the helpless lizards so that the child seems both the antithesis of the husband who has made her "suffer . . . under pressure and confinement" and he seems as vulnerable as these creatures are:

> How much a tone, a look, an almost imperceptible expression of countenance will awaken to new anguish an heart always oppressed like mine!—As, liberating his prisoners, he says this—I look round on him, his sweet sister, and his

baby-brother, and internally sighing, say, 'Oh! would I were sure, if ever your poor mamma is torn from you, that nobody will hurt *you*, poor little things!' (3:xi, 161)

Geraldine and her children are in danger because they are, according to the courts, the church, and the morality of the drawing room, bound to suffer the consequences of Verney's neglect or abuse of them.

The issue of the slave trade and its relevance to the marriage market are then, respectively, the explicit and implicit subjects of the third letter. Writing to Bethel, Desmond records a conversation with a member of Parliament who owns an estate in the West Indies. Desmond has been arguing the morality of treating human beings like cattle. The member of Parliament replies,

> You are young . . . and have but little considered the importance of this trade to the prosperity of the British nation; besides, give me leave to tell you, that you know nothing of the condition of the negroes neither, nor of their nature—They are not fit to be treated otherwise than as slaves, for they have not the same senses and feeling as we have. . . . They have no understanding to qualify them for any rank in society above slaves: and, indeed, are not to be called men—they are monkies. (3:xii, 162–63)

The reference to monkeys evokes earlier references to horses; between the two analogous allusions is the fablelike episode of the lizards. If the reader identifies with Geraldine's plight as a potential victim of the white slave trade, he or she has been given every reason to see the plight of a Negro slave from the same perspective. And, of course, the analogy works the other way as well; those who oppose the institution of slavery for political or moral reasons are invited to consider the position of women in so civilized a country as England.

In the letter that follows these three, Smith reveals the brutality that lies beneath the surface in polite society, a brutality that seems to be a natural consequence of equating human relationships—sexual relationships, in particular—with monetary values. Desmond's uncle, Mr. Danby, knowing something of his nephew's feelings for Geraldine Verney and suspecting that he has contributed to her support (albeit, without her knowledge), articulates a point of view about marital and extramarital relations usually suppressed in nineteenth-century fiction:

> If Mrs. Verney has a *penchant* for Lionel, with all my soul.—I know very well that if the stupid puppy, her husband, had as many horns as the beast in the Revelations, he deserves them all, and Desmond has as good a chance as

another, with any woman; but I think he's a fool to be at such a cursed expence
about it, and then to fancy himself so snug, like a woodcock that hides its head,
and believes itself secure,—Hah! ha! hah! (3:xii, 179)

Mr. Danby goes on to share his worldly wisdom with Desmond's friend,
Bethel, in a somewhat more refined tone. The result is, if anything, an even
more callous view of the pecuniary implications of Desmond's relations
with the Verneys. Mr. Danby asks Bethel,

When a young fellow lays down between three and four thousand pounds, to
release from execution the effects of a man he despises and contemns; when he
goes down *incog.* to the retirement of such a man's wife, and stays near a month
in her neighborhood; when he is known to have declined the most advantageous
offers of alliance from the families of some of the finest young women in England on her account; and, when he is actually, at this time, gone abroad with
her; or, however, concealed somewhere or other, how the plague can you suppose the world will *not* talk? It is well enough known, that Verney is a savage and
a scoundrel, who will sell his wife to the best bidder—Why don't Lionel offer him
her price at once, for now you may depend upon it he'll be sued, and Verney will
get devilish damages. (3:xiii, 180)

Danby is not worried that Geraldine might refuse. He sees as clearly in his
way as Mary Wollstonecraft does in hers that the odds are in favor of
acquiescence from a woman who "must be dependent on her husband's
bounty for her subsistence during his life or support after his death—for
how can a being . . . be virtuous, who is not free?"[24] Comments on Geraldine Verney's situation in *Desmond* are as radically feminist in their implications as anything in *A Vindication of the Rights of Woman*, also published in 1792.

Mr. Danby's suggestion for an equitable solution to the problem of
Desmond's relationship to the Verneys presupposes the existence of a covert and discreet form of "white slave trade" operating in upper-class English society.[25] In a novel that is so much about the French Revolution, and
so sympathetic to those in France who suffered as a result of the unconstrained tyranny of the French aristocracy, evidence that individuals in
England are treated as negotiable property in the manner Danby suggests
becomes part of the larger political argument of the novel. Danby's dissatisfaction with Desmond is, at the core, political. He is annoyed that,
"instead of sporting his money like a man of spirit, on the turf, or with the
bones, [Desmond] goes piping about, and talks of unequal representation,
and the weight of taxes" (3:xiii, 177–78). Sex, like riding and gambling, is
for him one of the avocations proper for a man of Desmond's class. Adul-

tery (especially if Geraldine is reluctant) would be a sign of political or-
thodoxy, as Danby views it. As Smith seems to see it, one of the key subjects in the kind of romantic fiction she writes is what, in the twentieth
century, is often called "sexual politics" with considerably less justification.

As an experiment in political fiction, *Desmond* is at least as extraordinary as William Godwin's *Caleb Williams.*[26] The sophisticated use of juxtaposition and metaphoric connection described above is only one of several insidious and seditious strategies that Smith uses to make her point.
Unlike *Caleb Williams, Desmond* is not an exciting, suspenseful novel.
Both its "matter" and its "manner" are relatively untheatrical. Smith concedes to popular taste in Geraldine's bizarre adventures on her way to her
husband. When she does find Verney, he is fortuitously dying, repentant,
and anxious to charge Desmond with the responsibility for her care and
protection; the novel ends in a gush of sentiment.[27] Otherwise, *Desmond* is
almost entirely a discussion of questions raised by events in France and a
description of events in Geraldine's marriage: the two subjects reflecting on
each other by way of common themes, especially slavery.

Smith does not allow her treatment of marriage to take shape as articulated polemic, as the political issues she raises do. None of the correspondents, least of all Geraldine, takes an ideological position on the rights of
women or the iniquities of the law. Rather, Smith uses Geraldine's letters to
show her trying to come to terms with her situation. Insofar as the reader is
appalled at the consequences of such an attempt, the novel succeeds as
persuasion in the way fiction should: by effectively rendering the extremes
to which an individual might be driven by "things as they are."

Interesting in terms of what is possible within the epistolary form is the
psychological and moral confusion that Geraldine's letters betray. Smith
shows her reaching for and rationalizing a moral construct that will allow
her to keep some remnant of dignity in a world in which the law of the
country and her mother and brother agree that her husband has the right to
govern his affairs and his family however he sees fit. Geraldine's letters, in
the third volume of the novel, describe the terms on which she hopes to
salvage some degree of integrity even as the circumstances of her marriage
force her toward the ultimate degradation: that she be compelled by her
husband to bed with his friends. Having conceded as much to Verney's
demands as she feels she can, she finally decides that she will not allow him
to use her as property, that she cannot be made to consider herself "his
slave" (3:x, 142). Even so, she wills herself to serve Verney's needs in every
other way. She tells her sister that, although she is no longer prepared to
sacrifice herself to a man who shows no regard for her, she will devote
herself all the more rigorously to a principle of righteous behavior. "Being

now, however, but too sensible, that whatever share of tenderness my young heart once gave him, he had long since thrown away; and that duty alone bound me to him, I determined to fulfill what seemed to be my destiny—to be a complete martyr to that duty, and to follow withersoever it led" (3:xxiii, 271). She holds herself honor-bound to observe the formal obligations of her legal and social position as a wife under the force of a moral imperative, fully internalized, all the more pressing once she realizes that she will resist should Verney try to trade on her body. The closer she comes to overt rebellion, the more desperately she acts the exemplary wife.

Geraldine is indeed a Griselda, but finally for reasons so wrong that, although she stands as moral exemplar, her rectitude seems hollow and unwholesome. She admits that there is something perverse about her motives: "Had I loved Mr. Verney, as the possessor of my first affections—as the father of my children—in short, as almost any other man might have been beloved, I should not, perhaps, have felt so very strongly the impulse of duty *only*." Yet it is clear to her that only "in the consciousness of having done my *duty*" (3:xxiii, 271, 323) does she provide herself with a moral defense against a time when her sordid marriage comes to a scandalous end. Hence, when Verney is wounded and sends for her, she undertakes a very dangerous journey alone into the lawless French countryside. In doing so, she is uncharacteristically reckless.

If Geraldine seems to nobly brave danger for her husband's sake, in fact, the emotional impetus driving her is suicidal despair. Trying to describe the consequences of having lived too long with shame and fear, she tells her sister:

> A wretch, who is compelled to tremble on the brink of a precipice, has often been known to throw himself headlong from it, and rush to death rather than endure the dread of it—This sort of sensation was, I think, what I felt. (3:xxiii, 271–72)

Having at first resolved to be a martyr to duty, Geraldine finds herself rushing toward a more absolute form of martyrdom, impelled toward total self-annihilation to escape an untenuous denial of self.

Although Smith then brings her story to a close with Geraldine safely in Desmond's protection, her virtue in every respect intact—that is, although she provides the happy ending that reviewers and readers found morally and aesthetically satisfying—there is a nagging dissonance that runs through the last volume of this novel. Smith suggests a much darker variant of the story, in which women like Geraldine, having contracted bad marriages, destroy themselves trying to reconcile notions of personal honor and virtue with the behavior required of them by the men who govern their lives. By way of Geraldine, Smith reveals the psychological disintegration that is the likely consequence.

Although Smith does not show Geraldine engaged in an overt act of rebellion against Verney, the radicalization of her heroine is complete by the end of the novel, and must be taken as its central action, although it is a psychological, moral, and political reversal rather than a dramatic one.[28] She understands that she has been taken for "property" and that she must not again seem a willing slave. Having extended her sympathies for French peasants and slaves to include a perception of her own position as wife, she allies herself in her second marriage to a man of the right political principles. Smith intends her readers to see that the security of Geraldine's position in the household Desmond governs depends on his honest intention to translate his ideological opposition to political autocracy into reasonably democratic domestic policies.

Because the plot involves so little dramatic action, *Desmond* is very much out of the mainstream of the English novel as that channel was carved out during the nineteenth century. It is easy to understand why *Desmond* has until now been neglected. It is difficult to understand why those interested in political, and especially feminist, literature have turned their attention recently so exclusively to Mary Wollstonecraft's clumsy, stridently partisan fiction when there is also Charlotte Smith's decorous and devastating *Desmond* to speak for the times.[29]

NOTES

1. All references to the text are to the Garland reprint. *Desmond* was first published in Dublin in 1792. There were two London editions in the same year and a French edition in 1793.

2. Eliot, "Silly Novels by Lady Novelists," in Pinney, *Essays of George Eliot*, 302–03. Eliot describes what had become a conventional plot by the mid 1850s.

3. Before *Desmond*, Smith published three novels: *Emmeline, the Orphan of the Castle* (1788); *Ethelinde, or The Recluse of the Lake* (1789); *Celestina, A Novel* (1791). All are heroine-centered, third-person narratives.

4. Individual letters that appear in Smith's other novels are almost always ironic devices, reflecting the writer's idiosyncrasies and affectations. Like the letters here, however, they always reflect conscious thoughts and seldom attempt to show psychological ambivalence.

5. Gregory, *The French Revolution and the English Novel*, 215.

6. Unsigned review of *Desmond. A Novel, in Three Volumes*, by Charlotte Smith, *European Magazine* 22 (1792): 21.

7. Unsigned review of *Desmond. A Novel*, by Charlotte Smith, *Monthly Review*, 2d ser., 9 (1972): 406.

8. Unsigned review of *Desmond. A Novel*, by Charlotte Smith, *Critical Review*, 2d ser., 6 (1792): 100.

9. Signed "M.," review of *Desmond. A Novel*, by Charlotte Smith, *Analytical Review* 13 (1792): 428 (italics mine).

10. *Critical Review*, 99.

11. *Analytical Review*, 428. The *Critical Review* remarks, "If an aristocrat is introduced, he is either to be confuted or ridiculed" (100).

12. Similarly, variants on the issue of game laws occur in 1:xii, 208–10, and in the interpolated narrative, the story of a Breton (2:xii, 251–70), which was excerpted and printed in full in the *Analytical Review*, 430–35.

13. Typical is a range of contrasting couples, as in Smith's own courtship novel, *Emmeline*, in D'Arblay's *Camilla* (1796), and in Austen's *Pride and Prejudice* (1813).

14. Desmond tells her he is totally committed to Geraldine; she has been in love with a man now a naval officer since childhood (3:xxv, 338–40).

15. *Critical Review*, 99.

16. *European Magazine*, 23.

17. Ibid.

18. *Monthly Review*, 412.

19. *Critical Review*, 99.

20. Ibid., 100.

21. William Makepeace Thackery, *The History of Pendennis: His Fortunes and Misfortunes, His Friends, and His Greatest Enemy, The Complete Works*, 3:xiv.

22. Charlotte Smith, *Beachy Head with Other Poems*, 139–40.

23. Eliot, "Silly Novels by Lady Novelists," 302–03.

24. Wollstonecraft, *A Vindication of the Rights of Women*, 120.

25. Danby suggests in fact that, if the sale is not secretly negotiated with Verney, he will claim his price publicly, as did Theophilus Cibber in 1738 and 1739 when he brought charges of "criminal conversation" against the man who enjoyed Mrs. Cibber's services. Because there was evidence of collusion, Cibber received only £10 of the £5,000 he claimed in the first suit; he received £500 of the £10,000 he asked for in the second (s.v. "Cibber, Theophilus," *Dictionary of National Biography* [1938]). The *Oxford English Dictionary* offers the following example of usage under " 'Conversation,' 3, Sexual intercourse or intimacy": "1809 Tomlins *Law Dictionary* [2d ed.], s.v. *Adultery*, the usual mode of punishing adulterers at present is by action of *crim. con.* (as it is commonly expressed), to recover damages." Thus, a husband commonly received compensation for the sins of his wife in cash during the late eighteenth century, and many were not above arranging to secure funds in this way.

26. In *Studies in the Literary Backgrounds of English Radicalism*, Adams points out that the "work of no literary period in English history has been more deeply affected by political discussion and an examination of the principles and conduct of government than the last decade of the eighteenth century. Around Burke's *Reflections* [*on the French Revolution* (1790)] developed a whole literature of protest in defense of revolutionary principles" (506). *Desmond* is part of that

body of literature: letters vi and x in volume 2 are, in part, a refutation of Burke, Desmond having just finished reading the *Reflections*. The debate was finally won by "counter-revolutionary writers" according to Palmer. For a catalogue of their publications, see *The World of the French Revolution*, 210.

27. The end of the novel seemed effective and commendable to the *European Magazine's* reviewer, who observed that "the *denouement*, or rather conclusion of the story is unembarrassed by a crowd of improbabilities huddled together; a fault too common in the last volumes of novels" (22). He is thinking of clusters of contrived reunions and recognition devices, such as strawberry marks.

28. The evidence of Smith's decision to use letters for this particular novel does not support Goldknopf's contention, in *The Life of the Novel*, that the epistolary novel is not as closely related to drama as Day (in *Told in Letters*) claims. Goldknopf's assumption, that "the novel typically organizes itself through the medium of action," is a questionable one, in part because his use of the word "action" seems too restrictive. Nevertheless, these are his conclusions:

> To the extent . . . that the novel became structured by a pattern of action, the epistolary novel became increasingly disadvantaged. Its life, like that of certain prehistoric animals, had to be confined to an age when its weaknesses were not decisive. In this light, Jane Austen's abandonment of the epistolary format becomes significant, because she was the first novelist to balance and coordinate structured action, empirical realism, and psychological insight into a design—on a cameo scale, to be sure—which is familiar even today (65).

I maintain that the form lost its peculiar advantages as soon as novelists in the 1790s, from whom Jane Austen learned her craft, became adept at using interior monologue. Smith, in electing to use the epistolary form in this novel, demonstrates that, when letters are used as a vehicle for communicating "sentiments," fully formulated conscious ideas and opinions, the epistolary form is not handicapped as it is when doing what is better done by means of narrative or interior monologue: presenting as yet unformulated thoughts and latent emotions. The letters in this novel manifestly do the work of speeches; thus, *Desmond* approaches the drama, albeit closet drama, in one of the ways Day suggests is significant to the evolution of the genre. See *Told in Letters*, 194–95.

29. *Desmond* has not entirely escaped notice. In *The Epistolary Novel*, Singer observes that Smith need not have doubted her ability "to make a novel go as well in letters as in the narrative which was her accustomed medium in her earlier work. When one has read the book . . . any thought of her possible failure is dispersed" (112). But Singer does not explain the nature of her success. Among recent critics, some are not persuaded that the novel is at all successful. In "The Happy Marriage," Magee submits that the "marriage theme would be more effective if the story were told from Geraldine's point of view, but Charlotte Smith wanted to use Desmond to develop her unrelated political theme" (129).

Hannah More's Tracts
for the Times
Social Fiction and Female Ideology

MITZI MYERS

Remarking "the extreme activity of mind which showed itself in the later eighteenth century among women," Virginia Woolf urged the importance of a change, "which, if I were rewriting history, I should describe more fully and think of greater importance than the Crusades or the Wars of the Roses. The middle-class woman began to write." An eyewitness to that late-eighteenth- and early-nineteenth-century female literary efflorescence, the poet Samuel Rogers offers another perspective on the phenomenon: "How strange it is that while we men are modestly content to amuse by our writings, women must be didactic." For all its exaggeration, Rogers's witticism nonetheless identifies a key field of middle-class women's literary tillage which neither Woolf nor more recent feminist commentators have thus far garnered.[1] Yet educational genres like conduct books, moral tales, and the particular focus of this essay, cheap improving tracts read by multi-layered audiences of children and the poor—the newly literate—and by family circles of all classes, were female specialties from the late Georgian era on.

And in terms of what they reveal about women's standing, functions, and self-image and about their material impact on national life, an impact both literary and sociocultural, the popular forms of cottage, school, and nursery literature scarcely stand second to the canonical novel in interest and importance. Margaret Anne Doody has recently argued for the consequence of "minor" women novelists: the late-eighteenth-century "period we have seen as a blank space is precisely that which sees the development of the paradigm for women's fiction of the nineteenth century—something hardly less than the paradigm of the nineteenth-century novel itself."[2] But this revisionist paradigm wants expanding to include didactic genres intended to socialize juvenile and lower-class readers, for these, even beyond the popular novel, were modes in which female authors evaded cultural silencing to speak with teacherly force and sometimes technical innovation. Expressing with assurance their new sense of themselves as society's moral caretakers and maternal guardians, the period's didactic middle-class women impressed their values on English culture through pedagogic and philanthropic literature. Such narrations constitute a neglected female literary tradition—a woman writer's distinctive brand of social fiction.

Socializing literatures stand in close relation to the events and thought of their day; they are works animated by social issues. These cultural artifacts embody women's modes of response to the political crisis and social upheaval of a revolutionary era—the areas and answers they defined as their own, the themes and images through which their imaginations grasped and rendered historical transition. Here women tackle national problems in their own way; here they critique their society and express dissatisfaction with it; here they envision plots answerable to its dilemmas, solutions shaped by their historically conditioned locus and preconceptions. Acculturating narratives, this essay argues, served as significant channels of female reformist impulse and expressive power. Catering to an ever-expanding readership swelled by proliferating Sunday schools for the poor and by bourgeois preoccupations with molding youth, several generations of female writers (a "monstrous regiment" of women, one male historian of children's literature terms them) made moral tales and religious tracts their vehicles for reforming national manners and reformulating national morals.[3] Conventional, predictable, all their plots arguments pitting vice against virtue and all their characters boldly labeled, now a warning, now an exemplar, these print prescriptions frankly design to change their readers and their world. Not readily amenable to traditional critical appraisal, such "subliterary," patently didactic genres have largely remained the province of specialized literary historians. Yet sensitively read in context, simple tracts and tales can yield sophisticated insights to modern researchers in social history, women's history, and literary history.

Hannah More's Cheap Repository tracts (1795–98) are prime examples. Emblematic of women writers' increasingly confident handling of social questions, as well as historically important in itself, More's Repository project resonates with the cultural implications of woman's new didactic role. Arguably the most influential woman of her day, More enjoyed extraordinary success in several careers. As a witty, talented member of Bluestocking and Johnsonian circles, she was a much bepraised dramatist and versifier. After her conversion to Evangelicalism, she won international prominence as an educator, reformer, and magisterial arbiter of manners and morals, always specially concerned with "the morals of my own sex." From the ideological materials at hand, didactic women like More shaped a new ideal of educated and responsible womanhood. Through female influence and moral power, this cultural myth's new women would educate the young and illiterate, succor the unfortunate, amend the debased popular culture of the lower orders, reorient worldly men of every class, and set the national household in order. No one outlined woman's nurturing and re-formative assignment more clearly than More, and no one worked harder to elevate the moral reform central to emerging female ideology into a national mission. Women, she claimed, did not sufficiently know their own power; they must not be content to entertain and polish when they should awaken and reform. Times of revolutionary "alarm and peril" compelled women "to come forward and contribute their full and fair proportion to the saving of their country. . . . to raise the depressed tone of public morals."[4]

And More practiced what she taught. Skillfully modulating the mentorial persona of the female middling classes, she reproved the rich and improved the poor. Rooted in her "familiar acquaintance with vulgar life," the Repository tracts are the literary counterpart of her extensive educational philanthropies among the Somerset peasantry in the semicivilized Mendip Hills. To replace the "indecent songs, trials, and penny histories" cried about the streets "to the corruption of the lower class," the series offered monthly a lively moral tale or history (many of More's add up to short novels on the installment plan), a rollicking though reformative ballad cleverly set to a traditional melody, "to expel the poison of the old sort," and a special Sunday reading—a prayer, Bible story, or miniature sermon. More contributed almost one-half of the hundred odd pieces and exercised close editorial control over the project. Her aim was not just to revise popular literature, but to nudge novice readers toward an alternative mentality of self-discipline and self-improvement, to reform the work, leisure, and domestic patterns of popular culture through reeducation. Honoring her moral rescue work, the *Gentleman's Magazine* styled her "Hannah More, who takes the poor under her protection," and Charlotte Yonge rightly called her "the real originator of books written exclusively for the poor." But her fictions were also widely read by the middle classes and the gentry (whose demand necessitated separate editions on better paper), as well as by children of every class; they own a place in registries of children's literature.[5]

The tracts are also one of the great success stories in eighteenth-century female authorship. They sold 2 million English copies the first year alone, "besides great numbers in Ireland"—an astonishing record, the likes of which, as Richard D. Altick justly remarks, had never been seen before in the history of English books: "Tom Paine and Hannah More between them had opened the book to the common English reader." Lauding the good offices of the Cheap Repository, the *Christian Observer* located More's tracts "among the mighty barriers that, under God, checked the growth of infidelity and anarchy," a *cordon sanitaire* against French revolutionary principles, and the *Evangelical Magazine* asserted that to her pen, "the world, in its different ranks, owes perhaps greater obligations than to that of any other living author." Maybe, as some historians suggest, "the most successful propagandist of the 1790s," More was among the first to try her hand at interclass communication between England's "two nations."[6]

In these ways and more, the tracts helped change the face of the nation; they also helped change literary history. Indeed, More was a pioneer social novelist whose themes, techniques, and modes of part-publication and cheap, efficient distribution anticipate numerous nineteenth-century literary ventures. With good cause, recent Victorian scholars suggest that she was "the most influential British writer of fiction of her day" and that the Evangelical tract literature she launched "was a major shaping force in the development of the nineteenth-century English novel."[7] Her organized diffusion of instructive penny papers laid groundwork for subsequent tract publishing operations, like the Religious Tract Society's enormous Evangelical output (in which so much Victorian children's literature is grounded), or the secular efforts of the Whigs' Society for the Diffusion of Useful Knowledge and Harriet Martineau's novelistic *Illustrations of Political Economy*. Much reprinted and much imitated, More's fictive formulas interconnect several traditions of purposive fiction—the Puritan legacy of realistic religious narrative; the newer educative tale for youth; the nineties' philosophic novel of doctrine; the early-nineteenth-century regional chronicle of the laboring classes by such women as Maria Edgeworth, Elizabeth Hamilton, and Mary Leadbeater; and the Victorian social problem novel by Evangelical successors like Charlotte Elizabeth Tonna (whose *Wrongs of Woman* also echoes Wollstonecraft) or reformers like Dickens, whose working waifs are prefigured in such Repository tracts as *Betty Brown, the St. Giles's Orange Girl, with Some Account of Mrs. Sponge, the Money-Lender* and *The Lancashire Collier Girl*.[8]

Transcribing her society's exigent problems into fiction, More helped give the novel a new seriousness, relevance, and direction. Sometimes brutal, sometimes touching, always didactic, her fictions curiously mingle shrewdly observed social documentary and idealistic moral fable. They comprise a literature of instruction rendered with polemic verve, mimetic realism, and the formulaic fantasy that results when popular forms like chapbook romance are kidnapped for Christianity. Rich in sympathy and social concern, More's narratives repay analysis, make spirited reading even now. Here are hard facts and hard lives, vigorous, racy dialogue and homely domestic detail: the language of rat catchers, fortunetellers, post-boys, and shoemakers, the "poor old grate which scarcely held a handful of coals," the shirt "nearly as coarse as the sails of a ship," and the "fine plump cherry-cheek little girl" that make up the lot of the Shepherd of Salisbury Plain.[9] Here too are children and the poor as central, often individualized characters whose autonomous moral choices are accorded dignity and respect—that Wordsworthian locus thus enters fiction with More's cottage literature. She deftly utilizes everyday particulars, the tones and rhythms of common speech—fresh literary analogues of urgent social awareness; her thematic message of domestic heroism occasions a new domestic realism, ideas and aesthetic alike generated from the woman moralist's characteristic stance. In its complex mix of literary and cultural innovation, More's Repository illustrates how women's educative and caretaking role fed into new strains of social fiction, and her work exemplifies how women could translate female ideology's didactic imperative into an authoritative voice capable of documenting and interpreting historical realities.

More's 1801 Preface to her collected works outlines clearly the female educator's rationale and métier. Didacticism, she recognizes, implies self-confidence: "it furnishes little proof of the modesty of the woman to fancy that she can instruct." Saint Paul's fiat—"I suffer not a woman to teach"—hovers in the background. Yet virtue and usefulness justify assertion, activity, responsibility; ultimately, doing good even confers power. The female teacher makes no claims "to what is called learning." Rather, she studies life and manners, laboring "assiduously to make that kind of knowledge which is most indispensable to common life, familiar to the unlearned, and acceptable to the young." More images herself as the compassionate yet corrective maternal instructor of new reading publics—children, barely literate workers, rising and uncertain middling classes. The truths she offers are "obvious and familiar," the fruits of real everyday experience, of the woman moralist's characteristically pragmatic approach: little things, not showy and theoretical, but practical and generally useful. She pursues, not skill and renown, but " 'That which before us lies in daily life.' " This female specialty provides the inner organizing principle of More's work, indivisibly linking the intellectual substance of her tiny tracts, their aesthetic shape, and her carefully thought-out didactic theory. The commonplace details of domestic realism ground her considerable achievement, help make her indisputably a "tract writer of genius" who transmutes ephemeral journalism into creative art; the everyday discipline of domestic heroism is the way she measures psychic power and the key through which she seeks social regeneration.[10]

Thinking in terms of public legislation and political reform alone, some male historians say More's tracts exemplify the "fundamentally counter-revolutionary nature of the whole charitable and educational enterprise."[11] Once perceived as woman-determined texts, however, they reveal more complex configurations fashioned around private amelioration and women's religio-moral concerns. Woman's distinctive cultural situation provided the frame of reference for their themes, style, and structure; woman's belief systems and behavioral ideals shaped both their manner and their message. More's "Sunday school fiction" encodes reformist aims and reflects female cultural bias, disclosing as much about author as audience: about women's notions of selfhood and social institutions, about how the world is to be coped with and improved, about what kinds of power and achievement matter. Less reactionary than radical in its challenge to the customary bases of traditional society and in its normative insistence on unadulterated Christianity, More's Repository project proposes close to a total reconstruction of culture, a resocialization organized around the moral reform priorities of Evangelical womanhood. Rather than the common stereotype of her tracts as cunningly seasoned doses of class subordination for the lower orders, the Cheap Repository was, my argument goes, a much broader social endeavor, a meaty chapter in that bourgeois renovation of manners and morals which marks the transition from the eighteenth to the nineteenth century. As Gerald Newman contends, in a persuasive reexamination of emergent middle-class hegemony, neopuritans like More "should be regarded as moral and social revolutionaries," however impeccably loyalist their politics.[12] More's tracts present not so much a brief for Tory political stasis as for a woman's brand of bourgeois progressivism—pedagogy, philanthropy, and purification her cures for the old order's social ills.

The miniature social world that More presides over shows history through woman's eyes, focused on the problems she perceives and ordered by the values she defines. Blood abroad and anxieties at home—working-class illiteracy, improvidence, drunkenness, and poverty; luxury, immorality, and abdication of communal responsibility among the upper ranks; corruption rife from vendors of lewd chapbooks to poorhouse administrators; bad weather and scanty crops, escalating prices and spreading unrest like food riots. More shows herself keenly alert to these strains and fissures in the social fabric; they form the backdrop and the stuff of her stories, which are often, as with those concerning the great grain scarcity of 1795–96, intensely topical. She scales these large problems of the war years down to manageable size, grounding them in home, shop, or community, treats them in women's domestic terms. Her *Good Militia Man; or, The*

Man That Is Worth a Host, for example, is praised not for his manly murders overseas, but for his virtuous resistance to soldierly ways at home: he neither swills nor seduces.

Matters of political debate More usually approaches obliquely, although her initial venture in tractsmanship was an extremely successful counter to Paine's *Rights of Man*, written in 1792 before the Repository was launched. *Village Politics, Addressed to All the Mechanics, Journeymen, and Labourers, in Great Britain*, by "Will Chip, A Country Carpenter," is a dramatized political argument in dialogue form; here the questions and answers fly between Jack Anvil the blacksmith, with a head full of Paine and French reform, and Tom Hod the mason, who discountenances political involvement and applauds the values and liberties of English common life.[13] More used the characters again for another piece of overt commentary, *The Riot; or, Half a Loaf Is Better than No Bread*, which similarly vetoes political demonstration, counsels self-discipline, and promises relief from the classes above. Contemporary reports credited the singing of the ballad with having checked a formidable disorder near Bath, but More pronounced the mode of such work "a sort of writing repugnant to my nature," even if "rather a question of *peace* than of *politics*." She dreaded being branded "pert and political," and her woman's imagination bypassed democratic talk of the poor's rights for a maternal thinking oriented to needs and duties, to family feeling and domestic responsibilities.[14]

Yet More responds quickly and directly to social crisis according to her own lights. Abandoning a serialized tale in progress, she borrowed a title and incorporated current material from the London *Times* for her *Way to Plenty . . . Written in 1795, the Year of Scarcity*, and throughout the dearth, her tracts and her letters circle round food shortages and greedy monopolizers. "I should derive more gratification from being able to lower the price of bread than from having written the Iliad," she wrote to a friend. In lieu of that, exemplary Mrs. White in *The Way to Plenty* and the heroine of *The Cottage Cook; or, Mrs. Jones's Cheap Dishes* "give these poor women a little advice": recipes for rice milk and filling stew and "Friendly Hints" on domestic economy. Social problems here are not abstract issues, but local and immediate hungers which demand personal nurturing, the provision of physical and spiritual sustenance—soup kitchens and thrifty cookery, civilizing values and Christian ideals, practical "*helps to the poor for the better management of their families*" and "wholesome aliment" for their minds.[15]

More's womanly desire to ameliorate the lot of those less fortunate is crisply benevolent and quite unsentimental, given instead to sensible plans underwritten by her Christian social ethic: reforming popular literature and culture by channeling fledgling literacy toward a new social morality, teaching audiences how to make the most of what they had and socializing them in bourgeois strategies for gaining ground in the world and bourgeois notions of family life. Following a strict Evangelical logic of causes and consequences, the typical More plot sets improvident vice against tested virtue, rewarding spiritual self-examination and devotion to local obligations with a modest rise in the world. More did not expect to cure massive evils by her literature or her labors, but she did mean to advance social betterment through social fiction and to manifest a revisionist maternal stance: "That simple idea of being *cared for*, has always appeared to me a very cheering one," she wrote of her charities.[16]

Like her sister pedagogues, More is much exercised by society's victims: animals, slaves, orphans, poor illiterate children, laborers at subsistence level, mothers and children brought to destitution because the man drinks, girls seduced and abandoned. She indignantly scores the filthy ballads and romantic novels which warp the young and impressionable; the blood sports and callous customs which mutilate beasts and brutalize their practitioners; the male ethos that celebrates a lad of "spirit" whatever his crimes (he always gets his comeuppance in her tracts); the frauds and cheats imposed on ignorant and superstitious girls, like those of the female usurer in *Betty Brown* or of *Tawny Rachel, the Fortune Teller*—the witchlike pseudomothers of her tales. She presses for all the reforms urged by late-eighteenth-century critics of popular culture, but "Z" (the persona of the Repository tales she wrote herself) tailors the middle-class agenda to women's priorities. Take alcohol, for example.

Bourgeois reformers of the working class devoted much energy to attacking the public house for both practical and symbolic reasons. The eighteenth-century expansion of liquor outlets was widely blamed for increasing crime and poverty, and by the century's closing years, meliorists began to make headway in reducing the supply of drinking places to manageable order. Women writers like More and Sarah Trimmer expressed the struggle between middle-class reformism, which strove to regularize and privatize the pleasures of the poor, as a conflict between the male ethos of the "Blue Posts" or the "Tennis-Court" (More's tales are full of such taverns), rough, bawdy, untrammeled, and the orderly domesticity and family discipline of the home. In More's *Carpenter; or, The Dangers of Evil Company*, for instance, the exemplarily industrious husband is seduced from his hearth by the jocularities of a ne'er-do-well drinking companion. The wife finally reclaims her drunken mate when he demands food and she serves up a knife and his baby in a basket, the only "meat" the father's dissipation has left them. Restored to virtue, he pens a revealing motto:

> *The drunkard murders child and wife,*
> *Nor matters it a pin,*
> *Whether he stabs them with his knife,*
> *Or starves them with his gin.*

In *The Two Soldiers* by Hannah's sister Sally, the "Green Dragon" similarly serves as the "general rendezvous of all the fives-players and skittle-players in the country," introducing "beggary and famine among the wives and children in all the neighboring cottages." Thus, writes Hannah, "while the man is *enjoying himself*, as it is called, his wife and children are ragged and starving." Alcohol makes kind husbands into tyrants, brings on hunger and rags, and engenders prostitution. More worried that some would think her *Gin Shop; or, A Peep into a Prison* "too strict," but "that is the stronghold against which my chief artillery will be planted; all the evils of this country put together do not make up gin."[17]

Women reformers were not prohibitionists, however. More's fictions are punctuated with domestic vignettes of home-brewed beer and happy households, rosy children playing about the father's knees while he quaffs his cup beside his cheerful wife. Rather, the alehouse symbolized a whole way of life: the improvident orientation that middle-class adherents of rational and religious discipline abhorred in working-class culture—the earn-a-little-and-spend-it-promptly syndrome supposedly endemic among laborers, to the detriment of wife, child, and foresighted getting on in the world. As students of lower-class leisure observe, the alehouse was the central transmitter of popular culture, an emblem round which plebian custom and traditional ways rallied. But, warns More's spokesman, exemplary Farmer Worthy, "There is not perhaps a more dangerous snare to the souls of men than is to be found in that word *Custom*."[18] Good Tom White, risen from a poor postboy to righteous landed prosperity, anatomizes the customary usages, the traditional patterns of work and play, which impede the spiritual and material advancement of the working class. Opposed to the old mores stands the new "progressive" ideal of diligence and domesticity interweaving worldly prudence, familial affection, and spiritual piety. Trade in corrupt old customs for religion and respectability, urge White, Worthy, and their like: keep sober, serve God, work hard, "go and enjoy it with [your] wife and children."[19] More's good man is always a family man, thoroughly dedicated to wife and home. More's good woman redeems her unregenerate mate—"the unbelieving husband, shall be saved by the believing wife"—so that they soon "began to thrive prodigiously," achieving the real if modest social mobility she grants her upright characters, the kind of rise in the world sketched in such titles as *The Apprentice Turned Master*.[20]

England's maladies, then, More (like most sister moralists and like such fellow Evangelicals as Wilberforce) diagnoses as moral, not political. The transformations in human behavior necessitated by "these alarming times" are to be effected not by legislative act, but by internal change, a heroism Christian, private, and domestic. "The only way to become free is to turn Christian," pronounces Trueman, opposite number to *Mr. Fantom, The New Fashioned Philosopher*, whose denigration of household virtues and local benevolence marks him for a villain's demise. Or as the secularized catechism of *Village Politics* puts More's distrust of vast theoretical schemes:

Tom: I'm a friend to the people. I want a reform.
Jack: Then the shortest way is to mend thy self.
Tom: But I want a *general reform*.
Jack: Then let every one mend one.

For the criminal irresponsibility and "thoughtless profusion of some of the rich," for the "idleness and bad management of some of the poor," More repeats again Jack's cure, her favorite "good old maxim." No democrat except in religion, she proffers not political equality, but equal participation in sin and salvation. Even as the humblest *Hackney Coachman* has a reputation to maintain and "a soul to be sav'd," so the highest lord in the land is as guilty of sin, as subject to social dependence and duty as he.[21]

Regenerative power inheres in self-discipline and devotion, in submission to God's will for all, and, for the leisured classes, in unremitting endeavor to make the world conform to that will. This is the heroism of *The True Heroes; or, The Noble Army of Martyrs*; of the humble model protagonist of perhaps the most famous Repository tale, *The Shepherd of Salisbury Plain*; of the good ladies who salvage victimized orphan fruit vendors and overworked collier girls; and of *Hester Wilmot*, the Sunday school scholar who reclaims her drunken father and converts her family, becoming the prototype for many a nineteenth-century heroine, fictive or real. More's is a fictional world of no small sins, where small victories are similarly charged with meaning. Women and children or the poor have no public projects in their hands, but they can demonstrate their moral mastery and spiritual achievement through their control of what they wear and think or how they manage time and habits, outward emblems of victory over sin and error within. "A poor man like me," says the Shepherd, "is seldom called out to do great things, so that it is not by a few great deeds his character can be judged by his neighbours, but by the little round of daily customs he allows himself in." Tables "rubbed as bright as a looking-glass" or "some bits of cake lying in the slop of a pewter dish, with the brim melted off" signify their owners, just as "that Mud Cottage with the broken windows stuffed with dirty rags" economically places its wastrel possessor, who "did not know the value of such useful sayings, as that '*a tile in time saves nine.*' "[22]

Where dirt and congestion and idleness are translated as moral qualities, minutely particularized descriptions of clothing and interiors or contrasting scenes of sloth and industry mingle verisimilitude and iconographic force, blend domestic realism and domestic heroism. And the smallest autonomous ethical acts of the youngest and lowliest—the Lancashire collier girl's laboring "like a little independant woman" to support her whole family, Hester's praying for the father who has gambled away her hard-earned money toward a new gown, young Dick's telling the truth about who stole the Widow Brown's fine apples, even though it spells punishment for himself and his reprobate father—these too epitomize transfiguring power. Conventionally the property of the powerless—women, the poor—this Christian heroism More makes the sole power that can save England from external threat and internal disintegration. Hers is peculiarly a woman's answer, a domestic endurance derived from women's moral traditions, now deemed appropriate for poor and rich, female and male alike, an answer that takes account of economic and material conditions, but cannot see them as the ultimate reality. These are not our answers, but it needs to be recognized that for the female teachers who embraced them, such remedies signaled anything but quietism and social apathy. They located the only real ground of power.[23]

And they sanctioned female exercise of that power, of those prerogatives and permissions without which duties cannot be performed. Defining social problems as essentially moral and religious made woman's role focal. She was, in More's frequent phrase, God's instrument. Socializing the young and rehabilitating the laboring poor—two groups key to moral renovation—were woman's rightful obligation, her field of civic activism, in life and in literature. "The superintendence of the poor" is woman's "immediate office," More asserts: "*Charity is the calling of a lady; the care of the poor is her profession.*" Her vocation was "instructing the poor, as the grand means of saving the nation." But setting workers' houses in order was only half her educative task. The other was teaching an ethic of communal responsibility to, in More's sardonic phrase, "those persons who are pleased to called themselves their betters."[24] As the later division of her Repository fictions into *Tales for the Common People* and *Stories for Persons of the Middle Rank* indicates, schooling for the gentry and middling classes also informs these annals of the poor. Indeed, More's records of plebian life provide models for all classes and both sexes, a whole little world of instructive types from poorhouse inmates to rising tradesmen and farmers to pastors and patrons not above being tutored in Christian fundamentals by the objects of their care. With their conduct book patterns of interclass communication and reciprocity, her stories abound not only in virtuous villagers, but also in energetic philanthropists like her female moral reformer Mrs. Jones, heroine of a homily for bourgeois women, *A Cure for Melancholy: Showing the Way to Do Much Good with Little Money.* Like that autobiographical protagonist, they discover how "a more feeling kind of beneficence . . . literally brought 'the rich and poor to meet together.' " They embody a recurrent theme of More's letters and writings: the healing of class rifts through a newly vitalized Christianity which can reconcile opposing factions and forge them into a new collective unity, a respectable Christian middle class molding a respectable Christian working class.[25]

Reflecting women's standards for evaluating social behavior and women's ways of negotiating cultural crisis, evincing female social conscience and motherly models of the desirable society, More's narratives constitute a woman reformer's literature of community, and her moral answers assume (often literally) a woman's form. Few female characters in Georgian fiction make so decided an impact on their milieus as More's Mrs. Jones. Male historians usually describe her as a benevolent busybody, arrogant and intrusive, who patrols her parish looking for bad to correct and good to do. Like God, she always knows which is which. She is, they say, a moral policewoman in petticoats, a punitive social controller who sees to it that village women forsake tea drinking and idleness for industrious housewifery, that bakers who sell light loaves get punished, that the reluctant rich finance Sunday schools and the ignorant poor attend them, that superfluous public houses shut down and men betake themselves to their own firesides. But Mrs. Jones's ventures are meant to be read from a woman's point of view. She is the exemplary heroine of linked stories which graphically demonstrate exactly how an entire community can be remodeled through female enterprise and persuasive influence and exactly what improving impact such moral reform exerts on communal and family life. "Written *experimentally* and founded upon fact," *The Cure for Melancholy*, *The Sunday School*, and the latter's two-part sequel, *The History of Hester Wilmot* and *The New Gown*, offer role models of accomplishment for middle-class woman and cottage girl alike. May all who read these accounts *"go and do likewise!"*[26]

Mrs. Jones's story, like a number of other Repository tales, is a typological narrative which gains its social resonance by updating a biblical source, here Matthew 25, brimful with parables of wise virgins and well-used talents and with Christ's injunctions to charity. Mrs. Jones enacts what it means to "resemble your Saviour *by going about and doing good.*" She is, par excellence, didactic woman as socializer, educator of the young, and reformer of popular culture. Her projects are at once a lightly fictionalized representation of More's and her sister Patty's social welfare campaigns, Hannah the general and Patty the lieutenant (the terms are Hannah's), and an imaginative fantasy of feminine power, a telling rendition of the female teacher as surrogate mother, regulating and redeeming her microcosmic world. More tasted impressive success in her Somerset Sunday schools and other therapeutic operations, as a note to one of her tales reminds: "This story exhibits an accurate picture of that part of the country where the author then resided; and where, by her benevolent zeal, a great reformation was effected among the poor inhabitants of at least twenty parishes." All the same, More's own hard-won victories pale before the ease, speed, and authority with which Mrs. Jones orders and sanitizes her neighborhood. More's letters lament over social evils "I almost despair of seeing remedied"; Mrs. Jones infallibly acts and achieves.[27]

Unlike such other reforming women as Sarah Trimmer's village benefactor Mrs. Andrews, heroine of interconnected *Instructive Tales* from which More learned much, Mrs. Jones has neither wealth nor helpful husband; she is a widow in reduced circumstances. Doing good is not a matter of money, however, but of activity, judgment (for More insists on these "unfeminine" qualifications), and masterly management of the retrograde. These tracts, like many of More's, are neat little pieces of social analysis, each of Mrs. Jones's antagonists emblematizing a prevalent attitude thwarting the bourgeois reformist stance. There is Sir John, "thoughtless, lavish, and indolent," who indulgently supports traditional customs and stands for the old order; there is the legalistic squire, who thinks in terms of punishment rather than improvement; there is Farmer Hoskins, vulgar and materialistic, for whom education is another "new whim wham for getting the money out of one's pocket"; there is Rebecca Wilmot, the selfish village mother who has no use for religion or learning: "I would rather you would teach her to fear me, and keep my house clean." Some are cajoled: " 'Of all the foolish inventions, and new fangled devices to ruin the country, that of teaching the poor to read is the very worst.'—'And I, farmer, think that to teach good principles to the lower classes, is the most likely way to save the country. Now, in order to do this, we much teach them to read.' " Outmaneuvered, Hoskins gives his guinea. Some are coerced, for the maternal hand is firm: Mrs. Jones tells the villagers "not to bring any excuse to her which they could not bring to the day of judgment."[28] Benighted mothers doom their children, keeping them from the education that saves: "nobody shall hector over them but myself." Wise maternal stand ins like Mrs. Jones "instruct reasonable beings in the road to eternal life," transforming idle lasses like Hester Wilmot into ideal heroines, homespun symbols of a regenerate social order. Women's social service work is, More makes clear, indispensable to cultural rebirth: "The best clergyman cannot do every thing. This is ladies business."[29]

Not a solitary fantasy of female potency, Mrs. Jones has many congeners. Sally More's Repository tale of *The Good Mother's Legacy* points to a larger pattern: the Mrs. Teachwells, the Rational Dames, the Moral Mothers, the Female Guardians, Preceptors, and Instructors, as women writers of children's books like to call themselves (Wollstonecraft's strong-minded Mrs. Mason in *Original Stories*, 1788, is a typical type); the philanthropic matrons who purify entire communities like Trimmer's Mrs. Andrews or Elizabeth Hamilton's protagonist in *The Cottagers of Glenburnie* (1808); the charitable matriarchs who found female utopias, as in Sarah Scott's *Millenium Hall* (1762) and Clara Reeve's *Plans of Education* (1792); and even the Dorothea Brooke-like young women of popular fiction, fresh, eager, and generous, aglow with humanitarian plans rather than romantic passion. John G. Cawelti calls attention to the ways in which formulaic literary patterns shift in response to changing cultural values; all these helpful and high-minded heroines signal a new cultural mythology, moral fantasies of benevolent female power achieved through usefulness, not love, visions of domestically grounded heroism as potent for radicals like Wollstonecraft as for Evangelicals like More.[30] With their ticklish balance of independent behavior and domestic advice, altruistic women characters bespeak both compensatory thinking and real attainment.

Beilby Porteus, Bishop of London, revealingly teased his friend More about her "spiritual quixotism," this "magnificent and ambitious project of your's"—the Cheap Repository's expansion into a national institution for distributing educational material: "You pretended at your outset, that you were extremely humble and modest, and should try your wild experiment first within the precincts of your own neighbourhood. But behold, like a true female adventurer, you dash at once without fear into the wide world, and will be content with nothing but a complete conquest over all the vulgar vices in Great Britain." Illuminating by exaggeration, capturing the fervor of educators' imaginings, Porteus traces the trajectory of that modestly heroic enterprise which radiates out from the home and is justified by home values. His jest, like many, encodes truth, suggesting how didactic women writers could build on the nurturing and reformative bent native to female ideology, not passively mirroring cultural ascriptions but creatively translating them into the female idiom, purposefully appropriating them to serve woman-defined ends. For, whatever submerged fears and ulterior motives ideologies hedge, they are, as Clifford Geertz astutely observes, "most distinctively, maps of problematic social reality and matrices for the creation of collective conscience," so construing situations as to orient meaningful action.[31] If ideologies sometimes inhibit, they also liberate energy and catalyze event.

And their enabling force extends to women's literary contributions. More's resolute female characters, the tough social problems they tackle, and the minutely rendered, tidily structured world they inhabit testify to the powers that pedagogy confers. For if, on the one hand, the didactic slides toward moral fantasy—good readers learning to reshape their lives, good characters experiencing how virtue is rewarded, and useful authors, omnipotent in their microcosms, ordering, teaching, recompensing, and punishing as they please—on the other, didacticism makes for social realism, the particularized local color Henry James found endemic to women's family narratives, that Sunday reading which played so large a part in nineteenth-century culture. The shrewdly observant educative eye, trained in female minutiae, never misses the circumstantial details that effect concrete authenticity, from material fact and locale to folkways to vernacular mimicry: "merry as a grig," eyes "blue as butter-milk," shoulders "round as a tub." And tutelage urges this transcription, to woo its plebian readers with recognizable images of their own lives and to root its ideal behavioral patterns in convincingly gritty substantiality.[32]

More's carefully considered pedagogic theory underlines these artistic consequences of female guardianship. "Resolved, in trying to *reform* the poor, to *please* them too," she thought the well-meaning too often forgot that the poor have "the same tastes, appetites, and feelings with ourselves, ay, and the same good sense, too, though not refined by education." No need then to "lower the sense, but only the phraseology and style." Her philanthropic service in rural Somerset was a thorough schooling in working-class life, customs, and ways of thinking, and, rather surprisingly, she added to her reportorial skills and moral zeal a fascination with popular mores, what might be called an anthropological approach, and a "real enjoyment among these poor people." Hence, her mapping of new little fictive territories: her lively language, both down-to-earth and epigrammatic, her fresh subject matter and fast-paced plots, and her narrative centering of the young and the lowly.[33]

To educate and to edify, "safe books" had to entertain. "Dry morality or religion will not answer the end," More recognizes: the chapbooks' "pleasant poison" demanded a spirited antidote, the "novel and striking," rather than the "merely didactic." "Don't be frightened, Reader!" begins a typical tract like *Diligent Dick*: "Although I set out with a text, I am not going to preach a sermon, but to tell a story." More collected and analyzed an "immense variety of trash" to discover the sources of its appeal, and her canny catering to her public amuses by its inventiveness in co-opting penny literature for her own reformist purposes. Her series closely mimics standard chapbook format: small size, coarse paper, low price (a penny or half penny), and bulk discount to peddlars; crudely alluring woodcut; and jaunty title, like her *Black Giles the Poacher: With Some Account of a Family who Had Rather Live by Their Wits Than Their Work* and *Tawny Rachel; or, The Fortune Teller: With Some Account of Dreams, Omens, and Conjurors*. More's sheep wear wolves' clothing and often counterfeit wolves' ways. The larcenous pranks of Giles the parish rat-catcher emulate many a merry jest book, and Rachel's cheats and phony predictions of fated love build on Old Mother Bunch, most durable among the chapbooks' white witches. These spicy redactions and others like them More, paradoxically enfranchised by her didactic purpose, clearly enjoyed; indeed, so relishing is her satiric specificity on scams and seductions that one male critic thought such acquaintance with depravity "inconsistent with the innocent speculations of a female mind." No wonder staid Christopher Wordsworth, Master of Trinity, pronounced her tales too "novelish and exciting." As if anticipating such criticism, More explicitly justifies her focus on "tricks" and "faults": "It is the duty of a faithful historian to relate the evil with the good."[34] The didactic woman's pragmatic poetics of domesticity must be grounded in the substratum of quotidian reality. Instructive in richer ways than their creators envisioned, pedagogic fictions like these invite our attention to criticism's stepchild, to didactic narrative—to the complex ways in which ideology inheres in aesthetic form, in which literature is a social institution.

NOTES

1. Virginia Woolf, *A Room of One's Own* (1929; rpt. New York and Burlingame: Harcourt, Brace and World, n.d.), p. 68; *Henry Crabb Robinson on Books and their Writers*, ed. Edith J. Morley (London: J. M. Dent, 1938), I: 436 (Jan. 6, 1834); Ellen Moer's brief but suggestive treatment of "Educating Heroinism" in *Literary Women* (Garden City, New York: Doubleday, 1976) is to the point, as is Vineta Colby, *Yesterday's Woman: Domestic Realism in the English Novel* (Princeton: Princeton Univ. Press, 1974), Ch. 3.

2. Margaret Anne Doody, "George Eliot and the Eighteenth-Century Novel," *Nineteenth-Century Fiction*, 35, No. 3 (Dec. 1980), 267–68.

3. The tremendously successful bookseller Lackington early noted the impact

of Sunday school literacy on the growth of the reading public—*Memoirs of the Forty-Five First Years of the Life of James Lackington*, 13th ed. (London: Lackington, [1791]), pp. 257–58, 260—and such recent investigators as Thomas Walter Laqueur, *Religion and Respectability: Sunday Schools and Working Class Culture, 1780–1850* (New Haven and London: Yale Univ. Press, 1976), concur; Percy Muir, *English Children's Books 1600 to 1900* (New York and Washington: Frederick A. Praeger, 1954), p. 82.

4. *The Works of Hannah More* (New York: Harper, 1854), I, Preface; *Mendip Annals; or, A Narrative of the Charitable Labours of Hannah and Martha More in their Neighbourhood: Being the Journal of Martha More*, ed. Arthur Roberts (London: James Nisbet, 1859), p. 7; *Strictures on the Modern System of Female Education* (1799; rpt. New York and London: Garland, 1974), I, 3–4. For an analysis of Evangelical womanhood which relates More to Wollstonecraft's rational ideal, see my "Reform or Ruin: 'A Revolution in Female Manners,' " *Studies in Eighteenth-Century Culture*, vol. 11, ed. Harry C. Payne (Madison: Univ. of Wisconsin Press, 1982), 119–216.

5. *Memorials, Personal and Historical of Admiral Lord Gambier, with Original Letters*, ed. Georgiana, Lady Chatterton (London: Hurst and Blackett, 1861), I, 266; finding that among the gentry "they are full as much read as by common people," More began to issue two versions after a year's experience, *Memoirs of the Life and Correspondence of Mrs. Hannah More*, ed. William Roberts, II, 457–58; "The Lancashire Collier-Girl: A True Story," *Gentleman's Magazine*, 65, Pt. 1 (March 1795), 198; Miss [Charlotte M.] Yonge, "Children's Literature of the Last Century," *Macmillan's Magazine*, 20, No. 117 (July 1869), 231.

6. For the publication figures, see *Gentleman's Magazine*, 66, Pt. 1 (June 1796), 505; *Memoirs*, III, 61; More's friend James Stonhouse traced with awe the rising figures: "No such sale has ever been heard of in the annals of England," quoted in Ford K. Brown, *Fathers of the Victorians: The Age of Wilberforce* (Cambridge: Cambridge Univ. Press, 1961), p. 135; Richard D. Altick, *The English Common Reader: A Social History of the Mass Reading Public* (Chicago: Univ. of Chicago Press, 1957), pp. 75, 77; Review of Mary Leadbeater's *Cottage Dialogues among the Irish Peasantry*, *Christian Observer*, 13, No. 6 (June 1813), 390; *Review of More's Coelebs in Search of a Wife*, *Evangelical Magazine*, 17 (July 1809), 289; A. D. Harvey, *Britain in the Early Nineteenth Century* (London: B. T. Batsford, 1978), p. 106. Interestingly, the Repository was favorably reviewed by such liberal journals as the *Analytical Review*, for which Wollstonecraft often wrote, 25 (Jan. 1797), 92–93, and the *Critical Review*, 2nd Series, 21 (Oct. 1797), 238–39.

7. Samuel Pickering, Jr., *The Moral Tradition in English Fiction, 1785–1850* (Hanover, New Hampshire: Univ. Press of New England, 1976), p. 36; Colby, p. 153.

8. More's Repository was so popular that astute publishers issued spurious continuations when she left off; in his most recent discussion of More's tracts, *John Locke and Children's Books in Eighteenth-Century England* (Knoxville: Univ. of Tennessee Press, 1981), Ch. 4, Samuel F. Pickering, Jr. fails to discriminate these from her authentic work. In 1799 the Religious Tract Society was founded in imita-

tion of More; by 1849, it had issued over 500 million publications, William Jones, *The Jubilee Memorial of the Religious Tract Society* (London: Religious Tract Society, 1850), Appendix II.

9. Most, but not all, of the tracts More wrote herself are reprinted in the various editions of her works, as well as in numerous collected editions. A few have recently been made available in a Garland edition (New York and London, 1977) which preserves the original chapbook appearance, complete with crudely engaging woodcut—the Shepherd and his sheep, the seedy family of Black Giles the poacher, "who had rather live by their Wits than their Work." Because the tracts are so brief—the longest run about thirty small pages and most are shorter—and because they exist in so many forms, I have not cited page numbers. I owe thanks to Special Collections, University Research Library, UCLA, for facilitating my research in its fine tract collection and to the Osborne Collection of Early Children's Books, Toronto Public Library, for providing reproductions. Bibliographies of the Repository can be found in G. H. Spinney, "Cheap Repository Tracts: Hazard and Marshall Edition," *The Library*, 4th Series, 20, No. 3 (Dec. 1939), 295–340, and Harry B. Weiss, "Hannah More's Cheap Repository Tracts in America," *Bulletin of the New York Public Library*, 50, No. 7 (July 1946), 539–49; 50, No. 8 (August 1946), 634–41. Even Spinney, usually cited as authoritative, is incomplete, however, Based, like many of More's characters, on a real-life prototype, the two-part *Shepherd* was widely reprinted for a century and even translated into Russian and Romansch, Emanuel Green, *Bibliotheca Somersetensis* (Taunton: Barnicott and Pearce, 1901), III, 84–85. Quotes are from both parts.

10. 1 Timothy 2.12; *Works*, I, Preface; More quotes *Paradise Lost* VIII.193; M[argaret] Nancy Cutt, *Mrs. Sherwood and her Books for Children* (London: Oxford Univ. Press, 1974), p. 12. As early as 1777, More had staked out realistic domestic fiction as peculiarly suited to "the characteristics of female genius," *Essays on Various Subjects, Principally Designed for Young Ladies* (London: J. Wilkie and T. Cadell, 1777), p. 12.

11. Phillip McCann, "Popular Education, Socialization and Social Control: Spitalfields 1812–1824," *Popular Education and Socialization in the Nineteenth Century*, ed. Phillip McCann (London: Methuen, 1977), p. 18. The social control argument which provides the usual framework for discussion of More's tracts goes all the way back to Cobbett (a former admirer who had actually distributed the Repository in America) and forward from the Hammonds to Ford K. Brown and E. P. Thompson. The most recent exemplar is Roger Sales, *English Literature in History, 1780–1830: Pastoral and Politics* (New York: St. Martin's Press, 1983), Ch. 1.

12. Gerald Newman, "Anti-French Propaganda and British Liberal Nationalism in the Early Nineteenth Century: Suggestions toward a General Interpretation," *Victorian Studies*, 18, No. 4 (June 1975), 401. For further discussion of bourgeois progressivism, see also Catherine Hall, "The Early Foundation of Victorian Domestic Ideology," *Fit Work for Women*, ed. Sandra Burman (London: Croom Helm, 1979), pp. 15–32; and "Reform or Ruin" including the documentation in notes 15 and 19. See Jane Tompkins, "Sentimental Power: *Uncle Tom's Cabin* and

the Politics of Literary History," *Glyph*, 8 (1981), 79–102, for a parallel rescue of American women-centered reform from misreading.

13. The political arguments of this piece were in fact the work of a friend, *A Later Pepys: The Correspondence of Sir William Weller Pepys, Bart.*, ed. Alice C. C. Gaussen (London: J. Lane, 1904), II, 283–85. The dialogue enjoyed an incredible success (*Memoirs*, II, 346–47) and was reissued again and again for a quarter-century.

14. *Memoirs*, II, 386, 379, 361.

15. *Memorials*, I, 285–86; *Memoirs*, II, 386. More drew from recipes and advice in the *Times*, No. 3351 (11 July 1795) and No. 3362 (24 July 1975). *The Cottage Cook* was later retitled *A Cure for Melancholy* to reinforce its focus as a directive to bourgeois women. Many of More's ballads like *The Riot* and *The Honest Miller of Gloucestershire* and Sunday readings are also "moral economy" pieces, urging the well-off to fulfill their traditional responsibilities for maintaining food supplies, in opposition to the new capitalist market nexus. See E. P. Thompson, "The Moral Economy of the English Crowd in the Eighteenth Century," *Past and Present*, No. 50 (Feb. 1971), 76–136; and Walter M. Stern, "The Bread Crisis in Britain, 1795–96," *Economica*, NS, 31, No. 122 (May 1964), 168–87, for the relevant background. Significantly, More's domestic economy approach to aiding the poor became a staple of the middle-class woman's philanthropic tradition, as in Sarah Trimmer's second edition of *The Oeconomy of Charity* (1801), Mary Leadbeater's *Cottage Dialogues among the Irish Peasantry* (1811), and the later patterns described in Selma Barbara Kanner, "Victorian Institutional Patronage: Angela Burdett-Coutts, Charles Dickens and Urania Cottage, Reformatory for Women, 1846–1858," Diss. UCLA 1972.

16. *Memoirs*, II, 320.

17. *A Cure for Melancholy; Memorials*, I, 275. More's *Carpenter* reworks a tale from Berquin's *Children's Friend* to bring out the reform of popular culture motif that informs so many of her tracts; for the relevant background, see Robert W. Malcolmson, *Popular Recreations in English Society* (Cambridge: Cambridge Univ. Press, 1973), Chs. 7, 8; Peter Burke, *Popular Culture in Early Modern Europe* (New York: Harper and Row, 1978), Pt. 3; Hugh Cunningham, *Leisure in the Industrial Revolution c.1780–c.1880* (London: Croom Helm, 1980), Chs. 1, 3; Beatrice and Sidney Webb, *The History of Liquor Licensing in England, Principally from 1700 to 1830* (London: Longmans, Green, 1903), Ch. 3; T. G. Coffey, "Beer Street: Gin Lane, Some Views of 18th-Century Drinking," *Journal of Studies on Alcohol*, 27 (1966), 669–92.

18. *The Two Wealthy Farmers; or, The History of Mr. Bragwell*, Pt. 5. The Evangelical attack on custom often parallels rationalist-radical positions.

19. *The Way to Plenty; or, The History of Tom White, the Post Boy*, Pt. 2.

20. *Sorrowful Sam; or, The Two Blacksmiths* by Hannah's sister Sally here aggrandizes the wife's role beyond its model, 1 Corinthians 7.14. *The Apprentice Turned Master; or, the Second Part of the Two Shoemakers: Shewing How James Stock from a Parish Apprentice Became a Creditable Tradesman* demonstrates the pattern of numerous Repository tracts.

21. *Memoirs*, II, 472; *Mr. Fantom; Village Politics The Way to Plenty; The Hackney Coachman; or, The Way to Get a Good Fare*. Mr. Fantom, based in part on William Godwin and his philosophy of universal benevolence, "despised all those little acts of kindness and charity which every man is called to perform every day; and while he was contriving grand schemes, which lay quite out of his reach, he neglected the ordinary duties of life, which lay directly before him"; More took up the characters again in *The Death of Mr. Fantom, the Great Reformist* (1817) to reiterate the same woman's message.

22. *Shepherd*, Pt. 2; *Sorrowful Sam; Black Giles the Poacher: with Some Account of a Family who Had Rather Live by their Wits than their Work.*

23. Based on a real-life female miner, *The Lancashire Collier Girl* has recently been reprinted in Ivanka Kovačević, *Fact into Fiction: English Literature and the Industrial Scene 1750–1850* (Leicester: Leicester Univ. Press, 1975); *Black Giles the Poacher: with the History of Widow Brown's Apple Tree*; exemplifying new attitudes toward children as worthwhile, autonomous beings, *The History of Hester Wilmot* established the ministering child as a long-lived exemplary model; for a real-life Hester, see *British Sessional Papers, House of Commons* (1816), IV, 156. For similar patterns of domestic heroism established in America via More, see Joanna Bowen Gillespie, "An Almost Irresistible Enginery: Five Decades of Nineteenth Century Methodist Sunday School Library Books," *Phaedrus: An International Journal of Children's Literature Research*, 8, No. 1 (Spring/Summer 1980), 5–12.

24. *Strictures*, I, 117; *Coelebs in Search of a Wife: Comprehending Observations on Domestic Habits and Manners, Religion and Morals* (1808), *The Complete Works of Hannah More* (New York: J. C. Derby, 1856), II, 372; *Memoirs*; III, 107; *The Lancashire Collier Girl*, Kovačević, p. 174.

25. The Biblical source is Proverbs 22.2; for the larger background of More's thinking, see V. Kiernan, "Evangelicalism and the French Revolution," *Past and Present*, No. 1 (Feb. 1952), pp. 44–56.

26. For the usual masculine reading, see Maurice J. Quinlan, *Victorian Prelude: A History of English Manners* (1941; rpt. Hamden, Conn.: Archon Books, 1965), p. 87; and Ford K. Brown's heavily ironic Ch. 4; *Mendip Annals*, p. 10; *Cure* concludes with Luke 10.37 (the Good Samaritan).

27. *Cure; Black Giles*, Pt. 1; *Memorials*, I, 326.

28. *The Sunday School; The History of Hester Wilmot*; originally published in Trimmer's *Family Magazine* (1788–89, the first of its kind), the *Instructive Tales* were often reprinted. Like More's *Repository*, they create a thickly peopled and precisely rendered little communal world.

29. *Sorrowful Sam; The History of Hester Wilmot; Cure.*

30. John G. Cawelti, *Adventure, Mystery, and Romance: Formula Stories as Art and Popular Culture* (Chicago and London: Univ. of Chicago Press, 1976), p. 34. Such radical heroines as Thomas Holcroft's Dorothea-like *Anna St. Ives* (1792) and Wollstonecraft's Mrs. Mason realize their idealism through active virtue and benevolent endeavor. "Perhaps the greatest pleasure I have ever received, has arisen from the habitual exercise of charity in its various branches," declares Mrs. Mason,

Original Stories, from Real Life: with Conversations, Calculated to Regulate the Affections, and Form the Mind to Truth and Goodness (London: J. Johnson, 1788), p. 141, and Wollstonecraft's key exemplar of female heroism in the *Rights of Woman* is the widow who sacrifices self to maternal and domestic duties, *A Vindication of the Rights of Woman with Strictures on Political and Moral Subjects* (1792), ed. Charles W. Hagelman, Jr. (New York: W. W. Norton, 1967), pp. 90–91. For recent discussions of early female utopias, see R. S. Neale, *Class in English History 1680–1850* (Oxford: Basil Blackwell, 1981), pp. 201–05; and Barbara Brandon Schnorrenberg, "A Paradise Like Eve's: Three Eighteenth Century English Female Utopias," *Women's Studies*, 9, No. 3 (1982), 263–73.

31. *Memoirs*, II, 454; Clifford Geertz, "Ideology as a Cultural System," *The Interpretation of Cultures* (New York: Basic Books, 1973), p. 220.

32. *The Two Wealthy Farmers*, Pt. 2; *Tawny Rachel; or, the Fortune Teller*; James discusses local color realism and Sunday reading in "*The Schönberg-Cotta Family*" (1865), *Notes and Reviews* (Cambridge, Mass.: Dunster House, 1921), pp. 77–83. Like More, Maria Edgeworth insisted that "those who write for the people, and who aim at touching their hearts, must deal in particulars, and must produce distinct individual pictures," notes to Mary Leadbeater, *Cottage Dialogues among the Irish Peasantry* (London: Johnson, 1811), p. 307.

33. "I am not conscious of having, on any occasion, taken more pains," More wrote of her labors, *The Works of Hannah More* (London: T. Cadell, 1830), I, vi; *Memorials*, I, 275–76, 234.

34. *Mendip Annals*, p. 6; *Memorials*, I, 267; Henry Thornton, Treasurer, A Plan for Establishing by Subscriptions a Repository of Cheap Publications, on Religious & Moral Subjects [1795], p. 2 (by permission of Toronto Public Library); *The History of Diligent Dick; or, Truth Will Out, though It Be Hid in a Well*; letter to Elizabeth Montagu, H. F. B. Wheeler and A. M. Broadley, *Napolean and the Invasion of England* (London and New York: John Lane, 1908), I, 210; Sir Archibald Mac Sarcasm [Rev. William Shaw], *The Life of Hannah More, with a Critical Review of her Writings* (London: T. Hurst, 1802), p. 63; Wordsworth is quoted in Charlotte M. Yonge, *Hannah More* (Eminent Women Series) (London: W. H. Allen, 1888), pp. 121–22; John Ashton reprints numerous examples of the kinds of material More drew on, *Chap-Books of the Eighteenth Century* (1882; rpt. New York: Benjamin Blom, 1966); *Black Giles*, Pt. 2.

Jane Austen and the
English Novel of the 1790s

GARY KELLY

It is clear by now that whatever place they may occupy in the "Great Tradition" of English fiction, Jane Austen's novels are firmly situated in the debate, initiated in the 1790s in Britain in response to the French Revolution, between rights and duties, or between the claims of the individual self to freedom of action and authenticity of being and the claims of society on the individual to conform to social and institutional codes and conventions. Like most Romantic novels, Jane Austen's are concerned with exploring the relationship between the self and society, and in her exploration of that relationship Austen has been seen to take her place with the "Anti-Jacobin" rather than the "Jacobin" novelists of the 1790s. These issues and relationships have of course been dealt with by Marilyn Butler, Alistair Duckworth,[1] and others, but in this paper I want to re-examine them by re-examining the formal means by which the Jacobins, Anti-Jacobins, and Jane Austen conducted the debate on the relationship of self and society in their fiction.

It was largely on the issues that Edmund Burke had identified—the true "nature" of the individual as a member of society; the family as the basic social unit, and not the individual citizen; tradition and convention as the custodians, preservers, and propagators of social and cultural values; and the "domestic affections" as the "natural" ground for individual feeling—it was on these issues that the French Revolution debate in Britain was conducted in imaginative literature, that most important social institution for conducting ideological controversy, during the 1790s. The issues were embodied in fiction in a variety of ways, as particular authors with particular points of view drew on the already available repertory of formal elements and themes, elements such as images of the constricting force of social institutions and conventions, narrative mode, the form of the novel of education, and elements of melodrama and Gothic fiction. A brief review of these elements, as they were adapted for fiction during the 1790s, will help to clarify the relationship between the novels of that decade and those (in some cases begun during the 1790s) of Jane Austen.[2]

In the novels written by the "English Jacobins," for example, society itself was often imaged as a prison in which the individual protagonist was confined and isolated, as well as being deprived of his or her rights, as in William Godwin's *Caleb Williams*. This imagery was of course partly a carryover from the Sentimental novel. Of course, too, the liberal reforming element of the culture of Sensibility was clearly recognized as subversive by "Anti-Jacobin" British writers in the 1790s, and so they were at pains to satirize and expose it. However the significance of formal and thematic elements is not static and unchanging, but varies according to the way the element is used and the way it is combined with other elements, as well as according to the changing circumstances of the practice of reading. Thus the imprisonment motif had a sharper edge in English Jacobin fiction of the 1790s than hitherto, and a greater ambiguity, owing to the image of the Bastille, but also to the images of the Terror. Nevertheless, in Britain the prison image was usually employed as a means of protesting against what was seen by urban intellectuals, dissenters, and artisans as a social and political hegemony still unjustly exercised by a decadent aristocratic chivalric and feudal culture. The imprisonment motif also dramatized, even in the new and sharpened political consciousness of the 1790s, a continuation of the anxiety, also found in Sentimental fiction, about the survival of the individual self in the face of social convention, social institutions, and the demands of society on the individual generally. The point remains, however, that the evolving political issues of the 1790s brought about the conditions for a rereading of the motif of imprisonment and near-extinction of the individual self wherever it was found in the literature of the previous century and a half.[3]

Another aspect of seventeenth- and eighteenth-century literature to be appropriated by British novelists in the 1790s in the light of the political issues of their time was first-person and confessional narrative. This narrative mode had many varieties and functions from the late seventeenth century, through the fiction of Defoe and Richardson, and into Sentimental fiction and autobiography—that is, from spiritual autobiography to epistolary novel, and from witness to personal salvation in a fallen world, to conflict of self against self in a treacherous and deceptive social world, to mere self-authenticating self-expressiveness. But in the 1790s the first-person confessional narrative came to be an essential device in the fictional arguments of English Jacobin writers. In the first place it had the function of showing how an individual developed from personal experience a critical consciousness about his or her own "rights" in the face of social oppression. Second, it could exhibit the individual case as a representative one, so that in the fate of one individual is seen the potential fate of anyone—as is suggested in such titles as Godwin's *Things As They Are; or, The Adventures of Caleb Williams*, Robert Bage's *Hermsprong; or, Man As He is Not*, and Mary Wollstonecraft's *The Wrongs of Woman; or, Maria*. This kind of form, and this kind of title, were soon appropriated by Anti-Jacobins. Third, the nature of first-person confessional narration itself could have political and revolutionary implications: to the protagonist first of all, but then to listeners within and readers outside the novel, it may possess the force of a revelation or demystification of the system, normally concealed, of "things as they are". The first-person narration may also, as a tale told to others, participate in the "spread of truth" and thus in the eventual reform of society and social institutions. Such revelations and such spread of truth could of course be linked to revolutionary political rhetoric, which was designed both to educate its audience to political "truth," and to move them to action based on those "truths." The English Jacobin novels thus attempt to reveal to readers the necessity of radical social change, and, at the same time, through the emotive rhetorical immediacy of the first-person narration, to move them to revolutionary action based on the "truth" revealed in the narrative.

On the other hand, the rhetorical implications of the English Jacobin novelists' choice of narrative mode turned out to be more complicated than they perhaps intended. For the first-person narration could also have a socializing and merely reformative effect, altering the perceptions of the hearers (and readers), and drawing them into a sympathetic and thus a social relationship with the narrator. In other words, the potentially alienating and isolating effect of possession of the truth of "things as they are" may in fact lead to authentic or "natural" social relations with other critical consciousnesses rather than to revolutionary action, to pantisocracy rather than to the barricades, to intellectual elitism rather than to widespread social change. In this way, both conventional socialization and revolution could be avoided, for a minority, through the revelatory but socially self-redeeming force of confessional autobiography. Confession is therefore, and not surprisingly, also a characteristic form of narration in Romantic or post-Revolutionary fiction, in fiction written after the heroic decade (or rather half-decade) when Revolutionary action seemed both possible and desirable in the early 1790s.

A third element appropriated by English Jacobin novelists from earlier fiction is the form of the novel of education, or the form of fiction which is designed primarily to show how, for better or for worse, character is formed by circumstances or by education in either a narrow or a very broad meaning of the term. However, the English Jacobin novelists are concerned not so much with the mere formation and initial testing of individual character in society as with the testing of character which then leads to acts of conversion—more or less (usually more) dramatic reversals, enlightenments, transformations in individual character and point of view. Once again one recalls the importance of the (especially Nonconformist) literature of spiritual autobiography in the novel of the 1790s, the continuing force and popularity of the novel of sentimental education, and the concurrent revival of interest in the fictional narratives (as well as in the political and journalistic career) of Daniel Defoe.[4] But with the English Jacobin writers of course the point of conversion or enlightenment is not a recognition by the individual of a divine order, a transcendent (transcendent over merely social) reality, a Providential validation of the self (through personal salvation); this is material for Sentimental fiction. Rather, the English Jacobin novel focuses on a transformation from intra- to extra-social point of view, the desocialization of the individual so that society and its institutions may be viewed critically, for the purposes of advancing options for social change. In the Romantic novel, of course, this desocialized critical point of view is often posited as an innate tendency and permanent quality of the mind of the protagonist and is indulged for its own sake.[5]

Finally, then, the English Jacobin novel of the 1790s also had a pronounced tendency to rely upon dramatic or melodramatic incidents, settings, and characters, along with the immediate and thus also dramatic form of first-person narration, in order to mount its argument on the relationship between the individual and society. Appropriation from the Gothic was a common occurrence because the Gothic, with its fondness for exaggerated reversals, or peripeteia, could serve the novelist's interest in dramatic conversions. But the Gothic elements of intrigue, conspiracy, uncertainty, and exotic furniture also provided materials that could be reconstituted for the 1790s political debate, and which also could serve the need of the English Jacobin writers for the heightening (for illustrative and exemplary as well as for rhetorical purposes) of psychological processes and conflicting social relationships. It is important to emphasize, however, that the English Jacobin novelists did appropriate, rather than merely imitate, some elements of Gothic. It was not in their interests to create fiction that was too strange, or fictional worlds and settings too remote from the familiar world of their readers, for they wanted to unmask certain aspects of that world, not provide a temporary escape from it. English Jacobin writers were in fact as severe in their criticisms of Gothic fiction as were the Anti-Jacobins, but since writers such as Godwin, Thomas Holcroft, and Wollstonecraft did appropriate elements of Gothic, it is understandable that the

Anti-Jacobins should see some similarity, and also try to smear the Jacobins' work as merely Gothic.

Jane Austen's career as a mature writer is of course conventionally thought to have begun with her critique of the Gothic in *Northanger Abbey*; but as we know there is much more to *Northanger Abbey* than a critique of the Gothic, and in fact a moment's thought as to the themes and formal properties of *Northanger Abbey* and all of Jane Austen's mature fiction would produce a whole variety of ways in which her novels would seem to be Anti-Jacobin. But before considering what is, I believe, a rather more complex relationship between her fiction and that of the English Jacobins than has been advanced hitherto, it will be useful to review briefly just what the Anti-Jacobin novelists of the 1790s themselves did to contain and refute the fictional arguments of the English Jacobins. In the first place one might say that in general men Anti-Jacobins used wit and satire, whereas women Anti-Jacobins used domestic comedy or sentimental sincerity to attack fictional Jacobinism; and in general the women were far less obvious in their attacks. In satiric romances such as *Vaurien* (1797) by Isaac D'Israeli, *The Vagabond* (1799) by Charles Walker, and *The Infernal Quixote* (1800) by Charles Lucas, certain common features of the Anti-Jacobin novel as written by men are to be seen. Rather than a limited, learning, expressive, and "sentimental" first-person narrator, an omniscient and ironic narrator is frequently used to present the reader with an already wise and yet witty model consciousness, looking down on the follies of youth and the "New Philosophy." The plot of these satiric romances simply consists of a series of encounters between theory and practice, or theory and "reality," with practice and reality repeatedly exposing the inadequacy of mere theory to human experience; thus the plot form is the repetitive one of satiric revelation or exposure. This plot form is also often combined with the plot of romantic comedy, the plot, that is, in which human efforts to shape circumstances and the world to some ideal desired end are exposed as futile; yet it is also the plot in which goodness and virtue are finally rewarded and the vicious are punished, because that is how a comic universe operates. As Butler summarizes the form:

> The hero—often, quixote-like, deluded by revolutionary ideas—travels the country, meeting grotesque groups of troublemakers, and eventually learning to see society as it is. With the revolutionary novel, the central impulse of the story is the hero-victim's oppression by society. The Anti-Jacobin plot leads to a climax in which the hero is made aware of his presumption and learns to take his place in the world as it actually is.[6]

Given this kind of plot, and what it implies about human efforts to use reason for social progress, the reader is led to ask, what use revolution? And what hope for the English Jacobins' dream of human perfectibility? Virtue, good intentions, and perseverance suffice. In romantic comedy, too, the resolution and the closure is marriage, the entry of the individual into a personal and yet public bond and social institution. The characters are similarly those of romantic or sentimental comedy. There is a "normal" hero and heroine, that is, someone perhaps merely better looking than what the typical intended reader might suppose himself or herself to be—a hero and heroine who may err in the course of the plot but who are rewarded with each another in the end. There are the eccentrics, varieties of "Philosophers" from the silly to the vicious and malicious. There are the good friends, lesser versions of the hero and heroine. And then there are the obstacles, parents or false friends who use the "New Philosophy" to subvert "natural" social ties for their own selfish ends. In the linguistic world of such novels there is of course first the witty and educated style of the narrator, then the candid and sincere style of the hero and heroine and their friends (thus closest to the "standard" English of the narrator), and then there is the "characteristic" and thus variously deformed speech of the eccentrics and villains. In the thematic material of these novels there is also a tendency to use the rhetoric of "realism," a repeated reference to "facts," or "common sense," or "common experience," or plausibility, to counter what is thus cast as the "imaginary," or "romantic" or theoretical, or delusive, or eccentric in the fiction and the theories of the "New Philosophers." And of course the domestic is opposed to the exotic, the familiar to the strange, because it is precisely the familiar (in several senses) which the Anti-Jacobin novelists, following Burke, insist that their readers should cleave to, rather than to the strange and foreign (even in the precise sense of French) ideas and principles of the English Jacobins.

In fact, throughout Anti-Jacobin fiction there is a tendency not only to reduce large political and public issues to their domestic, everyday, commonplace consequences in individual domestic experience (a tendency found in Burke's *Reflections* and fully developed in the Romantic historical novels), but also actually to translate the political and public issues into private and domestic equivalents; this tendency is seen particularly in the Anti-Jacobin novels by women, described by Butler as "the feminine female-conduct novel."[7] These novels in part celebrate individual self-realization within society and within traditional social institutions, as do the novels of Jane Austen, and in them too much insistence on the rights of self is seen as menacing to "normal" domestic feelings, bonds, and institutions. Thus too, there is a celebration of the reality immediately to hand, the domestic and local scene, the particular and even mundane, in opposition to what are viewed as the merely abstract and theoretical principles of the English Jacobins and of their novels' tendency to treat the individual case as generally representative. As Charles Lloyd put it, in the Advertisement to his not at all virulently Anti-Jacobin novel *Edmund Oliver* (1798): "The following pages were written with the design of counteracting that generalizing spirit, which seems so much to have insinuated itself among modern philosophers." Thus the ties that bind in Anti-Jacobin novels are not those of general philanthropy and benevolence, seen as all too easily exploited by the selfish, but rather the "domestic affections," friendship, gratitude, family ties, love (though not merely passionate love) as an absolute, and the immediate and local claims of ethical action. As the virtuous friend of Edmund Oliver in Charles Lloyd's novel says, "We never can be happy till we forget ourselves, and, living in surrounding objects [of feeling], lose our own individuality in benefitting others."[8] Burke, along with many Sentimental novelists, would have agreed.

So too, however, would many English Jacobin novelists. William Godwin, for example, altered the ending of *Caleb Williams* to make the novel into a plea for social reconciliation, and in successive editions he added specific references to the joys of the domestic affections as the highest felicity known to human beings (for example, the Laura Denison episode in volume three, added after he became Mary Wollstonecraft's lover). His next novel *St. Leon* (1799) and its successor *Fleetwood* (1805) both specifically warned against sacrificing family ties for a personal obsession, even obsessions with truth and philanthropy. His and Mary Wollstonecraft's daughter developed the same idea in her first novel, which is compositionally and thematically the offspring of *Caleb Williams* and *The Wrongs of Woman*. No doubt the form and the themes of English Jacobin fiction evolved, but if *Frankenstein*, along with *Fleetwood, St. Leon*, and even the revised *Caleb Williams* are to be considered Anti-Jacobin novels, then it becomes very difficult to sketch a configuration of the novel of the 1790s and the early decades of the nineteenth century that has much coherence. Thus it would be wrong to say that the Anti-Jacobin novel was completely at odds, either thematically or compositionally, with the fictional social criticism of the English Jacobins. They both tend to venerate the "domestic affections" and stoic virtues, though for different reasons. They both tend to mount consistent satire on social conventions and social institutions of certain kinds, and on "Society" or fashionable social life in particular. In brief, they both show a tendency to attack aristocratic cultural and social hegemony by attacking the (to them decadent) institutions of aristocratic court culture. There is in both a persistent concern, inherited from the bourgeois Enlightenment, for seeing "things as they are," that is, in penetrating the delusive appearances and social conventions that mask moral reality (a theme taken over from the eighteenth-century satire); and so "philosophical" enthusiasm and theoretical delusions are classed and condemned with more long-standing kinds of delusive enthusiasm and extremes of belief and behavior.

For example, novels or "romances" themselves may be condemned by English Jacobin and Anti-Jacobin alike, as a form of reading (like theoretical philosophy) all too likely to give the young reader false ideas and expectations of reality, and false models for behavior in real life. And the concern of both Jacobin and Anti-Jacobin novelists is very much with the young person, first experiencing the "World" (that is, conventional organized social life), and therefore usually facing two major moral choices, in terms of the integration of the self into society, namely choice of a vocation and choice of a mate. In this romance journey (often actual journeying) in both Jacobin and Anti-Jacobin novels alike, then, there are mentors or good guides, and tempters or false guides. And in their own way, of course, the Anti-Jacobin novels are as concerned as the Jacobin ones with the ultimate value of the "enlightened," critical, clear-sighted, socially responsible, and active individual to the process of moral change in society, and thus to the process of social change itself.

The opposition between Jacobin and Anti-Jacobin novel was, then, to a large extent, a false one. For the Jacobin and Anti-Jacobin writers together represent the range of ideological attitudes of the rapidly expanding and increasingly powerful professional middle class, as that class was in the process of clarifying its own values, blending with while subverting the hegemonic gentry class, and defending its increasing power and privileges from attack from "beloe." In particular, Jacobin and Anti-Jacobin writers alike represent the increasing group of professional ideologues, the "men of letters," within the broader professional class. During the 1790s this group of "men of letters" and "women of letters" showed a degree and kind of political activity and commitment which they would rapidly decrease or translate into less dangerous activity after that decade. On the other hand, one can see that in some respects the opposition between Jacobin and Anti-Jacobin was real enough. The Jacobin novelists did belong to or sympathize with the culture of English Dissent. The Anti-Jacobin novelists all belonged to the mainstream of English culture and Anglicanism; while aware to some extent that society, social conventions, and social institutions were man-made and not natural, they still emphasized the importance of maintaining practical ties to those conventions and institutions, if one wished to have any effect as a moral agent—indeed, if one wished to have any social existence at all—since to have no social life was to have no being at all. This, then, is another important connection between Austen and the Anti-Jacobins, for to the Anti-Jacobins it was only as an active member of society (rather than as an alienated individual outside of it) that one could live a moral and religious life. They were right to recognize that even those English Jacobin novels that did not end with the protagonist alone, isolated, and often imprisoned—the cost of having an extrasocial critical perspective on society—even those English Jacobin novels that had a sentimental-romance ending of marriage and the prospect of happiness, often leave the happy couple or couples in a kind of utopian or pantisocratic isolated community, isolated, that is, from a society which is past gradualist moral reform. Even those English Jacobin novels that overtly argue for the "domestic affections" against the excesses of passion for truth and philanthropy (such as the novels of the Godwin family) seem to be fascinated by the excesses against which they argue. The Anti-Jacobin novels, for their part (often being written by men with a classical "gentleman's" education),[9] are usually true to the resolution of moral comedy which goes back to Greek New Comedy: the union of the young man and young woman at the end of the comedy resolves social conflicts, "cures" the errors of the older generation, and promises a propagation of one's virtues through the greater social power the young couple will have as a family, a social institution, and through their progeny who will, no doubt, combine the best moral qualities of both parents. Here we are very close already to the closure of Austen's novels.

Jacobin and Anti-Jacobin novelists alike, then, are reformists, their respective thematic preoccupations and formal practices embodying different versions of contemporary "progressive" bourgeois ideology. And yet it is true that for the Jacobin novelists—emphasizing rights though not neglecting the importance of duties—the point of ideological attack is the hegemony, political and cultural, of what they see as aristocratic court culture. Whereas for the Anti-Jacobin novelists—emphasizing duties though preoccupied with individuality rather than collective social being—the point of anxiety is that the attack on aristocratic and gentry hegemony may go too far; and in its demand for equal rights to selfhood in the face of society (a demand inherited from much Sentimental fiction), it may undermine traditional social institutions to the extent of unleashing half-understood (therefore all the more menacing) social movements from "below," from the artisan classes and especially from what are seen as their mistaken or vicious middle-class intellectual and professional allies, propagandists, and leaders. Thus the struggle in the English novel of the 1790s is to exert different sorts of ideological discipline in an increasingly important and popular form of ideological communication. But the struggle is really between different sectors or fractions of a bourgeoisie which had always been divided, but was now undergoing a new period of militancy. I am speaking here of the novel as properly so understood in the 1790s, and leave out of account, because it was in many ways a different cultural phenomenon, the fiction found in chapbooks and cheap novellas for the artisan and working classes. This fiction was of course taken up in the 1790s by Hannah More and her allies in the Cheap Repository project, in a virulently Anti-Jacobin kind of fiction of their own. But in general the novelists of the late eighteenth and early nineteenth century ignored this literature until Walter Scott made his attempts to appropriate parts of it—even so, Scott was writing for gentry and middle-class readers, and "fiction for the working man" continued on its merry way, as the studies of R. K. Webb, Richard Altick, Louis James, Victor Neuburg, and others demonstrate. The division between "serious" middle-class novelists revealed in the 1790s would widen during the first decades of the nineteenth century, but clearly, once the hegemony of aristocratic ideology had been permanently subverted, the attention of most novelists would have to turn to the social threat from "below" and the ideological "betrayal" from within the middle-class—this attending would play a large part in the history of the Victorian novel. This is one reason why the issue of lower-class literacy was such a hot one at the turn of the century. What both Jacobin and Anti-Jacobin novelists come to share in the 1790s and early 1800s is an anxiety as to how to expose to members of the middle class the nature of aristocratic and gentry hegemony without at the same time arousing the "lower orders" (actually the artisan class) to question all power exerted from above. It is because of this anxiety that both sides in the "war of ideas" in the 1790s actively seek to use fiction to advance different versions of an ideology of the reconciliation of rights and duties, of selfhood and social institutions, in a social harmony founded on the cultural, social, and economic values of the late eighteenth-century professional bourgeoisie.

How is Jane Austen's fiction to be situated in this sketch of the organization of the fiction of the 1790s?[10] More particularly, how is her fiction related to the anxiety mentioned at the end of the last paragraph? For although Austen wrote fiction in the 1790s, her mature—and her published—fiction is post-Revolutionary, situated after the major episodes of the fictional debate between Jacobins and Anti-Jacobins in Britain. A brief survey of Austen's formal practice will shed some light on these questions, although obviously Austen's thematic and stylistic repertory is too well known and has been described too often for any very original contribution to be made to that scholarship here. Nevertheless, a reading of that repertory may be advanced which will show how Austen's novels could stand for many readers at that time in significant relationship—that is, in a relationship productive of important significations—to the novels, both Jacobin and Anti-Jacobin, of the 1790s.

In the first place, Austen's novels obviously do employ many of the techniques and formal elements found in the Anti-Jacobin novels of the 1790s. Like those novels, hers too may signify in important ways through what they do not contain, what they avoid, what they counter, or what they reject through parody or inversion. Her novels clearly avoid, militantly avoid we might say, the melodramatic, the sensational, the exotic, the intensely personal—in other words, techniques of Sentimental fiction frequently adopted by the English Jacobin novelists in the 1790s, or else identified by Anti-Jacobins as characteristic of subversive fiction. Ironic references or allusions to such techniques are found in all of Austen's novels; in her novels, too, a character's ability to resist applying these "novelish" elements to real life is an index of clear-sightedness and avoidance of delusive fantasy, that is, an index of the extent to which a character possesses true judgment. And in Austen as in the Anti-Jacobins, true judgment is presented as a transcendent if embattled mental faculty above questions of class or social relativities of that kind. Austen also avoids dramatic conversions, and charts her characters' progress, if that is the right word, by a series of small but to the individual concerned important revelations about the "real" as opposed to the imagined state of affairs, and the revelations of course include self-revelations. In fact "progress" is not the right word to use in regard to Austen's technique of character development; it is part of her conservative and Anglican "mental philosophy" that such liberties are not available to the individual in a structured society. Thus too Austen's novels are not novels of education, or at least not in the sense used by English Jacobins, in which "circumstances form character" (to quote the "necessitarian" English Jacobin philosopher William Godwin). In Austen's novels, as in her eighteenth-century predecessors in comic fiction, in the Anti-Jacobin comic novels, and indeed in a great many Sentimental novels, character is given, and is merely unfolded; and if the character is capable of seeing "things as they are," then marriage to a clear-sighted, self-aware partner furnishes the insurance for the promise of further social expansion of the character's innate and now unfolded goodness. This, in a less fully developed and more conventional way, is just what happens to characters and to marriages in many Anti-Jacobin novels of the 1790s, and to the same end: to deny that individual human potential is unlimited and thus that people are "perfectible" by any social order devisable by humankind, to deny the possibility of any "revolution" (for that is what conversion is) in the individual life and thus in the life of society, and to assert that human nature ("temper" is another word often used) is just that, "natural," and not a social product and thus not susceptible of radical change and improvement in any individual case through radical change in society.

However, if human natures or tempers are given in Austen's novels, so too are society and social institutions. How then to resolve conflicts between the two, the conflicts fought out in the English Jacobin and Anti-Jacobin novels of the 1790s and repeated in Austen's novels? Jane Austen, country gentlewoman, dutiful daughter, sister and aunt, and good Anglican (that is, Arminian) that she was, argues that the individual must use free will, not to reject social conventions and institutions, but rather to re-create or revalidate them in her own social existence. In Austen's novels the good, the bad, and the silly remain very much as they are throughout, but the "naturally" good learn how to be so socially—or rather circumstances combine, through the divine grace of comic form, to enable them to be so. For reference to Providence or Fate or Destiny is also absent from Austen's novels, in marked contrast (so it might have seemed to readers at the time) to the novels of earnestly didactic authors, and in particularly marked contrast to the Jacobin novelists, who had appropriated Fate from Sentimental and Gothic fiction and used it to stand for their own notion of philosophic Necessity. In Austen's novels the "natural" goodness of the main characters seems rather to be implicitly conformable to the order of a Nature presided over by a benevolent deity and operating through what mere mortals denominate Chance (all of her plots rely on happy coincidences). And so in the romantic comedy resolutions of Austen's novels, there is the same combination of good nature (Fielding's transcendent human value) and Chance, issuing in an "earned" yet fortuitous or at least unlooked-for happy ending, which is found in the Anti-Jacobin novels of the 1790s, and this resolution is at once a rejection of the English Jacobin philosophy of Necessity, and a rejection of the English Jacobin philosophic hope that individual will, guided by individual reason, can shape circumstances to desired and reformative ends. Nevertheless, Austen does go beyond her Anti-Jacobin contemporaries, by developing and emphasizing alertness and correctness of judgment, of discrimination, in her central characters, showing that the mind must not only be gifted, but also cultivated so as to be able to respond in the "right" way to circumstances of a world ruled by Chance—that "right" response will be both morally right and circumstantially appropriate or decorous and will include both judgment and action, for in Austen the two are always joined for the properly moral individual. Only the most dangerous of her characters are seen to have separated judgment from will to act.[11] Austen, then, has added an important psychological—intellectual would be a better word—dimension to the Anti-Jacobin plot of romantic comedy; it was an addition that would be richly developed in the nineteenth-century "Great Tradition" novelists. To be fair, quite a number of Jacobin novels had also utilized the form of romantic comedy in their resolutions, utilized that is, in the proper sense— made available for their own use the form of romantic comedy, and thus used it differently or for different emphasis than did the Anti-Jacobin novels of the 1790s and the novels of Jane Austen. They used it to project the founding of an ideal social unit, ideal and "utopian" in itself and immediately reformative in its implications.

However, apart from plot form, character typology, and the thematic repertory, the most important and obvious shared formal property of Austen's novels and those of the Anti-Jacobins is the use of a third-person "omniscient" narrator. As I have already argued, in the Anti-Jacobin novels such a narrative voice is used militantly, against the first-person narration used by so many Jacobin novelists. Austen's use of third-person narration could be read as having many of the same implications: as resistant to unmediated confessional narrative, to effects of Sentimental immediacy, to the domination of the narrative by the individual voice of the novel's principal agent, and thus as implicitly rejecting the idea that individual experience can authenticate universal human and social principles. Instead, the third-person omniscient narrator serves as the "voice" of historical reflection and social overview, a point of view not on the same plane as the novel's action, but from above, looking down at an angle, and thus representing a point of view which is withdrawn and spectatorial, interested but amused—in an important sense properly "above it all," properly authorial and authoritative. It is this point of view that the reader is invited to share, and not the involved, acting, "*engagé*" point of view of a heated, candid, "enthusiastic," Sentimental first-person narrator. Even more important, however, is the fact that, while Austen shares use of third-person narrative point of view with many Anti-Jacobin novelists of the 1790s, her development of the technique again goes much further than theirs. For whereas the Anti-Jacobins' third-person narrators are very similar to those of numerous eighteenth-century novelists, Jane Austen's have a more active and flexible role to play in the whole fictional structure. In particular, it is her use of "free indirect discourse," or reported internal speech, which marks her breakthrough to a fictional technique that would dominate the novels of the "Great Tradition" in the nineteenth century; the narrator, in reporting the thoughts and describing the feelings of the central agent's consciousness, can move freely from almost complete identification with the central consciousness to fairly distant amused irony.

Furthermore, one could also argue that, in causing her novel's central consciousness, a potential first-person narrator, to be absorbed into the third-person omniscient narrator, Austen has effectively merged the favorite narrative mode of the English Jacobin and Sentimental novelists into that of their adversaries. For Austen seldom allows her central character, or indeed any character, to speak confessionally, to the reader or anyone else, for more than a few sentences, except of course in a letter; but even then the letter is always given a dramatic reading within the novel. Austen rejects even the inset first-person narrative which was used by some Anti-Jacobin novelists to lend a moment of immediacy to their fictions. Most important of all, however, Austen does not report her central characters' thoughts directly, but through "free indirect discourse," and thus her narrator retains control over the attitude to those thoughts, passed on through the narrative voice to the reader. In this way, her fusion of first- and third-person narrative does favor the latter.

Finally, and most important of all, the flexibility and yet the authority in this narrative method are only means to an end, the end of producing a reader who thinks like the narrator. The authority in the narrative voice, along with the plot and handling of character, are clearly designed to do what all novels do in some way, to instruct the reader in the "truths" of the book's world view. But the flexibility of Austen's narrative voice—the way the voice slides, sometimes even within one sentence from apparent identification with the thoughts and feelings of the central character to considerable ironic detachment—tests the reader's alertness and discrimination and memory; in short, it tests his or her judgment.[12] This testing does not of course go on all the time; if it did, Austen's novels would resemble the fictions of our own "postmodernism," or of postmodernism's supposed ancestors, such as Laurence Sterne. Austen tests the reader occasionally, but critically, in judging the exact relationship between the heroine's judgment and what can be discerned, from the evidence supplied by the narrative, to be the "correct" judgment. The test often involves tempting the reader to sympathize too much with the heroine, and thus to approve of her at the wrong time (as when Elizabeth rejects Darcy), or to miss the occasion for disapproval (as with Emma's rudeness at Box Hill); but the test often involves too the reader's tendency to read Austen's novels through the familiar fictional conventions—most noticeably in the early novels, but also strongly if less obviously in the later ones. It is in these ways that Austen's novels are, in a new way, "novels of education," the education of both heroine and reader.

Jane Austen's use of a shifting (and sometimes even shifty) ironic distance narrator and narrated world goes along with her technique for deploying character, a technique that continues the Anti-Jacobins' development of eighteenth-century characterization in comic fiction and drama. This technique, like the use of narrative voice, is a technique of discrimination. The use of characteristic speech, comic gesture, dominant obsessions or "hobby-horses," arrangement of characters in significant relationships of comparison and contrast are all found in the comic novels and plays of the eighteenth century, and were adapted by the Anti-Jacobin novelists of the 1790s. But in Austen's novels, the technique of discrimination in characterization combines with the technique of discrimination in narration, particularly if one considers her novels as a linguistic universe. The center of this universe is the style of the narrator; closest to the center is the style of thought and speech of the central consciousness; close to her are the several good or wise individuals—often mentors, as in the Anti-Jacobin novels— and often the chief romantic male character as well. Then come the various eccentrics, whose eccentricity, whose distance from the full and balanced and discriminating human voice at the center of the novel is indicated clearly by the distorted, peculiar, idiosyncratic style in which they express themselves; one thinks of Mrs. Elton or Miss Bates, in *Emma*, for examples.

Thus, to an extent not seen in third-person narrative and certainly not in third-person Anti-Jacobin narrative before her time, Austen constructs a linguistic universe which is embodied in characters as an ordered community of individuals each with his or her own idiolect, but all in relation to a clearly established "standard" and ordering center. This linguistic universe then reinforces, by furnishing the reader with a standing model as it were, the argument implicit in the plot, and which is already familiar enough in Austen criticism: the individual pursuing a proper human existence will find a way through exercise of individual judgment to reconcile the uniqueness of the self and the conventions and the institutions of society, a way, that is, to re-create convention and institution through moral self-awareness, rather than to revolutionize or overthrow convention and institution in the name of self-advancement, or merely personal "rights"; and so, by re-creating convention and institution, by filling it with the meaning that flows from the exercise of moral discrimination, the individual neither abandons rights, nor overrides duties. This ordered linguistic community is certainly present, in crude versions, in the Anti-Jacobin fiction of the 1790s, but even there the order is less firm for lacking the appropriated first-person narration which is "free indirect discourse."

It is, then, above all in their formal procedures, as well as in their themes and plots, that Jane Austen's novels represent a development and refinement of Anti-Jacobin fictional technique, as that technique was used to conduct a debate in the 1790s on the relation between rights and duties, self and society. But in their formal procedures, Austen's novels also represent an attempted resolution of the debate between Jacobin and Anti-Jacobin fiction, and thus she makes clear (in more than one sense) what is in fact the common ground on which Jacobin and Anti-Jacobin novels, for all their differences, are constructed. Austen obviously did recognize, as the Jacobin and Anti-Jacobin novelists recognized, that the novel was becoming the most important single vehicle of ideological communication amongst the middle and upper classes in Britain—in spite of the relatively high cost of novels, their low status as literature, and strong competition from newspapers and magazines. Given the limited circulation of novels (though not of fiction), largely through circulating libraries, with really very few individual purchasers, and given that artisan and working-class reading clubs were very likely to buy novels, there is considerable justification in calling all novels of this period, as Butler has called those of Austen herself, "novels for the gentry."[13] While little research has been done on the consumption (as opposed to production) of novels during Austen's day, it seems safe to say that their readers were not only gentry, but also the professional middle classes, and large parts of the well-to-do middle classes in general, for these were the only people able to pay for new novels or the subscription to a circulating library. However, if novel readers spanned the middle classes and gentry, most novel writers seem to have been situated well within the middle class, if not in fact the urban middle class. This general statement is certainly true if one concentrates on the Jacobin and Anti-Jacobin novelists of the 1790s; and here is an interesting relationship between Jane Austen and the majority of novelists of her day, for surely relatively few novelists had as genteel a background as the author of *Mansfield Park*. She came from a family well up in the clergy, the leading profession in her day, and she had one brother who was actually adopted into the landed gentry. There was Jane Austen, then, on the border between the professional classes and the gentry, the more so because she was a woman, and remained a spinster. It was this border between professional middle class and gentry that had produced the stability of eighteenth-century British society, and it was this border that would be the breeding ground for the leadership, political and social, of the coalition that would rule Britain for another century. But in order that this should be so, two elements in society had to be chastened (the lower orders were simply locked out)—the apparently decadent but libertarian Whig magnates and gentry against whom Burke railed in the 1790s as against class traitors (see his *Letter to a Noble Lord*, 1796), and their sometime allies, the dissident and usually Dissenting urban middle classes, led at that time by some of the most energetic intellectuals in the Western world. These intellectuals,

Godwin, Holcroft, and Bage among them, wrote novels attacking aristocratic and gentry hegemony; they often satirized members of the professional classes—corrupt lawyers (as in Charlotte Smith's novels), crooked estate agents (as in Maria Edgeworth's), and ignorant lazy clergymen (the antecedents of Austen's own Mr. Elton or Reverend Grant)—who were firmly and safely within the Establishment, and who were most closely associated with the country gentry. They attacked war, the field of play and of social and economic advancement for younger sons of the gentry and promising sons of the professional classes, and not incidentally the cause of greater prosperity for the landowning gentry and of distress to the rural and urban poor and the mercantile middle classes. They attacked dueling, the last vestige of the social badges separating the classes of a feudal society.

This is the social and cultural context of the "war of ideas" in the 1790s, as expressed in the Jacobin and Anti-Jacobin novel, and in the novels of Jane Austen. A coalition of gentry and professional and mercentile middle classes had run—even if an aristocratic court elite had ruled—England for a century. But urbanization, working-class literacy, and industrialization, not to mention "French principles," threatened their power and even their unity in the late eighteenth and early nineteenth century. The coalition had to be broadened without seeming to be so, and ideological control over outsiders had to be strengthened at the same time that consciousness and self-discipline were increased within the ranks of those who mattered.[14] The novel was a weapon in this "war of ideas," the war of ideas that really mattered and not the one about the nature of human beings, or sensibility, or individualism. A campaign of propaganda in all cultural products developed, one that was aimed almost entirely at members of the ruling orders and at potential recruits and followers. (The propaganda designed for those outside power, as suggested earlier, can be found in the Cheap Repository tracts and the like.) The "war of ideas" in the novel of the 1790s was a disturbing episode, but it would be wrong to think that the Jacobin faction amongst the middle-class and gentry writers was somehow defeated; most converted to the Anti-Jacobin side, or kept quiet; a few, like Godwin, joined Romanticism. Meanwhile, some writers attempted to formulate a compromise between gentry and middle-class ideologies, a compromise that would in fact become the dominant ideology of the nineteenth century. A liberal writer in this enterprise was Maria Edgeworth. Her more conservative counterpart was Jane Austen; but it is perfectly clear that however they may have differed in their conception of the relation between individual selfhood and society, both were calling in effect for the professionalization of the gentry, and the gentrification of the professional classes (see Edgeworth's *Tales of Fashionable Life*, 1809–12, especially "Ennui,"

"The Absentee," and "Vivian").[15] Edgeworth's call was immediately popular (if that is the right word); Austen's "popularity" took longer to mature,
outlasted Edgeworth's, and became part of the institution of Literature
that we still live with.

Of course it is precisely as Literature that Jane Austen's novels have
significance now, quite in contrast to the Jacobin and Anti-Jacobin novels
of her day (though *Caleb Williams* does seem to be nudging its way into the
canon). So it might be argued that to propose a significant relationship
between her novels and those of the 1790s, as I have done here, is to miss
what is really significant about her novels. On the contrary, however, it is
exactly in their "literariness," their evident possession of the attributes of
literature rather than of mere polemics, that Austen's novels reveal, I would
argue, the final aspect of their relationship to the novels of the 1790s, the
aspect which is irrecoverable in all its fullness without some such understanding of an intertextual relationship as that I have sketched in this essay.
The attributes of "literariness" are of course never fixed, but depend on the
understanding of verbal art held by a particular culture or group within a
culture. However, in the case of Austen's novels I take these attributes
to be an evident concern that the work be well-made and "finished" (the
reader is occasionally and teasingly reminded of this); an evident lining
up with the tradition of knowing and witty, worldly-wise (though by no
means cynical) narration classically represented by Fielding and somewhat
crudely grasped at by some of the Anti-Jacobins; a fairly high though by no
means obtrusive literary allusiveness; an evident concern for shapeliness of
plot and character grouping; and an aversion to insufficiently dramatized
essay—or sermon—matter, in contradistinction to the less well-made novels of the 1790s. Furthermore, many of these attributes are made obvious,
or even drawn attention to, so that the literariness of the novels is actually
advertised to the reader. The most important literary attribute of Austen's
novels, however, is that correct reading of their characters and plots, correct reading of their ideological import, in other words, is dependent on the
reader's knowledge of the literary conventions—the mere conventionalities
of "bad" novels—Austen's novels play off and thus transcend. It would not
be too far-fetched to say that Austen's transcendence of the terms and lines
of the fictional debate of the 1790s is accomplished by a knowing transformation of the hackneyed elements of conventional and especially conventionally didactic fiction. How true that is can be seen at once if one thinks of
all the characters in Austen's novels who act, consistently or only occasionally, as if they were characters in a bad novel. In fact, I can think of only one
fictional device which is original, and Austen's own, and that is the mode of
narrative voice, free indirect discourse, which, as I have already argued, is

itself a transformation and a transcendence of the opposing narrative modes of the novels of the 1790s. In effect, what Austen was doing in her instructive and reformative attention to the art of the novel was to chasten the too earnest professional intellectual (and Jacobin) novelists of the 1790s, as well as their Anti-Jacobin opponents, with their affected gentry values and (frequently) gentry-style slap-dash inartistry. On another level, the continuity between her fiction and that of the 1790s is in effect with the Anti-Jacobin novels of domestic realism written by other women writers, but writers who were not as genteel as she herself was, socially, and as a writer.

What Austen's novels do on every level, then, is to argue for or represent the social and cultural hegemony of a professionalized gentry class. Her novels do this precisely by transforming the ideas, arguments, and formal methods of the ideological novels of the 1790s. In terms of the "mental philosophy" of the 1790s debate, Austen effects her transformation by ex-hibiting a model of the individual mind as at once fixed, with its genetically inherited "temper," and improvable, through the education of self-reflection, social interaction, and acceptance of instruction and chastening from moral and intellectual superiors. Austen's model of society therefore is also both fixed and progressive, fixed in that social structures, conven-tions, and institutions are not questioned in their nature but only in their abuse, and progressive in that she shows society to be at least somewhat improvable by means of "enlightened," that is, self-critical and socially crit-ical individual leadership. With this argument Austen tries to bring to-gether the opposing emphases in the debate on self and society carried out in the novel in the 1790s, and reformulates the whole issue for the next century. Furthermore, in her strategic and ideological use of evident artis-try (the formal counterpart of her novels' ironic narrative mode) Austen demonstrates on the level of artist/artistic convention the argument she pursues on the level of self/society. What Austen does with the conven-tional language of fiction, and especially the language of fiction of the 1790s, is exactly what her principal characters must do with the social con-ventions and institutions which are *their* inheritance: they must revivify them by taking them on, inhabiting them, and instilling them with the force of chastened, disciplined, informed, and therefore supremely individual selfhood. Only in this can the professionalized gentry, and their new cultur-al and ideological advisors, the novelists, deserve and effect the social lead-ership and social power which they also have inherited. In carrying out her argument on self and society by superbly appropriate formal methods, Jane Austen attempted to transform the ideas, compositional elements, and formal procedures of the ideological novel of the 1790s into a new version of the art novel. To this extent, Austen's fiction revolutionized the potential of the novel as an instrument of ideological warfare, paradoxically by seeming to transform mere crude didacticism into conscious artistry. But in fact in Austen's novels art is not separable from or superior to ideological import; the artistry is the ideological import. The idea of the transcendence of art, like the older idea of the transcendence of irony, is not ideology-free; it is a leading element in the ideology of the class that was coming to dominate British culture and society in Austen's day, and which still does.[16] In her fiction Austen clearly demonstrated the potential place of the Novel in the wing of Literature in the Palace of Art—three of the principal institutions of gentry-professional culture in the nineteenth century. To that extent she did initiate the "Great Tradition" in the English novel.

Paradoxically again, however, she did so as a woman writer; and let this be the last point of this paper, in terms of the themes of this book, even though this point is really the starting point for another paper. Austen accomplished her ideological work with materials—the "serious" novel of the 1790s—which had been most obviously, though not at all exclusively, in men's hands, with issues which were thought to be beyond the intellectual range or interests of women, even though the novel, to its disgrace, was considered women's domain, as to both reading and writing. That is why it is also wonderfully appropriate that Austen should conceal her resolution and transcendence of the Jacobin *versus* Anti-Jacobin debate in the novel behind an apparent conformity with the women's novel of domestic realism of the 1790s. It was in fact Jane Austen, amongst others such as Sir Walter Scott and Mary Shelley, who made the novel an object of serious intellectual and cultural concern, and who made it the principal vehicle for social criticism and ideological education in the nineteenth century. Surely that was a vigorous unfettering and freeing, even if, after all, Austen did her work in the interests of a society and a culture which was and is decidedly paternalistic.

NOTES

1. Marilyn Butler, *Jane Austen and the War of Ideas* (Oxford: Clarendon Press, 1975); Alistair Duckworth, *The Improvement of the Estate* (Baltimore: Johns Hopkins University Press, 1971). Butler's book is a rich contribution to Austen studies, indeed to an understanding of the whole of Romantic fiction. However, I feel her argument, that Austen is an Anti-Jacobin by virtue of being an Anti-Sentimentalist, seriously skews the relationship between Austen and the nov-

elists of the 1790s by underplaying the force of bourgeois ideology in all the fiction of the period. Indeed, her account of the Jacobin novelists is the least satisfactory part of her book, even though she does recognize that in their way the Jacobins were Anti-Sentimentalists too.

2. See the different views on the composition of the novels in Q. D. Leavis *Scrutiny*, 10 (1941–42) 61–90, 114–42, 272–94; 12 (1944) 104–19; and Brian Southan, *Jane Austen's Literary Manuscripts* (London: Oxford University Press, 1964), 136–48.

3. W. Bliss Carnochan explores the images of confinement in *Caleb Williams*, but gives them a more mythic significance than I would; see his *Confinement and Flight* (Berkeley: University of California Press, 1977), 127–34 and cf. my *English Jacobin Novel* (Oxford: Clarendon Press, 1976), ch. 4 on "the myth of the Bastille"; see ch. 3 of Victor Brombert's *The Romantic Prison* (1975, tr. Victor Brombert, Princeton: Princeton University Press, 1978).

4. See Pat Rogers, ed., *Defoe: The Critical Heritage* (London: Routledge and Kegan Paul, 1972). William Godwin was one important and serious student of Defoe's novels.

5. For an interesting account of a similar literary phenomenon, see the third section of Jack Zipes's "The Romantic Fairy Tale in Germany," in his *Breaking the Magic Spell: Radical Theories of Folk and Fairy Tales* (London: Heinemann, 1979).

6. Butler, *Jane Austen and the War of Ideas*, 107.

7. Butler writes, "From about 1796, the typical anti-Jacobin novel is no longer the feminine conduct-novel by writers like Mrs. (Jane) West, with its domestic plot familiar since the days of Richardson. . . . A picaresque variant becomes fashionable, usually though not invariably written by a man, and with a male protagonist" (106–7). There is, however, the popular *Adeline Mowbray* (1804) by Amelia Opie, a former member of Godwin's circle, and there are other novels and tales of a similar kind, a kind which seems to have been more popular and widely read than the picaresque Anti-Jacobin novels, if numbers of editions are anything to go by.

8. Charles Lloyd, *Edmund Oliver* (Bristol: J. Cottle, 1798), 1:vii; 2:106.

9. A notable exception was Elizabeth Hamilton, author of *Letters of a Hindoo Rajah* (1796) and *Memoirs of Modern Philosophers* (1800).

10. There are many studies of the relationship of Austen's fiction to her great eighteenth-century predecessors, but again the point should be made that Austen read these predecessors in the light of her understanding of the fiction and the issues of her own day.

11. Fanny Price has true judgment and does not act; but this is because her social standing and her feminine variety of heroism require her to act, as it were, by refusing to act, in contrast, say, to Lady Bertram's inaction from mere indolence.

12. See the valuable remarks on this subject by Ioan Williams, in *The Realist Novel in England* (London: Macmillan, 1974), 20–23. Butler also describes this aspect of Austen's achievement with proper emphasis on its significance, but she fails, I think, fully to relate it to Jacobin fiction.

13. Marilyn Butler, *Romantics, Rebels and Reactionaries: English Literature and its Background, 1760–1830* (Oxford, New York, Toronto, Melbourne: Oxford University Press, 1981), chap. 4. See also, Thomas Kelly, *Early Public Libraries: A History of Public Libraries in Great Britain before 1850* (London: The Library Association, 1966), 127. See also the thesis by A. Varley, "A History of Libraries in Cheltenham from 1780 to 1900," reported on in *Library History* (London) 1 (1969); 197–98.

14. G. E. Mingay, *The Gentry: The Rise and Fall of a Ruling Class* (London and New York: Longman, 1976).

15. I would include Sir Walter Scott in this project; D. D. Devlin, for example, argues that Scott was essentially a reconciler, in *The Author of Waverley* (London: Macmillan, 1971).

16. See the description of the relationship of the gentry and the professional classes in Martin J. Wiener, *English Culture and the Decline of the Industrial Spirit 1850–1980* (Cambridge: Cambridge University Press, 1981). On the role of the writer, see Thomas W. Heyck, *The Transformation of Intellectual Life in Victorian England* (London: Croom Helm, 1982).

V. FICTIONAL STRATEGIES

Springing the Trap
Subtexts and Subversions

DEBORAH DOWNS-MIERS

Sarah Fielding (1710–68), like Virginia Woolf two hundred years later, was a popular novelist, a conscious experimenter in the art of fiction, a journalist, a self-taught classicist, and a feminist. Her works reveal two primary concerns; the exploration of one becomes the various assertions of the other. These concerns are "the labyrinths of the mind" and the absolute necessity that women be equal with men in education and in marriage. Sarah Fielding presents and explains these issues in all her works in a great variety of ways. Any woman who insists upon equality for women recognizes the inequalities. Fielding's recognition becomes her work; intrigued by the processes of the human psyche, she realizes that the inequality suffered by women results from deep and elusive feelings in both female and male consciousness and is manifested primarily in language.

From Woolf's musing about "the woman's sentence" to Gilbert and Gubar's recent work, the language problem has fascinated and frustrated women writers and critics. Nancy K. Miller asks, "How is it that women, a statistical majority in our culture, perform as a literary subculture?"[1] Sarah Fielding, a very early representative of that subculture, consciously battles the dragon of her culture as manifested through its language. "But the puzzling mazes into which we shall throw our heroine, are the perverse interpretations made upon her words, the lions, tigers, and giants, from which we endeavour to rescue her, are the spiteful and malicious tongues of her enemies. . . ."[2] Like Spenser's Una and her own re-creation of that truth (*The Cry*), Fielding very quickly masters the language, befriends it, and sets it to work with and for her.

Through her particular use of language, experimenting with form and extending the range of content, Fielding explores the lives of women. In each of her works, she addresses the problem of women's parallel reality, that other-world state in which women live, relative in all ways to the real reality, the world of men. Fielding's intent is to help explain the cultural, historical context of women's lives through the descriptions and actions of fiction while also analyzing the ways women's minds work. As she explains in her introduction to *The Cry*: "we beg to inform our readers, that our intention in the following pages is . . . to paint the inward mind" (p. 8). Fielding is aware that others have attempted the same task. She gently insists, however, that her efforts go further and that because they do so, she must use methods which may discomfit some, particularly critics. The introduction to *The Cry* (1754) may be regarded as a kind of credo, in which Fielding announces her intentions as a writer and also reveals that she is aware that her methods may be unorthodox.

> Thoroughly to unfold the labyrinths of the human mind is an arduous task; and not withstanding the many skillful and penetrating strokes which are to be found in the best authors, there seem yet to remain some intricate and unopened recesses in the heart of man. In order to dive into those recesses and lay them open to the reader in a striking and intelligible manner, it is necessary to assume a certain freedom in writing, not strictly perhaps within the limits prescribed by rules. (p. 8)

The recesses of the heart, the labyrinths of the mind, are secrets which require secret, delicate expression. In fact, these truths are so potent that they frequently must be uttered while seeming to remain unsaid, still hidden in the recesses and labyrinths. It is the liminality of women, the suspension of their consciousness between being-object and becoming subject, a psychological basis of their cultural marginality, which constitutes the real subject of Fielding's work. This liminality also provides the structure and methodology for Fielding's work. She knows women speak in a subtext, often placing their real meanings and intentions into a variety of what I call "parenthetical forms," forms not prescribed by the limits of the rules.

Fielding is perhaps the first of British women writers who has *consciously* "long used a wide range of tactics to obscure but not obliterate their subversive impulses" by "presenting acceptable facades for private and dangerous visions."[3] The task Fielding sets for herself is formidable; she wants to write stories about the real lives of women. That reality includes the external context of everyday life, most particularly in Fielding's novels, the problems of achieving equality in education and marriage. And it includes the interior life of women's minds, which she understands requires creating and employing a wide range of tactics. Moreover, her strategies must allow her to present acceptable, marketable fiction while also addressing issues which are, at best, unpopular. Fielding's work in many subgenres of fiction is an effort not only to make money and to exercise her talent and intellect; each subgenre allows her to address those unpopular issues while appearing to be merely working in a somewhat new form. She brilliantly uses the tool of the majority culture against them. Her understanding of the language of fiction (and the language of the society) allows her to write metafiction before Sterne and gothic fiction before Walpole, the first novel in English intended for children, and much more— all as efforts to speak her real truth *and* to persuade others to believe and follow. Fielding's parenthetical forms exist as two primary categories, each containing several variations. The first category is that of treatment of characters. She creates actual protagonists (female) versus ostensible ones (male), so that unless a reader is particularly alert and interested, the ideas and actions of the female protagonist will not be greatly heeded. A strategy Fielding employs frequently is the splitting and/or doubling of the female protagonist so as to create a "bad" heroine while avoiding censure since there is clearly a "good" female model in the text as well. As Fielding becomes more certain of her craft and of her convictions, she becomes more daring, creating a fully drawn bad heroine and refusing to make absolutely clear that such a wicked woman will certainly be punished. All these characters Fielding employs to subversive ends. She also creates subversion through the structuring of the novels. She uses parallel texts—fairy tales, dream visions, fables—which actually function as subtexts because their intent is subversive, and she, like many eighteenth-century authors, obscures the line between fiction and nonfiction. The result is that the non-sympathetic reader, having been disarmed by a preface, reads in the text proper only what he has been told is there. Many critics highly disapprove of this technique, but she has achieved her intent; though risking critical disapprobation, she effectively obscures her real text from the wrong readers while presenting it clearly to her more important audience: other women and sympathetic men.

Just as the introduction to *The Cry* announces Fielding's awareness of the need to experiment with forms, her consciousness of employing subversive tactics via structural strategies is unquestionably revealed in a letter from her collaborator Jane Collier to Samuel Richardson. The great novelist and printer had questioned the advisability of leaving implicit the specific punishment received by the brawling little girls in *The Governess* (1749). Mrs. Collier explains, "As this book is not so much designed as a direction to governesses for their management of their scholars (though many a sly hint for that is to be found, if attended to) as for girls how to behave to each other, and to their teachers, it is, I think, rather better that the girls (her readers) should not know what this punishment was that Mrs. Teachum inflicts. . . ." Collier goes on to say Fielding is opposed to "corporeal severities" but that the work is more effective psychologically if each reader thinks the punishment to be the same she has suffered. Moreover, Fielding is quite aware "elder readers" will be among her audience and will have divided opinions as to the merits of corporal punishment. Mrs. Collier reveals that if the punishment is not explicit, then "all the party of the Thwackums" will be as disposed as the other party to give her the "very chance of a fair reading. . . ."[4] Fielding uses her knowledge of the human heart and labyrinths of the human mind to produce fiction which operates on several levels, for a wide and varied audience. Her devices of self-in-parenthesis are rich in variety; that they are so confirms my idea that women's language, in all its necessary variety and variation, bears a common feature: an effort to speak one's truth as oneself.

Fielding employs parenthetical forms as subversive strategies from her first novel to her last. Her strategies become increasingly subtle as her convictions become increasingly the content as well as the form of the novels. Analysis of the characters and structuring of the novels reveal a treasure of artful subversions, hidden within parentheses. In the first novel, *The Adventures of David Simple* (1744) and its two sequels, the ostensible protagonist is indicated by the title. The real protagonist of all three volumes is a woman, Cynthia. The ostensible subject of the novel is friendship; the real subject is the necessity for true friendship within marriage and how that is to be achieved. Thus, from the very beginning, Fielding puts her real concern into parenthesis. The energy of this extended work focuses on Cynthia. Indeed, she *is* the energy, so much so that in *Volume the Last* Fielding must banish the too-fascinating Cynthia to the West Indies in order to present the grim fable of the naive ostensible hero's fall. At the end of this volume, however, Fielding brings Cynthia home. Her husband and child have died, as have David and his entire family except the eldest child, a daughter whom we are told is just like Cynthia. It is Cynthia who remains at the end, strong, consciously articulate about the real and the ideal, passing her legacy to another woman.

Cynthia had entered the novel in precisely the same way. She speaks for and about the intelligent, intellectual young women of the time:

> I cannot say, I ever had any Happiness in my Life; for while I was young, I was bred up with my Father and Mother, who, without designing me any harm, were continually teazing me. I loved Reading, and had a great Desire of attaining Knowledge; but whenever I asked Questions of any kind whatsoever, I was always told, *such Things are not proper for Girls of my Age to know*: If I was pleased with any Book above the most silly Story or Romance, it was taken from me. for Miss must not enquire too far into things, it would turn her Brain; she had better mind her Needle-work, and such Things as were useful for Women; reading and poring on Books, would never get me a Husband.[5]

This speech is hardly beneath the surface. It is, however, an effective sub-versive strategy, a parenthetical form, in two ways. First, Cynthia's history is structured as a digression from the "real" story; hence, many readers will pay less attention to its content, hurrying through it in order to get back to David's adventures. This section is not a conventional subplot, so it func-tions more as a sub*text*, even though it appears to be on the surface. The second and more complex parenthesis is Fielding's strategy for displaying the unhappy situation of the intellectual woman in her society while using it to utter her important and unpopular convictions. She puts all this into the speech of a young woman cast out by parents and despised by society be-cause of the very views she nonetheless continues to voice. Cynthia lives in the subculture, that other less real reality of women's lives, but because she has a clear self-image, she articulates that reality clearly. Moreover, be-cause she is doubly disenfranchised (not only a woman, but also a "trouble-some" one), her speeches can function as subtexts, the contents of which are subversive. Cynthia persistently voices Fielding's views, for example, insisting upon equality for women in marriage and maintaining that equal-ity in education is prerequisite for women to be equal with men in marriage:

> I could not help reflecting on the Folly of those Women who *prostitute* them-selves (for I shall always call it Prostitution, for a Woman who has Sense, and has been tolerably educated, to marry a Clown and a Fool), and give up that Enjoyment, which everyone who has taste enough to know how to employ their time, can procure for themselves, tho' they should be obliged to live ever so retired, only to know they have married a Man who has an Estate, for they very often have no more Commend of it, than if they were Perfect Strangers. (2:vi, 205–06)

Fielding repeats this view in each novel, varying not the message but the character who speaks it. Always pronounced by a woman of great under-standing and significant formal education, the speaker is sometimes a "good" woman, sometimes one unaccepted by her society. The fact that Fielding makes these women virtually interchangeable but for their places in society indicates that she believes all women can and ought to be prop-erly educated. It also indicates her desire to reach as wide an audience as possible. In *The Cry*, both the good woman and the fallen one refuse to marry someone who is not proper for them—according to *their* definitions of propriety. The "good" heroine, Portia, initially refuses Ferdinand's proposal and retires into the country, convinced that she must make good her vow that if she does not "meet with any man that had discernment enough to know, that real well-chosen learning and true understanding must as surely direct the mind to a proper behaviour" she will never marry (pp. 162–63). Cylinda, the fallen woman, also refuses to marry, seeing it as bondage: "I was resolved that I would not for the enjoyment of his company pay such a tax as matrimony" (p. 115). It is significant to note that neither woman is punished for her view; Portia does marry Ferdinand, after reforming his silly sentimentalism, and Cylinda retires with them, devoting herself not only to good works, but also to the study of philosophy.

So intent is Fielding upon presenting her view of education and marriage that she expresses her notions even through the pagan heroine, Octavia, of *The Lives of Cleopatra and Octavia,* 1757.[6]

> I considered with myself, that my Sentiments of a married State would not suffer me to lead a Life of Deceit or Hypocrisy and therefore, if married at all, it was requisite for my Peace of Mind, that I should be united to a Man who was the Object of my Inclinations, and whose Disposition would make an artful Behaviour on my Part totally needless to obtain good Usage, or to secure his Esteem. I had formed and represented to myself the Character of the Man who would please me best; and resolved that (unless Considerations of State obliged me to be a Sacrifice) I would live single, if I found it impossible to meet with the Counterpart of the Picture which dwelt in my Imagination.

Fielding continues to explore this complex issue in her last novels, employing a variety of parenthetical forms to do so. Charlotte Lucum, the Countess in *The History of the Countess of Dellwyn* (1759), is an adulteress. She has fallen to such a state, Fielding makes very clear, because of the greed and ambition of her father who has married her off, against her wishes, for the prestige of the count's title. Before being betrayed by her father, Charlotte displays the same integrity as her predecessors in Fielding's works: "Lord Dellwyn was highly disagreeable in her Sight; and she chose rather to submit to any State of Life, than to shine in the highest Sphere on such terms; she called it Prostitution, and heroically defied all such Temptations."[7] Again, these statements are explicit; however, they are uttered by women who are disenfranchised. That each of these women, despite their social castes and with complete consciousness of how their views will be regarded, continues to speak her truth, constitutes a most clever subversion of the reader. The unsympathetic and nonsympathetic readers will be entertained by the women's plights and/or charmed and gratified by these models of virtue or its obverse, just as the prefaces and introductions have encouraged. The sympathetic readers, on the other hand, will hear repeatedly Fielding's female characters articulating her most cherished idea: the absolute necessity of equality for women in education and marriage.

The second major category of parenthetical forms Fielding employs is the structuring of her novels. Her commitment to the feminist issues of education and marriage while exploring the relationship to them of the "labyrinths of the mind" provided the impetus for her experiments in structuring, just as need had impelled her to write her first novel. By avoiding the trap of becoming a male impersonator as a writer through her creation of Cynthia as the real protagonist of the David Simple volumes, Fielding initiates her strategies of parentheses. The character and structure strategies often constitute one another, but it is possible to observe how Fielding's formal experiments have subversive intent. Fielding was working during the first great flowering of the English novel; in addition to having the great good sense to recognize and capitalize upon the exuberant development of fiction itself, she was also highly self-conscious, as a woman and as an artist. In 1749, Fielding published *The Governess; or, The Little Female Academy*,[8] regarded as the first novel in English intended for children. With this novel, Fielding establishes a system and a pattern variations of which constitute the rest of her corpus. *The Governess* is an intentional heuristic, a conscious teaching device. The very fact that the work is set in a school and is about education allows Fielding to be subversive. It is a case of forest and trees. Because Fielding understands that children's books will be read by children's parents, she creates characters who appeal not only to children, but to their parents as well. Fielding saw and seized an opportunity to teach adults as well as children; both the parts and the whole of the novel contain wise and effective ideas about the nature of teaching and the use of teaching devices. Very few adults could resist the combined models of Mrs. Teachum and Jenny Peace, her star pupil, and surely most of them would feel a desire to help their children become more like Miss Jenny—by applying those methods Mrs. Teachum, through Jenny, employs. Middle-class adults, with their increasing power to effect change, are being given a delightful model of *education for girls*, Fielding's absolute prerequisite for a healthy society. Her brilliance goes further: through the interpolations— fairy tales, dream visions, and so forth—Fielding deepens the impact of her message. Each of the tales emphasizes the importance of honest friendships, most particularly within marriage, to the creation and maintenance of a healthy society. Furthermore, the interpolations dramatize the imperative of a good, equal education for girls, demonstrating that honest friendship is impossible without equality of education. In a single text, Fielding manages to present her views implicitly and explicitly, avoiding that monotony which can become polemicizing via the tales, each of which is in miniature an example of a subgenre of fiction. At the same time, Fielding's book does precisely what its content is about: using materials pupils were likely to study at school, the stories *become* those very materials and serve as the vehicles through which the pupils, and thereby, the readers, are taught.

Many critics regard all Fielding's inset texts as being the same. It is true they all have overt didactic intent. However, some of them have only a thematic connection with the text proper (the tales within *The Governess*, the story of Isabelle in *David Simple*), while others have a structural connection. These stories function as subplots. At the same time, however, they are literally subtexts, or more accurately, they are parallel texts which function subtextually, subversively. Fielding employs this device often, but two instances will serve to reveal how she uses this parenthetical form to spring the trap of the traditionally structured novel. The Cylinda subplot parallel text in *The Cry* is an example of Fielding using a character to create a structure that subverts. Apparently a foil for the good heroine, Portia, Cylinda appears to be the wicked, knowing woman of the world who must surely be punished, just as Portia, the innocent but wise virgin, will be rewarded. The attentive reader, however, will quickly realize the parallels in the characters of the two women. These parallels, already rehearsed above, in turn call attention not to the differences in the characters of the women, but to the differences in their *circumstances*, which, as Fielding creates their psyches, motivate them to behave differently. Instead of showing a single character driven to immorality by misfortune and then reforming—the traditional treatment—Fielding economically, and more believably, because more realistically, presents us two versions of a single character. Moreover, the older Cylinda is as attractive as Portia; the younger woman (and the reader) is attracted to her at once. Fielding appeals to the good sense of her readers by creating very similar, likable characters. She forces us to be active in choosing to identify with the *more* proper model. Nor is Portia the least bit vapid. She is as good as she is intelligent, and she also welcomes sex and sensuality as she refuses to marry the wrong person or for the wrong reasons.

In *The Countess of Dellwyn* Fielding employs the same parenthetical form, but reverses the emphasis. Charlotte Lucum, the adulterous countess, is the protagonist of the novel, one of the first "bad" heroines in our literature to be created by a woman. Charlotte is balanced by the virtuous Mrs. Bilson, whose goodness of heart and sweetness of disposition reform her profligate husband and rescue Cleveland, a young man who is eventually allowed to marry the Bilsons' charming and virtuous daughter. Although this novel concludes with a paean to virtue as embodied in generations of Bilsons, Charlotte is allowed to repent, having learned wisdom through her suffering. (The novel is subtitled *A Domestic Tragedy*.) In this novel, the story of the virtuous characters parallels the primary text's focus on the fall of the protagonist. That the proper moral model is relegated to the subplot indicates two things: Fielding does insist that virtue is its own reward and vice its own punishment, but also, it is clear she wishes her readers to be aware that women are routinely victimized by circumstances over which they have no control and should be shown compassion. Implicit in the novel, then, through its structuring, is Fielding's insistence that women must be allowed to choose the proper man to marry and that they must be properly educated in order to make the right choice. At the same time that she uses traditional fictional forms, she shapes them to her own ends, by making the subplot reflect and challenge the ostensible assumptions purposely set up in the readers' minds by the main plot—a strategy which forces the readers into active moral deliberations. As readers ponder the moral choices of the characters, they are forced to engage as well the issues Fielding presents, issues they might otherwise avoid. Using parenthetical forms that are similar to those in *The Governess* and which operate in similar ways, Fielding once again not only instructs through delight— she subverts.

Fielding employs a final parenthetical form through which she speaks her truth and forces the reader to participate rather than merely observe. As usual, this form has variations and is rather complex, combining manipulation of structure and reader response. Other great eighteenth-century writers exploited the relationship of fiction and nonfiction. Fielding is not only an early and very self-conscious experimenter in this realm; she also is perhaps more clearly than many experimenting because of her commitment to the political and social statements of her content. One of the variations of this parenthetical form is her use of introductory material. In her typical fashion, while working within the convention of the Preface, she so blurs and obscures the distinctions between it and the fiction following that she invents a kind of metafiction. In *Familiar Letters between the Characters of David Simple* (1753), Fielding employs the epistolary form of *Clarissa* to tell stories of "real" incidents in the lives of the characters which they then comment upon via fables either recalled or invented by the correspondents. This structure constitutes a "courtesy book" for women. Such texts proliferated in the eighteenth century; Fielding's is the only one I know of which is a sequel to a novel, though in a different form from the parent text, while prefaced by an explicit intent to be a courtesy book. In this text, the conventions of the novel are sprung by being *overtly* used to teach, while the conventions of the courtesy books (most of them at mid-century written by men) are transformed into fiction, but rendered highly realistic because the fiction is in the form of correspondence.

The next year, with *The Cry*, Fielding employs much the same strategy, but makes it more complicated. Her long introduction to the novel and the prologues to each part make explicit the form of the work, explaining that the action of the plot will be interrupted for debate between Portia and the Cry, in an effort to discern "the truth." In the introduction, the authors state: "The motives to action, and the inward turns of mind, seem in our opinion more necessary to be known than the actions themselves; and much rather would we chuse that our reader should clearly understand what our principal actors think, than what they do" (p. 11). By making their intentions so explicit in the introduction, the authors spring the criticism trap awaiting them—the charge that their characters think (talk) too much and act too little. Moreover, revealing the plan of the form helps set up the sympathetic reading of the two parallel female characters, Portia and Cylinda. Finally, the introduction introduces a fiction which is structured and reads like a play but which also has narratives within it, thus obscuring even more the line between "real" and fictive. I contend that Fielding initiates and refines this strategy as a rhetorical ploy similar in intent to the shrewdness revealed in Collier's letter to Richardson. That is, the nonsympathetic readers will simply read fiction; the open-minded readers will be more alert to the structuring and thereby more receptive to the subversive message within it.

By making fictional characters part of a script, the very formal structure of drama, Fielding attempted to make them more immediate, more real. In her next work, *The Lives of Cleopatra and Octavia*, she uses essentially the same parenthetical form, but in reverse, just as she had reversed the emphases of the same strategy between *The Cry* and *The Countess of Dellwyn*. Her characters in *The Lives of Cleopatra and Octavia* are actual historical figures; in the work they speak to us with their own voices, yet almost because the women were real but are being made to speak to us out of the past and from Hades, they seem in a sense more fictional than Portia and Cylinda. However, Cleopatra and Octavia are not less real; they are real in a different way, demonstrating Fielding's abilities to manipulate her craft. The brief introduction is consistent with Fielding's prefaces in other works, in that it contains critical comment but also moves to become part of that very fiction it introduces. Thus she plays a game of intrigue with the readers, just as Cleopatra and even Octavia manipulate and fascinate *their* audience—Antony and the readers. Fielding almost audaciously explains that she is writing *fictional* autobiography and why, while at the same time, she fictionalizes her own nonfiction statements, thus adroitly drawing the readers even further into the suspension of disbelief that makes fiction work as fiction so that it may indeed instruct through delight. What happens to the readers is precisely what Fielding says she disavows by choosing "real" characters rather than imagined ones. Once again she appeals to the readers' moral, upright selves, while handily involving us in the fiction she has cautioned us to beware. Fielding establishes her customary dialectic between the apparent moral poles in the work; as always, they are women. Her supralevel dialectic, in essence a dialogue between the nonfictive and fictive structures and thus a most subtle parenthetical form, operates between the Preface and the novel itself. She goes further: the third level is the interaction similar to that intended by drama and created much as it is in *The Cry*. One of the most subversive effects of Fielding's work is that her readers could follow the development of her strategies from novel to novel, as each employs tactics of previous efforts, but always in a more refined and subtle fashion.

Nowhere is this development more evident than in Fielding's final novel, *The History of Ophelia* (1760).[9] On the surface, *Ophelia* is Fielding's attempt at a truly "popular" novel, after all her overt experimentation. She announces in the introduction that what follows is a work "as well calculated for Instruction and Amusement," persuading her readers she is working squarely in a tradition with which they are most familiar. Again she goes further: "the author of *David Simple*" explains that she has found in an old bureau a letter which is the present novel. Varying the fiction of the discovered manuscript, she announces that although the work is a letter, she feels it must have been intended for publication. This ploy demonstrates that she appreciates the increased sophistication of the reading public and lures them into playing the game of blurring distinctions between fiction and nonfiction. Although we read only one letter, and thereby receive the action ostensibly from only one viewpoint, the heroine is very conscious that she is, after all, writing a letter, to the extent that she breaks her narrative several times to comment on it or to continue the fiction of herself as a character, integrating her narration of her past with her present life as in the end of volume 1, chapter 6: "He then bid me a goodnight, and left me to take some rest, as I shall your ladyship, bidding you adieu for a little time." Chapter 7 then begins, "After a short rest, you are ready to proceed with me on my journey" (p. 15). The single-letter form also allows Fielding to work again with a technique, subgenre, and parenthetical form she had used before, the fictional autobiography. The fiction of the letter found in a bureau also makes it easier for her to continue the strategy of integrating the prefatory material of a work with the work, so the reader is in the fictional world before realizing it.

Ophelia only appears to be a typical popular novel, in part because of the very conventions Fielding seems content to perpetuate; in reality, however, it is the same as all her works, an experiment in the art of fiction which allows her to assert her belief in the necessary equality for women in education and marriage. The effort to create a popular novel was in itself perhaps one of her most subversive acts. One of the causes of *Ophelia*'s popularity with the common reader is that it is very funny. Fielding writes what the audience expects, but makes sly fun of both the content and its readers throughout while at the same time remarking upon injustice, especially that suffered by women and "mad" people. She continues to uphold her political and philosophical views, often humorously, and in the process creates a sustained exercise in Gothic fiction four years before Walpole published *The Castle of Otranto*. Fielding did achieve her intent; *Ophelia* was printed several times in her own century in England and on the Continent. Containing language, action, and characters absent on the whole from her other works, partly from her efforts to reach the general public, *Ophelia* also contains the germ of the Gothic romance. The kidnapping of Ophelia who languishes in a drafty, decaying castle until she manages to escape through the use of her wits and because she is protected by her beauty and virtue initiates a subgenre that remains not only vastly popular, but also quite unchanged from its eighteenth-century beginnings. More importantly, partly through this aspect of her "popular" novel, Fielding continues to address significant issues by exploring the labyrinths of the mind in the content of the novel and also via her unique parenthetical strategies of integrating her introductory material with the novel itself and of creating intriguing models of virtue. Ophelia teaches Dorchester *to allow himself* to be good. This novel's focus on Dorchester through the lenses of the parenthetical forms may be Fielding's most ambitious subversive act. It certainly is a daring departure for her; she has always chosen to direct her messages primarily to women and essentially to those who are already sympathetic with her views. Dorchester is neither. The parenthetical form of Dorchester's letters within the letter of Ophelia's which is *Ophelia*, and which are reports of conversations, so that we are several times removed from the action, allows readers simultaneously to see Dorchester from the inside as well as from the outside. This device causes readers, especially men, to identify more closely with Dorchester and to follow him more actively through his development from a cynical seducer to a devoted husband. Fielding insists in this novel that Dorchester must will himself to be good, for his own sake, rather than merely to win Ophelia. Such insistence pushes the tradition of the reformed rake far beyond that of the sentimentalists, appealing to men and women of sense as well as of sensibility. Moreover, by having Ophelia write her letter some time after she and Dorchester have married, Fielding further extends the tradition: we do not often see happy, content, successfully married couples in fiction as we do in this novel.

Fielding's persistent exploration of the labyrinths of the mind in order to support her demand for equality for women caused her to use parenthetical forms which allow her to demonstrate her views. This rhetorically astute combination of appeals increases her chances of being truly heard. Intriguing and impressive to twentieth-century readers, many of her structural devices constitute the creation or early practice of several subgenres of fiction, such as the Gothic, the school tale, and metafiction. Fielding is a conscious feminist whose expressed intent is to improve the lives of women. She knows she must appeal to persons in power (men) and employs all her craft to do so—without alienating them. Hence the need for parenthetical forms. She also knows she must educate women to understand the reality of their place in eighteenth-century society and then encourage them to work for change. The most effective way of doing so is to create positive models, women characters who have avoided or sprung the trap of male overdetermination of their lives. For Sarah Fielding, it was not sufficient merely to represent the plight of women, nor merely to assert that said plight must be cured.

The development of her art as a writer is actually her development as a creator of women characters who embody more and more specifically her own steadily growing and increasingly radical ideas. Fielding was a theorist, critic, philosopher, as well as a mimetic artist; for her it was imperative to analyze that which she represented, and vice versa. She always presents her ideas as a kind of literary Moebius-strip, a double helix of mimesis and analysis. That is why she explicitly states that her intent is to examine and expose the labyrinths of the mind; that is why she does so from a double perspective, her theoretical, critical approach, and her manifestation of that in the fiction itself, all of which constitutes parentheses. *The Cry* is perhaps the most obvious example of Fielding's unique deployment of characterization and structure, theory and mimesis.

The Cry is about true friendship, but unlike Fielding's first novel with its picaresque, episodic structure and many transparent apologues, this one explores friendship, particularly friendship in marriage, in a much more complex fashion, both in content and in structure. Several couples, some of them treacherous, some of them mediocre, and some of them struggling valiantly to be wise, strong, and good, interact via several subplots. The heroine, Portia, has been reared by her mother to be good, but also has been given a superior education. Cylinda, the apparent "bad" woman, also has a superior education, but she did not have the balance of a mother's wisdom, training her as well in virtue. Each woman encounters several suitors, interacting with the men according to, as Fielding paints it, their respective backgrounds, which means Portia remains virtuous while Cylinda, out of her intellectual beliefs, becomes what society regards as promiscuous. When Portia is an adolescent, she encounters Cylinda, then in her early twenties and going through a recluse period. The two women become friends and Cylinda, who is a most gifted philosopher and teacher, helps Portia in her studies until the younger girl's mother learns of Cylinda's reputation. At the same time, two other young people, Ferdinand and his sister, are cheated out of their inheritance by their brother and the conniving young woman who becomes his wife, because she wants Oliver's money, although she lusts after Ferdinand, who, of course, is in love with Portia. The treacherous couple contrive to make Ferdinand believe the worst of Portia, but he at least determines to "test" her. Portia, oblivious to perfidy, is not however insensitive to being insulted and, despite her love for Ferdinand, refuses to accept him after his treatment of her. Through the efforts of Cylinda, Portia and Ferdinand are reunited and Cylinda rewarded by becoming part of their household. Portia and Cylinda meet in the outer, dramatized structure of the work, bringing together the plot and the subplot of the narrative structure, which unites the abstract—the search for truth in the dramatized sections—and the concrete—the actions which manifest the truth in the narrative sections. This meeting brings resolution to the inner, narrated structure.

Most significant to Fielding's work as an artist and as a feminist is that within that resolution is another, personal one—the completion of the unfinished business of the two women's previous friendship, one which was both a sharing—because of their intellectual interests and abilities—and a discipleship—because of the difference in their ages. With this resolution, Fielding raises and addresses a problem with which twentieth century women have only begun to struggle. Portia's mother took her away from Cylinda because she wished her daughter not to be initiated into the more complete knowledge the older woman held because of her education and experience. But Portia's mother dies. Ultimately Cylinda returns to live from middle age to death in the home of her intellectual daughter. The daughter becomes the mother of the mother. Fielding does posit Portia as the ideal woman. Her strategy of making Cylinda parallel with Portia, though in the subplot, is a brilliant springing of the trap of female enslavement to male ideas of virtue and propriety. Through the structural strategies, we see that Cylinda is not the villainess—she is, rather, the *real* woman. She is so actual, so realistic, that Fielding must present her in parentheses. The most important and fascinating fact about Cylinda is that she *is* Portia, and Portia *is* Cylinda, because both of them are Sarah Fielding, a woman who had found her voice, who was compelled to speak herself, but who, in her wisdom, knew she must do so as a ventriloquist.

There is more evidence for Cylinda and Portia constituting one woman and for them to be Sarah herself. *The Cry*, almost invisibly, is autobiography, for it is Portia's and Cylinda's stories, told by themselves. Within the content of this novel are other similarities between the characters themselves and to their creator. Cylinda and Portia have received almost identical educations; each was reared primarily by a single parent; each prefers the study of philosophy to any other, but study in general to any other labor. Although on the surface their attitudes toward marriage seem different, they are essentially the same: both wish to retain their integrity (pp. 7, 8). Only Portia, because she lived longer with both parents, who had a loving marriage, and because she was reared primarily by her mother, sees that her integrity can be retained in marriage—if it is the proper kind. Cylinda, however, reared only by her father, has had to learn much too late the possibilities for integrity within marriage. Sarah Fielding's mother died when she was seven and a half. Until she lived with her brother Henry and his first wife, whose marriage is renowned for the mutual love of the partners, she had no model for a good marriage. And, being an intellectual like Cylinda, she was certainly capable of imagining a life like hers. Given her writing, it would not be surprising if we were to learn that Sarah wished for an independent income and an independent life, one that might very well include lovers. What is very likely, given Fielding's interest in the mind, is that in order to cope with the split in her own (so forceful is the impact of society even upon those who understand its traps), she created two versions of her self: the self she thought she ought to be—Portia—and the self she sometimes wished she could be—Cylinda.

I have dwelled on this point because we know so little about Sarah Fielding. What we do know about her life has been obscured by those who insist on maintaining that because she was unmarried, she was a bookish, rather unappealing (despite extensive evidence to the contrary) spinster. What we learn about Sarah Fielding from her works reveals a woman who was very real—wise, passionate as well as compassionate, and shrewd. The picture she paints of her women characters who are unmarried or who are perfectly willing never to marry—indeed, who *will not* marry unless the marriage is one of integrity according to *their* definitions—springs the ultimate trap. The marriage trap has been ensnaring women for eons; Fielding springs it by revealing it for what it is, especially as opposed to what marriage could and should be, a relationship based on true love: "A sympathetic liking, excited by fancy; directed by judgment; and to which is joyn'd also a most sincere desire of the good and happiness of its object," as she says in *The*

Cry (p. 65). Fielding's women characters indicate that while she was most likely very sorry not to have met a man who could meet her requirements, she was much happier being single, and writing about it. Moreover, through the technique of characterization, especially as it works parenthetically, Fielding not only springs traps; she also teaches her audience and herself that in order to be fully human, a woman must be free.

NOTES

1. Nancy K. Miller, "Emphasis Added: Plots and Plausibilities in Women's Fiction" *PMLA* 96 (January 1981): 38.

2. Sarah Fielding, *The Cry*, 3 vols. (London: R. and J. Dodsley, 1754), 1:i, 1:8. Further references appear in parentheses in the text.

3. Gilbert, Sandra, and Susan Gubar, *The Madwoman in the Attic: A Study of Women and the Literary Imagination in the Nineteenth Century* (New Haven: Yale University Press, 1979), 13.

4. Anna Barbauld, *The Correspondence of Samuel Richardson*, 6 vols. (London: Richard Phillips, 1804; reprint, New York: AMS Press, 1966), 2: 61–65.

5. Sarah Fielding, *The Adventures of David Simple*, 2 vols., 2d ed. (London: A. Millar, 1744), 1: ii, 6: 188–89. Further references appear in parentheses in the text.

6. Sarah Fielding, *The Lives of Cleopatra and Octavia* (London: A. Millar, 1757), 148–49.

7. Sarah Fielding, *The History of the Countess of Dellwyn: A Domestic Tragedy*, 2 vols. (London: A. Miller, 1759), 300.

8. Richardson's *Familiar Letters* was certainly a model. However, Richardson's "courtesy book" is intended only as such; he writes *Pamela* afterwards, a separate fiction. Only Fielding combines and plays against each other in the same text the fictions of fiction and nonfiction.

9. Sarah Fielding, *The History of Ophelia*, 2 vols. (London: R. Baldwin, 1760). References appear in parentheses in the text.

10. Certainly this device is present in some French novels, for example, *La Vie de Marianne, Histoire au Miss Jenny*.

11. Deborah Downs-Miers, "Masking the Face, Unmasking the Mind: The Gothic Masquerade" (Paper presented at Northeast Society for Eighteenth-Century Studies, October 1982).

Frances Sheridan
Morality and Annihilated Time

MARGARET ANNE DOODY

It may well seem so, answered Cadiga, buried as your senses have been in forgetfulness, and every faculty consigned to oblivion, that the interval of time so past must be quite annihilated. . . .

(Francis Sheridan, *The History of Nourjahad.*)

Our own age seems an auspicious time for an attempt to rescue Frances Sheridan from oblivion, and her works from the annihilation of forgetfulness. Feminists—and not only feminists—could find her interesting, this spirited and pleasant Anglo-Irish woman who won her husband, Thomas Sheridan (if report can be believed) by writing a poem and a pamphlet in his defense when riots rocked the theatrical and social life of Dublin.[1] According to the *Memoirs* published by the author's granddaughter, Alicia LeFanu, Frances Chamberlaine's father had an antipathy to learning or even literacy in a women. "He was with difficulty prevailed on to allow his daughter to learn to read; and to write, he affirmed to be perfectly superfluous in the education of a female. The Doctor considered the possession of this art, as tending to nothing but the multiplication of love letters. . . ." Fortunately, Frances's "affectionate brothers"—how important brothers have been in the lives of English women writers!—"vied with each other in averting the effects of her father's injudicious prohibitions."[2] She achieved not only literacy, but also a measure of learning; her scholarly eldest brother taught her Latin, as Sir George, the brother of the novelist's heroine Sidney Bidulph, was to do for his sister.

So defiant was Frances of her father's ban on women's writing that she secretly wrote a romance, *Eugenia and Adelaide*, by the time she was fifteen. Later, during her residence in London with her husband, Frances caught the attention and gained the friendship of Samuel Richardson, and she showed the eminent novelist the romance she had composed in her teens.

With Richardson, to whom she had first been introduced in Huntingdonshire, Mrs. Sheridan had frequent opportunities of conversing, both at her own house and at Parson's Green: and it was in consequence of the admiration he expressed upon the perusal of her manuscript novel, Eugenia and Adelaide, that she was first encouraged to try her powers in a work of higher importance and greater length.

Richardson was not just a literary mentor, but a personal friend; Alicia LeFanu says that the daughter born to the Sheridans while they were living in Covent Garden (an interesting location for a Richardsonian) was named Anne "in compliment to Anne, daughter of Samuel Richardson."[3] The elderly Richardson lived to see the literary fruit of his encouragement of Frances Sheridan, though we do not know if he ever read the whole of her first novel. The work "of higher importance and greater length" which she wrote was *The Memoirs of Miss Sidney Bidulph*, published in March 1761, a few months before Richardson's death.

Richardson seems to have read part of the novel in progress as early as the autumn or winter of 1756, but its writing extended over some time. And Mrs. Sheridan was fairly secretive in this bid for fame. The author's husband did not know about the work until it was completed. Alicia LeFanu explains that Frances was "unwilling that any hopes raised in the partial mind of her husband . . . should be blighted," and therefore she popped the manuscript into "a small trunk or chest placed beside her . . . if Mr. Sheridan chanced to enter the room"[4]—a very cautious proceeding in one whose novelistic talents has been encouraged by one of the most celebrated novelists of the day. Probably she was still not certain her husband would approve. Mrs. Sheridan hoped to make some money by her fiction; the family was in straitened circumstances, and for her, as for so many female writers, the needs of the family provided an excuse for venturing into publication. *The Memoirs of Miss Sidney Bidulph* was warmly received by the public (despite some critical doubts as to its moral tendencies); it was like Richardson's *Clarissa*, translated into French by the Abbé Prevost.

Mrs. Sheridan then boldly ventured into writing comedies for the stage. Her plays, *The Discovery* (1763) and *The Dupe* (1764) met with considerable success.[5] Both David Garrick and Thomas Sheridan acted in *The Discovery*, and the play continued to be put on for some years after its author's death. Mrs. Sheridan then turned again to prose fiction. When the Sheridans were in France for the sake of both Frances's health and family economy, she wrote a second part of *Miss Sidney Bidulph* and an oriental tale, *The History of Nourjahad*. Frances Sheridan died in 1776, and did not live to see the publication and popularity of these last works (both published in 1767).

Frances Sheridan's reputation—and indeed, that of her husband—has been overshadowed by the greater fame of her son, Richard Brinsley Sheridan, but any scholar of the eighteenth century should be happy at least to find out what R. B. Sheridan's mother wrote. A Richardsonian (like myself) is always interested in seeing how Richardson's influence worked upon his successors. Furthermore, our developing interest in works of the eighteenth century which have been less well known, and our interest in works by women, make Frances Sheridan's fiction an interesting case for investigation. The investigation would be worthwhile, as she made a real contribution to fiction. The main body of this present essay consists of an investigation of each of her works of prose fiction (*Sidney Bidulph I, Sidney Bidulph II* and *Nourjahad*) in order, with attention to Mrs. Sheridan's talents as a writer of fiction and to her characteristic and unusual themes. Such a discussion involves—necessarily—much account of plot and summary of action, for I cannot expect readers will be familiar with these works, but the plot summaries, although inescapable, are subordinate to the work of clarifying Mrs. Sheridan's moral views and fictional techniques. In particular, I wish to show that her apparently realistic novel (Sidney Bidulph, a life work in two parts) and her short Oriental tale are intimately related to each other, and that in the themes which connect them we may read something of the eighteenth century's preoccupations, as well as tracing new developments foreshadowing Romantic and modern fiction.

It was of the 1761 *Memoirs of Miss Sidney Bidulph* that Johnson said to the author, "I know not, Madam! that you have a right, upon moral principles, to make your readers suffer so much."[6] *Memoirs of Miss Sidney Bidulph* is a tale of distress, and the reader cannot avoid knowing at the outset that the story will not end happily. In "The Editor's Introduction," the nameless editor (a more obtrusive character than Richardson's) tells how he came to be acquainted with an old lady (Sidney's friend and confidante, Cecilia) who gave him the epistles which compose the *Memoirs* and commented on the meeting of her friend's sad story. The aged Cecilia argues that literary presentations of virtue which is not rewarded in this life are "justified . . . from every day's experience" and that Christians should not be taught to expect reward in this transitory existence but should learn to look to heaven "where . . . our lot is to be unchangeable" (1:5–7).[7] The old lady (who dies before the youthful editor has the chance to talk over with her what he has read) has written a comment at the beginning of the journals, advising the reader that they "may serve for an example, to prove that neither prudence, foresight, nor even the best disposition that the human heart is capable of, are of themselves sufficient to defend us against the inevitable ills that sometimes are allotted, even to the best"

(1:15). Changeableness and disappointment are thus announced as subjects. Frances Sheridan is a not unworthy follower of Richardson, to whom the novel is dedicated,[8] but the immediacy we associate with a Richardson narrative "to the moment" is softened; there is greater distancing and detachment in the presentation of this epistolary novel than in any of Richardson's tales in letters. The editorial material emphasizes that the outcome of this sad story is well known, that most of the major characters are deceased (indeed the last survivor dies during the introduction) and above all, that the events happened long, long ago. As is not the case with *Clarissa* (whose events are dated vaguely about twenty years ago) the first letters in this novel are headed according to year, as well as month and day. The year at the heading of the first letter is 1703—that is, the action begins fifty-eight years before the date of the novel's publication. There is a gap of time separating reader from characters; we observe them across that space. Needless to say, the historical difference between that time and contemporary time is scarcely dwelt upon; manners and idiom are those of the 1760s rather than of the beginning of the Age of Anne. We are not offered historicity, but are given the detachment of distance which makes bearable the somberness of affliction.

Yet, after the sober warnings of the beginning, and the distancing effects, the characters are unexpectedly lively and entertaining, particularly the youthful Sidney displayed in correspondence with her friend Cecilia. Sidney's bluff brother, Sir George, introduces the girl to his best friend, Orlando Faulkland—thus initiating one of the most extraordinary love affairs in English fiction of the eighteenth century. Sidney knows her brother hopes she and the eligible Orlando will make a match of it, and she is attracted. "He is neither like an Adonis nor an Apollo . . . he has no hyacinthine curls flowing down his back; no eyes like suns, whose brightness and majesty strike the beholders dumb; nor, in short, no rays of divinity about him; yet he is the handsomest mortal man that I ever saw" (1:31).

The language here indicates authorial awareness not only of the style of romance, but also of the descriptions of Fielding's heroes, and Richardson's—there is a touch of parody of the heroic descriptions of *Sir Charles Grandison*. Orlando is no hero of romance; still less he is a dashing rake-villain, but only "mortal man," a mixed character, like all Sheridan's best and central personages. Sidney, knowing her brother expects her to attract his friend, is restive and self-conscious about her position: "I thought of the conversations we had so often had about Mr. Faulkland, and could not help considering myself like a piece of goods that was to be shewn to the best advantage to the purchaser" (1:33). Lady Bidulph, Sidney's mother, praises modest reserve which is "among the chief recommendations of a woman," and comically remembers her own courtship: "I am sure, when I married Sir Robert, he never heard me speak twenty sentences" (1:34). Lady Bidulph is a well-drawn character from the beginning, when we naturally but mistakenly consider her a minor character in the background of a love story involving the young generation. Lady Bidulph seems kind, well-disposed, somewhat literal-minded; her anxiety for her child's happiness, and her pleasure in forwarding this excellent match, seems all we could expect from a mother. The courtship progresses; Orlando declares himself, and visits as a professed suitor. Sidney falls in love, though she assures herself that her affections are still bounded by reason.

> Yet certain as the event of our marriage appears . . . I still endeavour to keep a sort of guard over my wishes . . . and therefore cannot rank myself among the first-rate lovers, who have neither eyes, nor ears, nor sensations, but for one object. This Mr. Faulkland says, is his case, in regard to me. But I think we women should not love at such a rate, till duty makes the passion a virtue; and till *that* becomes my case . . . I am determined not to let it absorb any of the other cordial affections. . . . (1:51)

This conscientious observation is, in the context of the whole narrative, highly ironic, it is hard to find any other eighteenth-century heroine haunted for so long by one love and its effects. The seeds of destruction are already present, unknown to all. It is during Faulkland's courtship, as affairs seem to be drawing toward a happy wedding, that we (and Sidney) first hear Lady Bidulph's story. In marrying Sir Robert Bidulph, after the ladylike laconic courtship, she did not marry her first love. At the age of twenty-one she was courted by a young man she loved. After a year's courtship (she was proud of being "not very easily won") the wedding day was fixed. But on the day of the wedding she received, not the bridegroom but a distraught letter from him, telling her that he had been engaged to another girl before he ever saw her, and this other woman he had seduced under promise of marriage. Overtaken by guilt, he has decided that he must keep his promise to "the person who had his first vows; and whom, he declared, his infidelity had almost brought to the grave" (1:59). Lady Bidulph (not Lady Bidulph then) bore her afflicting disappointment "with a becoming resolution"; she too felt that the seduced woman had a prior claim. The distracted lover fell into melancholy, and was subsequently confined as a madman; the other young lady (still unmarried) died "of a broken heart" (1:60). Lady Bidulph insists that she had a fortunate escape from the marriage, for "had these fatal events happened in consequence of my marriage with him . . . I should never have survived it" (1:61). Lady Bidulph's unhappy story seems, when we first hear of it, like a mere episode, one of the recollected tales of experience so often interpolated in eighteenth-century novels to act as example, and to widen our own (and the characters') experience of life. But Lady Bidulph's story is no mere interpolated episode. Her experience and her reaction to it—that action so long antecedent to the time of the novel's story—really form the major action of the story. From this event all else springs.

Sidney's wedding date is fixed, and the girl is caught up in the amusing bustle of wedding preparations. There are a few signs that her happiness may be disturbed. Faulkland exhibits a tendency to violent temper when provoked; he strikes with his whip a footman who whipped a young horse. Yet Sidney refuses to allow herself to be perturbed. "This little incident convinces me that Mr. Faulkland is of too warm a temper; yet I am not alarmed at this discovery; you know I am the very reverse; and I hope in time, by gentle methods, in some measure to subdue it in Mr. Faulkland." Her complacency is shored up by her brother's assurances that Orlando Faulkland is aware of his own fault, and has "taken infinite pains to get the better of it" (1:67). That Faulkland is not perfectly faultless seems no cause for alarm.

But then Sidney's happiness is shattered. The family receives an anonymous letter revealing that Orlando Faulkland had seduced a young lady at Bath, and the girl is now pregnant. As proof, the letter encloses another signed "A.B.," to Faulkland from the young lady in question. The lady calls herself "the most unfortunate woman in the world," laments her "present condition," and asks Faulkland's pity. She also reproaches him with his intended marriage to Sidney, of which she appears to have heard: "Are you then really going to be married? There wants but this to complete my destruction!" (1:82). As Sidney has been ill with a sore throat and fever, the business of receiving the letters and delving into the truth of the matter falls upon her horrified mother. Sir George takes the matter lightly; he "smiled and said, he knew of that foolish business before." He insists that the matter is "a trivial affair" (1:85). Orlando never courted the girl in Bath, who was "thrown in his way by a vile designing woman that had the care of her" (1:86). Sir George is more interested in the source of the anonymous letter; he (rightly) believes it must have come from the vengeful footman who robbed Orlando's pocketbook before he left, and must have made use of some papers he found there. Sir George Bidulph gives his mother a letter formerly written to him by Faulkland from Bath, giving an account of the matter, an account which Sir George feels must largely exonerate his friend. In her indignant account to Sidney of this epistle, Lady Bidulph admits "I own I had not patience to read the letter through. To say the truth, I but run my eye in a cursory manner over it; I was afraid of meeting, at every line, something offensive to decency" (1:91). As far as she is concerned, Orlando's libertinism and the vicious rakishness of men are merely confirmed by that letter, which Sidney herself is not given to read. Lady Bidulph is indignant at her son's attempt "to convince me that it was such a *trifling* affair," believing he thinks so only "because that loose man treats the subject as lightly as he does" (1:90). Sir George and his mother are totally at odds over the issue. Lady Bidulph cannot bear to hear the seduction of a young woman treated as a trivial concern. Masculine and feminine views of sexual morals are totally at loggerheads. Lady Bidulph tells Sidney that Sir George said to her that "if I kept you unmarried till I found such a man as *I* should *not* call a rake, you were likely to live and die a maid" (1:92). Taking up the fight for her own sex, Lady Bidulph gains the victory. It is she who dismisses Orlando, telling him "I will never bring down the curses of an injured maid upon my daughter's head, nor purchase her worldly prosperity at the expence of the shame and sorrow of another woman, for aught I know, as well born, as tenderly bred, and, till she knew you, perhaps as innocent as herself" (1:96).

It is apparent to the reader that Lady Bidulph, although she may be morally right, is reliving her own deepest experience over again. "Little did I think, my Sidney, when I told you the story of my first disappointment, that a case so parallel would soon be your own" (1:100). It is the "parallel" which is foremost in Lady Bidulph's mind, reanimating memories and complex feelings. As she herself had been (by her bridegroom's decision) deprived of any real choice save passive and dignified acquiescence in her loss, she is the more inclined to think passive if high-minded resignation the only suitable course for Sidney, and gives the girl only a nominal right to choose what to do—as the mother has done everything. Sidney's own feelings are mixed. She is disgusted at the tale, and horrified, but she does not have quite her mother's reaction.

Sidney is weak in health and depressed already when this blow falls on her. Her affection is still engaged, and she enjoys none of the triumphant consolations of heroic virtue. In her account of the matter to Cecilia, most of Sidney's energy is devoted to an analysis of her mother—the most important person in her world, still, and certainly the major factor in her fate.

> You may recollect, my dear, that my mother, tho' nice in every particular, has a sort of partiality to her own sex, and where there is the least room for it, throws the whole of the blame upon the *man's* side; who, from her own early prepossessions, she is always inclined to think are deceivers of women. I am not surprised at this bias in her; her early disappointment, with the attending circumstances, gave her this impression. She is warm, and sometimes sudden, in her attachments; and yet it is not always difficult to turn her from them. The integrity of her own heart makes her liable to be imposed on by a plausible outside; and yet

the dear good woman takes a sort of pride in her sagacity. She had admired and esteemed Mr. Faulkland prodigiously; her vexation was the greater, in finding her expectations disappointed; and could I have been so unjust to the pretensions of another, or so indelicate in regard to myself, as to have overlooked Mr. Faulkland's fault, I knew my mother would be inflexible. (1:102–103)

Sidney tries to bring herself to share her mother's view, even though Faulkland's image still intrudes into her thoughts. She tries to make herself think, as her mother does, that Faulkland ought to marry the girl. "I wish I knew her name, but what is it to me; *mine* will never be Faulkland, *hers* ought. Perhaps Mr. Faulkland may be induced to marry her, when he sees her in her present interesting situation" (1:110).

Lady Bidulph herself seems a heroic moralist. Going against the current of ordinary opinion at the time (so well represented by Sir George), she insists not only on the rights of a delicate woman to the love of an uncorrupted man, but also, and most unusually, on the *rights* of the woman seduced. If all women combined in such solidarity, then the men would not be able to continue their career of rakishness, would not be able to treat seduction as a light and laughable matter. Lady Bidulph's "partiality to her own sex" makes her a kind of feminist. She has decided that in cases of sexual misconduct, the blame rests "on the man's side," and she feels not disgust but sympathy for the woman in the case—an unusual attitude. There is something admirable in Lady Bidulph's unconventional feminist stand. The irony is that she is the one taking this stand in her daughter's case, leaving the daughter no room to absorb her own reactions and decide for herself. Her moral position also has, very clearly, particular psychological roots which Lady Bidulph does not want to examine. She has had to justify the wronged woman in order to justify her lover's choice to have her, while at the same her anger at her lover, which she has never allowed herself to express fully, has emerged in her quick reaction of hostility at another man who allowed himself to get sexually entangled. It is all the man's fault. Her complicated feelings regarding her own rival (another deserted and unhappy woman) have resulted in an identification, although at the same time we may wonder if subdued feelings of resentment, not permitted and not acknowledged, may have emerged in an elaborate and compensatory desire for kindness and fair play to the seduced woman. The novel invites such psychological readings, as it constantly focuses our attention on psychological events and reactions. Lady Bidulph's ability to make sudden emotional swings, from attachment to disgust (a quality perhaps acquired and certainly strengthened in her own early experience) makes the mother capable—as her daughter is not—of withdrawing all feeling from Orlando, and of refusing to hear any explanation. He doesn't deny the existence of the young pregnant girl at Bath. And that is enough. And perhaps it is—or should be, but then again, perhaps it should not. Frances Sheridan deals best with ambiguities and questions. The novel is not only a story of loss and disappointment. Its real strength arises from the fact that loss and sorrow have ambivalent causes. The story is interesting not just because it is the story of affliction. It is the story of a life lived around a moral problem. The ensuing action multiplies the questions surrounding this original moral problem. The characters are interesting because they are capable of moral thought; prefiguring characters in George Eliot, they live in moral complexity.

Orlando Faulkland goes to Germany, but not before telling the Bidulphs that he has been taking care of the seduced "Miss B." who will soon come to lodgings in Putney that he has engaged for her. He has, he says, appealed to Miss B. to do him justice, and explain the situation; he wants Sidney to meet the girl and talk to her. Sidney believes, however, that no matter what Miss B. might say Lady Bidulph would never consent to a resumption of the engagement between Sidney and Orlando: "My mother's piety, genuine and rational as it is, is notwithstanding a little trinctured with superstition . . . so that I know the universe would not induce her to change her resolution in regard to Mr. Faulkland. She thinks he *ought* to marry Miss B. and she will *ever* think so" (1:126). The acquaintance with Miss B., now urged upon the Bidulphs by Faulkland, will, however, later take place, with important effects not anticipated by Faulkland or Sidney.

Meanwhile, Lady Bidulph takes Sidney away with her, on a visit to an old friend, Lady Grimston. A dull manor house in the depths of Essex and the company of the antiquated Lady Grimston do nothing to relieve the sadness of Sidney's days, though the girl has recovered spirits enough to make amusing descriptions of the place and its mistress.

> She . . . renders herself a still more unpleasing figure, by the oddity of her dress; you would take her for a lady of Charles the First's court at least. . . . I believe she sleeps in her cloths, for she comes down ruffled, and towered, and flounced, and fardingal'd, even to breakfast. My mother has a *very* high opinion of her, and says, she *knows more of the world* than any one of her acquaintance. It may be so; but it must be of the old world. . . . (1:129)

Lady Grimston has high notions of the obedience owed by children to parents (especially to mothers). She quarreled with her husband about the marriage of their daughter (who wished to marry a man approved by the father, but not by the mother), and now she treats the widowed daughter with contempt, and even insists on referring to the daughter, when she speaks of her at all, by her maiden name. Sidney thinks Lady Grimston "a

tyrant" (1:163). In such a bastion of female supremacy, Lady Bidulph finds
a reassurance for her own notions and is tempted to exercise her own authority over Sidney for the daughter's good. A neighbor, Mr. Arnold, begins to pay his attentions to Sidney; he is quiet and reserved, and the girl
knows little about him. Mr. Arnold declares himself to Sidney in a scene
which beautifully suggests the quiet monotony of her surroundings at
Grimston Hall, and of the occupations of a woman's life—and Sidney's
attempt to escape from those conventional limitations:

> I was sitting in the little drawing-room, reading, when he came in. . . . The
> book happened to be Horace; upon his entering the room, I laid it by; he asked
> me politely enough, what were my studies. When I named the author, he took
> the book up, and opening the leaves, started, and looked me full in the face; I
> coloured. My charming Miss Bidulph, said he, do you prefer this to the agree-
> able entertainment of finishing this beautiful rose here, that seems to blush at
> your neglect of it? He spoke this, pointing to a little piece of embroidery that lay
> in a frame before me. I was nettled at the question; it was too assuming. Sir, I
> hope I was as innocently, and as usefully employed; and I assure you, I give a
> greater portion of my time to my needle, than to my book.
> You are so lovely, madam, that nothing you can do needs an apology. An
> apology, I'll assure you! did not this look, my dear, as if the man thought I ought
> to beg his pardon for understanding Latin? (1:170–71)

This memorable scene may perhaps have been partly drawn from a recol-
lection of the poem by the Countess of Winchilsea so admired by Virginia
Woolf.[9] Sidney is bored with the feminine task, "Nor will in fading Silks
compose,/Faintly th'inimitable Rose." At least, she wishes to find more
than this for the life of her mind. Reading Horace (in the original) provides
escape into the life of the mind, an area considered so masculine that Mr.
Arnold is startled. He wishes Sidney to return to what he insists must be
"the agreeable entertainment" (agreeable for her, a woman, who should not
find Horace agreeable) of completing her embroidery, and he wants to keep
her attention fixed on the rose, the flower of love. Love, not thought,
should concern a woman. In the illustration of this scene by Edward Francesco Burney in figure 1, the artist has nicely caught this idea, and the rose
motif is repeated several times in the picture.[10] Mr. Arnold's surprise and
condescending rebuke give us another insight into the war between the
sexes, the conflict on which the novel is based and which Lady Bidulph
takes so to heart. Even more telling is his ability to inspire an almost guilty
self-defensiveness in Sidney, and his notation of the victory in seizing on
her remarks as "an apology"—an idea which Sidney resents with spirit, but
inwardly. It is immediately after this that Mr. Arnold "proceeded to tell me

Untitled engraving, courtesy of the Bodleian Library.

how much he admired, how much he loved me!" (1:171). Though Sidney
tells him she can offer him no hopes, their colloquy is interrupted before she
has made her position clear. Indeed, Mr. Arnold is being egged on by Lady
Grimston, who persuades Lady Bidulph that the only way to rid her daughter of any danger of an alliance with Faulkland is to marry her off to a
respectable man. Arnold's proposal takes place only two months after
Faulkland's, and Sidney is still suffering from feelings she dare not confess
to her mother; she can scarcely admit to herself how much she still thinks of
Faulkland, for that would be indelicate, and a treachery to her own sex.
Faulkland still appeals to Sidney, through Sir George, to meet "Miss B."
who may exculpate him, but Sidney sees this as unjust and defusive.

> How ungenrous these men are, even the best of them, in love matters! He knows
> the poor girl doats on her destroyer, and might perhaps take shame to *herself*,
> rather than throw as much blame on him as he deserves. I think this is all the
> justice that can be expected from her. . . . It would only add to the merit of *her*
> sufferings, without lessening his fault. (1:177–78)

A sense of sisterhood prevents the heroine from hoping for any éclaircisse-
ment. Her own moral sense interferes with her wishes. Lady Bidulph, anxious to assert her own authority and good sense in the eyes of Lady Grimston, presses the match with Mr. Arnold upon her daughter. Mr. Arnold is
handsome and serious, has a good reputation and good estates; the mother
is sure he is ideally designed to banish Faulkland from her daughter's mind
and heart, and settle her in a satisfactory way of life. Since the Horace
scene, the reader of course knows that this match must be highly unsuit-
able. Sidney herself had thought there could be no doubt of her steadfast
refusal. But she finds herself advised, scolded, harried on all sides, until her
own decision not to accept Mr. Arnold begins to crumble. "Fain would I
bring myself chearfully to conform to my mother's will, for I have no will of
my own. I never knew what it was to have one, and never shall, I believe; for
I am sure I will not contend with a husband. . . . I am treated like a baby,
that knows not what is fit for it to choose or to reject" (1:183). Sidney
convinces herself that a decision founded on obedience can be her own
decision, made in prudence for the ultimate good of herself, Arnold, Faulkland, and the unknown Miss B. At least she will have nothing with which to
reproach herself, whereas if she married Faulkland she might find herself
deserted. "Who knows but he might . . . return to his neglected mistress"
(1:187). There seems to be nothing of that sort to fear from the staid and
stiff Mr. Arnold, whose life appears to promise perpetual lack of surprise.
There can be no skeletons in his closet, no hope that this wedding may be
aborted like the last.

Who knows what may still happen to frustrate our present designs?—No—there
is not another Miss B. to interpose. Mr. Arnold seems to be one of those who are
born to pass quietly through life. He has already attained to the age of thirty,
without one event happening to him, but such as happen to every man every day.
(1:208)

Sidney is married—to the disgust of Sir George, who never left off planning
his sister's union with his friend. Besides, Sir George himself was never
consulted as to this match; he refuses to attend the wedding. Forever after
he treats Sidney's marriage to Arnold as a mistake.

It is after Sidney is safely transformed into Mrs. Arnold that the Bidulphs meet the mysterious Miss B. Lady Bidulph goes to Putney to see the
seduced girl, now nearing her confinement. The young woman confides in
Lady Bidulph, telling her she was "*indeed* seduced" (1:220). She reveals her
real name—she is Miss Burchell. Miss Burchell seems quite charming,
though her indications of joy at hearing of Sidney's marriage irritate Sidney when she hears of the interview. "I cannot help thinking, that there was
something like art in Miss Burchell's behaviour . . . something evasive
and disingenuous in her conduct" (1:222–23). But Lady Bidulph becomes
Miss Burchell's warm champion and defender; she is present at the birth of
the baby, a boy, privately baptized by the name of Orlando. Lady Bidulph
takes the young mother down to Sidney castle, after the boy is put out to
nurse. The invitation arouses all Sir George's contempt for the "wench"
and irritation at his mother's quixotry: "He says his mother ought not to be
surprized at Faulkland's falling into the girl's snares, since she herself has
done the same" (1:243). Sir George does, however, consent to escort his
mother and Miss Burchell to Sidney castle, and remains in his mother's
home for a while. So that breach is apparently healed.

Faulkland returns to England, and is a guest of the Arnold's neighbour
in Kent, Lord V. Sidney is agitated at finding herself "now under an almost
unavoidable necessity of sometimes seeing and conversing with a man, who
once had such convincing proofs that he was not indifferent to me" (1:282).
She now regrets that she never told Mr. Arnold of her former connection
with Faulkland; she fears if she were to tell Arnold now he would "think me
disingenuous for never having mentioned it" (1:284). So much of her mental energy is devoted to keeping her secret, and to observing with anxious
guilt her husband's growing coldness, that she does not notice all the evident signs that Mr. Arnold is having an affair with a dashing new neighbor,
the attractive young widow Mrs. Gerrarde.

Sidney was mistaken in assuming that Mr. Arnold was "born to pass
quietly through life"; after an existence of sober uneventfulness he is at last
having his fling. The acute Mrs. Gerrarde detects Faulkland's interest in

Sidney, and uses it to her own advantage, persuading Arnold that his wife is guilty of adultery. Arnold is evidently glad to cover his own guilt by flying into righteous indignation, though he also suffers from real jealousy. He orders Sidney out of his house; he himself keeps the children (they now have two little daughters). Sidney returns to her mother, who is greatly distressed, and reproaches herself "for her own soliciting this fatal marriage" (1:333).

It is on this miserable visit to her mother that Sidney at last meets the mysterious Miss Burchell. "She is really a very lovely young woman; and there is something so insinuating in her manner, that there is no seeing her without being prejudiced in her favour. She changed colour when my mother presented me to her by my name; but, at the same time, surveyed me with a scrutinous eye" (2:2). Lady Bidulph is as ardent a champion as ever of Miss Burchell's cause. "My mother told her, that as Mr. Faulkland was returned again, probably to continue in England, she did not despair of his being brought to do her justice; especially as she must suppose the sight of the child had made an impression on him" (2:3). To Sidney's embarrassment, Lady Bidulph has no notion of keeping any secret from her protégée; she tells Miss Burchell the whole of Sidney's unhappy story. As Sidney notes regretfully, her mother is "of a very communicative temper" and "made no scruple to inform Miss Burchell of every particular" (2:3). Miss Burchell is affected, not perhaps as ingenuously as the unsuspecting Lady Bidulph believes. Miss Burchell has a real reason to express personal regret, since the designing Mrs. Gerrarde is (as Sidney has already discovered) Miss Burchell's vicious aunt, from whom the seduced girl has long separated herself. "She exclaimed against her barbarity, reproached Mr. Arnold for his injurious suspicions, and condoled obligingly with me on the wrongs I had received; and yet, my Cecilia, would you believe it, I thought I could discover, through all this, that Miss Burchell was not entirely free from doubt in regard to my innocence" (2:4). Miss Burchell always recognizes in Sidney a rival for Faulkland. The young woman might herself contribute to clearing Sidney in her husband's eyes, or at least to removing the threat of Mrs. Gerrarde, by telling her own story to Mr. Arnold, thus revealing Mrs. Gerrarde's vicious habits and tendency to deceit. But Sidney generously admits that to expect Miss Burchell to do so would be unfairly demanding. Nor would Sidney try to purchase happiness by betraying another woman. "I cannot think of exposing the poor Miss Burchell by giving up her secret. Though it might contribute to clear me, by turning Mr. Arnold's suspicions on Mrs. Gerrarde, yet would she have great reason to resent it; more especially, as she is now, by a blameless life, endeavouring to blot out the memory of her fault" (2:9).

Miss Burchell, who has inherited some money, lives in a very respectable, genteel and comfortable manner—not at all, one might note, like the conventional seduced woman of most contemporary fiction, who has nothing to do but die or turn common prostitute. Sidney, with some kindness and some of the rationalization of unconscious wishing, hopes Miss Burchell "may yet retrieve her error by an advantageous match, should Mr. Faulkland still continue averse to to her" (2:6).

But how is the deluded and fascinated Mr. Arnold to be pried away from Mrs. Gerrarde? The removal of Mrs. Gerrarde is accomplished by an unexpected agent. Faulkland elopes with the adventurous widow, expressly in order that Mr. Arnold may be undeceived in her. He entices the eager Mrs. Gerrarde over to the Continent, and there confounds her with his explanation: he does not intend to make love to her, but he will settle money on her if she marries his valet and consents to live in France. As Orlando notes to Sir George, "it has cost me more to make one woman honest, than it need have done to have made half a dozen—otherwise" (2:177).

Freed of the fascination exercised by Mrs. Gerrarde, the now undeluded Arnold is anxious for reconciliation with his wife. They are reconciled, and have a brief interval of happiness before Mr. Arnold dies in a hunting accident. It is then revealed that his financial affairs have been sadly involved, and Sidney is left almost penniless. Sir George has married a wealthy and miserly woman, and is no longer likely to aid his sister very substantially, but he thinks his sister's problems will be solved by a marriage to Faulkland, which he again urges. Faulkland proposes, and the widowed Sidney rejects him; acceptance "would, indeed, be acknowledging that the humiliating change had levelled me to those principles which I formerly condemned; would lay me under mortifying obligations to Mr. Faulkland, and destroy the merit of that refusal which proceeded from such justifiable motives" (2:327). Like Gwendolen Harleth in *Daniel Deronda*, Sidney is faced a second time with a moral choice once decided on principle. Unlike Gwendolen, Sidney does not weaken on the second occasion and accept the second proposal; she remains loyal to her principles, and to the obligation to another woman. By now, Sidney is firmly committed to her mother's party, to the hopes that Miss Burchell will eventually marry Faulkland. She has given Miss Burchell her promise that she will assist her and not stand in her way.

Miss Burchell interests Sidney as an example of a female heart involved in the deepest and most extravagant love for one man; yet she is a puzzle too.

> She acknowledges that Mr. Faulkland's being disappointed in espousing me, gave the first encouragement to her hopes; for, she said, she had reason to believe

that I was the only woman in the world that stood between her and her happiness. . . . Then the generous attention that he paid to her welfare . . . my mother's constantly indulging her in the belief that she would one day recover Mr. Faulkland's affections: all these circumstances, I say, joined together, have kept alive the warmest and most romantic love I ever saw or heard of. . . . There is something to me unaccountable in this; but Miss Burchell is all made up of languishments and softness. I have heard her speak of Mr. Faulkland in so rapturous a strain as has amazed me; and she once owned to me, that she is sure she must have died, if he had not returned her love. Return it! Ah, my Cecilia, how did he return it? How mortifying is her situation! to be compelled to court the man who flies her, and to make use of a rival's mediation too! but let me forget that name; I am no longer so to her, and shall do my best to prove it. (2:330–32)

Yet the more Sidney learns of Miss Burchell's original history, the more murky it appears; it seems that she did not tell Sidney's mother the whole truth. Miss Burchell resists any pressure by her gentle languishings and tears: "She is made up of tears, and sighs, and romantic wishes" (2:352). Sidney appeals to Faulkland for her, and endeavors to promote the other woman's happiness, while feeling "Yet Faulkland deserves—oh, he deserves a worthier lot! (2:357).

Faulkland does at last consent to marry Miss Burchell, to the delight of Lady Bidulph. Faulkland is at last going to make himself perfectly virtuous; a forsaken woman will be restored, an old wrong made right. Sidney and her mother have really pushed Faulkland into marrying Miss Burchell, to the outrage of Sir George; "You will hardly be able to answer it to yourself, if you find that you have condemned one of the noblest fellows in the world to the arms of a prostitute" (2:40). Sidney feels that Faulkland has shown himself truly noble, in his sacrifice to "reason and humanity" as well as in his disinterested love and generous behavior. He has raised himself far above her: "He has left me, my dear, to gaze after him with grateful admiration!" (3:55). The man who once seemed a rake, meriting only the scorn of good women, has become a martyr to both love and reason, a model, like Sir Charles Grandison, of all that is admirable. In forcing him up to these Grandisonian heights, Sidney has depressed herself.

Consciousness of doing right does not make Sidney truly happy inwardly, a fact noted in defiance of much of the dominant eighteenth-century morality, which insisted on the satisfactions of virtue. In an unguarded moment of confidence, after enduring the wedding of Miss Burchell and Orlando, Sidney confesses as much to Cecilia: "I see . . . that you think my heart has *again* done itself some violence. . . . I own to you honestly I now feel my own unhappiness to its full extent" (3:52). Rea-

son and conscience are powerless to create happiness, or even content and
self-approval.

> I acted agreeably to the dictates both of my reason, and my conscience, in per-
> suading Mr. Faulkland to make Miss Burchell his wife. . . . Yet how deceitful
> is the human heart! this very act which I laboured with so much assiduity to
> accomplish, and on the accomplishment of which, I had founded, I know not
> how, a sort of contentment for myself, has been the very means of destroying
> what little peace of mind I was beginning to taste before. (3:54–55)

Her mother's approval is the only renewed source of consolation. But
soon after having accomplished her object, Lady Bidulph dies, and Sidney
is left without her mother's emotional support. Furthermore, Sidney, in going through her mother's papers, comes upon the old letter, never before
seen by her, the one written by Faulkland from Bath describing to Sir
George the course of the affair with Miss Burchell. This was the letter Lady
Bidulph only glanced at, her mind already made up. Sidney (and we) at last
see and read it. It would appear from this evidence that Faulkland was indeed inveigled into an affair by a young woman without scruples or inhibitions, and Sidney undergoes a revulsion of feeling. "*Had* I seen it but in
time—Oh what anguish of heart might we all have been spared! Miss Burchell singly as she *ought*, would have borne the punishment of her folly"
(3:67).

But it is too late now. Lady Bidulph's ideas had disdained the vagaries of
the individual case, or the niceties of evidence. Indeed, most of the main
characters in *Sidney Bidulph* are fallible when it comes to the use or misuse
of evidence—there is always too much, and at the same time not enough.
Lady Bidulph went by principles, and her principles allowed but one belief
in the case of "seduction": the woman is innocent, the *man* is to blame.
Sidney's own delicacy, generosity, prudence, and principle have contributed to her own—and Faulkland's—undoing. The well-meaning and refined moral sense of both mother and daughter have led to two disastrous
marriages. The marriage of Sidney to Mr. Arnold was a mistake, fostered
by a maternal cabal and by false notions of safety and respectability. That
Arnold and Sidney were incompatible was evident from the outset. Nor
was Arnold's appearance of sober carefulness and dignified respectability
to be trusted—though Arnold was no hypocrite. The man himself did not
know he was going to break out into extravagance and adultery. Sidney
could hardly have fared worse if she had married the most notorious rake
and wastrel. The widowed Mrs. Arnold, whose husband left his affairs so
entangled that she received nearly nothing, struggles along through illness

and poverty, until she is rescued by her wealthy relative, Mr. Warner, who appears suddenly from the West Indies and in effect adopts her. That Sidney can now fortunately live in relative affluence is, however, not thanks to prudence or safe arrangements, still less to Mr. Arnold. And material well-being, though a relief, never compensates for the loss of love.

The marriage of Faulkland and Miss Burchell seems a somber parallel to the mistaken marriage of Arnold and Sidney. It bears the seeds of its own destruction. Sidney has less and less reason to think complacently of it, or of her part in it as a good deed, particularly after Sir George confides to Sidney that he and Miss Burchell had an affair. That is how he came to know she was a "female libertine." Miss Burchell made advances to him at the time of his visit to Sidney castle, after Miss Burchell had borne Faulkland's child. Miss Burchell made Sir George promise never to tell Faulkland of this liaison; she assured Faulkland's friend that she had no wish or hope to be Faulkland's wife, but that she feared he might stop financial support for her and her baby son. Sidney now realizes the point of Miss Burchell's anxiety that Sir George should not be let into the secret of the marriage plan. Sir George Bidulph, on whom the affair has left a bitter impression, asserts that Miss Burchell is deceitful, and drifts from man to man; she is capable of deluding each victim: "Had I been as credulous as Faulkland, I should have thought myself the idol of her soul, so lavish was she in her expressions of tenderness." That she didn't have Faulkland long enough to weary of him perhaps preserved her attention. Sidney accuses herself privately: "What a fatal wretch have I been to Mr. Faulkland!" (3:168, 177). She is reduced to reliance on mere hope that Miss Burchell's oft-expressed love for Faulkland will keep her faithful, and make the marriage happy despite the past.

But the marriage between Miss Burchell and Faulkland is a first-rate disaster. Suddenly, Faulkland arrives at Sidney's house in a state of distraction, saying "My wife is dead—and by my hand—" (3:242). It appears that after slightly over a year of happy marriage in Ireland, Mrs. Faulkland engaged, without her husband's suspicion, in what may have been a fairly lengthy affair with one Major Smyth, the fiancé of her best friend among the neighbors. The affair was carried on in all the elaborate artifice of country house visits and sleeping arrangements. The unsuspecting Mr. Faulkland came upon his wife and Major Smyth in bed together; the major seized one of a pair of his pistols on the table, and Faulkland grabbed the other weapon. Smyth shot and missed fire; Mrs. Faulkland was rushing between the two men, just as Faulkland returned the shot. She shrieked and fell to the floor. The major also fell, crying out, "He has killed us both" (3:263). Faulkland rushed away from his friends' house and was followed by a servant, who told him that his lady was killed, and Smyth mortally wounded—though not too ill to make up a story covering the woman and laying the entire blame on Faulkland.

Faulkland's life is in danger from the law; he managed to make his way from Ireland to England, but of course he is no safer there. Sir George urges him to go at once to Holland, but the frenzied Faulkland, clearly in a suicidal frame of mind, refuses to go unless Sidney will marry him. He demands this as a kind of mad right: "What recompense then can you make the man, whom you have brought to misery, shame and death?" (3:243). Sidney is reluctant, as she sees the dangers that attend Faulkland's case if he increases suspicious circumstances by marrying another woman just after he has killed his wife. She lets herself be persuaded, since there seems no other way to save a man who insists his life now depends on her. She loves him more than ever, but at the same time feels afraid, and ironically the wedding she once so much desired is now tempered by the horrors of the situation and fears for Faulkland's sanity. After a private wedding, Faulkland goes off immediately to Holland, to await there the arrival of Sidney and his little boy. But after a week or so, delayed news from Ireland arrives. The wretched Mrs. Faulkland is not *dead*, nor is she even wounded. The major died and the erring wife, hearing of her lover's death, was shaken enough to confess the truth. Faulkland's life is now in no real danger from the law, as he would certainly be acquitted by a court. But of course the marriage between him and Sidney (presumably unconsummated) is a total mockery, as the real (if false) Mrs. Faulkland is still in existence. The wedding is and always has been completely void. Faulkland, hearing of this news in Holland, assumes a calm resignation, such as Sidney had urged in her farewell letter, in which she also explained that she would never meet him again. He is soon found dead in his bed, apparently by suicide though there is no suspicious sympton or any mark on his person, and Sir George is careful not to press inquiries. Faulkland's young son, Master Orlando Faulkland, inherits his personal fortune, but his relatives prove the boy's illegitimacy, and eagerly and legally take over the estate. The former Miss Burchell returns to England and lives in obscurity for several years before her own unlamented demise.

Nothing has stayed constant—as this donouement, with its melodramatic whirlwind of ironies, intends to prove. The girl who seemed so obsessively in love threw away that love once she had it. The man who at one point seemed Grandisonian in perfection becomes an innocent murderer, a crazed sufferer, a miserable suicide. Virtue is not rewarded, even by personal development. Moral decisions based on high principles of honor and the nicest scruples turn out wrong. All judgments err. Impressions are unstable; judgments of prudence are, after all, founded on assumptions and impressions, and these may betray.

Through Cecilia and her editor, Frances Sheridan assures us several times of her moral; Sidney's constant afflictions "may serve to show that it is not *here* that true virtue is to look for its reward" (3:338). But we may ask if that is *the* moral, the only or even the central theme illustrated by the extraordinary story.

What is Frances Sheridan doing? She seems perhaps to be betraying the cause of women, and even of morality—those causes that Richardson said were the same. In some ways the novel seems to be an answer back to *Sir Charles Grandison*; we have here a quasi-rake vindicated as a Grandisonian man, and that Grandisonian figure in turn reduced to chaos and self-destruction. Women assert, as Richardson advised, their detestation of rakes, and lo! that detestation is, in the particular instance, misplaced. The cause of women against rakes and rakishness, against the prevailing male ethos to which women are by custom expected to accede, is valiantly supported by Lady Bidulph and her daughter, but their crusade against the double standard comes to grief. Their new and singular feminine code ceases to be for Sidney (if indeed it ever was for her) simply and self-evidently valid. Sisterhood, and the responsibility of women to and for each other against a doctrine of male exploitation of women, seem right. Yet sisterhood comes on the rocks in the association with Miss Burchell, whose own piratical code has nothing of the generosity of sisterhood, though she is quick to notice her advantage in dealing with the magnanimous Bidulphs. Miss Burchell, one of the best drawn and most interesting characters in the novel—though we see her only from a distance—is a wonderfully mixed character, capable of being variously interpreted. She is herself an exploiter; she uses others ruthlessly and has no allegiance to inconvenient truth. Yet her "love" for Faulkland seems in some sense real, if only kind of monomania with a romantic tinge—though the selfish romanticism, like the "tears and languishments," is both genuine and theatrical. She had a claim on Faulkland and used it to advantage, in effect turning the tables by getting him "into trouble," though he would have had no trouble in shunting her off if it weren't for the Bidulph women. Miss Burchell was able to manipulate a (false) position as Woman wronged, acting for the eyes of the Bidulph women the role of Woman as Eternal Victim. Confronted by a woman who is extremely feminine but not womanly, the Bidulph ladies do not know what to make of her. They proceed by assumption, and, in Lady Bidulph's case, by enthusiasm *partly* arising from self-vindication. Miss Burchell made herself into a kind of cliché that the women (particularly Lady Bidulph) can accept because it is so recognizable.

Yet, as the novel of course shows, there is no satisfactory alternative to the Bidulph women's romantic code, to their "feminism," in the world as it is. Sir George, bluff, bossy and insensitive, is right, but only accidentally. He adheres to his own accepted masculine code, propped up by society in general, and his judgment is always crude. His views allow no room for women, and little for morality; that his attitudes don't make for happiness or virtue is illustrated in his own life. He can only reveal the truth about Miss Burchell (too late) because he slept with her, and then was disgusted and disturbed to find he had been used by "a sly rake in petticoats" (3:169). (We may choose not to trust entirely his account of that affair; he says that he wearied of Miss Burchell, but we are, I think free to wonder if she didn't tire of him first.) Society of course exacts no penalty of Sir George for his concupiscence, and he is free to marry the "virtuous," stupid, and miserly Lady Sarah; he can bear being tied for life to an ignorant shrew only because he has in general such a low opinion of women. Mr. Arnold, who so disapproved of Sidney's reading Horace, illustrates all the limitations of the male world that allows women neither freedom nor intelligence. His low opinion of women does not prevent his being made a fool of by a woman who can size him up and flatter him, drawing out the silly and empty fellow who lurked behind the rigid exterior.

The masculine views of women and sex do not make for sexual or emotional happiness for either men or women. The novel satirizes the crudity of masculine views, and of the world's views of family life, sexuality, and society's claims. It makes us feel that it *is* time someone took a feminist stand against the restrictions and debasements, time that someone worked through these limitations. That is what the Bidulph women try to do. But their new "feminist" view is also shown as limited by human fallibility. It is something to have characters—in the world and in a novel—who are capable of living according to a moral idea, of making a moral problem the center of life. Then, Frances Sheridan wants us to acknowledge, it must also be seen that this higher feminine understanding, these moral views, have their own limitations which in turn must be transcended in a larger comprehension. Above all, it must be seen that all moral life is intensely fragile, that even the highest decisions are founded partly on guesswork and prejudice, and that "worthy" acts have another side. Sidney's high-principled endeavor to assist Miss Burchell to marriage with Faulkland arises from a mixture of motives, and has its reverse side. (To some readers it has seemed as crazily obsessed and absurd as Miss Burchell's incessant hoping.) Principles themselves are founded on shaky judgments and beliefs, and, if we had known the effect in advance, our "prudent" actions would have been prudently different. It can, one observes, even be argued that Sidney, not Miss Burchell, is the final cause of Faulkland's death; the novel is constructed so that we can ask that question too (it would have been easy enough to engineer the ending so that Faulkland died in a duel). We never know quite how to place our shots—as illustrated in the night scene with the pistols. Sidney's letter to Faulkland, prudent, heartfelt, high-principled, struck the final blow.

The women's world is a real world, with both good and evil in it. Like Grimston Hall, it is not a sanctuary, and must not be made into an illusory perfection. In some respects—to the puzzlement of readers then and now—Frances Sheridan has, in what looks like a feminist novel, taken us beyond feminism, opening out the complexities that arise in human life whenever human beings try to do right. To wish to be right is a noble wish, but it may be as unreasonable as more worldly wishes.

Yet the debate over the cause of women, over sexual morality, or even over the real nature of morality is only part of the novel's subject. What seems to interest Frances Sheridan above all is the effect of the past on the present. Her whole novel, in both parts, is constructed (if that is the right word) around the idea that no act exists singly, in itself. The past never ceases, a past action is never cleared out of the way; the past never stops having an effect on the present. In a novel that pays so much attention to the idea of principle as abstract moral axiom guiding action, it is interesting to note the counteracting attention to the sources or origins of action—but one meaning of "principle" is fundamental basis or ultimate cause. In the novel the two meanings of "principle" intersect, creating tensions or ironies. The whole of *Miss Sidney Bidulph* circles about and repeatedly returns to the original experience of Lady Bidulph on her abortive wedding day. Lady Bidulph as a young woman did not make the primary decision (it was made for her, done to her); her decision is a reaction internalizing a meaning in what was done to her. She turned rejection into active sacrifice, elaborating a moral motif suggested by her wretched bridegroom into a governing law. The Bidulph women in general, and Sidney most especially, rarely initiate important action; their strength is that of reaction. Refusing to take initiative, they also refuse to be mere passive objects of the percussion of experience. They have a talent for transmuting experience into law. It may be that Sheridan saw this as at once the strength and the weakness of the female in her time, cut off from the power of original action and the force of positive law in the external social world. Emotionally reacting, woman turns into private lawmaker and lawgiver; her laws are transmissible, but only in company with emotional responses.

The original action or reaction of Lady Bidulph is a predetermining event. Her decision sets up in herself and later in her family currents of thought, patterns of action, that affect the lives of a number of people in the next two generations. Lady Bidulph, having accomplished her heroic and disastrous mission, dies, but the effects of all her acts, including primarily her original response to her original problem, remain. People die, but the past does not die.

It is doubtless this interest in the influence of the past that led Frances Sheridan to continue her novel in a second part, which appeared in 1767 (the year of her death). This second novel traces the effect of previous acts and responses on a third generation. The central characters here are Sidney's daughters, Dolly and Cecilia, and Faulkland's son, the next Orlando Falkland (for some reason the name "Faulkland" is throughout the second part spelled without the "u"). As far as I know, *Miss Sidney Bidulph* is the only English novel before Elizabeth Inchbald's *A Simple Story* (1791) to deal with the interlocking life of two generations, with parents the heroes of the first half of the story and those parents' children the central characters in the second. *Miss Sidney Bidulph*, like *A Simple Story*, may well have been an influence on *Wuthering Heights*. I believe also that the second part of Sidney Bidulph was an influence on Jane Austen's *Mansfield Park*.

When part 2 begins, Sidney is living in the country with her two daughters, Dolly and Cecilia, both of whom have been bequeathed handsome legacies by the rich and now defunct Mr. Warner, expressly so that they, unlike their mother, may be able to marry whom they choose. Young Orlando is still, as he was at the end of part 1, domiciled with Sidney as part of her family. In part 1 he was young Master Falkland, an innocent and babbling infant; now he and the Arnold girls are all in their late teens. Sidney has, in effect, though not legally, adopted Orlando, making the girls call him "brother."

> This idea I inculcated early amongst them; for having taken the dear unhappy orphan into my protection . . . I thought that precaution would sufficiently guard the young people from ever entertaining a thought, much less a wish, that any other tie should ever take place; and indeed it has succeeded to my expectations; fraternal affection there is between them . . . but nothing like a particular preference. To say the truth, I believe it seldom happens that persons brought up together from childhood, conceive a passion for each other. (4:20).

Like the prudence of Sir Thomas Bertram and Mrs. Norris (who might almost have been quoting Sidney),[11] Sidney's complacency is mistaken. The fraternal plan does not answer; through the course of the story both of the daughters fall in love with Orlando, who seems to inherit the fatal charm of both his parents. Indeed, there is a suggestion that Sidney feels unacknowledged psychological perturbation at the idea of this second Orlando being taken from her by a rival in the form of a daughter, as the (apparently) ingenuous Miss Burchell took the first Orlando from her. The rational grounds for disapproving any connection between either Arnold daughter and young Falkland are Orlando's illegitimate birth, and his penury. Moreover, Sir George (who is the same as ever) loudly declares that he dislikes the young man. "I own I could never have a very cordial regard for that youth, on his vile mother's account; it is an unwarrantable prejudice I grant; but as my mother used to say of hers, (which by the way she would never allow to *be* prejudices) it is *unconquerable*" (4:27).

The tranquil life Sidney has chosen for herself and her children is deliberately stirred up, and latent sexual tensions activated, by two other young people who come into the neighborhood. Sir Edward Audley and his sister Sophy are charming and worldly false friends. (These are the only really new characters of importance in the story—the others are people we have heard of in part 1.) Sir Edward, who is hard up, is determined to marry one of the Arnold girls for her inheritance, and he uses his sister as his willing agent in his plans to attract one of them. The Audley brother and sister are two charmers, gay, worldly plotters who despise the dull life, sober views, and moral scruples of the Arnold ménage, even though they feel some genuine liking for the girls and for Orlando. The pair have a strong resemblance to Mary and Henry Crawford in *Mansfield Park* (though Sheridan's characters are more villainous); a reading of the continuation of *Miss Sidney Bidulph* should disabuse us of the notion that the Crawfords represent modern Regency types in contrast to the dying breed of old-fashioned country gentry nostalgically enclosed in Mansfield—such contrasts were the stuff of eighteenth-century fiction.

Sophy and Sir Edward combine in an elaborate plot to encourage a clandestine love affair between Orlando and one of the Arnold girls, believing that when one of the girls has trespassed against filial obedience and when Orlando has been disposed of as a rival, the other sister will be the more willing to defy authority and engage herself to Sir Edward without the consent of her relatives. Orlando seems to be easy material to work on, given such a shrewd analyst of character as Sir Edward, who comments on his presumed friend:

He has no strong lines in his soul, and if I may use the expression, all the features of it are faint. I do not think him capable of a manly or steady friendship towards one of his own sex, or of a violent or constant attachment towards one of yours. . . . He has an infinite deal of vanity; but he has still more art in concealing it, and I believe that I am the first who ever discovered that he had either, with all this he has very good sense, and an address insinuating beyond any thing I ever met with. His faults seem all complexional, so are his virtues too . . . and it appears a moot point whether nature intended him for an angel or a devil. (4:100–101)

Wavering Orlando is brought to confess love (which he doesn't really feel) to Dolly, once the Audleys have discovered that Dolly is already se-cretly in love with Orlando and thus that Edward has no chance with her. Dolly and Orlando enter into an engagement, but then Orlando transfers his affections to Cecilia, without letting the other sister know. Sir Edward finally attempts to win Dolly in a Lovelacean abduction which has the appearance of a willful elopement. Dolly escapes, returning home in time to prevent the private wedding of her sister and Orlando, a match to which Sidney has finally given reluctant consent.

Dolly, mentally distracted, enters the room just after Mr. Price the clergy-man has made the solemn exhortation "*I require and charge you both . . . that if either of you know of any impediment*," and so forth—at which Orlando trembles and turns pale. When Mr. Price "was . . . making that solemn demand of *Wilt thou have this woman to be thy wedded wife*? She gave a piercing shriek, and flying to Falkland, seized his hand, This hand is *mine*, said she: Oh, Falkland, you cannot till my eyes are closed give it to another!—Falkland dropped senseless at her feet" (5:248, 259). This scene of an interrupted wedding prefigures that in Burney's *Cecilia* (1782) and in Radcliffe's *The Italian* (1797), not to mention that in *Jane Eyre*. In the novel's own context it is a repetition with variation of the original nonwed-ding of Lady Bidulph, and of the null and void wedding ceremony of Faulk-land and Sidney (even the clergyman here is the same as in that empty wedding). The ceremony is again nullified by the existence of a counter-claimant for the position of wife.

Faced with her lover's perfidy to her sister, Cecilia nobly refuses Falk-land, and Orlando has nothing left to do but to fight (and kill) Sir Edward in a duel. These trials and excitements are literally the death of Sidney, who, exhausted by emotion, makes a pious exit, dying at age thirty-eight. (She thus leaves her daughters, one might note, as her mother left her, to grapple on their own with the aftermath of crisis). Dolly slowly recovers her intellects, and she admits there was a selfishness in her endeavor to keep Orlando to his promise (they were, after all, engaged only, not married). Like all the characters' most dramatic acts, Dolly's interruption of Orlan-do's wedding (pathetic victim though the girl may be) is ambiguous and questionable.

What is most noticeable about the second part of *Miss Sidney Bidulph* is not its pathos, or its plots, or the witty machinations of the Audleys. Its most signal quality is the reiterated presence of the past. There are constant allusions to the history and deeds of the preceding two generations. Sir George refers several times to what he considers his mother's folly, and remembers the Arnold marriage with great scorn—a scorn which he ironically transfers to the idea of Cecilia Arnold's marriage with Faulkland's son: "That young fellow inherits all the art of his d—n'd mother," "is the curse of worthless husbands to be entailed on the family!" (5:20, 24–25). Sir George, who even yet regrets what he considers Sidney's excessive obedience to her mother, inconsistently exhorts Sidney to exert her authority over Cecilia, to demand obedience and make the girl marry his favored candidate, Lord V—. All the central characters, including young Lord V— (whose father appeared in part 1) are aware of the old story. Sir George (in a private *volte-face*) bids Sidney and Lord V: "Recollect that you, Madam [Sidney], who had not only married without inclination, but, as he believed, with strong prepossessions in favour of another, had made a most exemplary wife even in the most trying circumstances" (5:9–10). He attempts to argue in the same fashion to young Cecilia, but the girl has got Lord V—on her side, against his own interests, and she is well provided with illustrative argument from *her* knowledge of the past, and her interpretation of it.

> For Heaven's sake, my dear Sir George, said my Lord V—, consider a little of the merit of your niece's conduct . . . where will you find a young creature tenderly attached as she acknowledges herself to be, who would forego such a privilege, and sacrifice her own happiness to gratify a mere punctilio?—Her mother did so, interrupted my uncle—And how often, Sir, (as I have heard my mama say) did you reproach her for that? answered I; and what pains did you not take to persuade her to stick to her first engagements? The cases are very different, said my uncle; Mr. Falkland was a match of which the first woman in the kingdom might have been proud to accept. . . .—Oh, Sir, cried Mr. Falkland, I know how much he was superior to me in every thing; yet there was a time when you saw him stripped of his fortune, his character stained by a dreadful event, robbed almost of his reason, and obliged to abandon his family and his country; yet even then, under those circumstances of complicated misery, you thought him worthy of your sister . . . how can you then, Sir, reject the unhappy son of him whom you once preferred to all mankind? (5:58–59)

In an endeavor not to repeat what they consider the mistakes of the past generation, lively Cecilia and weak Orlando bring about new misery. Yet the new misery is parallel to the old. The old decisions and the old actions and reactions are the final causes of renewed unhappiness, to which the

Audleys merely contribute as ignorant external agents. Cecilia unwittingly commits the "sin" which her grandmother and her mother had struggled so strenuously to avoid. She takes another woman's man—in this case, a man "belonging" to a literal sister. The shy and intensely emotional Dolly was not physically but emotionally seduced, and betrayed by her belief in a promise of marriage. She is a victim—or she casts herself in that role. But this victim who prevents the marriage of lovers is also unwittingly cast in the role of Miss Burchell, the interrupter of joy. The past refuses to die.

The undying past is transmitted partly through heredity. Young Orlando visibly inherits the qualities of both parents, in a confused mixture that makes for the lack of "strong lines in his soul." He has his father's impatience and susceptibility, and his mother's softness, tears and languishments, "insinuating address," and dishonesty. The Arnold girls, too, take after both parents, inheriting in uneven mixtures both Sidney's romantic principles and sensibility, and Mr. Arnold's dogged self-will. They may be new actors on the scene, and they think that they improvise, but they also inherit old roles with temperaments that prove inescapable.

The past is also transmitted in the conditions it creates. Out of the past came both the estrangement of Sidney and Faulkland, and their lasting attachment. Out of the past came thus the Bidulphs' and Arnolds' involvement with the young Orlando. The past sets up psychological patterns; Sidney's reluctance to see any sexual attachment between her girls and Orlando has psychological rather than objective material causes; young Orlando is at once her lover returned, and the child that she never had by Orlando (which would make marriage to her daughters appear to her unconscious mind as a form of incest). Most important, out of the past came the self-consciousness of the characters about right and wrong, fear of old failure, and caution about self-denying decisions that lead to misery, as well as a continuing penchant for self-denial. The past repeats itself with every attempt to escape it.

The investigation of past and present was Sheridan's contribution to the novel as a genre. She took much from Richardson, who is good on families, but even Richardson never presented this tight patterning of generational interrelation. For Sheridan, past and present lapse into one another, conflate. Memory takes precedence of experience. It is as if consciousness lapses into intervals of dreamlike, if vivid, activity, only to awaken and return to some inevitable and more solid (if terrible) recurrence of the past, which is reality. It is no wonder that a critic of part 1 of *Miss Sidney Bidulph* worried lest "the too popular doctrine of predestination seems here to be encouraged."[12] There is some kind of predestination at work, though it seems less Providential than psychological, and less psychological than visionary. Actions are related to powerful "spots of time" which are conditioning but not redemptive.

The elements that I have extrapolated from *Miss Sidney Bidulph* appear in full force in Mrs. Sheridan's Oriental tale, *The History of Nourjahad*. Published anonymously in 1767, this tale was written at the same time as the continuation of *Miss Sidney Bidulph*. According to Sheridan's granddaughter, the idea of the tale came to its author after a sleepless night spent "reflecting upon the inequality in the conditions of men" and the dependence of happiness or misery upon "the due regulation of the passions, rather than on the outward dispensations of Providence." The idea for her story then occurred to her.

> Mrs. Sheridan represented it as entering her mind like a kind of vision or dream, between sleep and waking; and though this account is very extraordinary, persons of a fertile and poetical imagination themselves, will see nothing impossible in it. She communicated the sketch of the story the next morning to her eldest daughter. . . .[13]

At the outset of the story, Nourjahad, the friend and contemporary of the young Sultan of Persia, Schemzeddin, seems destined for great office in the state, but the sultan, to test him, asks him what he would like if any of his wishes could be granted. Nourjahad honestly answers, with his boundless wishes: "I should desire to be possessed of inexhaustible riches, and to enable me to enjoy them to the utmost, to have my life prolonged to eternity."[14] Seeing the sultan's displeasure with his fantasy, Nourjahad hastily makes a more prudent statement, but to himself, when again alone, he admits that his first wishes were his real desires. In the dead of night an apparition comes like a dream to his bedchamber; a gloriously handsome angelic youth tells Nourjahad he is his guardian genius, and that his wishes can be granted. He confers upon him a boundless treasure, and offers him also a vial whose contents confer eternal existence. But the genius warns Nourjahad that if he behaves iniquitously and abuses his gifts, he will be punished by "the temporary death of sleep" (p. 22)—a sleep that may last for months, years, or centuries. Nourjahad rejoices next morning to find his dream is true, transfers his treasure of gold and gems to a secret cave, and begins a course of extravagance.

The young man is somewhat disconcerted to find that the sultan, in displeasure with him and his suspicious access of wealth, soon has him put under house arrest, but with so many pleasures at his disposal within his own palatial mansion and grounds, Nourjahad endures the privation of liberty, flattering himself that he will soon—given his immortality—outlive the sultan. He acquires a seraglio of exotic beauties, and falls in love with one of his women, the lovely Mandana. He neglects the poets and sages he had first hired, and gives himself entirely to physical pleasure. At the end of one banquet, in defiance of Mohammedan law, he drinks wine and gets drunk. He awakens to find he has slept for four years and twenty days; his beloved Mandana is dead, having died well over three years ago in giving birth to his little son.

Regret makes Nourjahad keener than ever to give a loose to appetite. With the sultan's permission he acquires a summer palace, and enhances his seraglio with new purchases. Flown with delight and pride, he appoints a festival day in which his establishment will be called Paradise. His seraglio, led by his new favorite, Cadiga, will personate the houris, while he enacts the part of Mohammed. Taking a short nap before the festivities begin, he wakens to find that he has slept for forty years and eleven months. The withered hags who greet his awakening with joy are the ladies of his seraglio. Cadiga, who was entrusted with Nourjahad's secret by his faithful slave Hasem and has thus kept the palace in order until his restoration, tries to expostulate with him on his immoral life. But self-indulgence, loneliness, and disorientation have made Nourjahad cruel: "Go tell thy prophet so!" he cries and stabs Cadiga (p. 136).

Next morning he awakens to find that he has slept twenty years. Cadiga's brother, Cozro, to whom she entrusted the secret before she expired of the dagger thrust, had faithfully looked after Nourjahad's interests. Cozro kept his promise to Cadiga, refraining, as she made him swear, from revenge. Impressed by the moral strength of Cozro, and by the knowledge of his own wickedness, Nourjahad reforms. He will spend his money on aiding the poor. His reward for this charity is to be arrested by the officers of the new sultan, Schemzeddin's late-born Schemerzad. In his charitable pursuits Nourjahad has broken the laws of mourning for the old sultan, the late Schemzeddin, and is suspected of a treasonable attempt to gain popularity and raise a revolt among the people. Believing that Cozro, his agent in giving alms and now more friend than slave, has been executed, Nourjahad in prison prays to Mohammed that the fatal gifts be taken back; his guardian genius appears and assures him that this is done.

Now mortal once again, Nourjahad confronts the enraged young sultan and expresses his willingness to die. But the old sultan's son turns out to be none other than Schemzeddin himself; old Hasem appears as the vizier, and Mandana, still living—and young and beautiful—is recognizable as the guardian genius also, though she now appears to be in her true role as a member of Schemzeddin's harem. The sultan had arranged all in order to reform his friend. Nourjahad has lived in illusion, and the actions which he had supposed took place over a period of more than sixty years have all happened within fourteen months. He did not kill Cadiga. The young beauties of his seraglio and the withered hags were different persons. Mandana's son (who later went to the bad) was imaginary. Most of the treasure was fake.

The story of Nourjahad teaches "the folly of unreasonable wishes" (the subtitle of the tale in a children's version),[15] as well as the unreason of letting appetite triumph over humanity. Like so much Augustan literature, this tale preaches the need of acknowledging limitations and mortality in order to be fully human. Nourjahad's fantasies resemble Gulliver's ecstatic imaginings when he first hears of the immortal Struldbruggs in book 3 of *Gulliver's Travels*—that work by another Irish writer, a friend of Frances Sheridan's father-in-law. Nourjahad also bears a marked relationship to *Rasselas*, without resembling Johnson's story—there are, for instance, erotic elements completely absent in Johnson's work.

If *Nourjahad* is an Augustan piece, it is also a Romantic one; its influence can be felt in the exoticism of *Vathek* (1784), and in the fantastic elements in stories by William Godwin and Mary Shelley, authors who are also interested in the movement of time and in the psychological effects of peculiar immortalities.

What is really significantly new about Frances Sheridan's tale is its playing with time. Nourjahad experiences two time spans at once—but he is aware only of the longer one. His illusory protracted experience seems in duration and complexity more like real human life than does his saner existence, the shorter "real time" operated in by Schemzeddin. Nourjahad is for instance, made to experience, comically, the vicissitudes of fashion; when he tries to create yet another seraglio, after his forty-year sleep, he can find no girls to his taste—where, oh where, are the beauties of yesteryear? Cadiga the old informs him that "the taste for beauty is quite altered since that time: You may assure yourself that none will be offered to your acceptance that will exceed these. Were I and my companions, whom you once so much admired, to be restored to our youth again, we should not now be looked upon: such is the fantastic turn of the age" (p. 124).

Perhaps only a woman could have thought of this, but it should be pointed out that *Nourjahad* is consistent in maintaining a masculine point of view, just as it is consistent—and respectful—in its use of Mohammedanism. The main characters are male (women have only a subordinate walk-on part to play in the narrative) and masculine views, ambitions, and sexuality are sympathetically treated. This marks a change from *Miss Sidney Bidulph*, in which female experience and views are paramount, though in both novels the male characters are led to discover the power and importance of heterosexual love which mingles friendship and affection with erotic desire . . . the eighteenth-century ideal. Both novels, however, show a sympathy with men of strong sex drives who are tempted into excess. Nourjahad, given the license of the Persian seraglio, can discover his true love, Mandana, without suffering as Faulkland does for other adventures. And of course, Mandana, given the license of her position as member of a seraglio, does not worry about seduction nor in the conclusion stick at any scruples or "punctilio" regarding Nourjahad's connections with Cadiga & Co. It is noticeable that the excessively indulgent hero of the moral tale wins his true love, for all his debauchery, while the more virtuous hero of the romantic novel remains eternally denied consummation with his beloved, who is likewise his Nemesis as well as guardian genius.

What goes wrong in *Miss Sidney Bidulph* would seem at first glance to go even more wrong in *Nourjahad*, but in the latter work the road of excess leads not only to the palace of wisdom, but also to happiness and fulfillment. Nourjahad's unreasonable wishes only *appear* to wreak havoc for a time; morally, they are easily identifiable and corrigible. *Miss Sidney Bidulph* too is a story of unreasonable wishes, but the most unreasonable wishes are precisely the moral ideals. Lady Bidulph's—and Sidney's—wishes to do right, to behave with heroic justice to other women and, like the sultan, to mete out just returns to lascivious men, are destined for unsuccess. Only life's experience over time can prove to the would-be doer of right the disparity between external reality and private judgment. The true difficulty of doing right can be known only over a lifetime, just as the true difficulty of achieving pleasure can be proved to Nourjahad only after what seems a span of two generations' worth of time. Nourjahad can have a second chance; Sidney cannot.

Yet, until the end and the surprise turning of the closure with the sudden revelation of the sultan's trick, Nourjahad's experience is very like Sidney's after all. Both characters learn melancholy, and find everything they have hoped and worked for with apparent prudence slipping through their fingers. Experience changes them; indeed, perhaps Nourjahad's processes of psychological change are deeper and more interesting than Sidney's. Yet they cannot escape the consequences of the past, in external situation and in internal condition. A reviewer in the *Monthly Review* had doubts about *Miss Sidney Bidulph*, wondering whether such pictures of unhappiness could have a moral end: "It is much to be questioned if such pictures of human life, however justly they may be copied from nature, are well adapted to serve the cause of virtue."[16] *Nourjahad* met more unreserved critical admiration because its overt morality is simpler, more acceptable and cheerful than that of the long novel. Yet we can doubt whether morality—or rather, the "moral"—interested Sheridan primarily. In both the somber-shaded novel and the optimistic tale similar themes can be traced.

As I have indicated, Sheridan's new contribution in both narratives is found in her handling of *time*. In the apparently realistic *Miss Sidney Bidulph* as in the dreamlike and dream-originated *Nourjahad*, time proceeds in a spiral, or rather a helix, doubling back on itself. In both, the inner meaning of a series of actions or happenings can be understood only by circling back to an original point or time, a point of departure. Sidney's (and her daughters') periods of activity and pseudodecision (moral and social activity) are as vivid, lengthy and ironic as Nourjahad's pleasure seeking. The major decisive actions of characters in *Miss Sidney Bidulph* (for example, Sidney's first rejection of Faulkland, her marriage to Arnold, Dolly's interruption of her sister's wedding) take place in dreamlike states. These "realities" seem like illusions; they scatter and reform, as in a lapse of consciousness, and they return like recurring dreams. However far the Bidulph women may seem to advance in time (and they do proceed from cradle to grave in moral time) the characters all return, as if subject to reiterated and inevitable sleep of reason, to the condition in which individual desires or decisions are blotted out. Progressive time is annihilated.

The whole narrative of *Miss Sidney Bidulph* can be seen metaphorically in the light of what *Nourjahad* is literally—the story of a continuing consciousness (in this case a kind of group consciousness which endures through three generations of women) doomed to "the temporary death of sleep," as well as to the sleep of death. Which is more real—the activity or the dreamlike return to reenactment? Consciousness itself cannot triumph over the reiterated fate—the past—which makes almost every character succumb in a deathly reversion to Lady Bidulph's story. Characters awaken after this lapse and find everything altered, and yet after they have tried to cope with the disorienting and puzzling new conditions, they are still eventually doomed to fall again into that lacuna in time. They are constantly immobilized and rendered oblivious at that a-temporal point to which all their actions, however ambitious or frenetic, tend. Time is conflated in *Miss Sidney Bidulph*, as it is more happily in *Nourjahad*. The past is simultaneous with the present. But in *Nourjahad*, the past time, the time the sultan knows, the "real" time, is redemptive, whereas in *Miss Sidney Bidulph* the past can never be redeemed, and cannot heal or be healed.

Sheridan's view of time and the effect of the past is a somber one, however cheerfully she tried to render it at the end of *Nourjahad*. And in the Oriental tale, too, the most vivid effects concern the hero's fatiguing immortality of error, stuck at age twenty-three over a period of sixty years, and his bewilderment after each fit of oblivion. That Sheridan's views are somber does not mean that they are unattractive. Her handling of time is quite exciting, and it brings something new to fiction. I believe that her works were an influence on the Brontës' novels. One of her later, indirect, inheritors is Virginia Woolf (one thinks of *The Years*). Sheridan's novels were translated into French, and may have had an effect on the French novel; perhaps ultimately, indirectly and among many other influences, her novel was to affect *A La Recherche du Temps Perdu*.

Yet I believe too that that grave sense of time, and the sense of helplessness in relation to time and the past, are feminine insights, or at least in the eighteenth century could have been expressed only by a female writer. Such insights, that is, could have been expressed only by a sensibility with a deep knowledge of the meaning of powerlessness, and of lack of control over fate, as well as a comprehension of the hardship involved in encountering the outside world with moral ideals, or with warm desires. It is in her larger aesthetic view of the nature of time, rather than in particular opinions about female education or sexual morality, that Sheridan is truly a "feminist," and her treatment of time is her contribution—not only to feminism but to the Novel at large—that is, to humanism and humane experience.

NOTES

1. According to family tradition, Frances Chamberlaine's poem on Thomas Sheridan was written at the time of the Kelly riots in 1746. But Esther K. Sheldon insists that the poem was first published in 1745 and is related to the *Cato* riots, which arose after difficulties in a particular performance of Addison's *Cato* led to open rivalry between Theophilus Cibber and Thomas Sheridan as actors, and sparked conflict among their supporters. See Esther K. Sheldon, *Thomas Sheridan of Smock-Alley, 1719–1788* (Princeton: Princeton University Press, 1967), 4–5; 44 n.58. See also Alicia LeFanu, *Memoirs of the Life and Writings of Mrs. Frances Sheridan* (London: G. and W. B. Whittaker, 1824), 22–24.

2. LeFanu, *Memoirs*, 4–5.

3. *Ibid.*, 86–87; 88.

4. *Ibid.*, 109. For Richardson's reading some part of *Sidney Bidulph* (or an early version of it) in 1756, see T. C. Duncan Eaves and Ben D. Kimpel, *Samuel Richardson. A Biography* (Oxford: Clarendon Press, 1971), 454.

5. Frances Sheridan's attractively lively plays provide an interesting discussion of sexual relations. In *The Discovery*, the domestic tyrant Lord Medway is proud of his own free-living, and, in his approving reference to the Spartans, exhibits an interest in wife-swapping: "If their laws were in force here, my wife should be at your service, and I dare say I should be as welcome to yours" *The Discovery: A Comedy* (London: T. Davies, R. and J. Dodsley, *et al.*, 1763) Act 1, scene 2, p. 12.

The play traces the overthrow of Lord Medway's plans both to force his son and daughter to marry people they do not care for and also to seduce young Lady Flutter, the wife of his guest Sir Harry. Thomas Sheridan, the author's husband, acted Lord Medway, and was thus reformed nightly by his wife's authority.

The Dupe involves the discomfiture of another middle-aged rake, Sir John Woodall, who makes the mistake of marrying his kept mistress of many years; ultimately, he is forced to admit his own folly and the fallacy of his notions of manliness before he can admit that he needs the cold comforts of divorce. In her plays, Mrs. Sheridan seems, rather like Lady Bidulph, to be keen on educating men out of their rakish masculinist code. Her most comic male character is Sir Anthony Branville of *The Discovery* (a part taken by David Garrick). Sir Anthony, conceited and slow, talks at length of his unsuccessful love; the main fault was in his ladies: "I never could get any of them to be serious" Act 3, scene 2, p. 91. Pompous Sir Anthony is a forerunner of Jane Austen's Mr. Collins.

For new editions and a discussion of the plays see Robert Hogan and Jerry C. Beasley, *The Plays of Frances Sheridan* (Newark: University of Delaware Press; London & Toronto: Associated University Presses, 1984).

6. See LeFanu, *Memoirs*, 113, and James Boswell, *Life of Johnson*, ed. George Birkbeck Hill and L. F. Powell, 6 vols (Oxford: Clarendon Press, 1950), 1:390. Johnson wrote to Bennet Langton in 1760 "I wish him [Thomas Sheridan] well; and, among other reasons, because I like his wife" (358).

7. Quotations from the first part of the novel are taken from *Memoirs of Miss Sidney Bidulph. Extracted from Her Own Journal, And Now First Published*, 3 vols. (London: R. and J. Dodsley, 1761). Quotations from the latter part are taken from *Conclusion of the Memoirs of Miss Sidney Bidulph, As Prepared for the Press By the Late Editor of the Former Part* (London: J. Dodsley, 1767). The *Conclusion* is printed as volumes 4 and 5 of a continuous set. In my text, references to volume and page appear in parentheses after quotations.

8. "The Editor of the following sheets takes this opportunity of paying the tribute due to exemplary Goodness and distinguished Genius, when found united in One Person, by inscribing these Memoirs to The Author of Clarissa and Sir Charles Grandison."

9. See Virginia Woolf, *A Room of One's Own* (New York and London: Harcourt Brace Jovanovich, 1963), 63. Woolf's essay, first published by Harcourt Brace in 1929, undoubtedly contains this reference because Middleton Murry's 1928 edition of a selection of the poems of Anne Finch, Countess of Winchilsea, had brought Lady Winchilsea's work back into notice. The whole passage in which the lines appear is as follows:

> Thro' thy black Jaundice I all Objects see,
>   As Dark, and Terrible as Thee,
> My Lines decry'd, and my Employment thought
> An useless Folly, or presumptuous Fault:
>   Whilst in the *Muses* Paths I stray,
> Whilst in their Groves, and by their secret Springs
> My Hand delights to trace unusual Things,

> And deviates from the known, and common way;
>   Nor will in fading Silks compose
>   Faintly th'inimitable *Rose*,
> Fill up an ill-drawn-B*ird*, or paint on Glass
> The *Sov'reign's* blurred and undistinguish'd Face,
> The threatning *Angel*, and the speaking *Ass*.

(Anne Finch, Countess of Winchilsea, "The Spleen. A Pindarick Poem," *Miscellany Poems on Several Occasions*. Written by a Lady [London: J. B., and Benj. Tooke, 1713], 92–93.)

10. See figure 1. Edward Francesco Burney's picture was one of several illustrations of the novel commissioned from him by the *Novelists Magazine*. See *Novelists Magazine* vol. 22, containing *Lydia* and *Sidney Bidulph* (London: Harrison & Co., 1786), vol. 1, of *Sidney Bidulph*, facing p. 43. Some kind of rose is growing out of the pot or tub beside Sidney, and the heroine (drawn rather smirkingly) wears an enormous bunch of roses at her bosom. She is thus sitting in what seems a bower of rosy girlish love or loveableness, and Mr. Arnold, startled at the foreign element of her book, points emphatically to the unfinished needlework rose in its frame.

11. "You are thinking of your sons—but do not you know that of all things upon earth *that* is the least likely to happen; brought up, as they would be, always together like brothers and sisters? It is morally impossible. I never knew an instance of it. It is, in fact, the only sure way of providing against the connection," says Mrs. Norris in chapter 1 of *Mansfield Park*, proving at least that she is no novel-reader. See Jane Austen, *Mansfield Park*, ed. R. W. Chapman (London: Oxford University Press, 1966), 6–7.

12. *London Magazine* 30 (March 1761): 168.

13. LeFanu, *Memoirs*, 295, 295–96.

14. The edition used is *The History of Nourjahad*. By the Editor of *Sidney Bidulph* (London: J. Dodsley, 1767). References to page numbers appear in parentheses in my text after quotations.

15. *Nourjahad; or, The Folly of Unreasonable Wishes*, an Eastern Tale with Three Coloured Engravings (London: Printed for Tabart and Co. at the Juvenile and School Library, 1805). This is a greatly abridged and simplified version of the tale, priced at sixpence; the erotic touches, such as the rose-bud birthmark on Cadiga's breast, are omitted in this version for the very young. The pictures are attractive, if crude.

16. *Monthly Review* 37 (September 1768): 238.

A Near-Miss on the Psychological Novel

Maria Edgeworth's Harrington

TWILA YATES PAPAY

After this view, how can I return to speak of myself and of my works? In truth I have nothing to say of them but what my dear father has said for me in his prefaces to each of them as they came out. These sufficiently explain the moral design; they require no national explanations, and I have nothing personal to add. As a woman, my life, wholly domestic, cannot afford anything interesting to the public. (Frances Anne Edgeworth, *A Memoir of Maria Edgeworth*, 3:159).

Thus Maria Edgeworth spoke of her work in a letter to her publishers in August of 1847, less than two years before her death. In declining to write prefaces for later editions of her own works such as those supplied by Scott for the Waverly novels, she suggested that her fiction, unlike Scott's, was neither regional nor national, was not the product of genius, and did not inspire an interest in the life of the author. Content with her unusually happy domestic life and her success as a moralist, it did not occur to her to question her role or lament the status of her sex.

Was Maria Edgeworth fettered . . . or free? She would surely have dismissed the question. For her women were fettered, not by domesticity or societal conditioning, but (like men) by ignorance. The domestic life in which she flourished, and which she recommended to all women through the medium of her educative fiction (see, for example, *Belinda, Patronage, Helen*, and the children's tales), was a life in which the rational, intelligent, well-educated woman provided a focal point around which the family gathered for education, for entertainment, for intellectual as well as emotional sustenance. Given this image, her own international notoriety, and her satisfaction as a prominent and successful member of her father's large household, it is not surprising that Edgeworth simply assumed woman's importance in the intellectual activity of the day. (Indeed, in *Letters for Literary Ladies* she satirizes family friend Thomas Day and others who would question the intellectual ascendancy of women in society.) Her own success, then, surely blinded her to the lack of opportunity in which so many of her sisters foundered.

Intellectually, therefore, Edgeworth's position was secured, although there are still critics who quibble over her collaboration with her father.[1] Yet in artistic matters she was perhaps more severely fettered than many of her fellow authors by the very educational theories which motivated her to write. Indeed, in many of her educational novels (the novels of English manners), she seems to be on the very brink of a new and startling creation, only to draw back in order to underscore the particular lesson she wishes to teach. Nowhere is this phenomenon more evident than in *Harrington*, where a superb psychological analysis falls victim to Edgeworth's unrelenting focus upon the educative process that leads her hero into and back out of his society's pervasive prejudice against Jews.

Of Maria Edgeworth's major educative novels, *Harrington* (1817) has undoubtedly received the least attention, for most critics comment only upon the origin of the novel. *Harrington* was written because an American correspondent of Edgeworth's expressed her regret that such a novelist of morals should perpetuate the traditional anti-Jewish stereotype in her writings.[2] The justice of the observation is evident in light of the writer's long line of Jewish usurers and thieves, ranging from the miserly Jewish lady whom Sir Kit Rackrent marries in *Castle Rackrent* (1800) to the vicious Mr. Mordicai who pursues his debtors to the deathbed in *The Absentee* (1812), not to mention a whole host of bogeyman Jews in the children's tales. As Montagu Frank Modder observes, before *Harrington*, Edgeworth had supplied not "one honest Jew to redeem the race."[3]

Indeed, even in *Harrington* Edgeworth's attitude toward Jews is questionable in light of the story's conclusion. Perhaps the neglect of the novel is due in part to a critical objection, first put forward by Maria Edgeworth herself, to the last-minute transformation of the heroine from Jew to Christian.[4] In fact, critics who go beyond observing that a Jewish lady suggested the topic address themselves precisely to this point. Typical of such commentary is W. L. Renwick's dismissal of *Harrington* with the observation that in *Ivanhoe* "Scott displayed better manners as well as better art," or P. H. Newby's conclusion, based upon the same point, that "*Harrington* is not a novel to take very seriously. . . ."[5]

However, notwithstanding the contrived disclosure of the heroine's religion, *Harrington* is far more significant in Edgeworth's canon than the paucity of critical commentary would suggest. Only James Newcomer has recognized Edgeworth's accomplishment in producing a psychological novel: "She has received less than appropriate credit for an achievement in *Harrington* that she accomplished only to a lesser degree in other novels: a sharpened psychological study that would do credit to a twentieth-century analyst in fiction."[6] But in noting the hero's psychological progression, even Newcomer fails to place it in Maria Edgeworth's characteristic educational context. As a work of educative fiction, *Harrington* illustrates the doctrines of *Practical Education* (1798) in focusing upon what people learn, the principles that evolve out of the learning process. Thus, it is a psychological study of the external influences and internal habits of mind that bring about the formation of the hero's values. Throughout the novel Maria Edgeworth illustrates the external influences at work on Harrington at home and in school, explores the habits of mind he acquires through heredity or develops according to the dictates of environment, and examines the conflicting ethical codes he encounters.

Harrington's external influences begin at home when his wicked nurse, Fowler, initiates a series of events that lead to his strange preoccupation with Jews. Thus, in the opening scene, he first concludes that Simon, the Jewish rag-man, "had a good-natured countenance,"[7] but when the nurse threatens to have Harrington carried away in the man's bag, "the look of his eyes and his whole face had changed in an instant" (p. 2). Thereafter his fear increases with Fowler's nightly recounting of the cruel practices of Jews in roasting young children to sell the flesh as pork pies. The psychological terrors thus instilled soon lead to nightmare: "I saw faces around me grinning, glaring, receding, advancing, all turning at last into the same face of the Jew with the long beard and the terrible eyes; and that bag, in which I fancied were mangled limbs of the children . . ." (pp. 3–4).

But the nurse is only one of several influences on Harrington's life at home. More damaging, perhaps, is his mother's attitude when she learns of his problem. Proud of her son's "genuine temperament of genius" she exhibits his "positively natural antipathy to the sight or bare idea of a Jew" (p. 6) before her friends until he grows proud of his fears. Having encouraged the very fears she might have alleviated, his mother develops a complex theory of the effects of sympathies and antipathies, and bribes Jews to avoid her delicate son.

After being rewarded by his mother for his irrational fears, Harrington is next laughed at by his father, who teaches him that "Jews were all rascals" (p. 11), a race to be, not feared, but scorned. This antipathy is magnified in the pride the father, a member of Parliament, takes in opposing the naturalization of Jews in England. As Harrington observes the anti-Jewish campaign conducted through dinners in his father's house, he absorbs more

and more prejudice until his indoctrination is complete, and he proudly
drinks his father's toast, "No Naturalization Bill!—No Jews!" (p. 17). At
home as a child, then, Harrington is indulged in his irrationality and merely
laughed at for his foolish fears. His thought processes have not developed
through reasonable channels.

When Harrington goes to school at the age of ten, his companions once
again affect his education. Secure at first in his childhood prejudices, he
joins Lord Mowbray, an arrogant older child, in oppressing Jacob, a Jewish peddler boy. Reflecting upon that period as a man, Harrington realizes
the extent to which Mowbray led him into wrongdoing: "In looking back
upon this disgraceful scene of our boyish days . . . I have but one comfort. But I have one: I think I should never have done so *much* wrong, had it
not been for Mowbray" (p. 20). Yet Mowbray's influence works in the
opposite direction also. When the young lord turns to physical abuse, Harrington, realizing that the anti-Jewish schoolboys have been wrong, helps
Jacob escape. He insists that he has simply been " 'more of a Christian' "
(p. 26) by doing as he would be done by, but he has taken the first step in
reversing his opinion of Jews.

The influence of companions is even stronger when Harrington goes to
Cambridge, for he is befriended by Israel Lyons, a brilliant young rabbi
and teacher of Hebrew, who immediately engages him in intellectual discussion and cultural pursuits with a proper set of companions. But Harrington also learns from Israel Lyons that a man can be a Jew and still a
gentleman. As he observes his new friend's brilliance and humanity, popularity and refinement, the young man decides that Jews have been vastly
misrepresented. He begins to reconstruct his value system. "I may truly
say," he concludes, "that these three years, which I spent at Cambridge,
fixed my character, and the whole tone and colour of my future life" (p. 34).
Thus, Harrington uses both the reasoning powers he has acquired at school
and his newfound knowledge to reject the values instilled in him as a child.
As Newcomer points out, "He draws his own conclusions from what he
sees, identifies the psychological source of his own aversions, judges according to the facts, and comes to a just appraisal of his fellow human
beings."[8]

How Harrington manages to strengthen and adhere to his new code of
values in the face of parental and societal prejudices takes up the remaining
chapters of the novel. Thus, he befriends the noble and cultured Mr. Montenero, a Jewish acquaintance of Israel Lyons, despite his mother's con-
certed attempts to disrupt the relationship. Again, he rejects the insipid
Lady Anne Mowbray and falls in love with Berenice Montenero, the good
and beautiful daughter of his new friend. Having defeated Lord Mowbray

for the lady's favor, he proposes marriage despite his father's threat to disinherit him, and he perseveres in his suit despite Mr. Montenero's regretful assertion that an obstacle greater than religion exists. When the obstacle is discovered to be a fraud (Lord Mowbray had sought to prevent the match by assuring the Monteneros that Harrington suffers from fits of insanity), Harrington prepares to sacrifice his inheritance by marrying a Jew, thereby demonstrating the strength of his newfound convictions.

Harrington's learning process, then, is influenced both by the negative experiences of his childhood and early adolescence, and by the positive experiences he undergoes as a young man. Yet his companions are not entirely responsible for his formulation of values. The habits of mind he either acquires through heredity or develops according to the dictates of environment must also be considered. The question of heredity is introduced early in the novel when Harrington's mother laments that her son has inherited her "exquisite sensibility of the nervous system" (p. 6). Much later, when Harrington displays impatience at waiting to inform his beloved Berenice that the obstacle to marriage no longer exists, his father exclaims, " 'For you see the poor fellow is burning with impatience—he would not be my son if he were not' " (p. 204).

Harrington himself, however, is more cautious in claiming his emotional inheritance: "But it must be observed that, with my mother's warmth of imagination, I also had, I will not say, I inherited, some of my father's '*intensity of will*' " (p. 35). Indeed, whether he acquires certain habits of mind through hereditary gift or environmental conditioning, Harrington owes certain qualities to his parents. Yet it should be noted that Edgeworth herself dismisses the important question of hereditary versus environmental influence on character formation as a theoretical quibble. Clearly aware of both influences, she suggests that defects resulting from either may be corrected through the use of reason or the guidance of wise educators. As a writer of educative fiction, then, she dodges the question and focuses rather upon corrective measures.

Neither Mr. Harrington nor his wife is totally rational, the former being strong-willed and the latter weak-minded. The father's character is first established when he advances his irrational position against Jewish naturalization and then takes pride in his small son's adopting an attitude without understanding it. But Mr. Harrington's irrationality goes deeper than a single issue, for he seldom thinks before he takes a stand, and once something is sworn to, his pride in consistency forbids him to back down: "Now it was well known in our house, that a sentence of my father's beginning and ending '*by Jupiter Ammon*' admitted of no reply from any mortal—it was the stamp of fate; no hope of any reversion of the decree: it seemed to bind even him who uttered the oath beyond his own power of revocation" (p. 17). Nor is Mr. Harrington's temperament improved by age, for he is still denouncing Jews when his son returns from Cambridge, and his "intensity of will" has led to several attacks of the gout. His total irrationality is displayed again when he hears vague rumors that Harrington is engaged to Miss Montenero. Refusing to listen to the young man's denials, he swears to disinherit his son.

Despite his perpetual shifts in mood, Mr. Harrington still prides himself on consistency (p. 171), a trait which becomes a curse when he begins to admire Berenice and Mr. Montenero, who eventually helps him save the family fortune from possible bank failure. He cannot take back the threat of disinheritance, but he does concede that Harrington's friends "both deserved to be Christians" (p. 176) and wonders if Berenice cannot be converted. Although he tries to overcome his prejudices at the end, his character remains consistent as he questions how Jews can find "an obstacle on their side" (p. 177) and rejoices when Mr. Montenero announces that Berenice has been raised as an English Protestant. His last speech provides Edgeworth the opportunity for one of her best bits of humor: " 'Not a Jewess!' cried my father, starting from his seat: 'Not a Jewess! Then my Jupiter Ammon may go to the devil! Not a Jewess!—give you joy, Harrington, my boy!—give me joy, my dear Mrs. Harrington—give me joy, excellent—(*Jew*, he was on the point of saying) excellent Mr. Montenero; but, is she not your daughter?' " (p. 203). Mr. Harrington's exuberant enthusiasm is as strong as his other passions, and this trait, along with his "intensity of will," he shares with his son.

Mrs. Harrington, on the other hand, suffers more from a lack of spirit. Her "weak health, delicate nerves, and . . . morbid sensibility" (p. 6) render her unfit for intelligent discussion, and, due to her weakness of mind, she inevitably prefers feeling to reason. " 'Every body's feelings must be the best judge' " (p. 52), she insists in defense of Lady Anne's fits of bad temper. Similarly, instead of inquiring into rational causes for Harrington's early dislike of Jews, she develops her theory of sympathies and antipathies and later applies the same hypothesis to justify her own rejection of Mr. Montenero (p. 71). Further, she tries to discourage her son's friendship with Jews by describing her superstitions: "I dreamed last night—but I know you won't listen to dreams; I have a *presentiment*—but you have no faith in *presentiments*: what shall I say to you?" (p. 72). These superstitions, the narrator implies, are the result of a weak mind coupled to an overly active imagination.

Although Harrington does not share many of his mother's weaknesses, he certainly participates in her "warmth of imagination" (p. 35). As a child he was also said to possess her delicate sensibilities, and only good training at school rendered him more reasonable. To the extent that he is different from his parents, he learns from their mistakes, and their presence enables Edgeworth to illustrate the errors of irrationality. But in those characteristics in which he most closely resembles them—imagination and enthusiasm—lie Harrington's greatest faults and most eminent dangers. Through Harrington's more excitable qualities Edgeworth presents her most subtle and understated attack on irrationality.

The importance of governing the imagination is early announced as a major theme in the novel. From the first, Harrington is stimulated by his nurse's frightening tales, and the narrator frequently speculates upon the dangers of misguided imagination. He explains his focus upon the topic at the end of chapter 1, where he notes the need for further scientific study:

> Shall I be pardoned for having dwelt so long on this history of the mental and corporeal ills of my childhood? . . . Bacon . . . point[s] out as one of the most important subjects of human inquiry, equally necessary to the science of morals and medicine, 'The history of the power and influence of the imagination. . . .' This history, so much desired and so necessary, has been but little advanced. (pp. 8–9)

Suggesting that we must "discover or recollect those small causes which early influence the imagination, and afterwards become strong habits, prejudices, and passions" (p. 9), he offers his own anecdotes of childhood as early influences on the imagination, which in turn deeply affects a person's later life. Understanding the power of the imagination in the formation of values is essential, argues the mature Harrington, to the study of morals. Certainly Maria Edgeworth agrees.

The psychological effects on the mind of various habits of imagination are explored throughout *Harrington*. When Mrs. Harrington develops her superstition concerning presentiments, for example, the narrator observes that her "peculiarities of opinion and feeling" (p. 36), once assumed only as an affectation, had taken hold in her imagination and become reality. Similarly, Harrington tells Mr. Montenero of the unnecessary pain he suffers because of an overactive imagination: " 'You must know, that all my life, my quickness of perception of the slightest change in the countenance and manner of those I love, has ever been a curse to me; for my restless imagination always set to work to invent causes—and my causes, though ingenious unluckily, seldom happen to be the real causes. Many a vain alarm, many a miserable hour, has this superfluous activity of imagination cost me—so I am determined to cure myself' " (p. 139). The excesses of his imagination make him waste in useless speculation time and energy which might be better spent and deny him total self-control.

Harrington's "lively imagination" (p. 35) is closely tied to his excessive enthusiasm. At first his spirits are well controlled and suggest only youthful enjoyment of life. Indeed, Mr. Montenero praises him for the quality: "You have a great deal of enthusiasm, I see, Mr. Harrington: so much the better, in my opinion—I love generous enthusiasm" (p. 90). But the wise gentleman is quick to add the reasonable qualifier, "Enthusiasm well-governed, of course, I mean . . ." (p. 90). And so long as the excitement remains in check, Harrington continues to appear admirable and full of life.

But his enthusiasm, while often refreshing, can sometimes be ridiculous as well. He is not particularly admirable, for example, when he kneels in the Tower of London to do homage to the empty armor of the Black Prince. Yet O. Elizabeth Mc Whorter Harden exaggerates in her observation: "The scene in which Harrington rants Clarence's dream from Shakespeare is successful only in marking the major character as a contemptible blockhead, if not a madman."[9] Harrington is too interesting, agreeable, and lively to turn blockhead suddenly over a single speech. This particular episode occurs after his enthusiasm has been praised by Montenero and encouraged by Mowbray. Edgeworth allows her character these excesses in order to demonstrate the hazards into which he is led by unchecked enthusiasm. When he allows his excitement to control his mind, he becomes ridiculous.

But Harrington stands to suffer more than ridicule as the result of his unbridled excesses. His nearly fatal lack of self-control enables Mowbray to manipulate events and imply to the Monteneros that Harrington is edging toward insanity. Thus, Mowbray avidly encourages Harrington's enthusiasm, alludes in Montenero's presence to a tapestry of a Jew being scourged which terrified Harrington as a child and still distresses him, and arranges for Harrington to view the horrible portrait, *Dentition of a Jew*.

Having led the Monteneros into suspecting Harrington's stability, Mowbray then bribes Fowler the nurse to spread rumors concerning the young man's supposed insanity. In declaring this key episode to be "revolting," "trifling," and "irrelevant to the general design,"[10] Harden fails to recognize the illustration of mistaken values. This sequence of events establishes Edgeworth's point that self-control is an essential human value. Mowbray's scheme could not have succeeded had Harrington made his reason govern his enthusiasm.

The excesses of enthusiasm, then, have exposed Harrington both to ridicule and to the unscrupulous manipulations of his supposed friend. Fortunately for Harrington, he has long been developing the use of reason, and by the end of the novel he masters self-control. Other positive values first develop when he is sent away to school. There he first learns the use of reason, which he later tries on his mother without success. When she opposes his friendship with Jews, for example, he endeavors to explain how his own irrational prejudices have been overcome: "I laboured to show that no natural antipathy could have existed, since it had been completely conquered by humanity and reason . . ." (p. 37). Indeed, humanity and reason are the ideals he pursues throughout the novel. For these qualities Mr. Montenero (and presumably Berenice) admire him, as well as for his good temper, prudence, generosity, and liberal spirit (pp. 141–42). But one essential virtue is still missing. When Harrington first learns of the existence of an obstacle to his union with Berenice, Mr. Montenero urges him to practice self-control (p. 143), and this is one of the hardest lessons he must learn. He may visit the Monteneros as the father's friend, but not as Berenice's suitor, and as he disciplines himself to this cruel necessity, he learns to control his emotions. When the lovers are finally united, Mr. Montenero praises Harrington's discipline as a major source of all the young man's good qualities: "To this power over yourself you owe many of your virtues, and all the strength of character, and . . . the sanity of mind . . ." (p. 208).

And so Harrington has completed a remarkable intellectual and psychological journey. Of the many things he has accomplished, most prominent are his discovery of the nature of prejudice and his newfound ability to enjoy the companionship of intelligent Jewish people. In one sense *Harrington* is a book about Jews, written to appease a Jewish lady. As such, it is at least partially a failure, for it provides no information concerning Jewish life and customs. Indeed, as both Patrick Murray and Modder suggest, the Jews in the novel are actually "crypto-Christian," reflecting Edgeworth's own lack of information. And yet with all its faults as a representation of Jewish people, it is still an important step in the right direction, for as Modder insists, "The obvious hope of the novelist is to drive out the ancient and intolerant conceptions of the Jew as a repulsive and horror-provoking creature, and to substitute a new and more flattering portrait. The novel thus deserves notice because it marks a departure in the interpretation of Jews in the everyday life of modern England."[11]

In addition to setting forth intelligent and successful Jewish gentlemen, Edgeworth further atones for former errors by causing Harrington to criticize her own presentation of Jews in previous works. Speaking of the bad influence of the reading he did during his formative years, the narrator goes on to comment upon the literary stereotype presently in vogue and actually refers to Maria Edgeworth's own *Moral Tales* (1801): "I have met with books by authors professing candour and toleration—books written expressly for the rising generation, called, if I mistake not, Moral Tales for Young People; and even in these, wherever the Jews are introduced, I find that they are invariably represented as beings of a mean, avaricious, unprincipled, treacherous character" (p. 13). Of course, Harrington is quick to add that the nasty portraits must have been accidental and to suggest that authors try to avoid such errors in future works.

However, *Harrington* is more than an interesting, if abortive, attempt at a Jewish novel. As an early psychological study of the external influences and internal habits of mind that pervade a young man's moral education and generate his system of values, *Harrington* is a remarkable achievement. But just as the hero's attitude toward Jews is merely the vehicle the author employs to teach her value system, so the use of psychology is subordinated to the educative purpose which so plainly fetters Edgeworth in all her educative fiction. Harrington's early terrors and prejudices, so ably narrated, are presented for no other reason than to illustrate the effects of a bad education. Similarly, the question of heredity and environment is swept aside as irrelevant to human development since the Edgeworth educational system is calculated to correct hereditary defects as well as to overcome environmental influences. Thus, the novel is primarily a work of educative fiction intended both to illustrate the steps by which individuals establish their codes of ethics, and to teach the reader to adopt the same values. In maintaining her focus upon education, Maria Edgeworth narrowly misses the opportunity to free herself, to produce a first-rate psychological study of the nature of prejudice.

NOTES

1. For a full analysis of the "literary partnership" and a laying to rest of many myths derogatory to Richard Lovell Edgeworth, see Marilyn Butler, *Maria Edgeworth: A Literary Biography* (Oxford: Oxford University Press, 1972), 273–89.

2. For Maria Edgeworth's own account of this correspondence, see Frances Anne Edgeworth, *A Memoir of Maria Edgeworth with a Selection from Her Letters*, 3 vols. (London: Joseph Masters and Son, 1867), 2:286–87.

3. Montagu Frank Modder, *The Jew in the Literature of England* (1939; reprint, New York: Meridan Books, 1960), 132.

4. Edgeworth, *Memoir*, 287.

5. W. L. Renwick, *English Literature, 1789–1915*, vol. 9 of *The Oxford History of English Literature*, 12 vols., ed. F. P. Wilson and Bonamy Dobree (Oxford: Clarendon Press, 1960), 71; P. H. Newby, *Maria Edgeworth* (London: A. Barker, 1950), 71.

6. James Newcomer, *Maria Edgeworth* (Lewisburg, Pa.: Bucknell University Press, 1973), 78.

7. Maria Edgeworth, *Harrington*, vol. 9 of *Tales and Novels* (1817; reprint, New York: AMS Press, 1967), 2. Further references appear in page numbers in parentheses in the text.

8. Newcomer, *Maria Edgeworth*, 78.

9. O. Elizabeth McWhorter Harden, *Maria Edgeworth's Art of Prose Fiction* (The Hague: Mouton, 1971), 200.

10. Ibid., 200.

11. Patrick Murray, Maria Edgeworth: A Study of the Novelist (Cork: Mercier Press, 1971), 63; Modder, *The Jew in the Literature of England*, 136–37.

VI. THE NOVEL AND BEYOND:
CRITICAL ASSESSMENTS

Aphra Behn and the
Works of the Intellect

ROBERT ADAMS DAY

Those who have considered the life and works of Aphra Behn more than superficially have been rewarded by discovering the remarkable quality and quantity of her literary achievements, all the more astonishing since she had to struggle against the formidable compounded obstacles of being a woman while living in Restoration England, lacking formal education, and trying to earn her living as a writer. She has been revealed as a clever and successful playwright, a competent lyric poet, and an innovator in the technique of prose fiction; some biographers have viewed her as a militant feminist and a pioneer in exposing the evils of slavery. I shall try to show, by means of an almost unknown work of hers, written late in life, that at least potentially she was equally remarkable in three fields that are distinctly intellectual or learned: as a theorist of language and translation; a defender, even if belated, of the Copernican system against that of Ptolemy; and a pioneer practitioner of what would later be called the "higher criticism" of Scripture. I shall also argue that her sex, and therefore her lack of a grammar school and university education, together with the age in which she lived, not only conspired against these last achievements and made them all the more remarkable, but at the same time, paradoxically, made them possible.

The operation of this paradox can be seen in Mrs. Behn's earliest literary efforts. To be a playwright she needed no education beyond learning to read and write her mother tongue, and no resources beyond inexpensive playbooks and tickets to the playhouse to see performances. Her models were ready to hand, and plays (even Shakespeare's) were not regarded in the Restoration as serious literature. Here was a realm of potentially lucrative writing which a woman might enter merely by crossing the threshold, so to speak; the learned world would take no notice, and the playhouse was a social limbo, wholly alien to the conventions that governed the conduct of gentlefolk and the nobility.[1] Once a woman, such as Aphra Behn, had taken the simple but momentous step of deciding to do something that women had never done before, once she had succeeded (we do not know how) in persuading Thomas Betterton to accept *The Forc'd Marriage* for production in 1670, the preliminaries were over.[2] The novelty of a female playwright might, for all anyone knew, insure by itself the success of her first play, and after that the progress of her career would depend solely on her native talents. These, fortunately, Mrs. Behn possessed in plenty, and her plays appeared with varying success for the next twelve years. She herself was well aware of all these facts, as the prefaces and dedications to her plays make abundantly clear.[3]

Aphra Behn wrote for money; and when in 1682 her career as playwright came virtually to an end[4] she turned immediately to prose fiction, another literary form that for her age was not serious literature, and also one which a woman might undertake without formal preparation beyond the reading that any literate woman of the time might have done. The financial rewards were far less than the theater promised, but what else was Mrs. Behn to do?[5] Again, however, her native talents came to her aid, and in the first part of *Love-Letters between a Nobleman and His Sister* (1683) she produced an astonishing tour de force of epistolary technique, literally unprecedented in either French or English prose fiction.[6] The technical innovations and achievements of this work and of her later short novels have been amply discussed by various critics and do not need recapitulation here. The epistolary feats of *Love-Letters*, the breezy colloquial quality and Defoe-like "I was there" technique of her novellas (for which there were few if any close models either in English or French), and the astonishing innovations of *Oroonoko* (which is entirely original for its time in its clashing levels of diction, setting, plot, description, narrative voice—the reader's expectations are constantly being aroused and defeated in the most surprising ways) are remarkable enough as they stand. But one can argue that these fictional achievements owe their existence to Mrs. Behn's originality, in a sense quite beyond the usual hackneyed implications of that word. Could she have written in her own native voice, and in modes which she virtually invented, if she had been hampered by the dead weight of tradition, and merely imitated the ponderous French romances or the prose narratives of antiquity? Unlike her plays, her fictions did not depend greatly on models, for the simple reason that models scarcely existed. Again, the denial of the "higher" literary forms to a woman writer who wanted to earn money by her work operated paradoxically to free her natural talents and enable them to flourish in the literary limbo of vernacular prose fiction.

But Mrs. Behn was active as well on the fringes of "serious" literature, though at one remove. We have no proven facts about her early life or her education;[7] but we cannot avoid concluding that the latter was as good as a woman was likely to get in her day. She certainly acquired a very competent knowledge of French, and the frequency of references in her works to convents and nuns, together with the apparent fact that she was a Roman Catholic,[8] permits us at least to speculate that she may have been reared in a French or Belgian convent. When her career as playwright ended, she supplemented her meager income from fiction by turning to translation from the French as a means of livelihood. In addition to frothy trifles like *The Lover's Watch* (1685) and *The Isle of Love* (1688), she translated La Rochefoucauld ("Seneca Unmasq'd" in her *Miscellanies* of 1685) and two fairly demanding works of Fontenelle—the *Entretiens sur la pluralité des mondes* and the *Histoire des oracles* (1688), the latter in turn a translation from the Latin of a Dutch scholar. It may well have been the bookseller and not she who suggested the choice of Fontenelle for translation (such was the custom); and one must admit that the *Discovery of New Worlds* is popularized science, astronomy for ladies in a series of dialogues between a philosopher and a marquise. Nevertheless, these three are solid works, presupposing in the reader both some erudition and the capacity for sustained reasoning, and the bookseller must have felt that Mrs. Behn could give male competitors a run for their money without risk to his sales. In fact, a modern student finds her version of the *Entretiens* superior to that of John Glanvill in the same year, and of William Gardiner in 1715.[9]

Not content with merely rendering her author, Mrs. Behn provided a dividend in the form of an "Essay on Translated Prose" to accompany the *Discovery of New Worlds*. This must have been a labor of love, for it would not have been a very salable pamphlet (it is separately paginated as printed in the second volume of her *Works*, called *Histories, Novels, and Translations*, in 1700),[10] and it is in no sense a dedication, though she wrote plenty of those for the few pounds they might bring from a patron. So far as I know, the "Essay on Translated Prose" has never received attention from scholars except for passing mention in two articles printed 29 and 120 years ago;[11] yet for intellectual history (to say nothing of the history of women writers) it is a remarkable document. True to its designation as an essay, it rambles; there is first a discussion of the relative ease of translation among various languages, with notes on the history of their development; next a reconciliation of the Copernican system with Biblical cosmology; and lastly a beginning, if no more, of a reasoned attack on the factual reliability of Scripture. The incidental information revealed in these discussions, the positions the author takes, and what we may call their methodology, all attest to an astonishing intellectual feat for an uneducated woman who a few years before had modestly pointed out in a preface that in writing plays, at least, a woman did not need what men might freely have, "that is, learning."[12]

The word "uneducated" may cause the reader's hackles to rise; but we have proof positive that Mrs. Behn was uneducated as her age understood the term. In the preface to his collection of Ovid's heroic epistles, Dryden remarked of her contribution, the epistle of Oenone to Paris, "I was asked to say that the author, who is of the fair sex, understood not Latin."[13] And that, for his time and hers, meant that true education was forever closed to her; indeed, "Oenone to Paris" moved Matthew Prior to characterize her waspishly as "our blind translatress *Behn*, / The female wit."[14] But one may do much without going to a university. We know from her letters, prefaces, and dedications that Mrs. Behn was on familiar terms with many of London's leading wits (if they were our contemporaries we should justly style them intellectuals),[15] and we may presume that their conversations ranged widely and often included serious consideration of topics familiar to the learned, to say nothing of matters of current intellectual controversy. These men may have been Latinate, but they did not argue in Latin; and Mrs. Behn, living in the Restoration equivalent of Bohemia, was thereby admitted to an intellectual feast denied to her respectable sisters, confined to the tea-table and the drawing-room. Moreover, the age of translation was well under way by the later seventeenth century. Not only the major Greek and Latin classics, but numerous contemporary philosophical and scientific works in Latin, had appeared in English by the 1680's; and Mrs. Behn had certainly studied at least two of the latter with significant results, as we shall see. Again we find the paradox of her unusual status in operation: her connection with the playhouse and the wits liberated her talents in a way that compensated, to a degree unique among the women of her time, for her lack of conventional learning. She was a prophetic example of the shrewd observation made in the anonymous *Defence of the Female Sex* (1696):

> I have often thought, that the not teaching Women Latin and Greek, was an advantage to them, if it were rightly consider'd, and might be improv'd to a great height.[16]

In the course of her essay Mrs. Behn refers familiarly to the Roman emperors Theodosius, Arcadius, Honorius; Froissart's chronicles; Descartes' cosmological theory of vortices and his calculation of the depth of the earth's atmosphere; Copernicus and Ptolemy, with details of their systems; Josephus on Hebrew antiquity; Thomas Burnet's radical and shocking *Sacred Theory of the Earth*, translated but four years earlier, which proposed purely natural explanations for seemingly miraculous events, such as Noah's flood; the correspondence of St. Jerome with Bishop Vitalis; the edition of the Bible "published in a small folio by *Buck* at Cambridge;"[17] the arguments of the contemporary Jesuit mathematician Tacquet; and Antoine Godeau, bishop of Vence, who in his *Histoire de l'église* (1654) had treated of Biblical chronology.[18] She also shows a very competent knowledge for her age, with its often fantastic theories of etymology, of the formation of French, Spanish, and Italian from Vulgar Latin, with the admixture of Celtic, Teutonic, Arabic, and "Basbriton and Biscagne" (pp. 2–3). If, as scholars are professionally obliged to wonder, she may have borrowed here from someone else's writings, she at least took the trouble to rework the material thoroughly into her own idiom and progression of thought; the style is uniform throughout.

But is this "Essay on Translated Prose" truly remarkable? Was Mrs. Behn merely parroting what, by the time she wrote, had become commonplaces among the wits of the town? No. We should remember that only two decades before, Milton, no ignoramus, had decided in *Paradise Lost* to hedge on Ptolemy versus Copernicus; and as for science, cosmology, and Bible study in the Restoration, a recent authoritative work sums it up thus:

> The study of Descartes had been introduced at Cambridge by John Smith and encouraged by Henry More, but these men were brilliant innovators, and the average teachers still subscribed to the scholastic outlook. . . . The Bible . . . possessed an unapproachable authority. . . . Biblical criticism had not yet been born; all portions of Scripture were treated alike, and every passage possessed an authority equal to that of any other. . . . it still remains a marvel that men could know the Bible so well and understand it so little.[19]

Mrs. Behn, however, did not frequent the studies of divines and academics. If Milton may be said to open her era, Swift closes it with *A Tale of a Tub*; and the reader will not need to be told what so learned yet so conservative a writer as Swift thought of Descartes and his follower and popularizer Pierre Gassendi.[20] Aphra Behn must be rated as distinctly advanced in her ideas, even when set against the male writers of her period.

She begins her essay disarmingly enough, remarking on the first page, "I thought an *English* Woman might venture to translate any thing, a *French* Woman may be suppos'd to have spoken," but she soon plunges into a learned disquisition on the various languages that entered into the formation of the Romance tongues, and the periods when they entered. Her discourse on language, however, is less remarkable for the value of its observations than for what it shows of the breadth of her information on historical linguistics, and more importantly for the fact that when she gets to the characteristics of the French language she is specific and practical, not vague and dependent on theory. She notes, with what we should call surprising modernity of attitude, that while Italian had scarcely changed in several centuries, French had altered remarkably in the last hundred years,

"So that I am confident a *French* Man a hundred Years hence will no more understand an old Edition of *Froisard's* History, than he will understand *Arabick*"; that the present universality of French is merely owing to "an Accident . . . the French Arms, Mony [sic] and Intrigues" (p. 3), not to any mysterious superiority of the language itself. She also discusses French elision between words at some length, noting for instance, but without argument, that *son épouse* is illogical (p. 5). But the important point for us to note is that she merely records these matters, not bewailing the facts as a scholar of her day might do (or even Swift, with his obsessive desire to freeze English and prevent all innovation). Like Dr. Johnson half a century later, and like more recent dictionaries, she is historical and descriptive, not prescriptive, in her treatment of language.

But her Biblical criticism is even more interesting for the modern reader. She proposes to defend Fontenelle's Copernican astronomy "as far as a Woman's Reasoning can go" (p. 8). And therefore she is constrained to do two things that are as rare for learned discourse in her own time as they are (or should be) commonplace for us; she uses common sense, and she closely examines and compares texts. A learned Jesuit, she has heard, has used Joshua's making the sun stand still as Scriptural and therefore irrefutable evidence against Copernicus; but she discovers that according to "*Buck's* edition of the Bible, published . . . at Cambridge," the Hebrew word formerly translated "stand" means "be silent" (p. 14). She knows that the true formula for the circumference of a circle is $2\ pi\ r$, therefore that the circumference of Solomon's sea of molten brass could not be exactly thirty cubits if its diameter was ten cubits (p. 10). She does not hesitate to equate the text of the secular historian Josephus with the sacred text of Scripture, pointing out that Josephus must be right and the Holy Ghost wrong (or at least inconsistent), for Solomon reigned eighty years, not forty: "I would not presume to name this famous Historian in contradiction to the Holy Scriptures, if it were not easie to prove by the Scriptures, that Solomon reigned almost twice forty years" (p. 12). This she proceeds laboriously to do, by citing all the relevant texts. Again, both St. Paul and I Kings say that Solomon built the Temple four hundred and eighty years after the Exodus; but by carefully doing her Biblical sums Mrs. Behn demonstrates that the interval must have been about *five* hundred and eighty years (p. 11).

This is not to say that she takes the position of a rampant freethinker. Far from it: whatever her real opinions may have been, she either speaks sincerely (or hedges discreetly) as follows:

I hope I may be allowed to say, That the Design of the Bible was not to instruct Mankind in Astronomy, Geometry, or Chronology, but in the Law of God, to lead us to Eternal Life; and the Spirit of God has been so condescending to our

Weakness, that through the whole Bible, when any thing of that kind is mentioned, the Expressions are always turned to fit our Capacities, and to fit the common Acceptance, or Appearances of Things to the Vulgar. (pp. 9–10)

What could be more modern? Indeed, in view of current attempts to exchange messages by radio with other inhabited worlds, and Immanuel Velikovsky's speculations about the possible material causes of Joshua's miracle,[21] Mrs. Behn is positively prophetic of our own times. The demands of brevity preclude our going into further details about the contents of her essay, though they are fascinating; its style is often somewhat crabbed and its syntax far from lucid in its low spots, however impressive its high spots may be. My principal purpose, as I have said, is to show that, remarkable as is Mrs. Behn's tentative achievement in this essay, that performance paradoxically owes its existence as much to her "disadvantages" as to her superior talents. What was going on in her mind was also "modern" in the sense of the "quarrel of the Ancients and the Moderns," for the Moderns were pointing out, to the annoyance of Swift and others, that, for instance, Homer had his defects—errors and inconsistencies: how were these to be explained? Not until seventy-five years after Mrs. Behn's essay did the person often considered to be the first scientific Biblical critic, the French physician Jean Astruc, discover from such evidence as the creation of Eve from Adam's rib on one hand and "male and female created he them" on the other, the existence of the "J" and "E" or Jahvistic and Elohistic versions of Genesis; the disintegration of the Bible had begun.[22] But how could the "uneducated" Mrs. Behn so remarkably have anticipated his achievement? The answer, I think, lies in part in what we now understand, thanks to such writers as Walter J. Ong and the classicist Eric Havelock, of the significance of orality in Western culture.

Havelock, in his seminal *Preface to Plato*, argues that Plato's famous and puzzling opposition to the poets lay essentially in this: in an illiterate and therefore oral culture one merely absorbs, or mentally entertains or holds the text, though very tenaciously; one does not *analyze* it—and Plato knew that any genuine advance in thought must come from analysis.[23] But a written or printed text, unlike sounds that decay instantly in the air, will sit still forever, so to speak, while one analyzes it; yet that is not the whole story. Classical (and therefore Latin and Greek) education, admired by Swift and the Ancients, significantly preserved orality, as Walter Ong has shown, but in an ossified, artificial form.[24] It was the same with Scripture; one absorbed it like a sponge, memorized it, used its texts to prove points, but in a culture still conceptually oral and with a divinely inspired text, one did not analyze or comparatively examine it. (We ourselves have not lost the habit: how many of us have wondered who was standing by taking notes during the Temptation in the Wilderness, or what a herd of swine was doing in Hebrew Galilee? They are not said to have belonged to the Greco-Roman occupation troops.) When Pope and Swift attacked what they considered the nit-picking methods of so great a classical scholar as Richard Bentley, it was the minute examination and comparison of parts rather than the admiring and uncritical retention of the whole text in the mind that they really hated so much.

We may say that the Moderns had reached a point in the decay of popular orality when, seeing rather than hearing, without much deliberate effort they could regard a text analytically and perceive where Homer nodded. Similarly Mrs. Behn in her reading of Scripture. We often note today how many important discoveries in science or the humanities are made by "naive" yet brilliant newcomers (Wittgenstein is an example), partly because they lack the standard traditional preparation in a given discipline that will automatically inhibit them from asking basic questions. Such, I venture, was the case with this "uneducated" female scholar. Fortunately, her methodology was none at all; ignorance allowed her to use mother-wit on the emperor's invisible clothes. Unhampered by classical and scholastic training, she could readily see things to which far more learned persons were blind.

Two small qualifications are necessary. First, it has been pointed out that a suppressed passage in the original dedication of *Oroonoko* to Lord Maitland indicates that Mrs. Behn was or had become a Catholic.[25] Catholic apologists in her day had begun to argue that the text of Scripture, which must of necessity have been orally transmitted in the days of the Patriarchs, and its translations, which were often based on a faulty knowledge of Hebrew, contained many uncertainties, necessitating a dependence on Church tradition; and Mrs. Behn, who was at least a peripheral member of Dryden's circle, probably knew the English translation (1682) of Père Richard Simon's *Critical History of the Old Testament*, which led to the writing of Dryden's skeptical *Religio Laici*.[26] But neither her arguments nor her examples are borrowed from Simon's book, so far as I can discover from an examination of its text; she carefully steers clear of matters of faith and doctrine, and she seems to be working on her own.

Second, we have indubitable evidence that Mrs. Behn had knowledge, in translation, of a particular Latin classic which could not but contribute to skeptical and iconoclastic thought—Lucretius' *De Rerum Natura*. She was a close friend and admirer of the precocious and brilliant Thomas Creech, whose translation of Lucretius produced a sensation in 1683, and she contributed a commendatory poem to the volume.[27] Lucretius, atomist and atheist, was of course anathema to Ancients and to all right-thinking persons alike, as a believer in the random formation of the universe from the inherent properties of matter alone. This is why Swift as a parody-Modern prefixes a "presumptuous" Lucretian passage to *A Tale of a Tub*, and in its digressions refers to and quotes Lucretius with ironic admiration. The Roman poet's philosophical doctrines, regarded as deadly intellectual poison by the orthodox, but exactly conformable to the latest scientific positions that we hold today on the nature and origin of the physical universe, were thus available without hindrance to the inquiring and unprejudiced mind of a woman who had neither the pressure of academic authorities nor the sanctions of respectable society to inhibit her access to these newly-available ideas; she could judge them, so far as her natural talents permitted, on their own merits.

The significance of this fact is not at all diminished by a conjecture that may occur to a skeptical reader who knows the details of Aphra Behn's later life. It is possible that the clarity of vision leading to Mrs. Behn's daring innovations in Biblical criticism came from informal instruction administered during her long relationship with the raffish, Cambridge-educated, and erudite John Hoyle, to whom she probably wrote the *Love-Letters to a Gentleman*.[28] We know relatively little of him, but we do know that he was "A Wit uncommon and facetious, / A great admirer of Lucretius," as Mrs. Behn wrote in a jocular letter to Creech.[29] And Lucretius' admirer might well, during their Platonic conversations, have steered her into strange seas of thought. But one fact remains: Hoyle did not write an essay involving the embryonic Higher Criticism. Aphra Behn did.

NOTES

An earlier version of the present essay was read at a session on Aphra Behn during the December 1979 meeting of the Modern Language Association in San Francisco.

1. For a fuller discussion of this point, see Robert Adams Day, "Muses in the Mud: The Female Wits Anthropologically Considered," *Women's Studies* 7 (Spring 1980): 61–74.

2. See Angeline Goreau, *Reconstructing Aphra: A Social Biography of Aphra Behn* (New York: Dial Press, 1980), pp. 117–24. (Two recent biographies of Aphra Behn, Goreau's and Maureen Duffy's *The Passionate Shepherdess* (New York: Humanities Press, 1977) are readily available. Both contain numerous minor inaccuracies; Goreau's, however, is more thorough in its use of primary and secondary materials, more up-to-date, and more copious and detailed in its quotation from relevant documents and its coverage of the events of Mrs. Behn's life; it will therefore be used for documentation in the present study in preference to other sources.

3. See, for example, those quoted in Goreau, pp. 123–26, 132–33, 135–36, 209–10, 234.

4. Mrs. Behn left the theater as a means of livelihood for several reasons, both specific and general; see Goreau, pp. 251–53.

5. For a general account of the financial situation of women authors, playwrights, and writers of fiction at this time see Robert Adams Day, *Told in Letters: Epistolary Fiction Before Richardson* (Ann Arbor: Univ. of Michigan Press, 1966), pp. 69–83, 255–56.

6. Detailed discussions of the novel's technique are found in *Told in Letters*, pp. 159–64, and Ruth Perry, *Women, Letters, and the Novel* (New York: AMS Press, 1980), pp. 24–26, 157–59; its text is reproduced in Natascha Würzbach, *The Novel in Letters* (London: Routledge and Kegan Paul, 1969), pp. 197–282.

7. Despite the conjectures of Duffy and Goreau, no reliable evidence has been uncovered since that summarized in Robert Adams Day, "Aphra Behn's First Biography," *Studies in Bibliography* 22 (1969): 227–40, and given in the references cited therein.

8. See Gerald Duchovnay, "Aphra Behn's Religion," *Notes & Queries* 221 (May-June 1976): 235–37.

9. Margaret Turner, "A Note on the Standard of English Translations from the French, 1685–1720," *Notes & Queries* 199 (December 1954): 517. (Mrs. Behn's is the first known translation of La Rochefoucauld into English.)

10. This volume, issued by Samuel Briscoe (Wing 1711A), is probably composed of unsold sheets bound up. In the Huntington and British Library copies the "Essay" is sandwiched between the two works of Fontenelle, occupies sigs. I2–K3^v, and is paginated 1–20. It will be cited parenthetically in the text.

11. Turner, and an anonymous article in the *St. James's Magazine* for 1863, mentioned in Duchovnay, pp. 235–36.

12. Preface to *The Dutch Lover*, quoted in Goreau, p. 135.

13. *Ovid's Epistles Translated by Several Hands* (3rd ed., 1683), sig. A2^v. Dryden added, however: "But if she does not, I am afraid she has given us occasion to be ashamed who do."

14. "A satyr on the Modern Translators" in *The Literary Works of Matthew Prior*, ed. H. Bunker Wright and Monroe K. Spears, 2 vols. (Oxford: Oxford Univ. Press, 1959), 1:21.

15. See Goreau, pp. 140–42, 189–206, 211–16, 243, 254, 258–60, 264, for her principal connections with the wits; there is evidence also that she was on friendly terms with Dryden.

16. Reprinted (New York, 1970), p. 63.

17. *STC* 2285 (1629 ed.) or 2331 (1638 ed.).

18. The text reads (p. 13), "*Anthony Godean*, Lord and Bishop of *Venice*," but since Mrs. Behn discusses a passage in Godeau's history in detail, the error is presumably the printer's.

19. G. R. Cragg, *From Puritanism to the Age of Reason* (Cambridge, Eng.: Cambridge Univ. Press, 1966), pp. 6–7.

20. For an account of Gassendi's work and influence see Richard H. Popkin, *The History of Scepticism from Erasmus to Spinoza* (Berkeley: Univ. of California

Press, 1979), pp. 99–109, 141–46. The complex background (including political and religious factors) of the opposition to Descartes' ideas in England is excellently discussed by Margaret C. Jacob, *The Newtonians and the English Revolution: 1689–1720* (Ithaca: Cornell Univ. Press, 1976).

21. The humanist reader who may consider Velikovsky reliable should consult Carl Sagan, *Broca's Brain* (New York: Random House, 1979), 81–127, 317–27.

22. The *Conjectures* of Astruc (1684–1766) did not appear in print until 1763; see the article on him in the *Catholic Encyclopedia*.

23. Eric Havelock, *Preface to Plato* (Cambridge, Mass: Belknap Press, 1963).

24. Walter J. Ong, *The Presence of the Word* (New Haven: Yale Univ. Press, 1967), chs. 2, 5.

25. See Duchovnay (note 8, above).

26. The most recent extended discussion of this work and its influence on Dryden is in Sanford Budick, *Dryden and the Abyss of Light* (New Haven: Yale Univ. Press, 1970); see also Popkin, pp. 236–37, and Philip Harth, *Contexts of Dryden's Thought* (Chicago: Univ. of Chicago Press, 1968).

27. See Goreau, p. 254. One passage of this prefatory epistle is particularly significant in the context of the present essay:

> Till now, I curst my birth, my education,
> And more the scanted customs of the nation:
> Permitting not the female sex to tread
> The mighty paths of learned heroes dead.
> The God-like Virgil, and great Homers verse,
> Like divine mysteries are concealed from us.
>
> . . . .
>
> The fulsom gingle of the times,
> Is all we are allowed to understand or hear.
> So thou by this translation dost advance
> Our knowledge from the state of ignorance,
> And equal us to man!

28. See Goreau, pp. 189–206.

29. Quoted in Goreau, p. 192.

"Ladies . . . Taking the Pen in Hand"

Mrs. Barbauld's Criticism of Eighteenth-Century Women Novelists

CATHERINE E. MOORE

A versatile woman—poet, essayist, polemicist, hymnwriter, children's writer, educator, critic—Anna Laetitia Barbauld (1743–1825) never wrote a novel. As an avid reader of novels, as well as a respected writer for nearly forty years, and the editor of Samuel Richardson's *Correspondence* (1804), she was well-qualified in 1810 to serve as editor of the fifty-volume *British Novelists, with an Essay and Prefaces, Biographical and Critical*, published that year. This collection includes twenty-one novelists, twenty-eight novels, and twenty essays by Mrs. Barbauld, including a long introductory essay, "On the Origin and Progress of Novel-Writing." The purpose of this edition, she says in her introduction, is to present a "series of the most approved novels, from the first regular productions of the kind to the present time."[1] The titles offered in this collection confirm her judgment, for all the major eighteenth-century novelists (with the exception of Sterne—an unexplained omission) and many of the best and most popular minor novelists are represented.[2] The essays, though varying in length and in thoroughness, collectively constitute a defense of novels as a genre and an attempt to define and illustrate literary principles in novel writing.

This useful collection of essays has received remarkably little attention over the past two centuries. Indeed, Lucy Aikin's reference to it as the "humbler offices of literature" may reflect the attitude of her aunt, Mrs. Barbauld, and certainly Aikin's explanation that the task was undertaken to assuage grief over Mr. Barbauld's suicide in 1808 points to something less than Mrs. Barbauld's total commitment to the project on its own merit.[3] Since then, although scholars frequently have cited Mrs. Barbauld's prefatory remarks on novels in her edition of Richardson's *Correspon-*

dence, few have ever alluded to the prefaces to *British Novelists*.[4] Yet these are important for several reasons. Mrs. Barbauld has been justly praised for having written "the most complete and the most accurate history of prose fiction to appear during the years intervening between the publication of John Moore's *A View of the Commencement and Progress of Romance* (1797) and John Colin Dunlop's *History of Fiction* (1814)."[5] Equally significant is her assertion of the artistic values of the novel at a time when the literary reputation of the genre had not yet entirely outgrown the widespread disapproval common in eighteenth-century criticism. A third important feature is her advocacy of women novelists, who as a group were yet to be taken seriously.

As historian and theoretician of the novel, Mrs. Barbauld synthesizes current ideas and information. She had been preceded not only by John Moore in 1797 but also by Clara Reeve, whose "The Progress of Romance" had appeared in 1785. Criticism of novels, however, was fragmented because most of it appeared incidentally in magazine reviews of individual novels. Nevertheless, from the scattered observations of authors and critics, a distinct body of criticism was emerging, and Mrs. Barbauld's achievement was to give coherent voice to it, through the introductory essay, which provides a historical background and a statement of principles, and through the individual prefaces, which draw upon those principles.

The work reveals Mrs. Barbauld's thorough assimilation of contemporary criticism of novels. J. M. S. Tompkins says of the period from 1770 to the end of the century that "the two chief facts about the novel are its popularity as a form of entertainment and its inferiority as a form of art."[6] The opening sentence of Mrs. Barbauld's introductory essay demonstrates her awareness of these facts: "A collection of Novels has a better chance of giving pleasure than of commanding respect" ("Origin," 1:1). She even adopts the conciliatory tone which champions of the novel considered necessary to combat the moralistic opposition,[7] as, for example, in her tentatively worded thesis: "It might not perhaps be difficult to show that this species of composition is entitled to a higher rank than has been generally assigned it" ("Origin and Progress," 1:1). But concession is only a strategy which strengthens her defense of the novel. She addresses the main critical issues: defining the novel, defending it against the moralists, and asserting its authenticity as a literary form.[8] Her formal definition is obviously adapted from Fielding: "A good novel is an epic in prose, with more of character and less (indeed in modern novels nothing) of the supernatural machinery" ("Origin," 1:2). But as Mrs. Barbauld traces the history of fiction, she reveals her bias in favor of realism—"the closer imitation of nature"—as the crucial trait of the "modern" novel. Thus, in England the "modern" novel begins with Defoe because he was the "first author amongst us who distinguished himself by natural painting" ("Origin," 1:37). The account of the evolution of the novel has a twofold purpose: to show that "Fictitious adventures in one form or other, have made a part of polite literature of every age and nation" ("Origin," 1:1) and to show that the popular contemporary form, the novel, has a superior moral advantage because of its closer imitation of nature. She argues, "If the stage is a mirror of life, so is the novel, and perhaps a more accurate one, as less is sacrificed to effect and representation" ("Origin," 1:51). Moreover, she shrewdly connects the moral significance of the novel with its great popularity.

> Some perhaps may think that too much importance has been already given to a subject so frivolous, but a discriminating taste is no where more called for than with regard to a species of books which every body reads. It was said by Fletcher of Saltoun, 'Let me make the ballads of a nation, and I care not who makes the laws.' Might it not be said with as much propriety, Let me make the novels of a country, and let who will make the system? ("Origin," 1:61–62)

On the other hand, Mrs. Barbauld is at odds with even the defenders of the novel[9] in her defiant dismissal of the traditional idea that the "end and object of this species of writing" is "to call in fancy to the aid of reason, to deceive the mind into embracing truth under the guise of fiction" and in her personal endorsement of pleasure as the chief purpose of novels. "I scruple not to confess," she declares, "that when I take up a novel, my end and object is entertainment; and as I suspect that to be the case with most readers, I hesitate not to say that entertainment is their legitimate end and object" ("Origin," 1:46).

On the subject of the art of fiction, Mrs. Barbauld suggests some theoretical principles, but without much elaboration. Her introductory essay seems to illustrate Frederick R. Karl's observation of the later eighteenth century that criticism of the novel "remained rudimentary" although "the novel was becoming an acceptable part of critical vocabulary" and thus "without any conscious development of novel theory, the novel [was entering] the literary consciousness."[10] Mrs. Barbauld's summary of the required talents for a novelist implies what might be called rudimentary awareness of novelistic art. She simply lists "the invention of a story, the choice of proper incidents, the ordonnance of the plan, occasional beauties of description, and above all, the power exercised over the reader's heart by filling it with the successive emotions of love, pity, joy, anguish, transport, or indignation, together with the grave impressive moral resulting from the whole" ("Origin," 1:2–3). On the other hand, her perception that the novel

is an art form goes beyond the rudimentary. When she calls upon the novelist to attend to the truth of "real life and manners" because the novel must
in "some respects give false ideas, from the very nature of fictitious writing," her concern is moral, but her subsequent comments are aesthetic:

> Every such work is a *whole*, in which the fates and fortunes of the personages are
> brought to a conclusion, agreeably to the author's own preconceived idea. Every
> incident in a well written composition is introduced for a certain purpose, and
> made to forward a certain plan. . . . it is a fault in *his* composition if every
> circumstance does not answer the reasonable expectations of the reader.
> ("Origin," 1:55–56)

The "sagacious reader" actively "lays hold" on some "prominent circumstance" in the novel and interprets its meaning, often predicts the outcome
of the story: "And why does he foresee all this? Not from the real tendencies
of things, but from what he has discovered of the author's intentions"
("Origin," 1:57). Fiction, then, is an ordered arrangement by the author,
unlike real life, which is "a kind of chance-medley consisting of many un-
connected scenes," and probability is not so much related to reality as it is
to the successful execution of the novelist's design for the whole.

Not only is Mrs. Barbauld sensitive to artistic manipulation of material
behind the illusion of reality, but she is also aware of some of the problems
of narrative technique. In her earlier preface to Richardson's *Correspondence*, she had considered at length the methods of presenting the story,
suggesting that the novelist has available three narrative points of view: (1)
"narrative or epic," in which the "author relates himself the whole adventure"; (2) "memoirs," in which the "subject of the adventure relates his own
story"; and (3) "*epistolary corrrespondence*, carried on between the characters in the novel." Her analysis displays considerable insight into the limits
of each strategy. The omniscient narrator not only can "reveal the secret
springs of action" and provide "knowledge which would not properly belong to any of the characters," but can also stand as a barrier between the
fiction and the reader unless "he frequently drops himself and runs into
dialogue." The method of the "memoirs" solves the problem of the too-
intrusive narrator, communicates the "warmth and interest a person may
be supposed to feel in his own affairs," and permits the narrator to "dwell
upon minute circumstances which have affected him." Yet the first-person
narration is most difficult, for the novelist must maintain a style suitable to
the "supposed talents and capacity of the imaginary narrator," must write
under the restriction that "what the hero cannot say, the author cannot
tell," and also must create, in effect, "two characters"—the hero "at the

time of the events to be related," and, simultaneously, the hero "at the time he is relating them." She concludes that the first-person point of view is the "least perfect mode." The epistolary method gives the illusion of immediacy; it is dramatic because all characters speak "in their own persons"; it can present multiple points of view; it can even supply information furnished by the omniscient narrator through such devices as omitted or lost letters and elaborations or digressions within letters. Nevertheless, it is unlikely that letters should be so voluminously and conveniently produced and preserved so as to present a "connected story"; the "insipid confidant" is an irritating literary expedient; in sum, the epistolary method is "the most natural and the least probable way of telling a story."[11] All her remarks reveal a preference for the technique that best permits the author to "drop himself"—unless the narrator is like Fielding, in whose narrative everything is "continually heightened by the contrast between the author's style and his view of things, and the characters he is holding up to ridicule" ("Fielding," 18:v). Theoretical discussions of the various narrative points of view were rare at the time, and, as Miriam Allott comments: "It says much for Mrs. Barbauld's perspicacity that subsequent novelists' views on narrative technique coincide at so many points with hers."[12] Mrs. Barbauld does not repeat her theories on point of view in the introductory essay to *British Novelists*, but they are evident in practice in a number of the prefatory essays.

If, on the whole, Mrs. Barbauld pays more attention to defending the moral value of novels and less to novelistic theory in the introductory essay, she is at least addressing the most urgent problem her contemporaries saw in the novel. Moreover, she has more theoretical insight than one might expect. The individual prefaces to *British Novelists* similarly include much that is generalized and conventional in the way of criticism, but also a good deal that is specific and technical. Perhaps rudimentary as criticism, the prefaces also confirm Tompkins's observation that despite primary emphasis in later eighteenth-century criticism on the "moral, probability and characterization of a novel" and on style, there appeared "a growing interest in form."[13] A summing up of Mrs. Barbauld's contribution to the theory of the novel must acknowledge that her views were mostly derivative and general, yet not entirely conventional and often quite perspicacious and pointed.

It is not especially surprising that a widely read, experienced writer like Mrs. Barbauld, once she had accepted her task, could sort out and unify critical assessments of her day, particularly on a subject as congenial as novels. Somewhat more surprising is the importance she accords women writers, for her reputation today—and in her time—is not that of an ardent feminist. A spokeswoman for radical dissenters in such human rights issues as movements to repeal the Corporation and Test Acts and to abolish the slave trade, she was not notably interested in specifically feminist causes, although she numbered a few women writers among her friends—Hannah More, Joanna Baillie, and Maria Edgeworth, particularly. Her own uncomfortable experience as a remarkably well-educated woman taught her that women "ought only to have such a general tincture of knowledge as to make them agreeable companions to a man of sense"; indeed, "to have a too great fondness for books is little favorable to the happiness of a woman."[14] Her most direct comment on the feminist issue is a poem entitled "The Rights of Woman," which opens with an ironic address to "injured Woman" and concludes with the assertion that women ought to "abandon each ambitious thought" and accept the "soft maxims" of "Nature's school," which teach that "separate rights are lost in mutual love."[15] Although Mrs. Barbauld was occasionally grouped with feminists, even her political enemies knew better, as a critic for the *Anti-Jacobin Review* indicated when he disputed her inclusion in a political satire upon certain "sisters in femality" and argued, quite correctly, that Mrs. Barbauld "must reprobate with me the alarming eccentricities of Miss Wollstonecraft."[16] A. R. Humphreys has classified Mrs. Barbauld as belonging among conservative Bluestockings who "contented themselves with enhancing the prestige of women by a peaceful penetration of male preserves, rather than by blowing trumpets for independence."[17] This estimate of her position seems much more accurate than a recent study which has included Mrs. Barbauld among those who "discriminated against [their] own sex."[18]

In the *British Novelists*, if Mrs. Barbauld does not quite blow trumpets for the advent of women novelists, she comes very close to doing so. Not only does she recognize the dominance of women novelists, but she also welcomes it, as one paragraph, devoted to that point, states:

> And indeed . . . it may safely be affirmed that we have more good writers in this walk living at the present time, than at any period since the days of Richardson and Fielding. A very great proportion of these are ladies: and surely it will not be said that either taste or morals have been losers by their taking the pen in hand. The names of D'Arblay, Edgeworth, Inchbald, Radcliffe, and a number more, will vindicate the assertion. ("Origin," 1:58–59)

Several features signify Mrs. Barbauld's efforts to do justice to the women novelists. Of the twenty-one authors in *British Novelists*, eight are women, and of the twenty-eight novels, twelve are by women.[19] But it is not simply numerical apportionment that reveals her respect for these women, nor is her interest compelled by the common opinion she shares that the typical novel reader is female, often "a young woman in the retired scenes of life," for whom good novels proffer sound moral education, especially with respect to people "whom it is safer to read of than to meet" ("Origin," 1:51). Rather, the evidence is in the prefaces, in which she evaluates the work of the writers, and to some extent in the account of the history of the novel.

The recognition of women in the history of the novel is a significant point in Mrs. Barbauld's long introductory essay. Assuming realism to be the distinguishing trait of the developing novel, she marks its beginning from the period when "a closer imitation of nature began to be called for" ("Origin," 1:17). This landmark in the history of the novel is displayed by the work of Madeleine de Scudéry, along with that of La Calprenède, who "in the construction of the story, came nearer to real life" ("Origin," 1:14-15). The next important figure of the developing genre is also a woman, Mme de la Fayette, whose fiction is the first to depict truthfully "the manners of cultivated life and natural incidents related with elegance" and thereby the first to "approach the modern novel of the serious kind" ("Origin," 1:18).[20] In England, of course, she recognizes Defoe's realism as marking the beginning of the genre, after which "in the reign of George the Second, Richardson, Fielding, and Smollet, appeared in quick succession; and their success raised . . . a demand for this kind of entertainment" ("Origin," 1:38). Nevertheless, she includes male and female novelists impartially, with no divisions by gender or even by such rankings as "major" and "minor." She mentions Mrs. Behn and Mrs. Manly, citing some moral objections to their novels; more approvingly, Mrs. Haywood, Mrs. Sheridan, Mrs. West, Miss Fielding, and Mrs. Opie; and most enthusiastically, Miss Edgeworth, Miss Burney, Mrs. Inchbald, and Mrs. Radcliffe.

While not discriminating against women writers, Mrs. Barbauld does ponder the differences between men and women novelists. Women, she observes, give a more "melancholy tinge" and less humor to their works than men. The chief reason, she thinks, is circumstance: "Men, mixing at large in society, have a brisker flow of ideas." In addition, she suggests that only "the stronger powers of man" have the ability to produce humor, the "scarcer product of the mind." The product of woman's mind, in contrast, is "sentiment," resulting from the societally imposed necessity to "nurse those feelings in secrecy and silence" which men usually experience only "transiently" and "with fewer modifications of delicacy." Women, therefore, unlike men, "diversify the expression of [feelings] with endless shades of sentiment." Thus, she perceptively notes, it is isolation that gives a distinctive color to the creations of the feminine imagination ("Origin," 1:44-45).

The women whose works are represented in the collection of novels—

and who are thus treated more fully—are Clara Reeve, Charlotte Lennox, Frances Moore Brooke, Elizabeth Inchbald, Charlotte Turner Smith, Fanny Burney, Ann Radcliffe, and Maria Edgeworth—certainly a stellar group. Mrs. Barbauld deals with them justly and generously. In addition to biographical information, the prefaces include general assessments of the work of the authors and more detailed comments on a variety of matters such as structure and style and theme.

In each preface, usually at the beginning, Mrs. Barbauld summarizes in a few words the general reputation of the novelist. In the "Origin and Progress," though not applying any systematic rankings, she indicates that some novels are noteworthy for "excellence," some for "singularity," and some for moderate popularity "though not of high celebrity." These somewhat unequal categories roughly guide her overall assessments. Essentially they are subjective, but they also reflect popular critical opinions. Sometimes she evaluates in broad terms, as in the case of Clara Reeve who can claim only "a moderate degree of merit" ("Clara Reeve," 22:i), or Charlotte Lennox, who is "very respectable" ("Mrs. Lennox," 24:i), or even Fanny Burney, of whom she declares: "Scarcely any name, if any, stands higher in the list of novel-writers than that of Miss BURNEY" ("Miss Burney," 38:i). Maria Edgeworth is a novelist "fully in possession of the esteem and admiration of the public" ("Miss Edgeworth," 49:i). In other cases, style is the telling trait, as with Mrs. Brooke and Mrs. Smith, whose novels are characterized by "elegance" ("Mrs. Brooke," 27:i; "Mrs. Charlotte Smith," 36:i). Mrs. Barbauld also gives high marks for innovation. She admires Mrs. Inchbald's originality ("Mrs. Inchbald," 28:i), and especially Mrs. Radcliffe's: "Though every production which is good in its kind entitles its author to praise, a greater distinction is due to those which stand at the head of a class; and such are undoubtedly the novels of Mrs. Radcliffe—which exhibit a genius of no common stamp" ("Mrs. Radcliffe," 43:i). On the whole, Mrs. Barbauld's rankings hold good even today.

Mrs. Barbauld sometimes accords the individual elements of fiction the cursory treatment typical of the times, especially with respect to plot. For example, she complains that Frances Brooke's *Emily Montague* is not "interesting in the story" because descriptive passages predominate. But her criteria of coherence and unity are implicit in her praise of Brooke's *Lady Julia Mandeville* as a "simple, well connected story" (both in "Mrs. Brooke," 27:i) and of Clara Reeve's *Old English Baron* as a "simple and well connected" story ("Clara Reeve," 22:i). By the same standard she censures as "a fault in the story" the "unravelling" of *The Mysteries of Udolpho*, which "depends but little on the circumstances that previously engaged our attention" ("Mrs. Radcliffe," 43:v). Frederick R. Karl notes that the concept of coherent plot structures in eighteenth-century novels evolved from the effort to counteract and control the episodic nature of earlier fiction, largely by focusing more on character than on events.[21] Something of this attitude is evident in many of Mrs. Barbauld's remarks about plot. The objection to the loose episodic plot is clear in her criticism that *The Female Quixote* is "spun out too much" ("Mrs. Lennox," 24:iii). A feeling that plot should be subordinate to other elements lies behind her identification of the problem with stories characterized by the "strong charm of suspense and mystery," which is that at "the end of the story, the charm is dissolved, we have no wish to read it again" ("Mrs. Radcliffe," 43:viii).

Mrs. Barbauld's approval of the originality of the women novelists often focuses around their efforts to work out plots that center on character or theme more than events. She admires as "a new circumstance" the marital situation in Burney's *Cecilia* which "forms, very happily, the plot of the piece." She likes the characterization of the miser, Briggs, because "it is not the common idea of a miser . . . an originality is given to it" ("Miss Burney," 38:iv–v). Inchbald's "originality both in the characters and the situation" is illustrated by *A Simple Story*, which is not a *"simple story"* but "two distinct stories, connected indeed by the character of Dorriforth, which they successfully serve to illustrate" ("Mrs. Inchbald," 28:i).

Burney and Inchbald also represent laudable achievement in narrative technique. Significantly, both are praised for experimenting with points of view that conceal the authorial presence. Mrs. Barbauld praises Burney for dialogue "pointedly distinguished from the elegant and dignified style of the author herself." She is not simply addressing the issue of decorum. Fanny Burney's technique has the effect of drama: "every thing seems to pass before the reader's eyes." In *Cecilia*, for example, "We almost hear and feel the report of the pistol" ("Miss Burney," 38:iv, vi–vii). Similarly, she finds it "a particular beauty" of the novels of Elizabeth Inchbald that they are "thrown so much into the dramatic form" that there is "little of mere narrative." What Mrs. Barbauld likes is that "we see and hear the persons themselves; we are but little led to think of the author" ("Mrs. Inchbald," 28:iii).

Another example of Mrs. Barbauld's interest in the developing techniques is her responsiveness to Inchbald's manipulation of time in *A Simple Story*. "The break between the first and second parts of the story has a singularly fine effect. We pass over in a moment a large space of years, and find everything changed. . . . This sudden shifting of the scene has an effect which no continued narrative could produce; an effect which even the scenes of real life could not produce" ("Mrs. Inchbald," 28:ii). This is a remarkable concession from a proponent of realism.

Such a concession is, of course, prepared for by the discussion in the

introductory essay of the novel as an aesthetic form, determined by the
author's controlling hand in accordance with his or her design rather than
the chance-medley of real life. Mrs. Barbauld's analysis of Ann Radcliffe's
novels provides her the opportunity to illustrate her theory very clearly. As
a rationalist, she always preferred sense to sensibility, and Gothic novels
did not naturally appeal to her. Yet her recognition of Mrs. Radcliffe in one
of her longer prefaces is accorded to a writer breaking new ground and
carrying out successfully the design of the whole, no matter how different
the design is from fiction which is based in realism or how jarring some
elements seem in the execution.

   She accepts readily the assumption that Mrs. Radcliffe "seems to scorn
to move those passions which form the interests of common novels." Her
purposes are otherwise: Radcliffe "alarms the soul with terror; agitates it
with suspense, prolonged and wrought up to the most intense feeling"
("Mrs. Radcliffe," 43:i). A consequence of these different purposes is
clearly different methods. Mrs. Barbauld connects them with the idea of
the sublime and, citing Edmund Burke, praises the novelist for being able
"perfectly to understand that obscurity . . . is a strong ingredient in the
sublime" ("Mrs. Radcliffe," 43:vi). This focus on obscurity is central; it is
the reason for a setting of "vast uninhabited castles, winding stair-cases,
long echoing aisles . . . lonely heaths, gloomy forests . . . the canvass
and the figures of Salvator Rosa," or for an atmosphere of "solitude, darkness, low whispered sounds, obscure glimpses of objects" ("Mrs. Radcliffe," 43:i–ii). Characterization grows out of these assumptions, too: the
"living characters correspond to the scenery:—their wicked projects are
dark, singular, atrocious" ("Mrs. Radcliffe," 43:i). Mrs. Barbauld's main
criticism is aimed only at Mrs. Radcliffe's disruption of such unity, particularly manifest in this Gothic novelist's habit of finally revealing mysteries as
merely natural phenomena. The reader is not only disappointed at the kind
of explanation offered, but also resistant to any explanation, for the reader
has been "affected so repeatedly, the suspense has been so long protracted,
and expectations raised so high, that no explanation can satisfy, no imagery of horrors can equal the vague shapings of our imagination" ("Mrs.
Radcliffe," 43:iv–v).

   The criterion of "real life," nevertheless, weighs heavily in Mrs. Barbauld's judgment of other novelists. Thanks to a "discerning eye," Fanny
Burney "draws from life, and exhibits not only the passions of human nature, but the manners of the age and the affectations of the day" ("Fanny
Burney," 38:viii, vii). A virtue of Charlotte Smith's novels is "that they
show a knowledge of life," usually of "genteel life," but sometimes of
"common life" ("Mrs. Charlotte Smith," 36:vi, viii). Comments like these

are more usual, partly because they reflect a basic tenet, partly because when selecting representative novels, Mrs. Barbauld chose novels grounded in realism.

Mrs. Barbauld's essays are full of comments on a miscellany of fictional elements, for she is not a systematic critic. She likes good beginnings, which, as in Radcliffe's *The Sicilian Romance*, remind her of "the tuning of an instrument by a skillful hand" ("Mrs. Radcliffe," 43:v). She dislikes improbable or protracted endings, and she dislikes ambiguous endings, such as those in Fanny Burney's later novels, for though it is "true that in human life" one cannot "say whether the story ends happily or unhappily," in fiction there should be no doubt ("Miss Burney," 38:v–vi). On the other hand, though certainly a moralist herself, Mrs. Barbauld does not like novels that preach or teach too much, a fault she finds in Mrs. Inchbald's *Nature and Art*, which seems to her less a novel than a vehicle for "reflections on the political and moral state of society" ("Mrs. Inchbald," 28:iii). Moreover, Mrs. Barbauld may seem to give first importance to the "very moral and instructive story of the *Harrels*," for example, but her elaboration of the comment gives greater weight to Burney's ability to dramatize effectively the theme of "the mean rapacity of the fashionable spendthrift" ("Miss Burney," 38:vi). Inappropriate tone jars Mrs. Barbauld's sensibility, as, for example, the "bitter and querulous tone of complaint" that pervades much of the unhappy Charlotte Smith's writings ("Mrs. Charlotte Smith," 36:ii). Similarly, she objects to the "low humour" which "strongly characterizes, sometimes perhaps blemishes," Burney's "genius" ("Miss Burney," 38:iii). She personally enjoys both the "beauties of description" and original verse at which some of these writers excel—Smith, Brooke, and Radcliffe, particularly—but she thinks these elements are a hindrance to "a novel of high interest." On the other hand, such decorative passages may be "very properly placed, at judicious intervals, in compositions of which variety rather than deep pathos, and elegance rather than strength, are the characteristics" ("Mrs. Charlotte Smith," 35:vi–viii). Again, these elements are judged in terms of the whole design.

Mrs. Barbauld has never received adequate credit for her work as a critic. Yet she fully appreciated the novel and argued skillfully for its status as an important literary form. Although her theories about realistic representation of character, coherent plot structure, the design of the whole, dramatic narrative techniques, and moral tendency were not at all original, they were nowhere else at the time brought together; nor was there a single, extensive, thorough defense of the novel such as hers. But Mrs. Barbauld had always championed the novel, even as a young writer, for one of her earliest essays argues from the same premise that undergirds her later defense of the novel, that it "exhibits life in its true state" and that "every one can relish the author who represents common life because every one can refer to the originals from whence his ideas were taken."[22] Her history of fiction is important as an attempt to give the novel the prestige of literary tradition, then still a relatively rare concept, and it is a creditable history, even by today's standards.

Finally, Mrs. Barbauld leaves no doubts about the significant role of women in the development of this still young and mistrusted literary form, which, nonetheless, calls upon "talents of the highest order" ("Origin," 1:3). The introductory essay displays her appreciation of women writers throughout, not only by her references to English novelists, but also by her knowledgeable observations about various contemporary French women novelists, such as the Comtesse de Genlis, Sophie Cottin, Mme de Staël, Marie Jeanne Riccoboni, and Mme Élie de Beaumont. Subtly emphatic is her casual manner of giving the works of male and female novelists equal billing: "Many a young woman has caught from such works as *Clarissa* and *Cecilia*, ideas of delicacy and refinement" ("Origin," 1:48). At other times she simply offers women novelists as typical examples of responsible authorship: "The more severe and homely virtues of prudence and oeconomy have been enforced in the writings of a Burney and an Edgeworth" ("Origin," 1:50). Admirable, too, is Mrs. Barbauld's sensitivity to the different but powerful direction represented by Mrs. Radcliffe's novels. The more detailed analysis of the novels of Radcliffe and Burney signify the higher estimate she accords their work. She does a service, however, to all the women novelists, for she praises them freely and criticizes them seriously. She honestly ponders their distinctions both as novelists and as women novelists, and she grants them their own value as serious writers. Her introductory tribute to the work of the "ladies" who were "taking the pen in hand" is a fitting preamble to the critical and biographical prefaces which follow. They constitute a remarkable, enlightened, and even, to some degree, systematic criticism of the eighteenth-century novel and perhaps the first extended criticism of the woman novelist.

NOTES

1. [Anna Laetitia Barbauld], *An Essay on the Origin and Progress of Novel-Writing and Prefaces Biographical and Critical, from the British Novelists* (London: F. C. & J. Rivington, 1810), 61. This unique volume in the Library of Congress is made up of the essays taken from the fifty-volume set and bound into a single volume, retaining the original volume numbering and pagination, but using a var-

iant title. "An Essay on the Origin and Progress of Novel-Writing," 1:1–62, is in part a verbatim copy of Mrs. Barbauld's earlier preface to *The Correspondence of Samuel Richardson*, 6 vols. (London: Richard Phillips, 1804), but it also contains much additional material. Subsequent references to the "Essay on the Origin and Progress of Novel-Writing" ("Origin") and to the prefaces to individual novelists will appear in parentheses in the text.

2. The authors and novels, listed in order of appearance, are these: Richardson, *The History of Clarissa Harlow* and *The History of Sir Charles Grandison*; Defoe, *The Life and Surprising Adventures of Robinson Crusoe*; Fielding, *The History of the Adventures of Joseph Andrews* and *The History of Tom Jones*; Reeve, *The Old English Baron*; Walpole, *The Castle of Otranto*; Coventry, *The History of Pompey the Little*; Goldsmith, *The Vicar of Wakefield*; Lennox, *The Female Quixote*; Johnson, *Rasselas, Prince of Abissinia*; Hawkesworth, *Almoral and Hamet*; Brooke, *The History of Lady Julia Mandeville*; Inchbald, *Nature and Art* and *A Simple Story*; Mackenzie, *Julia de Roubigné* and *The Man of Feeling*; Smollett, *The Expedition of Humphry Clinker*; Graves, *The Spiritual Quixote*; Moore, *Zeluco*; Smith, *The Old Manor House*; Burney, *Evelina* and *Cecilia*; Radcliffe, *Romance of the Forest* and *The Mysteries of Udolpho*; Bage, *Hermsprong, or Man as He Is Not*; Edgeworth, *Belinda* and *Modern Griselda*. Only the two novels by Edgeworth were published in the nineteenth century; all the others are eighteenth-century novels. Sterne is discussed at some length in the introductory essay ("Origin," 1:40–42).

3. Lucy Aikin, ed., *The Works of Anna Laetitia Barbauld, with a Memoir*, 2 vols. (London: Longman, Hurst, Rees, Orme, Brown & Green, 1825). 1:xliii–xliv.

4. For an exception see Miriam Allott, *Novelists on the Novel* (New York: Columbia University Press, Columbia Paperback, 1966), xv. Allott states: "I have included one writer, Mrs. Anna Barbauld, who is not a novelist, for her admirable and too much neglected editorial work in her series, *British Novelists*."

5. Byron Hall Gibson, "The History from 1800 to 1832 of English Criticism of Prose Fiction: Part 1, English Criticism of Prose Fiction from 1800–1814" (Ph.D. diss., University of Illinois, 1931), no pagination.

6. J. M. S. Tompkins, *The Popular Novel in England, 1770–1800* (Lincoln: University of Nebraska Press, Bison Books, 1961), 1.

7. Robert D. Mayo, *The English Novel in the Magazines, 1740–1815* (Evanston, Ill.: Northwestern University Press, 1962), 265. W. F. Galloway, Jr., "Conservative Attitudes Toward Fiction, 1770–1830," *Publications of the Modern Language Association of America* 55 (December 1940): 1041–59, states that although Mrs. Barbauld "defended a few exceptional novelists . . . she was compelled to conclude that most novels were trivial and a waste of time" (1049). In fact, she concedes the trivial and worthless only to build her case for the value of novels as a genre.

8. On the state of the novel at the end of the eighteenth century, see Tompkins, *Popular Novel*, 1–33; Mayo, *English Novel in the Magazines*, 262–72; and John Tinnon Taylor, *Early Opposition to the English Novel: The Popular Reaction from 1760 to 1830* (New York: King's Crown, 1943), 1–20. See also Joseph Bunn Heidler,

The History from 1700 to 1800 of English Criticism of Prose Fiction, University of Illinois Studies in Language and Literature, vol. 13 (Urbana, Ill.: University of Illinois Press, 1928).

9. On the issue of edification versus entertainment, see Mayo, *English Novel in the Magazines*, 265–66, and Taylor, *Early Opposition to the English Novel*, 88–89, 111–12.

10. Frederick R. Karl, *The Adversary Literature: The English Novel in the Eighteenth Century: A Study of Genre* (New York: Farrar, Straus & Giroux, 1974), 326–27.

11. Anna Laetitia Barbauld, ed., *The Correspondence of Samuel Richardson, Selected from the Original Manuscripts, To Which Are Prefixed, a Biographical Account of That Author, and Observations on His Writing*, 6 vols. (London: Richard Phillips, 1804; reprint, New York: AMS Press, 1966), 1:xxiii–xxviii.

12. Allott, *Novelists on the Novel*, 187.

13. Tompkins, *Popular Novel*, 330.

14. Aikin, *Works of Anna Laetitia Barbauld*, 1:xvii–xix.

15. *Ibid.*, 1:185–87.

16. Review of *The Unsexed Females; A Poem: Addressed to the Author of "The Pursuits of Literature,"* *Anti-Jacobin Review* 3 (May 1799): 27–29.

17. A. R. Humphreys, "The 'Rights of Woman' in the Age of Reason," *Modern Language Review* 41 (July 1946): 261–62.

18. Lynn Agress, *The Feminine Irony: Women on Women in Early Nineteenth-Century English Literature* (Rutherford, N.J.: Fairleigh Dickinson University Press, 1978), 110.

19. The eight prefaces, which will be cited in the text, are the following "Clara Reeve," 22:i–iii; "Mrs. Lennox," 24:i–iv; "Mrs. Brooke," 27:i–iii; "Mrs. Inchbald," 28:i–iii; "Mrs. Charlotte Smith," 36:i–viii; "Miss Burney," 38:i–xi; "Mrs. Radcliffe," 43:i–viii; and "Miss Edgeworth," 49:i. The last title is not really a prefatory essay but merely a note identifying the two Edgeworth novels to follow and stating that comments on the "excellencies" of the author would be "superfluous." Edgeworth revised *Belinda* for this edition and was corresponding regularly with Mrs. Barbauld at that time.

20. A more typical comment about these seventeenth-century French authors and their heroic romances is that of Walter Allen, *The English Novel: A Short Critical History* (New York: E. P. Dutton, Dutton Paperback, 1954), 16, who sees their "high-flown artificiality" as the opposite of realism. On the other hand, Ernest A. Baker, *The History of the English Novel: The Later Romances and the Establishment of Realism* (London: H. F. & G. Witherby, 1929), 25–27, seems to agree with Mrs. Barbauld's recognition of "real life" in such traits as the "verisimilitude" of a "reasonable psychology," "complicated but carefully articulated plots," and convincing depiction of "the mental atmosphere of the salons."

21. Karl, *Adversary Literature*, 318–27.

22. Barbauld, "On Romances: An Imitation," *Works of Anna Laetitia Barbauld*, 2:171–75. This essay in style and partially in content is an imitation of Samuel Johnson's essay on the same subject in the *Rambler*, 4. Mrs. Barbauld's

essay was originally published in a collection of her brother's and her own prose pieces: J. & A. L. Aikin, *Miscellaneous Pieces, in Prose* (London: Joseph Johnson, 1773). Heidler, *History from 1700 to 1800*, 132–33, treats this essay as the "most pertinent criticism on the novel in general critical works of this period [1765–1778]."

The Modern Reader and the
"Truly Feminine Novel," 1660–1815
A Critical Reading List

ROGER D. LUND

In a critique of Mrs. Elizabeth Norman's *The Child of Woe. A Novel* (1789), the *Analytical Review* (February 1789)[1] remarked that having no other virtues to recommend it, the book could only be termed "a truly feminine novel," the "generality" of which were "so near akin to each other, that with a few trifling alterations, the same review would serve for almost all of them." The *Analytical Review*'s rather arch dismissal of novels by women has all too often been reflected in the histories of English fiction, where it has been popular to view the rise of the novel as the exclusive history of "*les cinq grands*" (McKillop's phrase for Defoe, Richardson, Fielding, Smollett, and Sterne) and to ignore or at best to minimize the contributions of eighteenth-century women novelists. Serious readers of eighteenth-century fiction have finally come to admit, however, that the realistic novel did not spring Athena-like from the head of Richardson, but was the child of many parents and the outgrowth of narrative techniques and fictional conventions first developed by writers of popular fiction, many of them women. In short, literary historians and critics have begun to give eighteenth-century women novelists their due, a process of reassessment outlined in the following annotated reading list. Of course, such a review must necessarily be selective. Because of space constraints, I have included only those works published within the last twenty years or so, a period in which the rise of women's studies has converged with the growing interest in eighteenth-century fiction. In addition, I have chosen to emphasize those books and articles that most clearly articulate the relationships between women novelists themselves, or which serve to clarify their contributions to the development of the novel in general. Taken together, these modern responses to the "feminine novel" suggest that in one sense the *Analytical Review* was right; women novelists of the eighteenth century were "akin to each other," sharing common interests, common themes, common techniques, and as women of the eighteenth century, a common fate. But the *Analytical Review* was also quite mistaken; for if, as popular writers, eighteenth-century women produced a large body of eminently forgettable (if not unreadable) works, modern readers remind us that eighteenth-century women novelists also created an abundance of works marked by their quality and originality, as well as their historical interest. If nothing else, the sheer variety of modern responses to the "feminine novel" proves beyond question that never again will the same review "serve for almost all of them."

There will be general agreement, I suspect, that among the greatest contributions to the growing interest in eighteenth-century women novelists have been the various Garland Reprint Series which have made accessible for the first time dozens of works by women writers previously obtainable only in the largest research libraries. Of particular value as well has been the publication of *An Annotated Bibliography of Twentieth-Century Critical Studies of Women and Literature, 1660–1800*, edited by Paula Backsheider and Felicity Nussbaum (New York and London: Garland, 1977). To these one might add a number of other studies of women and the novel relevant to the subject here, among them Hazel Mews's *Frail Vessels: Woman's Role in Women's Novels from Fanny Burney to George Eliot* (London: Athlone Press, 1969) and Anthea Zeman's *Presumptuous Girls: Women and Their World in the Serious Woman's Novel* (London: Weidenfeld and Nicolson, 1977), both of which provide discussions of Burney, Edgeworth, and Austen. Madeleine Blondel's *Images de la femme dans le roman anglais de 1740 à 1771*, 2 vols (Paris: H. Champion, 1976) offers a wealth of miscellaneous information about women and the novel, while Janet M. Todd's *Women's Friendship in Literature* (New York: Columbia University Press, 1980) outlines the "form and ideology" of sentimental, erotic, manipulative, political, and social friendships between women as represented in novels by Haywood, Lennox, Burney, Scott, and Manley. Worthy of special notice is the recently published *Women, Power, and Subversion: Social Strategies in British Fiction, 1778–1860* (Athens: University of Georgia Press, 1981) by Judith Lowder Newton, a complex and carefully crafted examination of the theme of women's power and influence as it emerges (often in covert and cleverly disguised ways) in novels by women, Burney and Austen in particular. Finally, we come to two excellent anthologies: *The Female Spectator: English Women Writers before 1800*, edited by Mary R. Mahl and Helene Koon (Bloomington: Indiana University Press; Old Westbury, NY: Feminist Press, 1977), and Katherine M. Rogers's *Before Their Time: Six Women Writers of the Eighteenth Century* (New York: Ungar, 1976).

Among recent studies treating the peculiar status of women in eighteenth-century fiction, several deserve special notice as well. In " 'Only a Boy': Notes on Sentimental Novels," *Genre* 10 (1977): 501–27, G.A. Starr points out that whereas the relative weakness and passivity of the man of feeling as a central character created problems for writers of sentimental novels, the "glorification of sentimental heroines posed no such artistic or ideological challenge as the idealization of sentimental heroes," since they are not expected to develop or attain their independence in the same ways that a hero would. Susan Staves carefully examines one of the central themes of eighteenth-century fiction in "British Seduced Maidens," *Eighteenth-Century Studies* 14 (1980–81): 109–34, while Dieter Schulz discusses one of the age's most familiar character types, the coquette, in "The Coquette's Progress from Satire to Sentimental Novel," *Literatur in Wissenschaft* 6 (1973): 77–87. R.F. Brissenden's *Virtue in Distress: Studies in the Novel of Sentiment from Richardson to Sade* (New York: Barnes & Noble, 1974) explores the aesthetic and philosophical premises of that benevolism and sentimentalism which so heavily influenced eighteenth-century fiction, and in particular gauges the significance of the theme of distressed heroism in the novel. Brissenden concludes that sentimental heroes/heroines suffer because they refuse to compromise their principles, but also because they "are somehow necessarily weak." And according to Brissenden, the vulnerability of virtue in a corrupt world is particularly acute when the character in question is a woman. This fundamental weakness experienced by eighteenth-century heroines (the necessity of influencing the men around them by tears, fainting, or violence) is explored in even greater detail by Paula R. Backscheider in "Woman's Influence," *Studies in the Novel* 11 (1979): 3–22. In *Feminism in Eighteenth-Century England* (Urbana, Chicago, London: University of Illinois Press, 1982), Katherine M. Rogers provides a sort of Baedeker to the "feminist feeling in practically all the innumerable women writers of the period, even the most timid and conventional." In the chapter devoted to the "Feminine Novel," Rogers discusses the importance of this new literary form as a vehicle for female wish-fulfillment, where women characters "enjoyed freedom real women never had," but which also adumbrated a whole realm of other submerged feminist values. Particularly useful is the "Appendix: Women Writers in Britain, 1660–1800" containing brief biographies of over eighty women writers.

Nowhere, however, is the position of women in the eighteenth century, their quest for identity, their sense of isolation and uncertainty about themselves, more clearly or more eloquently articulated than in a series of works by Patricia Meyer Spacks. In *The Female Imagination* (New York: Alfred A. Knopf, 1975) she traces characteristic themes of adolescent heroism, of "self-control and concealment" in works by Burney and Austen. In "Every Woman is at Heart a Rake," *Eighteenth-Century Studies* 8 (1974–75): 27–46, Spacks explores women's attitudes towards their own sexuality and the "ambiguities of women's condition," in particular the demands for feminine innocence so prevalent in novels written by women. In *Imagining a Self: Autobiography and the Novel in Eighteenth-Century England* (Cambridge: Harvard University Press, 1976) Spacks argues that eighteenth-century women writers employed "the writing of novels to affirm the social order that limits them." Such fiction simultaneously provides a kind of wish fulfillment while it reemphasizes such restrictions on women's freedom as the necessity of marriage, a punitive and absolute sexual morality, and a long-inculcated sense of their own weakness and helplessness. Women's novels express in various ways the "energy of defeat," and yet female novelists "upholding the established system, find images and actions to express profound ambivalence," about that system, narrative patterns and complexities of feeling that often contradict the didactic moral. Beneath the surface of novels by women, moreover, there is always the possibility of latent female anger and the implicit recognition of women's plight. As if by a kind of private language, "through the conventions of romance women tell themselves and one another the meaning of their fate."

The purely historical importance of early women novelists is emphasized by Dieter Schulz in " 'Novel,' 'Romance,' and Popular Fiction in the First Half of the Eighteenth Century," *Studies in Philology* 70 (1973): 77–91, and by Jerry C. Beasley, "English Fiction in the 1740's: Some Glances at the Major and Minor Novels," *Studies in the Novel* 5 (1973): 151–73. The influence and importance of eighteenth-century popular fiction has been most fully explored, however, in three well-known studies: Robert Adams Day's *Told in Letters: Epistolary Fiction before Richardson* (Ann Arbor: University Michigan Press, 1966), Ruth Perry's *Women, Letters, and the Novel* (New York: AMS Press, 1980), and John J. Richetti's *Popular Fiction before Richardson: Narrative Patterns, 1700–1739* (Oxford: Clarendon Press, 1969). *Told in Letters* is, of course, the point of departure for any study of the epistolary tradition in English fiction. Based upon a wide reading of various epistolary forms (an appendix lists over two hundred examples of letter fiction written between 1660 and 1740) the book provides a generic study of the kinds and uses of letters—real letters, fictional letters, found letters, letters from the dead to the living—which coalesced in the epistolary novel, and it discusses those epistolary techniques—writing to the moment, writing in dialect and so forth—which were to be absorbed into realistic fiction generally.

Where Day emphasizes the formal development of the epistolary novel,

Ruth Perry focuses on the social and economic matrix which gave rise to the novel of letters, and that made it a form peculiarly suited to the interests of women who seemed to have a "special affinity for this personal one-to-one format." *Women, Letters, and the Novel* argues that epistolary fiction came most easily to women because it "required no formal education," and because letter writing was "one of the few kinds of writing which had long been encouraged in women." Alienated from a society which denied their economic and political rights, women became increasingly isolated, an isolation strongly reflected in the epistolary novel, where women are consistently cut off from immediate contact with others and even forcibly imprisoned, having only pen and paper to provide a lifeline to the greater world of human affairs. The purpose of letters then, is "not to communicate anything but to slake some psychological thirst for externalized consciousness." Thus the written word does not merely express relationships; it brings them into being. According to Perry, the epistolary novel also made possible a new kind of heroine, "literate, isolated, unhappy—who symbolized in a purer form the dilemmas of the current culture than the heroines of earlier romances and epics," heroines who assumed that their highest happiness lay in marriage and who perpetuated the myth of romance by allowing ordinary readers to participate in the fantasy.

The sharing of such fantasies is the subject of Richetti's *Popular Fiction before Richardson*, a study examining the psychological "uses" of fiction by a mass audience which saw in the popular novel a source of escapist fantasies that would "allow pleasurable identification and projection." Preeminent among these fantasies was "the fable of persecuted innocence" exploited by such novelists as Eliza Haywood and Delariviere Manley. According to Richetti, Manley's *romans à clef* succeeded so well because they drew upon the myth of "the destruction of female innocence by a representative of the aristocratic world of male corruption," allowing readers "to participate vicariously in an erotically exciting and glittering fantasy world of aristocratic corruption and promiscuity." Haywood, whose interests were less political than sensational, repeated the same underlying fable of persecuted innocence, the same "erotic-pathetic clichés, and the same rhetoric of love's power," in order to imply the existence of a "tragic and compulsive dramatic universe" where all heroines are "victims of a world which sees them simply as opportunities for lust and avarice." Penelope Aubin, Jane Barker, and Elizabeth Rowe invert these same narrative patterns and conventions, but for more salutary purposes. For Aubin "the major purpose of her consistent combination of fictional patterns is to provide the ideological satisfactions of innocence preserved and atheism confuted," while Barker's heroines serve as pristine moral exemplars whose actions only gain meaning against the backdrop of a "moral world outlined by the ideology of beleaguered virtue." In his remarks on Rowe (first published as "Mrs. Elizabeth Rowe: The Novel as Polemic," *PMLA* 82 (1967): 522–29), Richetti argues that she molds the romantic clichés of the novella and the scandalous history into "fiction which is essentially a dramatization of the plight of an embattled and self-consciously 'virtuous' individual in a hostile and innately vicious world." By developing the oppositions between religion and infidelity, embattled virtue and conspicuous vice, "the English novel derives the ideological matrix in which Richardson's Clarissa may be said to achieve a heroism close to sainthood."

To these works by Day, Perry, and Richetti, one must add Jerry C. Beasley's *Novels of the 1740s* (Athens: University of Georgia Press, 1982). Although Beasley is primarily concerned with the major novelists of the decade 1740–1750, he pays particular attention to the importance of such novelists as Jane Barker, Penelope Aubin, Eliza Haywood, Mary Davys and Mary Collyer and their contribution to the development of the various forms of eighteenth-century popular fiction. A number of other scholars and critics have produced more specialized studies of the popular women novelists of the late seventeenth and early eighteenth centuries. Henry F. Strecher, *Elizabeth Singer Rowe, the Poetess of Frome: A Study in Eighteenth-Century English Pietism* (Bern and Frankfurt: Herbert Lang and Peter Lang, 1973) provides a useful chronology of Rowe's career and a list of editions of all her works printed in English. Robert Adams Day provides introductions to Catherine Trotter's *Olinda's Adventures: Or, The Amours of a Young Lady* (Los Angeles: Augustan Reprint Society, 1969) and Mary Davys's *Familiar Letters Betwixt a Gentleman and a Lady* (Los Angeles: Augustan Reprint Society, 1955), both of which, according to Day, are marked by their wit and a mature realism that anticipates the development of the English domestic and realistic novel, arguments more fully elaborated by William H. McBurney in "Mrs. Mary Davys: Forerunner of Fielding," *PMLA* 74 (1959): 348–55. McBurney also discusses the importance of Penelope Aubin and Jane Barker in "Mrs. Penelope Aubin and the Early Eighteenth-Century English Novel," *Huntington Library Quarterly* 20 (1956–57): 245–67, and in "Edmund Curll, Mrs. Jane Barker, and the English Novel," *Philological Quarterly* 37 (1958): 385–99. Aubin's position as the first popular Roman Catholic novelist of the eighteenth century is explored in Roger B. Dooley's "Penelope Aubin, Forgotten Catholic Novelist," *Renascence* 11, no. 2 (1959): 65–71. "The Sincerest Form of Flattery: Imitation in the Early Eighteenth-Century Novel," *South Atlantic Quarterly* 70 (1971): 248–55, by Michael F. Shugrue explores the degree to which novels by Barker, Aubin and Haywood consciously imitated the themes and conventions of such popular genres as crime narratives and such popular novels as *Robinson Crusoe*.

Considerably more attention has been paid to the life and works of Delariviere Manley in recent years. Patricia Köster's "Delariviere Manley and the *DNB*: A Cautionary Tale About Following Black Sheep, with a Challenge to Cataloguers," *Eighteenth-Century Life* 3 (1977): 106–11; and "New Light on Maria Williamina Manley," *Philological Quarterly* 57 (1978): 133–36 (a response to Henry L. Snyder's "New Light on Mrs. Manley," *Philological Quarterly* 52 [1973]: 767–70); as well as Calhoun Winton's "Steele, Mrs. Manley, and John Lacy," *Philological Quarterly* 42 (1963): 272–75, all help to clarify Manley's rather murky biography. To this list one must add the reprint of the *Memoirs of the Life of Mrs. Manley* . . . (1717) (New York: AMS Press, 1976). Of course the best source of information about Manley and her works is Patricia Köster's extensive critical introduction to *The Novels of Mary Delariviere Manley*, 2 vols. (Gainesville: Scholars' Facsimiles & Reprints, 1971). In addition to these studies, one might note two recent articles focusing on Manley's significance as an early feminist. In "Humanism, Feminism, Sensationalism: Mrs. Manley vs. Society," *Transactions of the Samuel Johnson Society of the Northwest* 4 (1972): 42–53, Patricia Köster examines the theme of women's education in Manley's novels, *Almyna, or the Arabian Vow* (1706) in particular. A far less enlightening article is Dolores Polomo's "A Woman Writer and the Scholars: A Review of Mary Manley's Reputation," *Women and Literature* 6, no. 1 (1978): 36–46, a rather tendentious argument which insists that Manley's reputation as a scandalous writer results from the insensitivity of male critics, and asserts in apparent defiance of the evidence that the sexual explicitness of Manley's fiction is not intentionally prurient but only "a knowing parody of romance style."

A happier performance is George Woodcock's "Mary Manley and Eliza Haywood," *Room of One's Own* 2, no. 4 (1977): 49–65, which compares these two writers with Aphra Behn. Several other articles on Eliza Haywood should also be noted. "Mme. De Gomez and La Belle Assemblée," *Revue de Litterature Comparée* 34 (1960): 212–25 by Charles C. Mish, and "Crébillon Fils, Mrs. Eliza Haywood and *Les heureux orphelins*: A Problem of Authorship," *Romance Notes* 11 (1969–70): 326–32 by John P. Kent discuss Haywood's borrowings from and contributions to the works of other women novelists. Helene Koon, "Eliza Haywood and the *Female Spectator*," *Huntington Library Quarterly* 42 (1978–79): 43–55 defends Haywood's skills as a journalist and praises her for her unique contribution to eighteenth-century periodical literature, while John R. Elwood, "Henry Fielding and Eliza Haywood: A Twenty Year War," *Albion* 5, no. 3 (1973):

184–92 reviews the injuries (both real and imagined) that Fielding presumably inflicted upon Haywood thus inciting her to attack him in *The History of Betsy Thoughtless*. Haywood's heroines are briefly discussed in Mary Anne Schofield's "Expose of the Popular Heroine: The Female Protagonists of Eliza Haywood," *Studies in Eighteenth-Century Culture* 12 (1983): 93–103, a subject treated in fuller form in Schofield's *Quiet Rebellion: The Fictional Heroines of Eliza Fowler Haywood* (Washington, D.C.: University Press of America, 1982), the most extensive and sympathetic treatment of Haywood's achievement as a popular novelist. Schofield provides a "taxonomy" of Haywood's many heroines who, taken together, offer "the most accurate and comprehensive presentation of the question of woman in the early decades of the eighteenth century." According to Schofield, all of Haywood's heroines merge into one portrait of the "sexually exploited and victimized eighteenth-century woman," and what emerges from this vast array of novels and romances is an "almost mythic female" who represents "woman's fall from innocence into the world of experience." While Haywood could be considered as an early feminist who dealt consistently with the problems of women, she could only explore those problems indirectly and "surreptitiously, under cover of romance techniques and modes."

Of all the popular women novelists of the late seventeenth and early eighteenth centuries, however, none has excited more interest among modern scholars than Aphra Behn, and much of the energy devoted to Behn studies has been directed toward dispelling the myths surrounding Behn's biography and defending the "realism" of her novels. Ruthe T. Sheffey's "Some Evidence for a New Source of Aphra Behn's *Oroonoko*," *Studies in Philology* 59 (1962): 52–63; R.A. Ramsaran's "*Oroonoko*: A Study of the Factual Elements," *Notes and Queries* 205 (1960): 142–45; H.A. Hargreaves's "New Evidence of the Realism of Mrs. Behn's *Oroonoko*," *Bulletin of the New York Public Library* 74 (1970); 437–44; "The Birth of Mrs. Behn," *Humanities Association Review* 16, no. 1 (1965): 19–20; and "A Case for Mister Behn," *Notes and Queries* 207 (1962): 203–05, all fall into this category. Of greater note is Robert Adams Day's article "Aphra Behn's First Biography," *Studies in Bibliography* 22 (1969): 227–40 which works out the detailed publishing history of Behn's "Life and Memoirs," and suggests that they were probably written by Behn herself. *New Light on Aphra Behn* (University of Auckland, 1961) by W.J. Cameron carefully traces Behn's adventures in Surinam and Flanders and includes reprints of nineteen documents from the Public Records Office, many originally written in Behn's own hand, related to her activities in Flanders.

Three full-length studies of Behn have also been recently published:

Frederick M. Link, *Aphra Behn* (New York: Twayne, 1968); Maureen Duffy, *The Passionate Shepherdess: Aphra Behn, 1640–89* (London: Jonathan Cape, 1977); and Angeline Goreau, *Reconstructing Aphra: A Social Biography of Aphra Behn* (New York: Dial Press, 1980). None of these biographies treats Behn's novels at any length or takes them seriously as works of fiction. Link, who seems primarily concerned with Behn's career as a dramatist, provides brief plot summaries of several of her novels, but concludes that "she made no significant contribution to the development of the form, and even her role in the sentimental and primitivist movements has been exaggerated." Unfortunately, Duffy and Goreau add little more to our appreciation of Behn the novelist. Written for a popular audience, Duffy's biography traces Behn's career in some detail, but she treats all Behn's works (both fictional and dramatic) as veiled autobiography, reveals only the most general knowledge of Restoration literature, and provides no clear estimate of Behn's place in the literary life of her time. *Reconstructing Aphra* seems more carefully researched than Duffy's biography, but it traces much the same route, discussing the novels merely as autobiographical documents. Goreau's claims to have written "a new kind of biography" seem overstated, but she does describe the importance of Behn's social context, reconstructing what it meant for Behn to be a woman writer in the seventeenth century, working out the social, marital, educational and economic options that Behn would have had as a woman in the strange profession of writing. In short, Goreau tries to recreate not merely the events but the texture of Behn's life, and does so successfully.

Although the primary interest in Behn's career has focused on the exciting events of her flamboyant life or on her acomplishments as a playwright, a few critics have examined the specific features of Behn's fiction. In "Aphra Behn and the First Epistolary Novel in English," *Publications of the Arkansas Philological Association* 3, no. 2 (1977): 29–33, Carol A. Lindquist discusses the significance of *Love Letters between a Nobleman and His Sister*, while Gary Kelly traces the French sources of Behn's fiction in " 'Intrigue' and 'Gallantry': The Seventeenth-Century French *Nouvelle* and the 'Novels' of Aphra Behn," *Revue de Litterature Comparée* 55 (1981): 184–94. Martine Watson Brownley defends Behn's narrative technique in "The Narrator in *Oroonoko*," *Essays in Literature* 4 (1977): 174–81, arguing that the personal narrative voice "unifies the novel, enhances the tenuous realism of the basically heroic story, and offers a viable standard of judgment for the readers." This argument is seconded by Lore Metzger whose introduction to the Norton Library Edition of *Oroonoko, or, The Royal Slave* (New York: Norton, 1973) praises Behn's narrative technique for its "flexibility," fusing "romance motifs with novelistic verisimilitude," blending the marvelous and the familiar. Perhaps the most challenging interpretation of *Oroonoko* is George Guffey's "*Oroonoko*: Occasion and Accomplishment," in *Two English Novelists: Aphra Behn and Anthony Trollope* (Los Angeles: William Andrews Clark Memorial Library, 1975), which interprets the novel as a subtle but clearly recognizable political allegory defending monarchy, and draws a parallel between the fate of the slave "Caesar" and the imperiled position of James II in 1688, the year of *Oroonoko's* publication.

Behn's place as a feminist writer is the subject of three excellent articles. In "Aphra Behn: The Poet's Heart in a Woman's Body," *Papers on Language & Literature* 14 (1978): 414–24, Larry Carver concentrates on the woman's point of view in Behn's novels and prefaces, while Judith Kegan Gardiner's "Aphra Behn: Sexuality and Self-Respect," *Women's Studies* 7, nos. 1 & 2 (1980): 67–78, suggests that Behn's single dominant theme is "human sexuality—its powers and problems," and argues that Behn's conscious adoption of the cavalier pose "helps her define an autonomous position for herself as a bright, sexually-active woman." This ambiguity of roles is discussed by Robert Adams Day in a far more ambitious essay, "Muses in the Mud: The Female Wits Anthropologically Considered," *Women's Studies* 7 (1980): 61–74. Day argues that such early novelists as Aphra Behn, Catherine Trotter, and Delariviere Manley were rejected by society for much the same reasons that traditional systems of taboo label certain activities and persons unclean. In a sense, these women were writing in genres which were not part of the sacred system and made a living "by a profession which, though not criminal, was new, unclassified, and therefore taboo."

If the period before Richardson and Fielding was one of exploration and innovation for women novelists, the period following was largely one of elaboration on established models. As Robert B. Pierce points out in "Moral Education in the Novel of the 1750's," *Philological Quarterly* 44 (1965): 73–87, the main question confronting the novelists of the mid-eighteenth century was that of depicting character development and moral education, as heroes and heroines endowed with innate good nature, courage, and sensibility learned prudence by their entrance into the world. Although it is a rough generalization to be sure, one might argue that such novelists as Sarah Fielding, Sarah Scott, Frances Sheridan, Frances Brooke and Charlotte Lennox all follow this pattern to some degree in their novels. This is the contention of Gerard A. Barker in "*David Simple*: The Novel of Sensibility in Embryo," *Modern Language Studies* 12, no. 2 (1982): 69–80, who suggests that Sarah Fielding's novel reveals the "complex impact that benevolence and sensibility, ideals embodied in the Man of Feeling, were destined to have on the novel." In his introduction to *The Adventures of David Simple* (London: Oxford University Press, 1969), Malcolm Kelsall also stresses the moralism and naiveté of Fielding's writing. This same moral earnestness suffuses Sarah Scott's best-known novel, *A Description of Millenium Hall*, edited with an introduction by Walter M. Crittenden (New York: Bookman Associates, 1955). In "Sarah Scott: A Reconsideration," *Coranto* 9, no. 1 (1973): 9–15, L.M. Grow remarks on the "unremitting tendentiousness" of the novel, finding in Scott's letters (part of the Elizabeth Montagu Collection of the Huntington Library) those "devices conspicuously absent from her fiction: humor, figurative language, and the beginnings of satire," hints suggesting that Scott's time might have been better spent had she not insisted upon the creation of such exemplary fictions.

The works of Frances Sheridan and Frances Brooke have also been rediscovered by recent scholars. Norma H. Russell, "Some Uncollected Authors, XXXVIII: Frances Sheridan, 1724–1766," *Book Collector* 13 (1964): 196–205, provides a brief biographical sketch of Sheridan's life as well as a valuable checklist of her works, while *The History of Nourjahad* has been reprinted in a facsimile edition with a critical introduction by Maurice Johnson (n.p.: Norwood Editions, 1977). Sheridan's influence on Goldsmith has been briefly noted as well by Morris Golden in "Sidney Bidulph and *The Vicar of Wakefield*," *Modern Language Studies* 9, no. 2 (1979): 33–35. In "Frances Brooke's Early Fiction," *Canadian Literature* 86 (1980); 31–40, Lorraine McMullen traces the sentimentality of Brooke's first novel, *The History of Lady Julia Mandeville* (1763) to her reading and translation of Madame Riccoboni's *Lettres de Milady Juliette Catesby à Milady Henriette Campley, son Amie* (1759). Katherine M. Rogers's "Sensibility and Feminism: The Novels of Frances Brooke," *Genre* 11 (1978): 159–71, suggests that while Brooke owed obvious debts to the example of Richardson, she "shifted the balance of the Richardsonian novel away from pathos toward comedy."

This link between sensibility and comedy emerges most clearly in the novels of Charlotte Lennox. In *The Comic Spirit of Eighteenth-Century Novels* (Port Washington, NY: Kennikat, 1975), Susan G. Auty compares *The Female Quixote* with its original, arguing that both burlesques were "betrayed by their author's humanity into becoming comic novels," a theme further developed by Susan Staves in "Don Quixote in Eighteenth-Century England," *Comparative Literature* 24 (1972): 193–215, who suggests that as the century wore on, the quixotic hero became less comic, more "idealistic and noble." While we have no recent biography of Charlotte Lennox, her American background has been ably investigated by

Phillipe Séjourné in *The Mystery of Charlotte Lennox: First Novelist of Colonial America (1727?–1804)* (Aix-en-Provence: Publications des Annales de la Faculté des Lettres, 1967), a book that focuses on *The Life of Harriet Stuart* and *Euphemia*. Letters from such correspondents as Richardson, Reynolds, and Johnson either to or about Mrs. Lennox have been collected by Duncan Isles in "The Lennox Collection," *Harvard Library Bulletin* 18 (1970): 317–44; 19 (1971): 36–60, 165–86, 416–35. Isles also explores the relationship between Mrs. Lennox and Samuel Johnson in "Johnson and Charlotte Lennox," *New Rambler* 19 (1967): 34–38. James L. Clifford augments Isles's account in "Johnson's First Club," in *Evidence in Literary Scholarship: Essays in Memory of James Marshall Osborn*, ed. René Wellek and Alvaro Ribeiro (Oxford: Clarendon Press, 1979). Finally, Lennox's masterpiece, *The Female Quixote; Or, The Adventures of Arabella* has been edited with an introduction by Margaret Dalziel (London: Oxford University Press, 1970).

Of all the sentimental novelists of the eighteenth century, Fanny Burney has retained her popularity most consistently throughout all the vicissitudes of critical taste, a popularity which has increased over the last twenty years with the publication of *The Journals and Letters of Fanny Burney*, ed. Joyce Hemlow et al., 10 vols. (Oxford: Clarendon Press, 1972–80), and the publication in the Oxford English Novels Series of *Evelina; or, The History of a Young Lady's Entrance into the World*, edited with an introduction by Edward A. Bloom (London: Oxford University Press, 1968); and *Camilla; or, A Picture of Youth*, edited with an introduction by Edward A. Bloom and Lillian D. Bloom (London: Oxford University Press, 1972). To these primary sources one may add Joseph A. Gran's *Fanny Burney: An Annotated Bibliography* (New York: Garland, 1981). Eugene White's *Fanny Burney Novelist: A Study in Technique* (Hamden, Conn.: Shoestring Press; London: Mark Paterson, 1960), and Michael E. Adelstein's *Fanny Burney* (New York: Twayne, 1968) both provide general surveys of Burney's achievement as a novelist. Adelstein's critical observations are generally familiar and unexceptional: that Burney belongs in the second rank of eighteenth-century English novelists, that she advanced the novel by focusing on the social relationship between individuals and by so doing prepared the way for the novels of Austen, and that her talents deteriorated from *Evelina* to *The Wanderer* as she moved away from "writing about the world she knew to a world beyond her," abandoning successful first-person narrative for an "obtuse, stilted, verbose omniscient style."

This obvious stylistic decline has been most carefully examined by Edward A. Bloom and Lillian D. Bloom in "Fanny Burney's Novels: The Retreat from Wonder," *Novel* 12 (1979): 215–35, who argue that Burney's "creative spark" derived from a need to "fantasize a sense of self and to envision order out of potential disintegration." Once she had attained marriage and relative success, however, the need to deal with inner frustrations and inner pressures through her art no longer existed, and the "creative compulsion" dried up. This view of Burney's creative predicament is modified by Patricia Meyer Spacks in *Imagining a Self* which suggests that while Burney's style may have deteriorated, the underlying sense of feminine identity under attack remains from *Evelina* to *The Wanderer*, a novel Spacks describes as Burney's most overt expression of her "conscious resentment of the female condition." Burney's novels are pervaded by a sense of anxiety as her heroines "face endless struggle between what they want to have (independence, specific husbands, friends, pleasure, work) and what they want to be (angelically perfect): between impulses to action and to avoidance." This fear of wrongdoing so deftly outlined by Spacks is the subject of another excellent article, Susan Staves's "*Evelina*: or, Female Difficulties," *Modern Philology* 72 (1974): 368–81, which emphasizes Evelina's acute anxiety over the threat of violence (either physical or emotional). Staves pays particular attention to the importance of "female delicacy," suggesting that the "real tension in *Evelina* lies between the heroine's struggle to preserve her delicacy under these extraordinarily difficult conditions and the multitude of comic characters who constantly threaten it." The violence implicit in Burney's world is also emphasized by Judith Newton in "*Evelina*: or, The History of a Young Lady's Entrance into the Marriage Market," *Modern Language Studies* 6, no. 1 (1976): 48–56. According to Newton, *Evelina* "tells us much about the predicament of eighteenth-century middle class women," that they had to "display" themselves and wait to be chosen, that in order to succeed in the marriage market they had to enter a world where "men appear licensed to abuse women." In "Money in the Novels of Fanny Burney," *Studies in the Novel* 8 (1976): 24–37, Edward W. Copeland argues that "the insistent exploration of women's peculiar relationship to money defines the new female fiction" of the later eighteenth century. Many of these feminist themes are traced yet again (and rather less skillfully) by Rose Marie Cutting in "Defiant Woman: The Growth of Feminism in Fanny Burney's Novels," *Studies in English Literature, 1500–1900* 17 (1977): 518–30, and in "A Wreath for Fanny Burney's Last Novel: *The Wanderer*'s Contribution to Women's Studies," *Illinois Quarterly* 37, no. 3 (1975): 45–63 (also unaccountably published in *College Language Association Journal* 20 [1976]: 57–67).

Burney's unintentional irony in the treatment of Reverend Villars has been discussed in Emily H. Patterson's "Unearned Irony in Fanny Burney's

Evelina," *Durham University Journal* 36 (1975): 200–04; and in "From Precept to Proper Social Action: Empirical Maturation in Fanny Burney's *Evelina,*" *Eighteenth-Century Life* 3, no. 3 (1977): 85–88, by Jonathan Deitz and Sidonie Smith. The importance of family relationships in *Evelina* has also been examined in a series of recent articles: Toby A. Olshin, " 'To Whom I Most Belong': The Role of Family in *Evelina,*" *Eighteenth-Century Life* 6, no. 1 (1980): 29–42; Emily H. Patterson, "Family and Pilgrimage Themes in Burney's *Evelina,*" *New Rambler* 18 (1977): 41–48. The most interesting and challenging of the three, Mary Poovey's "Fathers and Daughters: The Trauma of Growing up Female," *Women and Literature* n.s. 2 (1982): 39–57, traces the "clash" between Evelina's "duty towards her father and her affection for a lover," a conflict which is never really solved because in Burney's "society no adequate social or psychological solution is possible."

Several other useful background studies and brief articles on Burney have also appeared in recent years. In "Manners, Morals, Magic and *Evelina,*" *Enlightenment Essays* 8, no. 1 (1977): 35–47; David K. Jeffrey compares Evelina with the heroines of *Pamela* and *Humphry Clinker*, while Gerard A. Barker, "The Two Mrs. Selwyns: *Evelina* and *The Man of the World,*" *Papers on Language & Literature* 13 (1977): 80–84, traces the origins of Burney's character to one of the same name in Mackenzie's novel. Burney's debts to Madame Riccoboni and Eliza Haywood have been noted in two articles: Sharon B. Footerman, "A Neglected Source for Fanny Burney's *Evelina,*" *Notes and Queries* 222 (1977): 274–76, and James P. Erickson, "*Evelina* and Betsy Thoughtless," *Texas Studies in Literature and Language* 6 (1964–65): 96–103. Lillian D. Bloom, "Fanny Burney's *Camilla*: The Author as Editor," *Bulletin of Research in the Humanities* 82 (1979): 367–93 chronicles Burney's revisions of the novel, describing in great detail the maturation of her style as she edited and reedited it. Kemp Malone, "*Evelina* Revisited," *Papers on Language & Literature* 1 (1965): 3–19, provides a brief sketch of character and plot in the novel. At the polar extreme from Malone's brevity and concision is Patricia Voss-Clesly's *Tendencies of Character Depiction in the Domestic Novels of Burney, Edgeworth, and Austen: A Consideration of Subjective and Objective Worlds*, 3 vols. (Salzburg: Institut für Anglistik and Amerikanistik, 1979), a voluminous, ill-digested and jargon-ridden compendium that nevertheless contains interesting observations on the art of characterization in Burney's works. Worthy of note also are several articles whose titles seem reasonably self-explanatory: James B. Vopat, "*Evelina*: Life as Art—Notes Toward Becoming a Performer on the Stage of Life," *Essays in Literature* 2 (1975): 42–52; Waldo S. Glock, "Appearance and Reality: The Education of Evelina," *Essays in Literature* 2 (1975): 32–41; and Jill Rubenstein, "The Crisis of Identity in Fanny Burney's *Evelina*," *New Rambler* 112 (1972): 45–50.

It is perhaps surprising that Elizabeth Inchbald has not inspired more critical attention in recent years, since as J. M. S. Tompkins observes in her critical introduction to *A Simple Story* (London: Oxford University Press, 1967), it is "one of the few minor novels of the late eighteenth century to have had an unbroken life." A few appreciative articles have appeared, however. In "Elizabeth Inchbald's Treatment of the Family and Pilgrimage in *A Simple Story*," *Etudes Anglaise* 29 (1976): 196–98, Emily H. Patterson argues that unlike many other novelists of the eighteenth century, "Mrs. Inchbald built *A Simple Story* around aberrations in the traditional structure of the family and the pilgrimage." Katherine M. Rogers traces Inchbald's defiance of other conventions (the heroine who is refined, above reproach, yet nonetheless pitiable, abandoned, but not actually illegitimate) in "Inhibitions on Eighteenth-Century Women Novelists: Elizabeth Inchbald and Charlotte Smith," *Eighteenth-Century Studies* 11 (1978): 63–78. Although Miss Milner rebels against all of these expectations she remains "a lovable as well as attractive person." Yet, Rogers argues, the rebellion doesn't last long, for in Part 2 Inchbald lapses back into the conventional pattern of treating the adulterous Lady Elmwood as a common fallen woman and her daughter Matilda as the prototypical virtuous and colorless heroine.

Although several of the editorical questions raised by *Nature and Art* have been answered by Janice Marie Cauwels in "Authorial 'Caprice' vs. Editorial 'Calculation': The Text of Elizabeth Inchbald's *Nature and Art*," *Papers of the Bibliographical Society of America* 72 (1978): 169–85; and in Patricia M. Taylor's "Authorial Amendments in Mrs. Inchbald's *Nature and Art*," *Notes and Queries* 223 (1978): 68–70, we still do not have a modern edition of the novel in print. Nor do we have a good modern biography of Inchbald herself, although some of the problems of Inchbald's biography are addressed in Cecilia Macheski's "Not a Simple Story: James Boaden's *Memoirs of Mrs. Inchbald*," *Transactions of the Samuel Johnson Society of the Northwest* 11 (1980): 99–112. In *Elizabeth Inchbald et le revendication féminine aux dix-huitième siècle* (Lille: Encyclopedie universitaire: Universite de Lille III, 1973), a French translation of *Wives as They Were and Maids as They Are*, Françoise Moreux provides a biographical introduction, but one marred by factual errors. Equally unsatisfactory is P. D. Tripathi's treatment of *Nature and Art* in *The Doctrinal English Novel* (Calcutta: K. P. Bagchi, 1977), a superficial analysis of the influence of wealth and poverty in *Nature and Art*, a novel that Tripathi interprets as a "panegyric on the advantages of religious resignation" to one's material lot in life.

Although Tripathi's argument often seems jumbled and simplistic, happily nothing of the sort applies to Gary Kelly's *The English Jacobin Novel, 1780–1805* (Oxford: Clarendon Press, 1976), the most extensive and sophisticated treatment of Inchbald's novels in print. Kelly places Inchbald within the tradition of those other "Jacobin" novelists—Bage, Holcroft, and Godwin—and traces a number of significant themes in *A Simple Story*, including the contrast between the "ill-educated" and the well-educated woman, a theme of "increasing interest to various women authors amongst the English Jacobins, as they strove to raise the dignity of woman above the merely domestic circle." Although Kelly treats *A Simple Story* as a novel of ideas, he does not portray Inchbald as primarily an ideological writer, but as a psychological realist who showed the other Jacobin novelists what could be made of personal experience. "Her description of states of mind and feeling is, in effect, 'philosophical' in a way which anticipates the English Jacobin novel without participating in its didactic excesses." Unfortunately, Kelly suggests, excessive didacticism is one of the flaws of *Nature and Art*, Inchbald's satire on her own times. Here the contrasts between corrupt society and innocent nature are more sharply drawn, but less convincingly dramatized. "In *Nature and Art*," writes Kelly, "she was not . . . writing about her feelings but about her ideas, and she was neither a deep nor an original thinker." Neither, apparently, was Hannah More, but her masterpiece, *Coelebs in Search of a Wife* (1808) was a more successful attempt to marry fiction with a didactic program. In *The Moral Tradition in English Fiction, 1785–1850* (Hanover, NH: University Press of New England, 1976), Samuel Pickering, Jr., outlines the importance of this now-forgotten best-seller, a work hailed in its time as "a new literary genre," combining "religion and the novel," and a shining example of how fiction could serve the cause of virtue. The importance of Hannah More as a religious novelist is also traced in A.G. Newell's "Early Evangelical Fiction," *Evangelical Quarterly* 38 (1966): 3–21, 81–98.

Of course, the woman novelist most notable for her attempts to use fiction as a didactic instrument, and the single novelist of the eighteenth century who has received the greatest attention as the result of the burgeoning women's studies movement is Mary Wollstonecraft. Nowhere is this new interest in Wollstonecraft more clearly documented than in Janet M. Todd's *Mary Wollstonecraft: An Annotated Bibliography* (New York: Garland, 1976), the critical introduction of which was also published as "Mary Wollstonecraft: A Review of Research and Comment," *British Studies Monitor* 8, no. 3 (1977): 3–23. Wollstonecraft's novels themselves have been made available in modern editions including a facsimile reprint of the 1788 edition of *Mary: A Fiction*, edited with an introduction by Gina Luria (New York: Garland, 1974); *Maria, or, the Wrongs of Woman*, edited with an introduction by Moira Ferguson (New York: Norton, 1975); and perhaps most significant, *Mary, A Fiction and the Wrongs of Woman*, edited with an introduction by Gary Kelly (London: Oxford University Press, 1976). To this list of texts one might also add Janet M. Todd's *A Wollstonecraft Anthology* (Bloomington: Indiana University Press, 1977). Three new collections of Wollstonecraft letters have recently been published: Ralph Wardle's *Godwin & Mary: Letters of William Godwin and Mary Wollstonecraft* (Lawrence: University of Kansas Press, 1966); *The Collected Letters of Mary Wollstonecraft* (Ithaca and London: Cornell University Press, 1979); along with *Letters Written during a Short Residence in Sweden, Norway and Denmark*, edited with an introduction by Carol H. Poston (Lincoln and London: University of Nebraska Press, 1976).

Wollstonecraft's biographers have also been busy. Eleanor Flexner, *Mary Wollstonecraft: A Biography* (New York: Coward, McCann and Geoghegan, 1972) provides perhaps the best of the lot, in some respects superseding Ralph Wardle's excellent biography of 1951. Of Wollstonecraft's most recent biographers, Flexner takes her achievements as a novelist most seriously, at least attempting to evaluate her contributions to the art of fiction in comparison with the other women novelists of the eighteenth century. The same cannot be said of Claire Tomalin's *The Life and Death of Mary Wollstonecraft* (New York: Harcourt, Brace Jovanovitch, 1974) which pays almost no attention to Wollstonecraft's novels, and when it does, treats them as unfortunate mistakes which "sidetracked" her from writing another "volume of polemics." Emily W. Sunstein, *A Different Face: The Life of Mary Wollstonecraft* (New York: Harper and Row, 1975), presents a fuller and more sympathetic account of Wollstonecraft's life, but she has little more to say about the novels, mining them only as lodes of autobiographical information. Not really intended to serve as a full biography of Wollstonecraft, Margaret George's *One Woman's Situation: A Study of Mary Wollstonecraft* (Urbana: University of Illinois Press, 1970) is a more avowedly feminist "interpretation" of Wollstonecraft's history as an emblem of the "situation" of women in the eighteenth century. As biographical sources she finds the novels useful; as art she finds them to be the "essence of sentimental nonsense." Fortunately, the reputation of the novels has fared somewhat better in two recent articles: Marilyn Butler's "The Woman at the Window: Ann Radcliffe in the Novels of Mary Wollstonecraft and Jane Austen," *Women and Literature* 1 (1980): 128–48; and Mitzi

Myers's "Unfinished Business: Wollstonecraft's *Maria*," *Wordsworth Circle* 11 (1980): 107–14. Myers sees *Maria* as the "culmination" of Wollstonecraft's career, in some measure reconciling the "tension between a rational, radical philosophy and a passionate personal need that characterizes her life and achievement." Myers views Wollstonecraft as an innovator in the art of fiction who created a new kind of heroine who had been granted "the masculine privilege of maturation through error." Indeed, Myers argues that Wollstonecraft endeavored to "rehabilitate feminine fiction, to endow female suffering with philosophical significance."

Whether freighted with philosophical signficance or not, female suffering has remained the stock in trade of the Gothic novelist for the last two centuries. The Gothic, that fictional form most often connected with the women novelists of the eighteenth century, has acquired a new popularity in recent years. This growing fascination with the eighteenth-century Gothic novel is witnessed by the Arno Gothic Novels reprint series and by Arno's institution of a new series entitled "Gothic Studies and Dissertations," reprinting previously unpublished dissertations and monographs on the Gothic. There are other evidences of serious scholarly interest, including the publication of Elizabeth MacAndrew's *The Gothic Tradition in Fiction* (New York: Columbia University Press, 1979), a work which characterizes the eighteenth-century Gothic tale as a "vehicle for ideas about psychological evil," evil as a "distortion, a warping" of the human mind. MacAndrew also emphasizes the quasi-allegorical character of the Gothic novel and the ways it employs dream fantasy and submerged sexual symbolism to deal with preoccupations with evil and secret sin. Like works of sentimental fiction, Gothic novels are meant to educate the reader, to "show the world its own dreams, drawing the reader into their closed worlds, playing on his emotions, and preventing him from denying that what he experiences in the novel may also be within himself." In "Deserts, Ruins, and Troubled Waters: Female Dreams in Fiction and the Development of the Gothic Novel," *Genre* 10 (1977): 529–72, Margaret Anne Doody suggests that the achievement of Lee, Smith, Radcliffe and other female Gothicists was that they brought this submerged world of dream and nightmare to the surface; indeed, "the 'real world' for characters in a Gothic novel is one of nightmare." Radcliffe in particular makes "accessible what was strange and elusive, and so paying full attention to what had been underdeveloped in the work of earlier novelists."

Among these earlier Gothic novelists, Sophia Lee, Charlotte Smith, and Clara Reeve have received critical notice. In Sophia Lee's *The Recess; or, A Tale of Other Times*, foreward by J. M. S. Tompkins with an introduction by Devendra P. Varma, 3 vols. (New York: Arno Press, 1972), Varma provides capsule summaries of Lee's various novels and suggests that her originality lay in rejecting the overly supernatural elements of Walpole and the "domesticated supernatural" of Clara Reeve, discovering instead the potentialities of the "historical-gothic," and expanding the uses of sentiment in Gothic fiction. In her editions of *Emmeline: The Orphan of the Castle* (London: Oxford University Press, 1971) and *The Old Manor House* (London: Oxford University Press, 1969), Anne Henry Ehrenpreis praises Charlotte Smith for her courage in handling delicate themes and for her social conscience so evident in the novels themselves. Ehrenpreis suggests that, like Fielding, Smith is "intolerant of cant and pretension in all forms." However, she argues that those who see Smith primarily as a Gothic novelist do so only by "ignoring three-quarters of her work." In "Character Description and Meaning in the Romantic Novel," *Studies in Romanticism* 5 (1966): 208–18, John Graham suggests that Charlotte Smith's peculiar form of characterization may have been influenced by Lavater's *Essays on Physiognomy* (1772) and that the shift in emphasis from exterior action to internal psychology particularly in the novels of sensibility resulted in a new emphasis on the face and its features as clues to moral character. Finally, although very little has been said about Clara Reeve in recent years, *The Old English Baron: A Gothic Tale* has been edited with an introduction by James Trainor (London: Oxford University Press, 1967).

Radcliffe, of course, is the name synonymous with the Gothic, and of all the eighteenth-century Gothicists, she is the most accessible in modern reprints and in scholarly editions. The Arno Reprints of *A Sicilian Romance; The Castles of Athlin and Dunbayne: A Highland Story; Gaston de Blondeville*; and *The Romance of the Forest* have all been published with new introductions by Devendra P. Varma. *The Italian: Or The Confessional of the Black Penitents*, edited with an introduction by Frederick Garber (London: Oxford University Press, 1968), and *The Mysteries of Udolpho*, edited with an introduction by Bonamy Dobrée (London: Oxford University Press, 1966) fill out the collection of modern Radcliffe editions. The only recent biography of Radcliffe is E.B. Murray's *Ann Radcliffe* (New York: Twayne, 1972) which includes chapters on each of the novels and discusses Radcliffe's synthesis of those elements—the Burkean sublime, the picturesque, and supernatural—inherited from earlier writers. In the chapter on Radcliffe's life and times, Murray suggests the importance of *A Journey Made in the Summer of 1794* as the link between Radcliffe's private responses to sublime landscape and the transformation of those feelings into art.

Of course Radcliffe's exploitation of various kinds of scenic tableaux has inspired considerable comment from recent critics. Malcolm Ware in particular has examined the topic in at least three different works: "Mrs. Radcliffe's 'Picturesque Embellishment,' " *Tennessee Studies in Literature* 5 (1960): 67–71; *Sublimity in the Novels of Ann Radcliffe: A Study of the Influence upon Her Craft of Edmund Burke's "Enquiry into the Origin of our Ideas of the Sublime and the Beautiful"* (Uppsala: Lundequist, 1963); and "The Telescope Reversed: Ann Radcliffe and Natural Scenery," in *A Provision of Human Nature*, edited by Donald Kay (University Ala.: University of Alabama Press, 1977), 169–89. The influence of such landscape painters as Claude, Rosa, and Poussin has been traced by Lynne Epstein in "Mrs. Radcliffe's Landscapes: The Influence of Three Landscape Painters on Her Nature Description," *University of Hartford Studies in Literature* 9 (1960): 107–20. The best treatment of the importance of landscape, however, is David S. Durant's "Aesthetic Heroism in *The Mysteries of Udolpho*," *The Eighteenth Century* 22 (1981): 175–88, which suggests that "in *Udolpho* morality is almost entirely a matter of aesthetics," an aesthetics based upon the discrimination of visual sensations. "Since the mind is so consistently described as a picture hoard in *Udolpho*, it is possible to judge the pictures which make up personality by aesthetic criteria," just as it is possible to judge the moral goodness of a character by the "sort of pictures one stores in his or her mind. Not only are moral criteria based upon a kind of pictoral aesthetic, but narrative structure as well: "The heroine's limited perspective necessitates a restriction of the narrative to outward appearances. And as we share Emily's perspective, we are gradually manipulated into taking this sense data as thought."

A number of other studies explore the relationship between sensibility, sexuality, and the supernatural in Radcliffe's version of the Gothic. In " 'A Constant Vicissitude of Interesting Passions': Ann Radcliffe's Perplexed Narratives," *Ariel* 10, no. 2 (1979): 45–64, Gary Kelly argues that the form of the Radcliffean Gothic is "unprogressive and repetitious," that its only strong organizing principle is that of "alternation" between feelings of "perplexity, terror and sensibility." While its form is expressed in a kind of "braided narrative" of changing passions, the primary didactic impulse is manifest in the narrative voice itself, which while it may describe the strange and unfamiliar, "expresses sensibility enlightened, tempered, and refined by reason, a kind of sensibility which she and her readers would have called taste." Robert Kiely notes a similar incongruity in *The Romantic Novel in England* (Cambridge: Harvard University Press, 1972), pointing to an implicit contradiction between the events of a Radcliffe novel and the moral principles that presumably govern them. Thus a heroine like Emily St. Aubert "may preach prudence, moderation, and universal harmony, but the potential fertility of that irrational state remains the most

original and convincing aspect of Mrs. Radcliffe's art." Kiely also emphasizes the internalization of terror in *Udolpho* as Emily, like all romantic
heroines, is gradually separated from the world and "imprisoned within her
own consciousness." In "Sense, Sensibility and Ann Radcliffe," *Studies in
English Literature, 1500–1900* 13 (1973): 577–90, Nelson C. Smith suggests that while Radcliffe certainly titillates the reader with the emotions of
terror and suspense, she also implicitly criticizes the "weaknesses and
flaws" of sensibility, among them the fact that it leads the mind away from
reason, leaving it prey to superstition and the vagaries of imagination. "The
Radcliffean Gothic Model: A Form for Feminine Sexuality," *Modern
Language Studies* 9 no. 3 (1979): 98–113, by Cynthia Griffin Wolff, deals
more directly with the question of sexuality in Radcliffe's fiction and the
ways in which Radcliffe created a narrative language and set of narrative
conventions "within which 'respectable' feminine sexuality might find expression." In a Radcliffe novel, Wolff suggests, we encounter an enduring
mythic configuration: a woman is caught between a "chaste" and a
"demon" lover, the one less potent and more controlled, the other "an in-
truder, dominating the fiction as its undeniable emotional focus." For a
female reader of the eighteenth century "the reading always provided a
forbidden pleasure by allowing her to indulge sexual feelings of immense
power (as she responded to the demon lover) and it always concluded by
reassuring her that these emotions were, in fact, under control." Thus the
Gothic might "rehearse the potent and complex elements of feminine sexuality while appearing to reinforce the social definition of women as basically 'pure' and 'passive'."

In *Love, Mystery and Misery: Feeling in Gothic Fiction* (London: Athlone Press, 1978), Coral Ann Howells also emphasizes the close connection
between "masochistic fantasy and repressed sexuality" in the Radcliffean
Gothic, arguing in more general terms that the Gothic is the antithesis of
the Augustan, representing a "fantasy world of neurosis and morbidity,"
and revealing the "darker side of awareness, the side to which sensibility
and imagination belong." Like Nelson C. Smith and Cynthia Griffin Wolff,
she also stresses Radcliffe's "double view" of emotional experience, that of
the sensitive and emotionally involved heroine as opposed to that of the
objective and rational author, "points of view that lead to two entirely
different conclusions." Radcliffe always poses the "antithesis between the
suggestions of imagination and the justifications of reason," and while she
entertains the emotionally titillating world of imagination, she feels compelled to return her readers to the safety and sanity of the rational world
they recognize. The result, Howells observes, is that the Gothic often "ends
by being totally reactionary—socially, politically, and morally."

This ambiguous social significance of the Gothic is noted and explored in depth by Mary Poovey in "Ideology and *The Mysteries of Udolpho*," *Criticism* 21 (1979): 307–30, the richest and most rewarding treatment of Radcliffe's art published in recent years. Like Brissenden, Poovey emphasizes the "paradoxical role sensibility plays in simultaneously restricting women and providing them power and an arena for action," simultaneously praising the virtues of passivity and dependence, while it indicates the essential helplessness of such a condition. Perhaps most important, the ideology of sensibility "preserved the valuable illusion of stability and continuity even after political and social turmoil undermined that ideal." In *Udolpho*, moreover, Radcliffe reveals that "sensibility *is* dangerous, as Emily's hysteria shows, because it encourages imaginative and libidinal excesses; but its more telling liability resides in its inability to resist the masculine version of desire—the lust of unregulated avarice" symbolized by Montoni, a character whose "purely materialistic appetite scorns the aesthetic rewards of sensibility." No satisfactory solution can be found, "for Radcliffe can imagine no force apart from sensibility's feminine principles to control this masculine force," a force "outside the moral universe" created and understood by the sensitive heart.

Although I have noted some of the major contributions to Radcliffe studies in the past two decades, there are a number of other articles that should also be included: Janet M. Todd, "Posture and Imposture: The Gothic Manservant in Ann Radcliffe's *The Italian*," *Women and Literature* n.s. 2 (1982), 25–38; Frederick S. Frank, "A Bibliography of Writings About Ann Radcliffe," *Extrapolation* 7 (1975): 54–62; Donald Thomas, "The First Poetess of Romantic Fiction: Ann Radcliffe," *English* 15 (1964): 91–95; F.W. Price, "Ann Radcliffe, Mrs. Siddons and the Character of Hamlet," *Notes and Queries* 221 (1976): 164–67; Elizabeth P. Broadwell, "The Veil Image in Ann Radcliffe's *The Italian*," *South Atlantic Bulletin* 40 (1975): 76–87; and Ford H. Swigart, Jr., "Ann Radcliffe's Veil Imagery," *Studies in the Humanities* 1, no. 1 (1969): 55–59. Of particular interest is Eugene P. Wright's "A Divine Analysis of *The Romance of the Forest*," *Discourse* 13 (1970): 379–87, an intriguing account of Joanna Southcott's bizarre interpretation of the novel as a divinely inspired allegory of "the situation of God's followers in the world at that time."

It may seem like a rather vertiginous leap from the frantic world of the Radcliffean Gothic to the more staid and decorous novels of Maria Edgeworth; yet like Radcliffe, she too has profited from the new interest in the women novelists of the eighteenth century. Thomas Flanagan's *The Irish Novelists, 1800–1850* (New York: Columbia University Press, 1958) is, of course, partially responsible for the Edgeworth revival, in particular the renewal of interest in Edgeworth as a regional novelist. A number of scholars have followed Flanagan's lead, among them W.B. Coley, "An Early 'Irish' Novelist," in *Minor British Novelists*, edited by Charles Alva Hoyt (Carbondale and Edwardsville: Southern Illinois University Press, 1967): 13–37; Patrick Murray, "The Irish Novels of Maria Edgeworth," *Studies* 59 (1970): 267–78; Joseph Kestner, "Defamiliarization in the Romantic Regional Novel: Maria Edgeworth, Walter Scott, John Gibson Lockhart, Susan Ferrier, and John Galt," *Wordsworth Circle* 10 (1979): 326–30; William Howard, "Regional Perspective in Early Nineteenth-Century Fiction: The Case of *Ormond*," *Wordsworth Circle* 10 (1979): 331–38; and A. Norman Jeffares, "Maria Edgeworth's *Ormond*," *English*, 8 (1969): 85–90. Of special note is Michael Hurst's *Maria Edgeworth and the Public Scene: Intellect, Fine-Feeling, and Landlordism in the Age of Reform* (Coral Gables: University of Miami Press, 1969), a social history of Ireland in the eighteenth and nineteenth centuries drawn from the works of Edgeworth. Also of significance have been the publication of *Castle Rackrent*, edited with an introduction by George Watson (London: Oxford University Press, 1965); *Letters for Literary Ladies*, edited with an introduction by Gina Luria (New York: Garland, 1974); and *Letters from England, 1813–1844*, edited by Christina Colvin, (Oxford: Clarendon Press, 1972).

Perhaps the most important addition to Edgeworth scholarship has been Marilyn Butler's *Maria Edgeworth: A Literary Biography* (Oxford: Clarendon Press, 1972), an extraordinarily fine work which is the first modern life based upon a thorough reexamination of all primary sources, particularly Edgeworth's unpublished correspondence. Butler sets out to determine how Edgeworth's novels "originated," and in so doing she not only provides a richly detailed account of Edgeworth's personal history, but also a vivid portrayal of that provincial life in eighteenth-century Ireland which was the wellspring of her finest fictional creations. Butler's biography deserves special praise for its balanced portrayal of the relationship between Maria and her extraordinary father, Richard Lovell Edgeworth, a man who has been accused of everything from balking his daughter's genius to ghostwriting the novels themselves.

Maria Edgeworth's novels have inspired two critical biographies as well. The first, O. Elizabeth McWhorter Harden's *Maria Edgeworth's Art of Prose Fiction* (The Hague: Mouton, 1971), is a general study of Edgeworth's career complete with brief discussions of all her works. James Newcomer's *Maria Edgeworth the Novelist: 1767–1849, A Bicentennial Study* (Fort Worth Texas: Texas Christian University Press, 1967), provides a more ambitious attempt to rehabilitate Edgeworth's critical reputation, defending her ability (often denied) to create credible plots, dismissing the notion that her father's influence "vitiated her novelistic powers," and suggesting that her didacticism has been over emphasized by unsympathetic readers. Newcomer presents close readings of *Ormond, Patronage, The Absentee, Belinda* and *Helen* (all treated as novels of manners), and in two final chapters on *Castle Rackrent* (previously published as "*Castle Rackrent*: Its Structure and Its Irony," *Criticism* 8 [1966]: 170–79; and "The Disingenuous Thady Quirk," *Studies in Short Fiction* 2 [1964]: 44–50), he suggests that what has often been admired as a work of "spontaneous ebullience," is actually a sophisticated structure as "balanced, formal, and restrained as anything that the eighteenth century has to offer." Newcomer also asserts that the narrator is not faithful old Thady, as he has often been portrayed, but a calculating, self-seeking, and disingenuous old rascal who actually connives with his son Jason in the downfall of the Rackrent family. This whole line of argument is forcefully disputed by Duane Edwards in "The Narrator of *Castle Rackrent*," *South Atlantic Quarterly* 71 (1972): 124–29, who denies that Thady Quirk is a purposeful schemer, suggesting instead that he is only a "sentimental, generally unreflective old man whose love of money causes him to ally himself with Jason, who for some unexplained reason abandons him." In "Ironic Perspective in Maria Edgeworth's *Castle Rackrent*," *Journal of Narrative Technique* 2, no. 1 (1972): 68–73, Stanley J. Solomon addresses the problem somewhat differently, arguing that Thady Quirk is "one of the earliest instances of unreliable narration," and that while Thady condemns the family for its impracticality, he "does not at all comprehend the ethical structure of moral values supposedly inherent in the society he represents." As such he becomes a symbol of that "indifference to evil" manifest throughout the novel.

Recent critics have also defended the apparent didacticism of Edgeworth's novels. In "Style and Purpose in Maria Edgeworth's Fiction," *Nineteenth-Century Fiction* 23 (1968): 265–78, Joanne Altieri discovers a mating of form and function in Edgeworth's narratives, arguing that she was totally dedicated to the exemplary method of characterization as a didactic strategy. Gerry H. Brookes, "The Didacticism of Edgeworth's *Castle Rackrent*," *Studies in English Literature, 1500–1900* 17 (1977): 593–605, suggests that in *Castle Rackrent* Edgeworth exploits "bulls" (the laughable confusion of ideas or actions) to articulate the confused state of the Irish mind as it is expressed in the language of the narrator. Brookes argues, moreover, that by reading the book as an apologue and not a real novel, we escape those expectations of organic unity often imposed upon the text, expectations, which according to Brookes, result in inevitable misreadings. In *Doubt and Dogma in Maria Edgeworth* (Gainesville: University of Florida Press, 1967), Mark D. Hawthorne tries to explain away Edgeworth's didacticism as a problem more apparent than real, contending that the surface moralism of Edgeworth's novels (included merely to please her father) is ironically undercut by a "coherent substructure of opinions that differ, often very radically, from the principles she appears to have been teaching." The presumed influence of Edgeworth's father, both moral and literary, is strongly defended in Patrick Murray's "Maria Edgeworth and Her Father: The Literary Partnership," *Eire* 6, no. 3 (1971): 39–50, which discounts the chilling effect on Maria's freedom of expression noted by Hawthorne. Two other works on Edgeworth's didacticism need to be mentioned here: Mark D. Hawthorne's "Maria Edgeworth's Unpleasant Lesson: The Shaping of Character," *Studies* 64 (1975): 167–77 (on *Belinda*); and in a more general vein, Vineta Colby's *Yesterday's Woman: Domestic Realism in the English Novel* (Princeton: Princeton University Press, 1974), which discusses the "novel of education" and its primary practitioners: Maria Edgeworth, Elizabeth Inchbald, Hannah More, Susan Ferrier, and Jane Austen.

In a sense, Austen closes that circle of women novelists begun by Behn, Manley, and Haywood, looking back to the women novelists of the eighteenth century even as she anticipates those of the nineteenth. The sheer plenitude of Austen criticism produced in the last twenty years demands a bibliography all its own, but in conclusion it seems appropriate at least to mention a few works that deal specifically with Austen's debt to the "feminine novel" of the eighteenth century and her development of the themes and conventions that were her inheritance. Foremost among these, of course, is Frank W. Bradbrook's *Jane Austen and Her Predecessors* (Cambridge: Cambridge University Press, 1966), a book outlining Austen's debts both general and specific to the plots, characters, and language of Burney, Lennox, Radcliffe, Inchbald and Edgeworth. These literary debts are also noted briefly in *Jane Austen: A Study of Her Artistic Development*, by Walton A. Litz (New York: Oxford University Press, 1965). In *Jane Austen: A Study in Fictional Conventions* (The Hague: Mouton, 1964), Henrietta Ten Harmsel discusses Austen's tendency to "burlesque the fiction" of the eighteenth century in her early works and to transform its conventions as her fiction matured. A more sophisticated approach to Austen's use of eighteenth-century conventions is Kenneth L. Moler's *Jane Austen's Art of Allusion* (Lincoln: University of Nebraska, 1968), which suggests that the Austen novel tends to "define itself" in relation to other works of literature. Thus "Jane Austen habitually expresses herself in terms of imitation, parody, correction of her predecessors and contemporaries." Her borrowings, therefore, are meant to be recognized as allusions, "implicit invitations to the reader to see relationships and make comparisons between her works and what they resemble." Moler also traces Austen's reworking and transformation of such familiar eighteenth-century themes as the pursuit of self-knowledge, the dichotomy between nature and art, the conflict of feeling and reason, and the tension between imagination and judgment.

These are among the major studies of Austen's use of eighteenth-century fictional modes and conventions, but a number of other source studies might also be mentioned here. In "Jane Austen and *The Female Quixote*," *Studies in the Novel* 2 (1970): 211–21, Elaine M. Kauvar discusses Austen's use of the quixotic theme to reinforce the more important coming-of-age theme in her novels. The importance of Fanny Burney's influence has been noted by Elaine Bender, "The Significance of Jane Austen's Reference to *Camilla* in *Sanditon*: A Note," *Notes and Queries* 223 (1978): 214–16; and by Jerry C. Beasley, "Fanny Burney and Jane Austen's *Pride and Prejudice*," *English Miscellany* 24 (1973): 153–66. Anne Henry Ehrenpreis's "*Northanger Abbey*: Jane Austen and Charlotte Smith," *Nineteenth-Century Fiction* 25 (1970): 343–48, traces the character of Isabella Thorpe to the influence of Clarinthia Ludford in Smith's *Ethelinde, Or The Recluse of the Lake* (1789), while William H. Magee, "The Happy Marriage: The Influence of Charlotte Smith on Jane Austen," *Studies in the Novel* 5 (1975): 120–32, argues that Austen's most important inheritance from Charlotte Smith was the "courtship and marriage convention," which she transformed into "a significant comment on the aims of civilized living." In "Sources of Jane Austen's Ideas about Nature in *Mansfield Park*," *Notes and Queries* 206 (1961): 222–24, Frank W. Bradbrook cites Gilpin's *Observations on the River Wye* and *The Mysteries of Udolpho*, while Kenneth L. Moler, "*Sense and Sensibility* and its Sources," *Review of English Studies* 17 (1966): 413–19, discusses the influence of Edgeworth's short story, "Mademoiselle Panache" (1795) and Mrs. West's novel *The Advantages of Education* (1793) on Austen's early fiction.

Austen's obvious parody of Gothic and sentimental conventions and clichés in *Northanger Abbey* has inspired a lively critical exchange over the apparent disunity created in the novel by Austen's satirical treatment of her predecessors. Among the participants in this debate have been Cecil S. Emden, "The Composition of *Northanger Abbey*," *Review of English Studies* 19 (1968): 279–87; and Everett Zimmerman, "The Function of Parody in *Northanger Abbey*," *Modern Language Quarterly* 30 (1969): 53–63. But by far the most artful (not to say Byzantine) discussion of Austen's inclusion of apparently "detachable" Gothic episodes and sentimental parodies in the novel is Frank J. Kearful's "Satire and the Form of the Novel: The

Problem of Aesthetic Unity in *Northanger Abbey*," *ELH* 32 (1965): 511–27, which suggests that Austen continually switches back and forth from the novelistic to the satirical mode, "turning the tables on the too secure reader," purposely combining burlesque, parody, comedy, tragedy, romance and antiromance "in such a fashion as to make us aware of the paradoxical nature of all illusion—even those illusions by which we master illusion." Less elaborate but perhaps more convincing is Cynthia Griffin's "The Development of Realism in Jane Austen's Early Novels," *ELH* 30 (1963): 36–52. Griffin argues that in her early novels Austen parodies and ridicules non-realistic fiction as a way of negatively defining reality and marking the boundaries between fiction and life, a habit she outgrew as she learned how to present a more positive view of reality through the interplay of varying points of view, thus eliminating the need for obvious parody.

Austen's role as a feminist writer has also occasioned some controversy. In "Emma Woodhouse and *A Vindication of the Rights of Woman*," *Wordsworth Circle* 7 (1976): 320–32, by Allison G. Sulloway; and "Jane Austen and the Feminist Tradition," *Nineteenth-Century Fiction* 28 (1973–74): 321–28, by Lloyd W. Brown, both critics place Austen in the feminist camp as an implicit (if not explicit) follower of Wollstonecraft. According to Sulloway, Austen's novels include similar themes and preoccupations: obsession with feminine humiliation and the way that "sex tends to influence both wealth and caste," and both Austen and Wollstonecraft emphasize reason as the only "power of improvement" for women. Brown is a bit more cautious in his assertions, but he also argues that "insofar as such feminism questioned certain masculine assumptions in society," assumptions about male domination of education, about women's special emotions, about the role of marriage, Austen was indeed a feminist in the mold of Wollstonecraft. These assertions are implicitly rejected by Marilyn Butler in *Jane Austen and the War of Ideas* (Oxford: Clarendon Press, 1975), who implies that while Austen is indeed a partisan writer, she is one who opposes most of what a revolutionary feminist like Wollstonecraft stood for. Austen's novels belong to a movement "that defines itself by opposition to revolution." In her earlier novels the "key virtues are prudence and concern for the evidence: the vices are romanticism, self-indulgence, conceit, and for Jane Austen, other subtle variations upon the broad anti-jacobin target of individualism." Such conspicuous disagreement is a healthy sign, I suspect, because it indicates that eighteenth-century women novelists are finally being judged as independent thinkers worthy of such consideration; and because it suggests that it is no longer *de rigeur* to find an implicit and often anachronistic modern feminism in all utterances made by eighteenth-century women.

As the preceding pages indicate, the debate over the role of women in the development of the eighteenth-century fiction has been as lively as it has been profitable. Of course, as in all areas of literary study, much has been written that was perhaps better left unsaid, some scholarship seems superfluous, some merely dull. But what seems clearest of all is that the rediscovery of the eighteenth-century woman novelist has inspired the skillful mapping of a territory which in the past had existed as a kind of literary Van Dieman's Land: known but infrequently visted and until recently largely unexplored.

NOTES

1. This review has been attributed to Mary Wollstonecraft by Janet M. Todd, A Wollstonecraft Anthology (Bloomington, London: Indiana University Press, 1977), 219.

Afterword
Jane Austen Looks Ahead

IRENE TAYLER

The social, philosophic, aesthetic, political, and economic revolution that characterized the late eighteenth century inevitably broke new ground for women as well as men, as Mary Wollstonecraft implied when she echoed Thomas Paine's famous "Rights of Man" (1791–92) in titling her own "Vindication of the Rights of Woman" (1792). Behind both titles, of course, lay the historic Declaration of the Rights of Man and of the Citizen, made by the French National Assembly in 1789. In the wave of this new and internationally felt sense of freedom, women novelists like Mary Hays in her controversial *Memoirs of Emma Courtney* (1796) began to claim with increasing boldness woman's right to economic and intellectual independence. And social critics like Priscilla Wakefield in her "Reflections on the Present Condition of the Female Sex; With Suggestions for its Improvement" (1798) and Mary Ann Radcliffe in "The Female Advocate, or, An Attempt to Recover the Rights of Women from Male Usurpation" (1799) spoke more openly and to a broader and more receptive audience than they could possibly have done in a time less alive with the ferment of fresh thought. On the continent the way was preparing for women like Madame de Stael, whose influence would grow so great as to make Napoleon take individual action against her; and like George Sand, whose name was to become synonymous with female sexual and intellectual daring and literary success.

England produced no Madame de Stael or George Sand, no woman of enormous personal flair who was also both a literary giant and an out-spoken feminist. Yet England did produce in Jane Austen one of the great female writers in any language of the nineteenth century; and from her vantage point as a woman she identified some of the key issues of the future. In *Persuasion*, the last novel she finished, Austen not only depicted, but also clearly approved the historic shift away from land or place (the house, family, and position into which one is born) and toward work or profession as the legitimate new way of defining the individual in relationship to society.

It is the new breed, the Crofts and Wentworths, who inherit the world of that book, the effete Elliots who must relinquish it. The story of the novel's heroine, Anne, is the story of her move from the periphery of the decaying world to the center of the rising one. Despite the "autumnal tone" that some critics have heard in the novel, its vision of the future is really quite bright. The Frederick Wentworth who was "nobody" at the outset is "no longer nobody" at the end, and "only Anne" departs the family that never honored her to join Frederick and his "brother officers" in developing a whole new concept of family, based on the idea of a profession dedicated at once to public service and private loyalties. Even the traditional sex roles are up for revision. It is the capable and energetic Mrs. Croft who takes the reins when she and her husband go driving, and as a Navy wife, she boldly and happily joins her husband when he is sent to sea.

But for a woman to join her husband at his place of work is not quite the same as having her own work to do; to hold the reins on an outing is not to hold down a job. Much must be undergone before changes of that magnitude can come. Similarly, a nation that has long depended on one system of domestic order and economic stability will not shift to new ones without dangerous disruption. Austen saw that these issues were interrelated. She saw that the uncertainty of woman's place in a new world defined by work connections rather than land connections was symptomatic of the more general problems of human displacement in time of change, and that although the "new" women might have opportunities that had been closed to their mothers, they would be correspondingly more vulnerable than their mothers had been.

Could the old values, eroded though they were to their very core, nonetheless provide some support for the new? Did there perhaps remain elements of the old stability that were healthy enough that a new English society might ground itself on them? Or, to put it in other terms, were there values of a perhaps transcendent kind that were not dependent on the economic and social conditions of the old world, values that were in danger of disappearing, and would be lost at society's peril? Indeed, might this new society not rediscover and renew them? Jane Austen was a devout Christian, and though she never proselytized, all her novels reflect her deep commitment to the idea of Christian service, of each person's moral obligation to the human community—an obligation always to attend quietly but generously to the needs of others. Persons acting on such values will have no trouble extending their understanding of the meaning of family to include mankind, no trouble moving from the idea of brother to brother officer and ultimately to brother man. Though it was more sisters than brothers that Austen wrote about, the way siblings treat one another in her novels serves regularly as an index to the moral character of each.

In her last work, however, Austen looked farther than ever beyond the context of the household. Having recognized that the concept of community was itself changing, and with it the place and role of women, she seemed prepared now in this final work to suggest that the experience of England's women would provide the test case for the whole new nation: that the problems and possibilities facing English women were paradigmatic of those that faced England herself.

When Austen undertook her last novel, *Sanditon,* she was suffering from Addison's disease and knew she was dying. With her face toward eternity, she drew her text, I would suggest, from the close of the Sermon on the Mount, where Jesus distinguished the wise person who "heareth these sayings of mine, and doeth them" from him who "heareth . . . and doeth them not." In Jesus' figure, the wise man "built his house upon a rock," whereas the foolish man "built his house upon the sand": "And the rain descended, and the floods came, and the winds blew, and beat upon that house; and it fell: and great was the fall of it" (Matt. 7:27). The house Austen had in mind was the one she saw post-Napoleanic England building for the future, and, as her title *Sanditon* suggests, she feared for its foundations.[1]

Although Austen died before the plot of *Sanditon* was fully established, the book's projected theme cannot be in doubt. The fifty or so pages she left us repeatedly depict houses both sand-built and solid. The people of Sanditon have left their solid houses behind, and the town of sand is inhabited by the restless, the unstable, by people of unfocused (or of misfocused) energies. It is a town economically grounded on speculation, built with venture capital, engaging entreprenurial energies fueled by the hope of private gain. Significantly, it is not a mere factory being built, but an entire community. It is moreover a community made up largely of women whose energies have no constructive outlet, or of men who have taken on dead-end feminine roles. Here in Sanditon we watch one man parading his sexual seductiveness in the hope of marrying money, another affecting delicate health as a mask for mere selfishness, and many who move with the restlessness of those who have nothing to do. Austen demonstrates that for both sexes, idleness breeds illness, both physical and moral; that the health of society depends on everyone's having meaningful work, and doing it— certainly women no less than men.

We may see that in a matter of a few pages Austen sketched her outline rapidly, in broad strokes. We see first her heroine's family background, the very model of old-fashioned English social solidity, and then the seaside resort of Sanditon, model of all that is hopeful and new but also restless, feckless, financially unsound, morally endangered. Both literally and figuratively, it is a health resort without a doctor.

Surely our young heroine is to be the doctor—though probably (given Austen's time and tone) only in the figurative sense. Yet the issue of women's profession, especially as it touches on matters of sickness and healing, threads through every portion of the fragment Austen left us. Charlotte Heywood is an ordinary young woman of twenty-two, who has been raised as one of a comfortable, large, cheerful, and very stable family. Her busy parents "never left home"; instead they have contentedly remained for the whole of their married life in the house into which Mr. Heywood was born, in aptly named Willingden—a stronghold of old-style family values, where each member has work to do and does it willingly, for the good of all. On the rare occasions when movement is absolutely required of the Heywoods, they employ "the old coach which had been new when they were married and fresh lined on their eldest son's coming of age ten years ago." Their property is comfortable enough to have allowed them more luxuries had they had fewer obligations. They might for example have afforded, Austen wryly suggests, "a new carriage and better roads . . . and symptoms of the gout and a winter at Bath." But no: "the maintenance, education, and fitting out of fourteen children demanded a very quiet, settled, careful course of life—and obliged them to be stationary and healthy at Willingden."

From this paradigm of old-fashioned British health, grounded on the virtues of family obligation and communal duty, Charlotte is taken to Sanditon—literally a town built on shifting sand, and figuratively too, in that its very life as a "spa" depends on people's illnesses, or on their self-centered affectations of invalidism. Charlotte's hosts at Sanditon are a Mr. and Mrs. Parker who have become acquainted with the Heywoods as a result of injuries received when, through an act of characteristic impulsiveness, they overturned their carriage at the Heywoods' door. Mr. Parker is a man of respectable background, and he is amiable and kindhearted. But he lives in a very shaky house. In him is literalized the large historic condition of a people no longer defined by the connections of land or family, yet lacking the security of a dependable new definition. Having observed that Mr. Parker has "no profession," Austen describes his situation with respect to his family and future without further comment: "Sanditon was a second wife and four children to him—hardly less dear—and certainly more engrossing. . . . it was his mine, his lottery, his speculation and his hobby horse; his occupation, his hope, and his futurity." Accordingly he is convinced of Sanditon's economic soundness and unique healing properties: but we, viewing it though Charlotte's more balanced intelligence, see it far otherwise.

Austen gathers at Sanditon a cross-section of England's ills—not medical ills but social ones. There we see commercial speculation that hazards small lives against the uncertainties of the future: the Stringers who have been encouraged to move their gardening business to a new location, and who are not doing very well; the shoemaker who has stocked "Blue shoes, and nankin boots" ("Civilization, civilization indeed!" in Mr. Parker's fond estimate) in the expectation of well-heeled visitors who have, however, not yet come; the newly smartened cottage windows announcing "Lodgings to let" to the still indifferent streets. In this context of uncertainty it is on women, and women's lives, that Austen focuses our attention.

For example, Mr. Parker's coadjutor in the Sanditon enterprise is a wealthy and childless widow, Lady Denham. Her consuming interest is money. Indeed, the interest is "consuming" in quite a punning sense, for the financial prosperity of the town depends on a consumerism whose rising importance Austen swiftly summarizes in her heroine's visit to the town library, where the lending of books now takes second place to the marketing of what Austen dryly characterizes as "all the useless things in the world that could not be done without." We have here, in short, that characteristic resort of the bored and useless modern woman: a gift shop. Lady Denham did not get her original capital by commerce of this kind, or by speculation, but rather in woman's old way—by marrying it. Indeed, she had negotiated the marriage market with a striking ability that she now hopes to demonstrate in the sale of farm commodities: "I do not think I was ever overreached in my life; and that is a good deal for a woman to say that has been married twice." In an ironic and suggestive reversal of gender roles, it is now the allotted employment of Lady Denham's nephew, Sir Edward, to marry into wealth. Appropriately, his "great objective in life was to be seductive," and (like many women before him) he has studied his trade with the masters of the sentimental novel. Aunt and nephew are equally self-absorbed, equally the symptoms of some national disease. But of the two, the aunt is by far the more capable and interesting; she is indeed a person of considerable potential—worthy, it seems to me, of being redeemed through some future turn of the plot.

Even more telling examples of social instability are Mr. Parker's sisters and youngest brother. As the Heywoods were too busy to be ill, so Susan and Diana Parker are ill because they are not busy. They are ill of frustration, ill because they have no constructive outlet for their enormous energies. They are a study in social waste.

Charlotte's first estimate of them—unspoken, of course—is "Unaccountable officiousness! Activity run mad!" But she soon reaches the juster judgment that must also be ours: their devastating illnesses and sudden recoveries "seemed more like the amusement of eager minds in want of employment than of actual afflictions and relief." Austen herself summarizes their case: "they must either be very busy for the good of others, or else extremely ill themselves." With their eldest brother, Charlotte's host, they share "charitable hearts and many amiable feelings—but a spirit of restless activity." Austen appears to concur with Diana's own judgment that "the body is better, for the refreshment the mind receives in doing its duty." But this new world does not yet offer appropriate duties for women like these, whose zeal, turned inward, can only sicken its source.

Finally, the disease of the youngest Parker brother, Arthur, is related by contrast to that of his sisters. Too sodden and lazy to work, he hides his indolence behind the pretense of delicate health. Even Mr. Parker, who in his aimiability always prefers to take people at their own best estimate, must fault his youngest brother's idleness: "It *is* bad;—it *is* bad that he should be fancying himself too sickly for any profession—and sit down at one and twenty on the interest of his own little fortune, without any idea of attempting to improve it, or of engaging in any occupation that may be of use to himself or others."

Sanditon, then, is a town where "the disease of activity" (a rejected phrase from the manuscript) stalks like a plague. And Sanditon was modern England, as Austen saw it in dying vision. The issues of wisdom and foolishness as depicted in Jesus' parable Austen twice summarizes: first in the contrast between the stable home lives of the Heywoods of Willingdon and the frenetic, dispersed family condition of the Parkers of Sanditon; then again within Sanditon itself in the contrast between Mr. Parker's old house and his new one. "Whose very snug-looking place is this?" Charlotte had asked as the company was first approaching the outskirts of Sanditon village, adding significantly, "It seems to have as many comforts about it as Willingdon." To which Mr. Parker had significantly responded, "This is my old house—the house of my forefathers—the house where I and all my brothers and sisters were born and bred—and where my own three eldest children were born. . . . I have given it up." Eagerly he had urged Charlotte to attend instead to his new house, whose location directly overlooking the sea gave it "a rather better situation," Mr. Parker was convinced. "You will not think I have made a bad exchange," he assures her, "when we reach Trafalgar House—which by the bye, I almost wish I had not named Trafalgar." Mr. Parker now thinks he might better have named his house for the more current "Waterloo." One trembles at the ironies.

Mrs. Parker, on the other hand, is sensible enough to miss the old house: its present occupants "did not seem to feel the storms last winter at all," she pointedly remarks, whereas "*we* had been literally rocked in our bed." But Mr. Parker dismisses her worries. He is satisfied that "*We* have all the grandeur of the storm, with less real danger, because the wind meeting with nothing to oppose or confine it around our house, simply rages and passes on."

We will never know whether Austen intended us later to see the rains descend and floods come and winds "beat upon the house . . . and great was the fall of it." Perhaps not literally, given her comic mode. What we do know is that she saw dangers that the Mr. Parkers of her world did not see (though their wives may have seen them), and that she viewed Charlotte's solid Willingdon foundations as offering one kind of protection against those dangers. This is not to argue that Austen favored stasis: significantly the Heywoods "staid at home, that their children *might* get out." Austen's emphasis on the conditional points to her recognition that activity in itself is no more wrong than building a house is wrong: it is activity without social function that is the moral equivalent of building on sand. Activity like Frederick Wentworth's, exercised in a "profession which is, if possible, more distinguished in its domestic virtues than in its national importance," is health itself. *That* is what is meant by building one's home on Jesus' rock.

How might Austen's quietly observant little heroine have functioned in this book? It seems clear that Austen intended Charlotte's Willingdon foundations somehow to shore up the sandy ones of her new friends, and by implication those of the new England. She might somehow have provided the good sense that could temper Parker enthusiams, the good heart that should moderate Lady Denham's zeal for gain and harness her financial power for the fulfillment of worthier goals than the narrowly selfish ones we witness her pursuing. Clear-eyed young Clara might have been given a chance of independence; Miss Lambe, one hopes, was not to have been sacrificed. (Just think, an octoroon in an Austen novel: this is a new world indeed!) It looks as if part of Charlotte's vocation would have been to re-claim one Parker—the interesting brother Sidney—from his habit of rov-ing. Mr. Parker acknowledges, "He lives too much in the world to be settled; that is his only fault.—He is here and there and everywhere."

For Austen, the disease of activity is a disease of the social spirit; in a healthy nation, activity itself is energy to be harnessed for the public good, a potential *national* resource. Clearly if Sidney Parker is to deserve Char-lotte, he will have to employ his energies more worthily, have to build for himself a solid place in life, probably by settling into a profession. Perhaps something concerning medicine? One would like to know whether Austen's vision extended so far as to discern "helping" professions for Susan and Diana Parker too, anticipating that great nineteenth-century burgeoning of woman's "good works" that became a route for many to both profession and political consciousness (such as abolition). Crafty Lady Denham might help set them up—it would not be a bad investment, after all: a speculation in moral health rather than in milch-ass futures.

However Austen might have unfolded the specifics of her plot, clearly her references to the houses of one's fathers—the Heywood house at Willingdon, the Parkers' original family home, now given up—are resonant with the concerns of one whose eye is on the houses of the eternal Father and of the enduring Mother land. How to begin a new national life, she seems to be asking? How to implement a social vision in which vigorous women no longer fulfill the traditional family roles, yet nonetheless find meaningful places for themselves? In a strangely prescient way, she suggests that an economy based on speculation and consumption is built on the sands of selfishness, and that narrowly private structures that are not in service to the community bring illness, and are doomed to fall when the rains descend, and the floods come, and the winds beat upon them. Only a society that can provide worthy professions to channel worthy energies can build for its members stable homes.

This is a novel whose larger ending could be written only by history. I do not wish so much to speculate about what Austen did not live to finish, as to emphasize something she had already achieved: a vision of the future presented with a sharpness of political acuity that critics have not often recognized in this woman whose eye is so often thought to be narrowly on the parlor. Whatever its projected ending, *Sanditon* already contains the elements of an analysis of the vast cultural changes that were taking place in the nineteenth century. Austen's eye was on such large issues as the new place of work and property, capital, speculation, and consumption, and on the social ills of alienation and rootlessness. For a more complete vision of these issues and their interconnections we will have to wait for the mid-nineteenth-century critiques of such social philosophers as Marx and Ruskin. And not even they saw as clearly as did Austen the meaning of these vast social changes as they bore, and bear, on the lives of women.

NOTES

1. Quotations are drawn from the text as printed in *Lady Susan/The Watsons/Sanditon* (edited, with an introduction by Margaret Drabble) Penguin Books, 1974.

Index to Authors and Works Cited

(NOTE: Further references to most works in this text can be found in the bibliography by Lund beginning at page 398)

434

Index

Index